Mastering®
Autodesk® Architectural Desktop 2006

Scott Onstott

SYBEX®

San Francisco   London

Publisher: Dan Brodnitz
Acquisitions Editor: Willem Knibbe
Developmental Editor: Pete Gaughan, Jim Compton
Production Editor: Rachel Gunn
Technical Editor: David Koch
Copyeditor: Nancy Sixsmith
Compositor: Laurie Stewart, Happenstance Type-O-Rama
DVD Technician: Kevin Ly
Proofreaders: Jim Brook, Nancy Riddiough
Indexer: Nancy Guenther
Cover Designer: Design Site
Cover Illustration: Jack T. Myers, Design Site

Library of Congress Card Number: 2005924242

ISBN: 0-7821-4429-2

Wiley Publishing, Inc.
End-User License Agreement

To Merlin Jasper Nelson, my son who entered this world with perfect timing, just as I finished this book.

Acknowledgments

This book wouldn't be what it is without the help of so many excellent people who have helped me bring it to you. I'd like to thank Willem Knibbe for supporting me early on and for convincing me to write this book. Thanks to Pete Gaughan for his excellent editoral work: I have learned a lot in the process. Thanks also to Jim Compton who assisted with developmental editing. David Koch has my sincere appreciation for doing a great job identifying my mistakes and suggesting solutions. I want to thank Rachel Gunn for keeping me on track and for helping me to meet deadlines. Nancy Sixsmith deserves credit for making the text more readable and has my gratitude for teaching me more about the English language. Thanks to Chris Yanchar at Autodesk for graciously writing the foreward to this book. Finally, thanks to my wife Jenn for her support during this intense and lengthy project.

About the Author

Born in California, Scott Onstott attended the University of California Berkeley and graduated with a bachelor's degree in Architecture. He began his career doing manual drafting and soon transitioned to AutoCAD. Scott discovered that he enjoyed using computers and fully embraced the change that technology brought to architecture.

Scott gained experience in several prominent engineering, architecture, and interiors firms in San Francisco, working as a draftsman, CAD designer, CAD manager, job captain, and programmer before becoming an independent consultant. He has taught dozens of semester courses at three San Francisco Bay Area colleges and has written or edited dozens of technical computer books, including his unique book *Enhancing CAD Drawings with Photoshop*.

In addition to writing and editing books, Scott also creates independent video courses on a variety of architectural software, including Autodesk VIZ, Revit, AutoCAD, Adobe Photoshop, and discreet 3ds max.

Foreword

As an architect, one of the most rewarding moments is when your building is completed and the occupants finally move in. Those of us in the software industry—specifically those who design, implement, test, and document the features—get our pleasure from the day we finally release the software to the world. However, software is intangible compared to a building that one can drive by and point out to your kids. So when an actual book is written on the product, this gives the Autodesk Architectural Desktop team much delight—especially a book that clearly communicates the design intent of the features, and even goes further in describing how to apply the tool from the point of view of an actual user. Scott Onstott's *Mastering Autodesk Architectural Desktop 2006* fits all of the above.

I first became aware of the author several years ago through his website, www.scotttonstott.com, where he began offering 3D content using i-Drop but in a very visual manner, which of course communicates best to architects. Scott's site, along with the myriad of eStores that started hitting the Internet in abundance, were in fact inspiration for the Content Browser feature introduced in Architectural Desktop 2004. His new book on Architectural Desktop 2006 follows suit in presenting the program's vast array of functionality in a clear, visual manner.

Scott begins the book with the most critical aspects of Architectural Desktop that make it unique, as well as those that are often misunderstood by new users. Starting with a basic history of AutoCAD to Architectural Desktop, he then segues into describing the design intent of the overall workspace of the product, what is where and why. Next he covers the logic of Display System, which is one of the main sub-systems that allow the architectural objects to display differently based on viewing direction (plan vs. reflected ceiling plan vs. model) as well as with varying levels of detail. He describes the Display System in such a way that the underlying complexity can be better understood by the casual observer and how it can be utilized appropriately for your benefit.

Scott delves into the other unique aspect of Architectural Desktop, the style-based method of defining the various objects. He explains how the objects can start off generic and then be progressively refined as your design progresses, just like the real-world process of architectural design, and as the system was originally intended to be utilized. Here he also shows how you can use the vast array of styles that you can create through tool catalogs and the Content Browser, allowing you to present content in a visual format that is manageable for your design team.

Scott's book goes on to cover all areas of Architectural Desktop in understandable detail, from annotation, to project standards, to rendering, to some of the other products Autodesk offers to help improve your business. Look for the sidebars that explain certain topics further or interject extra color commentary.

Whether you are an architect migrating from AutoCAD or another CAD application over to Architectural Desktop, or you're an experienced Architectural Desktop user, this book will help you understand the product in a manner that is clear and can be utilized at your own pace. It will surely be a valued addition to your library.

—*Chris Yanchar*
Desktops Product Planning Manager
Building Solutions Division, Autodesk

Contents at a Glance

Contents

Introduction

Welcome to *Mastering Autodesk Architectural Desktop 2006*. This book is a journey toward eventual mastery of this software. Should you choose to take this journey, the experiences you'll have will steadily build valuable skills and teach you new ways of thinking about designing architecture with a computer.

This book is for architects, designers, builders, developers, and all those who wish to design and document architecture using Architectural Desktop (ADT). Chances are if you are reading this Introduction, you will eventually work with ADT every day. ADT is an incredibly complex and powerful software: it can be intimidating setting off on this journey, knowing how much you'll have to assimilate to achieve mastery. But rest assured that to achieve stunning success with ADT, all you'll need is the desire to learn, the persistence to reach your goals, and time to practice.

This book focuses on first understanding how ADT works, then creating conceptual models, developing designs, producing construction documents, and communicating your designs to others. Because *Mastering Autodesk Architectural Desktop 2006* is focused on practical uses of the software, this book doesn't describe every single tool and feature that's available. You *will* find illuminating discussions and step-by-step tutorials covering everything you'll need to digitally design and document architecture.

How to Use This Book

If you are new to ADT, you'll want to read the chapters sequentially from front to back, doing the tutorial exercises as you go along. Each chapter builds on the skills from previous chapters, so you can use this book as a self-paced course on Architectural Desktop 2006. If you have used ADT before, you can jump directly to chapters that you need to work on. Each chapter has numerous references to other chapters, so you can let your interest guide you through the content once you know enough about how ADT works.

NOTE   Before you get started on the tutorials, make sure you've installed the sample files from the companion DVD. You'll need these files to work through the tutorials in almost every chapter. The DVD also contains a free, time-limited trial version of ADT.

The first three chapters form Part 1 of this book and help you to understand the nuts and bolts of how ADT works. Even if you are already familiar with ADT, you should skim through these chapters to become aware of the new features and to strengthen the foundations of your knowledge.

Chapters 4–6 show you how to create conceptual models both from the outside in and from the inside out. In addition, it is essential that you understand the concepts behind project management in Part 2 because they lay the foundation for subsequent phases in the continuing design process.

You'll study each object type in depth in Part 3, which contains Chapters 7–12. As you learn to use each type of architectural object, your skills to develop designs in ADT will improve tremendously. Once you have mastered those skills, you'll be prepared to confidently use ADT's rich set of tools in your own projects.

Chapters 13–17 comprise Part 4 of this book and delve into the complexities of generating construction documentation of the designs you have already developed. Here you'll learn to annotate, tag, dimension, generate schedules and display themes, calculate areas, create floor and ceiling plans, project sections and elevations, and finally make details and keynotes.

Part 5 contains the final two chapters (18 and 19) that teach you effective ways to communicate your design both digitally and on paper. You'll learn how to make impressive photo-realistic renderings using VIZ Render, and the ins and outs of printing and publishing.

At the back of the book you'll find an Appendix that describes the stand-alone utility programs that accompany ADT.

System Requirements

This book assumes you already have a PC on which to run the software. The following are the recommended hardware and software requirements:

◆ Intel® Pentium® 4 or AMD-K7™ processor, 1.4 GHz or higher

◆ Microsoft® Windows® XP (Professional, Home Edition, or Tablet PC Edition, SP2 or later) or Windows 2000 Professional (SP4 or later)

◆ 1 GB RAM

◆ 650 MB free hard disk space and 75 MB swap space; 1.3 GB for full installation

◆ 1024×768 VGA video display

◆ Microsoft Internet Explorer 6.0 or later

◆ Modem or other connection to the Internet

◆ Sound card for multimedia learning

◆ TCP/IP or IPX support (required only for multiuser or floating license configurations)

What's on the Companion DVD

As mentioned earlier, you'll want to make sure that you've installed the sample files from the companion DVD that's included with this book. They are needed for many of the exercises that you'll encounter. You'll find installation instructions for the sample files on the DVD. In addition, you'll find a trial version of Autodesk Architectural Desktop 2006 provided on the companion DVD.

WARNING This book's companion disc is not playable on a consumer electronics DVD player connected to a television. Instead, use a peripheral device attached to your computer that can read DVDs.

How to Contact the Author

I appreciate your feedback on this book. Let me know if you have any quick questions or comments. You can contact me using a form on my website: ScottOnstott.com

Sybex strives to keep you supplied with the latest tools and information you need for your work. Please check their website at www.sybex.com for additional content and updates that supplement this book. Enter the book's ISBN—4429—in the Search box (or type **architectural desktop**), and click Go to get to the book's update page.

Part 1

Understanding Architectural Desktop

- ◆ Chapter 1: The Basics
- ◆ Chapter 2: Object Display
- ◆ Chapter 3: Object Styles

Chapter 1

The Basics

Your journey begins here! You'll start with a mini-history lesson to put Architectural Desktop (ADT) in context and then move on for a quick review of the AutoCAD skills that you'll need to work with ADT. You'll learn the character of working in ADT by taking a look at its basic features and learn how you might need to change your work style if coming from an AutoCAD background. Then you'll identify workspace components, tools, palettes, and catalogs. Later in this chapter you'll be introduced to architecture, engineering, and construction (AEC) options; templates; drawing setup; and user interface customization.

◆ In the Beginning There Was AutoCAD

◆ Basic ADT Features

◆ The ADT Workspace

◆ CAD/ADT Management

In the Beginning There Was AutoCAD

A little history is in order to place Architectural Desktop—ADT—in a wider context. Understanding the evolution of digital architectural tools will help you appreciate where computer-aided drafting (CAD) came from, what ADT can do today, and where architectural technology is heading in the future. You'll need to have some facility with AutoCAD before trying to learn ADT.

Autodesk released its first version of AutoCAD in the early 1980s. At that time, the focus was on making manual drafting more efficient by simulating geometric entities (such as lines, arcs, and circles). Digital tools initially mirrored the physical aspects of manual drafting. For example, layers simulated sheets of acetate that building systems were traditionally drawn on.

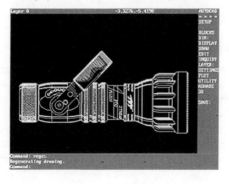

Design changes could theoretically be implemented much more quickly using AutoCAD, taking less time than on the old drawing board. Instead, much of the time to be supposedly saved was actually spent learning how to replace the pencil and triangle with a keyboard and mouse.

After a critical mass had learned how to use AutoCAD, new efficiencies were finally realized in the entire building industry. Those who were still drawing by hand were pressured to adopt CAD when their clients started specifically requesting electronic drawings. It took about a decade before CAD was adopted by almost everyone in the industry.

In the 1990s software developers realized that more could be done to advance digital tools beyond the simulation of traditional drafting. New data structures were invented to manage geometrical and nongeometric data such as blocks and attributes. External references (XRefs) split up the dataset to allow concurrent design input from multiple people. Geographical information systems (GIS) were built using all these new technologies. Three-dimensional (3D) modeling tools evolved to simulate surfaces and then solids. Around this time the acronym CAD came more to mean computer-aided *design*, showing that it had evolved beyond mundane computer-aided drafting.

AutoCAD has always been a generic product because it is used by a wide variety of industries. Its core functionality can be expanded with programming languages, and Autodesk's original intent was to open a market for third-party software developers to create custom tools as needed for each industry.

Many architects had CAD managers who would write AutoLISP routines or Visual Basic macros to automate tasks. As this customization market grew, many routines, menus, and macros were shared on the Internet, and more complex add-ons were and are available for sale by third parties and can be specifically created by consultants.

```
foreach n (eval (read "FF"))
    (setq b1 (tblsearch "block" n))
    (setq b2 (cdr (assoc -2 b1)))
    (setq b3 (entget b2))
    (setq ename (dxf -1 b3))
    (while (and ename (/= (dxf 0 (setq edata (entget ename))) "SEQEND"))
        (cond ((= (dxf 0 edata) "ATTDEF")
            (setq b4 (cdr (assoc 70 edata)))
            (setq b4 (rem b4 2))
            (cond ((= b4 0)
                (command ".insert" n "0,0" "1" "1" "0")
                (command ".zoom" "e")
                (setq check2 (ssget "L"))
                (if check2 (command ".explode" "l"))
                (setq check (ssget "P"))
                (if check (command ".block" n "0,0" "p" ""))
            ))
        ))
        (setq ename (entnext ename))
    )
)
```

Using CAD efficiently requires great discipline on the part of designers to adhere to standards and also requires enforcement by managers to maintain these standards. At this point, software developers found that increasing the efficiency of CAD required ever-greater programming effort for decreasing returns. Moving architectural technology forward required a fundamental change in thinking.

Building Information Modeling

At the end of the 20th century, software developers discovered that greater efficiencies could be realized with two strategies: keeping information digital and maintaining a single building model. Enter building information modeling (BIM). Autodesk's buzzword refers to an approach to building design, construction, and management, not a specific technology.

The concept of BIM springs from a deeper understanding of the digital medium and what software can ultimately do for the building industry. In the past, traditional drafting was replaced with CAD, and only now are we all realizing the greater potential of the digital medium.

The first half of BIM is the recognition that information is more efficiently utilized when stored, transmitted, and edited digitally. Each time drawings are printed out, an order of magnitude of efficiency is lost. In the past, designers would print out a digital drawing, mark it up, and enter the corrections (redlines) back into a digital form. This cycle usually repeats many more times with requests for information (RFI), change orders, and the generation of "as-built" plans. Printing out drawings made more sense when designers didn't themselves use CAD, but relied on CAD specialists to enter data. As designers adopted CAD directly, printing out drawings for every revision cycle became less viable.

Autodesk's DWF file format solves part of this problem by allowing digital redlines to be made and quickly integrated into the revised dataset (see Chapter 19, "Printing and Publishing"). Hand-held devices are used more frequently in the field, keeping information digital and lessening the need for printed drawings.

The other half of BIM is the single building model (SBM) concept, which is a single 3D model holding all the project data. All the deliverable 2D drawings are automatically generated from the SBM (see Figure 1.1). This concept has the potential to greatly increase coordination between drawings because they are all sourced from a single dataset.

FIGURE 1.1
Single building model

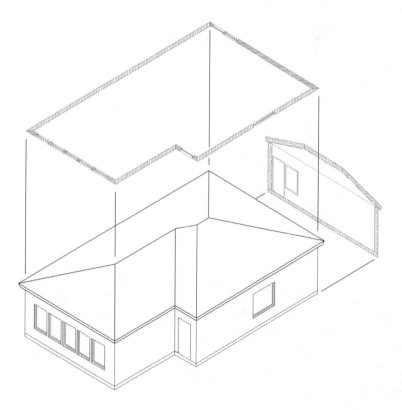

ADT implements the SBM concept by virtue of being based on *parametric objects* (also called *intelligent objects*). These digital objects can visually represent themselves differently in varying situations. Greater building complexity is more easily expressed when all the 2D drawings are generated automatically. Also, less time is spent doing repetitive drafting of the same geometric forms in plans, elevations, and sections.

In ADT, objects have extensive parameters built into them that allow schedules and inventories to be generated and areas to be automatically calculated. Construction documentation is streamlined because all the relevant data is already stored in the "smart" objects. ADT maintains links between plans, elevations, sections, details, schedules, sheet numbers, and annotation, making drawing coordination virtually automatic.

On the downside, many of ADT's connections are one-way links rather than live relationships. This is because ADT is based on AutoCAD, which was never intended to manage numerous interrelationships between geometric entities and their associated data. You have to be aware of how ADT works to ensure that changes are done in the right way to ensure coordination throughout the sheet set.

PARAMETRIC CHANGE MANAGEMENT TECHNOLOGY

Around the turn of the millennium, BIM was taken a step further with the development of Revit, which is fundamentally based on a relational database. This database-driven software maintains consistent interconnected relationships between all aspects of a building throughout its lifecycle. Revit integrates geometric data with complex behavioral models that allow objects to interact with different views, schedules, details, energy calculations, cost estimates, and much more. Changes made anywhere in Revit ("REVise IT") are certain to be coordinated everywhere.

Autodesk recognized that Revit was the future of BIM when it acquired the software. I see ADT as a bridging technology between AutoCAD and Revit. That said, it might take another decade before widespread adoption of parametric change management technology when people switch to Revit. Until then, ADT is getting more powerful and is in many ways becoming more like Revit.

On the plus side, ADT is built on AutoCAD, which means that it is more approachable if you've been using AutoCAD comfortably for years. Revit can be difficult to switch to because its different interface and way of working both require complete retraining from CAD.

Required AutoCAD Knowledge

Ideally, you should have some background using AutoCAD before learning ADT. Because ADT is based on AutoCAD, this book assumes you already know how to do basic drafting. If ADT is the first architectural program you are learning, I recommend studying AutoCAD first.

TIP See *Just Enough AutoCAD 2006* by George Omura (Sybex, 2005) for an excellent text on computer-aided design. Also check out ScottOnstott.com for computer video courses on AutoCAD.

You'll need to be quite familiar with basic drafting, not because you'll ever actually do any drafting after you learn ADT. Ironically, it is very rare to actually create geometric entities such as lines and circles in ADT. Instead, you'll use many of the same skills in new ways in ADT.

Architectural Desktop 2006 is based on AutoCAD 2006, so even veteran AutoCAD users will need to familiarize themselves with updates made to the basic drafting tools in the new AutoCAD release. In no particular order, here's a rundown of some of the most important skills and knowledge you will hopefully bring to the table from your AutoCAD experience:

Using Toolbars and Flyout Toolbars   Learn how to open hidden toolbars, and load and customize menus and keyboard shortcuts. You also need to know how to access hidden tools on flyout toolbars.

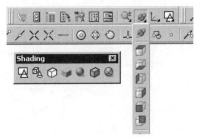

Polylines   Plines are used heavily in ADT, specifically the newer LWPolyline entity (the old style Polylines don't work in ADT). Review how to use the PEDIT command to join multiple line segments together and how to switch between straight line and arc segments.

Object Snaps   Good clean drafting comes from practicing for many hours drawing geometric entities with object snaps. Make sure that all your geometry snaps precisely together; accurate drafting is what CAD is all about, after all. This importance of this skill in AutoCAD and ADT cannot be overemphasized.

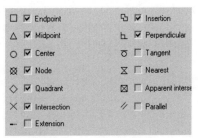

Polar and Object Tracking Modes   These drafting aids eliminate most reasons to draw temporary construction lines to layout geometry. Polar mode is more flexible than the old Ortho mode because many additional angles are involved. Understanding object tracking is essential for being a productive draftsperson.

Grip Editing   If you have shied away from using grips in previous versions of AutoCAD, now is the time to get into them; ADT makes extensive use of grips (see "Direct Editing" in the next section). Learn how to stretch, move, rotate, scale, and mirror entities using grips.

```
** STRETCH **
Specify stretch point or [Base point/Copy/Undo/eXit]:

** MOVE **
Specify move point or [Base point/Copy/Undo/eXit]:

** ROTATE **
Specify rotation angle or [Base point/Copy/Undo/Reference/eXit]:

** SCALE **
Specify scale factor or [Base point/Copy/Undo/Reference/eXit]:

** MIRROR **
Specify second point or [Base point/Copy/Undo/eXit]:
```

Blocks   Obviously blocks are an important part of AutoCAD. You'll need to know how to create, insert, redefine, and edit block references in-place.

Attributes   Attributes carry nongeometric data (often invisible) inside blocks. Learn how to create attribute definitions, encapsulate them in blocks, and edit attributed blocks. Extracting attribute data is not something you'll need because ADT does data extraction automatically.

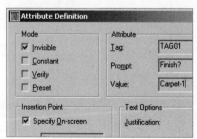

External References   You'll definitely need to understand how XRefs are manually attached, overlaid, detached, unloaded, and reloaded. Review how to edit XRefs in place as well.

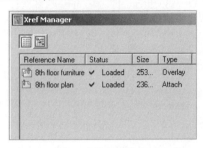

Paper Space Layouts   Understanding the relationships between model space, paper space, paper space layouts, floating viewports, and viewport scale is essential for preparing drawings for print in AutoCAD. Relatively new to AutoCAD are the maximize and minimize viewport commands (VPMAX and VPMIN) that you should review in the Help system. Review how to lock and unlock viewports and also how to use the Page Setup Manager.

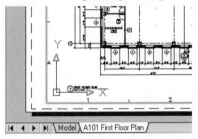

User Coordinate Systems   You'll need to understand and be able to manipulate user coordinate systems (UCS) in order to work with ADT 3D models.

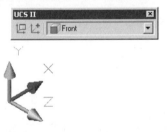

New!   There are numerous ease-of-use enhancements and new features in AutoCAD 2006. Because ADT is based on AutoCAD, the new AutoCAD features are integrated into ADT 2006. You'll want to review the new topics on your own in the AutoCAD Help that comes with ADT. Press F1 to access Help.

Basic ADT Features

Although ADT is built on AutoCAD, the way you'll end up working in ADT is quite different from how you might have worked in AutoCAD. If you've used AutoCAD for years, you might have to concentrate on changing old work styles, such as using the keyboard extensively. The topics in this section should give you a feel for the character of work in ADT.

Changing Your Work Style

Design is a process. ADT mirrors this process by enabling you to use one program to move from conceptual design, through design development, and on to documenting the design for construction. The best strategy is to start simply and progressively refine your ideas over time. ADT's intelligent objects are based on styles that offer parametric control at any stage of the design process.

This means that you can add a generic "wall" in the conceptual design phase without having to worry about what its final width and component structure will be. As the design progresses, you might change the wall's parameters many times without ever having to erase and redraw the wall. When the design starts coming together, you can add detail and documentation as required.

In AutoCAD, the command line is primary; most people are used to entering command names (or their abbreviations) on the keyboard. Many AutoCAD veterans have adopted a work style of keeping one hand on the mouse and the other on the keyboard. However, not everyone works this way; many people prefer using toolbars and menus, or some combination, to enter commands. In fact, some of the best things about the AutoCAD interface are all the numerous ways you can interact with the program.

Most of the commands in ADT have very long names that are not easily abbreviated (that is, WallToolToLinework, BldgElevationLineGenerate, or ApplyToolToObjects). If you try to abbreviate all the ADT commands and enter them on the keyboard you would be hopelessly confused with acronyms. Furthermore, there are too many commands in ADT, so it doesn't make sense to memorize their proper names as it does in AutoCAD.

```
Command: WallToolToLinework
Select lines, arcs, circles, or polylines to convert into walls:
```

Instead, you'll primarily interact in ADT by using tools and properties on palettes or by clicking an object and right-clicking to access its shortcut menu. The command line is still there and remains useful to see what is going on at the moment in ADT. But most of the options you select will be in dialog boxes, in palettes, or on-screen, rather than command line options as in old school AutoCAD.

Layers have a different role in ADT as compared with AutoCAD. You won't have to worry what layer objects are on for the most part in ADT because it's handled automatically. In AutoCAD, changing layer states is the main way to control object visibility. ADT has several of its own systems (in addition to layers) that manage object visibility. See Chapter 2, "Display Systems," for more on object display.

Instead of writing AutoLISP routines or including DIESEL macros in menus to create custom tools in AutoCAD, it is very easy to create custom tools in ADT without programming. Essentially all you have to do to create a custom tool is drag and drop an object to a palette and then customize the tool's properties. You'll learn how to store and access numerous custom tools in the Content Browser, which was designed for storing and sharing tools and palettes (see Chapter 3, "Object Styles").

ADT makes extensive use of styles to organize and control object parameters. This is quite different from AutoCAD, in which geometric entities stand alone and are not based on styles. You'll learn the intricacies of ADT's drawing default styles, style overrides, and object overrides in Chapter 3.

In AutoCAD, XRefs allow multiple people to work concurrently on a dataset. By splitting the entire dataset into smaller files, memory and computer resources are more efficiently utilized. XRefs are central to how project management works in ADT. The good news is that most of the mechanics behind managing XRefs is handled automatically by the Project Navigator in ADT (see Chapter 5, "Project Management").

Direct Editing

Much of the work you'll do with ADT objects will be done directly by editing objects with grips. In fact, you will rarely use basic AutoCAD modify tools when you see how intuitive direct editing is. ADT's grips are far more sophisticated than those in AutoCAD. Direct editing is the primary way to interact with objects in ADT.

GRIP COLORS

Change the default grip colors by choosing Format ➢ Options, thereby opening the Options dialog box. To control AutoCAD's entity grip colors, choose the Selection tab; control ADT's object grip colors using the AEC Editor tab (see Figure 1.2). Leave the default colors set as they are for now, but know where to find these settings should you need them.

GRIP SHAPES

Object grips have many different shapes that help identify their function. For example, a square grip means that you can edit it in two dimensions (by moving it in a plane). A triangular grip means that the range of motion is constrained to one dimension (along a line). Arrow grips are toggles that reverse an object's direction (such as flipping a door swing) when clicked. Figure 1.3 shows several different object grip shapes.

FIGURE 1.2
Grip colors in (left)
AutoCAD and
(right) ADT

FIGURE 1.3
Object grip shapes

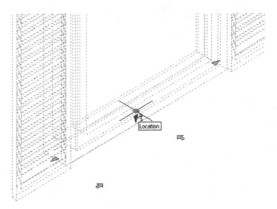

GRIP TIPS

Grip tips appear when you hover the mouse over any object grip. Depending on the type of object selected, grip tips might have multiple options that you can cycle through by pressing the Ctrl key. After selecting a grip with options, press the Ctrl key once and release it to toggle into the next editing mode. You might have to press the Ctrl key multiple times to access an option that is lower down in a grip tip list.

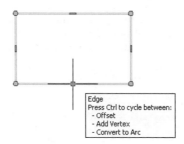

WARNING   Do not hold down the Ctrl key to choose a grip tip option.

TRIGGER GRIPS

Some types of objects have trigger grips that immediately perform an action when clicked. An example of this type of special grip is the round Edit In Place grip on Mass Groups that you'll learn about in Chapter 4, "Mass Modeling" (see Figure 1.4).

EDITING IN PLACE

After triggering an Edit In Place mode, you'll see a floating toolbar with tools specific to that mode (see Figure 1.5). Edit In Place activates a different set of grips on component objects, providing additional editing possibilities. Edit In Place modes are available for editing components in polyline-based and profile-based objects, as well as 3D body modifiers in walls and material surface hatches.

FIGURE 1.4
Edit In Place trigger grip

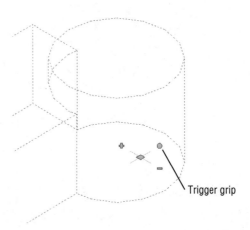

TEMPORARY UCS

Many objects have Height grips that automatically utilize a temporary UCS when clicked. You normally can't change the height of an object while working in an isometric viewpoint if you were working in a plan UCS. ADT streamlines this issue: The relevant grip can transparently alter the UCS as required to allow the desired edit. After the change is made, the UCS reverts to what it was before you made the edit. Pretty amazing stuff!

DYNAMIC DIMENSIONS

Grips that alter the dimensions of objects cause temporary dimensions that respond dynamically to appear. Unlike normal dimension objects, dynamic dimensions are temporary and cannot be used for documentation. Instead, they are used as aids in the design process to locate and size objects precisely, as shown on the Wall object in Figure 1.6. You'll learn how to use Wall objects in Chapter 8. For now, it is enough to be aware of how dynamic dimensions work; you'll get experience using them in Part 2 of this book.

There are three types of dynamic dimensions: noneditable, editable, and focal. The noneditable dimensions are for your information only and are displayed in gray. Editable dimensions are either displayed in a black or white box, automatically contrasting with the background color of the screen. Focal dimensions are displayed with highlighted editable text.

FIGURE 1.5
Editing in place

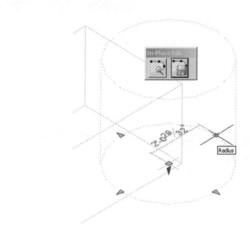

FIGURE 1.6
Dynamic dimensions

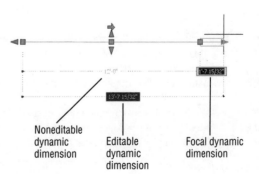

Noneditable dynamic dimension

Editable dynamic dimension

Focal dynamic dimension

Pressing the Tab key cycles through each editable dimension, giving one dynamic dimension focus at a time. To edit a focal dimension, simply start typing a value. Press Enter to input the property value and end the operation.

Dynamic dimensions eliminate the need to enter values on the command line. However, it is still possible to enter dimensions on the command line by turning dynamic input mode off by pressing its toggle button on the application status bar or by pressing F12.

TIP   Cycle backward through editable dynamic dimensions by pressing Shift+Tab.

New!   ### DYNAMIC INPUT

AutoCAD 2006 introduces dynamic input features, which provide a heads-up interface so you can focus more on the drawing window and less on the command line. Dynamic input features are similar to dynamic dimensions for ADT objects in how you see on-screen feedback, but dynamic input works on all AutoCAD commands. In addition, the new dynamic input system offers the dynamic prompt feature, which is activated by pressing the down arrow key whenever there are options on the command line.

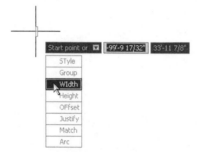

Drag and Drop, Right-Click, and the Clipboard

ADT's working style is more intuitive than classic AutoCAD, in which most commands are typed in on the command line. ADT expands the methods of user interaction by making heavy use of drag and drop, right-click shortcut menus, and the Windows Clipboard.

There are many instances in ADT where dragging and dropping objects, styles, tools, and palettes execute commands. For example, styles are loaded by dragging them into the drawing area from the Content Browser (see Chapter 3). The Project Navigator works primarily with a drag-and-drop interface (see Chapter 5). There are many more examples of this kind of interaction that you'll be learning in ADT.

The primary interface to objects is the *shortcut menu* (also known as the *context menu*). There are myriad kinds of shortcut menus in ADT that are opened by right-clicking. You'll get a different menu depending on what is selected, and where on the screen you right-click. When in doubt, right-click. Figure 1.7 shows a small part of the shortcut menu that is accessed by right-clicking when a wall is selected.

The Windows Clipboard is much more useful in ADT than it used to be because of the Paste to Original Coordinates, Copy with Base Point, and Paste as Block commands. Copying and pasting objects across drawings effectively replaces the old WBLOCK and INSERT commands from AutoCAD.

FIGURE 1.7
Right-click object menu

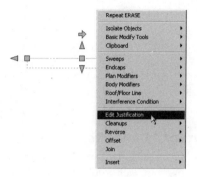

The ADT Workspace

A *workspace* is a set of user interface (UI) characteristics. You might want to change your workspace's layout, depending on what you're working on or according to your personal preferences and work style. You'll learn how to save a workspace layout in a user profile later in this section. But first, let's identify the many workspace components. It's important to learn the proper naming of components to be able to effectively communicate with other ADT users in your office, to communicate in discussion groups on the Internet, and to understand this book.

Figure 1.8 shows an overall view of the ADT workspace with many of its component parts labeled. These and additional components are described in the following sections.

FIGURE 1.8
The ADT Workspace

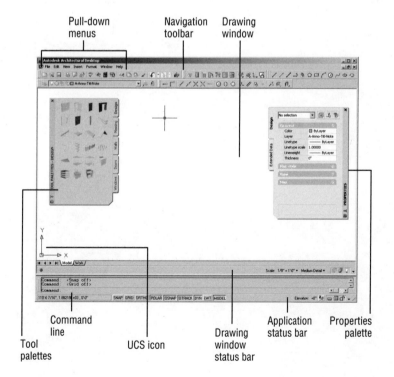

Windows Components

Almost all Windows programs have a title bar, pull-down menus, and a set of buttons to control minimizing, maximizing, and closing. Because ADT has a multiple document interface, it has two sets of Windows buttons to control both the application (on top) and the current drawing (below).

Figure 1.9 shows the Window menu open to its pull-down submenu. Use the options listed in this submenu to load and unload additional pull-downs for backward compatibility with earlier versions of ADT.

Toolbars and Dialog Boxes

ADT uses the same kinds of toolbars and dialog box interface elements as AutoCAD does. If you don't already know them well, you might want to review the proper names for these common components so you'll be aware of what I'll refer to in later chapters (see Figure 1.10).

Docked toolbars can be dragged by their handles and dropped as floating toolbars (or vice versa). The default workspace includes the Standard, Navigation, Layer Properties, and Shapes docked toolbars. Right-click on a blank part of the workspace adjacent to the toolbars to open the toolbar shortcut menu (just as in AutoCAD) to access additional toolbars.

TIP   Hold down the Ctrl key when dragging a floating toolbar or palette close to a workspace edge to avoid docking.

FIGURE 1.9
Standard Windows components

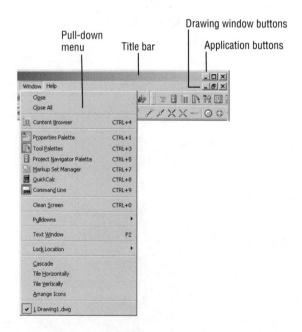

FIGURE 1.10

Common component names

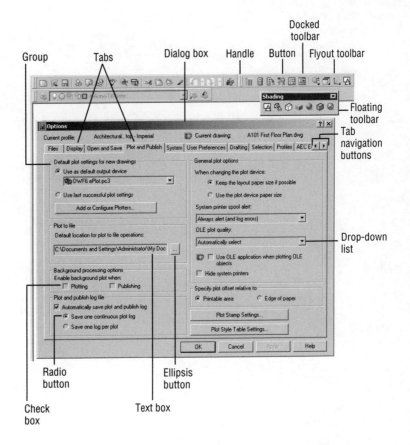

Shortcut Menus

As mentioned earlier, ADT makes heavy use of shortcut menus. Figure 1.11 is an amalgam of different common shortcut menus, but be aware that you'll only ever see one shortcut menu at a time when you right-click.

The application shortcut menu appears when you right-click in the drawing window without anything selected. Notice that the wall object shortcut menu contains most of the application shortcut menu items. Compare the two object shortcut menus and observe how the object-specific items are grouped in a similar way.

Application Status Bar

The application status bar has toggle buttons and settings (right-click a button to access) for many features that are constant across the entire drawing session (see Figure 1.12).

FIGURE 1.11

Shortcut menus from (left) the application, (center) a wall object, and (right) a door object

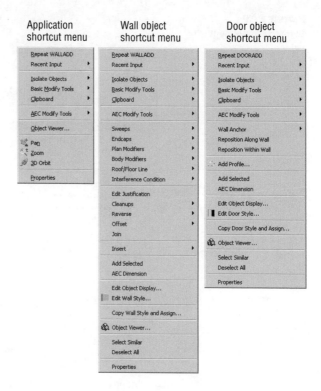

FIGURE 1.12

Application status bar features

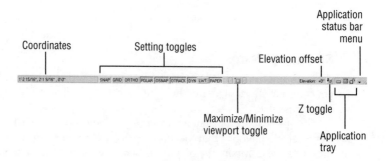

Many of the settings on the application status bar can also be toggled by pressing function keys (see Table 1.1).

The Maximize/Minimize viewport toggle is available only on layouts (see AutoCAD Help). The tray concept is a takeoff on the Windows system tray (on the right edge of the taskbar in Windows 2000 and XP where the clock is located). ADT has two trays; one managed by the application and one for the current drawing. The application tray might contain the communication center, drawing status bar toggle, clean screen mode toggle, and plot/publish details report features (see Figure 1.13). Not all these icons might be visible, depending on the options that are set.

FIGURE 1.13
Application tray icons

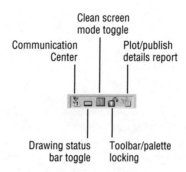

The Communication Center keeps you electronically connected with Autodesk and supplies general product and product support info, sends extension announcements (sorry, subscribers only), and tells you when articles and tips are available from Autodesk. This feature notifies you by displaying a balloon help message whenever something new is communicated. If you find it as annoying as I do, talk to your CAD manager and have it turned off.

TABLE 1.1: Function Keys and Their Effects

KEY	COMMAND
Esc	Cancel
F1	Help
F2	AutoCAD Text Window
F3	Object snap mode toggle
F4	Tablet input device toggle
F5	Cycle Isoplane
F6	Coordinate display toggle
F7	Grid toggle
F8	Ortho toggle
F9	Snap toggle
F10	Polar tracking toggle
F11	Object snap tracking toggle
F12	Dynamic input toggle

TIP See the Appendix, "Stand-Alone Utilities," to learn how to turn off the Communication Center feature using the CAD Manager Control Utility.

The drawing status bar toggle can be used to eliminate its namesake, merging the all the tray icons into one tray. The drawing status bar has some useful features (see the following), so I don't recommend that you ever toggle it off.

The clean screen mode toggle is useful when you're running short on screen real estate and want to eliminate clutter (at least temporarily); it hides all the toolbars and palettes, except for the Tool palettes. This feature is smart enough to remember all the positions and states of the toolbars and palettes and to restore them to their former glory when you toggle out of clean screen mode.

New!

Toolbar and palette locking is a new feature in ADT 2006. Right-click this icon to access its shortcut menu, in which you can lock and unlock floating and docked toolbars and/or palettes. It is convenient to be able to "freeze" your workspace layout after you are happy with its configuration.

The plot/publish details report icon appears when you need to debug plotting errors (see Chapter 19). Finally, the status bar menu options are along the extreme right edge of the application status bar. Click this arrow to open a shortcut menu that allows you to permanently remove toggles you never use and don't want to see again (I suggest removing the ancient Snap, Grid, and Ortho toggles).

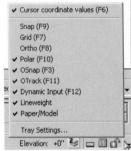

Drawing Window Status Bar

The drawing window status bar holds many controls and menus that are specific to the current drawing (see Figure 1.14). This bar isn't visible if you've toggled it off with the drawing status bar icon in the application status bar tray (refer to the preceding section); I recommend always leaving the drawing status bar on.

FIGURE 1.14
Drawing window status bar features

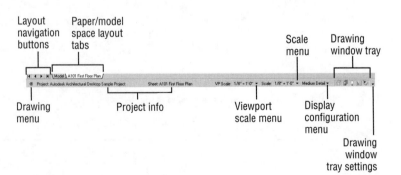

The paper space layout tabs and their navigation controls along the lower edge of the drawing window remain unchanged from AutoCAD. Just below this area you'll see the controls on the drawing window status bar. Starting on the left side, notice a small left-facing triangle inside a circle. This is the drawing menu that opens a shortcut menu when clicked. The drawing menu contains some frequently used commands.

Adjacent to the drawing menu you might see project information if the current drawing has been included in ADT's project management system (see Chapter 5). This read-only information identifies the project, drawing type, and name.

Moving to the right along the drawing status bar, you will see a VP Scale menu if you are in the floating model space of a viewport on a paper space layout. To the right of this menu another similar menu appears that controls annotation scale (labeled Scale). The Scale menu appears both in model and paper space. Figure 1.15 shows both scale menus.

FIGURE 1.15
Viewport and annotation scale menus

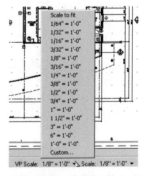

The last menu to the left of the tray is the display configuration menu. Notice that this menu is not labeled; it simply shows which display configuration is active. This menu is essential to managing ADT's display control system (see Chapter 2).

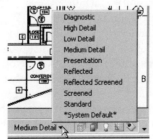

The drawing window tray is along the extreme right side of the drawing window status bar. Figure 1.16 identifies each of the tray's icons and the drawing window menu options arrow.

Each of the tray icons can be right-clicked to open each icon's shortcut menu. Surface hatches are part of material styles and are covered in Chapter 3. See Templates and Drawing Setup (following) for more information on Layer key overrides. Hiding and isolating objects is one of ADT's concurrent display systems (see Chapter 2).

FIGURE 1.16
Drawing window
tray icons

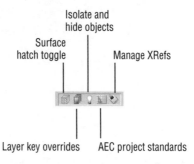

New!

AEC Project standards are a new feature in ADT 2006 (see Chapter 5). The AEC Project standards drawing tray icon can be used to configure or synchronize the drawing with project standards for each type of AEC object in ADT.

The Manage XRefs icon is an easy way to open the XRef Manager dialog box and is useful in project management (see Chapter 5). The tray settings open a menu that selects which features are available on the drawing window status bar. I recommend leaving all the drawing window tray features enabled.

Navigation Toolbar and Palette Access

The default ADT workspace is quite streamlined to reduce clutter and give you more screen real estate to work with. This streamlining is partly achieved through the Navigation toolbar, which encapsulates a great deal of content into a small area on-screen. The Navigation toolbar is docked in the default workspace along the top edge sandwiched between the Standard and Layer Properties toolbars. It's divided into two main areas: the left seven buttons open additional palettes and dialog boxes, and the right side contains four flyout toolbars (see Figure 1.17).

Hover your mouse over the buttons on the Navigation toolbar and notice the shortcut keys identified on each button's ToolTip. Five of the six navigation buttons can also be activated using Ctrl shortcut keys. Table 1.2 shows all the Ctrl+number shortcut keys. Note that some of the palettes listed in Table 1.2 are not on the Navigation toolbar; they are accessible only by pressing their Ctrl+number shortcut or from the pull-down menus. QuickCalc is also available from the Standard toolbar. Examine each one carefully. Notice that the Content Browser is not a palette but a separate task in Windows. You can run the Content Browser independently from ADT (it can also be used in VIZ Render; see Chapter 18, "Using VIZ Render").

FIGURE 1.17
Navigation toolbar

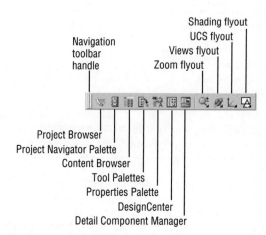

The Navigation toolbar also has a button for the Detail Component Manager, which doesn't have a shortcut key combination. You can also find the Detail Component Manager on the Insert pull-down menu. In a similar way, you'll find the Structural Member Catalog (see Chapter 7, "Parametric Layouts, Anchors, and Structural Members") on the Format menu, but not on any toolbar.

TABLE 1.2:   Ctrl+Number Shortcut Keys

COMMAND	SHORTCUT
Clean Screen	Ctrl+0
Properties palette	Ctrl+1
DesignCenter palette	Ctrl+2
Tool palettes	Ctrl+3
Content Browser	Ctrl+4
Project Navigator palette	Ctrl+5
DBConnect Manager palette	Ctrl+6
DWF Markup palette	Ctrl+7
QuickCalc palette	Ctrl+8
Command Line palette	Ctrl+9

Properties Palette

The Properties palette is second in importance after the Tool palettes (see Figure 1.18). The Properties palette starts displaying information after a tool is clicked while an object is in the process of being created. You can therefore alter the properties of an object before and after the actual object creation.

ADT Inherits New AutoCAD Palettes

Click the Calculator button on the Standard toolbar or type **QUICKCALC** on the command line to open AutoCAD's new palette-based calculator. The quick calculator does math with Imperial units and can be used transparently (while you're using another command). Handy unit conversions, scientific functions, and variable modes are included.

The Drawing Recovery Manager is another new palette that is helpful whenever ADT occasionally crashes and corrupts any of your files. Type **DRAWINGRECOVERY** to open this palette in ADT. Use it to track down and recover DWG, DWS, SV$, and/or BAK files from one convenient interface.

The Properties palette shows different information depending on what is selected. When you select multiple objects or entities, the Properties palette shows what all the members of the selection set have in common. For example, if you select two doors, you'll see more door-specific properties than if you select a door and a wall. The Properties palette is usually used to edit one object at a time.

Notice that there are two tabs along the edge of the Properties palette: Design and Extended Data. You'll be using the Design tab mostly; the Extended Data tab is used to manage hyperlinks, notes, reference documents, and property set data.

You can expand and collapse categories and subcategories by clicking their corresponding toggles. Likewise, many objects have illustrations that can be shown or hidden with a button in their subcategory. Illustrations show capital letters that correspond to specific labeled properties. Add-only properties appear only before an object is created and are identified with a starburst icon. Some properties might contain icons that open *worksheets*, which are dialog boxes containing information pertaining specifically to the selection.

NOTE   You won't find worksheets in pull-down menus because they are object-specific.

Resizing and Screen Real Estate

Almost every palette, dialog box, and worksheet can be resized by dragging its edges. As in most Windows programs, you can resize UI components when your cursor changes to any of a number of resize icons. Many headings, panes, and separator bars within dialog boxes and worksheets can be resized in an intuitive fashion.

After you resize a component, it will remain that way the next time you use it. Over time, you'll probably arrange and resize myriad components to your liking. The new toolbar and palette lock features (see the previous Application Status Bar topic) provide one level of protection for your tweaks made to the UI. See "Customizing the User Interface" later in this chapter for additional strategies.

ADT is really a screen hog with its numerous palettes and extremely large dialog boxes (such as the Display Manager and Style Manager that you'll learn about in Chapters 2 and 3). You can work with hidden and/or transparent palettes and resize components to your heart's content, but the best solution is to buy more screen real estate by using multiple monitors.

You can pick up a smaller CRT and used graphics card very affordably; in other words, screen real estate is becoming less expensive than it once was. A secondary monitor need not have much graphics power because it might be needed only for palettes and dialog boxes. Ideally, your primary monitor should maximize the size of the drawing window (and graphics power), and the secondary monitor(s) can hold ADT's numerous palettes and display large dialog boxes when needed.

FIGURE 1.18
Properties palette

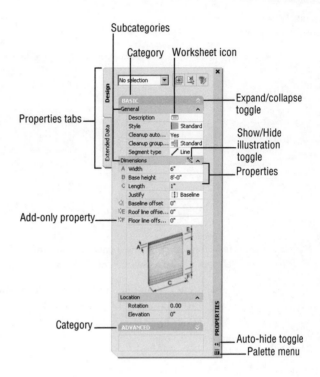

Subcategories

Category Worksheet icon

Properties tabs

Add-only property

Category

Expand/collapse toggle

Show/Hide illustration toggle

Properties

Auto-hide toggle
Palette menu

Tools, Tool Palettes, and Tool Palette Groups

The Tool palettes are accessible from the Navigation toolbar (or turn them on by pressing Ctrl+3 if they are not visible). Each one of the icons on the Tool palettes is called a *tool*. Tools are the primary way to create objects in ADT. Figure 1.19 identifies the main components of the Tool palettes.

Tools are like buttons on toolbars in that you click them to execute commands. Tools give you more visual feedback in comparison to toolbar buttons. The icons shown on tools are previews of the actual objects. You'll learn how to create custom tools, palettes, and palette groups in Chapter 3.

Tools are organized on palettes that are accessed by clicking the tabs along the edge of the Tool Palette interface. Multiple palettes are collected together into palette groups. Only one palette group is shown on the Tool palettes at a time. Figure 1.19 shows the Design palette group, which contains the Design, Massing, Walls, Doors, and Windows palettes. (You'll learn how to use the tools in the Design palette group in Parts 2 and 3 of this book.) Let's investigate how the Tool palettes work:

1. Click the Auto-hide toggle near the bottom of the Tool Palette title bar if the palettes are currently showing.

2. Move the mouse away from the Tool palettes and notice that they disappear after a few seconds. Only the title bar remains visible, so you have a place to hover the mouse to reopen the Tool palettes.

3. Toggle Auto-hide back off.

4. Click the palette properties menu button at the bottom of the Tool Palettes title bar.

FIGURE 1.19
Design palette group

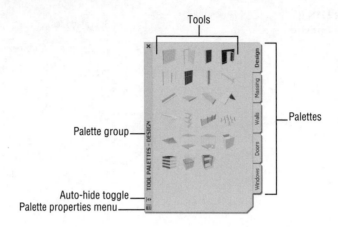

NOTE There are options to create new palettes and rename the palette group on the palette properties menu. Palettes are renamed by right-clicking the palette itself or the palette's tab.

5. Choose Transparency from the palette properties menu. Drag the slider to the middle of the range in the Transparency worksheet. Click OK.

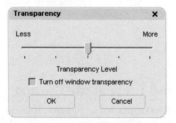

6. Open a sample drawing (it doesn't matter which drawing) and pan the drawing so it underlays the Tool palettes (see Figure 1.20). Notice that you partially see through the Tool palettes. Transparency is a feature available on most palettes, and the amount of transparency is maintained separately in each palette's properties menu.

FIGURE 1.20
Transparent palettes

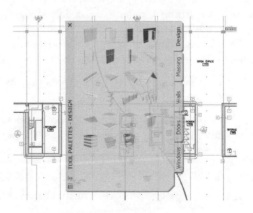

7. Open the palette properties menu and choose Transparency again to open the Transparency worksheet. Check Turn Off Window Transparency and click OK. This setting affects all palettes and turns off transparency globally.

8. Click the palette properties button again and choose Document from the bottom of the menu to swap palette groups.

9. Click each one of the palettes in the Document palette group: Annotation, Callouts, Scheduling, and Drafting (see Figure 1.21). You'll learn to use the tools on the Document palette group in Part 4 of this book. Notice the scrollbar that appears near the Tool Palettes title bar. Drag the scrollbar or roll the wheel on your mouse (if so equipped) to see all the tools on a palette.

TIP Right-click individual palettes' tabs to access a shortcut menu that allows the repositioning of palettes within a palette group.

The Annotation palette shows its tools in list view, displaying both a small icon and text in list format. You can change the way tools are displayed (and the icon size) separately on each palette by selecting View Options from the palette properties menu.

10. Click the palette properties button again and choose Detailing palette group. Investigate each palette in turn: Basic, Exterior, Roofing, Doors & Windows, Interiors, and Finishes (see Figure 1.22). You'll use the tools in this palette group in Chapter 17, "Details and Keynotes."

NOTE See Chapter 5 to see how to use the new project-specific palette group.

11. Change back to the Design palette group using the palette properties menu.

The aggregation of tools onto palettes and palettes into palette groups allows the Tool palettes to contain a large amount of content organized into an intuitive and efficient interface. This is good because tools are used for much more than the basic creation commands found in ADT.

FIGURE 1.21
Document palette group

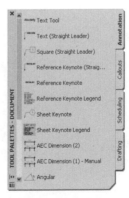

FIGURE 1.22
Detailing palette
group

You'll learn how to create tools for individual object styles in Chapter 3. You will probably end up working with hundreds of different tools in the course of a typical project. To handle the large number of tools and palettes, they are organized in catalogs that you access with the Content Browser. Let's see how this works:

1. Click the Content Browser button on the Navigation toolbar or press Ctrl+4. The Content Browser window appears (see Figure 1.23). Notice that a new task appeared on the Windows taskbar, indicating that the Content Browser is a separate process. This means you can run the Content Browser independently of ADT; content can be shared between ADT and VIZ Render by using the Content Browser as a go-between (see Chapter 18).

   The Content Browser's top-level catalogs are listed in Table 1.3.

2. Click the Preferences button to open the Content Browser Preferences dialog box (see Figure 1.24). Change the Library Name to **Catalog Library**. You could optionally name this with your company or personal name, for example. Click OK and notice that the title at the top of the Content Browser changed.

TIP Many of the catalogs are identified as Imperial or Metric, depending on the measurement systems installed. Right-click catalogs and delete them if you installed both measurement systems, but never plan to use one of them. It's good to simplify wherever possible to reduce screen clutter.

3. Click the Design Tool Catalog. Hover the mouse over Door and Windows in the navigation bar of the left. Click Doors.

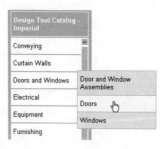

FIGURE 1.23
Content Browser

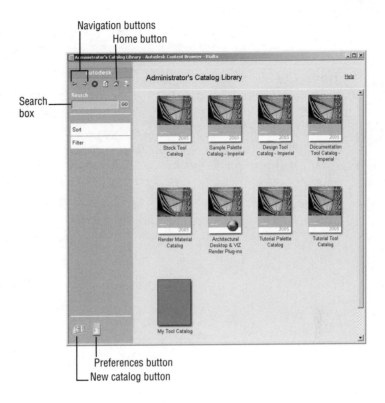

FIGURE 1.24
Content Browser
preferences

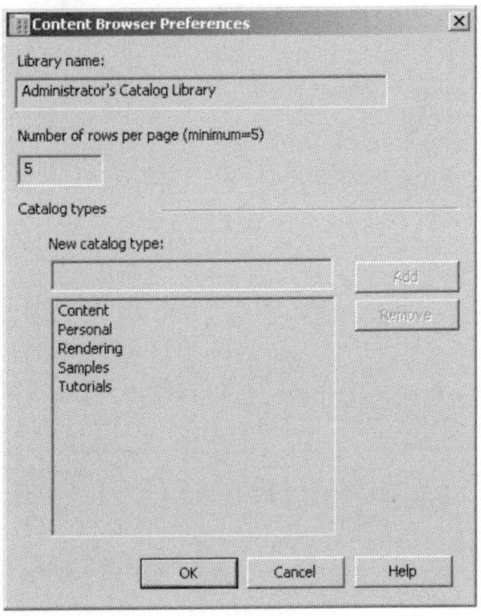

4. Browse through the five pages of door tools by clicking the navigation links at the bottom of the page (see Figure 1.25). Notice that each door tool has a preview of its object style and an *i-drop* icon that can be used to drag each tool into ADT (see Chapter 3).

NOTE Autodesk's proprietary i-drop technology seamlessly uses the Extensible Markup Language (XML) technology to insert content from the Web (or Content Browser) into ADT and/or your current drawing. See Chapter 19 to learn how to create custom i-drop-enabled web pages using the Publish To Web wizard.

5. Click the Home button in the Content Browser (refer to Figure 1.23) and investigate the other catalogs on your own. Close the Content Browser when done.

FIGURE 1.25
Tools available in the catalog

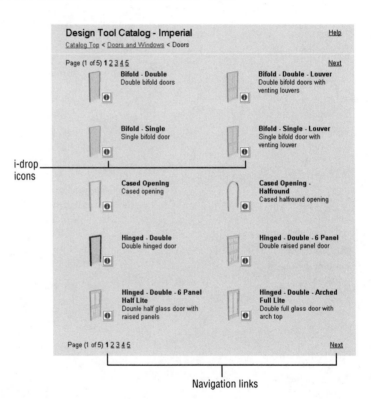

i-drop icons

Navigation links

TABLE 1.3: Tool and Palette Catalogs in Content Browser

CATALOG	CONTENT TYPE
Stock Tools	All standard tools
Sample Palettes	Factory-fresh palettes
Design Tools	Object styles and design content

TABLE 1.3:   Tool and Palette Catalogs in Content Browser *(CONTINUED)*

CATALOG	CONTENT TYPE
Documentation Tools	Documentation content
Render Materials	Material tools and palettes
Plug-Ins	Web links for ADT and VIZ Render
Tutorial Palettes	For ADT's built-in tutorial
Tutorial Tools	For ADT's built-in tutorial
My Tools	Blank catalog for custom tools

CAD/ADT Management

The role that a "CAD manager" plays is somewhat different in AutoCAD from the role played in ADT. (In fact, when using ADT, it's more appropriate to refer to an "ADT manager" than a "CAD manager," but I'll just call that person a manager from here on.) In AutoCAD, managers generally spend most of their time creating, documenting, and enforcing the use of company standards. It requires continued diligence on the part of designers to adhere to a company's standards. In the end, a manager often becomes a kind of police officer, charged with the enforcement of standards.

Thankfully, ADT 2006 can now enforce its own project standards, shifting the manager's role from police officer to tool fabricator. The manager ensures consistency by creating a project catalog with custom tools and palettes. Team members can then each link to a centrally stored project catalog using their Content Browsers, dragging out tools and palettes as needed. Any time the manager changes the tools or palettes, the new Project Standards feature can synchronize drawings with up-to-the-minute standards.

NOTE   Providing step-by-step procedures for managers goes beyond the scope of this book. Please refer to the ADT Help system for specific information.

In addition to creating project catalogs, the manager must also set AutoCAD and AEC options, populate templates, customize the UI, set up drawings, and configure project standards. All ADT users should generally understand these issues to ensure that work goes smoothly.

Options

The Options dialog box provides access to a plethora of settings, defaults, system variables, templates, file paths, printer drivers, databases, user profiles, and much more. Some options are stored in the current drawing, but most are stored in the system registry in a user profile. Before you change anything at all, it is best to create a new user profile. That way, if you make any undesired changes, you can roll back to the factory profile.

1. Choose Format ➤ Options to open the Options dialog box.

2. Click the Profiles tab. Notice which profile is current (displayed near the top of the Options dialog box). In my case, Architectural Desktop - Imperial is current (see Figure 1.26). Double-click this profile if it is not current. When you create a new profile, it will be based on the current profile.

FIGURE 1.26
Creating a user profile

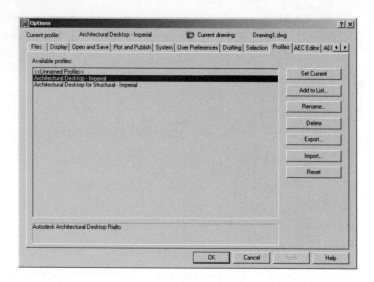

3. Click the Add to List button to open the Add Profile dialog box. Type **Custom ADT Profile** as the profile name and **My profile** as the Description. Click the Apply & Close button.

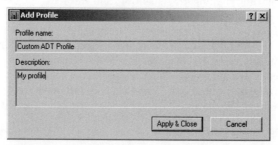

4. Set the new profile current. Do this by double-clicking Custom ADT Profile or by clicking its name and then clicking the Set Current button. Now you are set to make changes because they will be stored in the custom profile.

NOTE   You can export and import profile data stored in the system registry as .ARG files. The .ARG file is the mechanism to transfer profiles between machines.

5. Click the Display tab in the Options dialog box.

6. Click the Colors button in the Window Elements group to open the Color Options dialog box.

TIP   Contrary to longstanding AutoCAD practice, consider changing the model tab background to white in ADT. Many of ADT's colors look best against a white background.

7. Verify that the Window Element pop-up list is set to Model tab background and change the Color pop-up to White (see Figure 1.27). This book will use a white background for maximum readability in print. Click Apply & Close and then OK to close both dialog boxes.

FIGURE 1.27
Setting color options

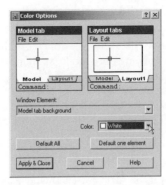

Now that you have created a new profile, you'll want to create a launch icon that references this profile. That way, whenever you launch ADT, you are sure to have your user profile current. You can create different launch icons for each profile. For example, you might have one launch icon for running ADT as AutoCAD and another that references a specific user profile within ADT. Let's create the latter:

1. Use the Windows Explorer to locate the ADT icon on the desktop.

2. Right-click the desktop shortcut and choose Properties.

3. Enter the following in the Target text box:

   ```
   "C:\Program Files\Autodesk Architectural Desktop 2006\acad.exe" /ld "C:\Program
   Files\Common Files\Autodesk Shared\AecBase47.dbx" /p "Custom ADT Profile"
   ```

4. Enter the following in the Start In text box:

   ```
   "C:\Program Files\Autodesk Architectural Desktop 2006\UserDataCache\"
   ```

5. Click Apply and OK (see Figure 1.28).

FIGURE 1.28
Customizing ADT
launch icon

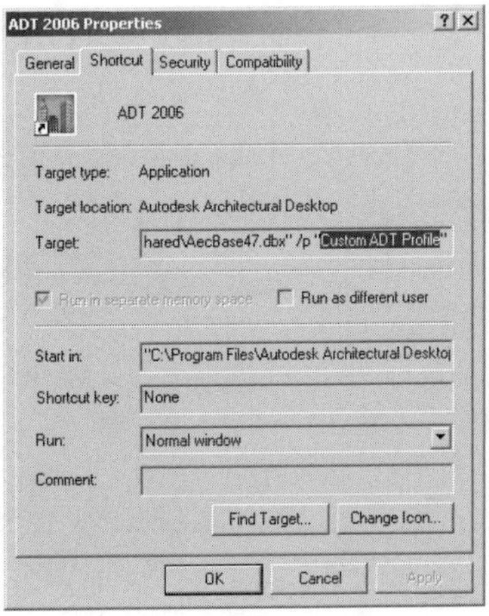

Templates and Drawing Setup

Template files contain settings used to create new drawings with the same settings. ADT uses multiple template files for different types of files in the project management system (see Chapter 5). Template files contain drawing units, scale, annotation plot size, display configurations, layouts, and drawing-specific options.

In general, templates no longer contain object styles as they once did in early versions of ADT. The template file locations are managed in the Options dialog box on the Files and AEC Project Defaults tabs. The default template file location on a single machine installation is in the following folder:

```
C:\Documents and Settings\All Users\Application Data\Autodesk\ADT 2006\enu\Template
```

TIP Managers on ADT projects should change template locations to a centralized folder on a file server to maintain a single set of templates.

To see how templates work, let's make a few changes to ADT's default template file.

1. Choose File ➢ Open to open the Select File dialog box. Change the Files Of Type pop-up to Drawing Template (*.dwt) (see Figure 1.29).

2. Open the file called Aec Model (Imperial Stb).dwt; the name indicates that this is a model space template using Imperial units and named plot styles.

3. Toggle off Grid and Ortho on the application status bar. You will remove these outdated functions from your interface.

4. Open the application status bar menu, and uncheck Grid and Ortho, one at a time. These toggles disappear from the application status bar, making a slightly more simplified UI.

NOTE Application status bar toggles' visibility is stored in the registry, not in a template. It makes sense to address these basic setup issues when you are in a template, however.

FIGURE 1.29
Opening template file

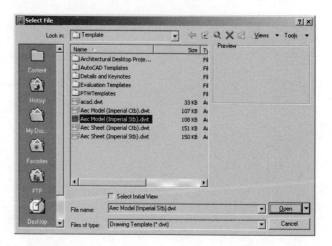

5. From the menu bar, choose Format ➢ Drawing Setup to open the Drawing Setup dialog box (see Figure 1.30).

6. On the Units tab, verify that the Drawing Units are set to Inches. Change the Precision pop-up in the Length group to $1/16''$.

WARNING This book uses Imperial units. If you use Metric units, please consider changing your units temporarily to maintain consistency with the tutorials.

7. Click the Scale tab and verify that $1/8''=1'-0''$ is the default scale. Change the annotation plot size to $1/8''$.

8. Click the Layering tab and verify that AECLayerStd.dwg is selected as the Layer Standards/ Key File to Auto-Import and that AIA (256 Color) is selected in the Layer Key Style pop-up. Check the "Always import Layer Key Style when first used in drawing" box. This setting is essential to maintain layer consistency in legacy drawings.

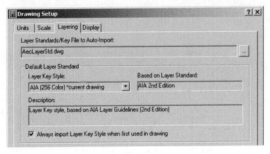

NOTE Layers are not stored in templates in ADT. Instead, layers are auto-created as needed according to the layer key defined in the Layer Standards/Key File.

FIGURE 1.30
Drawing Setup
dialog box

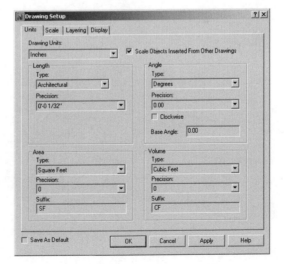

9. Before you save the template, you might want to make a backup copy of the original template file for safekeeping. Check Save As Default at the bottom of the Drawing Setup dialog box and click OK to close. If you are working in a networked environment and do not have write access to the template directory, save your altered template in another folder.

10. Be careful not to create any objects while working in the template file (or else their styles would become part of the template). Save and close the template.

Customizing the User Interface

New!

The UI customization system has been overhauled in ADT 2006. Now ADT uses an XML-based system that integrates most customization possibilities into a single interface in which you can control workspaces, toolbars, pull-down menus, shortcut menus, keyboard shortcuts, mouse buttons, LISP files, tablet menus, screen menus, and image tile menus. Figure 1.31 illustrates this new interface.

Before ADT 2006, you could customize the UI only by manually editing files such as menu MNU or MNS files in an ASCII text editor. This system was tedious and difficult to debug because any misplaced characters in the text files could invalidate the entire menu. In addition, there was a separate interface for editing toolbars and buttons.

FIGURE 1.31

Customize User
Interface dialog box

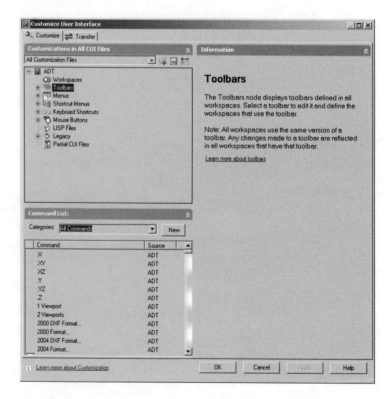

In ADT 2006 the new Customize User Interface dialog box greatly simplifies the process by integrating all forms of customization into one dialog box. You can drag commands from the Command List and drop them into toolbars, menus, and shortcut menus with the corresponding nodes in the dialog box's tree view. Any errors that occur are caught within the interface, and you are prompted to fix them without invalidating any menus.

All your customizations are saved in a single XML-based `.cui` file. The XML format is backward compatible—the customizations you make in ADT 2006 can be transferred to older versions of the software by using the Customize User Interface dialog box's Transfer tab. Managers should read the AutoCAD documentation on Customizing the User Interface to plan customization strategies for the entire enterprise.

Summary

In this chapter you learned about ADT's place in the progression of architectural software from CAD to BIM. You were exposed to topics you might need to review from AutoCAD before diving deeper into ADT. Also, you became acquainted with ADT's unique work style learning—the intuitive nature and the intricacies of direct editing.

Hopefully you also learned the jargon to properly identify ADT's interface components so you'll understand my references in subsequent chapters. Finally, this chapter touched on management options, templates, and customization issues. In Chapter 2 you'll learn the complexities of the object display system.

Chapter 2

Display Systems

As you learned in Chapter 1, "The Basics," ADT (Architectural Desktop) is based on the single building model concept whereby objects are drawn once per project. ADT's object display system makes this possible by allowing objects to be represented differently in each required view. You'll learn how the display system works by studying the relationships between its representations, sets, configurations, and viewpoints.

Layers offer another level of display control combined with ADT's object display system. This chapter reveals how layers play a different role in ADT compared with AutoCAD. Here you'll learn how to use a layer standard that keys objects to layers automatically. In addition, you'll analyze many tools that manage layers, including filters, key overrides, and snapshots.

You'll explore additional display controls that go beyond what the object display system and layers have to offer. In particular, you'll edit in view, isolate objects, use the Object Viewer, and more. This chapter's topics include

◆ Understanding the Object Display System

◆ Displaying with Layers

◆ Additional Display Controls

Understanding the Object Display System

ADT's object display system is both wonderful and *amazingly* complex. It's wonderful because of how much descriptive power the system has, as you'll be seeing later in this section. The display system's complexity will probably be overwhelming at first; stick with it and you'll be able to appreciate and understand the genius behind its logic.

The single building model (SBM) concept at the core of Autodesk's much-hyped building information modeling (BIM) approach (refer to Chapter 1) requires that the entire building model consist of one—and only one—dataset. This means that the floor plans, reflected ceiling plans, elevations, sections, 3D geometry, and much more must be stored in one "model." The thinking behind this is that if everything could be stored once, it would eliminate the coordination errors so common in architectural drawing sets.

NOTE   The single building model is not stored in one file. Chapter 5, "Project Management," discusses the way the Project Navigator manages the relationships between all the files in a project dataset.

In the old way of thinking (computer-aided design), the requirement for the building model to consist of one dataset is virtually impossible. In AutoCAD, 3D geometry is separate from the 2D linework used to generate plans, elevations, and sections. Although you can certainly model 3D geometry in AutoCAD, having to also include all the necessary linework, dimensions, and layers in a single building model would be an organizational nightmare. Furthermore, design changes could not be automatically coordinated between 2D and 3D geometry, making the single building model strategy unworkable in AutoCAD.

ADT's display system evolved out of the desire to represent the same objects differently in varying contexts. For example, if a door could at the same time be represented differently in plan, elevation, and in a 3D model, all three representations of the door could be stored in the same "AEC object" (see Figure 2.1).

NOTE This book refers to the proper name *AEC object* simply as *object*. AEC stands for the architecture, engineering, and construction disciplines of the building industry.

ADT's object display system does what it advertises; it displays objects differently in a variety of contexts. This eliminates the need for duplication of entities in different drawings; the data objects therefore become more like the real-world objects that we experience. A door is placed once in the model and displayed in as many different ways as needs dictate.

FIGURE 2.1
Different representations of the same object

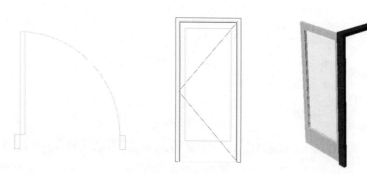

Using Display Configurations

The object display system is based on hierarchical relationships. At the top of this hierarchy is the primary means of interacting with the object display system by changing display configurations and viewpoints.

NOTE You'll work upward from the bottom of the object display system hierarchy in the section "Exploring the Display Manager," later in this chapter.

Let's first take a look at display configurations by exploring a sample file.

1. Open Floor Plan.dwg from this chapter's folder on the companion DVD (see Figure 2.2).

FIGURE 2.2

Floor plan sample file

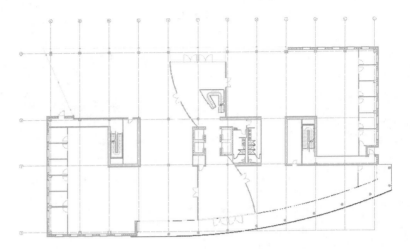

2. Click the Layer Properties Manager button on the Layer Properties toolbar, or type **LAYER** on the command line and press Enter. Take a look at the Layer Manager dialog box and get a general sense for how many layers there are, and which layers are off and frozen. Don't worry about memorizing the layer properties perfectly (you can refer to Figure 2.3).

NOTE   You'll learn more about the Layer Manager later in this chapter.

FIGURE 2.3

Layer Manager

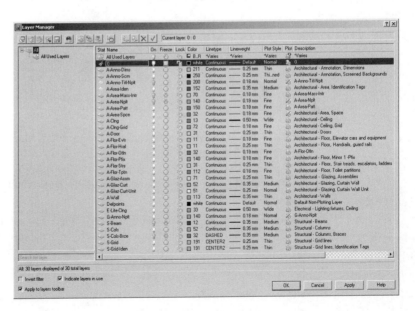

3. Open the display configuration menu on the drawing status bar (refer to Chapter 1). Notice that it is currently set to Medium Detail.

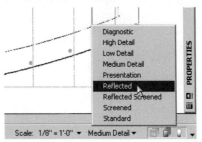

4. Select the Reflected display configuration. After waiting a few moments, you'll see a markedly different picture in the drawing window as the reflected ceiling representations of the objects are displayed (see Figure 2.4). Notice that only one display configuration is active at any time.

5. Reopen the Layer Manager and examine the layer properties again. Notice that they are identical to those in Figure 2.3.

None of the layer properties was changed, yet the floor plan changed into a reflected ceiling plan. Comparing the layer properties before and after you changed the display configuration reveals a very important fact: The object display system works independently of layers. Let's check out some additional display configurations.

1. Open the display configuration menu on the drawing status bar.

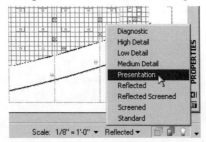

2. Set Presentation as the current display configuration. After a few moments you'll see a drawing dominated by large solid-filled spaces (see Figure 2.5). This configuration is intended for general-purpose plan review, presentation, and marketing. In this display configuration, the walls are filled with solid poché, and none of the wall's internal components is visible, greatly simplifying the display.

3. Set Low Detail as the current display configuration. The solid-filled spaces disappear and the walls display only their boundaries without any internal components (see Figure 2.6). This level of detail is appropriate for site plans or other small-scale drawings ($1/16''=1'\text{-}0''$, for example).

4. Zoom in closer to the elevator core to get a closer look at the objects.

5. Set High Detail as the current display configuration (see Figure 2.7). Notice the additional wall components and hatch patterns that appear, giving this drawing a high level of detail. This display configuration is appropriate for enlarged plans and details at $1/4''=1'\text{-}0''$ or higher scales.

FIGURE 2.4
Reflected display
configuration

FIGURE 2.5
Presentation display
configuration

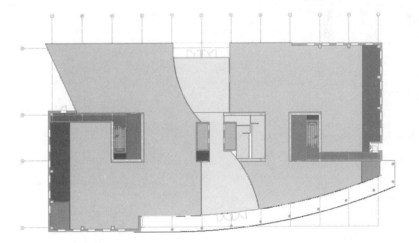

6. Try out all the display configurations on your own while zoomed in closely to the building core. Pay special attention to the differences between the three levels of detail in the template's display configurations.

7. Close the sample file without saving (you will return to it later).

The object display system is completely customizable. It is worthwhile to make your own display configurations that better suit your office standards and working style.

FIGURE 2.6
Low Detail display
configuration

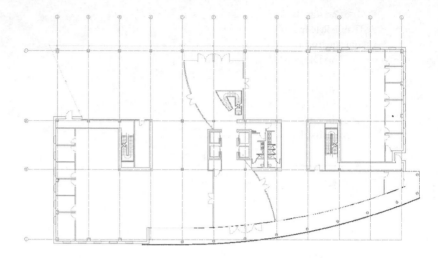

FIGURE 2.7
High Detail display
configuration

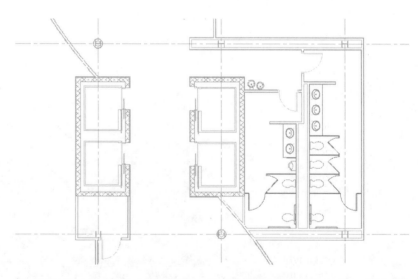

All the display configurations you've been using so far are defined in default templates that ship
with ADT. After you read this entire book, you'll be in a position to make intelligent alterations to the
templates to suit your specific needs. Until then, my advice is to definitely stick with the default templates. The object display system is so intertwined with everything else in ADT that you can't safely
alter templates until you have a full understanding of how ADT works.

TIP See "Templates and Drawing Setup" in Chapter 1. Also see "Establishing Project Standards" in
Chapter 5 for specifying project display settings with a standard drawing.

The `Aec Model (Imperial Stb).dwt` template defines eight display configurations, as shown in Table 2.1. In addition, there will always be a Standard display configuration because, like layer 0, it is required for ADT to function.

The Diagnostic display configuration is designed to help you troubleshoot wall cleanup (see Chapter 8, "Walls") and is not intended for printing. The Reflected Screened and Screened display configurations both display objects using screened plot styles that print with less than full ink intensity. Screened plans, which help to visually differentiate objects and focus attention in directed areas, are often used on the background plan on engineering drawings. The Standard Detail and Medium Detail display configurations are identical by default.

TABLE 2.1:   Default Display Configurations

CONFIGURATION	DESCRIPTION
Diagnostic	Used for analysis and troubleshooting (not for printing)
High Detail	Plans, models, and details (in $1/4$" scale or larger)
Low Detail	Site plans and models (in $1/16$" scale or smaller)
Medium Detail	Typical drawings (in $1/8$" scale)
Presentation	Solid-filled presentation plans
Reflected	Typical ceiling plans
Reflected Screened	Ceiling plans with low ink intensity
Screened	Plans with low ink intensity
Standard	Default display configuration

Changing Viewpoints

You have seen how changing display configurations alters the display, but that doesn't explain how objects might display differently in varying orientations. Changing your *viewpoint* (also called *view direction*) automatically affects the object display system. To see how this works, let's investigate another example.

1. Open `Viewpoints.dwg` from the Chapter 2 folder on the companion DVD (see Figure 2.8). Notice that the file opens in the Top view with the Medium Detail display configuration active, the most typical combination for a floor plan.

2. Right-click a blank portion of any toolbar and open the shortcut menu. Choose Views to display the toolbar (see Figure 2.9).

FIGURE 2.8
Viewpoints sample file
shown in the Top view
using Medium Detail
display configuration

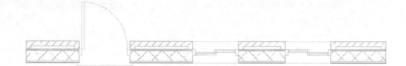

FIGURE 2.9
Views toolbar

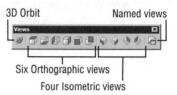

3D Orbit   Named views

Six Orthographic views

Four Isometric views

TIP   Try to develop a habit of using the Views flyout menu on the Navigation toolbar instead of the Views toolbar. The buttons are identical in both cases, but flyout menus take much less screen real estate. The Views toolbar is used in the illustration for clarity.

3. Click the Front orthographic view button. When the viewpoint changes, the objects are represented differently (see Figure 2.10).

NOTE   The user coordinate system (UCS) automatically follows the view so that you can work appropriately in every viewpoint.

4. Click the NW Isometric button. Open the Shading flyout on the Navigation menu (see Chapter 1) and choose the Hidden button. Figure 2.11 shows a hidden-line isometric viewpoint. Notice that the objects are now represented by 3D geometry. Surface hatching appears on the brick side of the wall.

NOTE   Surface hatching is controlled by material definitions (see Chapter 3, "Object Styles").

5. Right-click the surface hatch toggle in the drawing status bar tray. Choose Off from its shortcut menu. The brick surface hatch pattern disappears from the wall.

The surface hatch toggle is useful, especially when you are working with complex drawings. Surface hatching can take a long time to display, so it's helpful to be able to toggle it off while you're working and changing viewpoints.

FIGURE 2.10
Front view displays
an elevation

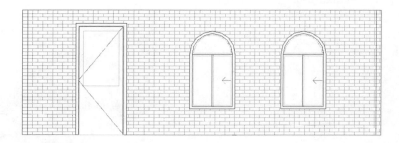

FIGURE 2.11
Isometric viewpoint dis-
plays 3D geometry

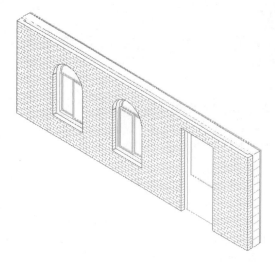

6. Choose Flat Shaded from the Shading flyout on the Navigation toolbar. The brick component of the wall is represented by a much more realistic shaded version (see Figure 2.12). The
shaded version displays render materials, which are also controlled by material definitions
(see Chapter 3).

7. Investigate each of the remaining preset orthogonal and isometric viewpoints. Use 3D Orbit to
arc rotate the model manually to oblique viewpoints. Notice that every isometric and oblique
viewpoint displays the model with 3D geometry. The bottom viewpoint shows a diagnostic
representation.

8. Switch back to the Top viewpoint, choose 2D Wireframe shading mode, and close the views
toolbar. Set the display configuration to Medium Detail.

FIGURE 2.12
Flat Shaded view
displays render
materials

Working Within Viewports

Now you are aware that changing the display configuration and/or changing your viewpoint alters what the object display system shows in model space. Taking it a step further, let's examine what happens in paper space.

1. Open Floor Plan.dwg from this chapter's folder on the companion DVD.

2. Click the Layout1 tab at the bottom of the drawing window (see Figure 2.13). Layout 1 has four viewports. The lower-right viewport is in $1/2''$=1'-0'' scale, whereas the others are in $1/16''$=1'-0'' scale.

FIGURE 2.13
Paper space layout

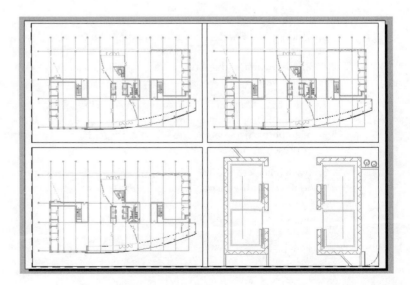

3. Double-click inside the upper-left viewport to switch into floating model space. Change the display configuration to Presentation. In a few moments you'll notice that only the active viewport's display changes.

4. Click inside the lower-left viewport and change its display configuration to Reflected.

5. Activate the upper-right viewport and change its viewpoint to NW Isometric. Change its shading mode to Hidden. It might take some time for ADT to make calculations and update the viewport.

6. Click inside the lower-right viewport and change its display configuration to High Detail. Figure 2.14 shows the results.

Each viewport holds its own display settings. Figure 2.14 shows many different representations of the same objects. The object display system enables content to be stored independently of representation.

7. Click the Model tab to exit the paper space layout and leave the file open for the next section.

FIGURE 2.14
Four viewports
showing different
display configurations
and viewpoints

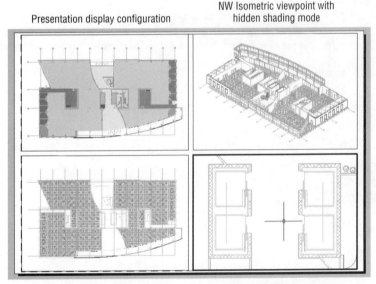

Presentation display configuration

NW Isometric viewpoint with
hidden shading mode

Reflected display configuration

Large-scale floor plan with
High Detail display configuration

Objects versus Entities

Objects (technically called *AEC objects*) are "intelligent" because they can display themselves differently according to varying needs. You have seen how the same objects can be shown in many different ways at the same time. This fact makes much of coordination between traditional drawings automatic because objects "know" how to display themselves consistently in all situations. You'll learn to customize the way objects are displayed in the next section.

Basic geometry such as lines, polylines, arcs, circles, ellipses, and splines are called *entities*. Entities are straightforward and as simple to use in ADT as they are in AutoCAD. Perhaps quite surprisingly, you'll discover that it is quite rare to use entities in ADT, with the exception of the occasional polyline. This is because entities have a different relationship to the object display system. Let's take a look.

1. If you left the sample file open from the last section, you can continue here. If not, open Floor Plan.dwg from this chapter's folder on the companion DVD.

2. Pan the floor plan over a bit in model space until you see some blank drawing area.

3. Draw a few entities off to the side—a circle, a polyline, and a spline. Do not worry about the size or location to draw the entities; they are intended only as an example.

4. Change the display configuration to Reflected.

5. Change the viewpoint to Bottom and then NW Isometric (see Figure 2.15). Notice how the entities are displayed each time. Change to the Top viewpoint and set the display configuration to Medium Detail.

6. Save and leave the sample file open for the next section.

No matter which display configuration you choose or which viewpoint you look at the entities from, they will be displayed in the same way. Entities are not affected by the object display system. Entity display is controlled by layers, and objects are as well (see the section "Displaying with Layers").

FIGURE 2.15

Entities shown in different viewpoints and display configurations

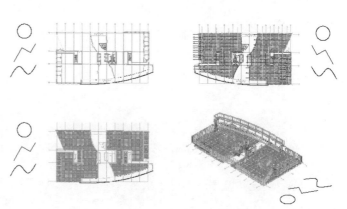

Exploring the Display Manager

The Display Manager is the control center for the object display system. It manages the hierarchical relationships that comprise the object display system. You started at the top of this hierarchy earlier by choosing the current display configuration and view direction for each viewport. Let's open the Display Manager.

1. If you left sample files open from the last sections, you can continue here. If not, open Viewpoints.dwg and Floor Plan.dwg from the Chapter 2 folder on the companion DVD.

2. Choose Format ➤ Display Manager to open a dialog box of the same name (see Figure 2.16). Leave this dialog box open.

The Display Manager is divided into the hierarchical (or tree) pane on the left side and the content pane on the right. You can drag the dividing bar to locate where the dialog box is divided. The content pane shows information according to which node in the tree pane is selected.

The tree pane shows nodes for each open drawing. You will also see a standard drawing node if the current drawing is part of a project (see Chapter 5). Each drawing has three folders that correspond to the hierarchy of the object display system: Configurations, Sets, and Representations By Object.

NOTE   Notice the floating object viewer in the bottom-left corner of the Display Manager. You will learn more about this later on.

Now let's take a look the bottom of the hierarchy, with the goal of understanding the basis of the entire object display system. You'll build on that knowledge and eventually arrive where we started—with a discussion of display configurations.

FIGURE 2.16
Display Manager
dialog box

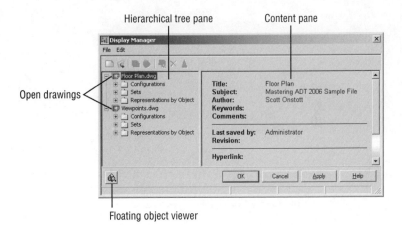

REPRESENTATIONS BY OBJECT

Objects can be graphically represented in many different ways (plan, elevation, model, and more). Each one of these "ways" is managed by a *display representation* in ADT. Most objects have multiple representations that each control the way an object is drawn in a specific situation. Only a few objects have single representations, causing them to appear the same in every view.

Objects are made of components. For example, a door object has component parts, including a frame, swing, and the door panel itself (plus many others). Representations manage the display properties of the object components. Let's take a look:

1. Expand `Viewpoints.dwg` and the Representation By Object nodes in the tree pane within the Display Manager. You'll see a long listing of all the object types in ADT.

2. Scroll down if necessary and expand the Door node in the tree pane. An indented list of its display representations appears below.

3. Click the Door's Plan representation node in the tree pane. Notice that there are two display properties tabs appearing at the top of the content pane. Verify that the Layer/Color/Linetype tab is selected (see Figure 2.17).

FIGURE 2.17
Display representations
by object

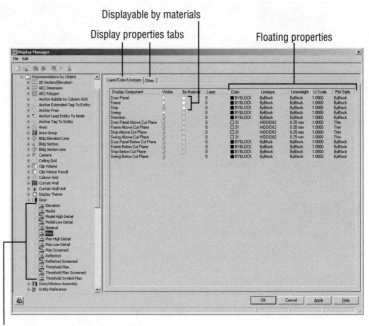

Displayable by materials

Display properties tabs

Floating properties

Representations for the door object

4. Set the Door Panel's By Material check box. After the check mark is placed, notice that the Door Panel's display properties are grayed-out. It is not possible to assign materials to those components that have gray check boxes.

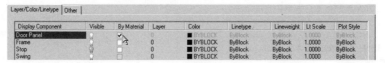

The Layer/Color/Linetype tab is really an abbreviation of all the display properties available, which include visibility, displayable by material setting, layer, color, linetype, lineweight, linetype scale, and named plot style. You'll manage many of the same display properties in the "Displaying with Layers" section.

NOTE All the display properties in the Display Manager work concurrently with those in the Layer Manager.

Display properties can either be assigned to an object directly in a representation or by material definition styles instead. The check box interface should tip you off that this is an either/or decision (see Chapter 3). When materials are assigned, they determine the appearance of an object.

Some of the components have specific display properties assigned such as color 31, HIDDEN2 linetype, 0.25mm lineweight, and others. Notice that many components are assigned *floating properties*. Floating properties are not assigned directly, but are inherited either ByLayer or ByBlock.

UNDERSTANDING FLOATING PROPERTIES (BYLAYER AND BYBLOCK)

Floating properties have been around almost as long as AutoCAD, yet they are often misunderstood. Floating properties were originally designed to work with the geometry of block definitions, but they work much the same for object components in ADT. Object components cannot exist on their own by being exploded like blocks, however.

If you want a block or object to inherit properties from the parent object's layer (such as layer, color, line-weight, linetype, and/or named plot style), create its components on layer 0 (zero) and set the component properties to ByLayer. If you want the component to inherit properties from a specific layer other than that of the parent object, create the components on that layer and set the component properties to ByLayer.

If you want a block or object to inherit properties from the parent object, create its components on any layer (0 is usually best), but set the component properties to ByBlock. If the parent object's properties are set to ByLayer, the component will inherit the properties from the parent object's layer. If the parent object has any properties set directly, the component will inherit them. In other words, the ByBlock setting does everything that ByLayer does and more; ByBlock also enables property overrides to be inherited.

Most object components are usually set to ByBlock unless they are directly specified.

Changes made to representations in the Display Manager affect only the default display properties of objects. You'll learn in Chapter 3 how it is possible for a style or even a specific object to override these properties. Let's take a look at some of the other representations in the Display Manager.

1. Click the Door's elevation representation in the tree pane. Look very closely at the representation icons and notice the differences. Some of the icons in Figure 2.18 show an arrow; others show a (red) square. The icons with arrows are custom representations, and the others are predefined.

   Predefined representations are permanent and are a basic part of ADT; custom representations are almost always defined in a template or standards drawing.

NOTE Custom representations are duplicates of predefined representations. It is not possible to create a custom representation from scratch.

FIGURE 2.18
Predefined and custom representations

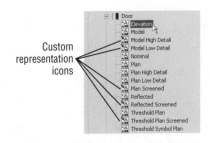

Custom representation icons

2. The elevation representation's information appears in the content pane. Notice that there is a different set of components in this representation. There is also an additional tab called Muntins. You'll explore this tab in Chapter 9, "Doors, Windows, and Openings."

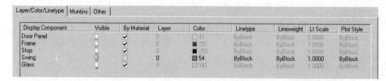

3. Click the Door's model representation in the tree pane. The content pane shows the same set of components compared to the elevation representation, but the display properties have different settings. Notice that most of the components in the model representation are controlled by materials. This makes sense because materials provide more realism and they are displayed in the 3D model.

4. Take a look at other representations by objects. Many representations have at least Layer/Color/Linetype, Hatching, and Other tabs, but there are many common and specialized representations with display properties tabs to discover. For now, open many of the specialized representations and tabs on your own to get a feel for how the disparate object display content is organized (see Table 2.2 for a start, but the table is not an exhaustive list).

Part 3, "Design Development," and Part 4, "Construction Documentation," of this book show how to use many of these representations in their proper context. You'll be amazed to see how much content is accessible inside the Display Manager.

TABLE 2.2: Selected Specialized Representations and Display Properties Tabs

OBJECT	REPRESENTATION	TAB(S)
Stair	Plan	Other, Riser Numbering
AEC Dimension	Plans	Contents, Other
AEC Polygon	True Color	Fill Properties
Area	Decomposed	Decomposition, Proof
Area Group	Any	Other
Door	Threshold Plan	Other

DISPLAY REPRESENTATION SETS

Display representation sets are commonly known as *sets*. Sets are what their formal name suggests, collections of display representations. Sets are at the midpoint of the hierarchy, forming relationships between representations and configurations. Sets don't depend on viewpoints as configurations do, nor component properties as representations do. Instead, sets collect all object representations together and determine which are used in a given context. Sets can be managed for individual objects and collectively for all objects. Let's explore both methods:

1. Open the Display Manager (if it is not already open).

2. In the tree pane, expand the `Floor Plan.dwg` and Representations By Object nodes if necessary, and click the Door node. The content pane displays a matrix interface, organized into rows and columns with many check boxes (see Figure 2.19).

   When you click directly on an object node in the tree pane (not on one of its representations) an interactive matrix appears that allows you to select how representations are organized into sets. Set names are the columns, and representations are the rows. The checks in the matrix assign specific representations to sets.

   Notice that some of the door object's sets have more than one representation assigned (Plan, Plan High Detail, Plan Presentation, and Plan Screened, in particular). Some sets have more than one representation because some representations are complementary and meant to be displayed concurrently. For example, look in the Plan set column and notice that the Plan and Threshold Plan representations are checked. Figure 2.20 shows components from both the Threshold Plan and Plan representations.

3. In the tree pane, click the Plan representation and notice that it contains the swing, panel, and frame components. Click the Threshold Plan representation and notice that it contains the Threshold B component.

NOTE   See Chapter 9 for more on doors and their components.

FIGURE 2.19
Door object's representation and set matrix

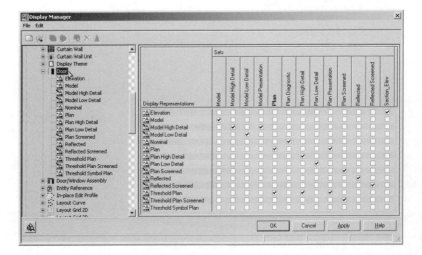

FIGURE 2.20
Door object's Plan set
displaying multiple
representations and
their components

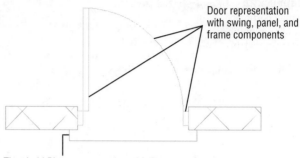

Door representation
with swing, panel, and
frame components

Threshold Plan representation with Threshold B component

4. Collapse the Door node in the tree pane of the Display Manager and then scroll down and select the Stair node (see Figure 2.21). Notice that the stair's representations are different from the door's representations, but the sets are the same as in Figure 2.19. All objects share the same sets.

5. Scroll up in the tree pane of the Display Manager and collapse the Representations By Object node. Then click the Representations By Object node. An immense matrix appears in the content pane, showing all the objects in rows and their collected representations in columns (see Figure 2.22). Notice that instead of check boxes, this matrix shows predefined and custom representation icons.

6. Scroll down the matrix and click the Door node. The row highlights, making it a bit easier to visually track across the matrix and see which icons correspond with which representations. Double-click the Door's predefined icon in the Plan column. This representation's display properties open in a dialog box interface (see Figure 2.23). Each icon in the matrix opens its own dialog box (there are more than 100).

You have seen the information in the Display Properties (Drawing Default) dialog box before, but in a different place in the Display Manager (refer to Figure 2.17).

TIP The benefit of using the Representations By Object matrix is that you can access all objects' display properties at once.

FIGURE 2.21
Stair object's set matrix

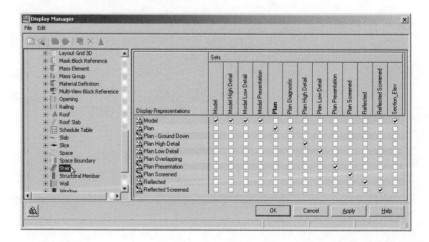

FIGURE 2.22
A small portion of the Representations By Object matrix

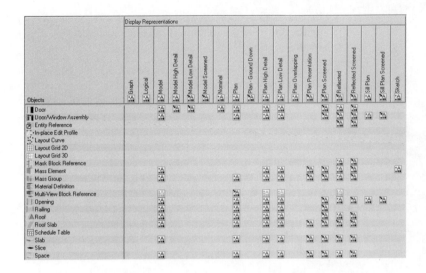

FIGURE 2.23
Display Properties (Drawing Default) dialog box

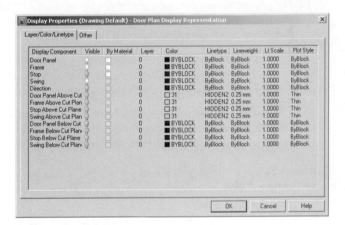

7. Click Cancel to close the Display Properties (Drawing Default) dialog box. Click the Sets node in the tree pane of the Display Manager. Read the content pane that describes the general purpose of each set. The last column allows you to ignore particular sets during standards synchronization (see Chapter 5).

Name	Description	Ignore During Standards Synchronization
Model	3D display turned on for all AEC objects	No
Model High Detail		No
Model Low Detail		No
Model Presentation	3D display turned on for all AEC objects	No
Plan	Medium display detail	No
Plan Diagnostic	Sketch, graph and diagnostic display configuration for troubles...	No
Plan High Detail	High display detail	No
Plan Low Detail	Low display detail	No
Plan Presentation	Presentation display style	No
Plan Screened	All AEC objects shown with a screened effect	No
Reflected	Reflected display for plots	No
Reflected Screened	For working in reflected ceiling plans, not intended for plotting	No
Section_Elev	Controls the display of AEC objects in sections and elevations	No

8. Expand the Sets node. Set names correspond to specific viewing directions (Plan, Model, Reflected, and Section_Elev), situations (Presentation, Diagnostic, and Screened), and levels of detail (Low, Medium, and High).

Notice that the Plan set shows in bold because it is currently in use (see Display Configurations). The set icons convey information: The red check mark indicates that a set is referenced by at least one configuration, and the green rectangle indicates a predefined set that cannot be deleted.

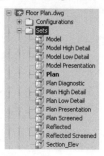

NOTE All drawings include the predefined Model, Model High Detail, Model Low Detail, Plan, Plan High Detail, Plan Low Detail, Reflected, and Section_Elev sets. It is possible to create a new set from scratch and assign representations to it as you see fit.

9. Click the Plan node under Sets in the tree pane of the Display Manager. The content pane shows a tabbed interface. The General tab holds the set name, description, and notes. Click the Display Representation Control tab to show another gigantic matrix (see Figure 2.24).

The Plan set matrix looks similar to the Representations By Object matrix because it lists all the objects in rows and representations in columns (compare it with Figure 2.22). The key difference you'll notice is that there are check boxes in the Plan set matrix.

FIGURE 2.24
A small portion of the
Plan set matrix

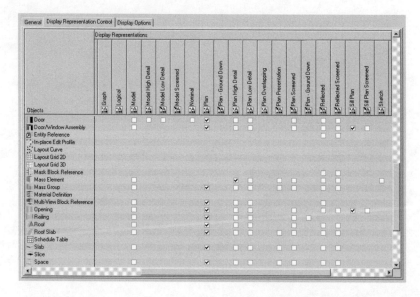

Figure 2.24 also has a resemblance to Figure 2.19 because of the many check boxes. The Plan set matrix does everything the Door object matrix does and much more. The Plan set matrix controls all objects; use it to determine which representations are included in the set.

NOTE   Objects having no representations selected in a set are not displayed. For example, the Ceiling Grid object is not displayed in the Plan set, so none of its representations is selected.

10. Click the Display Options tab in the content pane (see Figure 2.25). Here you'll find classification filters, which allow you to hide selected content from being displayed in the set (see Chapter 3). There are also some live section settings at the bottom of the tab (see Chapter 16, "Sections and Elevations"). The Hide Surface Hatching setting is controlled by the Surface Hatch Toggle you used earlier in this chapter.

FIGURE 2.25

Plan set's Display Options

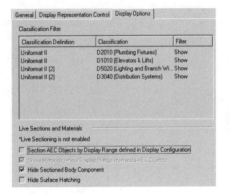

DISPLAY CONFIGURATIONS

We are finally coming full circle to discuss the display configurations you assigned earlier in the "Using Display Configurations" section. Now that you understand representations and sets, you can see how the hierarchy fits together. *Display configurations* assign sets to each possible view direction (viewpoint). In addition, configurations are where you assign cut plane heights. Let's have a look:

1. In the tree pane of the Display Manager, collapse the Sets node if it is still expanded and click the Configurations node. The content pane has a matrix that shows configurations in rows and sets in columns. You can't change anything in the configurations matrix; it is for your information only. Use it to study the configurations display system as a whole (see Figure 2.26).

The icons in the configurations matrix are similar to the buttons on the Views toolbar (refer to Figure 2.9), but with two exceptions. The solid box icon represents a multiview direction set; for example, Section_Elev is usually displayed in the Left, Right, Front, and Back view directions. The blank box icon represents a set that is displayed in the Viewport View direction, which means *any and all* isometric and oblique viewpoints.

The configuration icons along the left edge of the matrix are differentiated in several ways: The current configuration has the drawing crosshairs on its icon to set it apart from the others. Bold text also brings this important fact to your attention. In addition, there are two main types of icons along the left edge: one that shows a single sheet (for configurations with a fixed view direction; see the Diagnostic Display Configuration for example), and those that show two sheets (for configurations with multiple view directions).

TIP   Bold text indicates a configuration, set, or representation that is current or in use in both the Display Manager and the Style Manager (see Chapter 3). This helps by drawing your attention to editing settings that will be immediately displayed on-screen.

2. Expand the Configurations node and click the Medium Detail node in the tree pane. Click the Configuration tab in the content pane (see Figure 2.27). This is where you choose which sets will be displayed in particular view directions.

FIGURE 2.26
Configurations matrix

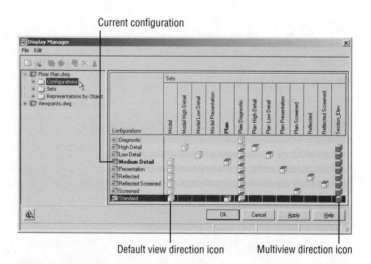

FIGURE 2.27
Editing a configuration in the Display Manager

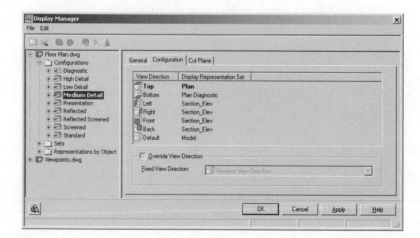

3. Click Plan Diagnostic next to the Bottom view direction. A pop-up appears, allowing you to select any one of the previously defined sets from a list.

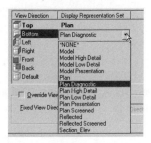

4. Click the Reflected node in the tree pane. Notice that the only difference compared with Medium Detail is the Top viewpoint. In the Reflected configuration, the Top view direction is obviously assigned the Reflected set.

5. Click the Diagnostic configuration in the tree pane. Notice that Override View Direction is checked, and Viewport View direction is assigned as a fixed view direction. This means that Plan Diagnostic is the only set that appears in the Diagnostic configuration, *regardless of the view direction.*

6. Click Medium Detail configuration in the tree pane and the Cut Plane tab at the top of the content pane. The cut height specifies the location of the global cut plane (relative to the building level) for the selected configuration. Plans are dynamically generated from the 3D model in ADT, so the location of the cut plane determines what is shown.

NOTE You can override the configuration's cut plane within individual objects, or in the object styles of walls, curtain walls, and slabs (see Part 3).

7. Expand the Medium Detail node in the tree pane. All the sets referenced by the configuration show up as children (indented) in the tree.

8. Click the Plan node under Medium Detail configuration in the tree pane. The content pane shows something you saw before: a set matrix (compare Figure 2.28 with Figure 2.24). This is merely an alternative way to access the same information.

9. It is possible to exchange configurations and sets between drawings within the Display Manager. Right-click the Configurations node and choose Import/Export from the shortcut menu (see Figure 2.29). Click Cancel after you see the possibilities.

WARNING Please hold off on actually changing any configurations or sets in the templates until you fully understand what you're doing. For now, it is enough to identify features with the goal of understanding how ADT works.

10. Be aware that changes you make anywhere in the Display Manager are updated immediately in every part of the dialog box. Click Cancel to finally close the Display Manager. You can leave the sample file open.

FIGURE 2.28
Alternative access to sets through a configuration's children

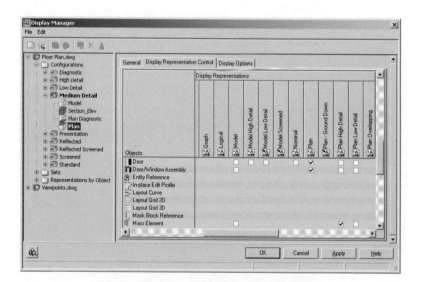

FIGURE 2.29
Import/Export dialog box

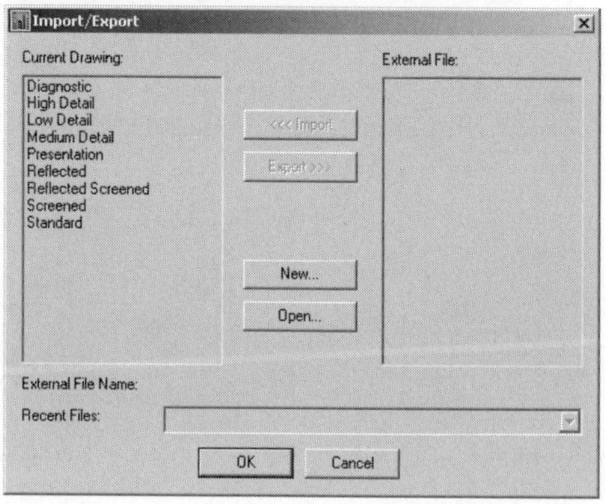

Now that you've studied the relationships between configurations, sets, and representations, you are well on your way to understanding how the object display system works. Now let's turn our attention to another display system that AutoCAD users will find familiar: layers. You'll find layers have been augmented in ADT.

Displaying with Layers

Layers are a time-tested display system that has been used in computer-aided design (CAD) for decades. You have already learned that layers are used concurrently with the object display system in ADT. In CAD and ADT, layers remain useful as a high-level categorization system used to organize architectural drawings. In addition, layers are the primary way data remains categorized when exporting ADT objects to other nonintelligent CAD systems.

Every entity and object resides on a layer. Every layer has its own set of properties that the objects on that layer generally inherit, although it is possible to override layer properties at the object or entity level. A major change from CAD is the way layers are automatically generated in ADT according to a layer key style that is itself determined by a layer standard. In this way, layers need not be stored in templates, as they are in AutoCAD and previous versions of ADT. In addition, there are many specialized tools that facilitate layer management that you'll learn about in this section.

Selecting a Default Layer Standard and Key Style

The first order of business when considering layers is to select a layer standard and its associated key style. A *layer standard* in ADT is a set of rules that determines a naming convention. A *layer key style* contains *keys* (code words), specific layer names, and their properties. The key style maps objects to layers that automatically conform to standards (you'll learn more about this in the following "Layer Key Styles" section).

Managers are generally the individuals responsible for selecting organization and/or project standards, including layer standards. The country in which your designs are built is likely to determine the layer standard, which is ultimately adopted. Check with your manager if applicable before changing layer standards in your projects.

Using a layer standard and its consistent naming convention ensures that the datasets you make will be useful to others in your organization and will be readable by others in your field for years to come.

1. Open `Layers.dwg` from the Layer Example subfolder inside this chapter's folder on the companion DVD. This file uses multiple XRefs that reside in subfolders seen in Figure 2.30. Do not move `Layers.dwg` relative to its subfolders or else the relative pathing will be broken. You'll be using this sample file for the duration of the "Displaying with Layers" topic, so please leave it open between sections.

2. Choose Format ➤ Layer Management ➤ Select Layer Standard (see Figure 2.31) to open the Drawing Setup dialog box (you can also access it from the Drawing menu on the drawings status bar; select the Layering tab if it's not already current).

3. Open the Layer Key Style pop-up in the Default Layer Standard group. Notice the array of standards that ship with ADT (they are defined in the `AecLayerStd.dwg` file). Verify that AIA (256 Color) is selected. Notice that the pop-up also says `*current drawing`, which indicates that the sample file already uses this standard.

NOTE   This book uses the *American Institute of Architects Layer Guidelines* (Second Edition with 256 colors). Please adopt this standard while using this book.

FIGURE 2.30
Layers sample file

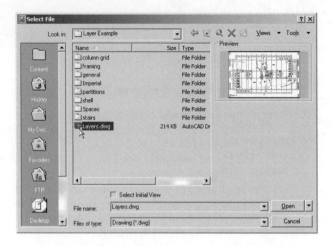

FIGURE 2.31
Selecting a layer
standard

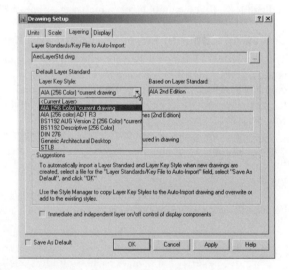

4. Check the only setting in the Default Layer Standard group. This setting always checks the current drawing to see whether the selected layer key style exists and then reimports it if it doesn't exist or if the external layer key style is newer.

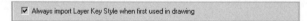

5. Check Save As Default at the bottom of the Drawing Setup dialog box. This saved default even overrides templates that can contain a different layer key style. Click OK to close the Drawing Setup dialog box.

Working with Layers

Most long-time CAD users already understand how to work with layers. I will summarize the most important concepts here in case you are new to both CAD and ADT. The Layer Properties toolbar is the primary interface to layers (see Figure 2.32).

The Layer Manager button opens the dialog box that is the subject of the next section. The Layer drop-down list is used to set the current layer, adjust selected layer states, and change entities and objects to different layers.

To change layer states in the layer drop-down list, click On/Off, Freeze/Thaw In All Viewports, Freeze/Thaw In Current Viewport, and/or Lock/Unlock Icons. The icons are shown in this order and have identifying ToolTips in the layer drop-down list.

You can also set the current layer by clicking on a layer's name (the text portion) in the layer drop-down list. XRef-dependent and frozen layers cannot be made current, and there can be only one current layer at any time. The current layer determines which layer new entities are created on, but objects get created on layers assigned by the layer key style (more on that later).

To change existing objects or entities to a different layer, select them and choose a layer name in the drop-down list. The layer to which an object or entity is assigned appears in the unopened drop-down list when there is a selection.

The Make object's layer current button does exactly what its name suggests, and is similar to Match Properties command. Layer Previous reverts layer properties to the previous settings, but does not affect added, renamed, or deleted layers (see the "Snapshots" section for a more powerful alternative).

The Properties toolbar (not open by default) is the key to changing an existing selection's layer properties and overriding creation settings for new objects/entities. Figure 2.33 shows the Properties toolbar and its drop-down lists that control color, linetype, lineweight, and plot style.

FIGURE 2.32
Layer Properties toolbar

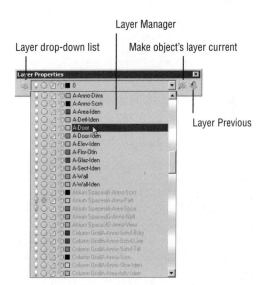

FIGURE 2.33
Properties toolbar

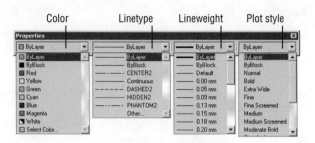

Normally, you'll assign properties such as color, linetype, lineweight, and plot style to layers (see the "Setting Layer Properties" section). Objects and entities usually assume the layer properties of the layer they reside on (using ByLayer). However, it is sometimes desirable to override these properties explicitly for a specific object or entity, thus creating a one-off situation.

To override a selection's layer properties, simply make the appropriate changes with the Properties toolbar's drop-down lists. The states that these drop-down lists show when nothing is selected control the *current properties* that affect newly created objects.

WARNING   Leave the current color, linetype, lineweight, and plot style drop-down lists on the Properties toolbar set to ByLayer. This setting gives layers more power to control the drawing.

Deconstructing the Layer Manager

The Layer Manager is one-stop shopping for layer standards, key styles, key overrides, filters, snapshots, and more. Let's analyze the many features of this dialog box to understand the plethora of tools available.

1. If you left the sample file open from the last section, you can continue here. If not, open Layers.dwg from the Layer Example subfolder inside this chapter's folder on the companion DVD.

2. Click the Layer Properties Manager button on the Layer Properties toolbar or type **LAYER** on the command line and press Enter (see Figure 2.34).

3. You'll want to refer to Figure 2.34 as you progress through the sections within this topic. Leave the Layer Manager dialog box open throughout this topic unless otherwise directed.

SETTING LAYER PROPERTIES

Each layer has numerous properties that it controls. These properties can be broken down into states and settings. States are toggles that have an either/or setting such as On/Off, Lock/Unlock, Freeze/Thaw In All Viewports, Freeze/Thaw In Current Viewport, Freeze/Thaw In New Viewports, and Plot/Non-Plot Status. Settings include color, linetype, lineweight, and plot style. Each layer, of course, has a name, and a description is optional (see Figure 2.35).

The current layer is indicated by the green check mark icon in the Status column. Figure 2.35 shows layer A-Anno-Dims current. The nodes above layer 0 in Figure 2.34 are filters that show indeterminate state icons that exhibit both states at once (for example, frozen and thawed). Filters often contain many layers having multiple states.

Setting layer properties is intuitive; just click the property to want to change and you'll either see its icon change or be presented with a drop-down list or dialog box, as the case may be.

FIGURE 2.34
Layer Properties

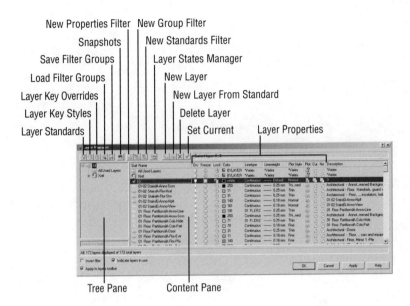

Tree Pane   Content Pane

FIGURE 2.35
Layer Manager
dialog box

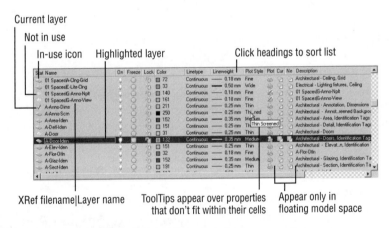

In no particular order, here are some important tips regarding layer properties:

◆ Layers that are in use show up as a blue layer icon in the status column, and layers not being used are white in the same column. Layer filters each have its own icon that appears in the status column and in the tree pane.

◆ You can sort long layer lists by clicking the property headings such as Status, Name, or On. Any heading you click sorts the entire list, much like the behavior of a spreadsheet in Microsoft Excel. You can also reverse the sorting direction by clicking the heading again. So clicking the Name heading twice sorts the list in reverse alphabetical order.

◆ Resize columns by dragging their headings.

◆ ToolTips appear when you hover the mouse over a cell whose contents are abbreviated because it doesn't fit.

◆ Highlighting a layer doesn't affect any properties; it just makes it easier to see which properties belong to a particular layer.

◆ Layers that are part of external references exhibit the XRef filename | Layer name convention, in which the delimiting vertical bar is the *pipe* character (vertical line).

◆ You'll only see the Current VP Freeze and New VP Freeze columns when you are on a paper space layout.

LAYER STANDARDS

Layer standards use highly structured naming conventions that separate layer names into fields with delimiters such as hyphens. Each field follows rules that ultimately determine the possible layer names that can be formed within the standard. Let's examine two different layer standards.

1. Click the Layer Standards button in the Layer Manager to open a dialog box of the same name.

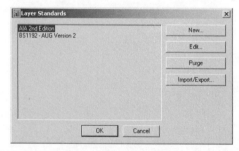

2. Verify that AIA 2nd Edition is highlighted and click the Edit button to open the Layer Standard Properties dialog box (see Figure 2.36). This is the interface for altering a naming convention's structure and its descriptions. The Wildcard column controls which characters and how many comprise each field.

FIGURE 2.36
Layer Standard
Properties

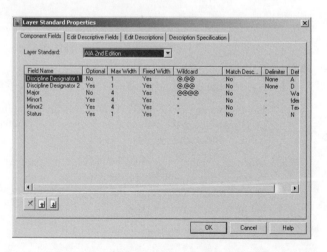

TIP See Table 2.3 under Layer Filters for a list of wildcard characters you can use in layer standard fields.

The AIA 2nd Edition layer standard has the following fields:

Discipline Designator 1-Discipline Designator 2-**Major**-Minor1-Minor2-Status

The fields in bold are required; the others are optional. An example of a layer conforming to this standard is A-Wall-Full-E, where A is for architectural (Discipline Designator 1), Wall represents the Major field, Full is for Full Height Partition (Minor), and E is for Existing Construction to Remain (Status). The optional Discipline Designator 2 and Minor 2 fields were skipped in this example.

1. Click the Edit Descriptions tab in the Layer Standards Properties dialog box. Change the Field To Edit drop-down list to Major. You see a list of the descriptions fitting within this field of the layer standard. It is possible to delete, edit, and add descriptions within this dialog box (see Figure 2.37).

2. Explore the other fields and descriptions within the AIA standard on your own. Click Cancel when you are done.

3. Select BS1192 - AUG Version 2 from the Layer Standard dialog box.

4. Click Edit and examine the fields comprising this naming convention. They are very different from the AIA 2nd Edition layer standard (see Figure 2.38).

NOTE Describing each layer standard goes beyond the scope of this book.

5. Click Cancel to close the Layer Standard Properties dialog box and click Cancel again to close the Layer Standards dialog box.

FIGURE 2.37
Editing descriptions
with a layer standard

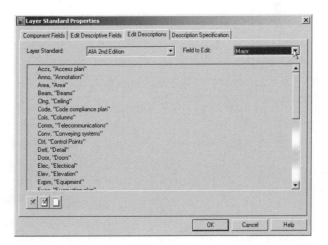

FIGURE 2.38

Examining the BS1192
layer standard

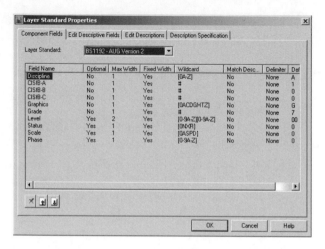

6. Right-click any in-use layer and examine the shortcut menu. Open the Change Layer Standard cascading submenu. Notice that you can change to Non Standard here. Do this only when you want a specific layer to deviate from your current layer standard.

WARNING   Do not make any changes to the layer standard until you consult with a manager.

CREATING A NEW LAYER FROM A STANDARD

The New layer button simply creates a blank nonstandard layer. Use the New Layer from Standard button to do as its name suggests. When you create a layer from a standard, you will be guided with dialog boxes in choosing a conforming layer name, and you'll be warned if you deviate from the pre-specified fields and values. Let's try this feature.

1. Click the New Layer From Standard button to open a dialog box of the same name (see Figure 2.39).

2. Click the ellipsis controlling the Major field's value. Scroll up, choose Door, and click OK (see Figure 2.40).

3. Scroll down in the New Layer From Standard dialog box and locate the Status field.

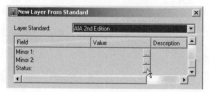

FIGURE 2.39
Creating a New Layer
From Standard

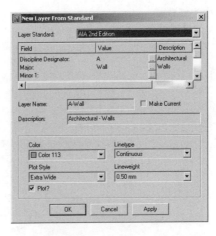

FIGURE 2.40
Choose a Pre-
Specified Value

4. Click the Status value ellipsis button and select N, "New Work" from a similar dialog box. The bottom half of the New Layer From Standard dialog box shows the full layer name we have created, A-Door-N, and its settings are filled in by the standard. Set the Lineweight to 0.25mm. Click OK to create the layer.

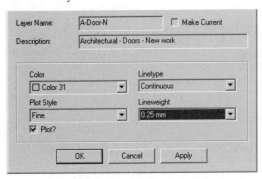

LAYER KEY STYLES

Layer keys are managed by styles (you'll learn about styles in Chapter 3). The Layer Manager's Layer Key Styles button conveniently opens the Style Manager so you can make changes while you're working on layers.

Click the Layer Key Styles button; the Style Manager opens, showing only the Layer Key Styles node. Click AIA (256 Color) in the tree pane and click the Keys tab in the content pane if it's not already selected (see Figure 2.41).

FIGURE 2.41
Editing Layer Key Styles

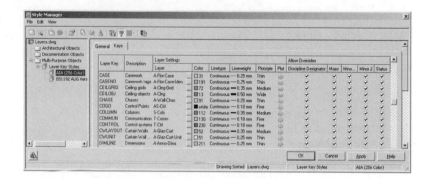

Now click BS1192 AUG Version in the tree pane and examine this standard's layer keys. Notice the layer names in this standard are different from the AIA standard, although both standards use the same keys. Observe that this standard doesn't allow overrides on all layers. Click Cancel when you're done.

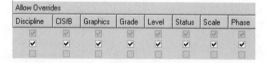

Layer keys are defined internally by ADT itself. Layer keys are used to map objects to appropriate layers using their internal layer key. The key style works hand-in-hand with a naming convention to generate compliant layer names.

Different standards obviously generate different layer names, but all standards work using the same keys. The Layer Key style also enables you to disallow overrides for chosen layer fields (see the next section).

LAYER KEY OVERRIDES

Layer key overrides allow you to make exceptions to the strict mappings of layer key styles. Let's say you create a Wall object but don't want it to appear on the A-Wall layer that the layer key says it should. Instead, suppose you want to create a wall on the A-Wall-E layer to identify it as existing construction to remain. This is where layer key overrides come in.

1. Click the Layer Key Override button in the Layer Manager (see Figure 2.42). By the way, you can also access this in the drawing status bar tray. It is more convenient to access overrides from the tray when you are drawing.

2. Click the ellipsis button for Status Override. Choose A Pre-Specified Value appears. Click E, "Existing To Remain," and click OK (see Figure 2.43).

NOTE You can override the layer key only with another layer name that conforms to standards. This ingenious safety feature ensures standards compliance.

3. Verify that Enable All Overrides is checked and click OK to close the Layer Key Overrides dialog box.

4. Click OK to close the Layer Manager.

5. Click the Layer Key Overrides icon in the drawing status bar tray. The same dialog box you saw in steps 1 and 3 appears.

Only one layer key override can be active at any time. You can toggle it on and off as needed, or change the layer set up to override whatever layer name suits your needs at the time.

TIP If you encounter objects that were created with a layer key override, but you no longer want them to diverge from the layer key, Remap Object Layers can fix it. Choose Format ➢ Layer Management ➢ Remap Object Layers, or use the AecRemapLayers command and select the divergent objects.

FIGURE 2.42
Layer Key Overrides

FIGURE 2.43
Choose a Pre-Specified Override

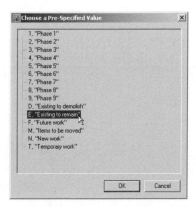

LAYER FILTERS

Layer filters help organize complex drawings into manageable categories. There are primarily three types of filters: those based on properties, groups, and standards. Let's take a look at each.

Property Filters

Use property filters when you want to filter layers together based on part of their names, property states, or settings.

1. Reopen the Layer Manager. Click the All node in the tree pane. Click the New Property Filter button to open the Layer Filter Properties dialog box

2. Click in the first row under the On column and select the yellow light bulb icon. Click under the Plot column and choose the plottable icon. Type **On And Plottable** in the Filter Name text box. The lower portion of the dialog box shows a dynamic preview of how this filter is working on the current drawing (see Figure 2.44). Click OK to close the dialog box.

3. Let's nest a filter: Right-click the On And Plottable node in the tree pane of the Layer Manager and choose New Property Filter from the shortcut menu.

NOTE The location of a filter in the tree pane hierarchy determines its scope.

FIGURE 2.44

Setting up a property filter

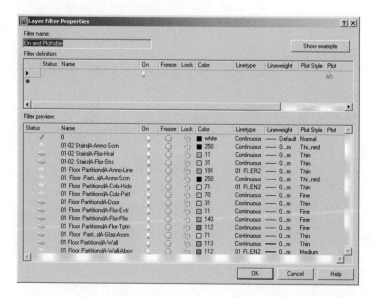

4. Click in the first row under the Name column and type ***door*** (see Table 2.3 for a description of wildcard characters such as the asterisk). Type **Doors** in the Filter Name text box and click OK to close the dialog box.

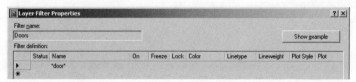

5. The results are property filters you can use to sort the long list of layers. Click the Doors node in the tree pane of the Layer Manager. Filtered layers appear in the content pane.

TABLE 2.3:   Wildcard Characters and Their Representations

WILDCARD	REPRESENTATION
#	Numeric character
@	Alphabetic character
.	Nonalphabetic character
?	Any specific character
*	Any string of characters
~	Any character but (logical NOT)
[ ]	Specific characters listed inside brackets
[-]	Range denoted by characters delimited by dash

Group Filters

Group filters are very simple in concept; they collect layers together that you decide for any reason to categorize together. This might be easier then trying to create an elaborate property filter to meet criteria that select your desired layers.

1. Click the New Group Filter button in the Layer Manager.

2. Type **My Group** to give the new filter a name in the tree pane.

3. Click the All node in the tree pane to display the layer list unfiltered.

4. Drag a few layers from the content pane onto the My Group node in the tree pane.

5. Click the My Group node to display the filter in the content pane.

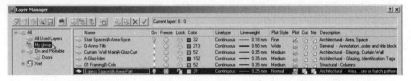

TIP Right-click any property filter and choose Convert To Group Filter if you want to have drag-and-drop control over which layers remain in a group filter.

Standards Filters

Standards filters automatically create multiple nodes in the tree pane corresponding to field values (categories) in a layer standard. They are a great way to add easy categorization to the Layer Manager.

1. Click the All node in the tree pane.

2. Click the New Standards Filter button. The Layer Standard Filter Properties dialog box appears. Type **Discipline** in the Filter Name text box. Click Discipline Designator in the Available Category(s) group and then click the Add button to move this field over to the Selected Category group (see Figure 2.45). Click OK.

3. Expand the Discipline node in the tree view of the Layer Manager. Notice that the filter is automatically populated with children based on the standard. Click on Architectural, and the content pane is filtered to show only this layer type.

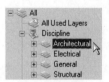

4. Repeat steps 1–3, adding individual standards filters for the Major, Minor 1, and Minor 2 categories of the layer standard.

5. Expand each standard filter node and examine the child nodes that represent the categorization inherent in the layer standard.

FIGURE 2.45
Setting layer standard
filter properties

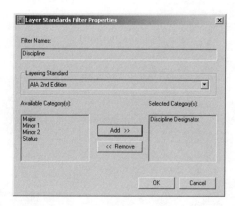

Additional Layer Filter Tools

There are a few other layer filter tools worth mentioning. Tools such as these might become some of your favorites if you routinely work with complex projects containing hundreds of layers.

All Used Layers   This property filter is created by default. You can nest additional property filters within the All Used Layers node at the top of the filter hierarchy.

XRef Filter   The XRef node in the tree pane contains a list of all the externally referenced drawings. This is a quick way to locate a layer based upon its drawing file membership.

Invert Filter   This unassuming check box at the bottom of the Layer Manager is a powerful tool because it inverts any conceivable filter you can make with a single click—that is, it hides the layers you're currently displaying and displays all hidden ones.

Load and Save Filter Groups   Here is a way to transfer all your hard work of setting up filters between drawing and users. There are buttons allowing you to save and load .lft files in the Layer Manager.

SNAPSHOTS

Snapshots are to layers what pictures are to the real world: Both are permanent records of a moment in time. Unlike photographs, layer snapshots can be used to restore layer properties back into the Layer Manager. You can also import and export snapshots for use with other drawings and people.

1. Click the Snapshot button in the Layer Manager to open a dialog box of the same name.

2. Click the New button, type **Snap 1,** and click OK (see Figure 2.46). Notice that at this moment the snapshot is reading the same as the drawing because you haven't had a chance to make the drawing's layer properties diverge from the snapshot you just took.

3. Click the Edit button and check out the Edit Snapshot dialog box. The properties you see here are the ones saved in the snapshot (see Figure 2.47). You can alter anything you like and then click OK.

4. Click OK in both the Snapshot and Layer Manager dialog boxes.

5. Close the Layers.dwg sample file.

FIGURE 2.46
Taking layer snapshots

FIGURE 2.47
Editing a snapshot

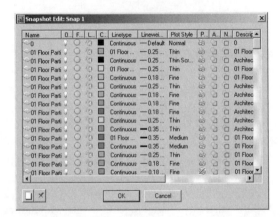

ADDITIONAL LAYER TOOLS

There are a few older layer tools I thought I'd mention here. These tools still work in ADT but have been around in previous versions and might still prove useful, especially when working with "legacy data" (meaning older drawings).

Layer States Manager   There is a button for the Layer States Manager in the Layer Manager. It provides essentially the same functionality as Snapshots, but is still in ADT 2006 in case you still have .las files hanging around (this is the Import/Export format for use with the Layer States Manager).

Layer Translator   This is now accessible only through the menu bar, under CAD Manager ≻ CAD Standard ≻ Layer Translator. The layer translator is useful in mapping nonstandard legacy drawings to standard layers. If you do not have the CAD Manager menu, add it by selecting Window ≻ Pulldowns ≻ CAD Manager Pulldown.

Express Layer Tools   Available as an option when you install ADT (see your installation CDs), the Express tools have numerous helpful layer features including Layer Off, which allows you to turn off a layer by clicking on an entity or object. If you work with layers a lot, consider installing the Express Layer Tools.

Additional Display Controls

There are a number of additional display controls that help make your job easier. The controls listed in this section work outside the object display and layer-management systems, but are just as important for you to learn how to use.

Editing In View

Editing In View is a new feature in ADT 2006. The "In View" concept is the ability to quickly display selected objects in a plan, elevation, or section. Of course, you could open a plan, elevation, or section drawing and accomplish the same things, but that would take far longer (especially if you haven't yet generated elevations or sections, for example). Edit In View allows you to quickly display objects in whichever view you prefer to get on with editing your work.

The Edit In View commands are accessible via a shortcut menu when there is an object selection. The three new commands are: Edit In Plan, Edit In Elevation, and Edit In Section.

1. Open House.dwg from this chapter's folder on the companion DVD.

2. Make a crossing selection of all the objects within the northern wall, including the wall, door, and windows.

TIP Don't focus on the objects themselves yet. You'll have time to explore these objects in Chapters 8 and 9.

3. Right-click and choose Isolate Objects ➤ Edit in Elevation from the shortcut menu.

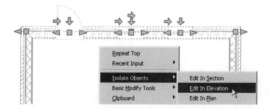

4. The command line says Select linework or face under the cursor or specify reference point for view direction. Hover the cursor over the exterior face of the wall. When you see the ToolTip saying View Direction Reference Line, click to establish the plane of the elevation.

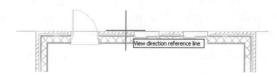

5. Move the cursor away from the reference line and notice that an elevation callout appears ghosted in the view. Click a point anywhere below the wall you want to elevate.

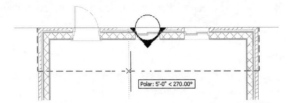

6. The elevation appears in the view (see Figure 2.48), allowing you to work on the objects where you might adjust the roofline of the wall, for example (see Chapter 8). Click the single button on the floating Edit In View toolbar to exit the mode.

7. Edit In Section and Edit In Plan work much the same way. Remember to read the command line when using these commands. Try these two on your own.

8. Leave the sample file open.

TIP Enter an isometric viewpoint before attempting Edit In Plan.

FIGURE 2.48
Editing In Elevation

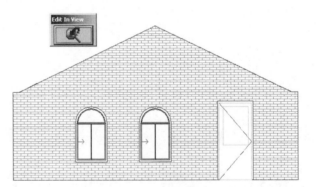

Hiding and Isolating Objects

You have learned how to control object visibility using both the display system and by managing layers, so you already have tools to hide and isolate objects. However, using either of these systems to isolate a few objects on the screen can be very difficult indeed.

Fortunately, a concurrent display control is available specifically to hide and isolate objects. That means you don't have to turn off dozens of layers, or create new display sets and configurations, to simply hide and isolate the few objects you are working on.

1. If you left the sample file open from the last section, you can continue here. If not, open House.dwg from the Chapter 2 folder on the companion DVD.

2. Select the north wall and its door by making a crossing selection.

3. Right-click the yellow light bulb icon in the drawing window status bar tray. Choose Isolate Objects from the shortcut menu.

4. All the other objects disappear, and you are left viewing only the wall and door, providing an opportunity to work on these objects without all the distraction from the rest of the scene. Notice that the light bulb icon has turned red, indicating that you are in isolation mode. Click the red light bulb and choose End Object Isolation.

TIP   You can choose to isolate additional objects once in isolation mode. This works like isolation within isolation, allowing you to pare down the display even more.

5. Select the door object, right-click the yellow light bulb icon in the tray, and choose Hide Objects. As you'd expect, only the door disappears.

6. Click the red light bulb icon in the drawing tray and choose End Object Isolation to restore the door object to the screen.

7. Leave the sample file open.

Before you start hunting through the object display system or wading through layers, remember to check to see whether the light bulb icon is red if you can't find an object.

It is possible to save the drawing with objects hidden or in isolation. Hiding and/or isolating can be a convenient way to draw someone's attention to a particular set of objects when they open a drawing.

WARNING   Hidden and/or isolated objects won't stay that way if someone with an older version of ADT or AutoCAD opens the file in question. Therefore, these modes aren't meant to display objects as a permanent record, but rather as a temporary convenience.

Using the Object Viewer

The Object Viewer is a floating interface that allows for more efficient viewing of the objects you select. You will find that ADT runs slowly in complex drawings when changing viewpoints, paper space layouts, shading modes, and display configurations. Each of these tasks taxes your computer's graphics card. You can save time by using the Object Viewer to visualize only those objects that you select.

1. If you left the sample file open from the last section, you can continue here. If not, open `House.dwg` from this chapter's folder on the companion DVD.

2. Make a crossing selection of all the objects within the northern wall, including the wall, door, and windows.

FIGURE 2.49
The Object Viewer

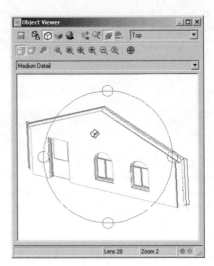

3. Right-click and choose Object Viewer from the shortcut menu. Figure 2.49 shows the Object Viewer dialog box.

4. Drag the mouse within the green circle to orbit. Use the zoom tool buttons and preset viewing direction drop-down list to navigate within the Object Viewer. Try different shading modes and display configurations to visualize the selected objects from all vantage points.

5. Close the Object Viewer to continue working in the drawing window. The Object Viewer is modal, meaning that you can't do anything else until you close the dialog box.

TIP   There are Object Viewer buttons in the corners of the Display Manager and Style Manager dialog boxes. Use the floating Object Viewer to preview representations by object and individual object styles without having to change display parameters or create objects in the drawing window.

Summary

This chapter taught you a lot about objects, entities, and display systems. You learned how changing viewpoints and configurations affect what you see in the viewport and drawing window. You studied the object display system and learned its hierarchy of representations, sets, and configurations. In addition, you know how layers work in ADT with properties, standards, keys, overrides, filters, snapshots, and more. Finally, you learned about a few additional display tools that will definitely come in handy as you progress with ADT. In the next chapter, we'll delve into the complexities of object styles.

Chapter 3

Object Styles

In this chapter, you'll see how objects are made intelligent with styles. You'll access a wealth of styled objects ready for use in the Content Browser, and learn how to organize and customize your content library and Tool palettes. Styles hold a vast array of information that you'll explore using the Style Manager, by editing object styles and the object display. Finally, you'll work with other nonobject styles such as material and classification definitions. This chapter's topics include the following:

- ◆ Intelligence with Style
- ◆ Setting Object Properties
- ◆ Using the Content Browser
- ◆ What's In a Style?
- ◆ Working with Definition Styles

Intelligence with Style

Styles make generic objects flexible by differentiating them into a plethora of specific real-world types. For example, styles are used to represent wall types such as those constructed with wooden studs, concrete masonry units (CMUs), brick, and many other combinations of components. Think of the wall and door types shown in a typical construction drawing as examples of object styles in Architectural Desktop (ADT).

Many aspects of real-world objects are encoded into styles including materials, classifications, display properties, dimensions, design rules, standard sizes, components, profile shapes, and much more. Each object has different kinds of information stored in its style, appropriate to the object's purpose.

Most importantly, styles offer global control over objects. If you make a series of objects in a particular style, say a number of brick walls, you can change them all at once by editing their style. By modifying the wall style to include an air gap, rigid insulation, a layer of CMU, and furring, all the objects assigned to that style would be immediately updated throughout the drawing.

TIP   You don't have to create all your styles from scratch. See "Using the Content Browser" later in this chapter to see how to take advantage of an extensive library of styles.

Creating Generic Objects

Let's start by creating a few generic objects such as a wall, door, and window. If you haven't played around with it yet, you'll find that the object-creation process is quite straightforward and intuitive.

1. Start a new blank drawing based on the standard template by clicking the QNew button on the Standard toolbar if you currently have another drawing open.

2. In the Tool palettes, switch to the Design palette group, and click the Design palette's tab if these aren't already selected.

3. Click the Wall tool (see Figure 3.1).

FIGURE 3.1
Generic object-creation tools

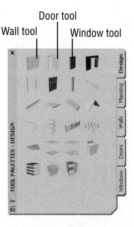

4. Click any point in the drawing window to set the first endpoint of the wall.

5. Make sure that the Polar and Dyn toggles are set to On in the application status bar and move the mouse horizontally to the right. Using the new dynamic input system, type **15′** and press Enter. Press either Esc or Enter to end the command.

WARNING Although it might be tempting, please don't get sidetracked into exploring all the object tools yet. Part 3 of this book, "Design Development," is devoted to exploring each object in depth.

6. Zoom and pan, if necessary, to focus on the new wall object. This generic object is currently assigned the Standard style, as all objects are when they are at a conceptual stage.

7. Click the Door tool and then click the wall. Notice that the door is ghosted and shows dynamic dimensions. Move your cursor around until the door is 6″ off the left start point of the wall and click again to place the door within the wall (see Figure 3.2). Press Esc to finish the command.

FIGURE 3.2
Placing a door within
a wall using dynamic
dimensions

8. Click the Window tool and then add it to the wall 6″ off the right end point of the wall, just as you did with the door in the last step.

9. Save as **Styles.dwg** in a working folder on your hard drive and leave the drawing open.

Creating Styled Objects

Creating objects with specific styles is just as easy as creating generic objects. If you already know which style an object should have, bypass creating a generic object. The Design palette group is pre-populated with common styled object tools on its Walls, Doors, and Windows palettes.

1. If you left the sample file open from the last section, you can continue here. If not, open `Styles.dwg` from the working folder on your hard drive.

2. Open the Walls palette and click the Brick-4 Brick-4 tool. The names of styled wall objects refer to their component part dimensions. Brick-4 Brick-4 is a wall style featuring two 4″ bricks making an 8″ thick wall (see Figure 3.3).

FIGURE 3.3
Styled wall tools

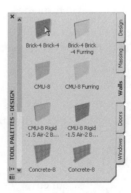

3. Create another 15′ horizontal wall under the first one. Switch to High Detail display configuration. Notice that this time, the styled object appears differently from the generic one.

4. Open the Doors palette and place a Bifold - Single door in the brick wall.

5. Open the Windows palette and place a Glider window in the brick wall (see Figure 3.4).

6. Create a series of styled walls, doors, and windows on your own. Explore various viewpoints and display configurations to learn more about the styles you have chosen.

7. Save the current drawing and leave it open to continue working.

FIGURE 3.4
Top: generic objects with Standard styles; bottom: styled objects each with its own style

Applying Tool Properties to Assign Styles

You can change the style of an object you've already created using any styled tool. To do this, you'll be using the tool shortcut menu and applying its tool properties to the object in question. It is also possible to convert entity and object types using tool properties. Let's see how this works.

1. If you left the sample file open from the last section, you can continue here. If not, open StyledObjects.dwg from the Chapter 3 folder on the companion DVD (see Figure 3.5).

2. Open the Walls palette and right-click the Brick-4 Brick-4 tool. Choose Apply Tool Properties To ➤ Wall from the shortcut menu (see Figure 3.6).

3. Select a few wall objects and press Enter to change their styles to Brick-4 Brick-4. Press Esc to exit grip mode.

NOTE See "Customizing Tools" in the "Using the Content Browser" section to learn how to edit tool properties.

4. Change the styles of a few doors and windows using this technique.

FIGURE 3.5
Styles differentiate and
control objects

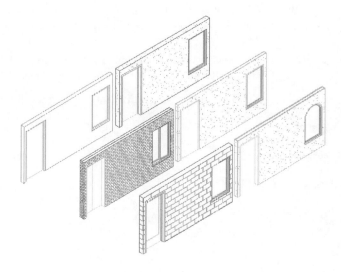

FIGURE 3.6
Changing styles by
applying tool properties

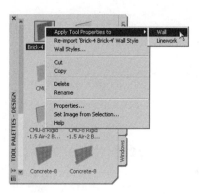

You can also assign tool properties to entities, and to other object types in some cases. In fact, this is a way to convert object types. Each tool offers different choices in its Apply Tool Properties To submenu.

1. Off to the side of the drawing window, draw a polyline with a few straight-line and arc segments. You can draw lines and arcs instead if you prefer.

2. On the Walls palette, right-click the Concrete-8 tool and choose Apply Tool Properties To ➤ Linework. Select the polyline and press Enter. Notice what the command line says.

```
Select lines, arcs, circles, or polylines to convert into walls:
Erase layout geometry? [Yes/No] <No>:
```

3. Press Y and then Enter to erase the layout geometry (polyline). The polyline is replaced with 8″ concrete walls (see Figure 3.7); imagine all that without formwork!

TIP   Occasionally objects may not appear correctly on-screen. Choosing View ➤ Regen Model will fix it. Note this is separate from the older Regen (entities) and Regen All (entities in viewports) commands.

4. Save the current drawing and leave it open to continue working.

FIGURE 3.7
Left, polyline used as lay-out geometry; right, wall objects after tool properties assigned to polyline.

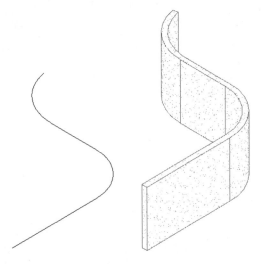

Setting Object Properties

Each object has properties specific to it alone that are called *object properties*. For example, each wall object has unique length property (among others) that is not controlled by its style. You determine the length property of a particular wall object as you create it by clicking its endpoints in the drawing window. Object properties are found quite naturally on the Properties palette.

1. If you left the sample file open from the last section, you can continue here. If not, open StyledObjects.dwg from the working folder on your hard drive.

2. Click one of the wall objects you drew in the last section; for example, select a concrete wall. Press Ctrl+1 to open the Properties palette if it's not already open. Click the Design tab to access object properties (see Figure 3.8). Expand the Basic category and its subcategories. Click the show illustration toggle to display it if necessary (see Chapter 1, "The Basics," for terminology).

TIP   You'll use the Properties palette so often that it makes sense to leave it open at all times.

FIGURE 3.8
Object properties on the
Properties palette

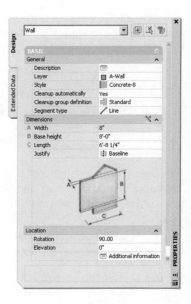

3. Click the Description worksheet icon in the General subcategory. You can type something into the worksheet if you want. Every object has a description property in which you can make any notes you like. Click OK to close the worksheet.

4. Notice that style is a property value currently set to Concrete-8. Click the value and it turns into a drop-down list. Choose Brick-4 Brick-4, and the wall style is changed. Note that you can change objects only to styles that already exist in the drawing.

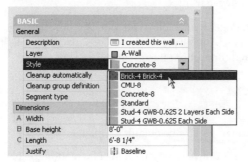

5. Select a second wall object. Now the Properties palette shows *VARIES* for several values. You can edit only properties that the selected objects have in common. Notice that many of the wall properties are still available (two wall objects selected).

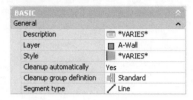

6. Select a Door object as well. Now there are only three properties that the selected objects have in common: Description, Layer, and Style. However, you can't set Style because the selection includes styles from different object types.

WARNING   The Properties palette's Design tab won't show anything at all if the selection includes both entities and objects. Entities and objects have no properties in common.

7. Press Esc and close the file without saving.

Using the Content Browser

Each one of the tools you've been using on the Walls, Doors, and Windows palettes represents a different styled object. In the course of a typical project, you'll probably end up using dozens or even hundreds of different tools to adequately document your design. To organize all this, tools are organized onto palettes, and palettes are organized into palette groups, but that is just the beginning.

The Content Browser allows you to interact with a customizable library of myriad tools. In this section, you'll learn how to bring tools from the library into your workspace and how to insert tools that you customize back into the library. In this way, the library becomes a dynamic storehouse of design data that evolves with each one of your projects.

In the Content Browser each designer has a personal library that contains many different *catalogs*, in which tools actually reside. Be aware that tool data is not physically stored in a designer's library. Instead, the library is merely a retrieval system that points to the location where the actual catalog data resides.

NOTE   Each designer can browse through the content of only one library at a time, even when using multiple Content Browsers.

In this way, networked organizations can centrally store catalogs and have each designer's library link to those catalogs on a file server. Modifications made to tools stored in centralized catalogs are then instantly updated throughout the organization.

Accessing Content

Let's take a look at some of the Content Browser features.

1. Start a new drawing with the default template.

2. Click the Content Browser button on the Navigation toolbar, or press Ctrl+4. The Content Browser window appears (see Figure 3.9). Notice that a new task appeared on the Windows

Taskbar, indicating that the Content Browser is a separate process. This means you can run the Content Browser independently of ADT; content can be shared between ADT and VIZ Render by using the Content Browser as a go-between (see Chapter 18, "Using Viz Render").

TIP   Right-click the Content Browser's title bar and choose Always on Top.

3. Click Preferences to open the Content Browser Preferences dialog box. Change the Library Name to **Content Library** (see Figure 3.10). You could optionally name this with your company or personal name, for example. Change the number of rows per page to 10, so you can see more tools in the Content Browser at once without having to navigate to the next page. Notice that there are five types defined by default for catalogs: Content, Personal, Rendering, Sample, and Tutorials. Add or delete types here as you see fit and click OK.

4. Right-click the Content Library title itself to open a shortcut menu. This is how you can select a different library. Library files have a `.cbl` file extension. You don't need to select a different library now; this step is just for your information.

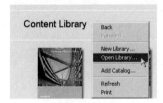

FIGURE 3.9
Content Browser

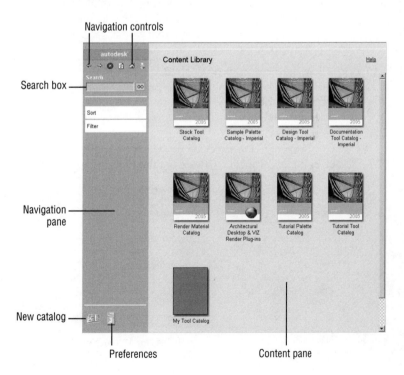

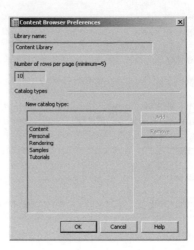

FIGURE 3.10
Content Browser
preferences

5. Hold your pointer over Sort in the navigation pane and watch as additional choices appear on a green rollover menu. Choose By Type, and the catalogs get rearranged in a different order.

6. Using the navigation pane, filter the catalogs by Content. You should see Documentation and Design Tool catalogs only now because they are assigned the Content type defined in step 3. Change the filter to All Catalogs.

7. Many of the catalogs are identified as either Imperial or Metric, depending on the measurement systems installed with ADT. If you don't plan to use the metric system, right-click those catalogs and remove them from your library. It's good to simplify wherever possible to reduce screen clutter.

Content in the browser is divided into different catalogs for organizational purposes, listed in Table 3.1. The Stock Tool catalog contains all the generic tools, so you don't have to worry about losing anything by altering the Tool palettes. Styled tools are stored in both the Design Tool and Documentation Tool catalogs.

TABLE 3.1:   Tool and Palette Catalogs In Content Browser

CATALOG NAME	PURPOSE
Stock Tools	Contains all generic tools
Sample Palettes	Factory-fresh palettes
Design Tools	Styled design tools
Documentation Tools	Styled Documentation tools
Render Materials	Render materials and palettes
Plug-Ins	Web links for ADT and VIZ Render

TABLE 3.1: Tool and Palette Catalogs In Content Browser *(CONTINUED)*

CATALOG NAME	PURPOSE
Tutorial Palettes	Used for ADT's built-in tutorial
Tutorial Tools	Used for ADT's built-in tutorial
My Tools	Blank catalog for custom tools

Let's explore some of the content in the Design Tool catalog.

1. Click the Design Tool Catalog. Hover the mouse over Walls and select the Stud category in the rollover menu.

2. Navigate through the pages of wall tools and locate Stud-3.625 GWB-0.625 Each Side. Notice that each door tool has a preview icon of its object style and an i-drop icon (see Figure 3.11).

3. Position your cursor over the i-drop icon and observe it change to an i-drop cursor. Click and hold the left mouse button and wait for the dropper icon to fill with black. While still holding down the left mouse button, move the filled i-drop cursor into the drawing window and release the button. (In the future, I'll refer to the above procedure as "dragging an i-drop tool.") Notice that the WallAdd command is running in the Command window.

4. Click two points to draw a horizontal wall. Press Esc to finish the command.

5. Click the Catalog Top navigation link in the content pane. Choose Doors and Windows ➢ Doors from the navigation pane.

6. Locate the Hinged - Single - Double Lite tool and drag its i-drop icon into ADT's drawing window.

TIP   If you can't see the ADT application window when you're dragging with the i-drop cursor, drag to the ADT task on the Taskbar first and then to the ADT window.

FIGURE 3.11
Tools available in catalog

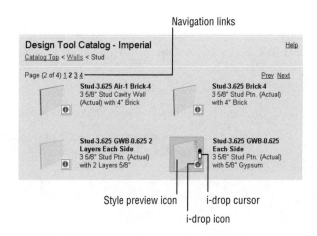

7. Place the door inside the wall.

8. Use a window tool from the Content Browser to insert a new style of your choosing into your drawing. Display the wall, door, and window from an isometric viewpoint and shaded view (see Figure 3.12).

TIP You can import a style into the current drawing by dragging a tool from the Content Browser into the drawing window and pressing Esc without creating an object. Be careful not to import styles into your drawing that you don't plan on using (they increase drawing file size).

9. Click the Home button in the Content Browser and investigate the other catalogs on your own.

FIGURE 3.12
Using tools in the Content Browser to bring new styles into a drawing

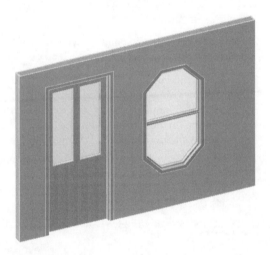

Customizing Tool Palettes and Your Library

You can do a lot more with the Content Browser than just dragging styled objects into a drawing. In this section you'll learn many ways to drag content back and forth between your drawing, the Tool palettes, and the Content Browser. To begin, let's open a catalog I've put together containing sample door styles.

1. Open the Content Browser if it is not already open.

2. Click the Home button to view all the catalogs in your library.

3. Click the New Catalog button to open the Add Catalog dialog box. Verify that the "Add an existing catalog or web site" radio button is selected and click this choice's Browse button (see Figure 3.13).

FIGURE 3.13
Add Door Catalog

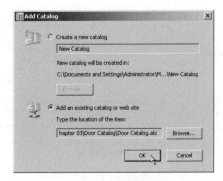

4. Navigate to the Chapter 3 folder on the DVD. Go into the `Door Catalog` subfolder and select the `Door Catalog.atc` file. Click OK. In a moment you'll see the Door Catalog appear in the Content Browser.

TIP Protect entire catalogs by making their `.atc` files read-only (visible in Content Browser's title bar). A more selective way to do this is to have a network administrator allow only certain designers permission to write files in the catalog folder.

5. Click the Door Catalog in the Content Browser and explore its content. Leave the Content Browser open for the duration of this section.

DRAGGING FROM THE CONTENT BROWSER TO ADT

The Door catalog contains categories, palettes, packages, and tools of sample door style content that you can drag into ADT. Table 3.2 shows all the different ways this can be done.

1. In ADT, open the Tool Palettes properties menu and select New Palette. Give the new palette a name by typing **My Pal** and pressing Enter.

2. Right-click the My Pal tab and choose Move Up in the shortcut menu. Now your new blank palette is at the top of the Tool palettes.

TIP Use an i-drop icon every time you drag anything in the Content Browser.

3. Switch to the Content Browser. Navigate to the Revolving category. Open the Revolving Doors package and drag the Revolving - Custom tool onto My Pal in ADT (see Figure 3.14).

TABLE 3.2:   Dragging From the Content Browser Into ADT

DRAG FROM	DRAG TO	EFFECT
Category	Tool palettes	Creates palette group
Package	Existing palette	Populates palette with tools
Palette	Tool palettes	Creates palette in current palette group
Tools	Existing palette	Stores tool on palette
Tools	Drawing	Inserts styled object into drawing
Tools	Drawing and Esc	Inserts style into drawing without object

4. Navigate to Catalog Top and then open the Sliding category. Drag the Sliding Doors package onto My Pal. The package deposited all its tools onto My Pal (see Figure 3.15).

5. Switch back to the Content Browser. Navigate to Catalog Top and click the Bifold category. Drag the Bifold Doors palette into the Tool palettes in ADT. It appears as a palette in the current palette group (Design). Notice that the new palette appears at the top of the palette group (see Figure 3.16).

FIGURE 3.14
Left to right: Category, Package, Palette, and Tool icons

FIGURE 3.15
My Pal with tool and package dragged from Content Browser

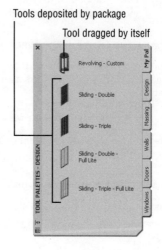

FIGURE 3.16
Dragging a palette into
current palette group

NOTE You can drag only categories containing at least one palette from the Content Browser into ADT's Tool palettes.

6. Switch once more to the Content Browser. Navigate to Catalog Top and open the Hinged category. You'll find two nested categories inside: Single Doors and Double Doors. It's a new feature in ADT 2006 to drag entire categories and subcategories into ADT to become palette groups. Drag the Single Doors subcategory into the Tool palettes in ADT. Notice that Single Doors does not appear as a tab in the current palette group in the Tool palettes because it has become its own set.

7. In ADT, open the Tool Palettes properties menu and select the Single Doors palette group. Hinged Single Doors is the only palette in the Single Doors palette group.

8. To edit palette groups you'll have to open the Customize dialog box. First make the Design palette group current again. Then open the Tool Palettes properties menu and choose Customize. Right-click Single in the right pane of the Customize dialog box and choose Delete from the context menu (see Figure 3.17). Click Close to exit the Customize dialog box.

FIGURE 3.17
Customizing palette
groups

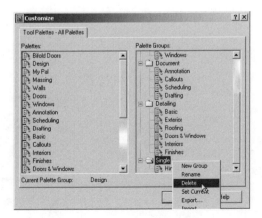

LINKING VERSUS COPYING

Content Browser links are to XRefs as Content Browser copies are to entities. In other words, links in the Tool palettes allow categories, palettes, packages, and tools to retain their association with the originals in the Content Browser (the link is one way, much like external references). Copies break association with their originals and become unique like entities.

New!

To link items from the Content Browser into the Tool palettes, you must first enable this feature in catalog properties. One-click palette refresh is new in ADT 2006. Let's get linking!

1. Click the Home button in the navigation pane of the Content Browser.

2. Right-click the Door Catalog to open the Catalog Properties dialog box (see Figure 3.18). Check "Link items when added to workspace" and click OK.

NOTE   All items dragged from the Stock Tool catalog are unlinked because linking is not enabled in this catalog by default. This behavior enables you to alter tool properties of any stock tool in the Tool palettes.

3. Open the Door Catalog and navigate to the Hinged category, in which you'll find the Double Doors and Single Doors subcategories. Drag the Double Doors subcategory into the Tool palettes in the workspace.

4. After perhaps 30 seconds (linking takes longer than copying), ADT will complete the linking process. Open the Tool Palettes properties menu and select the Double Doors palette group. Notice the refresh button in the lower-right corner of the Hinged Double Doors palette (see Figure 3.19).

5. Right-click a blank area (not on a tool) on the Hinged Double Doors palette to open the Palette Properties worksheet. Notice that both Refresh From and Enable Auto-refresh are checked (see Figure 3.20). The fact that Refresh From is checked indicates that this is a linked palette. Click Cancel to close the worksheet.

FIGURE 3.18
Editing the Door Catalog properties

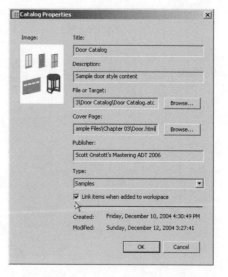

6. Switch back to the Design palette group. Switch to the Content Browser and navigate to the Overhead category. Hold down Alt and drag the Overhead Doors palette into the workspace.

7. Select the Overhead Doors tab on the Tool palettes. Notice that there is no Refresh button on this palette.

NOTE Holding down Alt before you select an i-drop icon forces copying behavior (even in a catalog set to link items) when dragging items from the Content Browser to the workspace.

8. Click the My Pal tab on the Tool palettes. Navigate to Catalog Top in the Content Browser. Choose the Pocket category and open the Pocket Doors package. Drag the Pocket - Single tool to the Tool palettes and drop it at the bottom of My Pal.

9. Right-click the Pocket - Single tool on My Pal. Choose Properties from the shortcut menu. The Tool Properties worksheet appears. Notice that Refresh From: Door Catalog is checked at the top of the worksheet, showing that individual tools can also be linked. You'll be learning more about Tool Properties in the Customizing Tool section. Close the worksheet.

NOTE You can link individual tools on unlinked palettes.

From this experience, you have learned that linked palettes and tools retain their association with their originals in the Content Browser. Be aware that links in the Tool palettes are not "live;" they must be refreshed to be updated with the originals in the Content Browser. Automatic refresh occurs only at program startup and is not an option for individual tools.

FIGURE 3.19
Linked palette group

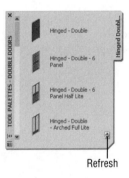

Refresh

FIGURE 3.20
Palette Properties
worksheet

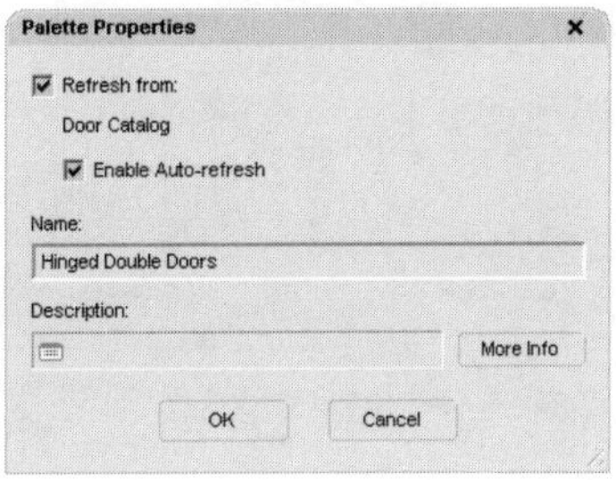

TIP   Automatic refresh is available only for palettes and can be a powerful method to synchronize all the computers in your organization with palettes stored in a centralized catalog. Be aware that it can also create a major delay when starting up ADT.

You can refresh links manually at any time, whether you are using auto-refresh or not. Linked palette groups and palettes have refresh buttons that overwrite tools with the originals in the Content Browser. New tools that are added to a source palette in the Content Browser will automatically appear on a linked palette when that palette is refreshed. Linked packages and tools on unlinked palettes can be refreshed by choosing Refresh Tool from their tool shortcut menus.

WARNING   If you ever encounter a Tool palette that will not accept a dragged tool, it is because that palette is linked. Linked palettes can accept only tools within the Content Browser.

DRAGGING OBJECTS FROM CONTENT DRAWING TO TOOL PALETTES

It's easy to create a new tool—simply drag an object from the drawing window to a tool palette. Keep in mind that there are a couple of rules to observe. First, you can only create a new tool from an object in a saved drawing because the new tool references its object style in the content drawing, and the file must be saved so you'll have access the next time you want to use the new tool.

The second rule applies to the mechanics of dragging objects to palettes. Do not use grips to drag a selected object to the Tool palettes. Instead, position the cursor anywhere over an object's representation (but not over a grip) and drag from there. Let's give it a try.

1. Open NewStyles.dwg from this chapter's folder on the companion DVD.

2. Select My Pal on the Tool palettes if it is not already open.

3. Click the Cased Opening (door) object to select it. Put your cursor over the door's 3D geometry. Drag and drop this object on My Pal between the Revolving - Custom and Sliding - Double tools (see Figure 3.21).

FIGURE 3.21
Dragging an object to the Tool palettes

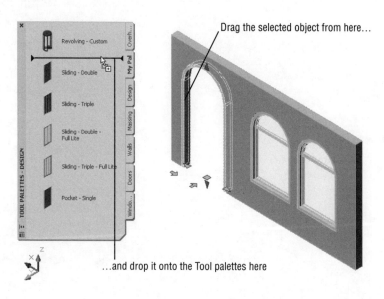

Drag the selected object from here…

…and drop it onto the Tool palettes here

Notice that before you drop the object, an insertion cursor appears in My Pal that indicates where the new tool will be placed. After you drop the object, a new tool appears on My Pal called Cased Opening - Halfround. The icon for this tool might show its plan representation, which is hard to see because this is a cased opening that doesn't show the actual door panel. See the "Customizing Tools" section to learn how to alter tool icons to your liking.

TIP You can drag object style nodes from the Style Manager and drop them in the Tool palettes to create tools.

DRAGGING FROM ADT TO THE CONTENT BROWSER AND BACK

After you make a tool, you can alter its properties (see "Customizing Tools") and/or drag it from the Tool palettes to the Content Browser. You can also drag palettes to the Content Browser by dragging them from their Tool palette tabs.

1. Navigate to the top of the Door Catalog so you see all its categories in the navigation pane.

2. Switch back to ADT and position your cursor on the My Pal tab of the Tool palettes. Drag this palette to the Content Browser and drop it at the top level of the Door Catalog. My Pal appears in the Content Browser (see Figure 3.22).

WARNING You can't drag objects directly from ADT to the Content Browser without first making them tools in the Tool palettes.

3. Switch back to ADT and right-click the My Pal tab. Choose Delete Palette from the shortcut menu. Click OK in the Confirm Palette Deletion dialog box.

FIGURE 3.22
Dragging a palette from ADT to the Content Browser

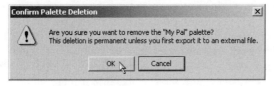

4. Coming full circle, switch back to the Content Browser and drag My Pal back into ADT. My Pal has a Refresh button because it is now linked from the Content Browser. This changes the relationship the tools on My Pal have with ADT. At the beginning of step 2 they were unique, and after step 4 the originals were stored in the Content Browser and linked back to the Tool palettes.

5. Now that you see how this works, go ahead and delete My Pal and the Overhead Doors palette. Open the Tool Palettes properties menu and choose Customize. Delete the Double Doors palette group.

6. Switch to the Tool palettes and delete My Pal from the Door Catalog.

TIP See Chapter 5, "Project Management," to learn about the new project-specific tool palettes.

ORGANIZING YOUR LIBRARY

The steps to organize your library are intuitive and straightforward. You can create catalogs, categories, packages, and palettes directly in the Content Browser. As you saw in the last topic, tools are initially created by dragging them from the Tool palettes into the Content Browser. You can also cut, copy, and paste existing tools anywhere within the Content Browser, including between catalogs.

When categories are nested they create subcategories that automatically get registered with the navigation pane in the Content Browser. When categories are dragged into ADT from the Content Browser, they become palette groups. Packages are containers for multiple tools that get unpacked when dragged onto a palette in ADT. Finally, palettes provide a way to organize related tools and can maintain linkages with the Tool palettes. These mechanisms should fulfill your organizational needs to arrange tools in a clear and logical fashion within your library. Buttons are available at the bottom of the navigation pane within catalogs to create categories, packages, and palettes (see Figure 3.23).

Categories have only a name property, but packages and palettes have additional optional properties—including description, keywords, and publisher (see Figure 2.24). These properties allow catalogs to be sorted by publisher and searched for by keywords in the Content Browser.

Catalogs also have a set of properties (refer to Figure 3.18) that include an optional cover page and a thumbnail image. The cover page must be in HTML format and appears at the top level of a catalog.

TIP Open Door.html from the Door Catalog in a web browser or design program to study an example cover page.

FIGURE 3.23
Creating categories, packages, and palettes

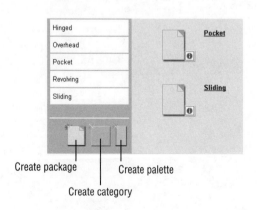

Create package   Create palette

Create category

FIGURE 3.24

Typical Package/Palette
Properties

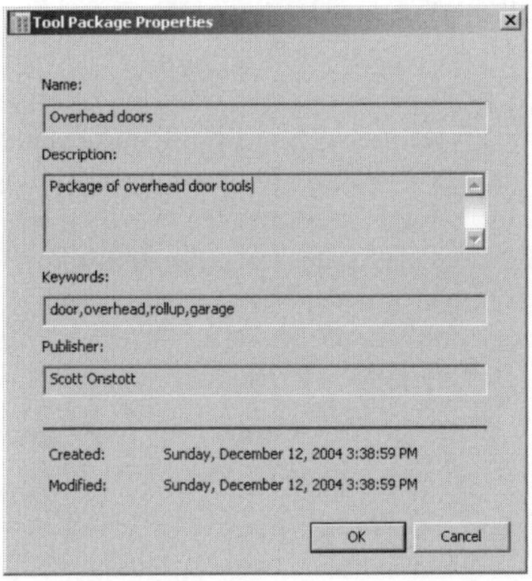

Click the image thumbnail itself in the Catalog Properties dialog box to enter a new image file
(`.jpg` or `.gif` are the recommended image file types). The catalog thumbnail should measure 90×120
pixels in size.

You can use multiple Content Browsers to aid in organizing your library. Instead of separate copy-
and-paste operations, drag items between two Content Browsers. To open an additional Content
Browser, press Ctrl+N in any open Content Browser. You can't drag entire libraries or catalogs, but
all other data structures can be dragged and dropped between open Content Browsers.

WHERE TO FIND CATALOGS

Here are the paths for the default tool catalogs found in the Content Browser:

```
C:\Documents and Settings\All Users\Application Data\Autodesk\ADT 2006\enu\Tool
Catalogs

C:\Documents and Settings\<username>\My Documents\Autodesk\My Content Browser Library

C:\Program Files\Autodesk Architectural Desktop 2006\Catalogs

C:\Program Files\Autodesk Architectural Desktop 2006\DefaultCatalogs

C:\Program Files\Autodesk Architectural Desktop 2006\Tutorial\Architectural
Desktop\TutorialToolCatalog

C:\Program Files\Autodesk Architectural Desktop 2006\Tutorial\Architectural
Desktop\TutorialPalettesCatalog

C:\Program Files\Autodesk Architectural Desktop 2006\Sample\Sample Palette Catalog -
Imperial

C:\Program Files\Autodesk Architectural Desktop 2006\Sample\Sample Palette Catalog -
Metric
```

PUBLISHING CATALOGS FOR TEAMS

After you're satisfied with the content and behavior of a custom catalog, you can publish it to a local file server or to a website, where teams of multiple people will be able to find it. Managers might be responsible for designing and publishing such catalogs. Publishing options are handled by a wizard that is launched by right-clicking a catalog in the Content Browser (see Figure 3.25).

Catalogs have dependent files in which tools reference their object styles. You'll get an error message if the dependent files are deleted or moved from their folders. Fortunately, the Publish Tool Catalog Wizard has options for automatically moving or copying dependent files along with the catalog that's being published (see Figure 3.26).

Here are the options in the four-step Publish Tool Catalog Wizard:

Step 1   Choose move, copy, or leave catalog in current location.

Step 2   Specify where you want to move or copy the catalog (this step is skipped if leaving catalog in current location).

FIGURE 3.25
Publishing a catalog

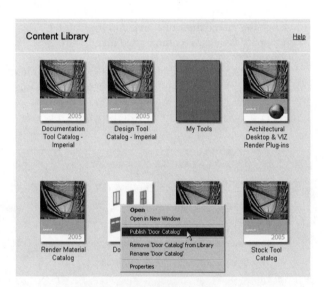

FIGURE 3.26
Publish Tool Catalog
Wizard

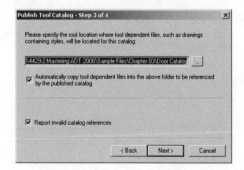

Step 3   Specify where the catalog's dependent files are located. Additional options include the following:

- Automatically move (or copy) tool dependent files into catalog folder
- Report invalid catalog references (this is a good way to identify dependent files)

Step 4   Choose whether to access catalog directly or from aliased location such as a website or mapped drive. Additional options include the following:

- Set catalog to be read-only
- Set catalog to unlinked status

CREATING WINDOWS REGISTRY FILES TO ADD CATALOGS TO DESIGNER LIBRARIES

Managers can install catalogs into designer Content Browser libraries more easily by converting catalogs to Registry files. Hold down Shift and right-click a catalog to convert it to a Registry file. Then copy the Registry file (.reg) to the file server. Double-click the Registry file on each designer's computer to add the catalog and its properties to their library.

Customizing Tools

Each tool can be customized with its own set of properties in the Tool palettes. Tool properties are what separate styled from generic tools. Tool properties can include the object style and the location of its dependent content drawing, layer key overrides, and/or specific dimensions and locations. Any tool properties you leave blank are left to be determined by the designer in the Properties palette after the object is created. Let's see how it works with an example.

1. Start a blank drawing with the default template.

2. Click the Doors palette within the Design set of the Tool palettes. Right-click the Hinged - Single tool and choose Properties from the shortcut menu. The Tool Properties worksheet appears (see Figure 3.27).

3. Click the Layer Overrides worksheet icon to open the Select Layer Overrides worksheet. Uncheck Do Not Specify Layer Overrides and then click the Status ellipsis button (see Figure 3.28).

4. Choose N, "New work" in the Choose a Pre-Specified Value dialog box and click OK. Click OK again to close the Select Layer Overrides worksheet. Notice how the Layer override appears in the Tool Properties worksheet: AIA (256 Color):,,,,N. This means that the letter N will be appended to the end of the layer as defined by the layer key for a door object.

FIGURE 3.27
Tool Properties
worksheet

FIGURE 3.28
Select Layer Overrides
worksheet

Uncheck this first   Status

5. Look in the Dimensions subcategory and notice that the values show up as double dashes (--) by default. This means that the value is generic and will be set when the object is created, or afterward in the Properties palette. Click the double dashes next to Standard sizes and choose 2´-6″ X 6´-8″ from the drop-down list that appears. Selecting values creates a more specific tool (although property values can always be changed during object creation or after objects are created in the Properties palette).

6. Scroll down in the Tool Properties worksheet to the Viewer category and right-click in the object viewer window. Choose Preset Views ➤ NW Isometric from the shortcut menu. Right-click again and choose Shading Modes ➤ Flat Shaded.

7. Right-click the image thumbnail at the top of the Tool Properties worksheet and choose Refresh Image from the shortcut menu. The thumbnail gets refreshed from the viewer (see Figure 3.29). Click OK to close the Tool Properties worksheet.

8. Use your newly customized tool to create a hinged single door in a wall. Notice its icon appears as you saved it in step 7 in the Tool palettes. Open the Properties palette and observe that the object was created on the A-Door-N layer (overridden from layer key), has a width of 2´-6˝, and has a height of 6´-8˝ as specified in its tool properties (see Figure 3.30). You can make changes in its properties like any other door object; the customized tool merely pre-populated the object's properties values.

9. Set the Hinged - Single door tool back to its defaults by replacing the version you customized with a copy from the sample palette catalog.

FIGURE 3.29
Adjusting the viewer within the Tool Properties worksheet

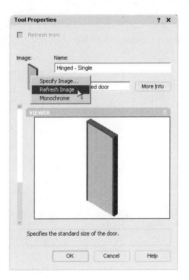

FIGURE 3.30
Properties after object was created from custom tool

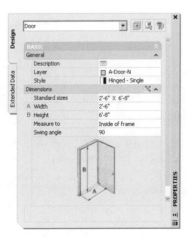

NOTE Being able to Ctrl-select multiple tools to set properties in the Tool palettes and Content Browser is a great new feature in ADT 2006. You can apply tool properties to a selection of tools or save time by dragging multiple selected tools at once.

Generating Tool Catalogs from Content Drawings

New!

You can have ADT 2006 create tool catalogs from existing drawings with the powerful new Tool Catalog Generator. The generator scans one or more content drawings for the object types you choose, creating catalogs, categories, and/or palettes based on existing styles.

The Tool Catalog Generator works from ADT, so you'll have to manually load the catalogs it generates into the Content Browser. Let's give it a try on one of the sample files that ships with ADT.

1. Choose Window ➢ Pulldowns ➢ CAD Manager Pulldown. This loads a new menu.

2. Choose CAD Manager ➢ Tool Catalog Generator to open the Populate Tool Catalog From Content Drawings dialog box (see Figure 3.31).

FIGURE 3.31

Populating a tool catalog from content drawings

3. In the Catalog group, click Create a New Catalog and type **Brick Wall Styles** for the catalog name. Click the Browser button and choose the following path in which the catalog will be created:

```
C:\Documents and Settings\All Users\Application Data\Autodesk\ADT 2006\enu\Tool
Catalogs\BrickWallCatalog
```

To do this, you will have to create a new folder in the Browse dialog box called `BrickWallCatalog`.

NOTE Notice the option to add styles to an existing catalog; this option is good for extending an existing catalog with additional tool palettes.

4. In the Content Source group, choose Create From Drawing and click its Browse button. Choose the following file containing sample object styles:

   ```
   C:\Documents and Settings\All Users\Application Data\Autodesk\ADT
   2006\enu\Styles\Imperial\Wall Styles - Brick (Imperial).dwg
   ```

WARNING Although it is possible to create a catalog from a folder, be aware that it can take a long time to process if the folder's drawings contain a lot of styles.

5. In the Tool Organization group, check Group Tools By Source Drawing and choose Create Tools In Palettes. Uncheck Group Tools By Object Type.

6. Click the Clear All button below the Create Tools For The Following Objects group. Then check Wall Styles only. Click OK to process your request and close the Populate Tool Catalog From Content Drawings dialog box. Be patient while ADT processes your request (you'll see progress bars appear on the application status bar).

After the Tool Catalog Generator completes its processing, you might be wondering what to do next because it does not automatically open the catalog in the Content Browser; you'll have to do it manually.

1. Open the Content Browser if it is not already open and click the Home button to return to the catalog level. Click the Add Or Create Catalog button at the bottom of the naviga tion pane.

2. Choose to Add An Existing Catalog and browse to the following location:

   ```
   C:\Program Files\Autodesk Architectural Desktop 2006\Catalogs\ BrickWallCatalog
   ```

   Choose the catalog file generated in the previous procedure called `Brick Wall Styles.atc` and click Open. Click OK to close the dialog box.

3. Enter the Brick Wall Styles catalog and open its Wall Styles - Brick (Imperial) palette. Figure 3.32 shows the tools that were generated from the content drawing.

4. Close the Content Browser when you are done.

FIGURE 3.32
Tools generated from a
content drawing shown
in Content Browser

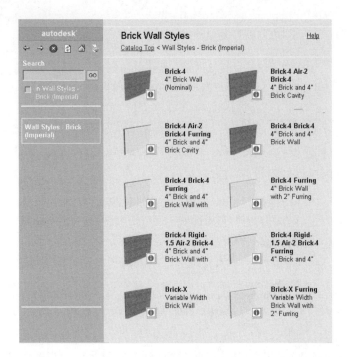

What's In a Style?

There are essentially five points of access to styles in ADT: the Content Browser, Tool palettes, Properties palette, Style Manager dialog box, and by choosing Edit Style in object shortcut menus. As you learned in the last section, the Content Browser gives access to a plethora of object styles represented by tools. The Tool palettes let you customize tools, but they allow you to assign only a particular preexisting style to a generic tool. The Properties palette is yet another place in which you can assign a style to an object, but not edit it. Thus far, you haven't learned how to edit styles—or what's in a style—which is what you'll learn in this important section.

The Style Manager is the main interface for working with the styles of all object types. In this section, you'll see how the Style Manager organizes object types into categories, lets you edit styles, and copies styles between drawings.

Almost all objects in ADT have styles (but not all). The most convenient way to work on a particular object type's style is to choose Edit Style (or Copy Style And Assign) in the object shortcut menu. In addition to styles, all objects have Edit Object Display as a choice in their shortcut menus. Object display allows you to override styles for particular objects (used only in exceptional cases).

Exploring the Style Manager

Like the Display Manager, the Style Manager is one-stop shopping within another potentially giant resizable dialog box. With the Style Manager, not only do you have access to all the styles in the current drawing, but to all open drawings and project standard drawings (see Chapter 5). You can also

UNDERSTANDING DISPLAY PROPERTY SOURCES

It's crucial to understand the hierarchy of display property sources that are at the center of how styles work in ADT.

First of all, what are display properties? In Chapter 2, "Object Display," you learned how display properties are managed by objects' display representations. Display properties include component visibility, material setting, layer, color, linetype, and more. Many objects have additional display property content arranged on tabs, for example, Hatching, Muntins, Contents, and so on (specific to the object type).

As if this weren't enough, display properties have the added complexity of being sourced at different levels of a hierarchy. However, this gives you tremendous power and flexibility to control exactly where display properties apply. Display property sources include the following levels:

Drawing Default   At the base of the hierarchy, this is what you see in the Display Manager's representations. The drawing default establishes the basis of all styles of a particular object type. For example, the drawing default is what all wall styles have in common. So far in this book, you've seen only the drawing default property source.

Style Override   Supercedes the drawing default with a style's own set of display properties, giving display control to the style itself. For example, you can apply a style override to the Concrete-8 style so that the display of all 8″ concrete walls is controlled independently from other styles in the drawing (see the section "Editing Object Styles").

Object Override   Supercedes both the drawing default and style override at the object level. An object override gives the complete set of display properties to a particular object, offering maximum control over its display (see the section "Editing Object Display"). Care should be taken to override only down to the object level in exceptional situations (when creating an additional style for a single object is not warranted).

open any drawing to access its styles within the Style Manager (without opening the drawing itself). Therefore, as its name suggests, the Style Manager is the central place to manage and exchange styles. Let's explore.

1. Open `StyledObjects.dwg` from this chapter's folder on the companion DVD (refer to Figure 3.5).

2. Choose Format ➢ Style Manager to open a dialog box of the same name. Notice that there are drawings open as nodes in Figure 3.33. Each drawing contains three object categories: architectural, documentation, and multipurpose.

3. In the current drawing, expand the Architectural Objects category. Expand the Door Styles node and observe that there are five custom styles defined in this drawing in addition to the ever-present Standard generic style. Click Bifold - Single and observe that the content pane shows a tabbed interface (see Figure 3.34). Click each tab to open a property sheet in which style content is further organized.

NOTE   Tabbed property sheets within the Style Manager itself are new in ADT 2006 (they used to open in a separate dialog box). You'll see the new Version History tab only when working on standards drawings in the Style Manager (see Chapter 5).

Figure 3.33
Style Manager's drawing and object categorization

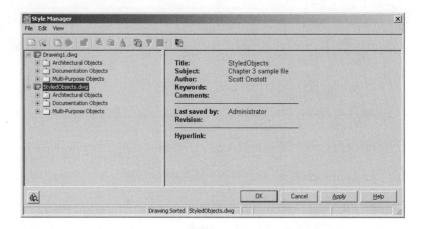

Figure 3.34
Accessing Door Styles

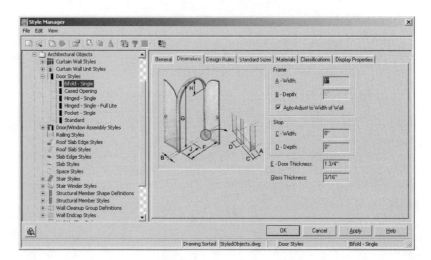

4. Scroll down in the tree pane and expand the Wall Styles node. Click the Brick-4 Brick-4 style. Notice how many of the property sheets are different in the wall as compared with the door (see Figure 3.35).

5. Take a few minutes and explore the many object types and their styles' property sheets to become familiar with the Style Manager interface. Close the Style Manager when you're done.

The property sheets that object types have in common are General, Materials, Classifications, Display Properties, and Version History (see preceding note). Many different property sheets appear in other object types, including Dimension, Design Rules, Standard Sizes, Components, Shape, Overrides, and Endcaps/Opening Endcaps. You'll learn specifically how to use each of these with step-by-step examples in Part 3, "Design Development" and Part 4, "Construction Documentation."

FIGURE 3.35
Wall Style property
sheets in the Style
Manager

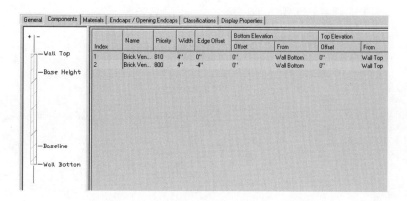

FILTERING STYLES WITH STYLE MANAGER

It is helpful to simplify the Style Manager by filtering it to display only one type of object, especially when you have many drawing nodes open. This allows you to focus on what you are working on, and makes it easier to copy and paste styles between drawings.

1. Click the Design palette if it is not already selected. Right-click the generic wall tool and choose Wall Styles from the shortcut menu (see Figure 3.36).

2. The Style Manager appears, showing only wall styles. Notice that the plus symbols next to other nodes are gone, allowing you to easily find and focus on your chosen object type. Expand the Architectural Object node in Drawing1.dwg; only the Wall Styles node appears inside. Click the Filter Style Type button (see Figure 3.37).

3. All the object type nodes appear after you toggle Filter Style Type off. Scroll up in the left pane and click the Door Styles node. Toggle Filter Style Type on. Again, the display is filtered showing only door styles.

FIGURE 3.36
Filtering the Style
Manager with the
Tool shortcut menu

FIGURE 3.37
Toggling the Filter Style
Type button

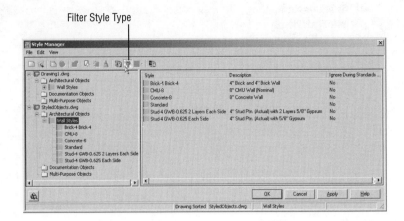

CREATING NEW OBJECT STYLES

Styles are almost never created from scratch. Instead, new styles are born from existing or standard styles that you first copy and then edit to your liking. When you create a so-called new style, it is actually a copy of that object type's standard style. You can copy and paste styles in the Style Manager to exchange styles between drawings. As in the Layer Manager, you can only purge (delete) a style if it is not being used anywhere in a particular drawing.

The easiest way to create a new style does not actually involve the Style Manager. There is an option in the object shortcut menu called Copy Style And Assign, which first duplicates the selected object's style and then assigns the duplicate style to the object. Let's give it a try.

1. Select a door and then right-click, opening its object shortcut menu. Choose Copy Door Style And Assign. The Door Style Properties dialog box appears, which has the same style property sheets you'd see for a door in the Style Manager.

2. Click the General tab and change the name ending in "(2)" to Double Door. This first thing you should always do when using Copy Style And Assign is change the name as it was just duplicated.

3. The next task is to edit the style in some way. Click the Design Rules tab. Select Double in the Door Type group. Notice that the new style name appears on the title bar (see Figure 3.38). Click OK to close the dialog box.

4. Open the Style Manager and verify that Double Door appears under the current drawing's Door Styles node.

TIP Right-click while in the Style Manager to access commands such as Copy, Paste, and Purge.

Editing Object Styles

You can edit styles either in the Style Manager or by selecting an object and choosing Edit Style from its shortcut menu. Using the Style Manager is appropriate when you plan to edit multiple styles, or when you are copying and pasting styles between drawings. Using Edit Style from the shortcut menu is better suited to working on one style at a time. In addition, use Copy Style And Assign in the object shortcut menu when you want to start editing a new style.

1. Start a new blank drawing with the default template.

2. In the Tool palettes, click the Doors palette and click the Hinged - Single door tool. Create a door in the drawing window.

3. Click the door and then right-click to open its shortcut menu. Choose Edit Door Style.

4. Click the General tab to open its property sheet. Notice that there is already information filled into this custom style. Every style must have a name, and changes made to the Name text box immediately appear on the Door Style Properties dialog box's title bar (see Figure 3.38). This style is assigned a keynote for documentation purposes (see Chapter 17, "Details and Keynotes").

FIGURE 3.38
Door Style Properties

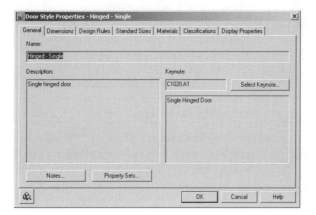

ON THE IMPORTANCE OF NAMING

In the long run, it really pays to give styles descriptive names. The drawing you are working on today might have styles that you or another designer uses tomorrow. For example, you can avoid a lot of confusion in the future by naming a wall style Brick-4 Brick-4 rather than Brick Wall. The former name gives more information (naming the component widths) and saves you time in comparison with the latter (you would have to edit to learn the widths of its component parts).

What benefit would the style name Standard(2) offer? It indicates that it is different from the generic style, but in what way? We don't know without having to spend time to investigate every time we encounter the style. So pay attention to naming—you'll be happy you did.

5. Click the Property Sets button. The Edit Property Set Data worksheet appears. Property sets are data structures that can be attached to object styles that are used in annotation tags and schedules (see Chapter 13, "Annotating, Tagging, and Dimensioning" and Chapter 14, "Schedules, Display Themes, and Areas"). Click Cancel to close the worksheet.

6. Click the Notes button to open the Notes dialog box in which you can access notes and reference documents on tabs of the same names (see Figure 3.39). Notes are anything you'd like to write about a particular style, in plain text (longer than a description). Reference documents can be in any file format and are attached to object styles with the straightforward interface in the Notes dialog box. Click Cancel for now.

NOTE Some examples of useful reference documents include product specification sheets in .pdf format, manufacturer contact information, product photos, and/or material sample images. You can attach anything to styles.

Every style has General, Materials, Classifications, and Display Properties property sheets. You'll learn about materials and classifications in the "Working with Definition Styles" section. The door object also has property sheets for Dimensions, Design Rules, and Standard Sizes that you'll learn how to use in Chapter 9, "Doors, Windows, and Openings." Display Properties control the way objects appear.

FIGURE 3.39
Accessing notes and
reference documents

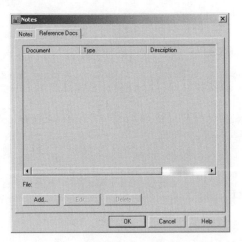

7. Click the Display Properties tab in the Door Style Properties dialog box. Notice that the display representations you see when editing the door style are the same as those seen in the Display Manager (refer to Chapter 2). Changes you make to the drawing default property source affect all styles of that object type (all door styles, for example).

8. Notice that two display representations are shown in bold: Plan and Threshold Plan, meaning that these representations are currently being displayed in the drawing window. Therefore, only the edits you make to the bold representations are immediately visible on-screen (without changing viewpoint or display configuration). Select the Plan representation and then click the Edit Display Properties button (see Figure 3.40).

9. The dialog box that appears has the following in its title bar:

```
Display Properties (Drawing Default) - Door Plan Display Representation
```

It is all spelled out for you in the title bar; pay attention to the title bar to be sure which display property source you are editing. Change the color of the Door Panel component from ByBlock to green (see Figure 3.41).

NOTE Notice that the Other tab is also available in the Display Property dialog box. Different tabs are available depending on the object type.

10. Click OK to close the Display properties dialog box and click OK again to close the Door Style Properties dialog box. Notice that the door object in the drawing window now has a green door panel. Create another door of a different style. Notice that its door panel is also green. Changing the default property source affects all styles of a given object type (all doors, in this case).

FIGURE 3.40
Comparing Display Properties in an object style with the same object type shown in the Display Manager

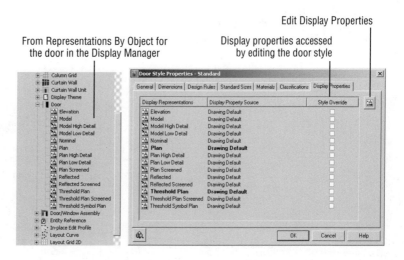

From Representations By Object for the door in the Display Manager

Display properties accessed by editing the door style

Edit Display Properties

FIGURE 3.41
Editing the drawing
default display proper-
ties of the door plan
representation

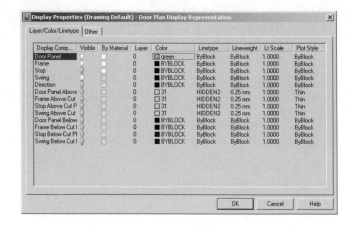

11. Open the Display Manager, expand Representations By Object, and then expand the Door node. Select the Door's Plan representation and change its Door Panel component color from green back to ByBlock (see Figure 3.42). Close the Select Color and Display Manager dialog boxes by clicking OK twice. Using the Display Manager is an alternative to editing the drawing default with the Edit Style command.

12. Select the first door you made (Hinged - Single style). Right-click and choose Edit Door Style. Choose the Display Properties tab in the Door Style Properties - Hinged - Single dialog box if it's not already selected. This time, check the box next to the Plan display representation in the Style Override column (see Figure 3.43).

13. As soon as you check the Style Override box, another Display Properties dialog box appears. Its title bar says the following:

```
Display Properties (Door Style Override - Hinged - Single) - Door Plan Display
Representation
```

FIGURE 3.42
Select Color dialog box

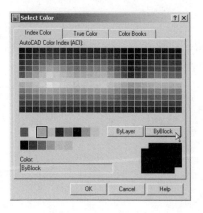

FIGURE 3.43
Making a Style Override

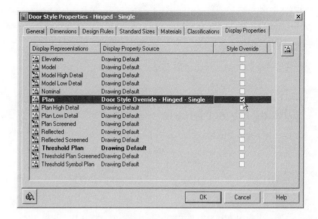

Always pay attention to what information the title bar is giving you. The dialog box shows the same set of properties as Figure 3.43, but this time its display properties override the drawing default at the style level. Change the Door Panel component color from ByBlock to blue (see Figure 3.44).

TIP Style overrides are also editable in the Style Manager.

14. Click OK twice to close out of the open dialog boxes. Notice that only the Hinged - Single door's panel is blue in the drawing window. Doors of all other styles are unaffected. This is what it means to override display properties at the style level. The Hinged - Single door style now has independent display control of the generic door object's Plan representation.

15. Go back to the Display Manager and verify that the Door object's Door Panel component still has its color property set to ByBlock. The color blue is accessible only through the Edit Style command as a style override. Close the Display Manager.

FIGURE 3.44
Editing display properties at the style level

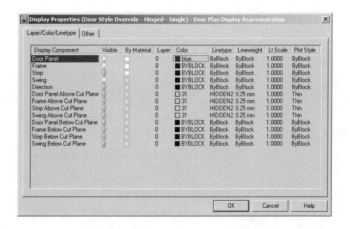

TIP If you want to edit an existing style override, don't uncheck it in the Style Properties dialog box (that clears it); just select the representation you are working on and click the Edit Display Properties button.

16. Save your work as **Overrides.dwg**. You can leave this file open if you plan to continue to the next section.

Editing Object Display

Objects form the lowest level of the display hierarchy (as was pointed out earlier in the "Understanding Display Property Sources" sidebar). In general, you should edit object display only in exceptional cases when you want to change the way a single object appears. It makes sense to edit object display when it's not worth it to you to create a new style or to change the way all objects appear in the drawing defaults.

1. If you left the sample file open from the last section, you can continue here. If not, open `Overrides.dwg` from the working folder on your hard drive or the companion DVD.

2. Make a copy of the door with the blue panel (it has the Hinged - Single style assigned).

3. Select the new door object, right-click, and choose Edit Object Display from the shortcut menu. The Object Display dialog box appears. It is organized with three tabs: Material, Display Properties, and General Properties. Click the Display Properties tab (see Figure 3.45).

NOTE See the "Working with Definition Styles" section to see how Material overrides can be applied in the Object Display dialog box.

4. Notice that the Plan representation already has a style override applied to it, whereas the other representations have drawing default as their display property source. Click the Threshold Plan representation and then click the Edit Display Properties button.

5. The dialog box that appears has the following title bar:

```
Display Properties (Drawing Default) - Door Threshold Plan Display
Representation
```

The important thing to recognize here is that you are looking at drawing default properties. Remember that you can also access the same thing in Edit Style, the Style Manager, and the Display Manager. Chances are you won't edit object display just to access the drawing default display properties. Click Cancel to close the dialog box and return to the Object Display dialog box.

6. Check the box next to the Plan display representation in the Object Override column. The Display Properties dialog box immediately appears and its title bar identifies it as a door override.

7. Change the Door Panel component's color from blue (set in the style override) to magenta. Click OK twice to close both dialog boxes.

The drawing window now has one door showing a magenta door panel. The three doors display differently because of style and object overrides.

8. Select the door with the magenta-colored panel and edit its object display again. The Plan representation shows up now as Door Override in the Display Property Source column.

9. Click the General Properties tab (see Figure 3.46). All objects have general properties, including color, layer, linetype, linetype scale, lineweight, and plot style (just as entities do in AutoCAD). The general properties are global and affect all object components. However, general properties override only the drawing default settings; style and object overrides are still visible. Leave these settings alone and close the dialog box.

WARNING   Avoid changing general properties for objects (leave them set to ByLayer). They are appropriate for overriding entity display properties in exceptional cases only. Layers should be used primarily to control entity display properties.

FIGURE 3.45
Editing object display

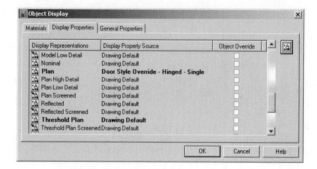

FIGURE 3.46
Object Display General
Properties

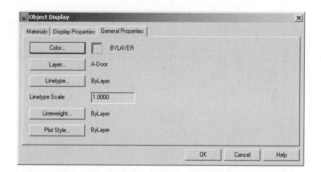

Working with Definition Styles

Definition styles aren't objects in themselves, but can be assigned within object styles. Think of them as styles within styles, if you will. We'll be looking at the multipurpose material and classification definition styles in this section. Property set definitions are another nonobject style you'll learn about in Chapter 14. See Chapter 8, "Walls, Blocks, and Anchors," to learn about Multi-View Block Definitions and Mask Block Definitions (both of them are inserted as objects in a drawing).

Assigning Materials

Materials represent real-world finishes such as glass, concrete, brick, or wood, and provide high level control of display properties with a definition style. For example, you can assign a glass material to windows, door lights (also known as "lites" to differentiate glazing from actual light sources), curtain walls, and furniture components. If in the course of the design process you decide to use frosted glass everywhere instead of transparent glass, changing one material definition updates all the object components that reference it from any number of object styles.

New!

Material definitions are assigned to specific object components, such as wood to a door panel and metal to the doorframe. ADT 2006 features a new material tool that makes assigning materials easier. As you learned in Chapter 2, most objects have the option to display selected components By Material rather than through object display properties. When this setting is checked, materials take over the job of displaying the component in question.

1. Create a new blank drawing with the default template.

2. Choose Format ➤ Material Definitions to open a filtered Style Manager. Click the Standard definition and click the Display Properties tab in the content pane. All of Standard's display representations already have style overrides applied (see Figure 3.47). Materials apply to all object types, so there is no such thing as a default property source for material definitions. Close the Style Manager.

FIGURE 3.47

Standard material definition in Style Manager

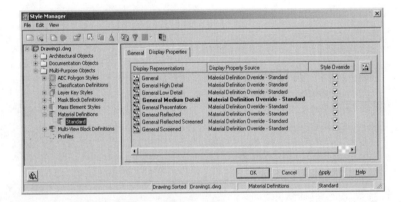

3. Create a generic wall, door, and window. Change to an isometric viewpoint and shaded view. The objects appear as a flat gray in the drawing window.

4. Click the Material tool on the Design palette.

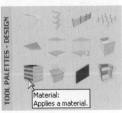

5. Clicking the Door object opens a worksheet. Choose Doors & Windows.Wood Doors.Ash from the drop-down list. Click Leave As Is in the Apply To column for the Panel component and choose Style from the drop-down list that appears (see Figure 3.48). Click OK to close the worksheet. The door appears wooden in the drawing window.

TIP You can also use the Material tool to apply materials to components as object overrides in exceptional cases. You can select multiple components and apply the same material to all of them in one step—use the standard Windows Shift and Ctrl selection techniques.

6. Use the Material tool to apply material definitions at the style level according to Table 3.3.

NOTE The Material tool automatically loads the material definitions you apply to components into the current drawing.

7. Select the door, right-click it, and choose Edit Door Style. Click the Display Properties tab, click the Model display representation (in bold because it's currently being used), and click the Edit Display Properties button. Notice that the Door Panel component has a check in its By Material column; this is part of the reason why we can see the material in the drawing window. Click Cancel to close the Display Properties dialog box, but leave the Door Style Properties dialog box open.

TIP If you still can't see materials, check the Display Manager and verify that the General Medium Detail representation for the Material Definition is checked in your current display set matrix.

8. Click the Materials tab in the Door Style Properties dialog box. This is another place to assign materials to components. Click any of the materials in the Material Definition column and notice that only materials defined in the current drawing appear in the drop-down lists (see Figure 3.49). You can't load new material definitions here as you can using the Material tool. Click OK to close the dialog box.

9. Save your work as **Materials.dwg**. You can leave this file open if you plan to continue to the next section.

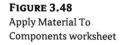

FIGURE 3.48
Apply Material To Components worksheet

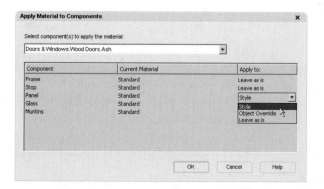

FIGURE 3.49
Material property
sheet of Window Style
Properties

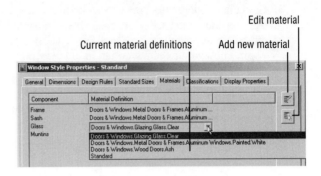

Edit material

Current material definitions

Add new material

TABLE 3.3: Objects, Components, and Material Definition Assignments

OBJECT	COMPONENT	MATERIAL DEFINITION
Window	Frame	Doors & Windows.Metal Doors & Frames.Aluminum Windows.Painted.White
Window	Sash	Doors & Windows.Metal Doors & Frames.Aluminum Windows.Painted.White
Window	Glass	Doors & Windows.Glazing.Glass.Clear
Door	Frame	Doors & Windows.Metal Doors & Frames.Aluminum Windows.Painted.White

Editing Material Definitions

Each material definition controls display components that appear in different kinds of drawings, including plans, elevations, sections, and 3D live sections. You can edit material definitions in the Style Manager or gain more specific access through the Material property sheet when editing object styles.

Material definitions are different from *rendering materials* (not architecture, engineering, and construction [AEC] objects), which determine the realistic shaded appearance of objects. VIZ Render uses rendering materials to create photo-realistic renderings (see Chapter 18). In this section you'll also learn how to access and assign VIZ Render's rendering materials within ADT material definitions.

1. If you left the sample file open from the last section, you can continue here. If not, open `Materials.dwg` from the working folder on your hard drive or the companion DVD.

2. Select the window object and edit its style. Click the Material tab and select the Glass component.

3. Click the Edit Material button (refer to Figure 3.49). A new dialog box appears called Material Definition Properties, which shows the display representations of the material definition on the Display Properties tab.

4. Select the General Medium Detail representation and click the Edit Display Properties button. A third dialog box opens that contains the display properties of the material definition override. This is the ultimate place in the display system to set properties such as visibility, layer, color, linetype, and so on.

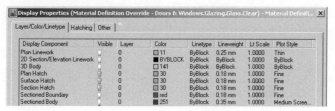

The display components of a material definition are never all seen in the same view. Instead, the components in Table 3.4 determine how the material will appear in many different types of drawings.

5. Click the Hatching tab. There are three hatching components for plan, surface, and section hatches. Click the icon for the pattern of the plan hatch and you'll see some familiar patterns from the Boundary Hatch AutoCAD command. Cancel out after you take a look.

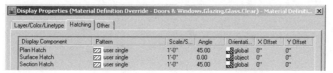

6. Click the Other tab in the material definition override display properties dialog box (see Figure 3.50). Here you can choose from the six orientations to display surface hatches, assign a rendering material and select its mapping type, assign live section render materials, and set section/elevation options (see Chapter 16, "Sections and Elevations").

TABLE 3.4: Material Definition Display Component Uses

DISPLAY COMPONENT	USE
Plan Linework	Linework in plan view
2D Section/Elevation	Linework in 2D section or elevation
3D Body	Linework in any 3D view
Plan Hatch	Appears only in plan view
Surface Hatch	Appears on surfaces in six possible orientations
Section Hatch	Appears on all faces cut by a section line
Sectioned Boundary	Outline of live section cut line
Sectioned Body	Parts of objects outside live section

7. Click the Browse button next to the surface rendering render material to open the Select Rendering Material dialog box. The only possibility here is to select a rendering material from those already loaded into the current drawing. Because rendering materials are not objects, you can't load them using the Style Manager. Cancel out of all the open dialog boxes.

8. Open the Content Browser and enter the Render Material catalog. Open the Doors and Windows, and Glazing categories. Drag the Doors & Windows.Glazing.Blue render material into ADT's drawing window.

TIP You can drag render materials you create in VIZ Render to the Content Browser and later drag them from the Content Browser into ADT.

9. The Create AEC Material worksheet appears. Choose Doors & Windows.Glazing.Glass.Clear from the drop-down list as your AEC Material to use as a template. Type **Doors & Windows .Glazing.Glass.Blue** for the New AEC Material Name (see Figure 3.51). Click OK.

10. Select the window object and edit its style. Assign Doors & Windows.Glazing.Glass.Blue to its Glass component. Repeat steps 3–7 and verify that Doors & Windows.Glazing.Blue is the assigned surface rendering material. Click OK in each dialog box to accept the changes.

FIGURE 3.50
The "Other" property sheet of a material definition

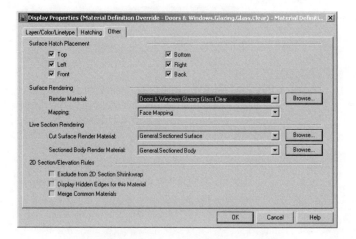

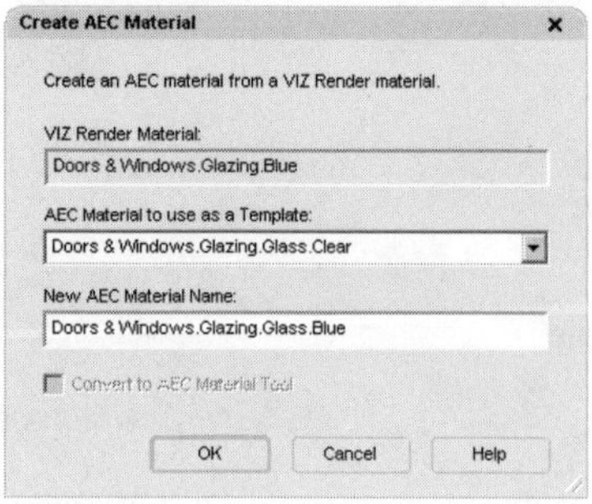

FIGURE 3.51
Create the AEC Material worksheet

TIP Check out the specialized MaterialList and MaterialQuery commands in ADT Help.

11. Another way to edit materials is to apply overrides at the object level. Click the door object and edit its object display. Click the Materials tab within the Object Display dialog box. Place a check in the Object Override column for the Panel component (see Figure 3.52).

12. Assign a different material to the Panel component in the Material Definition column's drop-down list. Remember that this override affects this object only (and not other members of the Hinged - Single style). You also have access to edit the material definition itself here as you did in step 4 when editing object style. Click OK and close the drawing.

FIGURE 3.52
Overriding material definitions within object display

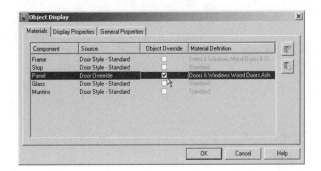

Defining Classifications

Classifications are an optional feature that allows you to create your own data structures. You'll create a construction status definition here with several classifications including new work, existing to remain, and existing to demolish. Classification definitions are used ultimately to filter the styles shown in display sets and schedule tables. Let's begin by creating a classification definition.

1. Create a new blank drawing with the default template.

2. Choose Format ➢ Classification Definitions to open a filtered Style Manager. Right-click the Classification Definitions node and choose New from its shortcut menu. A new node appears as follows; give it the name **Construction Status**. Click the new Construction Status node.

3. In the content pane of the Style Manager, click the Classifications tab. Click the Add button and type **N** in the Name field and **New work** in the Description field.

4. Click the Add button again and type **E** in the Name field and **Existing to remain** in the Description field.

5. Add another classification called **D** with the description **Existing to demolish**.

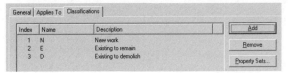

TIP You might eventually want to make classification definitions for door types including interior, exterior, screens, and toilet partition doors. You can also attach property set data to classifications. For example, a vendor property set could be attached to track additional information with the classification such as preferred vendor status. All of this can be put in a schedule table.

6. Click the Applies To tab. Check Door Style, Window Style, and Wall Style. Click OK to close the Style Manager.

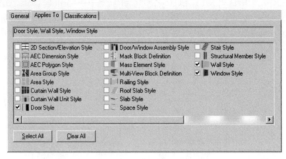

WARNING Classification definitions must apply to at least one object style type to function.

7. Save your work as **Classifications.dwg**. You can leave this file open if you plan to continue to the next section.

Using Classifications

Classifications can be used to filter objects in the display system and in schedule tables. You'll learn about schedule tables in Chapter 14. Here you'll learn how to show or hide objects in the drawing window using classifications.

1. If you left the sample file open from the last section, you can continue here. If not, open `Materials.dwg` from the working folder on your hard drive or the companion DVD.

2. Insert `StyledObjects.dwg` into the current drawing. Be sure to check Explode at the bottom of the Insert dialog box so you'll have access to the objects.

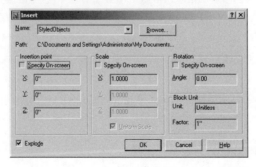

3. Select any one of the six wall objects. Edit its object style and click the Classifications tab. Change the drop-down for the Construction Status classification definition you made in the last section to D (Existing To Demolish). Click OK.

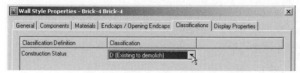

4. Select the door that is inside the wall you chose in the last step. Change its classification to D.

5. Select the window next to the door you just changed. Change its classification also to D.

6. Open the Display Manager. Expand the Sets node and select the Plan display set (it appears in bold because it is current).

7. In the content pane of the Display Manager, click the Display Options tab. Click Show in the Filter column for the D (Existing To Demolish) classification and change it to Hide (see Figure 3.53). Click OK.

WARNING   You may need to use the REGEN command to see changes on-screen.

The wall, door, and window disappear from the drawing window. You can make any classifications you need and filter the display system in this way. Be aware that classifications are attached to object styles, so it pays to plan ahead and make tools with classifications embedded before you create all the objects in your design. Otherwise, it can be very time-consuming after the fact to change classifications in every object style throughout a project.

FIGURE 3.53
Hiding objects with
classifications

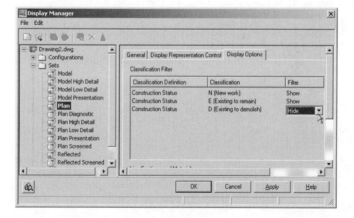

Summary

You have been exposed to perhaps an overwhelming amount of information in this chapter regarding object styles. From creating your first objects and setting their properties, to creating tool catalogs in the Content Browser and studying the intricacies of style, only now are you prepared to get to work with objects in ADT. The first three chapters of this book form a solid foundation for you to understand Architectural Desktop.

Part 2

Conceptual Design

Chapter 4

Mass Modeling

The design process often starts by considering the big picture. What are your client's needs? What sort of parti do you have in mind that fulfills the building program? How does the building respond to its site? Do you sketch schematic ideas in a notebook or have you ever been caught sketching important design ideas on a cocktail napkin during an inspiring conversation?

TIP   Check out SketchUp (www.SketchUp.com) and tablet computers for the ultimate portable digital conceptual design solution. SketchUp exports .dwg files that you can bring into ADT to continue with design development. Autodesk used to have a similar product called Architectural Studio that has been discontinued.

If you are designing an entire structure, creating a massing model in ADT might help you to work out spatial design ideas when they are still in the conceptual stage. Developing a massing model is an "outside-in" design process, in which you'll create overall exterior volumes called *mass elements* to determine the structure and proportion of a building.

In this chapter's tutorial approach, you'll organize mass elements into mass groups and learn techniques to better visualize and document the massing model. In the end, you'll slice *floorplates* from the massing model that determine the boundaries of the individual floors of the building. Finally, you'll convert floorplates to space boundaries that you'll use to develop a project structure in the next chapter. This chapter includes the following topics:

◆   Working with Mass Elements

◆   Working with Mass Groups

◆   Visualizing the Massing Model

◆   Slicing Floorplates from the Massing Model

Working with Mass Elements

Mass elements are geometric shapes that you use to define building volumes. ADT has a number of archetypal (also known as primitive) shapes, including the arch, barrel vault, box, cone, cylinder, dome, gable, pyramid, sphere, isosceles triangle, right triangle, and Doric column. Here's how a mass element gets started:

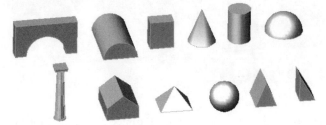

1. Create a new blank drawing with the default template.

2. Select the Massing palette in the Design palette group in Tool Palettes (see Figure 4.1).

3. Verify that the POLAR, OSNAP, OTRACK, and DYN toggles are on in the application status bar.

4. Click the Box tool and then click any point in the drawing window to set the location of this mass element's first corner.

5. Type @ to indicate that you'll be entering new coordinates relative to the first corner: The dynamic input display appears on-screen. Type **90´,60´** and press Enter.

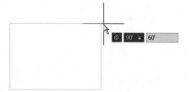

6. Notice that the command line asks for Height or [Shape/Undo]:. Type **20´** and press Enter.

7. The final step in creating a box mass element appears on the command line: Rotation or [Shape/Undo] <0.00>:. Press Enter to accept the default of 0 degrees to complete the command. Your first mass element appears in the drawing window as a hatched rectangle in top view. Press Esc to cancel the continuation of the MassElementAdd command.

FIGURE 4.1
Massing tool palette

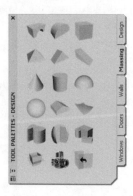

The color of the mass element is controlled by its object style (cyan by default). To help identify the volumes of the various mass elements that you'll be adding, create named styles that display different hatching colors for each portion of the building model. Here's some practice in using styles for easy identification:

1. Click the mass element to select it. Right-click and choose Copy Mass Element Style And Assign from the object shortcut menu. The Mass Element Style Properties dialog box appears.

2. Click the General tab and give this new style the name **Main Office**. I will refer to mass elements by their style names in this tutorial.

3. Click the Display Properties tab and notice that the Plan High Detail representation is shown in bold, meaning that it is currently being displayed in the drawing window. Somewhat unusually, the Mass Element style does not have a Plan representation as many other styles do. Instead, this style displays the Plan High Detail representation in the Medium Detail display configuration. Check to create a style override in the Plan High Detail representation (see Figure 4.2).

4. The Display Properties dialog box appears. Click the color property (set to 130 by default) for the Hatch component to open the Select Color dialog box. Choose blue and click OK (see Figure 4.3). Click OK twice more to close both remaining open dialog boxes.

FIGURE 4.2
Creating a style override

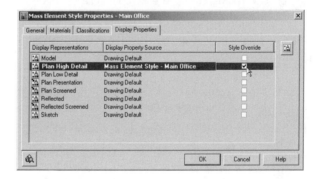

FIGURE 4.3
Setting display properties

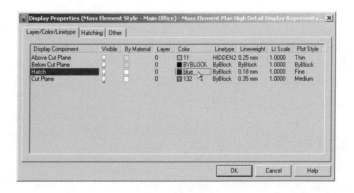

5. Switch to the SW Isometric viewpoint. Notice that the mass element's 3D representation is shown, but the hatch pattern is not displayed in this display set. Click the Main Office mass to reveal its grips. Hover the mouse over each grip, revealing their ToolTips: There is a location grip in the center; individual height, depth, width grips on opposite sides; plus width and depth grips on each corner. Click the top Height grip, type **39′** into the dynamic input text box and press Enter to resize the mass element. Press Esc to deselect.

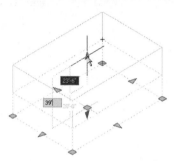

6. Switch to Gouraud Shaded, Edges On shading mode; the mass appears solid in the isometric viewpoint. Switch to Top view; the hatch pattern appears even while you are in a shaded mode.

The next mass element you'll add is at an angle to the first one. Of course, you could create another box and then rotate it, but rotating the z-axis and then creating the object directly in a user coordinate system (UCS) is a more attractive alternative when you plan to create multiple objects with the same rotation.

1. Draw a construction line vertically through the midpoint of Main Office (see Figure 4.4). I will refer to this construction line as the building's major axis.

2. Rotate the z-axis 45 degrees by typing **UCS↵ Z↵ 45↵**.

3. Start another box-shaped mass element where the construction line meets the lower edge of the Main Office mass element. Type **@50′,130′↵** to enter the width and depth; then type **25′↵** for the height, press Enter to accept the default rotation angle of 0.0, and press Esc.

FIGURE 4.4
Drawing a vertical
construction line

Main Office mass element

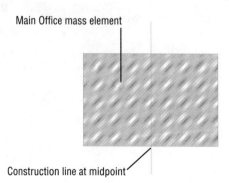

Construction line at midpoint

4. Select the new object, right-click and choose Copy Mass Element And Assign to open the Style Properties dialog box. Click the General tab, rename the style from Standard (2) to **Office Wing**, and click OK. You can leave this style with the drawing default hatch component color of 130.

5. Toggle OSNAP off so you won't have interference when you move. Move Office Wing down 12´ along the construction line so a corner of Office Wing symmetrically projects beyond Main Office.

The mass elements you are adding are three-dimensional. It is helpful to be able to see both plan and isometric views while you are working in model space to comprehend the masses you are adding. Tiled model space viewports are a very old AutoCAD feature that is perfect in this situation.

NOTE Veteran AutoCAD users will appreciate that some commands they might have learned 15 years ago still work in ADT.

1. Choose View ➤ Viewports ➤ 2 Viewports. The command line says Enter a configuration option [Horizontal/Vertical] <Vertical>:, so press **H**↵ to select the horizonal configuration. The model space drawing window divides into top and bottom tiled viewports.

2. Click in the top viewport and switch to a SW Isometric view (see Figure 4.5). Now you have the best of both worlds. You won't have to continually switch back and forth between different viewports to visualize what you are working on.

WARNING Tiled model space viewports all share the same display configuration, unlike paper space floating viewports.

3. Toggle OSNAP on by pressing the F3 key. Click in the bottom viewport and zoom into the area in which the major axis crosses the top edge of Main Office (see Figure 4.6). Add a cylindrical mass element, giving the cylinder a 12´ radius and 43´ height.

4. Click the top viewport and switch to a NE Isometric viewpoint. Change to Flat Shaded, Edges On shading mode and notice that the cylinder shows a series of flat facets. The facet spacing and number are determined by two options. Choose Format ➤ Options and click the AEC Object Settings tab. In the AEC Display Resolution group, verify that Facet Deviation (system variable: AECFACETDEV) is set to $1/2''$ and Facet Maximum (system variable: AECFACETMAX) is set to 128. Click OK to close the Options dialog box.

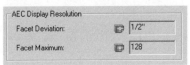

FIGURE 4.5
Using tiled model
space viewports

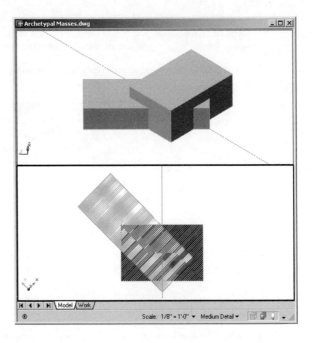

FIGURE 4.6
Adding a cylindrical
mass element

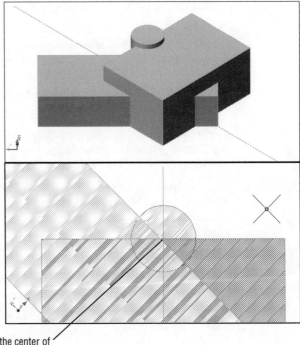

Locate the center of
a cylindrical mass here

5. Still in the top viewport, select the cylindrical mass element and choose Copy Mass Element Style And Assign from the object shortcut menu. In the Mass Element Style Properties dialog box, rename the style on the General tab to **Tower**.

6. Click the Display Properties tab and make a style override for the Plan High Detail representation. Notice that it does not appear in bold because Model is the current representation.

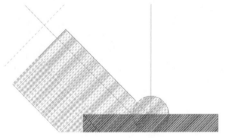

Display Representations	Display Property Source	Style Override
Model	**Drawing Default**	☐
Plan High Detail	Mass Element Style Override - Tower	☑
Plan Low Detail	Drawing Default	☐
Plan Presentation	Drawing Default	☐
Plan Screened	Drawing Default	☐
Reflected	Drawing Default	☐
Reflected Screened	Drawing Default	☐
Sketch	Drawing Default	☐

7. The Display Properties dialog box appears for the style override. Change the Hatch component property from color number 130 to green. Click OK in both open dialog boxes. The Tower appears with a green hatch pattern in the plan viewport.

8. Activate the plan viewport and pan over to the far right end of the Office Wing. Click the Construction Line tool on the Shapes toolbar. Click the right edge of Office Wing to establish the orientation for the construction line (parallel to the selected edge). Using polar tracking moves the cursor perpendicularly down from the point you clicked; type **8′**↵ (see Figure 4.7). Press Esc to cancel the continuation of the command.

9. Add another construction line offset 12′ outward from the left edge of the Office Wing.

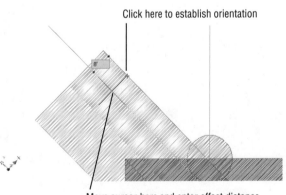

FIGURE 4.7
Adding and offsetting a
construction line

Click here to establish orientation

Move cursor here and enter offset distance

10. Using the Box tool on the Massing palette, click the intersection point of the two construction lines you just made to set its first corner. Type **@60´,-40´**⏎ to set the width and depth, type **29´**⏎ for the height, and press Enter again to accept the default rotation. Press Esc to end the command.

11. Select the box you created previously, right-click, and choose Copy Mass Element Style And Assign. Click the General tab in the Style Properties dialog box and rename the style to **Annex**. Click the Display Properties tab, create a style override in the Plan High Detail representation, and give its Hatch component the color magenta.

12. Verify that the Properties palette is open. Click the Cylinder tool on the Massing palette. Before you create the cylindrical mass, choose the style Annex in the Properties palette.

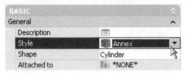

13. Click the insert point of the cylinder at the intersection of the major axis and the corner of Annex mass you created in step 10. Give the cylinder a radius of **2´** and a height of **26´** with default rotation. This is the last mass element you'll need to add in this tutorial.

FIGURE 4.8
Archetypal shapes and their mass element styles

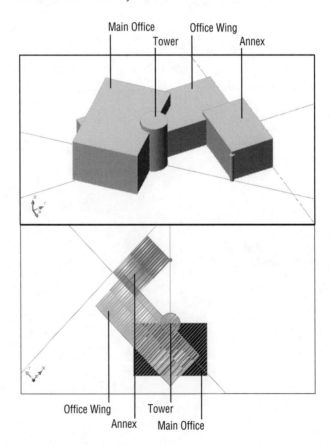

TIP Explore all the remaining mass element archetypal shapes on your own. The Doric (column) shape is available only in the Shape drop-down list on the Properties palette.

14. Click the top viewport and use the 3D Orbit command to set an oblique view in which you can see all the mass elements (see Figure 4.8).

15. Set the UCS back to the world coordinate system (WCS) and save your work as **Archetypal Masses.dwg**. You can leave this file open if you plan to continue now into the next section.

Editing Profile-Based Shapes

In addition to archetypal shapes, you can create extrusion and revolution mass element shapes that are based on profiles. *Profiles* are multipurpose object styles that are themselves defined by closed 2D polylines.

NOTE See Chapter 6, "Space Planning," to learn how to edit profile-based objects with the AEC Modify tools.

An *extrusion* is 3D geometry that results from sweeping a profile orthogonally upward in the z direction. A *revolution* is 3D geometry resulting from spinning a profile about its own x-axis. Figure 4.9 shows both the shapes and the profiles that were used to define them.

FIGURE 4.9
Revolution (top right) and extrusion (bottom right) mass elements, with the profiles that define their shapes shown at the left

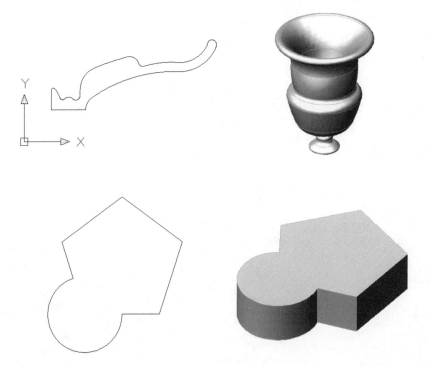

EXTRUSIONS

Extrusions have edge and vertex grips that allow you to alter their embedded profiles directly. Profile-based grips offer tremendous flexibility in terms of changing an extrusion's form compared with the archetypal shapes. All the archetypal shapes can be converted to extrusions at any time.

1. If you left the sample file open from the last section, you can continue here. If not, open `Archetypal Masses.dwg` from the working folder on your hard drive or from the Chapter 4 folder on the companion DVD.

2. In the plan viewport, select the Main Office. Open the Properties palette if it is not already open. Click the Box shape in the General subcategory. Choose Extrusion from the drop-down menu. Notice that the grips immediately change.

3. The width and height grips have been replaced with edge and vertex grips. Hold the cursor over the upper-right vertex grip and read the ToolTip. You have the option of removing this vertex by pressing the Ctrl key, but don't do it. Instead, click the vertex, and you'll default to the first item in the ToolTip's list, which is Move. Move the cursor horizontally to the left and type **12′**⏎.

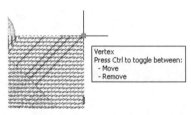

4. Notice that the grips appear on the "ground," or bottom surface of the Main Office—showing that the profile has been swept upward, forming the volume of this extrusion (see Figure 4.10). Look at the Properties palette and observe that Profile reads as *Embedded*, meaning that it comes from an object conversion. Press Esc to deselect.

NOTE It is possible to use a predefined profile style for an extrusion instead of an embedded profile: Draw a closed polyline, convert it to a profile style (use the object shortcut menu), and then assign the profile style within a mass element. Predefined profiles can be used in more than one object.

FIGURE 4.10
Extrusion grips on an embedded profile

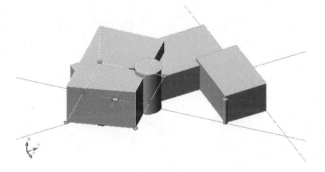

5. Turn your attention to the Annex. Draw a construction line oriented to the Annex's inner courtyard edge, and offset it 10′ into the building.

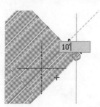

6. Convert the Annex mass element to the Extrusion shape by using the Properties palette. Hold the cursor over the edge grip along the courtyard. The ToolTip has three choices: Offset, Add Vertex, and Convert To Arc. Press the Ctrl key two times to select Convert To Arc.

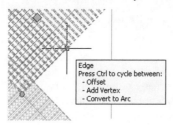

TIP Do not hold down the Ctrl button when cycling through ToolTip menus. Instead, press the Ctrl key repeatedly to move through the options. The ToolTip remains visible during the cycling process, even with DYN on (although you might have to move the cursor to get the ToolTip to display), so you can also keep track of which option is current that way. Pressing Ctrl again when you reach the bottom of a list cycles back to the first option.

7. Click the point where the edge of the new arc is perpendicular to the construction line you drew in step 5 (see Figure 4.11). Notice that the ToolTip menu is immediately updated with new options: Stretch and Convert To Line.

FIGURE 4.11
Converting a straight
profile edge to an arc

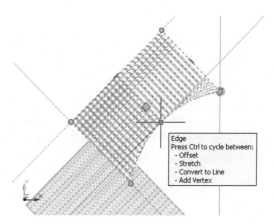

8. Click the lower edge and move the cursor perpendicularly down. Type **10´**↵ and hit Esc. The arc of the Annex extends further into the Office Wing.

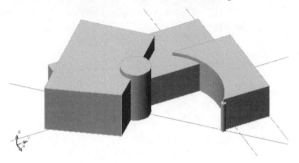

9. Save your work as **Extrusions.dwg** and close the file for now. You'll be returning to it in a later section.

REVOLUTIONS

A revolution mass element is made by turning a profile definition 360 degrees about its own x-axis. Remember the fact that profiles are turned around their x-axis in particular: This is the key to making a successful revolution. Let's give it a try.

1. Open the file `Polyline.dwg` from the companion DVD. This file contains the cross-sectional closed polyline shown in the upper-left image in Figure 4.9. It was designed to be spun around its lower edge—along the x-axis. This will form the center of a nineteenth century architectural urn.

2. The first step of creating a revolution is to define its profile from a closed polyline. Select the polyline, right-click, and choose Convert To ➢ Profile. The command line says:

```
Insertion Point or [Add ring/Centroid]:
```

Snap the insertion point at the lower-left corner of the polyline. This will form the bottom center of the urn.

3. Press Enter to accept the default option of creating a new profile: the New Profile Definition worksheet appears. Type **Urn** for the name and click OK. The worksheet closes, and the profile is defined. You can delete the polyline if you want because the profile definition is now part of the drawing.

4. On the Massing palette, click the Revolution tool. Click a point in the drawing window to insert the mass element. Press Enter once to accept zero as the rotation, and press Enter again to end the command.

5. Select the mass element, and in the Properties palette, change Profile to Urn. Switch to any isometric viewpoint and use a shaded display mode. The urn appears solid, as shown in the upper right of Figure 4.9.

6. Close the file without saving.

CONVERTING OBJECTS

A 3D Solid is a type of American Committee for Interoperable Systems (ACIS) modeling entity from AutoCAD; it is not an intelligent architecture, engineering, and construction (AEC) object. If you have built 3D models in the past based on these entities, you can bring them into ADT and convert them to mass elements. Just right-click a 3D Solid and choose Convert To Mass Element, or use the AecMassElementConvert command. You can also go the other way: Use AecConvertto3DSolids to convert a mass element into a 3D Solid.

Mass elements can also be converted into wall objects directly. Model the mass element into the form you want the custom wall to take and choose Convert To Wall from the object shortcut menu. You'll then be prompted to specify the wall's baseline. This is especially useful when making a nonstandard wall that has projections or cutouts. In addition, mass elements can be used to add 3D body modifiers to existing wall objects (see Chapter 8, "Walls"). The process can be reversed by using the MassElement command with its Convert option to go from a wall object back to a mass element.

Editing Free Form Masses

Free form mass elements offer different editing possibilities when compared with archetypal shapes and extrusions. All the mass element shapes can be converted into a free form that allows finer control over geometrical faces, edges, and vertices. Let's take a look by continuing our tutorial.

1. Open Extrusions.dwg from the working folder on your hard drive or from the Chapter 4 folder on the companion DVD.

2. Activate the top viewport and switch to SW Isometric view. Select the Main Office mass element, which is currently an extrusion.

3. In the Properties palette, click the Shape property—which is set to Extrusion—and select Free Form from the drop-down list.

4. Notice that the Main Office's grips have changed: The vertex and edge grips on the bottom of the object are gone. Now there are gray trigger grips on each face. Free form objects allow you to edit each face independently. Start editing by enabling one face for editing: Click the top face's trigger grip (see Figure 4.12).

FIGURE 4.12
Activating a free
form trigger grip

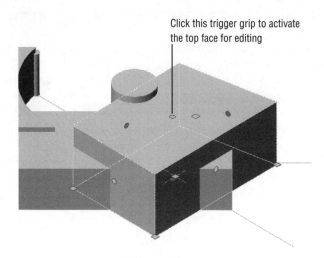

Click this trigger grip to activate
the top face for editing

5. Notice that the top grip has changed color from gray to cyan, indicating that it is active. Move the cursor over the top face grip to reveal the many ToolTip options, which include Move Ortho, Move, Move Plane, Pull Ortho, Pull, and Push Ortho. You can cycle through each one of these options by clicking the face grip and pressing the Ctrl key repeatedly as before. However, in this case, do not click the top face grip.

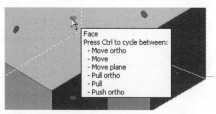

6. Notice that in addition to the top grip, four edge grips are also active on the top face. Click the front edge grip and move the cursor perpendicularly by using Polar tracking in toward the center of the top face. Type **12´↵** and press Esc. The front face of the building is now canted inward.

In addition to being able to edit all the edges of each face in free form mode, you can also create new edges. New edges can also be edited, giving you as fine a control over a mass element's *topology*, or 3D form as you desire.

1. Select the large Annex mass element and then right-click the light bulb icon in the drawing window tray. Choose Isolate Objects to get a better look at the Annex.

2. Use 3D Orbit to get a better view of the object. Select the Annex again and choose Split Face from the object shortcut menu.

3. Click the first point on the top face along the shorter of its two top side edges at its midpoint. Click the second point on the same face by snapping perpendicularly to the opposite edge (see Figure 4.13).

FIGURE 4.13
Splitting a face

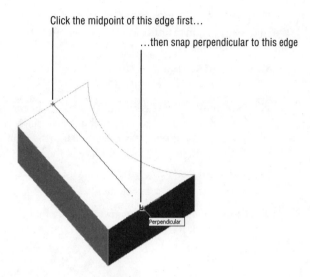

Click the midpoint of this edge first…

…then snap perpendicular to this edge

Perpendicular

NOTE Join Faces is available on the object shortcut menu only after you have split a face because it is the opposite command. You can rejoin faces that have already been split.

4. Right-click the light bulb icon in the drawing window tray and choose End Object Isolation from its shortcut menu.

5. Select the Annex and click the front face's trigger grip. Click this face's top edge grip. To move this edge down to match the height of another object, click the top endpoint of Office Wing (see Figure 4.14). Press Esc to deselect. The Annex's roof slopes down from the new edge to match the height of Office Wing.

FIGURE 4.14
Moving edge down
to match height of
Office Wing

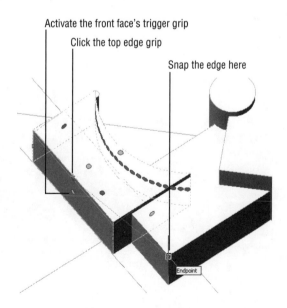

Activate the front face's trigger grip

Click the top edge grip

Snap the edge here

Endpoint

The last thing we'll need to do to the mass elements in terms of modeling is to split an object using a plane. The portion of Office Wing that penetrates through the Main Office can be split off and made into a separate mass element.

1. Switch to SW Isometric view and select the Office Wing mass element. Choose Split By Plane from the object shortcut menu.

2. The command line says `Specify divide plane start point [3points]:`, which means that you have the option to specify the divide plane with two or three points. If you divide by two points, the plane will be perpendicular to the ground plane. In our case, we want the divide plane to match the slope of the front face of the Main Office: type **3↵** to select the three-point option.

3. Click the three points shown in Figure 4.15 to specify the plane that is used to split Office Wing into two separate mass elements.

4. Select the new mass element and verify that it is separate from Office Wing. You'll be making the new object into a mass group in the next section called Entry.

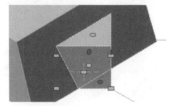

NOTE   Trim By Plane works the same as Split By Plane except that it deletes the portion split by the dividing plane.

5. Save your work as **Free Forms.dwg**. You can leave this file open if you plan to continue now into the next section.

FIGURE 4.15
Click these three points
to split by plane.

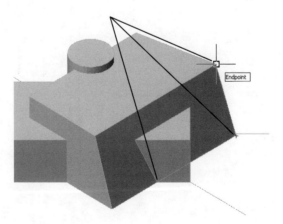

Modeling the Site

There is a special mass element tool that creates a surface draped over topographic contour lines, which is useful for modeling landforms. Let's use the Drape mass element tool to model the site in our tutorial.

1. If you left the sample file open from the last section, you can continue here. If not, open Free Forms.dwg from the working folder on your hard drive from the Chapter 4 folder on or the companion DVD.

2. Choose Insert ➤ Block to open AutoCAD's familiar Insert dialog box. Click the Browse button and select the file Contours.dwg from the companion DVD. Check Specify On Screen in the Insertion point group, check Explode in the bottom-left corner of the dialog box (see Figure 4.16), and click OK. Place the countour lines somewhere behind the building, as shown in Figure 4.16.

3. A series of contour lines appears in the form of 2D polylines, each moved to the appropriate elevation in the z direction. Use 3D Orbit to get a better look.

4. Hide all the existing mass elements. There is a hidden contour line following the structures at zero elevation along the courtyard edge.

5. Turn off layer G-Anno-Nplt to temporarily hide the construction lines.

6. Click the Drape tool on the Massing palette. Select all the contour lines and press Enter.

7. The command line asks whether you want to erase the selected contours: Choose No. Next, you are asked if you want to generate a regular mesh: Choose No. The next step asks whether you want to generate a rectangular mesh: Choose No. Press Enter to accept the base thickness of 10´.

```
Select objects representing contours:
Erase selected contours [Yes/No] <No>: n
Generate regular mesh [Yes/No] <Yes>: n
Generate rectangular mesh [Yes/No] <Yes>: n
Enter base thickness<10'-0">:
```

8. In a few moments, the free form mass element that was generated from the contour lines appears. Choose End Object Isolation from the light bulb icon in the drawing window tray. Choose View ➤ Viewports ➤ 1 Viewport. Use 3D Orbit to visualize the new 3D site model (see Figure 4.17).

TIP You could insert property lines, setbacks, sidewalk, and street boundaries into the site model if you had access to such data.

FIGURE 4.16
Inserting contour lines

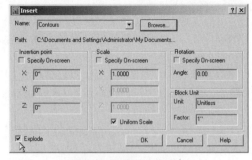

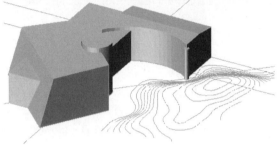

FIGURE 4.17
Site model

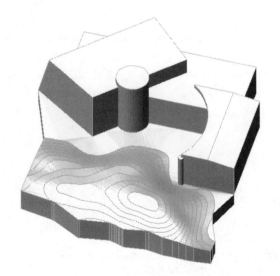

9. Copy the new massing element's style and assign it as the name Site. You don't need to make any changes to its display properties.

10. Save your work as **Site Model.dwg**. You can leave this file open if you plan to continue now into the next section.

Working with Mass Groups

After you've made some mass elements, you can combine them in mass groups. Mass groups offer several advantages, including a way to work with Booleans that retains editability into the future. You'll learn how to use the Model Explorer to work with mass groups in this section.

1. If you left the sample file open from the last section, you can continue here. If not, open `Site Model.dwg` from the working folder on your hard drive or from the Chapter 4 folder on the companion DVD.

2. Hide the site mass element. Switch to SW Isometric view.

3. Click the Mass Group tool on the Massing palette. Select the Main Office and Office Wing elements (but *not* the entry that was split off in an earlier section) and press Enter. Notice that the command line says `Location:` so click a point on the corner of the Main Office to complete the mass group. The location can be anywhere, but it makes sense to set the location of a mass group conveniently close to the mass elements that comprise it. Think of a mass group's location like a block's insertion point.

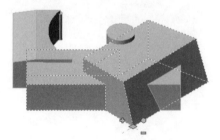

4. Select the Main Office again and notice that its grips have changed. Mass groups have Location, Attach, Detach, and Edit In Place grips. Press Esc to deselect.

5. Click the Mass Group tool again and select only the Tower. Locate the new mass group at the center of the base of the cylinder.

6. Create another mass group and select the "entry" mass element. This was the portion of Office Wing that was split off earlier. Locate this mass group on the corner point of the entry.

7. Make one final mass group that contains both the Annex and the tiny cylinder of the same mass element style. Locate this mass group on the back corner of the Annex. Figure 4.18 identifies the four mass groups and their location grips.

8. Switch to the Top view, select one of the mass groups, and choose Show Model Explorer to open the Model Explorer dialog box. Select the first MassGroup node in the tree pane and you'll see it shown in the Object Viewer pane on the right. Rename the nodes Office, Tower, Entry, and Annex. Click the Project node to display all four mass groups at once (see Figure 4.19). Close the Model Explorer. Now there are only four objects visible in the drawing window.

TIP　It is possible to nest mass groups within other mass groups in the Model Explorer for added organization. This could be helpful in highly complex massing models.

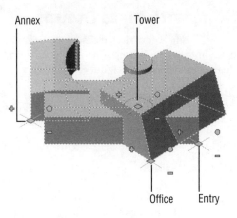

FIGURE 4.18
Making mass groups

FIGURE 4.19
Renaming mass groups
in the Model Explorer

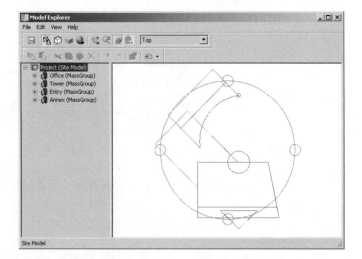

9. Create a new cylindrical mass element in the Main Office style off to the side with a radius of 12′ and height of 12′ (see Figure 4.20). Notice that the hatch pattern appears for the mass element but not the mass groups. Verify that mass groups do not have hatch display components in the Display Manager: Investigate the Plan display set and Plan representation in the Mass Group object (see Chapter 2, "Object Display").

10. Select the mass element and move it using its location grip. Place it on the bottom tip of the Entry group. Deselect it.

FIGURE 4.20

Creating a new
mass group

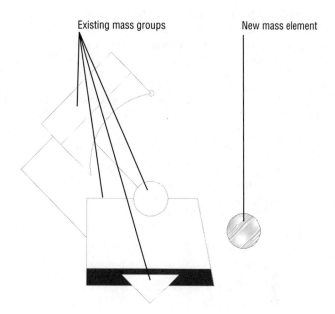

Existing mass groups   New mass element

11. Select the Entry mass group, click its Attach Elements grip, and select the new cylindrical mass element. Press Esc to deselect and switch to SW Isometric view.

12. Select the Entry mass group. Open the Model Explorer. Expand the Entry node in the tree pane. Right-click the Cylinder node inside the mass group. Choose Operation ➤ Subtractive from the shortcut menu (see Figure 4.21). Close the Model Explorer.

FIGURE 4.21

Making a mass
element subtractive
within a mass group

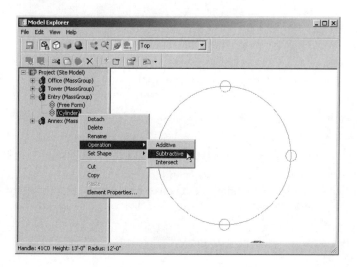

NOTE The advantage of specifying Boolean operations within the Model Explorer is that mass elements retain operation editability into the future. You can always change the operation from additive to subtractive or reorder nodes to change the effect, for example. On the other hand, applying Boolean commands (MassElementUnion, MassElementSubtract, and MassElementIntersect) directly to mass elements is convenient but you lose editability as the result is a free form element.

13. Select the Office mass group and notice that its boundary is an additive Boolean operation by default; you do not see the internal edges of the Office Wing or Main Office elements within the group. This is an important consideration because the Booleaned mass group boundary is what will be generating the floorplates in a later section. Press Esc to deselect.

14. Select the Entry mass group and click its Edit In Place trigger grip. The subtractive cylinder element appears; select it and notice its archetypal grips appear. Select the Height grip and type **13′**⏎ (see Figure 4.22). Click the Save All Changes button on the temporary In Place Edit toolbar to exit the mode.

TIP You still have access to all the editing features of mass elements inside mass groups when you Edit In Place.

15. End the object isolation for the site mass and save your work as **Mass groups.dwg**. You can leave this file open if you plan to continue now into the next section.

FIGURE 4.22
Editing the mass element inside the mass group

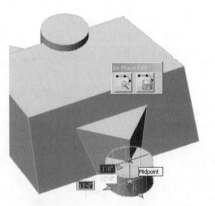

Visualizing the Massing Model

You can add a bit of realism to the massing model by applying real-world materials to masses. This can get you thinking about materiality, which might spark additional design ideas that you can feed back into your own massing models.

NOTE   Mass groups do not have object styles. Materials are applied to mass groups at the object override level, so each mass group object is unique.

In this section you'll add materials to your masses and then learn how to better visualize the model using a perspective camera.

1. If you left the sample file open from the last section, you can continue here. If not, open `Mass groups.dwg` from the working folder on your hard drive or from the Chapter 4 folder on the companion DVD.

2. Select the Design palette and choose the Material tool. Click the Office mass group to open the Apply Material To Component worksheet (see Chapter 3, "Object Styles"). Assign the material `Masonry.Unit Masonry.Brick.Modular` to the Body component as an Object override (see Figure 4.23). Click OK to close the worksheet.

3. Assign materials to the Annex, Tower, and Entry as follows.

Render Material	Mass Group
Masonry.Unit Masonry.Brick.Modular	Office
Concrete.Cast-in-Place.Panels.Reveal.Smooth	Annex
Metals.Ornamental Metals.Aluminum.Brushed.Blue-Silver	Tower
Doors & Windows.Glazing.Glass.Clear	Entry

4. Choose the Material tool and select the Site massing element. Assign the `Site Construction.Planting.Groundcover.Grass.Short` material to the Site massing element as a Style override. Figure 4.24 shows the results of applying materials to all the masses.

WARNING   You must be in an isometric or oblique viewpoint and in a shaded mode to see materials in the drawing window.

FIGURE 4.23
Assigning a material
to a mass group

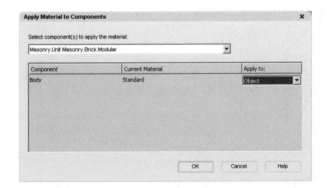

FIGURE 4.24
Material applied
to masses

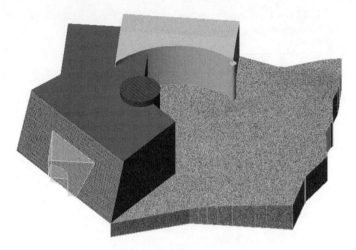

Use the Camera tool with the 3D Orbit command to prepare a perspective composition. We'll set up a view at eye level on the grass looking back at the building's courtyard.

1. Switch to the Top viewpoint in 2D Wireframe shading mode. You'll save time by staying out of shaded views while setting up your composition; you'll switch back later.

2. Type **Camera** on the command line and press Enter. (Don't select the Camera tool from the Massing palette; that's a different thing entirely.) Click the camera location near the top of the grassy knoll and click its target in front of the building (see Figure 4.25). Save the file in case ADT crashes—you can never be too careful.

3. The viewport will change after you've created the camera, but you still have a lot to do to set up the composition. Click on the Surface Hatch Toggle in the drawing window tray and turn it off. Right-click and choose Projection ➤ Perspective from the shortcut menu. Then choose 3D Orbit from the application shortcut menu.

4. Right-click and choose Zoom from the shortcut menu. Drag the mouse vertically down to zoom out. Zoom actually changes the field-of-view of the camera (not its position), making the composition more wide-angle. Drag the cursor down while holding the wheel button to raise the level of the camera above the contour lines. Right-click and choose Orbit and adjust the position of the camera if necessary. When you are satisfied with the composition, press Enter to end the 3D Orbit command. Switch to Gouraud Shaded, Edges On view (see Figure 4.26).

5. Type **View** on the command line and press Enter to open the View dialog box. Click the New button to open the New View dialog box. Type **Camera** in the View name text box (see Figure 4.27). Click OK twice to close both dialog boxes. You are saving your camera composition as a view so you can come back to it at any time (use the View command).

TIP Try making a napkin sketch of the massing model for an artistic type of line drawing that almost looks hand-sketched. See the ADT Help for more on Napkin Sketch, which you can find in the Stock Tool catalog.

6. Save your work as **Camera.dwg**. You can leave this file open if you plan to continue now into the last section.

FIGURE 4.25
Camera and target
locations

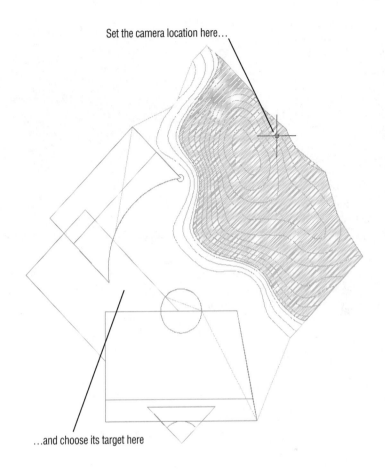

Set the camera location here…

…and choose its target here

FIGURE 4.26
Perspective composition
looking through camera

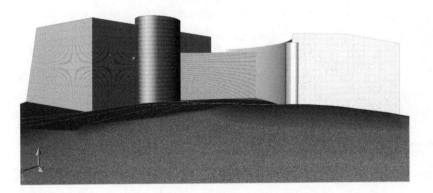

FIGURE 4.27
Saving a view name

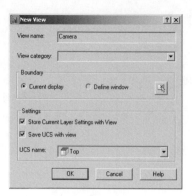

Slicing Floorplates from the Massing Model

After you have worked out your schematic design ideas with a massing model, use the Slice tool to generate floorplates. Floorplates can then be converted to polylines or space boundaries that will form the basis of your project in the space planning and design development phase. Floorplates are linked to the massing model, so any changes you make to mass groups or their contained mass elements are automatically updated in the floorplate boundaries.

After you convert floorplates to either polylines or space boundaries, the link to the massing model is broken. We will use space boundaries in Chapter 5, "Project Management," to set up the project structure, but changes made to either the massing model or space boundaries thereafter will not be coordinated with each other. Therefore, slicing floorplates marks the end of outside-in conceptual design, and you should cross this threshold only after you are satisfied with your massing model.

1. If you left the sample file open from the last section, you can continue here. If not, open Camera.dwg from the working folder on your hard drive or from the Chapter 4 folder on the companion DVD.

2. Switch to SW Isometric viewpoint. 3D Orbit until your viewpoint matches Figure 4.28 so you can see all the faces of the model. Isolate the four mass group objects. You don't want to slice through the site mass element or the contour lines as they won't be part of any floorplate.

3. Select the Office mass group and click its Attach Elements grip. Select the Annex and press Enter and then Esc. The Annex and Office masses are unified. This step is necessary if you want to avoid having space boundaries that separate the mass groups where they intersect.

4. Click the Slice tool on the Massing palette. You are prompted to enter the number of slices on the command line. The massing model calls for three floors, so type **3**↵.

5. Click two points to define a small rectangle off to the side of the massing model. This will locate the slice markers; they don't have to surround the building.

6. Type **0**↵ for the rotation and **0″**↵ for the starting height because you want the first floor to start at ground level. Type **13′**↵ for the distance between slices. Three slice markers will appear in the drawing window.

7. Select all three slice markers and right-click to open a shortcut menu: choose Attach Objects. Select the Office mass group and press Enter. Three floorplates are generated (see Figure 4.28).

WARNING Boolean operational characteristics (additive, subtractive, or intersect) are not respected when you attach slices to mass elements. Therefore, it is better to attach slices to mass groups.

8. Select the Design palette and right-click the Space Boundary tool. Choose Apply Tool Properties To ➤ Slice from the shortcut menu. Select all three slice markers and press Enter. Space boundaries are generated, conforming to the floorplate boundaries. Do not worry that the space boundaries do not follow the canted front wall of the Main Office mass group.

9. You will reuse the slice markers to generate a new floorplate in the Entry. Detach Office from the slice markers so you can use them again. Attach the first floor slice marker to the Entry mass group. Create another space boundary based on the first floor slice.

10. Finally, detach the first floor slice marker from the Entry and then attach it to the Tower mass group. Create a space boundary from this slice. Do not make additional space boundaries on levels 2 and 3 to represent the Tower; the single space boundary will become a construct that spans multiple levels in Chapter 5.

FIGURE 4.28
Generating floorplates
with slices

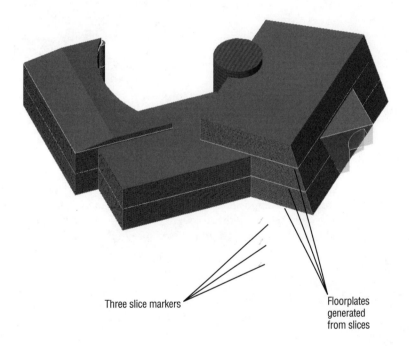

Three slice markers

Floorplates
generated
from slices

11. Notice that the Annex mistakenly has a third floor because the slice generated a floorplate there. Click the third floor space boundary of the Annex. Right-click and choose Split Boundary. Select the space inside the same space boundary, press Enter and then press Delete. You have removed the nonexistent third floor of the Annex. Figure 4.29 shows the space boundaries generated from the floorplates.

12. Delete the slice markers. They are no longer needed after you used them to generate space boundaries. Save your work as **Floorplates.dwg**. This file will be used in the next chapter (also provided on the DVD).

FIGURE 4.29
Space boundaries
generated from
floorplates

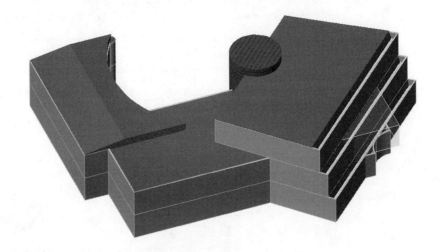

Summary

This chapter taught you skills for creating a massing model that is part of the outside-in design process. You have learned many techniques for working with mass elements and mass groups that make it easy to get your spatial ideas quickly into digital form. You learned how to add materials and create a perspective composition that helps to document your initial concepts about the evolving design. Finally, you sliced floorplates out of the massing model and turned them into the space boundaries essential for developing a project structure in the next chapter.

Chapter 5

Project Management

Drawing management is perhaps the most important system in Architectural Desktop (ADT) because it ties an entire building project dataset together. In this chapter you'll be learning how to use the Project Browser and Project Navigator, two interfaces that will be used by all your team members to manage the project dataset.

The project dataset will ultimately consist of myriad drawing files referenced into one another and Extensible Markup Language (XML) files that store the relationships each drawing file has within the project management system. In addition, ADT automatically manages your file system by creating folders and subfolders, organizing all the relevant project files within.

ADT makes heavy use of externally referenced files (XRefs) in project management because XRefs allow multiple people to work together simultaneously on the same dataset—just as they do in AutoCAD. However, there is more to the project management system than just XRefs between drawing files: XML files are also created that store project data. In ADT, project data (.xml and .apj) is stored separately from drawing data (.dwg). Therefore, you can reuse drawing files in different projects because the drawings themselves are not project-specific.

You'll create a sample project and study the relations between the many project components, including levels, divisions, categories, elements, constructs, views, and sheets. You'll use the massing model developed in Chapter 4, "Mass Modeling," to flesh out a project skeleton. Finally, you'll learn how to synchronize your object styles and display settings, drawings, and entire project with the standards you establish. This chapter's topics include:

- ◆ Creating a Project
- ◆ Defining Levels and Divisions
- ◆ Categories, Constructs, and Elements
- ◆ Working with Views
- ◆ Generating a Sheet Set
- ◆ Establishing Project Standards

Creating a Project

The first step in managing a building design campaign is to create a project. In ADT, think of a *project* as a framework that logically interconnects all the myriad drawing files you will make over the lifetime of your real-world building project. When I use the word *project* in this chapter, I'm referring to this notion of a logical framework. Projects maintain the building dataset in a centralized location so that everyone on your team has access to the most current drawings at all times. The project structure also ensures that all the drawings that belong to it are seamlessly interconnected in a logical and consistent interface.

NOTE   The Chapter 05 project is provided on the companion DVD for your reference. You can use the files there to follow along at every stage in this chapter.

Using the Project Browser

Projects are created and accessed from the Project Browser, which also acts as a bulletin board system for the use of the project team members. Your project manager might use the bulletin board feature to communicate important messages to the team and to post project-specific content. Let's take a look at some of these features and create a project that we can use throughout this chapter.

1. Choose the Project Navigator palette button from the Navigation toolbar, or press Ctrl+5. A small dialog box appears informing you that there is no current project, so you cannot use the Project Navigator until you set a current project in the Project Browser.

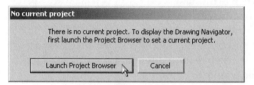

NOTE   You can have only one project active at any time. Use the Project Browser to create, change, and close projects.

2. Click the Launch Project Browser button to open the dialog box of the same name. Figure 5.1 identifies the parts of the Project Browser.

3. Open the Path drop down list and verify that for this tutorial you are in the following folder:

   `C:\Documents and Settings\`*`Administrator`*`\My Documents\Autodesk\My Projects`

   where *Administrator* is the name you logged into Windows. This is the default project location for a single machine (that path was created when you installed ADT) and the one I will use in this tutorial. You'll learn later how to set the default project location to a mapped drive on a file server. You might see the Tutorial Projects folder in the project selector if you chose to install the default tutorials when you installed ADT.

4. Let's create our first project by—you guessed it—clicking the new project button. Doing so opens the Add Project worksheet (see Figure 5.2). Many organizations identify projects on their file servers by project number, which is often a code for the project birth date. You don't have to enter a project number at all, but type **2006.04.22** for this tutorial. In the Project Name text box, type **Chapter 05** (using the leading zero to keep it sorted properly in the file system). Optionally enter the following as a project description: **Mastering ADT 2006 by Scott Onstott.⏎Sample Project**. Notice that there is an option to create the new project from a template project. This new feature in ADT 2006 is useful to save time by starting with all the same settings as one of your previous projects. Check Create from template project and use the ADT Template Project (Imperial), which is the default project template. Click OK to close the worksheet.

FIGURE 5.1
The Project Browser

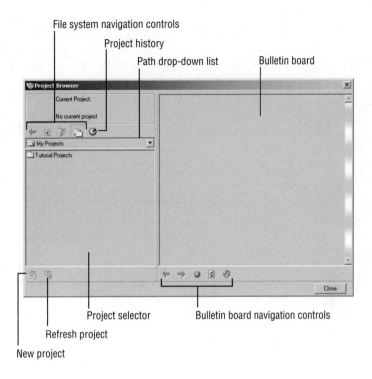

File system navigation controls

Project history

Path drop-down list

Bulletin board

Project selector

Bulletin board navigation controls

Refresh project

New project

FIGURE 5.2
Add Project worksheet

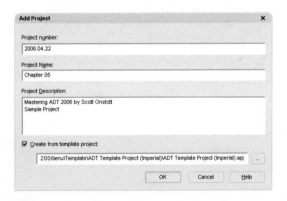

5. In a few moments the project file structure will be created on your hard drive. You'll see Autodesk's default project image and bulletin board, which we will change in the next section. But first click OK to close the Project Browser.

6. Use the Windows Explorer to open the following project folder:

```
C:\Documents and Settings\Administrator\My Documents\Autodesk\My
Projects\Chapter 05
```

When you created the project, ADT automatically made the following folders on your hard drive: Elements, Constructs, Views, Sheets, and Palettes; these are the project components you'll be learning about in the rest of this chapter. In addition, the project folder contains a project file (.apj), a project tool catalog file (.atc), a sheet set file (.dst), and a project-specific tool catalog. All this was created for a project that currently contains no data: it is the skeleton of your first project. Close the Windows Explorer and return to ADT.

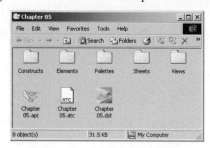

7. Notice that the Tool Palettes are showing only one palette: Project Tools (see Figure 5.3): this is a new feature in ADT 2006. Each project contains its own tool catalog and palette group. They are intended to be developed over time with custom tools that you can use to create the specific objects in your project. Your project manager or ADT manager might be responsible for such development. For now, change back to the Design palette group. Realize that every time you change projects in the Project Browser, you'll see a different project-specific palette group (that can contain as many palettes as you wish) in the Tool Palettes.

TIP The Project palette group might be linked as a shared workspace catalog for centralized tool management and distribution (see Chapter 3, "Object Styles"). This ensures that everyone on the team uses the same tools.

8. The Project Navigator palette (also known more succinctly as the *Navigator*) also appears immediately after you create a new project in the Project Browser (see Figure 5.4). The Navigator has four tabs: Project, Constructs, Views, and Sheets. We will start using the Navigator by setting project properties on the Project tab.

FIGURE 5.3

Project palette group

FIGURE 5.4

Project Navigator palette

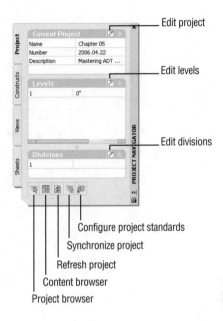

Edit project

Edit levels

Edit divisions

Configure project standards

Synchronize project

Refresh project

Content browser

Project browser

Setting Project Properties

The project (.apj) file contains high-level settings such as template locations, file prefixes, default paths, and project-specific data such as the client's name, the building address, contact information, financial data, and much more. You can set as much or as little of this information as your needs require with project properties. When creating a typical project, just fill in as much information as you know off-hand—you can always add more information later if need be. Let's set a few of the properties for our demonstration project:

1. Before you start editing project properties, copy the following files from the Chapter 5 folder on the companion DVD to your Chapter 05 project folder:

```
Sample Bulletin Board.htm
SampleProject.bmp
MassingThumbnail.jpg
```

   These sample files have been prepared using Adobe Photoshop and Macromedia Dreamweaver. You will need to use programs such as these, or learn how to hand-code HTML, to create project images and a bulletin board intranet if you choose to use these optional features of the Project Browser.

2. Click the Edit Project button on the Project tab of the Navigator. The Modify Project worksheet appears (see Figure 5.5). Click the path next to Bulletin Board, click the ellipsis button, and locate the file `Sample Bulletin Board.htm` in the project folder (this can be a single web page or the index to an entire site). Choose the file `SampleProject.bmp` as the project image (64×64 pixels). Change Use Relative XRef Paths to Yes so that you can move the project folder to another location in your file system without breaking links. Notice that you can also specify many different template file locations and tool catalog and palette options in this worksheet.

FIGURE 5.5
Modify Project
worksheet

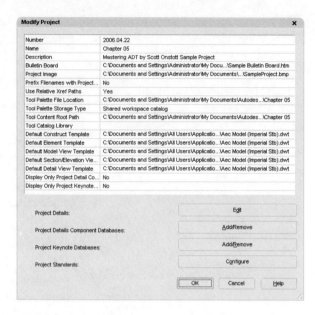

WARNING   The Project Sheet Set Template is only editable immediately after creating the project while the Project Browser is open for the first time by choosing Properties in the project selector. Afterward, this property value is set to read-only and is grayed-out in the worksheet.

3. Click the Edit button next to Project Details to open a worksheet of the same name (see Figure 5.6). Explore the worksheet by expanding and scrolling through its many categories and details of editable data. You can add as much or as little here as you want. Note that many of these fields are directly linked to the information that ultimately appears on your sheet title blocks, so it is a good idea to enter at least some relevant data in this worksheet. You can also add additional categories and details to suit your specific project. However, click OK without entering anything for now.

FIGURE 5.6
Editing project details

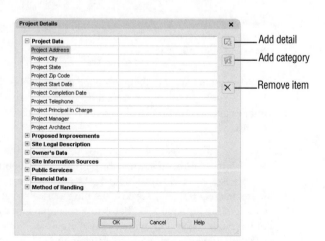

TIP   Consider storing all relevant general building information inside your ADT project instead of in another database. This minimizes the software you'll have to maintain over the lifetime of the project.

4. You can optionally specify project detail component and keynote databases with the buttons at the bottom of the Modify Project worksheet. ADT currently only supports Microsoft Access databases for these features (see Chapter 17, "Details and Keynotes"). Finally, you could jump to Project Standards from this worksheet (bottom button), but we'll get to that a bit later. Click OK to close the worksheet. A small warning dialog box appears, asking if you want to convert the existing XRefs in drawings to use relative paths. Click Yes.

NOTE   Relative path support is a new feature in ADT 2006 that allows you to move your project folder to another drive letter without breaking all the dependent references.

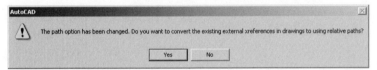

5. Choose File ➤ Project Browser. Chapter 05 appears in bold in the project selector because it is the current project. Notice that the project selector does not reveal any project subfolders: these are "under the hood" and managed internally by ADT. Right-click Chapter 05 and take a look at the project shortcut menu (see Figure 5.7). There are options to copy the project structure (as a template for future projects), close the current project, eTransmit and Archive (see Chapter 19, "Printing and Publishing"), and finally Project Properties. This last option opens the Modify Project worksheet (refer to Figure 5.5) and is an alternative to accessing the worksheet from the Navigator. Click Close after reviewing these features.

FIGURE 5.7

Shortcut menu in
Project Browser

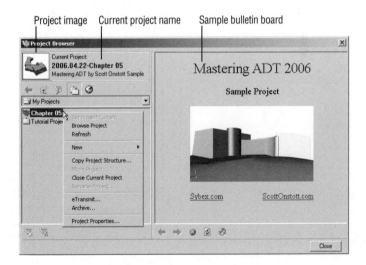

WARNING When working on a project, do not meddle with renaming or deleting files in the Windows Explorer. The danger is that you will break important project associations by making manual changes. Instead, use ADT's project-management features to do this low-level work for you.

If you are working in an organization using a file server, you'll want to change some architecture, engineering, and construction (AEC) options so your default paths will point to a centralized storage location for projects, templates, and so on. Check first with your ADT manager before changing any AEC options, but if you're ready to modify them, here's how to do so:

1. Right-click in the Command window and choose Options from the shortcut menu to open the Options dialog box (see Figure 5.8). ADT adds many AEC tabs to the Options dialog box that you can investigate on your own: so many, in fact, that navigation arrows had to be added to get all the tabs to fit inside. Use the tab navigation arrows to page over to the last sheet on the right called AEC Project Defaults.

2. Of particular interest is the AEC Project Location Search Path, which controls where your projects are stored. This book uses the default path on the local drive, but you might want to change it to a mapped drive on your file server.

NOTE Mapped drive support is new in ADT 2006.

3. If you are working on multiple projects every workday, check Show Project Browser at startup, so you'll be able to select the project you'll be working on in the morning when you launch ADT. Otherwise, you can always open the Project Browser from the File menu or the Navigator. Click Cancel to close the Options dialog box.

FIGURE 5.8
Accessing AEC Options

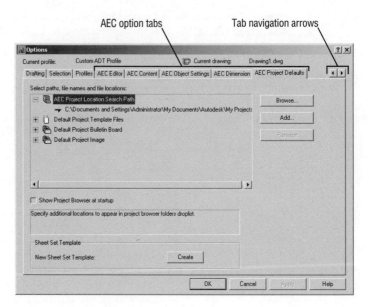

Defining Levels and Divisions

After you've made a conceptual model and created a project, it is time to define *levels* and *divisions*. Levels are the vertical segments of a building, and divisions are horizontal segments usually corresponding to an annex or wing of a building. Every project must have at least one level and division by default.

Determining how many levels to make is usually obvious: Count the number of floors in the building. You'll have to use your own judgment to determine whether mezzanines should be defined as levels; if you want to generate separate drawings for different floor planes, define them as separate levels. A level has a floor elevation and floor-to-floor height.

It is worthwhile to define divisions in projects that have clear spatial separations in the horizontal dimension, such as with detached structures, additions, annexed areas, or entire wings. If you want to generate separate drawings for structures on the same level, define those compartments as divisions. Be aware that not all projects have clear horizontal separations; so using the default division might be all that is required.

TIP Divisions can be creatively used to indicate a construction phase in which a clear spatial separation exists between the new construction and the existing construction to remain. Using classifications to indicate phase is more appropriate in renovations in which new and existing objects are spatially intermingled (see Chapter 3). Divisions can also be creatively used to hold options for a base design. For example, in residential design, one division could hold the common parts of a given level, and other divisions can be defined for various options. For example, separate divisions for a standard kitchen, a kitchen with a breakfast nook, a two-car garage, and a three-car garage can be created. By combining the base division with various combinations of optional divisions, you can create a final plan with a particular set of options.

Unlike levels, divisions are not explicitly given elevations, heights, or geometric boundaries. Instead, divisions are determined solely by the constructs you assign to them (as you'll see in the next section). Let's get started defining levels and divisions.

1. Click the Project tab in the Navigator if it is not already selected. Click the Edit Levels button to open the Levels worksheet. Change the Name of the default level to **Floor 1**, change its Floor To Floor Height to **13´-0˝**, and give it a description of **Ground Floor**. Make sure that Auto-Adjust Elevation is checked so you won't have to calculate floor heights as you add them. Click the Add Level button and give it the name **Floor 2**, and describe it as **Second Floor**. Add **Floor 3,** described most obviously as **Third Floor** (see Figure 5.9). Click OK.

FIGURE 5.9
Levels worksheet

2. A warning dialog box appears, asking if you want to regenerate all the views in this project: Choose Yes. This is really relevant only if you've made changes to levels after you've assigned constructs and views.

3. Click the Edit Divisions button in the Navigator to open the Divisions worksheet. Change the default division's name to **Office** and give it the description **Primary division**. Add another division and change it to **Annex**, ID to **2**, and describe it as **Secondary division** (see Figure 5.10). Click OK.

4. There is no need to save a drawing file because the levels and divisions you defined are automatically stored to the project (`.apj`) file in XML. Leave the sample file open if you plan to continue to the next section.

FIGURE 5.10
Navigator palette that shows the project's levels and divisions

NOTE   The cut planes that determine what is shown in plans, elevations, and section drawings are not set in levels. Instead, cut planes are typically controlled in views. Use the Display Manager to set the cut plane heights within view display configurations.

It's no problem to change level and division properties at any time in your project's lifecycle. However, changes made this high in the project structure might have far-reaching consequences in the design-development or construction-documentation phases such as changing the heights of all the walls, for example.

TIP   Levels can have negative elevations. For example, you might define a basement level with a negative elevation to maintain the ground floor at elevation zero. Always use a positive floor-to-floor height.

No geometry has yet been assigned to the levels and divisions you have defined. In the next section, you'll learn to assign skeletal constructs to the levels and divisions you defined here.

Categories, Constructs, and Elements

You'll be using the Constructs tab of the Project Navigator palette to work with *categories*, *elements*, and *constructs*. You'll use these data structures every day when doing design work, so it is critical that you understand how each one works. Categories mirror the project's folder structure in the file system and are used to organize elements, constructs, views, and sheets within the Project Navigator. Generally speaking, elements are for instanced collections of objects that will be reused multiple times. Constructs represent logically related collections of uniquely located objects in your building. In this section, we will use each data structure to create the skeleton of a project.

Creating Categories

Top-level categories were generated when you created the project: Elements, Constructs, Views, and Sheets. These top-level categories appear on their corresponding tabs in the Navigator. You explored the project folder earlier in this chapter; remember that there is a Palettes folder in there as well. However, the Palettes folder does not appear in the Navigator because palettes are managed by using the Tool Palettes and Content Browser instead.

You cannot create new top-level categories, nor can you alter their names or move their folders into a different folder structure; they must be located right in the folder that contains the project file. If your pre-ADT office standard folder structure differs from ADT's project-based structure—and it is very likely—you are out of luck. You must follow ADT's project folder structure or else it just won't work.

Thus, when you create categories in ADT, you are technically making user-defined subcategories that live inside the top-level categories—think of them simply as categories if it helps. You can make categories in two ways: by making a folder in the Windows Explorer and dragging it into the Project Navigator in ADT, or by using the built-in controls in the Navigator.

I recommend using the buttons on the Navigator to create categories. It is dangerous to meddle with the file system, in which you might inadvertently delete part of the project and break XML associations that could mess up the project for your entire team.

TIP Network administrators can offer additional security by using network permissions to limit delete rights to project subfolders, if at all.

There are different strategies to think about when creating categories; they depend on the type of project you're working on. In projects using construction-phase divisions, you might make New and Existing categories for elements and constructs. The complexity of some projects might warrant making categories for various disciplines such as Architectural, Structural, Mechanical, Electrical, and Plumbing. Still others might like to add subcategories by types such as Partitions, Shells, Grids, Slabs, and so on. Let's make a few categories using the Navigator:

1. Click the Elements category (it appears as a folder icon) on the Constructs tab of the Navigator. Click the Add Category button and name the new folder **Core**.

2. Click the Elements category again and add another subcategory called **Furniture** at the same level as Core. Note that adding a new category while Core is selected would make it a subfolder of Core (not what you want).

3. Continue adding categories under Constructs to match Figure 5.11. In all, you will be adding six more categories to the project.

4. Use Windows Explorer to verify the folder structure of your project; it should mirror the category structure in the Navigator. You can make this as simple or as complicated as your project dictates.

Having perfect foreknowledge of how a project will evolve and the categorization scheme it will ultimately require isn't necessary: You can always drag elements and constructs into categories later on as the design progresses.

FIGURE 5.11
Constructs tab of the
Project Navigator

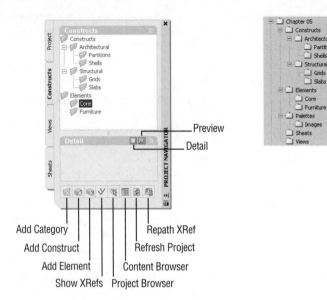

Preview
Detail

Add Category
Add Construct
Add Element
Show XRefs   Project Browser
Content Browser
Refresh Project
Repath XRef

Understanding Elements and Constructs

Elements and constructs are like building blocks that contain collections of objects. Constructs are associated with a specific level and division and are unique structures. In contrast, elements are not tied to a specific location and can thus be used multiple times in a project.

The Navigator saves elements and constructs on disk as separate dwg files and automatically associates xml files with these drawings that record their relationships to the project. You don't have to think about files when using the Navigator because it handles these low-level issues.

Instead, focus on the nodes in the Navigator; the nodes are related through hierarchical external reference relationships. Generally speaking, elements are referenced into constructs, which are in turn referenced into views, which are then referenced onto sheets (Element ➤ Construct ➤ View ➤ Sheet). You'll primarily use elements for building blocks, constructs for the building itself, views for annotation, and sheets for printing.

ELEMENTS

Let's start our journey through the project hierarchy by studying elements. Think of elements as the project version of AutoCAD blocks. Elements are meant to be defined once and instanced repeatedly. An element might contain any number of object types, such as walls, doors, and Multi-View Blocks. Examples of elements are washrooms, furniture groupings, cubicles, and the building core.

You can nest elements within other elements, such as a chair and desk within a cubicle. The cubicle elements could then be referenced in many locations within a construct. You can also reference the same element in many different constructs, such as the building core on all the levels of a building. Elements do not get assigned to specific levels and divisions.

When you change an element file, all instances of that element in the project are updated. This is great for design changes—for example, you might start by making a generic cubicle element and reference it into several constructs on different levels and divisions during space planning. When you get around to specifying the parts of the cubicle, just edit the element and save. The changes are available for immediate reloading into all the instances in which that element is referenced (within other elements, in constructs, in views, and in sheets).

Although you cannot directly reference an element into a view, you can reference an element into a sheet in some special situations. For example, you might define a title block drawing as an element and reference it into a sheet.

Elements do not have to be related to anything; they can exist as *orphans*. This is a good way to include stand-alone drawings in your project such as the massing model, napkin sketches, and the like. If you realize that an element is being used only once, you have the option of converting it directly to a construct; then you will have to associate it with a level and division.

CONSTRUCTS

Constructs are what you use to build the digital model. *Constructs* are unique portions of the building assigned to specific levels and divisions (for example, shells, partitions, ceilings, curtain walls, stair towers, and roofs). You might make a specific construct called **Partitions02**; assign it to the Floor 2/Annex; and then proceed to add its walls, doors, windows, and so on.

UNDERSTANDING XREF RELATIONSHIPS

External drawings can be referenced in two different ways: as *attachments* or *overlays*. In ADT's project hierarchy, XRefs are normally nested as attachments (Element > Construct > View > Sheet). When XRefs are attached to each other in this way, all nested elements and constructs appear in views and on the sheets.

If you choose to overlay an XRef in a drawing, it will not appear when that drawing is itself attached or overlaid as an XRef in another drawing. More succinctly: Overlaid constructs do not appear on sheets.

Here are some examples of when you should use XRef attachments (default):

◆ Elements attached to Elements

◆ Elements attached to Constructs

◆ Elements attached to Sheets

◆ Constructs attached to Views

◆ Views attached to Sheets

In rare cases, you might attach a construct to another construct if you want to see a roof construct appear below a higher-level floor plan in the same view.

There are two situations in which overlays might be useful:

◆ Constructs overlaid on Constructs

◆ Constructs overlaid on Elements

Constructs are not typically overlaid because confusion arises as to which level and division the constructs would be on (each has a different assignment). However, there are exceptional circumstances in which overlaying one construct over another construct or element might help you align structures vertically or to see what another designer is doing without permanently altering project relationships. Do not attach property set data to an overlaid construct, or else errors will result (see Chapter 14, "Schedules, Display Themes, and Areas").

Constructs might contain objects and referenced elements, as mentioned previously. As with all the other nodes in the project hierarchy, constructs are automatically stored as dwg and xml files by the Navigator.

Constructs are typically referenced into views for annotation, which you will learn about in "Working with Views," later in this chapter. Although a construct is normally assigned to one level and division, there are situations in which you'll need to assign a construct to multiple levels or divisions; this is called a *spanning construct*. Spanning constructs appear in multiple views and are appropriate for building features such as curtain walls, stair towers, and vertical shafts.

For buildings containing multiple similar floor plans, you can save time by defining a construct for one level and then copying it to multiple levels. The copies added to each level remain unique but start out life identically; perfect for high-rise buildings, for example.

TIP If you want to reuse a construct on the same level, convert it to an element and reference elements instead.

Adding Elements and Constructs to the Project

Now that you've had a chance to study elements and constructs, let's work with them in a practical situation. You'll get a chance to see how elements and constructs are created from various pieces of the space boundary cake. Delicious! In the end, the model will look the same, but it will be organized into the logical framework of the project.

PARTING-OUT SPACE BOUNDARIES INTO ELEMENTS AND CONSTRUCTS

You will use the Navigator's intuitive drag-and-drop interface to part-out the space boundaries from the massing model into appropriate constructs and elements.

1. Open the file SpaceBoundaries.dwg from this chapter's folder on the companion DVD.

2. Click the Constructs tab in the Navigator and select the Shells node. You will be adding a construct in this category.

3. Click the Add Construct button in the Navigator: the Add Construct worksheet appears. Type **Office Shell 01** in the Name text box. Click in the Description text area and type **Ground Floor Office Shell** in the small worksheet that appears; click OK. Assign this construct to the Floor 1 level and Office division by checking the appropriate box in the Assignments matrix (see Figure 5.12). Click OK to close the worksheet.

4. Select the ground floor space boundary of the office. Being careful not to select a grip, drag the space boundary and drop it on the Office Shell 01 construct in the Navigator (see Figure 5.13). After a moment the space boundary disappears.

5. Double-click the Office Shell 01 construct icon in the Navigator. ADT's title bar shows that you have opened the file Office Shell 01.dwg (see Figure 5.14). This file contains only the single space boundary you dragged into it. Zoom, pan, 3D orbit, and change shading modes to help you visualize what this construct file contains. When you are done, close the file.

TIP Set the TASKBAR system variable to 1 if you want ADT to show separate tasks for each drawing on the Windows taskbar.

FIGURE 5.12
Adding a construct and
assigning it to a level and
division

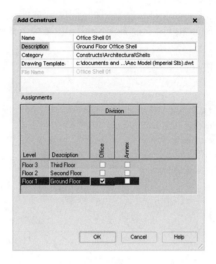

FIGURE 5.13
Drag space boundary
to construct.

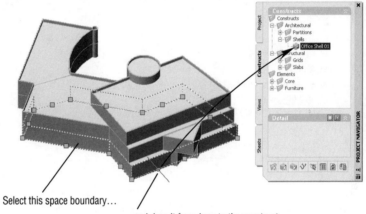

Select this space boundary…

…and drag it from here to the construct

FIGURE 5.14
Ground Floor Office
Shell

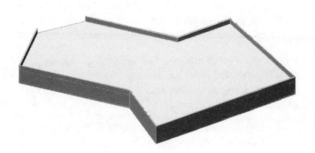

6. Create another construct in the Shells category called **Office Shell 02**. Give it a description of **Second Floor Office Shell** and assign it to the proper level and division (see Figure 5.15).

7. Double-click the Office Shell 02 construct and click the edge of the space boundary. In the Properties palette, notice that the Elevation is 13′-0″. Change this value to **0** (zero). Press Esc, save, and close the construct (see Figure 5.16).

FIGURE 5.15
After moving the second floor office shell to a construct

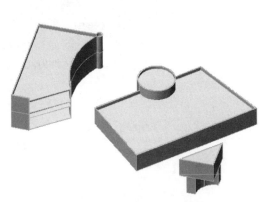

FIGURE 5.16
Change the elevation of the space boundary to zero in the construct.

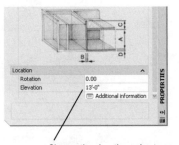

Change the elevation value to zero

WARNING Space boundaries contain spaces; both are object types that you'll learn more about in Chapter 6, "Space Planning." You can select a space boundary by clicking its edge; select its contained space by clicking inside. Be careful when selecting space boundaries to be sure that you haven't selected a contained space instead.

You must set the elevation of each space boundary to zero within each construct. After you move the objects generated from the massing model into constructs and elements, project levels are responsible for maintaining elevations and floor-to-floor height values instead of Z heights. Let's continue parting-out the space boundaries from the massing model into useful project constructs and elements.

1. Create a new construct for Office Shell 03, and drag and drop the appropriate space boundary into it in the Navigator. Open the new construct, select its space boundary, and set its elevation value to zero. Save and close Office Shell 03.dwg.

2. Repeat the same process twice more and create constructs for Annex Shell 01 and Annex Shell 02, moving the appropriate space boundaries to their corresponding constructs. Open the construct files and move their space boundaries to elevation zero. Save and close the constructs. You will be left with the few parts shown in Figure 5.17.

3. Create another construct in the Shells category called **Tower Shell** with the description **Tower spanning construct**. In the Add Construct worksheet, check all three levels in the Office division assignment matrix (see Figure 5.18). You create spanning constructs simply by checking more than one box in the assignment matrix. Note that spanning constructs are inserted at the lowest level checked and their objects are shared among all selected levels and/or divisions.

FIGURE 5.17
Remaining objects in SpaceBoundaries

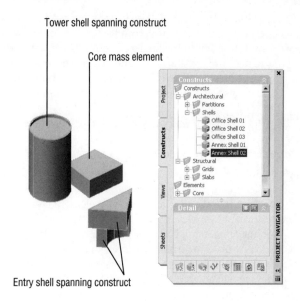

Tower shell spanning construct

Core mass element

Entry shell spanning construct

FIGURE 5.18
Adding a spanning construct

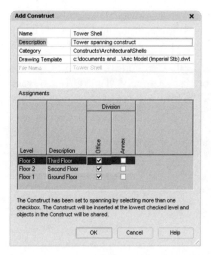

4. Select the Tower shell and then drag and drop it into the Tower Shell construct in the Navigator.

5. Make another construct called **Entry Shell 01** with a description of **First floor entry shell**. Assign it to Floor 1 in the Office division. Select and then drag and drop the space boundary into the construct.

6. Select the space boundary on the second floor and then drag and drop it into the Shells category folder. The Add Construct worksheet appears. Type the name **Entry Shell 02** and the description **Second floor entry shell**. Assign the space boundary to the Second Floor level and Office division and click OK, closing the worksheet. Open the construct and move its space boundary to elevation zero. Save and close `Entry Shell 02.dwg`.

7. The Core mass element is all that remains in the `SpaceBoundaries.dwg` file. This time you will create a construct differently: Select the core mass element, hold down the Ctrl key, and drag and drop it into the Shells category folder. The Add Construct worksheet appears. Type the name **Core** and the description **Office elevator and washroom core**. Assign the mass element to the First Floor level and Office division only and click OK, closing the worksheet. Notice that the mass element remains in the original file.

TIP Hold down Ctrl when dragging into the Navigator to copy objects rather than move them.

CONVERTING BETWEEN CONSTRUCTS AND ELEMENTS

After thinking more about it, you might realize that the core would be better suited as an element, rather than a construct. Typical building cores housing elevators and washrooms are usually identical on all levels. If you define the core as an element it can be referenced into each level's shell construct, and controlled from a single file.

If on the other hand, you anticipate the cores to be similar but different on each floor, it makes more sense to copy the core construct to levels so you'll have unique cores to customize on each level. Although we won't cover this in the tutorial, remember it as a possibility for your own projects.

Next we will convert a construct to an element simply and efficiently by using the Navigator's drag-and-drop interface.

1. Right-click the Core construct and take a look at its shortcut menu (see Figure 5.19). Notice that there are options to change the XRef to Attach or Overlay mode (see the earlier "Understanding XRef Relationships" sidebar). In addition, you can Copy Construct To Levels as was mentioned previously. In this case we will convert this construct to an element, so press Esc.

2. Drag the Core construct into the Core subcategory under the Elements category. The Add Element worksheet appears. Type **Office elevator and washroom core** for the description and click OK. You obviously lose the level and division assignment when converting a construct to an element.

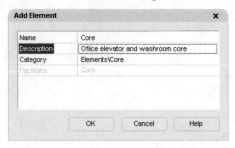

FIGURE 5.19
Construct shortcut
menu options

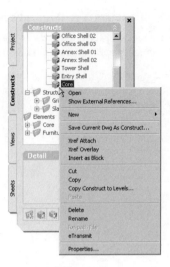

NOTE Convert elements to constructs by dragging them into a construct category. As you can see, drag and drop in the Navigator is very intuitive.

3. Close SpaceBoundaries.dwg without saving. It is essential that you discard changes because you have parted-out most of the objects of this file into constructs.

4. Reopen SpaceBoundaries.dwg. Right-click the Element category folder and choose Save Current Dwg As Element. Accept the default name and description in the worksheet and click OK; SpaceBoundaries appears as an element node (see Figure 5.20). Although you won't be referencing this element into other elements or constructs, it is good to include it as an orphan so it at least gets copied into the project folders. This way, the orphan file will get archived and backed up if and when the project does.

FIGURE 5.20
Constructs and Elements

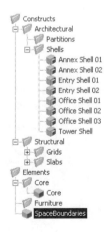

REFERENCING ELEMENTS INTO CONSTRUCTS

Now that you have completely parted-out the conceptual model, you are ready to start making references between the elements and constructs that you have created (this is done quite simply with the Navigator).

1. Double-click the Office Shell 01 construct in the Navigator to open it. Drag and drop the Core element from the Navigator into the drawing window. The core mass element appears correctly positioned at its original coordinates (see Figure 5.21).

FIGURE 5.21
Core element attached to
Shell construct

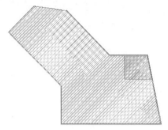

2. Click the Manage XRefs icon in the drawing tray: the XRef Manager dialog box appears. Notice that the Type is set to Attach by default (see Figure 5.22). Therefore, the core will ultimately appear in views and sheets. Click Cancel. Save and close Office Shell 01.dwg.

WARNING   Do not use the XRef Manager to create external drawing references in a project; use the Project Navigator instead. When you drag a drawing from the Project Navigator, it both XRefs and makes XML files that maintain the project database. However, it is OK to use the XRef Manager to change reference types, reload, unload, or detach XRefs in a project.

3. You can save time by attaching the core element to multiple constructs at once. Right-click the Core element and choose Attach Element To Constructs; a worksheet then appears. Notice that Office Shell 01 already has a grayed out check, indicating that it already has this element assigned to it. Check the boxes for Office Shell 02 and Office Shell 03 and click OK (see Figure 5.23).

4. Double-click to open the Office Shell 02 and Office Shell 03 constructs and verify that the Core mass element appears there; it is attached to these files by default.

5. Select the Office Shell 03 construct and click the Show External Reference button in the Navigator. A small worksheet appears, revealing the XRef relationships in this file. Right now there is only one reference, but this is a useful feature—complex projects might have multiple XRefs nested several levels deep, and it helps to visualize their relationships.

FIGURE 5.22
Examining the
XRef Manager for
reference type

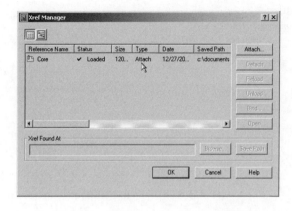

FIGURE 5.23
Attaching an element to
multiple constructs

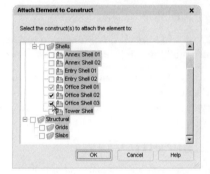

REFRESHING AND REPATHING THE PROJECT

If one of your team members makes changes to the project structure while you are working, such as adding categories or deleting constructs, your Project Navigator won't be up-to-date.

1. Click the Refresh Project button in the Navigator to reload all folder and XML data from disk.

TIP   It's a good idea to refresh periodically if you know that your team members might be making changes to the project while you are working.

2. Finally, before closing the project or ADT, be sure to re-path all project files. If your computer tends to crash, do this often. Click the Repath XRef button in the Navigator. The Reference File Re-path Queue worksheet appears (see Figure 5.24). Click Re-path and you'll see a progress bar as all the files in the queue are processed and incorrect paths are corrected.

WARNING   If you close ADT without re-pathing the project, you will lose all changed path infor-mation. The next time you launch ADT, some paths might be broken and will require manual updating in the XRef Manager.

FIGURE 5.24
Reference File Re-path
Queue worksheet

Re-pathing is required in the following situations:

◆ The project folder is moved to a different location (only required if relative pathing is off)

◆ Any node is moved to a different category in the Navigator

◆ Any subcategories are moved into different categories

◆ Any file is renamed

3. Close and save all open files. You can leave ADT running if you will continue on to the next section: otherwise it is safe to close it now.

My advice is to refresh and re-path often. Just do it every hour or so and you'll be sure to be up-to-date and safe path-wise if your computer crashes. We'll continue building this project's skeleton by attaching the constructs to views in the next section.

Working with Views

Views lie between constructs and sheets in the project hierarchy. Therefore you will tend not to do design work in views, nor will you plot views. Instead, a view is used to assemble selected constructs from any level and division into a drawing. You can include multiple constructs in a single view, such as floor plans from the first and second floors, for example. Think of views as traditional drawings such as floor plans, reflected ceiling plans, sections, elevations, and so on. Let's take a closer look.

Understanding Views

Views can be confusing for some because they are an intermediate abstraction layer in which you usually don't plot or do design work. Even if you have used XRefs before in AutoCAD to create plot sheets, you might never have come across this concept. Views are different from plot sheets and are essential to the drawing management system in ADT. Views are just what their name suggests: windows or reports on the "real" objects stored in constructs—all through the magic of external references and the many XRef-aware tools in ADT.

NOTE Elements cannot be directly referenced into views, but appear in views when they are themselves referenced by attachment into constructs.

The drawings you can assemble with views are specific to a level and division. In other words, views are where all the work you did assigning constructs to levels and divisions pays off. Views make it easy to assemble appropriate constructs into a typical drawing.

Views are the place where you will add annotation and dimensions to drawings before the views are laid out on sheets (see Chapter 13, "Annotating, Tagging, and Dimensioning"). In Chapter 2, "Object Display," you learned how entities do not use ADT's display system, but rely on layer management to control their visibility. If you need to add entities to views, you can keep layer management to a minimum. Entities in views are already in specific drawings and will not need to be hidden later in others. This eliminates paper space complexity and the need to freeze layers in the current viewport as is often done in AutoCAD.

What's in a View?

The term "view" can be easily confused with other commands in ADT. In this book I'll use the term *view* to describe those drawings that form a specific part of the hierarchy in the drawing management system. Views appear as nodes in the Views tab of the Project Navigator. Views are stored as dwg and xml files by the Navigator.

For many years there has been an AutoCAD command called VIEW that saves both model space and paper space view directions as named views and optionally records the layer state and user coordinate system (UCS) orientation. For clarity, I will always refer to them as *named views*.

What makes matters more confusing is that ADT also has a concept called *model space views* (MSVs)—and as you can guess—MSVs work only in model space. Incredibly, MSVs are used on views and themselves save named views—have you got that? We almost need a new language to speak "ADT." Pay attention to the jargon so you'll know what this book and other ADT users are talking about.

MSVs save the view direction, layer state, and UCS orientation in old-school named views. In addition, an MSV records a name, description, display configuration, layer snapshot, and drawing scale and ties it all together with a named view. Think of MSVs as ADT's answer to named views.

Views can contain multiple drawings, as is typical with exterior elevations. You will define one MSV for each drawing in a view. In the next section you'll see how a MSV is used to place a drawing correctly on a sheet.

Making views is handled by wizards that guide you in different ways depending on whether you are making a general view (covered in this chapter), section/elevation view (see Chapter 16, "Sections and Elevations"), or a detail view (see Chapter 17, "Details and Keynotes"). Let's gain some practical experience by making some general views and MSVs.

Making Views

There are three stages involved in making a view ready to be referenced onto a sheet: Create the view itself using a wizard, save a model space view, and add a title mark. Views should be created in a particular order. As you might intuit, plan views should be made first. Elevations and sections are themselves generated from plan views (see Chapter 16), so they must be created after plan views. Details also work in a similar way: You must have either a plan, elevation, or section view open before you can create a detail callout that generates yet another view (see Chapter 17). It actually makes a lot of sense, and the view workflow mirrors the design process.

CREATING A FLOOR PLAN VIEW

Let's create a general view for the first floor plan.

1. Click the Views tab of the Navigator. Right now there are no nodes here other than the top-level Views category. Right-click the Views folder icon and select New View Dwg ➢ General from the shortcut menu.

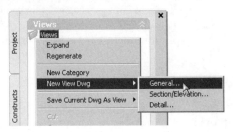

NOTE You can make categories on the Views tab if you want to organize a complex project that has a plethora of views.

2. The Add General View worksheet appears. Its wizard interface has three pages listed in the navigation pane: General, Context, and Content. Type **Floor 1 Office Plan** into the Name field and type **Construction plan** as its description. Notice that the view will be based on a template, which you have the option to select on this page (see Figure 5.25). Click Next to advance to the Context page.

3. Choose Floor 1 level and Office division as the context for this view by checking the appropriate box in the matrix (see Figure 5.26). Notice that the wizard lets you go back to the General tab if you change your mind about something you entered there. Click Next to advance to the Content page.

4. Only the categories and constructs appropriate to this context are displayed in the wizard. In other words, you can choose only from the constructs that belong to the Floor 1 Office. Because this is only a project skeleton at this point, you haven't created partition or structural constructs yet. Uncheck the top Constructs node to deselect all. Then check Shells to select all three shell constructs (see Figure 5.27). Click Finish to complete the wizard and close the Add General View worksheet.

FIGURE 5.25
General page of the
Add General View
Wizard

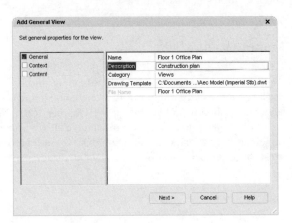

FIGURE 5.26
Context page of the Add
General View wizard

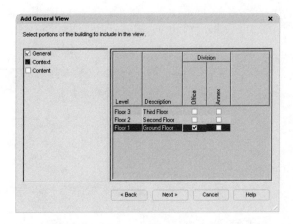

FIGURE 5.27
Content page of the Add
General View Wizard

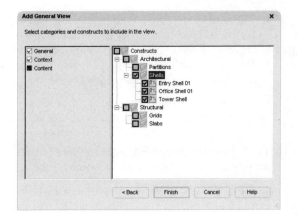

TIP   You can add additional constructs to a view later on.

SAVING A MODEL SPACE VIEW

The next step is to create an MSV in the view you made that represents the bounds of the drawing. The MSV will store all the information needed to properly reference this view into a sheet. Thus you do some prep work for a sheet within a view.

   1. Double-click the Floor 1 Office Plan view in the Navigator to open it. It contains the space boundary from the ground floor office, plus the core, stair tower, and entry in one drawing. Zoom out so you can see the whole drawing if necessary. Stay in the top view.

2. Click the Show External References button in the Navigator. A small worksheet reveals all the files that are referenced into the view. Click OK.

3. Right-click the Floor 1 Office Plan node in the Navigator and choose New Model Space View from the shortcut menu.

4. The Add Model Space View worksheet appears. Type **First Floor Construction Plan** in the Name field and type **Office ground floor** as a description. Leave the display configuration set to Medium Detail and the drawing scale set at $1/8''=1'-0''$. Notice that you could also choose a layer snapshot here if one had already been defined (see Chapter 2). Click the Define View Window button (see Figure 5.28).

5. Click two points of a rectangle that surrounds the floor plan. Click OK to close the worksheet. Notice that a new icon appears as a child of the view: This is the model space view (see Figure 5.29).

NOTE You will need to refresh the project or select the Views node; then select the Floor 1 Office Plan node to get the details of the newly created view file to show up in the Detail area of the Views tab.

6. Using the pop-up menu on the drawing window status bar, set the scale to $1/16''=1'-0''$. I'm asking you to do this to illustrate a point in the next step.

FIGURE 5.28
Add Model Space
View worksheet

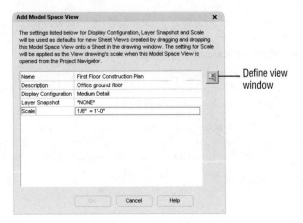

FIGURE 5.29
View and Model
Space View icons
in the Navigator

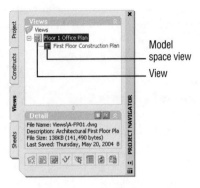

TIP It is sometimes helpful to work backward from the size of your sheet's title block to determine how much room you might have for a drawing in a particular scale. This information can help you define a view window that will make the drawing fit perfectly on a sheet. See Chapter 15, "Floor and Ceiling Plans" for a tutorial that takes this approach.

7. Double-click the First Floor Construction Plan MSV in the Navigator. The drawing immediately zooms to the view window you defined in step 5. Notice that the drawing scale has been set back to $1/8''=1'-0''$ by the MSV. Also the MSV extents are indicated by a rectangle, and the view name is displayed in blocky text at the top of the window; they are shown simply for your information. Pan slightly, and the view extents rectangle and blocky text disappear. Zoom out slightly.

8. Type **VIEW**↵ on the command line. Observe that First Floor Construction Plan is saved as a named view in the View dialog box; it was done automatically when you saved the MSV. Click Cancel.

ADDING A TITLE MARK

The last step to make this view sheet-ready is to add a *title mark* callout. The title mark is an attributed block that contains *fields* for view number, view title, and drawing scale. Fields display data that can be updated automatically. ADT's default title mark callout uses fields in its attribute definitions.

All we have to do is attach a title mark to our MSV. We can let ADT keep track of what information needs to appear in the title mark (it will be determined when we reference the view onto a sheet in the next section).

1. In the Tool Palettes, make the Document palette group current. Click the Callouts palette.

2. Click the title mark tool that has number, name, and scale (see Figure 5.30).

NOTE It is possible to make your own callouts. This advanced topic won't be covered in this book because of space limitations.

3. Move your cursor over the MSV and notice that its view window highlights. You must locate the title mark within the view window. Click a point within the highlighted circle to locate the symbol. Then click a second point toward the right to end the title mark's horizontal line (see Figure 5.31).

FIGURE 5.30
Title marks on Callouts palette

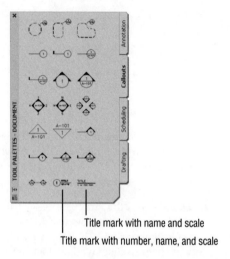

Title mark with name and scale

Title mark with number, name, and scale

FIGURE 5.31
Adding a title mark to an MSV

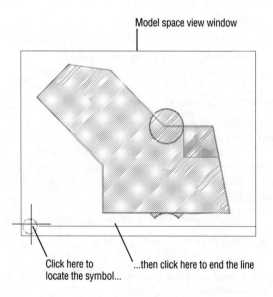

Model space view window

Click here to locate the symbol...

...then click here to end the line

4. Zoom in on the new title mark. Its title reads with the name of the MSV: First Floor Construction Plan. The scale also comes from the MSV. Notice that the number appears as a question mark because it is yet to be determined.

TIP You can drag an existing title mark onto an MSV in the Navigator to update its fields if changes to the MSV make this necessary. This process is called post-linking.

5. Make views, MSVs, and title marks for the second and third floors of the office. Then do the same for the two floors of the Annex. It should go much faster now that you've been all the way though the process.

6. Save all the view files you created.

CREATING A COMPOSITE MODEL VIEW

Let's make one more view that is a composite of the entire 3D model. This view will be useful to have in the future so you can see how the design progresses for the building as a whole. The composite view will contain all constructs, so be careful later on when opening the composite view because it might take a long time.

1. In the Navigator, click the Views category, and then click the Add View button. Choose General View from the Add View worksheet and click OK.

2. The Add General View Wizard appears. On the General page, type the name **Composite View** with a description of **3D model**. Click Next.

3. On the Context page, select all check boxes in the assignment matrix. Click Next.

4. On the Content page, leave all constructs selected. Click Finish.

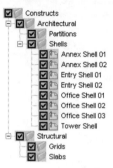

5. Double-click the Composite View node in the Navigator to open its file. Switch to an isometric view in shaded mode (see Figure 5.32). We have come full circle: Consider where you started, back at the beginning of "Defining Levels and Divisions," with space boundaries generated from massing model. The only visible difference is the core element poking out of the top of the third floor in the office division. However, select an object and verify that it now appears as an External Reference in the Properties palette, rather than a space boundary at an elevated Z height.

To complete the drawing management workflow, you'll learn how to generate a sheet set in the next section. Then you'll be able to populate sheets with your views and be ready to print at any time.

FIGURE 5.32
Composite View
showing 3D Model

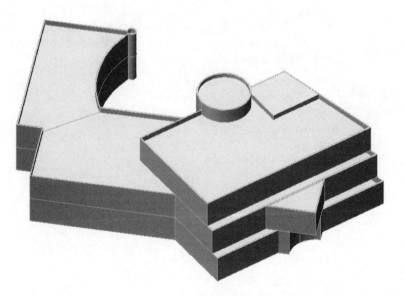

REGENERATING VIEWS

Views are composed of externally referenced constructs and elements. If your team members change any of these files while you are working in a view, you might not have the most up-to-date changes loaded.

One way to make sure that you have the latest changes is to save, close, and reopen your view drawings because XRefs are reloaded when the file they are referenced into is opened.

A more elegant solution is to click the button on the Views tab of the Navigator called Regenerate Views. When you click this button (or use AecRegenerateProjectViews on the command line) all the XRefs in all the open views in the project are reloaded on your computer.

Generating a Sheet Set

A *sheet set* is traditionally thought of as a collection of bound drawings, colloquially known as blueprints. You can publish a sheet set to a plotter or to the digital dwf format (see Chapter 19). In ADT, sheets are used exclusively to publish drawings.

The Sheets tab of the Project Navigator allows you to create and manage the following:

Sheet Set This contains a collection of sheet drawings comprising the entire set of documentation for the project.

Sheet Drawings These are the actual dwg and xml files that are stored on disk. A sheet drawing contains one or more sheets.

Sheets These are paper space layout tabs in sheet drawings. Think of sheets as pieces of paper. The U.S. National CAD Standards (NCS) recommend having one sheet per sheet drawing, and this is the standard this book uses. Sheets can contain title blocks, referenced views and elements, and schedule tables (see Chapter 14). No content resides on the sheet itself; only referenced content that lives elsewhere in the project.

Sheet Views These are what MSVs become when they are placed on sheets. Sheet views use the information stored in MSVs to format each view for publishing. Sheets can have multiple sheet views.

WARNING Although it is possible to work in sheets, I do not recommend it. The drawing management system is designed for sheets to act solely as reports of the building model for up-to-date printing at any time. You jeopardize the integrity of this system by harboring content in sheets and you can waste print media as a result.

There are two modes available on the Sheets tab of the Navigator: Explorer View and Sheet Set View—don't confuse these with views. Explorer View shows the categories that mirror the physical folder structure on disk. The Views and Constructs tabs of the Navigator also show Explorer View modes. Sheets also have Sheet Set View, which offers logical categories called subsets that do not necessarily mirror the physical folder structure.

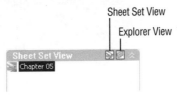

Sheet Set View

Explorer View

Sheets are made using templates that contain ready to use title blocks. The default sheet template's title blocks have fields that display relevant project details automatically. You might have entered project details in the Project Browser near the beginning of this chapter (refer to Figure 5.6). In addition, each subset in Sheet Set View can hold a different sheet template. Let's get started making sheets.

1. Click the Sheets tab in the Navigator if you haven't already. Switch to Sheet Set View.

2. Right-click the top-level node that has the project name: Chapter 05. Choose Properties from the shortcut menu. The Sheet Set Properties dialog box appears. Type your name in the Drawn By field (see Figure 5.33).

3. Click the Browse button in the Sheet Creation template field (scroll down if necessary to see it). The Select Layout as Sheet Template dialog box appears. Choose Arch D (24 x 36) and click OK (see Figure 5.34). Click OK again to close the Sheet Set Properties dialog box.

FIGURE 5.33

Sheet Set Properties

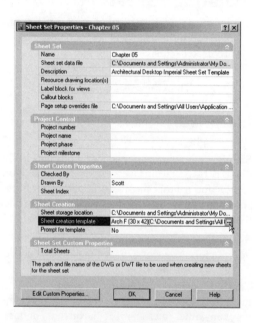

FIGURE 5.34

Choosing a sheet template layout

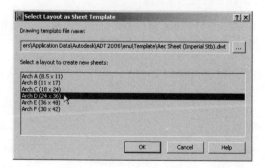

4. Right-click the Chapter 05 node and choose New ➤ Subset. The Subset Properties dialog box appears. Type **Plans** as the Subset name and check Create Folders Relative To Parent Subset Storage Location (see Figure 5.35). Checking it means that your subset will make a corresponding folder on disk. I recommend doing this to avoid confusion when you're working in Explorer View. Notice that you have the option to select a different template or sheet size for the sheets in this subset; this is great when you also want to make $8^1/2 \times 11$ sheets in your sheets set. Click OK.

FIGURE 5.35

Entering the number and title for a new sheet

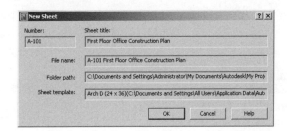

5. Click the Add Sheet button in the Navigator. Type **A-101** in the Number text box and **First Floor Office Construction Plan** as the Sheet title (see Figure 5.36). None of the other fields are editable in this dialog box. Click OK.

6. Double-click the A-101 First Floor Office Construction Plan node under the Plans subset in the Navigator to open the sheet file. Zoom into the title block and check out the data that has been automatically entered into the fields (see Figure 5.37).

7. The final step after making a sheet is to drag and drop an MSV onto it. Zoom out so you can see the whole title block. Switch to the Views tab in the Navigator. Drag the only MSV of the Floor 1 Office Plan from the Navigator and drop it onto the open sheet (see Figure 5.38). Notice the ToolTip, which gives you a chance to right-click change the scale if the MSV doesn't fit on the sheet.

8. Switch back to the Sheets tab of the Navigator. The MSV you referenced has become known as a sheet view when it hit the sheet. Now all sheet set nodes display in the Navigator (see Figure 5.39). Zoom into the title mark and observe that the number now correctly reads as 1 because it is the only sheet view on the sheet. Subsequent title marks will be numbered correctly as MSVs are dragged onto sheets.

9. Go ahead and make one sheet for each of the four remaining MSVs you have defined in this project in the Plans subset. Both Annex construction plans can fit on one sheet. Number the sheets sequentially.

FIGURE 5.36
Entering Subset
Properties

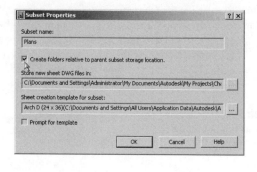

FIGURE 5.37
Examining field data in
new sheet's title block

FIGURE 5.38
Drag and drop a
model space view
onto the sheet.

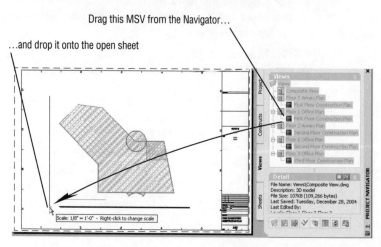

FIGURE 5.39
Sheet Set View nodes in
the Navigator

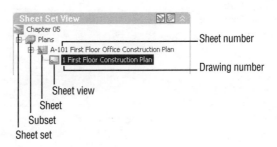

TIP   After you complete your entire sheet set, have ADT generate a sheet list for you that you can
place on a cover sheet. Do this by right-clicking the Sheet set node and choosing Insert Sheet List.

Congratulations! Now you have converted the massing model to a project skeleton! The project's
levels, divisions, elements, constructs, views, and sheets are ready to be used in a team environment.
Team members should remember to use elements and constructs for design work, views for annotation, and sheets to publish up-to-date information.

Establishing Project Standards

Project standards are new in ADT 2006. Standards are rules that keep all team members' drawings consistent within a project's sheet set, and in the long run standards enforce consistency between projects.
Establishing and synchronizing standards as the project evolves ensures the integrity of your deliver-
ables at all times. Even if project standards are usually set up by a manager, it is important for all team
members to understand how standards work in ADT. You'll start by configuring standards and then
move on to study synchronization options.

You can configure project standards to include any number of display properties, object styles, layers,
and AutoCAD entity styles that have been identified in *standards drawings*. Standards drawings are any
collection of drawings (.dwg), drawing templates (.dwt), and/or legacy AutoCAD drawing standards
(.dws) files.

Configuring Standards

Standards fall into two overall categories: ADT standards and AutoCAD standards. *ADT standards*
specify object styles and display settings. *AutoCAD standards* specify layers, linetypes, dimension
styles, and text styles. You might use AutoCAD standards if you have legacy CAD standards that you
want to bring forward into ADT. Otherwise, ADT standards are probably all you need to consider.

SELECTING STANDARD STYLES FROM STANDARDS DRAWINGS

You'll choose standards drawings and configure which object styles to use as standards for your
project from them.

1. Open the Project Browser and verify that Chapter 05 is selected as the current project, as was
   done in the last section. Close the Project Browser.

2. Select the Project tab in the Navigator. Click the Configure Project Standards button in the Navigator or right-click the project standards icon in the drawing window tray (see Figure 5.40).

FIGURE 5.40
Configuring Project
Standards

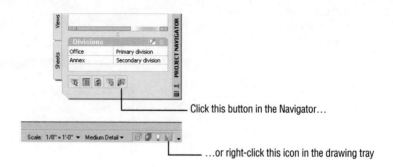

Click this button in the Navigator…

…or right-click this icon in the drawing tray

3. In the Configure AEC Project Standards dialog box that appears, check "Enable project standards for project 2006.04.22 - Chapter 05". Leave this dialog box open until you are done configuring the project standards.

WARNING You can't use standards unless a project is set current in the Project Browser. Standards do not affect drawings that are not part of the current project.

4. Click the Add Drawing button on the Standard Styles tab, and the Select Standards Drawing dialog box appears. Select StudWallStyles.dwg from the Chapter 5 folder on your hard drive or the companion DVD and then click Open.

WARNING If you path standards drawings to a DVD, you will need that disc in your computer whenever you work with drawings that reference those standards.

5. Choose Architectural Objects from the Object Type drop-down list, scroll to the bottom of the list of object styles and check all the wall-related styles (see Figure 5.41). You have now indicated that the styles in the selected file will act as standards for your project.

6. Click the Add Drawing button, and the Select Standards Drawing dialog box appears again. This time, change the Files Of Type drop-down list to AutoCAD Drawing Template (*.dwt), navigate to this chapter's folder on the companion DVD, and choose LayerKeyStyle.dwt (see Figure 5.42). Click Open to close the dialog box.

7. Change the Object Type drop down list to Multi-Purpose Objects and check Layer Key Styles in the DWT column (see Figure 5.43). Use the matrix in the Configure AEC Project Standards dialog box to match up the object styles you choose with definitions in specific standards drawings. You can add as many drawing standards files as you like, and they will appear as new columns: it doesn't matter which file type you choose, be it dwg, dwt, or dws.

TIP The Copy Standards From Project button allows you to scavenge the entire configuration matrix from another project.

FIGURE 5.41
Configuring project standards

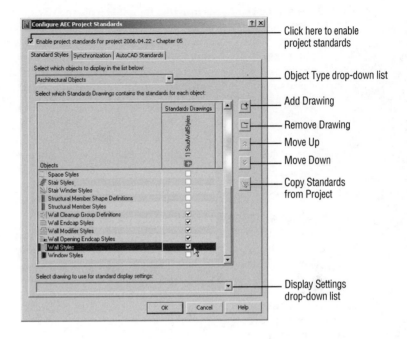

Click here to enable project standards

Object Type drop-down list

Add Drawing

Remove Drawing

Move Up

Move Down

Copy Standards from Project

Display Settings drop-down list

FIGURE 5.42
Selecting a standards drawing template file

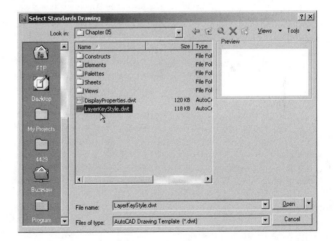

8. Click the standards drawing template icon and notice that the Move Up button is enabled. Standards drawings are synchronized in a linear order from left to right. The Move Up button actually advances a standards drawing to the left. The precedence that each drawing has is listed by number in the Configure AEC Project Standards dialog box (refer to Figure 5.43). You don't need to worry about synchronization order unless you have more than one standards drawing checked for a particular object type (because a conflict would occur). Synchronization order solves the problem, and only one standard is allowed for a given object type.

9. Open the display settings drop-down list and choose Browse. Select `DisplayProperties.dwt` from the companion DVD. All the display configurations, sets, and representations in this single file will act as standards for your project. It is not possible to split these display settings up into separate files. Leave the dialog box open.

TIP Managers: Reference project-specific standards from the `Project Root\Standards\Styles` folder (whose standards drawings can be copied and changed from project to project), and reference unchanging organization-wide standards that are used in many projects from a write-protected folder on the file server.

FIGURE 5.43
Assigning both DWG and DWT files to act as standards drawings

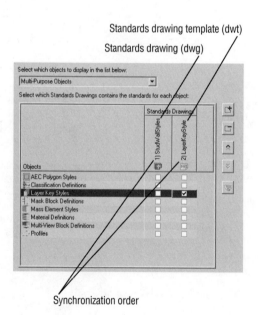

INCLUDING AUTOCAD STANDARDS IN PROJECT STANDARDS

So far, you have been configuring only standards for ADT's object styles. AutoCAD standards control layers, linetypes, dimension styles, and text styles. For many years now, AutoCAD standards have traditionally been stored in dws files; you can still use these in ADT.

1. Click the AutoCAD Standards tab. Click the Add Drawing button, and the Select Standards File dialog box appears.

2. Double-click AutoCADStandards.dws from the companion DVD. Notice that there is no option for selecting which dws file you want to load a dimension style from, for example, because you cannot define different dws files as standards for different standard components. Therefore, lump all your layers, linetypes, dimension styles, and text styles together in one dws file to act as standards for the current project.

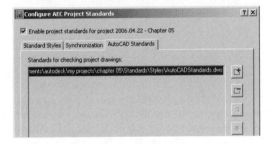

3. Click OK to close the Configure AEC Project Standards dialog box.

4. The Version Comment dialog box will appear, asking for you to add a comment for the initial standard version. Type something here if you want, such as **First Version,** and then click OK. You have established some standards for the project. You can always go back and configure additional standards drawings to represent object styles as the project develops.

ACCESSING STANDARD STYLES

Standard object styles are never automatically copied into your project drawings. Instead, as you work in elements and constructs, plan to create objects that adhere to the standards that were configured for the project. Your manager should populate the project tool palette with tools that adhere to the project standards, so you'll be sure to be on track as you flesh out the design.

In case your tool palettes haven't been completely "standardized," you can access standard object styles in the Style Manager and Display Manager now that standards have been configured for the project. Let's take a look.

1. Open Walls.dwg from this chapter's folder on the companion DVD. It contains three wall objects, and each has a different wall style.

2. Switch to the Constructs tab in the Navigator. Right-click the Elements node and select Save Current Dwg As Element. Click OK in the worksheet that appears to accept the name Walls as the name of the element you're adding to the project.

WARNING Unless a drawing is defined as an element or construct, it will not be synchronized with project standards.

3. Open the Style Manager. Notice that in addition to the current drawing, there is a node that has the project name. Expand this node. Inside you'll find nodes for the two configured standards drawings. You have access to each one of the standards drawing's object categories.

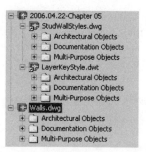

4. Expand the node for Architectural Objects under the StudWallStyles.dwg node. Notice that all the object style nodes have a blue color—this is new and indicates that these nodes are in a standards drawing. Expand the Wall Styles node. You'll find more than 70 wall styles inside. These standard styles live in the standard drawing. You have access to them at any time. You can drag and drop or cut and paste styles from standards drawings into the current drawing or any other drawings you care to open in the Style Manager.

5. Expand the Walls node to access the current drawing. Expand Architectural Objects and Wall Styles. MyWallStyle's icon is gray, indicating that it is a nonstandard style (not defined in any standards drawings). Nonstandard styles are not synchronized with standards. There are also three blue Wall Style icons with exclamation marks on them; the blue icons indicate that they are standard styles, and the exclamation marks mean that they need updating (see Figure 5.44). These icons would be blue without an exclamation mark if they were already synchronized with the project standards (see the next section).

WARNING Be careful when using the Style Manager to copy standard object styles from the "right" drawings. For example, although you configured StudWallStyles.dwg to represent all related wall styles in the project, you are not using it to represent door styles. Therefore, if you copied a door style out of the StudWallStyles standards drawing, it would (somewhat confusingly) be a nonstandard style. In my opinion, only the object styles specifically configured as standards should have blue icons, but we'll have to wait for the next version of ADT for that.

6. Click Cancel to close the Style Manager. Open the Display Manager. In addition to the current drawing, notice that there is also a project node in the Display Manager.

7. Expand the project node and the DisplayProperties.dwt node. Remember that this was the drawing template you configured to hold the display settings for the project standards.

8. Expand the DisplayProperties.dwt node's Configurations, Sets, and Representation nodes. Look around and verify that all the display configurations, sets and representations appear with blue icons. Note that it is the representations themselves that are blue, not the Representation by Object nodes. Although it is possible to copy and paste these nodes between drawings in the Display Manager, you learn to synchronize all this more efficiently in the next section.

9. Expand the nodes of the current drawing. Notice that they all appear as standard styles that need updating (blue with an exclamation mark). Click Cancel to close the Display Manager.

10. Leave the sample file open if you plan to continue to the next section.

Synchronizing Standards

If you've gone to the trouble of configuring standards, synchronizing standards is where your effort pays off. ADT 2006 features a new versioning system that appears as the Version History tab in the Style Manager. The Version History tab automatically stamps the date and time standard drawing styles are changed. This allows you to synchronize the latest standard changes across the entire project dataset.

FIGURE 5.44
Accessing standard styles in Style Manager

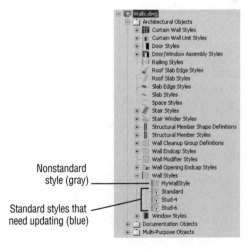

Nonstandard style (gray)

Standard styles that need updating (blue)

Managers can choose from three different synchronization behaviors: manual, semi-automatic, and automatic. There are many synchronization features that go beyond the scope of this book, including auditing, versioning, synchronizing with AutoCAD Standards, changing project standards, and more. I recommend reading this entire book first and then studying the ADT Help before coming to any conclusions about the best practices for your organization.

Something that all designers should know is how to synchronize objects, drawings, and the entire project with the configured standards. Check with your manager about their policies before synchronizing anything!

1. If it is not already open, open `Walls.dwg` from the Chapter 5 folder on the companion DVD.

2. You can synchronize object styles with standards one-by-one in the Style Manager. Open the Style Manager and expand nodes until you find Stud-4 wall style in the current drawing. Right-click this node and witness the shortcut menu option Synchronize With Project Standards. This is for the selected style only and gives you maximum control. Close the Style Manager. As you might expect, similar functionality exists in the Display Manager.

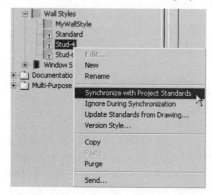

3. The next more -global method is to synchronize the entire drawing. Right-click the AEC Project Standards icon in the drawing window tray and choose Synchronize Drawing. The aptly titled Synchronize Drawing With Project Standards dialog box (Figure 5.45) is one-stop shopping for all the styles in this drawing. You can change the Action for each style as you desire: Update From Standard, Do Not Update, or Ignore. Nonstandardized styles appear below for your information. Click Cancel.

4. The most far-reaching synchronization applies to all the drawings in the entire project. Obviously, do not perform this task unless you are certain about its consequences in a real project. Choose Window ➢ Pulldowns ➢ CAD Manager Pulldown. This should give you a hint about who should be doing this!

5. Look at—but don't click—CAD Manager ➢ AEC Project Standards ➢ Synchronize Project With Standards (see Figure 5.46). It would take quite some time to synchronize the entire project with standards, so you don't need to do it because this is a sample project, anyway. Notice the other options in this pull-down list: there are many powerful tools here available to the CAD manager. Unfortunately, space doesn't permit me to elaborate on them in this book.

6. Close the `Walls.dwg` file.

FIGURE 5.45
Plan your
synchronicity here.

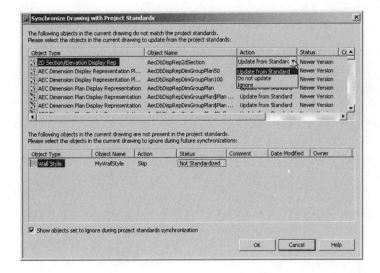

FIGURE 5.46
Don't do this unless you
have some time to wait.

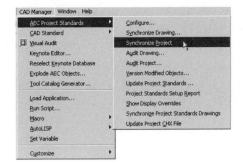

Summary

In this chapter you learned how to use the drawing management system to organize and prepare you to work with projects. You learned how to use the Project Browser and Project Navigator to manage project data structures such as projects, levels, divisions, elements, constructs, views, and sheets. You studied XRef overlays and attachments that create the relationships that tie a project together. Finally, you took a look at the new project standards and understand how they work in ADT. In the next chapter, we will begin the inside-out design process known as space planning.

Chapter 6

Space Planning

Space planning (also known as bubble diagramming in 2D) is the art of inside-out building design. It proceeds by first identifying the programmatic requirements of your design and then representing them as volumes called *spaces*. Spaces can be placed, shaped, sized, and oriented as inspiration moves you.

Space planning is the opposite of, and complement to, mass modeling (which was described in Chapter 4, "Mass Modeling"). Balancing the interplay between the container and the contained can be approached from either direction, and your design is usually solved somewhere in the middle.

Spaces can be separated with *space boundaries* that represent conceptual partitions between volumes. As you continue to develop your design with more specific detail, you'll convert space boundaries to walls. In the end, walls are what ultimately define and bound spaces (see Chapter 8, "Walls"); you'll learn how to automatically generate and update spaces from walls. This chapter's topics include:

- Working with Spaces
- Working with Space Boundaries
- Converting Space Boundaries and Walls

Working with Spaces

Think of spaces as rooms—or more precisely as volumes—that might or might not be separated by physical boundaries. By themselves, spaces do not have boundaries; they have areas instead. Space boundaries are separate objects that can contain spaces, as you'll see later in this chapter. Adjacent spaces not separated by boundaries designate different uses, such as work and circulation areas in an open office (also called a department).

In this topic you'll learn to create spaces from scratch, modify their shapes using vertex and edge grips, and use powerful architecture, engineering, and construction (AEC) Modify tools. In addition, you'll see how to export the information stored in spaces to make an area report.

TIP It isn't necessary to draw spaces before boundaries, or vice versa. Either way works, but I show spaces before space boundaries because I use a bottom-up approach in this chapter.

Like other objects, spaces have styles that control their dimensions and display properties. You'll learn how to use styles to create and represent each space differently—altering the display system to present and visualize spatial volumes.

Spaces have different display components in Plan (2D) and Model (3D) representations (see Figure 6.1). In all plan representations, as seen from the top viewpoint, spaces have net and gross boundaries, plus a hatch display component. The *net boundary* defines the space's usable floor area, whereas the *gross boundary* allows additional room for partitions between spaces. By default, the gross boundary is not displayed; it is normally used only to provide room for partitions when spaces are placed adjacent to one another.

The net-to-gross offset is a distance value that separates these two defined edges and carries around the entire perimeter of the space. The hatch component is contained within the net boundary and can alternately be displayed as a solid. Solid hatch components are often used to present space plans in color.

In all other viewpoints, the model representation displays space objects with floor and ceiling components that can optionally have materials and/or floor patterns applied (see Chapter 3, "Object Styles"). It is also possible to represent the void between the floor and ceiling as part of a solid form encompassing the entire volume of the space.

FIGURE 6.1

Space objects display components in 2D (left) and 3D (right) representations

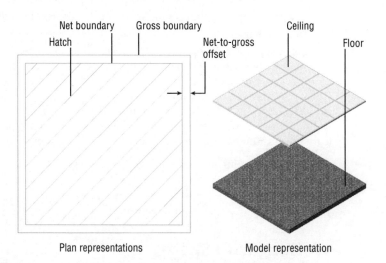

Creating Spaces

You might create spaces from scratch if you are approaching design from the inside out (the opposite of what you did in Chapter 4). There are three modes in which you can create spaces: rectangle, polygon, and insert. As the first two mode names suggest, you can draw a rectangle or polygon to define the shape of a space. Rectangles are defined by opposite corners and are rectilinear. Space polygons can have both line and arc segments, as Polyline entities do in AutoCAD. Let's get started creating spaces in all three modes.

1. Create a new drawing with the default template.

2. Choose the Design palette in the Design palette group on the Tool Palettes. Click the Space tool (see Figure 6.2).

3. In the Properties palette, change the Create Type to Rectangle (see Figure 6.3). Show the illustration in the Component Dimensions group if it does not already show. Study the illustration; notice that there are four object components labeled A–D. Three of the components control the "room" itself: floor, space, and ceiling thickness (A–C). If nonzero, component D allows you to define a height above the ceiling that belongs to the space volume. This might be used for the plenum space above a suspended ceiling.

ENABLING USABLE AND GROSS BOUNDARIES FOR SPACE OBJECTS

In ADT 2006, there is a new space settings feature that is unfortunately not compatible with previous versions. To enable this setting, choose Format ➤ Options and select the AEC Object Settings tab. Check Enable Usable and Gross Boundaries. When this feature is enabled, space objects get enhanced display components. Remember that they won't work in previous versions—even though ADT 2006 uses the AutoCAD 2004 file format. If you aren't concerned with backward compatibility, you'll probably want to enable the enhanced display components for space objects.

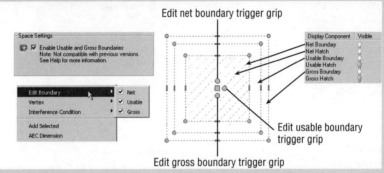

Enhanced display components include net, usable, and gross boundaries:

Net area is measured to the inside of exterior walls and to the inside of the interior walls—typically used in facility management and space planning.

Usable area is measured to the inside of the exterior wall and to the centerline of interior walls below a certain width—typically used to calculate rentable area. Check your local building codes to determine the legal definition of this area.

Gross area is measured to the outside of the exterior wall and to the centerline of interior walls—typically used in cost calculation and price estimation.

Each type of boundary has a corresponding hatch component, although you will probably want to display only one hatch component at a time to avoid confusion. To use these enhanced features, right-click any space object and choose Edit Boundary; you'll see a cascading submenu that lets you toggle on Net, Usable, and/or Gross boundaries for any space object.

After these boundaries are toggled on for a particular space object, new grips appear surrounding the space. There are also trigger grips corresponding to net, usable, and gross boundaries that enable or disable each boundary in the drawing window. Therefore, you can turn on just the components you are concerned with and avoid cluttering the drawing.

NOTE   The top surface of the floor is where the space height (A) and floor boundary thickness (B) object components meet. By default, B extends below ground; the top of the floor surface is at elevation zero.

4. Click two points in the drawing window to create your first rectangular space. Draw a few more nonoverlapping rectangular spaces.

FIGURE 6.2
Space Planning tools

Space tool   Space Boundary tool

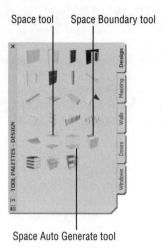

Space Auto Generate tool

FIGURE 6.3
Creating spaces in
Rectangle mode. The
starburst icon at left
is a parameter that is
available only during
object creation.

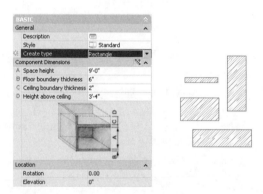

5. Click the Space tool again. In the Properties palette, change the Create Type to Polygon. After you change modes, a starburst icon appears next to a new parameter that lets you set the Segment type. Choose Arc as the segment type (see Figure 6.4).

6. Click three points in the drawing window to draw an arc. Switch to Line as the segment type and draw two more lines; each segment is connected to the previous one, as in a polyline. Type C↵ to close and complete the polygonal space.

Insert mode is the most powerful creation mode because it allows you to dynamically constrain a space using areas, lengths, or widths as you create. This is the way to go if you already have specific dimensions or an overall area in mind; for example a 100-square-foot office. Let's see how it works.

1. Click the Space tool and change the create type to Insert. While in Insert mode, notice two additional starburst icons appear in the Properties palette: Specify On Screen, and Constrain. Toggle on the illustration in the Actual Dimensions group if it is not already displayed. This illustration is similar to the previous one, but the Actual Dimensions illustration has different labeled parts A and B: Length, and Width.

FIGURE 6.4
Creating spaces
in Polygon mode

2. Verify that Specify On Screen is set to Yes. When it is set to No, the Length and Width parameters are enabled; right now they are grayed-out but read with values of 10′ each. Verify also that Constrain is set to Area; other choices include Length, Width, and *NONE* (see Figure 6.5).

3. Click a point in the drawing window and move the cursor. With the settings you specified in the previous two steps, the new space you are in the process of creating is constrained to 100 square feet. Moving the cursor controls whether the space is tall and narrow, squarish, short and wide, or anywhere in-between (see Figure 6.6). Click again to insert the shape you are looking for. Read the command line:

```
Rotation or [Style/Area/Length/Width/Height/Move/Size/Drag point/Match/Undo]
<0.00>:
```

Press Enter to accept the default of zero degrees. Notice all the other options that are available on the command line; many of them are mirrored in the Properties palette.

FIGURE 6.5
Creating spaces
in Insert mode

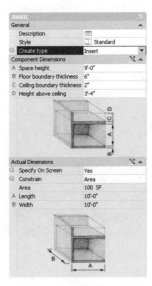

FIGURE 6.6
Constraining by Area
adjusts the shape of
your space as you drag.

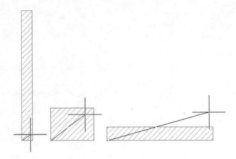

TIP   The Space tool's drag point option rotates the space 90 degrees each time you use it. Use drag point before you insert a space to get it oriented the way you want it.

4. Right-click the Space tool in the Tool Palettes. Open the Apply Tool Properties To submenu; it contains Space, AEC Polygon, Area, Polyline, and Slab. Being able to convert areas and slabs into spaces is new in ADT 2006.

5. Practice by inserting a few more spaces of different proportions, each with 100 square feet areas. Leave the file open for the next section.

Modifying Space Objects

After a space object is created, there are two ways to edit its shape: with edge and/or vertex grips, or with AEC Modify tools.

EDITING SPACES WITH GRIPS

Edge and vertex grips are available on many profile-based objects, such as spaces, mass element extrusions, AEC Polygons, slabs, and more. Let's take a look at these with a conceptual tutorial.

1. Click one of the spaces you made in the last section. Once selected, the space shows edge and vertex grips.

2. Move the cursor over one of the vertex grips. Pay attention to the ToolTip choices: You can move or remove vertices, or offset edges. Click the vertex to select it and click again to move it.

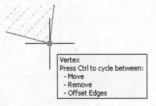

WARNING   Space objects that are edited with grips might no longer fit within the maximum or minimum areas defined in their styles.

3. Move the cursor over an edge grip. Once again, pay attention to the choices listed on the ToolTip: Offset, Add Vertex, Convert to Arc, and Offset All.

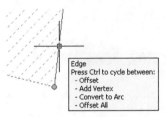

4. Press Ctrl twice and click to locate the midpoint of the converted arc segment. The result is a space similar to one made in Polygon mode. Continue practicing editing vertex and edge grips. The process is quite simple and intuitive. Press Esc when you are done.

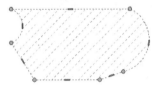

5. Draw a closed polyline. Right-click the Space tool in the Tool Palettes. Expand the Apply Tool Properties to submenu where choices include other profile-based objects: Space, AEC Polygon, Area, Polyline, and Slab. Choose Polyline and click the one you drew before, and choose Yes on the command line to erase the layout geometry. This is another alternative to drawing a space directly in Polygon mode. As you can see, shaping spaces is very easy.

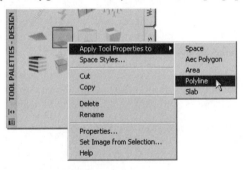

EDITING SPACES WITH AEC MODIFY TOOLS

AEC Modify tools are powerful commands that go beyond the tools you might have used in AutoCAD to edit entities. The AEC Modify tools work on spaces, mass element extrusions, areas, AEC polygons, detail components, and blocks when any of them are embedded in blocks.

1. Click a space object to select it. Right-click and expend the AEC Modify Tools submenu. A number of tools appear above a separator bar: Trim, Divide, Subtract, Merge, and Crop. Although the tools below the bar technically can be used on spaces, they are more suited

to arranging multiple objects in relation to each other (see Chapter 9, "Doors, Windows, and Openings").

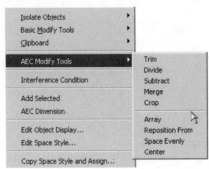

2. Choose Trim from the AEC Modify Tools submenu. Read the command line:

```
Command: LineworkTrim
Select the first point of the trim lime or ENTER to pick on screen:
```

Click a point outside but near to the selected space to start the cutting edge. Click a second point to establish the cutting edge.

3. A red cutting edge appears. Click anywhere to the right of the cutting edge to delete this portion of the space (see Figure 6.7). Trim is great for lopping off spaces within a line.

TIP   You can also use AEC Modify tools on many basic drafting AutoCAD entities, including polylines, circles, arcs, text, and hatches.

4. Select the space, right-click, and choose AEC Modify Tools ➢ Divide from the shortcut menu. Divide works just like trim, except it doesn't delete the trimmed portion. Divide the space into two portions using a dividing line (see Figure 6.8).

5. Select the left space and move on top of the right one. Select the right space, right-click, and choose AEC Modify Tools ➢ Subtract from the shortcut menu. Notice that the command line version is called LineworkSubtract. Click the left space and press Enter. Type **Y**↵ to erase the selected space object.

FIGURE 6.7
Using LineworkTrim: left, during the operation; right, the result.

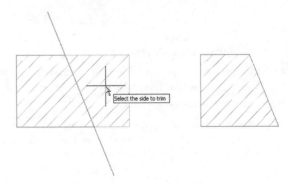

FIGURE 6.8

Dividing and subtracting a space: left, after applying the Divide tool; center, during the LineworkSubtract operation; right, the result.

 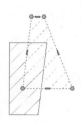

NOTE The object that is selected before you use LineworkSubtract is the object that will remain afterward.

6. Create another overlapping space object using any method you please. Select the right space and type **LineworkMerge**⏎. Select the overlapping space and press Enter. The command line says the following:

```
Erase selected linework? [Yes/No] <No>:
```

Type **Y**⏎, and the two spaces are merged (see Figure 6.9). This is conceptually identical to performing a Boolean union with region entities.

7. The last AEC Modify tool to consider using with spaces is Crop. As the name suggests, the `LineworkCrop` command lets you truncate a space object by drawing a rectangle (or by using another space object to act as the crop boundary). Select the space object and choose Crop from the shortcut menu. Read the command line:

```
Select objects(s) to form crop boundary or NONE to pick rectangle:
```

Press Enter to default to NONE. Draw an overlapping rectangle around the space (see Figure 6.10). The portions of the space outside the rectangle are cropped away.

8. Practice using the AEC Modify tools on spaces until you feel quite comfortable with their functionality. It might take awhile to break old habits if you are used to using AutoCAD's Modify tools.

FIGURE 6.9

Using LineworkMerge: left, during the operation; right, the result.

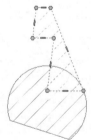 

FIGURE 6.10
Using LineworkCrop:
left, during the opera-
tion; right, the result.

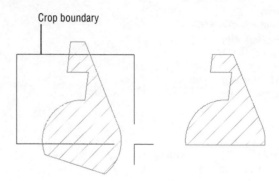

9. Switch into an isometric viewpoint. Remember that the modifications you make in plan simultaneously affect the 3D model's floor and ceiling components. Close the file you have been
   experimenting with without saving.

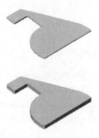

With a little practice, you will be able to perform every conceivable type of modification to space
shapes with grips and AEC Modify tools. This will hold you in good stead in the future when you'll
apply these same skills to modifying other object types.

Making Styled Spaces

The space objects you made earlier were constrained to 100 square feet by the Standard space style.
You'll be able to set up different sizes by specifying target, minimum, and maximum areas in space
styles. In addition, the default display properties can be overridden, giving you the opportunity to
give each space style a unique color. Let's style some spaces.

1. Start a new blank drawing with the default template.

2. Choose Format ≻ Style Manager. Expand Architectural Objects and right-click Space
   Styles. Choose New from the shortcut menu and type the name **Reception**.

3. Click the Dimensions tab and type target, minimum, and maximum areas of **500**, **300**, and **800** SF
   (square feet). Type in Length target, minimum, and maximum values of **25′**, **5′**, and **40′**. Finally
   type in Width values of **20′**, **5′**, and **40′**. Leave Net to Gross Offset at zero (see Figure 6.11).

FIGURE 6.11
Entering target
dimensions for
a space style

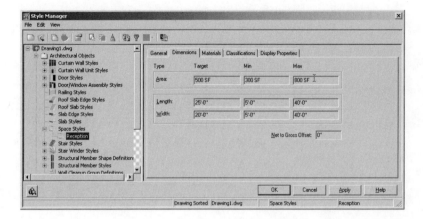

4. Switch to the Display Properties tab. Remember from Chapter 3 that the drawing default display property sources are common to all space styles—in other words, changes you make to the drawing defaults affect all space objects. Therefore, to give each style unique colors, you'll have to create style overrides. Place a check in the Style Override column next to the Plan representation. The Display Properties dialog box appears.

5. You'll use the Net Hatch display component to identify this space style by color. Click the Color swatch in the Hatch row and choose color 40 from the Select Color Dialog box that appears. For your information, click the Hatching tab and notice that the selected pattern is user single with a scale of 1´-0˝ at a 45-degree angle; this is what you see in the Top viewpoint. Click OK to close the dialog box, but leave the Style Manager open.

Display Component	Visible	By Mat...	Layer	Color	Linetype	Lineweight	Lt Scale
Net Boundary			0	■ BYBLOCK	ByBlock	ByBlock	1.0000
Net Hatch			0	□ 30	ByBlock	0.18 mm	1.0000
Gross Boundary			0	■ BYBLOCK	ByBlock	ByBlock	1.0000

6. Make a style override for the Plan Presentation display representation. On the Hatching tab, notice that this representation uses the SOLID pattern; this is perfect for making color space plans. Click the Layer/Color/Linetype tab and then click the Hatch component's color swatch. Choose color 40 from the picker and click OK; click OK again to close both dialog boxes. Figure 6.12 shows the Style Manager after making two style overrides in the Reception space style.

FIGURE 6.12
Making style
overrides in a
space style

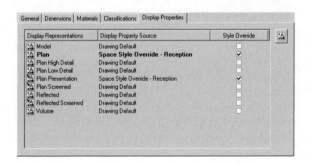

7. Referring to Table 6.1, repeat steps 3–5 for each style listed. Enter the appropriate areas, lengths, and widths, and then make style overrides for the Hatch component color in both Plan and Plan Presentation representations.

8. Save your work as **SpaceStyles.dwg**. You can leave this file open if you are continuing to the next section.

TABLE 6.1: Space Styles Matrix

| STYLE NAME | COLOR | AREA | | | | LENGTH | | | WIDTH | |
		TARGET	MIN	MAX	TARGET	MIN	MAX	TARGET	MIN	MAX
Break Room	Brown	175	150	200	14	5	30	12	5	30
Conference	Yellow	350	300	400	24	5	40	14	5	30
Elev Lobby	Aqua	80	50	120	16	5	30	5	5	20
Large Office	Magenta	240	180	275	18	5	30	12	5	30
Men	Cyan	130	100	165	18	5	40	8	5	20
Reception	Orange	500	300	800	25	5	40	20	5	40
Small Office	Blue	130	100	160	13	5	30	10	5	25
Stairwell	Violet	150	100	175	20	5	40	8	5	20
Utility Room	Gray	35	25	50	6	5	20	6	5	20
Women	Pink	130	100	165	18	5	40	8	5	20
Workstation	Green	75	60	90	9	5	20	8	5	20

Using Net to Gross Offsets

Using net to gross offsets is a quick way of laying out spaces while leaving room for future walls between spaces. Space styles have a gross boundary component that is larger than the net boundary that is used to calculate the usable floor area. The distance that the gross boundary is away from the net boundary is controlled by the Net To Gross Offset parameter (refer to Figure 6.1). What makes this feature useful is the fact that nodes are placed along the gross boundary opposite net boundary vertices. By using node object snap, you can place adjacent spaces precisely next to one another, leaving exactly the right amount of room for partitions between the spaces. Let's give this a try.

1. If you left the sample file open from the last section, you can continue here. If not, open SpaceStyles.dwg from the working folder on your hard drive or from the Chapter 6 folder on the companion DVD.

2. Open the Style Manager and select the Small Office space style. Click the Dimensions tab in the content pane. Let's assume that partitions between spaces will have a thickness of 6″. Type **6″** in the Net To Gross Offset text box and click OK to close the Style Manager.

3. Click the Space tool in the Tool palettes. On the Properties palette, change the style to Small Office and verify that the Create type is Insert.

4. Verify that the OSNAP toggle is on in the drawing status bar. Right-click the OSNAP toggle and choose Settings. Click the Clear All button in the Drafting Settings dialog box. Check Node object snap mode and click OK. Note that Drafting Settings was invoked transparently—in other words, it didn't interrupt the SpaceAdd command.

5. Create a small office space object by clicking one point in the drawing window. Notice that the shape of the rectangle initially mirrors the Target dimensions you entered in its style. As you move the cursor, you can dynamically size the space within the min and max tolerances specified earlier. Click a second point to add a small office. Press Enter to accept the default rotation of zero.

6. Move the cursor just outside the net boundary of the space you made previously. The node object snap icon appears. Click a node to locate the new space so as to leave exactly enough room for a partition (6″, in this case). Click again to determine the size of the new space and press Enter. Create yet another small office using node snap (see Figure 6.13).

NOTE When you create space objects using a net to gross offset, space boundaries applied to these spaces will automatically receive solid form boundaries (also known as partitions) that precisely fill the areas in between spaces.

7. Save your work as Spaces.dwg. You can leave this file open if you are continuing to the next section.

FIGURE 6.13
Snapping new spaces to nodes

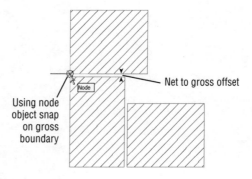

Net to gross offset

Node

Using node object snap on gross boundary

Using the Display System with Spaces

Spaces can be displayed in a variety of ways—each is helpful in different situations. On the most basic level, spaces are displayed with hatch patterns in their plan representations. As you saw in the previous section, the hatch patterns can have unique colors through the use of style overrides. Colored hatches help to differentiate spaces on-screen, but are less useful in hard copy, in which colored linework is often hard to read. On the other hand, solid filled boundaries read much better when presented in color. Let's see how to use the Presentation display configuration to make an attractive space plan.

1. If you left the sample file open from the last section, you can continue here. If not, open Spaces.dwg from the working folder on your hard drive or from the Chapter 6 folder on the companion DVD.

2. Using the pop-up menu on the drawing status bar, change to the Presentation display configuration. Notice that the spaces you already made appear with solid "hatching."

3. Create additional spaces using the space styles you set up in the preceding section. Play with the relationships between spaces by changing their shapes, sizes, locations, and orientations until you have designed an office floor plan from the inside out. Figure 6.14 shows one possible office configuration. There is no need to copy the figure exactly—design your own office.

TIP Use Net To Gross offsets while laying out adjacent spaces to leave room for future partitions. Do not use a Net To Gross offset on the workstations, however. Instead, snap the workstation spaces together in clusters.

4. Save your work as **SpacePlan.dwg**.

Three-dimensional aspects of spaces can be better visualized by adding materials to the floor and ceiling components in the Model representation.

1. Switch to an isometric viewpoint. Switch to Gouraud Shaded, Edges On mode.

FIGURE 6.14
Space planning using Presentation display configuration

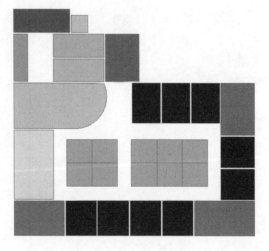

2. Click the Material tool and click a space object. Assign appropriate materials to floor and ceiling components. You can choose to apply the material either as a style override or object override (see Figure 6.15)—choose object override only if the materials are unique to one space.

3. Add materials to floors and ceilings where you like. It does help to visualize the model.

4. Select the Reception space and increase its height to **11´** in the Properties palette (see Figure 6.16). Spaces are great for designing changes in ceiling plane.

Spatial volumes might also help you to visualize how the spaces of your design interrelate. Space objects have a Volume display representation that is provided for this purpose. To work efficiently with volumes, you'll make a new display configuration and set.

1. Choose Format ➢ Display Manager. Expand the Sets node.

2. Right-click the Model display representation and choose Copy from the shortcut menu. Give the copied set the name **Volumes**.

3. Click the Volumes set and switch to the Display Representation Control tab. Scroll down and click the Space object type to highlight it. Uncheck its Model representation. Scroll all the way over to the right and place a check in the Volume display representation column (see Figure 6.17).

FIGURE 6.15
Assigning a material as a style override

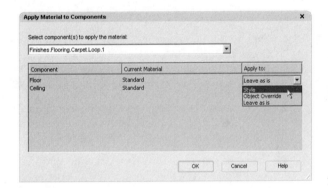

FIGURE 6.16
Working with materials and ceiling heights

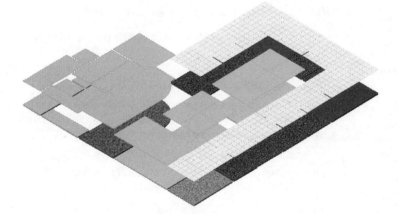

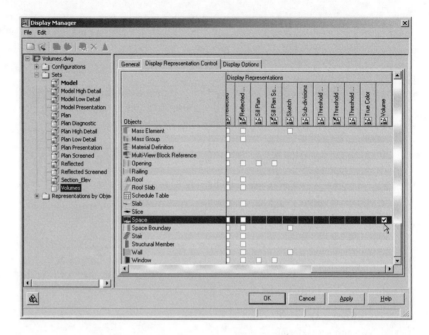

4. Expand the Configurations node. Right-click the Medium Detail configuration and choose Copy from the shortcut menu. Open the shortcut menu again and choose Paste. Right-click the new configuration, choose Rename and type **Space Volumes**. Type the following description below: **3D volume turned on for space objects**.

5. Click the Space Volumes node in the tree pane. In the content pane, click the Configuration tab. Click the set for the Default view direction and open its drop-down menu. Choose the Volumes display representation set (see Figure 6.18). Click OK to close the Display Manager.

6. Using the pop-up menu on the drawing status bar, change to the Space Volumes display configuration. Notice that the spaces you already made appear as volumes—the floors and ceilings are no longer distinct, but are merged into solids filling the spaces (see Figure 6.19).

NOTE You cannot display materials on space volumes.

7. Save your work as **Volumes.dwg**. Leave this file open if you plan on continuing to the next section.

Reporting on Space Information

You can have ADT create a report based on the space objects in your drawing. This report can optionally be exported to a Microsoft Access database (an mdb file) for further study and possible integration with other project management software you might be using.

1. If you left the sample file open from the last section, you can continue here. If not, open Volumes.dwg from the working folder on your hard drive or from the companion DVD.

FIGURE 6.18
Setting up the Space
Volumes configuration

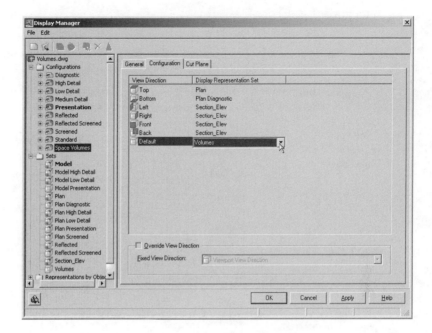

FIGURE 6.19
Displaying Space
Volumes

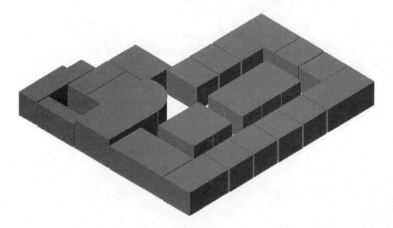

2. On the command line, type **Space ↵ Q ↵**, where Q is for the Query option. The Space Information dialog box appears (see Figure 6.20). The Space Info Total tab displays the space style name and lists the quantity of space objects and the total area they comprise. Click the Space Information tab, which shows data broken down per space object, with the actual, minimum, and maximum areas of each space listed.

TIP Use area objects instead of space objects for more powerful area calculation and reporting options. Area objects, which are covered in Chapter 14, "Schedules, Display Themes, and Areas," can export data to Microsoft Excel.

3. Click the Create MDB button and type the name **Spaces.mdb** in the Database File dialog box that appears. Click Save.

4. If you have Access installed, locate the Spaces.mdb file on your hard drive (or the companion DVD) and double-click it to launch Access. Double-click the spaces table (see Figure 6.21).

5. You can use Access to format and report on this data, but doing so goes beyond the scope of this book. Close Access and the Volumes.dwg file in ADT.

FIGURE 6.20

Space Information and Area Totals

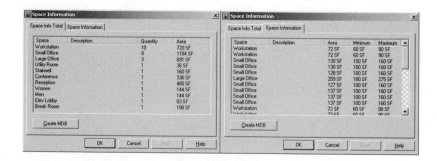

FIGURE 6.21

Space data shown in database table

NAME	DESCRIPTION	SPACEID	GROUPID	AREA_TARGET	AREA_CONSTI	AREA_CONSTI	LENGTH_TARC	LE
Standard		1CFB	0	249.7712157362	0.5	10000	120	
Workstation		1CFE	0	72	60	90	108	
Workstation		1CFD	0	72	60	90	108	
Small Office		1CFC	0	130	100	160	156	
Small Office		1CFB	0	130	100	160	156	
Small Office		1CF5	0	128.1059277632	100	160	156	
Large Office		1CF4	0	258.5543753798	180	275	216	
Small Office		1CF3	0	126.7474368505	100	160	156	
Small Office		1CF2	0	136.5414284568	100	160	156	
Small Office		1CF1	0	136.5414284568	100	160	156	
Small Office		1CEF	0	136.5414284568	100	160	156	
Workstation		1CEE	0	72	60	90	108	
Workstation		1CED	0	72	60	90	108	
Workstation		1CEC	0	72	60	90	108	
Workstation		1CEB	0	72	60	90	108	
Utility Room		1CEA	0	36	25	50	72	
Stairwell		1CE9	0	160	100	175	240	
Large Office		1CE8	0	216	180	275	216	
Small Office		1CE7	0	130	100	160	156	
Small Office		1CE6	0	130	100	160	156	
Workstation		1CE5	0	72	60	90	108	

Record: 1 of 31

Working with Space Boundaries

Space boundaries are a separate type of object from spaces. Although space boundaries can technically stand alone, they are intended to contain spaces, and you will almost always use them together. In fact, spaces and space boundaries are so interconnected that the base height of a space boundary is actually controlled by the space it contains. This is so that the ceiling height set in a space updates its container.

Unlike spaces, space boundaries do not have object styles. Instead, space boundaries are controlled solely by editing their object properties and object display. In this section you'll learn specialized commands that apply to space boundaries and the spaces they contain.

Creating Space Boundaries

Space boundaries have two boundary types: *solid*, and *separation*. Solid boundaries are conceptual partitions with thickness, height, and justification parameters that ultimately can be converted to generic wall objects, as you'll see in the next section. Separation boundaries do not have any parameters and cannot be converted to wall objects. Instead, separations do as their name suggests: they conceptually separate space boundaries, but they do so without partitions. Let's try making both boundary types.

1. Start a blank new drawing with the default template.

2. Click the Space Boundary tool in the Tool Palettes. Take a look at the Properties palette (see Figure 6.22). Two parameters have starburst icons: Segment Type and Baseline Offset. Verify that Boundary Type is set to Solid, Segment Type is Line, and Baseline Offset is zero. Remember that the starburst parameters are available only before you create the object. Notice that the Base Height property is not editable.

WARNING The base height property cannot be set from the space boundary; edit the space height of the enclosed space instead.

3. Click several points in the drawing window: it is just like drawing a polyline. The space boundary edges stay connected and remain part of the same object. Draw three sides of an enclosure and type **C↵** to close the boundary.

4. Make another space boundary next to the first one, but make the new object using the Separation boundary type.

TIP You can also create space boundaries by first drawing polylines, lines, and/or arcs. To do this, apply space boundary tool properties to the edges you drew previously.

5. Switch into a 3D viewpoint and shaded mode. Both objects are space boundaries containing spaces (four objects total). The space boundary with the Solid boundary type appears as partitions surrounding the space in both plan and model representations. The Separation boundary type is more confusing because it looks exactly like a space. However, there are two objects on the right in Figure 6.23. The space and space boundary are coincident, so there will be two objects no matter what shape you have drawn for the space boundary.

FIGURE 6.22
Space boundary
object properties

FIGURE 6.23
Space boundaries and
contained spaces

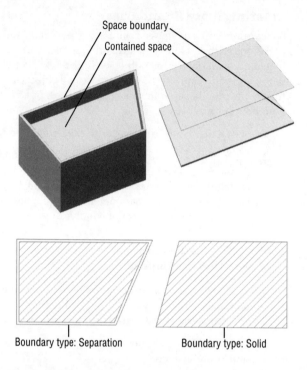

CONTROLLING HOW SPACE BOUNDARIES MANAGE SPACES

Each space boundary has the option to manage contained spaces. When selected, this links the container to the contained, so that changes to the shape of a space boundary affect the shape of its contained spaces.

1. Hold down Ctrl and click the space boundary separation/contained space objects (such as those on the right of Figure 6.23). The Command line reads <Cycle on>, which means you have entered Cycle selection mode. Notice that the entire floor and ceiling are selected: this means the space object is selected. Click again on the floor. Only the top of the floor surface is selected, meaning that the space boundary is selected (see Figure 6.24). Press Enter to end Cycle selection mode.

FIGURE 6.24
The space boundary
is selected.

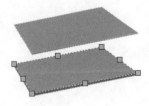

TIP   You can also use Quick Select to select space boundaries of the separation type. The Quick Select button is at the upper-right corner of the Properties palette. Refer to AutoCAD help to learn how to use this feature.

2. Space boundary grips appear in the drawing window. Click one of the corner grips and move it to a new location. The contained space updates to this new boundary.

3. On the Properties palette in the Dimensions group, change the Manage contained spaces to No.

4. Using the space boundary's grips, move one of the corners to a new location. The space inside does not update to the new boundary (see Figure 6.25).

5. Change Manage Contained Spaces to Yes in the Properties palette. Now a second space appears within the space boundary, filling it completely. The original space overlaps the new boundary.

WARNING   Do not overlap spaces unless you plan to merge, subtract, or crop them. Overlapping spaces will throw off your area calculations, among other things.

6. Select the old contained space and delete it. It is best to delete contained spaces if they are not being managed by their surrounding space boundary, or else confusion will result.

SETTING SPACE BOUNDARY CONDITIONS

Solid space boundary objects have boundary conditions that you can set to determine where the ceiling and floor stop in relation to the wall.

1. Select the space boundary with the solid boundary type.

2. In the Properties palettes, locate the Boundary conditions subgroup. Change the Ceiling Condition drop-down list to Ceiling Stops At Boundary. Notice that the labeled parameter C (Upper Extension) appears below the drop-down list. You can use C to control how far the walls extend above the ceiling (from top of ceiling to top of boundary).

FIGURE 6.25
Not managing
contained spaces

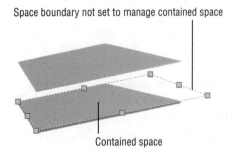

Space boundary not set to manage contained space

Contained space

3. Change the Floor Condition drop-down to Floor Stops At Boundary. Likewise, a labeled parameter D (Lower Extension) appears below. Use D to control how far the wall extends below the top of the floor (from bottom of wall to top of floor).

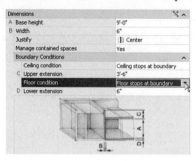

Boundary conditions describe exactly where the wall stops at ceiling and floor. Refer to Table 6.2 for all boundary conditions.

4. Experiment with boundary conditions on your own and then close the file without saving.

TABLE 6.2: Space Boundary Conditions Control where Walls Meet Ceilings and Floors

BOUNDARY CONDITION	CHOICE	DESCRIPTION
Ceiling condition	Ceiling stops at boundary	Extends walls above top of ceiling
Ceiling condition	Boundary stops at ceiling	Locates bottom of ceiling at top of wall
Floor condition	Floor stops at boundary	Extends bottom of wall below top of floor
Floor condition	Boundary stops at floor	Locates bottom of wall at top of floor

CREATING SPACE BOUNDARIES FROM SPACES

You've already seen how to draw a space boundary from scratch, clicking each vertex to make an enclosure. That method is good if you happen to be starting your project from scratch. If, on the other hand, you followed the inside-out design process and created spaces first, create space boundaries to contain the existing spaces.

1. Open SpacePlan.dwg from the working folder on your hard drive or from the Chapter 6 folder on the companion DVD. Notice that most of the spaces were made by using net to gross offsets that left room for the space boundaries (refer to Figure 6.14).

2. Right-click the Space boundary tool and choose Apply Tool Properties To ➤ Space.

3. Select all the spaces and press Enter. Space boundaries appear everywhere (see Figure 6.26).

WARNING   Although one space boundary can surround noncontiguous spaces, it might be confusing and probably should be avoided unless you have a good reason to do so.

FIGURE 6.26
Applying space
boundaries to
existing spaces

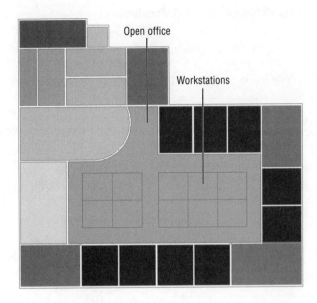

There are no partitions between the workstations and the open office because the workstation space style did not use a net to gross offset. The space boundaries surrounding the workstations got separation type boundaries automatically. By using Presentation display configuration, you'll notice that the open office is the same color (green) as the workstations—this happened because the open office was not defined as a space style (refer to Table 6.1). Instead, a space was generated for the open office because it was itself contained within the larger space boundary object. For the purposes of tracking spaces in the future, it would be best to differentiate the open office with a new space style.

1. Click the open office space.

2. Choose Copy Space Style And Assign from the shortcut menu.

3. Click the General tab in the Space Style Properties dialog box that appears. Type **Open Office** as its name and then click the Display Properties tab. Edit the style overrides for both Plan and Plan Presentation representations and change the Hatch color to dark green. Click OK.

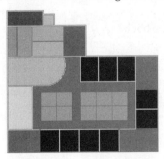

4. Save your work as **SpacePlanBoundaries.dwg**. Leave this file open if you plan to continue to the next section.

Modifying Space Boundaries

There are several specialized commands for modifying space boundaries. They fall into two categories: those that affect the entire boundary and those that affect each segment of a space boundary, called *space boundary edges*. All the space boundary edges together constitute the entire boundary. These specialized commands are accessed from the object shortcut menu.

EDITING ENTIRE BOUNDARIES

Space boundary commands include Attach Spaces To Boundary, Merge Boundaries, Split Boundary, and Anchor To Boundary. Let's try each command with an example.

1. If you left the sample file open from the last section, you can continue here. If not, open `SpacePlanBoundaries.dwg` from the working folder on your hard drive or from the companion DVD.

2. Create a new conference space adjacent to reception.

3. Select the space boundary, right-click, and choose Attach Spaces To Boundary. Select the new conference space and press Enter. The space boundaries extend to contain the space.

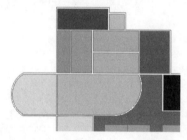

WARNING   You can attach spaces only to space boundaries that already manage contained spaces.

4. Click the Space Boundary tool and set Justify to Left in the Properties palette. Draw a rectangular space boundary above the new conference space, snapping to the existing space boundary along the edges (see Figure 6.27). The new space boundary contains a space that uses the Standard style by default.

5. Select the existing space boundary, right-click, and choose Merge Boundaries from the shortcut menu. Select the new space boundary and press Enter.

6. Select the new space that was added in step 4. Change its style to Large Office.

7. Select the space boundary, right-click, and choose Split Boundary. Choose the Stairwell space and press Enter. The space and its container are split off from the rest of the space boundary, as shown in Figure 6.28.

NOTE   Split Boundary is the opposite of Merge Boundary. You can clearly only split a boundary that contains multiple spaces.

FIGURE 6.27
Drawing a new space
boundary adjacent
to an existing one

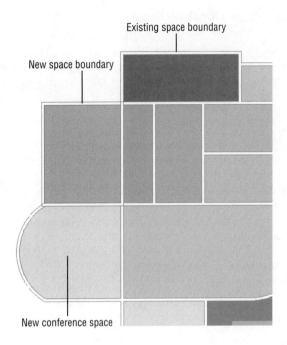

Existing space boundary

New space boundary

New conference space

FIGURE 6.28
Splitting off a space
boundary from the
whole

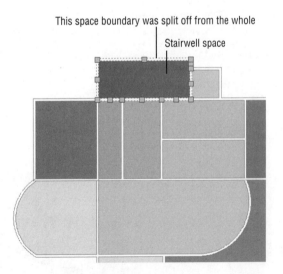

This space boundary was split off from the whole

Stairwell space

8. Create a box mass element roughly positioned and sized according to Figure 6.29.

9. Select the new space boundary that was separated in step 7. Right-click and choose Anchor To Boundary. Type **A.⏎** for the Attach Objects option (Free Objects is the opposite). Click the mass element that was added previously. Click the new space boundary at the location in which you want to anchor the mass element.

10. Select the mass element and try to move it away from the space boundary using its location grip. You will find that it is impossible to do so. Try moving the mass element along the space boundary or even around the corner; the mass element always stays linked to the space boundary edges.

11. Leave the file open.

You'll learn more about anchors in Chapter 7, "Parametric Layouts, Anchors, and Structural Members." Being able to attach mass elements to space boundaries might be helpful as placeholders for objects that you plan to add to walls in the future. Examples might be doors or 3D Body modifiers such as a fireplace or pilasters that thicken the wall. Anchoring objects to the space boundary is the best way to represent these conditions in the conceptual stage of the design process. However, you might also find it expedient just to ignore these details until a later date, when you can add them directly to walls in the design development stage of the project.

EDITING SPACE BOUNDARY EDGES

You can modify each space boundary edge independently. The specialized commands that affect edges are Add Edges, Remove Edges, Edit Edges, and Insert Joint. As we did before, let's try each command with an example.

1. Select the large space boundary, right-click, and choose Add Edges from the shortcut menu. Shift+right-click and choose Nearest from the menu that appears. Click a nearest point on the outer edge of the boundary where indicated in Figure 6.30. Using object tracking, snap the second point perpendicular to the other wall as shown and press Enter.

2. Note that the new edges do not enclose a space by default—you would have to add that manually if desired. Let's get rid of the edges added previously. Select the large space boundary, right-click, and choose Remove Edges. Click the two edges and poof!

FIGURE 6.29
Creating a mass
element placeholder

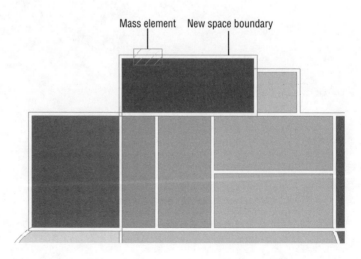

Mass element   New space boundary

FIGURE 6.30
Adding new
boundary edges

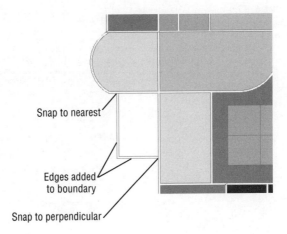

Snap to nearest

Edges added
to boundary

Snap to perpendicular

3. Switch into an isometric and shaded view. Select the large boundary edge, right-click, and select Edit Edges. Select the three edges identified in Figure 6.31.

4. Press Enter and the Boundary Edge Properties dialog box appears. On the Dimensions tab, change the Segment Type to B - Area Separation (see Figure 6.32). Click OK and the selected edges disappear.

5. Edit the edge between the new conference room and reception. Click the Design Rules tab of the Boundary Edge Properties dialog box. In the Boundary Condition(s) At Ceiling group, uncheck Automatically Determine From Spaces. Choose the Wall Stops At Ceiling radio button and click OK (see Figure 6.33). This dialog box allows you to store independent boundary conditions for each edge.

NOTE   Many of the walls already stop at the ceiling—boundary conditions were automatically assigned per edge when you generated the space boundary from the original spaces.

6. Select the large space boundary, right-click, and choose Insert Joint. Click a memorable point along the boundary edge.

FIGURE 6.31
Editing boundary edges

Select these three edges

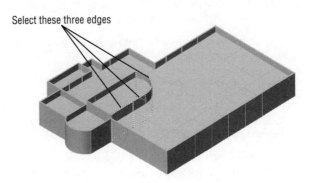

FIGURE 6.32
Changing segment types

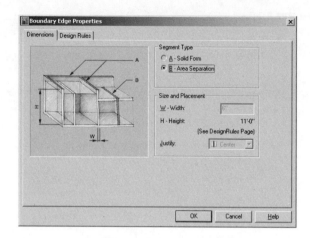

FIGURE 6.33
Editing boundary
conditions per edge

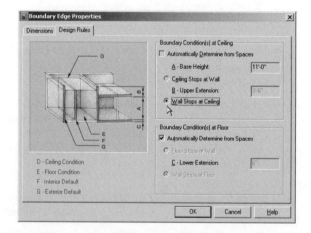

7. Select the space boundary. Notice that a new grip appears where you clicked in the previous step. This joint can be used to manipulate the space boundary. You can add as many joints as needed to get the shape you are trying to achieve. Note that you can't delete joints after they are added, so add only as many as you need.

8. Save your work as **EditedSpacePlanBoundaries.dwg**. You can leave this file open if you plan on continuing to the next section.

Editing Contained Spaces

There are several commands available to spaces that are contained within space boundaries: Join Spaces, Swap Spaces, Divide Spaces, and Interference Condition. The interesting thing is that these commands are not available to spaces by themselves (with the exception of Interference Condition).

1. If you left the sample file open from the last section, you can continue here. If not, open EditedSpacePlanBoundaries.dwg from the working folder on your hard drive or from the companion DVD.

2. Switch back to the Top viewpoint in 2D wireframe shading mode.

3. Select the reception space, right-click, and choose Divide Spaces from the shortcut menu. Click the two points of the dividing line, as shown in Figure 6.34. The reception is divided and the new space is randomly assigned a style.

4. Select the open office space, right-click, and choose Join Spaces from the shortcut menu. Select the new space from the previous step and press Enter. The open office space expands and fills the area divided off of reception.

5. Select the Men washroom space, right-click, and choose Swap Spaces from the shortcut menu. Click the Women space and press Enter. As you should expect, the space styles are swapped.

6. Create a small cylindrical mass element somewhere in the open office, which will represent a column in the conceptual model (see Figure 6.35).

7. Select the open office space, right-click, and choose Interference Condition ➢ Add. Select the mass element and press Enter. Switch into a 3D viewpoint to get a better view of where the mass element penetrates through the ceiling. Figure 6.36 shows the result.

NOTE   The interference condition automatically subtracts the area of what interferes from the affected space; in our example the ceiling was subtracted. Area calculations will reflect this condition only if the interference penetrates through the floor of the space object.

8. Save your work as **CompletedSpacePlan.dwg**. You can leave this file open if you plan to continue to the next section.

FIGURE 6.34
Dividing contained space

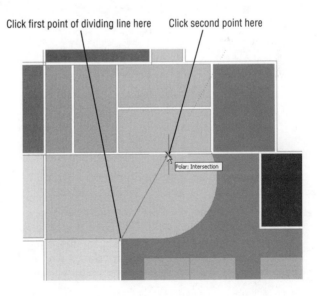

Click first point of dividing line here   Click second point here

Polar: Intersection

FIGURE 6.35
Adding a cylindrical
mass element

Cylindrical mass element to act as interference condition

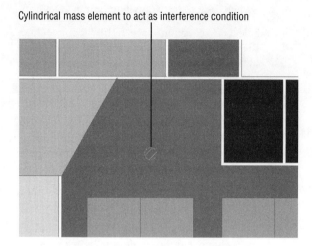

FIGURE 6.36
Interference condition
slicing through space

Cylindrical mass element

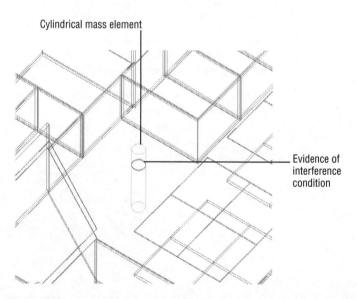

Evidence of
interference
condition

You might hold off on making interference conditions until later in the design process (for example with a column grid, as discussed in Chapter 7, "Parametric Layouts, Anchors, and Structural Members"). It's really a question of how much effort you want to put into the conceptual model. It might be more helpful to add interference conditions later on in design development when they will be respected by ceiling grids (see Chapter 15, "Floor and Ceiling Plans"), and so on. However, adding interference conditions would be important if you are doing careful accounting of areas in the space planning phase.

Converting between Space Boundaries, Walls, and Spaces

When you have completed space planning and feel that you have reached the maximum benefit that the inside-out design process offers, it is time to convert your space boundaries to walls. As I mentioned earlier, only space boundaries of the solid type can be converted to walls. They are converted to generic wall objects using the Standard style, copying the base height, width, and justification parameters from space boundaries to walls. Adding to the interconnectedness of intelligent objects, spaces can also be automatically generated from walls.

Generating Walls from Space Boundaries

There is no link between space boundaries and the walls generated from them. After walls are generated, subsequent changes that you make to the space boundaries are not updated in the walls. This transition marks both the end of the conceptual design phase and the beginning of the design development phase.

1. If you left the sample file open from the last section, you can continue here. If not, open `CompletedSpacePlan.dwg` from the working folder on your hard drive or from the companion DVD.

2. Select the large space boundary, right-click, and choose Generate Walls. Wall objects appear (in green) on top of the space boundaries.

3. Notice there are a few defect warnings that appear on some of the new wall objects (see Figure 6.37). Defect warnings appear when walls overlap; you'll learn to fix them in Chapter 8, "Walls." Zoom in on one of these defect symbols. For now it is enough to be aware of the potential for space boundaries to create defective walls.

TIP   Collinear space boundary edges are joined together into a single wall object upon conversion. You can force separate wall objects to be generated by giving each edge a different width.

FIGURE 6.37
Wall defect warnings

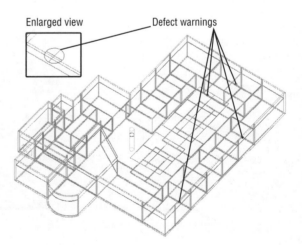

4. You'll need to separate space boundaries from walls to work on either of them. You can use Quick Select to select only the space boundaries. Press Ctrl+A to select all. Click the Quick Select button on the Properties palette 🔧.

5. Choose Space Boundary from the Object type drop-down list (see Figure 6.38). Click the Operator drop-down list and choose Select All; then click OK. Now only the space boundaries are selected.

6. If you are working with a project structure, the space boundaries can now be dragged into a new construct. On the other hand, you might want to delete them and then save the current file with a new name. If you deleted the space boundaries now, their contained spaces would also be erased. Change the Manage Contained Spaces property to No. Then press the delete key. The spaces and walls remain.

WARNING   Spaces are not linked to walls.

7. Save the file as **WallsAndSpaces.dwg**.

Generating Spaces from Walls

The generic walls you generated from space boundaries are by no means final, and you will certainly make many changes to walls and other objects during the design development stage. Therefore, there probably will not be a perfect correspondence between walls and your original spaces later in the design process.

To reestablish this correspondence, the Space Auto Generate tool is used to generate spaces from walls. You might use this tool to create spaces for the first time if you skipped the conceptual design phase altogether. Let's give this tool a try.

NOTE   Spaces are not just for conceptual design. In the construction documentation stage, spaces have many uses including generating space tags (see Chapter 13, "Annotating, Tagging, and Dimensioning") and schedules (see Chapter 14, "Schedules, Display Themes, and Areas"). In addition, ceiling grids are usually anchored to spaces (see Chapter 15, "Floor and Ceiling Plans").

FIGURE 6.38
Using Quick Select to grab the walls only

1. Open WallsAndSpaces.dwg if it's not already open.

2. Switch to the Top viewpoint and delete the large office and conference space. We are simulating what might happen later in the design development stage. You might also have altered the walls so they no longer correspond with their space. Although you can change a space's shape to fit a new wall configuration, the Space Auto Generate tool is faster.

3. Click the Space Auto Generate tool. An old-style modal dialog box (from early versions of ADT) appears, called Generate Spaces. This dialog box works like a palette in that you can change its options while working with the tool in the drawing window. It's called *modal* because you must work in this "mode" until you close the dialog box.

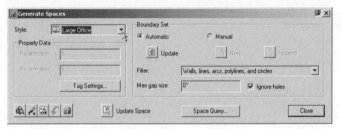

4. Change the Style drop-down list to Large Office and leave the Boundary Set radio button set at Automatic. Verify that the Filter drop-down list is set to "Walls, lines, arcs, polylines, and circles." Click a point inside the large office, and a new space appears.

5. Change the Style drop-down list to Conference and click inside the conference room. A new space appears instantly! The Space Auto Generate tool works a lot like the Hatch command in how it analyzes the screen to discover boundaries automatically.

6. Click Close or press Enter to exit the Generate Spaces mode.

7. Close the file without saving.

WARNING   The Space Auto Generate tool does not recognize boundaries in XRefs more than one level deep. Therefore, you might need to work in a construct, rather than a view, to add spaces to elements.

Summary

In this chapter you learned skills for effective space planning. You created spaces that express programmatic requirements of a design. You modified and played with spatial possibilities in 2D and in 3D, and you reported on areas using space objects.

When you worked with space boundaries, you designed rooms, indicating where partitions were placed and how areas were separated. After the solid boundaries were converted to walls, you came to the end of the conceptual design phase.

Part 3

Design Development

Chapter 7

Parametric Layouts, Anchors, and Structural Members

Parametric layout is the formal name of what is more commonly called a layout—the word parametric is added to distinguish the term from *paper space layouts*, a well-known AutoCAD concept. *Layouts* in this context refer to objects whose purpose is to literally lay out objects that will ultimately be anchored to them.

Layouts are structures forming a logical spatial arrangement controlled by parameters. For example, a column grid is a specialized kind of layout that column objects can be anchored to and controlled from. *Anchors* are fixed relationships that bind objects such as columns to a column grid.

After you understand layouts and anchors, you'll be able to work effectively with structural members, the first real building objects you will encounter in the design development phase of any project. ADT's structural member object type includes columns, beams, and braces. Here you'll learn to model structural members so you can work in conjunction with a structural engineer. This chapter's topics include the following:

- ◆ Using Parametric Layouts
- ◆ Anchoring Objects
- ◆ Working with Structural Members

Using Parametric Layouts

There are three types of layouts on which you can anchor objects: curves (1D), grids (2D), and volume grids (3D). You might use a layout curve to arrange light fixtures on a ceiling track, lavatories along a washroom wall, or an array of planter boxes in a site plan. Layout grids are commonly used to lay out columns, either radially or in rectangular fashion. Volume grids organize space using rectilinear cells, as in a Chicago-style structural steel cage.

Layout Curves

Layout curves are defined only along their length, so in a sense they are one-dimensional. Seemingly paradoxically, layout curves can themselves be drawn in either two or three dimensions, similar to the way polylines and 3D polylines work. There's actually no paradox here, however, because objects anchored to a 2D or 3D layout curve are attached to nodes on the one-dimensional layout curve edge.

Layout and anchor tools are located in the Content Browser. You'll have to drag tools into a tool palette to prepare for using the tools in this section and the following one. Here's how:

1. Open the Tool palettes Properties menu and choose New Palette. Give the new blank palette the name **MyPal**. Right-click MyPal and move it up to the top of the list of palette tabs.

2. Open the Content Browser by pressing Ctrl+4 and enter the Stock Tool Catalog. Click the Parametric Layout & Anchoring Tools category (see Figure 7.1).

FIGURE 7.1

Parametric Layout & Anchoring Tools, in the Stock Tool catalog and added to the palette

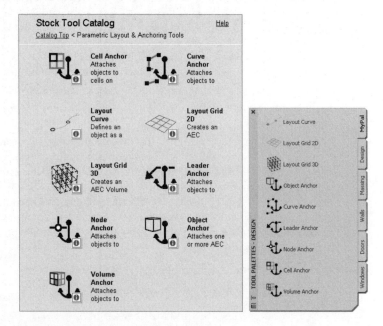

3. Right-click inside MyPal and choose View Options from the shortcut menu. Select the List View radio button for View Style. Adjust the Image Size slider if you prefer, and click OK.

4. Using the i-drop icons, drag and drop each tool to MyPal in the following order: Layout Curve, Layout Grid 2D, Layout Grid 3D, Object Anchor, Curve Anchor, Leader Anchor, Node Anchor, Cell Anchor, and Volume Anchor.

Unlike the other types of parametric layouts, layout curves cannot be created directly. Instead, you first draw some curving or straight-line geometry (such as a polyline or spline) and then add a layout curve to what you already drew.

The layout curve controls where *nodes* are placed on the selected geometry. Nodes are where objects can be anchored (see the section "Anchoring Objects" later in this chapter). Although the layout curve's purpose is to locate nodes for anchoring objects, it is ironic that the layout curve is itself anchored to geometry.

1. Start a new blank drawing based on the default template.

2. Use the Spline command to draw a 2D curving entity approximately 20´ in length. The exact shape of your curve isn't important; but size matters because layout curves create measured nodes.

NOTE   You can add layout curves to the following objects and entities: Walls, Curtain Walls, Door/Window Assemblies, Spaces, Mass Elements, Roofs, Lines, Arcs, Circles, Ellipses, Polygons, Polylines (PEDIT Spline option not supported), and Splines.

3. Click the Layout Curve tool in MyPal. Select the spline you drew previously.

4. Read the command line:

```
Select node layout mode [Manual/Repeat/Space evenly] <Manual>
```

There are three modes to choose from: Manual, Repeat, and Space Evenly. Press Enter to accept the default of Manual, in which you will explicitly specify distances from the start point along the layout curve where nodes will be placed.

5. Type 5↵ to enter the number of nodes.

6. Enter the appropriate positions for each of five nodes. Press Enter after each entry:

Node	Position
0	2´
1	4´
2	5´
3	8´
4	12´

7. The nodes appear as magenta circles with broken linetype. Click one of the nodes and study the layout curve grips (see Figure 7.2).

8. Click the last Add Node trigger grip (nearest the end of the layout curve). A new node appears there. Click the Remove Node grip corresponding to node 1 (second from start of layout curve); it disappears.

FIGURE 7.2

Layout curve grips

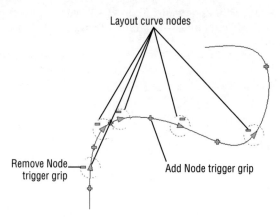

9. Open the Properties palette if it's not already open and click the Nodes worksheet icon. The Nodes worksheet gives more explicit control over distances. Note that node zero is never listed. Change the Distance To Line value of node 4 to 15´ and click OK. The last node moved slightly.

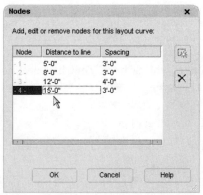

10. Press Esc to deselect the layout curve. Select the spline entity. Click one of its grips and reposition it. The nodes of the layout curve move with the spline because the layout curve is attached to it. Press Esc.

TIP If you reposition spline grips up or down in the Z direction in 3D space, the layout curve will stay anchored.

In addition to Manual, there are two more layout modes worth understanding: Repeat and Space Evenly. These modes allow you to space nodes (or bays) according to the number of conditions you want to specify and/or have ADT calculate (see Table 7.1).

TABLE 7.1: Layout Modes

MODE	SPACING	NUMBER OF NODES/BAYS
Manual	You specify	You specify
Repeat	You specify	Calculated
Space Evenly	Calculated	You specify

1. Draw a horizontal line 10′ in length.

2. Click the Layout Curve tool and select the line you just drew.

3. Press **R**↵ to select the Repeat option. Enter Start Offset of **3′**, zero End Offset, and a Spacing of **4′**. Two nodes appear on the line.

4. Select a layout curve node. In the Properties palette, change Start Offset to zero. A third node appears along the line because the number of nodes is calculated from the spacing and offsets in this mode.

5. Change the Layout type property to Space Evenly. Change the Number of Bays to **5**. The Spacing is immediately calculated at 2′-6″.

6. Deselect the layout curve and select the line entity. Click the line's right grip, move the mouse to the right using polar object tracking, and type **5′** to lengthen the line. Deselect the line and select the layout curve. Verify that the Spacing parameter in the Properties palette now reads as 3′-9″; it was calculated when you changed the line to which the layout curve is anchored.

TIP You can right-click and hold for a couple of seconds instead of pressing Esc.

7. Save your work as **LayoutCurve.dwg**. Leave this file open if you plan to continue to the next section.

Layout Grids

There are three layout grid shapes: Rectangular, Radial, and Custom. Both Rectangular and Radial layout grids are controlled parametrically and are used to anchor objects in 2D patterns. For example, you might use a layout grid to anchor plywood divisions within casework or bollards in a parking garage. Use layout grids in any way your creativity inspires you.

NOTE   Column grids are a specialized kind of layout grid with additional options including automatic labeling. See the section "Column Grids" later in this chapter.

CREATING LAYOUT GRIDS

Layout grids are organized into any number of x-axis (horizontal) and y-axis (vertical) bays. Layout grids have *nodes* at the intersections of axis lines and *cells* at the center of each bay. You'll learn to anchor objects to nodes and/or to cells in the next section. Parametrically changing the size of the layout grid immediately affects the spacing of anchored objects. Let's get started here by creating layout grids.

1. You can continue here if you left `LayoutCurve.dwg` open from the last section. If not, open the file from your hard drive or the companion DVD.

2. Click the Layout Grid 2D tool on MyPal.

3. In the Properties palette, change Shape to Radial. Verify that the creation parameter (with the starburst icon) Specify On Screen is set to No. Change X - Width to **30′** and A - Angle to **90** degrees.

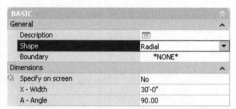

4. Click a point to the right of the existing layout curves to locate the new radial layout grid. Press Enter twice to accept the default rotation and finish the command. The radial layout grid appears (see Figure 7.3). In radial layout grids, the x-axis bays emerge concentrically from the center and the y-axis bays follow the circumference.

5. Click the Layout Grid 2D tool again. Change the Shape property to Rectangular. Click a point directly below the radial layout grid to place the rectangular one. Press Enter twice more to complete the command.

6. Select the rectangular layout grid. Right-click and choose Edit Object Display from the shortcut menu. Layout grids do not have styles. Check Object Override for the one and only General representation to override the default property source for this object only.

7. In the Display Properties dialog box, make this layout grid's Node and Cell display components visible (see Figure 7.4). Click OK and OK again to close both dialog boxes.

FIGURE 7.3
Creating a radial
layout grid

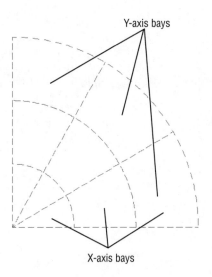

Y-axis bays

X-axis bays

FIGURE 7.4
Turning on the Node and
Cell display components
with an object override

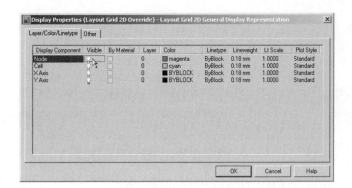

8. Select the layout grid and zoom in to get a closer look. Nodes and cells now appear on each bay in the rectangular layout grid (see Figure 7.5). You'll be attaching objects to nodes and cells later in this chapter. Notice also that the layout grid appears with dashed linetype on the G-Grid-Nplt layer.

WARNING Layout grids do not plot by default. The normal behavior is for anchored objects to plot, but the layout grids that control them remain hidden.

9. Save your work as **LayoutGrid.dwg**.

FIGURE 7.5
Rectangular layout
displaying nodes
and cells

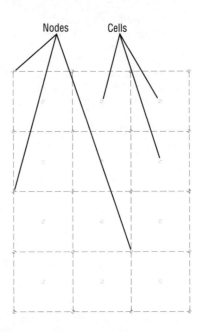

ADJUSTING LAYOUT GRIDS

It is easy to adjust layout grids parametrically. Here you'll use the same layout modes you used with layout curves: Manual, Repeat, and Space Evenly (refer to Table 7.1).

1. Select the rectangular layout grid you made previously.

2. In the Properties palette, change X Axis Bay Size to **12′**. The layout grid immediately changes to two horizontal bays instead of three. This happened because in Repeat layout mode the number of bays is calculated from how many whole times the Bay Size divides into the X - Width or Y - Depth dimensions. In this case, 30′ divided by 12′ equals 2 bays and a remainder that is ignored. The grid now measures 24′ horizontally across, even though the X - Width has a value of 30′.

3. In the Y Axis group, change Layout Type to Space Evenly. Right-click and choose Y Axis ➤ Remove Grid Line. The command line reads as follows:

   ```
   Enter approximate Y length to remove <10'-0">:
   ```

   Press Enter to accept the default length, which equals one bay. The layout grid now shows three bays rather than four in the vertical dimension.

WARNING   You cannot add or remove grid lines using the shortcut menu when in Repeat layout mode. The menu options to do so are still present but fail to execute.

4. In the Y Axis group, change Layout Type to Manual. The layout grid spacing does not change but new grips appear so that each bay has its own grips in the y-axis.

5. Click the bottom left grip and move it vertically up **3′** using Polar drafting mode. Click the grip in the second row and move it down **6′**. You can arrange bays any way you see fit in Manual layout mode (Figure 7.6).

6. With the rectangular layout grid still selected, right-click and choose Y Axis ➢ Add Grid Line. The command line reads as follows:

```
Enter Y Length <10'-0">:
```

Type **25′** and press Enter. A new grid horizontal line appears 25′ from the bottom of the layout grid.

7. In the Y Axis group, click the Bays worksheet icon. The Bays Along The Y Axis worksheet appears, in which you can alter the absolute distances to the y-axis lines of the layout grid (from the bottom), or adjust the spacing between each bay. Note that these are exactly the same controls you would see had you created the layout grid manually from the beginning. Click Cancel and press Esc to deselect.

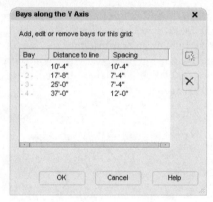

FIGURE 7.6
Making manual
alterations to layout grid

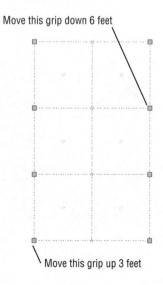

TIP It is often quicker to create a layout grid in Repeat or Space Evenly mode and then switch into Manual mode to alter its regular structure, than to start in Manual mode in the beginning.

CREATING CUSTOM LAYOUT GRIDS WITH LINEWORK

Sometimes the bays you need for your design don't follow a rectangular or polar grid. In these cases you can create a custom grid from linework.

1. Draw a few lines on one side of the existing rectangular grid (see Figure 7.7). The exact placement and spacing of the lines is not important to this example. Note that you could draw an entire layout grid from scratch in this way.

2. In MyPal in the Tool Palettes, right-click the Layout Grid 2D tool, and choose Apply Tool Properties To ➢ Linework from the tool menu. Select the linework you drew previously and press Enter.

3. The command line asks if you want to `Erase Selected linework? [Yes/No] <no>:` Type **Yes** and press Enter.

4. Select the new layout grid and notice that it is separate from the existing rectangular layout grid object. Look at the Properties palette: the Shape parameter is listed as Custom and is not editable. You cannot change a custom grid into another type. The number of parameters for the Custom layout type is quite limited because it is not controlled parametrically, but by the linework you drew previously. You can alter existing custom grids with grips, and add and remove additional linework as needed.

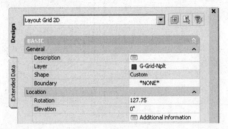

FIGURE 7.7
Drawing linework (solid lines) to add to an existing grid (dashed lines)

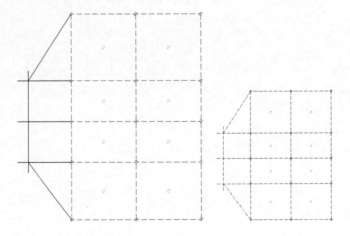

NOTE Custom grids have node markers but no cell markers. Also, custom grids do not respond to node object snap at grid intersections like parametric grids do.

CLIPPING BOUNDARIES AND HOLES FROM LAYOUT GRIDS

Sometimes grids are interrupted by conditions like a building's core or shell. The core constitutes a hole in the grid, whereas the shell defines the grid's outer boundary. Both of these conditions are handled with *clipping profiles*. You define what is clipped away from a layout grid by drawing a closed polyline for the outer boundary and closed polylines for any holes that may be required.

1. Draw a closed polyline representing the outer boundary, beyond which the layout grid will be clipped away (see Figure 7.8). Make this polyline smaller than the size of the grid you already drew. Again, the exact shape does not matter for this tutorial.

2. Select one of the layout grids, right click, and choose Clip from the shortcut menu. Read the command line:

   ```
   Layout grid clip [Set boundary/Add hole/Remove hole]:
   ```

   Press S to select the Set Boundary option and press Enter.

3. Select both adjacent layout grids and press Enter.

4. Select the polyline you drew in step 1 and press Enter. The layout grids outside the boundary are hidden.

5. Click the polyline and use a grip to move a vertex. The clipping boundary is immediately updated because the polyline is "live." If you erased the boundary, both entire layout grids would reappear.

TIP Place the clipping boundary on a non-plotting layer if you want to hide it.

6. Draw another closed polyline inside the boundary to represent a hole.

7. Type **LayoutGridClip** on the command line and press Enter. Choose the Add Hole option.

8. Select the layout grids and then the interior closed polyline. A hole appears in the grid (see Figure 7.9). The clipping boundary, hole, and layout grids are all live and editable.

9. Save your work as **ClippedLayouts.dwg**. Leave this file open if you plan to continue to the next section.

FIGURE 7.8
Drawing a polyline to serve as a clipping profile

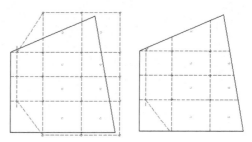

FIGURE 7.9
Adding clipping profiles to layout grids

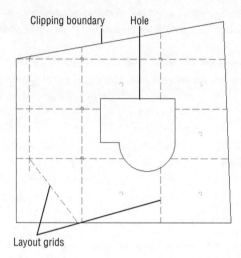

Volume Grids

Volume grids are the 3D equivalent of rectangular layout grids. Volume grids have nodes at the intersections of their grid lines and cells on each grid "surface." However, there aren't components at the centroids of the bay volumes. Use volume grids to construct the space frames common in many high-rise buildings.

1. You can continue here if you left LayoutCurve.dwg open from the last section. If not, open the file from your hard drive or the companion DVD.

2. Switch into an isometric viewpoint.

3. Click the Layout Grid 3D tool. Click a point to insert this object and press Enter twice to complete the command. You might want to 3D Orbit a bit so you can see all the lines of the volume grid better at an oblique angle (see Figure 7.10).

NOTE   There is no volume equivalent of the radial layout grid. You can achieve something similar by manually layering multiple radial layout grids on top of one another in the z-axis.

FIGURE 7.10
Layouts: left, layout curves; center, layout grids; right, a volume grid

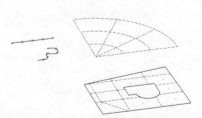
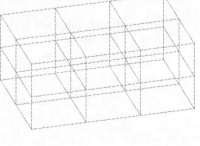

4. Select the volume grid and change the Layout Type to Manual in the X Axis group in the Properties palette. Grips appear on all bays in the x direction.

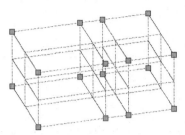

5. Close the sample file without saving.

Volume grids work exactly the same as rectangular layout grids but with Z Axis controls added. You have the same Manual, Repeat, and Space Evenly layout modes for each axis.

Anchoring Objects

The mechanism of anchoring objects is fundamental to how ADT works. For example, in Chapter 9, "Doors, Windows, and Openings," you'll see how doors, windows, and openings are anchored to walls. When an object is anchored, it can still be moved but only in a more limited sense—for example, doors, windows, and openings can move along a wall (or even around a corner), but they can't move outside the object to which they are anchored. When you move the wall, its anchored doors, windows, and openings move with it. These relationships are expressions of *automatic anchoring* that is built into ADT's core functionality.

Therefore, when we speak of anchoring objects, we refer instead to *user-defined anchoring*, unless otherwise noted. User-defined anchors are intentionally placed and include the following types of anchors: Object, Curve, Leader, Node, Cell, and Volume. Each anchor relationship is formed between an *anchoring* object and its *anchored* object. The uses for anchors are limited only by your project and imagination. We will take a look at all six types of anchors in turn.

Object Anchor

You might choose to anchor objects to maintain specific spatial relationships, such as light fixtures in a ceiling track, lavatories along a washroom wall, or partitions relative to each other to maintain a clear dimension. Let's experiment using mass elements to understand how it works.

1. Start a new blank drawing using the default template.

2. Select the Massing palette in the Tool Palettes. Create a Box and a Sphere; it doesn't matter what size or where you place them. Switch to an isometric viewpoint and a shaded mode.

3. Select MyPal in the Tool Palettes. Click the Object Anchor tool. The command line reads as follows:

```
Select objects to be anchored:
```

Click the Sphere and press Enter.

4. Select the Box as the object to anchor to (anchoring object) and press Enter. The command ends with seemingly nothing changing. However, an anchor relationship has been made.

5. Click the Box object to select it. Click the Box's location grip and move it to a new location. The Sphere moves with the Box. Press Esc to deselect.

6. Select the Sphere. Click the Sphere's location grip and move it; it moves independently of the Box. Notice that the Sphere is connected to the Box with an anchor chain (see Figure 7.11).

7. Select the Box again and move it. The position of the Sphere relative to the Box is maintained when the anchoring object is moved. This is what it means to be anchored.

8. Select the Sphere if it's not already and click its Release Object Anchor trigger grip. When the relationship is broken, the chain disappears (there is a joke here somewhere). You can now move both objects independently.

NOTE Anchors work much like forward kinematic chains do in Autodesk VIZ.

FIGURE 7.11
Object anchor

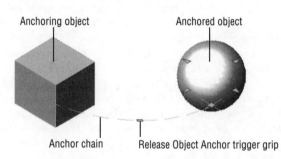

Anchoring object   Anchored object

Anchor chain   Release Object Anchor trigger grip

Curve Anchor

Curve anchors form a relationship between an object and a curve such that the anchored object cannot move off the curve. The object is said to be *constrained* to the curve when a Curve anchor is used.

NOTE Curve anchors are an alternative to using layout curves in which the anchored object is constrained anywhere along the curve (see "Node Anchor" to learn how to anchor objects to layout curves).

1. Draw a Spline entity.

2. Click the Curve Anchor tool. Type **AT↵** to use the Attach Object option.

3. Click the Sphere as the object to be anchored.

4. Select the spline you drew in step 1 and press Enter to end the command.

5. The Sphere moved to the point you clicked previously. Select the Sphere and try to move it away from the curve; you cannot do it. The Sphere can move anywhere along the length of the curve. The Sphere is constrained by the curve.

6. Select the spline and move some of its grips to change the curve shape. The Sphere stays attached (see Figure 7.12).

7. Press Esc and then select the anchored object. Right-click and take a look at the Curve Anchor submenu. Here is where you might choose to Release the anchor, among other options. Press Esc.

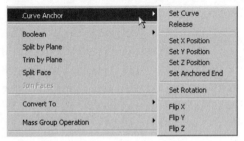

8. In the Properties palette, click the Anchor worksheet icon in the Location On Curve group. The Anchor worksheet gives the most detailed options for managing this anchor relationship (see Figure 7.13). In the Position Within (Y) group, change the To drop-down list to Front Of Object and click OK. The Sphere moves relative to the curve so its radius lines up with the curve edge.

FIGURE 7.12
Curve anchor

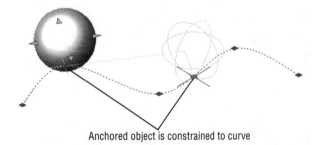

Anchored object is constrained to curve

FIGURE 7.13
Anchor worksheet for the
Curve anchor

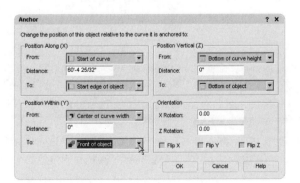

Leader Anchor

Although the Leader anchor is technically a user-defined anchor, it is seldom used as such. Instead, Leader anchors are automatically made by Column grid bubbles (see the section "Labeling the Column Grid" later in this chapter). Leader anchors keep grid bubbles attached to column grids with flexible leaders.

If you want to see the way Leader anchors work, create a rectangular layout grid and box mass element. Attach the Box as the object to be anchored and then click a node on the layout grid to connect them with a flexible leader.

Use the Anchor worksheet to control the options. You can have two different extension distances and an angle for the leader if desired (see Figure 7.14).

WARNING AutoCAD entities cannot be anchored.

FIGURE 7.14
Anchor options for Leader Anchors

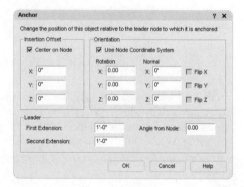

Node Anchor

The Node anchor is perhaps the most commonly used anchoring tool. As you learned in the last section, layouts have nodes that can be controlled parametrically. Use the Node anchor to attach objects to these nodes. Let's use the node anchor on a layout curve; it works exactly the same on layout grids and layout volumes.

1. Reopen LayoutCurve.dwg from your hard drive or companion DVD.

2. Create a Cylindrical mass element.

3. Click the Node Anchor tool and use the Attach option.

4. Select the Cylindrical mass element as the object to be anchored.

5. Click one of the nodes on the spline to select a layout curve as the anchoring object, and press Enter to end the command. The Cylinder appears at the selected node (see Figure 7.15).

6. Select the attached object and try to move it; you can only make it jump to other nodes on the same layout. Press Esc to deselect.

7. Select the layout curve you anchored the Cylinder to in step 5. Change the Layout Type to Space Evenly; the Cylinder moves to the new node position.

FIGURE 7.15
Node anchor

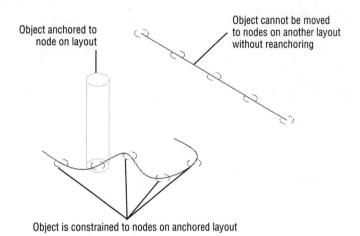

Object anchored to
node on layout

Object cannot be moved
to nodes on another layout
without reanchoring

Object is constrained to nodes on anchored layout

8. Change the Number of Nodes to 4. The Cylinder moves again because it is anchored to node 2 (nodes numbering starts at zero). You get the idea.

WARNING Deleting an anchoring object also deletes its anchored objects.

9. Close the file without saving.

Cell Anchor

Remember that layout grids have cell components (refer to Figure 7.5). Cell anchors let you anchor objects to these components, much as you anchored objects to nodes previously. The real twist with cell anchors is that the anchored objects are resized to fill the cell by default.

1. Reopen LayoutGrid.dwg from your hard drive or companion DVD.

2. Create a Box mass element.

3. Click the Cell Anchor tool and use the Attach option.

4. Select the Box mass element as the object to be anchored.

5. Click one of the cells to select the layout grid as the anchoring object. The Box appears at the selected cell and was resized to fill the area of the bay (see Figure 7.16).

6. Select the attached object and try to move it; you can make quantum jumps to other cells only on the same layout. Press Esc to deselect.

7. Select the layout grid you anchored the Box to in step 5. Change the Y Axis Layout Type to Space Evenly. Change the Number of Nodes to 5: the Box dimensions change to fit the new cell size. Control the anchored objects using the layout.

WARNING Be careful not to move multiple anchored objects into the same cell because you cannot tell that there are duplicates because of overlap.

FIGURE 7.16
Cell anchor

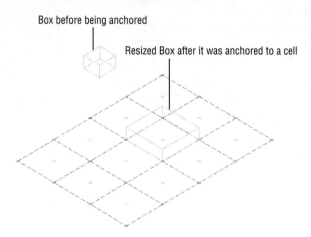

Box before being anchored

Resized Box after it was anchored to a cell

Volume Anchor

By now you can probably guess how this last type of anchor works: Much like the Cell anchor, but it works on volume grids instead. Objects are resized to fill a 3D bay when attached with the Volume anchor.

1. Create a volume grid.

2. Create a Box mass element.

3. Click the Volume Anchor tool and use the Attach option.

4. Select the Box mass element as the object to be anchored.

5. Click the edge of a bay in one of the volumes to select the volume grid as the anchoring object. The Box appears at the selected volume and was resized to fill the entire volume of the bay. Switch to shaded view because it might be difficult to see the mass element overlapping the volume grid otherwise (see Figure 7.17).

6. Select the Box and click its Anchoring worksheet icon in the Properties palette. Notice that there are Apply Resize and Size Offset options in the worksheet. You can decouple automatic resizing by unchecking Apply Resize when you alter the volume grid. You can also offset the attached object evenly by using Size Offset. These two options are also available for Cell Anchored objects.

7. Close the file without saving.

FIGURE 7.17
Volume anchor

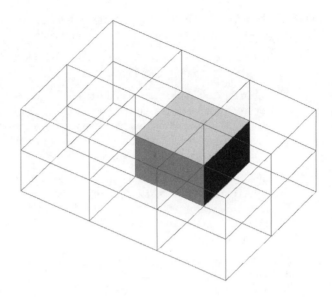

FIGURE 7.17
Volume anchor

Working with Structural Members

Structural members include columns, beams, and braces. All three of these structural member types share the same object style because they have similar components. Members are composed of one or more shapes extruded along a path. The orientation of the path is essentially what determines whether to use a Column (vertical), Beam (horizontal), or Brace (angled) tool.

NOTE   Structural members are constructed much like Lofts are in Autodesk VIZ.

Structural members bearing building loads are usually made of steel, concrete, timber, or composite materials. Load-bearing walls are generally not considered to be structural members in ADT's object hierarchy (see Chapter 8, "Walls" for more on walls).

Adding Structural Member Styles

Generally the first step when working with structural members is to add one or more styles to your drawing. Structural member styles are used to create structural member objects and are themselves based upon structural member shape definitions, which you'll learn to create later in "Designing Structural Member Styles." ADT has two convenient interfaces for adding structural member styles (and the shape definitions they are based on): the Structural Member Catalog and the Structural Member Style Wizard.

USING THE STRUCTURAL MEMBER CATALOG

The catalog hosts an extensive database containing industry standard specifications, shapes, and sizes of all the most common concrete, steel, and timber members. Let's take a look.

1. Start a new blank drawing using the default template.

2. Choose Format ➤ Structural Members ➤ Catalog. The Structural Member Catalog dialog box appears, which is organized into tree and content panes like many other ADT dialog boxes.

3. In the tree pane on the left, expand Imperial ➤ Steel ➤ AISC ➤ I-Shaped. Click the `W1n, Wide-Flange Shapes` node (see Figure 7.18).

4. Notice the design illustration at the top of the content pane. It has labeled features A–D that are represented below with specific values for each shape designation. Scroll down and double-click W14x43. The Structural Member Style worksheet appears, suggesting the shape designation as a new style name. Click OK to create a new structural member style (and the corresponding structural member shape definition) in your drawing.

5. Click the `Wn, Wide Flange Shapes` node in the tree pane. In the content pane, scroll over to the right and take a look at the extensive set of engineering specifications stored for each shape designation; this data might help a structural engineer select members. Scroll back and double-click W8x31. Click OK in the worksheet to make a new member style. Click the catalog's close box.

6. To see what the catalog did for you, choose Format ➤ Style Manager. Expand the Architectural Objects, Structural Member Shape Definitions, and Structural Member Styles nodes. Notice that W14x43 and W8x31 appear as styles in two areas, as shown in Figure 7.19. The member styles are based upon shape definitions, which contain the actual profile. Close the Style Manager dialog box.

NOTE   Having structural member shape definitions available in the Style Manager is a new feature in ADT 2006.

FIGURE 7.18
Structural Member
Catalog

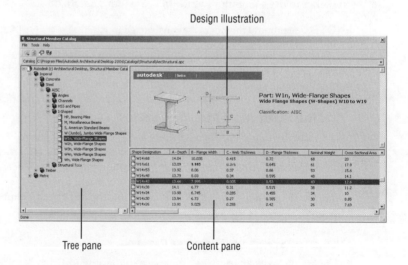

Design illustration

Tree pane

Content pane

FIGURE 7.19
Structural
Member Styles

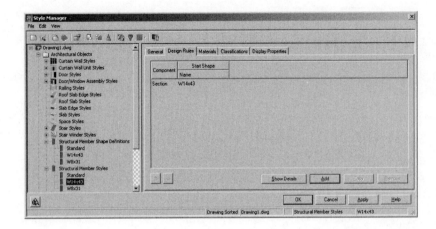

USING THE STRUCTURAL MEMBER STYLE WIZARD

The Structural Member Style Wizard is another way to create member styles and shape definitions. Use the wizard when you only know the shape and size of the member style you want to create. It is better to use the wizard rather than the catalog if you aren't ready to specify a proper shape designation (before consulting a structural engineer, for example). You can always change structural members' styles when you get more specific information later in the design process.

1. Choose Format ➢ Structural Members ➢ Wizard. The Structural Member Style Wizard dialog box appears. It is organized into pages with Next and Back buttons like other wizards.

2. Expand the nodes for Concrete, Steel, and Wood and click each of the different member shapes to see their design illustrations on the left. After you explore the 20 preset possibilities, choose Concrete ➢ Circular Column (see Figure 7.20).

FIGURE 7.20
Structural Member
Style Wizard

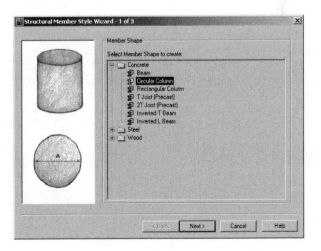

TIP   You'll learn how to create custom structural shapes later in this chapter.

3. Click the Next button. The circular concrete shape has only one dimension: its diameter. Enter a value of **1´-6˝** and click the Next button.

4. The third page of the wizard is where you must name the style. Type **ConcreteColumn** as the name and click the Finish button.

5. Open the Style Manager and verify that ConcreteColumn is listed both as a Structural Member Style and as a Structural Member Shape Definition. Close the Style Manager.

6. Save your work as **StructuralStyles.dwg**. Leave this file open if you plan to continue to the next section.

Making Structural Members

Now that you have added structural member styles to your drawing, you can make member objects such as freestanding columns, column grids, beams, braces, and curved members. All these member objects can share the same styles and shape definitions if required. On the other hand, you can always make generic structural member objects first, and then add and assign member styles to them later on if you prefer.

FREESTANDING COLUMNS

Columns are structural members with shape definitions lofted along vertical paths. Make freestanding columns when the overhead of making a column grid isn't warranted—best when you only have a few columns or when the columns aren't arranged in a regular grid. In this section you'll also learn how to display varying levels of detail and will use several AEC Modify Tools to arrange freestanding members.

1. You can continue here if you left StructuralStyles.dwg open from the last section. If not, open the file from your hard drive or the companion DVD.

2. In the Design tool palette, click the Structural Column tool.

3. In the Properties palette, notice that there are two creation parameters that appear with starburst icons (these appear only before you create the object): Trim Automatically and Specify Roll On Screen. Specify No for both. Columns can be trimmed automatically when they intersect with other beams or braces. In most cases you'll want to trim the beams or braces, not the columns. Roll is the rotation in the z-axis. Choose W14x43 from the Style drop-down list and study the design illustration and the labeled parameters A, B, C, and E (see Figure 7.21).

4. Click a point in the drawing window, and a freestanding column appears. You could keep adding columns by clicking, but press Esc to end the command.

FIGURE 7.21
Column creation
properties

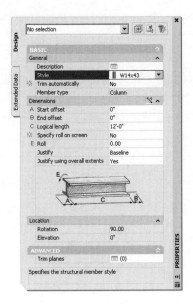

Displaying Levels of Detail

The default templates include display configurations for low, medium, and high levels of detail that work with structural members. These display configurations have a one-to-one correspondence with three possible levels of detail in structural member shape definitions. Use the Low Detail configurations for framing plans where members are drawn with single-line representations. Use Medium Detail for general-purpose work (double line representations) and High Detail for large-scale detail drawings. Let's take a look at the three levels of detail using the freestanding column as an example.

1. Zoom in on the freestanding column. Note that you are in the Medium Detail display configuration by default, in which this structural steel column is represented by double lines.

2. Click the display configuration pop-up on the drawing status bar and choose Low Detail. The column appears with a single line representation. Traditional framing plans use this level of detail.

3. Select the High Detail configuration and observe the column revert back to a double-line representation. Look closely to discern the differences in this level of detail: A hatch pattern appears in the cross sectional area of the steel, and there are inner fillets where the web meets the flanges (see Figure 7.22).

4. Switch to an isometric viewpoint. Zoom in on the top of the column.

5. Change to Low Detail and then Medium Detail configurations (see Figure 7.23); there is no difference between them in the model representation. Change to a shaded mode and the High Detail configuration: it shows fillets in the model representation.

WARNING   The High Detail configuration might take a long time to display complex models. It is better to work in 3D with a medium level of detail.

6. Switch back to 2D Wireframe shading mode and the Top viewpoint. Select the Presentation configuration; the column is filled with a solid hatch pattern. Change back to Medium Detail.

FIGURE 7.22
Levels of detail in plan representation

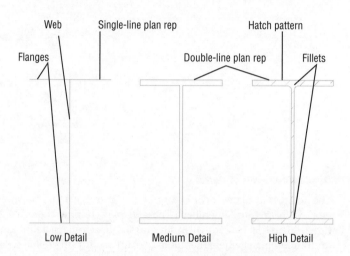

FIGURE 7.23
Levels of detail in model representation

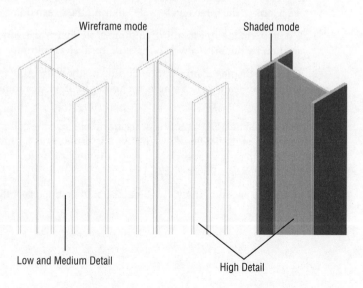

Using AEC Modify Tools with Structural Members

New!

There are several new AEC Modify tools: Array, Center, and Space Evenly. You can use these AEC Modify tools with any objects, but they are particularly helpful for laying out freestanding columns. Let's examine each of these tools in turn.

1. To give yourself more space to work in, type **Z.⏎0.01X.⏎**. This zooms you out to 1 percent of the original size, regenerates, and recalculates the drawing limits. Zoom back in close to the single freestanding column. Verify that POLAR, OSNAP, and DYN modes are toggled on in the application status bar.

2. Select the column, right-click, and choose AEC Modify Tools ➤ Array.

3. Position the cursor along the right edge of the flange and click when you see a vertical construction line appear.

4. Zoom out by turning the wheel on your mouse or by typing '**Z.⏎0.01X.⏎**. Move the cursor horizontally to the right and type **10′** to set the array distance. Click when you see a ToolTip reading Array Count (8). Eight freestanding columns appear (see Figure 7.24). The advantage to making an array with this AEC Modify Tool, rather than the AutoCAD ARRAY command, is the interactive feedback you get on the screen. You can preview how many objects you are arraying simply by moving the cursor.

5. Draw a horizontal line measuring 100′ in length just below the leftmost freestanding column.

6. Select all eight columns. Right-click and choose AEC Modify Tools ➤ Center from the shortcut menu.

7. Click the horizontal line you drew in step 5 to select it as the axis upon which you will center the columns.

8. Click the left and right endpoints of the line; the columns are immediately centered on it. This is a useful command whenever you need to center objects—but be aware that it doesn't adjust the spacing between objects; it only centers the selection.

FIGURE 7.24
AEC Modify Tool: Array

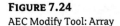

9. Select all eight columns, right-click, and choose AEC Modify Tools ➢ Space Evenly. Click the horizontal line you drew in step 5 to select it as the axis.

10. Click the left and right endpoints of the line; the column spacing is adjusted slightly so the distance between the center of each column and the endpoints of the line are all the same: $11'\text{-}1\ ^{11}/_{32}''$ in this case. Delete the line.

COLUMN GRIDS

The disadvantage of using freestanding columns is that their spacing is not parametrically controlled. Although you could create a layout grid and anchor columns to it by using node or cell anchors, the Structural Column Grid tool has some additional functionality that makes it the tool of choice for laying out columns.

Creating Column Grids with Columns

Column grids are layout tools with a twist. Unlike the other layout tools, column grids can also create columns anchored to the nodes of the grid automatically. Let's give that a try.

1. Click the Structural Column Grid tool on the Design palette. Look at the Properties palette; there are two starburst icons: Specify On Screen and Style. Choose Yes for Specify On Screen (otherwise, you can use the X - Width and Y- Depth parameters). Choose the ConcreteColumn style to have column structural members automatically anchored to the column grid (see Figure 7.25).

FIGURE 7.25
Creating a Structural Column grid: Select a style to automatically anchor columns to the nodes of the grid.

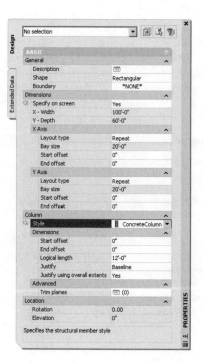

TIP You have the opportunity to predetermine the dimensions of column objects anchored to a column grid. Look in the Dimensions subgroup under Style in the Properties panel before creating a column grid.

2. Click a point in the drawing window to insert the lower-left corner of the column grid. It is like drawing a rectangle: Click the opposite corner some distance to the right and above the first point you clicked.

3. Move the cursor closer to the first point you clicked in the previous step; this determines the bay size. Click a point when you have a 4x3 column grid. Of course, you could type in relative coordinates if you were drawing this to a particular size.

4. Switch to an isometric viewpoint. Concrete columns appear on the column grid.

5. Select the column grid and change both X and Y Axis Layout Types to Manual. Use grips to move grid lines around. Notice that the columns move with the grid lines because they are anchored to its nodes.

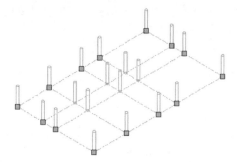

NOTE Column grids are on layer S-Grid by default; it is a plotting layer. Unlike layout grids, you typically will see column grids in drawings.

Labeling the Column Grid

After you have created a column grid, you can use a built-in command to automatically label it with grid bubbles. You'll have control over labeling rules and many other parameters.

1. Switch to the Top viewpoint. Select the column grid, right-click, and choose Label from the shortcut menu. The Column Grid Labeling dialog box appears. Click the two dashes (--) in the first number field. Type **A** and press Enter. The remaining fields are automatically labeled in ascending order A though E (see Figure 7.26).

2. Click the Y - Labeling tab of the Column Grid Labeling dialog box. Type **1** in the first field and press Enter. The remaining fields are numbered sequentially, 1 through 4 in this case. Click OK. Labeled grid bubbles appear on top and bottom, left and right of the column grid.

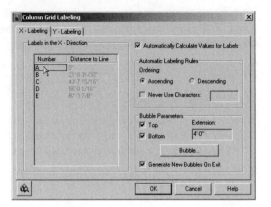

FIGURE 7.26
Column Grid Labeling

3. Zoom in and click one of the grid bubbles. Notice that it is listed as a Multi-View Block Reference in the Properties palette. It has two grips: one centered on the bubble and one on the line connecting the bubble to the column grid. This latter grip controls the leader. Click the leader grip and move it diagonally. A third grip appears. It can be helpful to move grid bubbles when things get crowded on drawings.

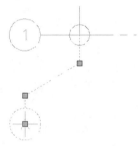

4. With the grid bubble still selected, click the Anchor worksheet icon in the Properties palette. You'll see the same worksheet as in Figure 7.14 where you learned about Leader Anchors. So now you see how sophisticated the Structural Column Grid tool really is: Not only does it make a layout grid, but it can also anchor columns to nodes and bubbles to leaders quite easily. Click Cancel.

TIP You can label two sides of a column grid and have grid lines extend beyond the column grid rectangle (without grid bubbles) on the opposite sides. The procedure to do this involves making a custom Multi-View block definition. See also ADT help.

BEAMS

Beams are structural members with shape definitions extruded along horizontal paths. You can create a beam by clicking two points that determine its start point and endpoint, or you can use two different modes (Edge and Fill) to lay out beams quickly by clicking within a column grid.

New!   ADT 2006 has a new Z elevation toggle feature that is very helpful when laying out beams. You can set the elevation (above the ground plane in the Z direction) on the application status bar, and then place beams at the correct height as you create them.

Edge Mode

Edge mode places beams along column grid edges. Beams can be automatically trimmed as they are created to fit precisely between columns.

1. Select all the columns anchored to the column grid; they are currently using the ConcreteColumn style. Change the style assigned to all the columns to W14x43.

2. Switch to an isometric viewpoint in shaded mode. Zoom in on the grid from columns A1 to B2.

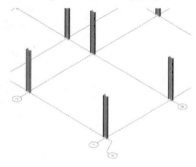

3. Double-click the elevation value on the application status bar (Figure 7.27). You want to create beams at the top of the existing columns, so type **12′-0″** in the Set Elevation Offset worksheet that appears and click OK. Toggle the Z button on in the application status bar (this activates the elevation value).

FIGURE 7.27
Double-click the elevation value on the status bar to open the worksheet.

4. Click the Structural Beam tool on the Design tool palette. In the Properties palette, change the Style to W8x31 and set Trim Automatically to Yes. If necessary, change the Layout Type to Edge, and Justify to Top Center (see Figure 7.28). Notice that beams have many justification options (like Text entities do). The justification options control the placement of the beam relative to its shape definition. We want the top center of the beam to be at an elevation of 12′.

5. Press F3 to toggle OSNAP off: it can distract you from selecting edges. Position the cursor over the column grid edge between columns A1 and A2. Read the ToolTip; you can add the beam

to a single segment, one grid line, or all grid lines. Press Ctrl once and click. Three beams were added along the A grid line.

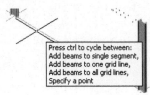

6. Move the cursor over the B grid line and click again. Press Esc three times to exit the command. Three more beams were added (see Figure 7.29).

FIGURE 7.28
Creating a
structural beam

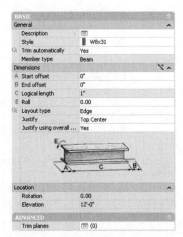

FIGURE 7.29
Laying out structural
beams using Edge mode

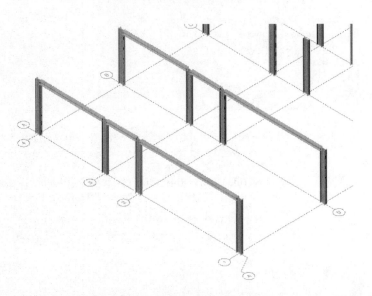

TIP You can create beams along the edges of column grids, walls, slabs, and polylines.

Fill Mode

Fill mode spans beams across bays. Fill mode arrays multiple beams by repeating them across a specified bay size or by spacing a number of beams evenly across a bay.

1. Click the Structural Beam tool on the Design tool palette.

2. On the Properties palette, change the Layout Type to Fill. Verify that the Style is still set to W8x31 and Trim Automatically is set to Yes. In the Layout group, set Array to Yes, Layout Method to Space Evenly, and Number of Bays to 4.

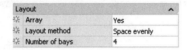

Layout		⌃
❊ Array	Yes	
❊ Layout method	Space evenly	
❊ Number of bays	4	

3. Hold the cursor over the grid line extending between grid intersections B1 and B2. The ToolTip indicates that you can create beams in this cell or in all cells at once. Take the former option and click the grid line. Three new beams appear transverse to the beams you created earlier.

4. Change the Number of Bays to 3 and click the grid line between intersections B3 and B4. Two more beams appear.

5. Change Array to No and click midway along the grid line between bubbles A2 and A3. One beam is created (see Figure 7.30).

6. Save your work as **StructuralBeams.dwg**. Leave this file open.

FIGURE 7.30
Laying out structural
beams using Fill mode

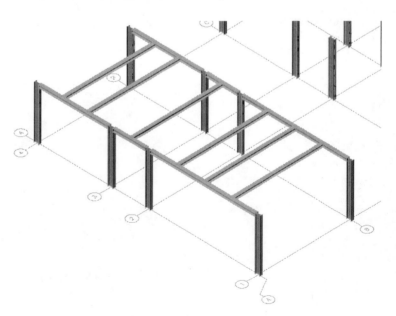

TIP You can create structural members in Edge or Fill modes in the current drawing by clicking a column grid in an XRef. For example, you might make structural members in a construct that references a column grid in an externally referenced element. These beams will not be anchored to the grid in the XRef, however.

BRACES

Braces are structural members with shape definitions lofted along angled paths. Braces, which connect with columns and beams, give rigidity to the structural system. The Diagnostic display configuration is a great aid in laying out braces in 3D. You can also use point filters (look up this AutoCAD topic in help if you need a review) to specify 3D coordinates in plan. I favor the 3D approach.

1. Open the file `StructuralBeams.dwg` if you are jumping in here.

2. Switch to Diagnostic display configuration. Columns appear as single vertical lines and you can see single horizontal lines at the centers of each beam. There are green circles where members intersect.

3. Toggle the Z elevation off on the application status bar. Toggle OSNAP on by pressing F3.

4. Click the Structural Brace tool in the Design tool palette.

5. In the Properties palette, verify that Trim Automatically is set to Yes and the Style is W8x31. Set Justify to Middle Center. Change the Specify Rise On Screen creation parameter to Yes. You will click points in the 3D diagnostic view to locate the start points and endpoints of braces.

6. Click the start point of the brace on the ground at the base of column A1. Click the endpoint of the brace where the beams meet the top of column A2 and press Enter (see Figure 7.31).

7. Draw another symmetrical brace connecting the base of column A4 with the top of column A3.

FIGURE 7.31
Creating a Structural
Brace in Diagnostic
display configuration

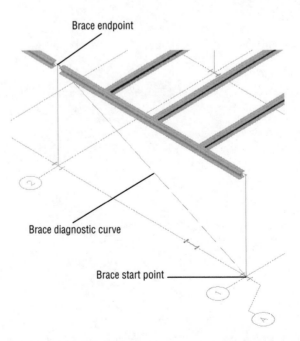

Brace endpoint

Brace diagnostic curve

Brace start point

WARNING   It is tricky to snap braces correctly in 3D. Zoom in closely and make sure that your braces snap to the center of each intersection or else the braces will actually be slightly askew in relation to the column grid. Node object snap is most helpful here.

8. Switch back to the Medium Detail display configuration. Notice that the braces were trimmed on the top where they meet the beams. You'll learn how to manually add trim planes later so you can clean up the intersections of the braces with the bases of the columns (see Figure 7.32).

9. Save your work as **StructuralBraces.dwg**. Leave this file open.

FIGURE 7.32
Completed structural members

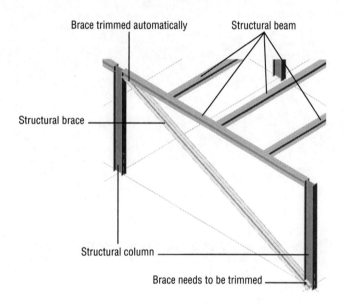

CURVED MEMBERS

Curved members are a possibility for all three structural types. Make curved members by first drawing an arc or polyline with arc segments. By applying tool properties to linework, you can create curved members.

1. Open the file `StructuralBraces.dwg` if you are jumping in here.

2. Draw a 2-point circle between the centers of columns A2 and A3. Trim the circle in half using the column grid as the cutting object. You are left with an arc. Move this arc up to an elevation of 12'.

3. Right-click in the Command window and choose Options from the shortcut menu. Use the tab navigation buttons in the Options dialog box to advance tabs to the right. Click the AEC Object Settings tab. There are two settings in the AEC Display Resolution group that apply to curved objects: Facet Deviation and Facet Maximum. Type ¼″ in the Facet Deviation text box and click OK (see Figure 7.33).

FIGURE 7.33
Setting display-resolution options

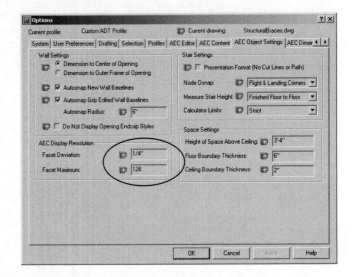

TIP   FACETDEV and FACETMAX are system variables affecting curved objects. Leave FACETMAX set to a low number (128 is the default) to avoid long refresh times.

4. Right-click the Structural Beam tool and choose Apply Tool Properties To ➤ Linework. Select the arc you drew in step 2 and press Enter. Check Erase Layout Geometry and click OK in the Convert to Beam worksheet. If you had selected a polyline, you would have the option to create one member per segment.

5. In the Properties palette, change Style to W8x31 and Justify to Top Center. Notice that there is a curved member design illustration labeled A–E. There are no starburst icons because the object already exists by the time you see its properties by virtue of being converted from linework. There is no other way to create curved members.

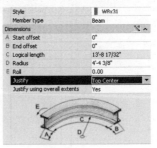

6. Press Esc to deselect and zoom in. You can make curved column and braces like you made the curved beam (see Figure 7.34).

7. Save your work as **CurvedMembers.dwg**. Leave this file open if you plan to continue to the next section.

FIGURE 7.34
Curved structural beam

Editing Structural Members

New!

It is generally very easy to edit structural members using the column grid and member grips. You'll learn how to do these common tasks and observe the new stretch behavior that connected structural members exhibit in ADT 2006. In addition, you learn how to add trim planes and miter structural members together.

1. You can continue here if you left CurvedMembers.dwg open from the last section. If not, open the file from your hard drive or the companion DVD.

2. Select the column grid and click the grip at column grid intersection A1. Move this grip **3′** along the A grid line. Not only did all the columns on grid line 1 move, but all the beams and the brace connected to these columns were instantly resized. Now you can appreciate how powerful the column grid is—editing it affects all anchored structural members and instantly affects all members connected to these columns.

3. Select column B1. Right-click and choose Node Anchor ➢ Release from the shortcut menu. This particular column is released from the column grid, even if it remains in the same place.

4. Click column B1's location grip, which is right in the middle of the column. Verify that POLAR is toggled on in the application status bar. Move column B1 along grid line 1 a distance of **6′** toward grid line C. The beams connected to the column stretch and remain connected.

5. Click the Lengthen grip at the very top of column B1. Move the cursor vertically up and press Tab once to switch to the partial dynamic dimension. Type **3′** and press Enter (see Figure 7.35). Not only does column B1 get taller, but all the beams connected to it stretch and remain connected (this behavior is new in ADT 2006).

6. Draw a freestanding column and beam. Select both and study their grips (see Figure 7.36). You use location grips to move members, and there are several options in the ToolTip that can be cycled through using the Ctrl key. Lengthen grips are constrained to work only along the path, making the member longer in either direction. The Roll grip rotates a member about its path axis.

FIGURE 7.35
Members stretched by editing column B1

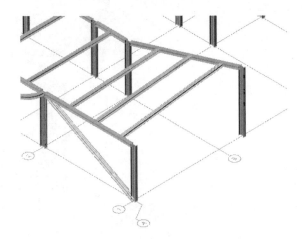

FIGURE 7.36
Structural member grips

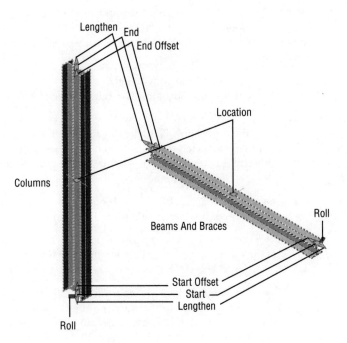

Use the Start and End grips to reposition a member in 3D space; this is especially appropriate for a brace. The Start Offset and End Offset grips are a way to introduce a distance between the Start or End grips where the member does not exist. This might be useful when you want a column to start at the ground level, but actually be offset to appear above a slab, for example.

7. Save your work as **AlteredMembers.dwg**. Leave this file open.

You have already seen how members can be automatically trimmed when they are created. For example, the beams were trimmed to fit between the columns when you created them in Edge mode. The braces also got trimmed just under the beams, but automatic trimming did not occur at the bottom of the braces. Let's clean this up now.

1. Open AlteredMembers.dwg if it is not already open.

2. Zoom in on the bottom of column A4.

3. Select the brace, right-click, and choose Trim Planes ➤ Add Trim Plane. Move the cursor over the column web and notice the ToolTip that reads Press Ctrl To Toggle Trim To Face as the second option. Press Ctrl once to use the second option (the first option is the default) and then click the column. The brace is trimmed to this face (see Figure 7.37).

4. Pan to the top of column A4. Select the beam, right-click, and choose Trim Planes ➤ Miter. Select the column and press Enter. Trim planes are added to both members and the angle is split evenly (see Figure 7.38).

FIGURE 7.37
Trimming structural members: left, before trim; right, after a trim plane is added to the brace

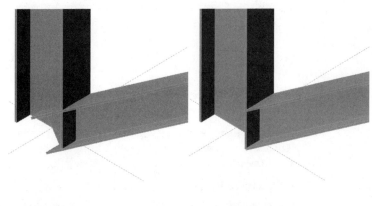

FIGURE 7.38
Mitering structural members: left, before mitering; right, after the column and beam are mitered together

5. Select the brace and click its Trim Plane worksheet icon in the Advanced group of the Properties palette. The worksheet that appears lets you control each trim plane's offsets and rotations in detail. Click Cancel.

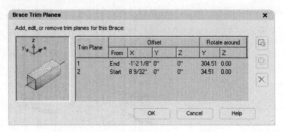

6. Save your work as **TrimMiterStructuralMembers.dwg**. Leave this file open if you plan to continuing to the last section.

Designing Structural Member Styles

If you want to create a structural member that isn't in the catalog or wizard, you have to learn how to design structural member styles. Remember that every structural member style is based upon shapes, and these shapes are controlled by structural member shape definitions. That is the place to start designing custom styles.

CREATING CUSTOM STRUCTURAL MEMBER SHAPE DEFINITIONS

Remember that shape definitions were created automatically when you used the catalog or wizard. Each shape definition has three levels of detail that correspond with the three display configurations you experimented with earlier in this chapter. Structural member shape definitions appear in the Style Manager.

1. You can continue here if you left `TrimMiterStructuralMembers.dwg` open from the last section. If not, open the file from your hard drive or the companion DVD.

2. To start a shape definition, you need to draw at least one closed polyline. In this tutorial, you will insert one that is already drawn. Choose Insert ➢ Block to open the Insert dialog box. Click the Browse button and locate the `Shape.dwg` file on the companion DVD.

3. Uncheck Specify On-Screen in the Insertion Point group and check Explode. Click OK.

4. Switch into the Top viewpoint and zoom in on the polylines you just inserted into your drawing.

5. Choose Format ➢ Style Manager. Expand the Architectural Objects and right-click the Structural Member Shape Definitions node. Choose New from the shortcut menu and give the new definition the name **Precast**.

6. Click the Precast definition in the tree pane and click the Specify Rings button on the Design Rules tab in the content pane. Select the outer ring. The default shape geometry selection is for Medium Detail.

7. The command line reads:

   ```
   Insertion point or [Add ring/Centriod]:
   ```

   Choose **A** for Add Ring and press Enter. Select the first inner ring.

8. Repeat step 7 four more times, adding each inner ring. When you are done press C to indicate that the insertion point for the entire shape will be its *centroid* (the center of its area). The Style Manager reappears.

9. Click Low Detail shape designation and then click the Specify Rings button (see Figure 7.39). Select the outer ring. Notice there is a new option in brackets on the command line. Press **P**↵ to use the Previous Point option to designate the insertion point.

10. Toggle back and forth between the Low Detail and Medium Detail shape designations; the current shape highlights in green in the Style Manager. Click Apply and OK.

11. Erase the polylines you inserted in step 2; they are no longer needed now that the shapes have been defined. Save the file as **CustomShape.dwg**.

NOTE Each structural member shape definition must have at least a Medium Detail shape designation. Adding Low and High shape designations is optional. You can insert a polyline representation of a Structural Member Shape Definition by using the MemberShapeInsert command or by choosing Format ➢ Structural Members ➢ Insert Member Shape. This can be handy if you want to use an existing member shape as the starting point for a new one.

FIGURE 7.39
Creating a Structural Member Shape Definition

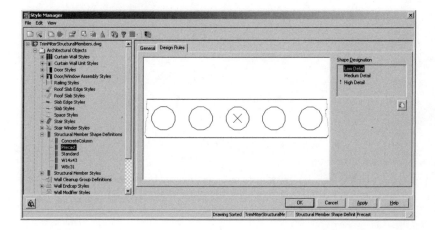

DEFINING DESIGN RULES

After you have defined the necessary structural member shape designations to work with, you are finally ready to specify the design rules of the structural member style itself. You can loft shape definitions straight along their paths, they can optionally be tapered, or you can create additional components to make composite member styles (such as a steel member encased in concrete).

Straight member styles merely need to be assigned a shape definition. That's all there is to it; most of the work went into creating the shape definition.

Tapered member styles increase or decrease their cross-sectional area along the length of the structural member. These styles are useful for creating columns with simple capitals, for example. Make tapered member styles by changing the scale of the end shape. Use X offset to control where the member shape begins tapering.

Composite member styles are made with more than one component using different shape definitions simultaneously. For example, we will make a concrete-encased steel column style by copying and editing an existing style.

1. Reopen the Style Manager. Right-click the W14x43 style and choose Copy from the shortcut menu. Click the Structural Member Styles node, right-click, and choose Paste. Rename the pasted style **ConcreteSteel**.

2. On the Design Rules tab in the content pane, click the Show Details button. Rename the Section component to **Steel**. Click the Add button and name the new component **Concrete**.

3. Select the Start Shape Name of ConcreteColumn and the Start Shape Scale to 1.5. There is no need to change anything else because you want both components to loft from start to end. Click OK.

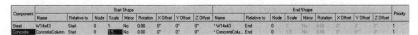

| Component | Start Shape | | | | | | | | | End Shape | | | | | | | | | Priority |
	Name	Relative to	Node	Scale	Mirror	Rotation	X Offset	Y Offset	Z Offset	Name	Relative to	Node	Scale	Mirror	Rotation	X Offset	Y Offset	Z Offset	
Steel	W14x43	Start	0	1	No	0.00	0"	0"	0"	*W14x43	End	0		No	0.00	0"	0"	0"	1
Concrete	ConcreteColumn	Start	0	1.5	No	0.00	0"	0"	0"	*ConcreteColu...	End	0	1.5	No	0.00	0"	0"	0"	1

4. Create a column and assign the ConcreteSteel style to it. Switch to the 2D Wireframe shading mode so you can see through the object; the composite column has a concrete encased steel core.

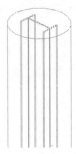

5. Save your work as **CustomStyles.dwg**. Leave this file open.

NOTE It is possible to make segmented member styles using the Nodes design rule feature. You can make trusses that have different component features at each node. Read ADT help for more information on this.

DISPLAYING CUSTOM BLOCKS

Custom blocks allow you to add forms along the length of structural members such as stiffener plates. Let's explore this final aspect of structural members.

1. You can continue here if you left `CustomStyles.dwg` open from the last section. If not, open the file from your hard drive or the companion DVD.

2. Custom blocks can be made from anything, but extruded mass elements are ideal for making stiffener plates. We will insert two plates that have already been fitted to the W14x43 style steel columns as a block. Choose Insert ➤ Block to open the Insert dialog box. Click the Browse button and locate the `StiffenerPlates.dwg` file on the companion DVD.

3. Check Specify On-Screen in the Insertion Point group, and uncheck Explode because this time we want it inserted as a block. Click OK and then press Esc. Even if you didn't actually insert the block into the drawing area, it is defined as a block in the drawing database.

4. Zoom in on column E4. Select the column, right-click, and choose Edit Object Display from the shortcut menu. In this case we will assign custom display block as an object override, but it could work just as well as a style override. In the Object Display dialog box, click the Display Properties tab. Place a check mark in the Object Override column for the Model representation.

5. The Display Properties dialog box appears. Click the Other tab. In the Custom Block Display group, click the Add button.

6. In the Custom Block dialog box, click the Select Block button. Choose StiffenerPlates from the Select A Block dialog box that appears. Click OK to close it.

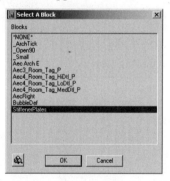

7. In the Custom Block dialog box, change the X Insertion Offset to **1´-6˝**. Check Repeat Block Display in the Repeat Mode group. Type **3´** in the Space Between text box. (See Figure 7.40.) Click OK three times to close all the dialog boxes.

8. Switch to a shaded view and check out the new stiffener plates arrayed along the column's path (see Figure 7.41). You can add anything to a structural member in this way.

9. If you like, save your work as **CustomDisplayBlocks.dwg**—however, we won't need this file again. This file is provided on the DVD for you to check out.

TIP Rotate masses about the world y-axis when trying to align them as custom display blocks with columns. Try inserting the StiffenerPlates block into the drawing to see where its insertion point is and how it is rotated about the y-axis. This will help you visualize how you have to define your own custom blocks.

FIGURE 7.40
Defining a Custom
Display Block

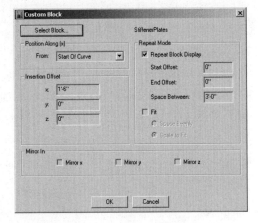

FIGURE 7.41
Custom display blocks
added as an object
override

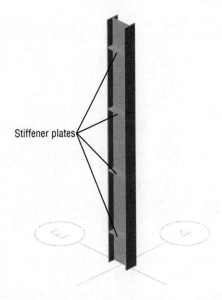

Summary

In this chapter you learned how parametric layouts, anchors, and structural members are all closely interconnected in ADT. Hopefully, now you can appreciate the beauty of the way these tools work together, giving you great parametric control over the entire structural system of a building. You have explored all the tools for creating structural members and have gained experience making, editing, and designing custom styles. As with all things in ADT, practice makes perfect. You might want to spend time building structural members for one of your own projects or forge ahead and start learning about walls. It should become easier to absorb additional ADT concepts the more you work with the program.

Chapter 8

Walls

You will probably use walls more than any other type of object as you develop your designs. Therefore, it is critical to learn all the dimensions of this multifaceted object if you are going to use ADT successfully.

Much more than the solid space boundaries described in Chapter 6, "Space Planning," walls are complex beasts that represent interior and exterior partitions in almost every conceivable architectural situation. Like other objects, walls are controlled by styles that define their subcomponents and display properties, among other things. Beyond style, you will learn numerous additional techniques to lay out walls, clean up intersections between walls, and alter wall form both in 2D and 3D. This chapter's topics include the following:

◆ Understanding Wall Components

◆ Laying Out Walls

◆ Cleaning Up Walls

◆ Working with Wall Styles

◆ Altering Wall Form

Understanding Wall Components

Like solid space boundaries, walls partition space: but they do a lot more—having components representing the actual sandwich of real-world materials constructed in the field, such as stud, brick, concrete, and masonry walls. In AutoCAD you might have been accustomed to drawing double lines to represent walls, tagging the linework to identify wall type, and listing the components of wall types in a schedule table. In ADT, all the information about walls comes from objects and their styles: tags and schedules merely report on this data (see Chapter 14, "Schedules, Display Themes, and Areas").

Walls don't have to be monolithic; they can be straight or curved, and can have gables, steps, cutouts, projections, *fenestrations* (penetrations through the wall), and much more. You'll learn how to alter wall form later in this chapter. To begin, let's start by drawing a few wall objects. Drawing walls is a lot like drawing lines. Straight walls are defined by their start points and endpoints; curving walls have them plus a radius. Walls have a width appropriate to accommodate all their components as defined in the wall style.

1. Start a new blank drawing with the default template.

2. Draw a horizontal line **17′** in length. You will use this line to compare justification options.

3. Click the Walls tool palette.

4. Click the CMU-8 Rigid-1.5 Air-2 Brick-4 Furring-2 tool. Wall tools are often named after their components. In the Basic group of the properties palette, verify that all three creation parameters (with starburst icons) are set to zero. Set Justify to Baseline (see Figure 8.1).

NOTE   Notice that the Width parameter is gray, meaning that it is not editable in the properties palette; some wall styles have fixed widths. When wall styles have components with variable widths, the Width parameter in the properties palette is editable.

5. Snap to the left endpoint of the line you drew in step 2 to locate the start point. Make sure that DYN and POLAR are toggled on in the application status bar. Move the cursor along the line to the right, type **3´**, and press Enter twice. You have drawn a short straight wall segment. Figure 8.2 shows the wall components visible in this style: brick, an air gap, rigid insulation, concrete masonry unit (CMU), furring, and sheetrock. Each component is hatched separately, and you can also see an example of an endcap in which the brick component turns the corner at the outer edges of the wall segment. You'll learn about how to set up components later in "Working with Wall Styles."

6. Change the display configuration to Low Detail. The components disappear, and you see only a double-line representation of the wall. Switch to High Detail; the hatch patterns appear in a smaller scale (appropriate for making detail drawings). The levels of detail are controlled by the display properties of the wall object's display representations. Switch back to Medium Detail.

7. Move the wall object **1´** horizontally to the right, exposing some of the line you drew in step 2 on the left.

8. Select the wall object, right-click, and choose AEC Modify Tools ➢ Array from the shortcut menu. Click the right vertical edge to array from, type **4´**, and move the cursor to the right until you see four wall objects. Click to complete the array; four wall objects are equally spaced along the line.

FIGURE 8.1
Wall creation properties

BASIC	
General	
Description	
Style	CMU-8 Rigid-1.5 …
Cleanup automatically	Yes
Cleanup group definition	Standard
Segment type	Line
Dimensions	
A Width	1'-5"
B Base height	8'-0"
C Length	1"
Justify	Baseline
Baseline offset	0"
E Roof line offset from base height	0"
F Floor line offset from baseline	0"
Location	
Rotation	0.00
Elevation	0"

FIGURE 8.2

Wall components visible inside wall object

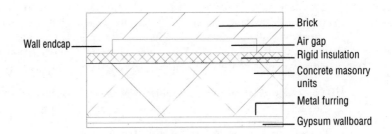

Justification is very important with walls because it determines the location of the wall in the width dimension from the points used to draw the wall. You have four Justify choices: Baseline, Center, Left, and Right. In generic walls, baseline is the same as centerline. Baseline is the zero point of the wall components and is determined in the wall style. In the case of our example wall, you'll see that baseline and centerline are in different locations; it is very important to understand this distinction.

Click the second wall object from the left. Change Justify to Center; the wall moves slightly. Zoom in and observe the second wall's offset from the line you drew originally. The wall style defines the baseline at the junction of the rigid insulation and CMU components. The centerline is slightly off this mark because the center is determined from the thickness of all the components put together.

Select the third wall object and change its justification to Left. Justify the last wall Right (see Figure 8.3). In the left-justified wall, its exterior face rests on the line; it's just the opposite for the right-justified wall.

The direction in which a wall is drawn is very significant because it determines which side is exterior and which is interior. Click the first wall object you drew on the left. Zoom in closely and take a look at its grips (see Figure 8.4). There are start and end grips, two lengthen grips, the location grip, and a reverse direction trigger grip. Press Esc.

Draw two short horizontal line segments off the top and bottom-left corners of the wall to record where the object is currently located.

Select the same wall and click its Reverse Direction trigger grip. Notice that the exterior and interior sides are swapped: the gypsum wallboard (GWB) is on top, and brick is on the bottom. This method of reversing a wall in called an *in-place reversal* because the outer edges of the wall are in the same place where you drew the lines previously. This method is preferable when you don't want to change the position of the wall in the drawing.

Notice that the baseline no longer aligns with your original line. Hover the cursor over the grips; notice that the start grip is on the right, and end is on the left now. Reversing direction swaps start points and endpoints.

FIGURE 8.3

Wall justify options

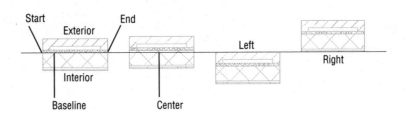

Click the Reverse Direction trigger grip again, performing another in-place reversal. The wall returns to its original orientation. Hold down the Ctrl key and click the Reverse Direction trigger grip again. This time the wall flips, maintaining its baseline, and its outer edges no longer align with the lines you drew in step 4 (see Figure 8.5). This method is preferable when you are creating walls from spaces or polylines where the baseline location determines areas of spaces, for example.

NOTE An in-place reversal maintains the position of a wall's outer edges. A baseline reversal flips the wall about its baseline, not necessarily respecting its outer edges.

There is another way to adjust justification with the possibility of maintaining the baseline by using trigger grips. Right-click and choose Edit Justification from the object shortcut menu. Four diamond-shaped trigger grips appear. The current justification is shown by the gray trigger grip, which acts like an exit trigger. Hold the cursor over the Set To Left trigger grip and read its ToolTip. Hold Ctrl and click Set To Left (see Figure 8.6).

FIGURE 8.4
Wall grips in plan

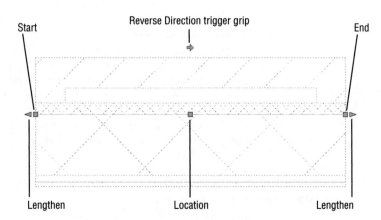

FIGURE 8.5
Reversing a wall and maintaining its baseline

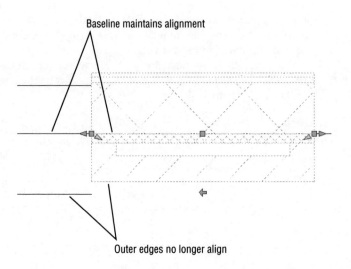

The grips moved to the left side of the object. Ctrl+clicking justification trigger grips is the only way to do this. The preview of the wall position is where the wall would have ended up had you not held down the Ctrl key in the last step. In that case, the wall would have moved so that its left edge aligned with the original baseline.

TIP I recommend using Baseline justification for exterior and load-bearing walls because the base-line represents the edge of the load-bearing components and is helpful for alignment. In general, use Center justification for interior partitions, and use Left and Right justification in cases where you want to align the outside or inside face of a wall with a particular edge.

FIGURE 8.6
Justification trigger grips, before (left) and after (right) using Set To Left

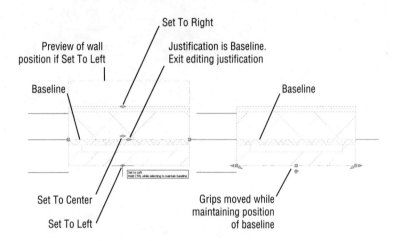

Laying Out Walls

You will probably spend most of your production time working on floor plans and laying out walls in constructs, and elements might be one of your most common tasks. Aside from clean drafting techniques, which you hopefully picked up during your AutoCAD experience, there are several techniques that you'll learn in this section that will help you to arrange walls efficiently in a floor plan.

ADT ships with a large number of preconfigured wall styles. Although you'll be learning how to make your own wall styles later in this chapter, it doesn't make sense to reinvent the wheel. You can use many wall styles out of the box or adapt the default styles slightly to meet your own project's needs.

You have already used a few wall tools on the Walls palette. There are pages and pages of wall tools in the Content Browser's Design Tool Catalog. Simply drag out the appropriate tools into one of the tool palettes for use in your project.

Another way to access wall styles is using the Style Manager. Choose Format ➤ Style Manager; in the menu bar inside the Style Manager dialog, choose File ➤ Open Drawing. In the Open Drawing dialog box that appears, click the Content folder in the Places pane.

Double-click Styles ➤ Imperial to see a list of style drawings that ship with ADT. Select Wall Styles - Brick (Imperial).dwg and click Open (see Figure 8.7).

FIGURE 8.7
Opening drawings in
Style Manager

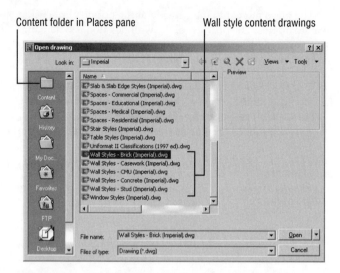

Content folder in Places pane

Wall style content drawings

Click the Wall Styles node. Check out all the brick styles that you have access to. You can copy and paste any of these styles into your drawings or define them as Standards drawings in your project standards (see Chapter 5, "Project Management"). You can also drag styles from the Style Manager to the Tool Palettes. Close the Style Manager.

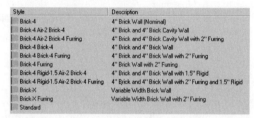

After a wall style is defined in your drawing, you can reassign existing wall objects to use the style in the properties palette. You can also reassign styles by applying tool properties to selected objects. Close the file without saving.

Creating Walls

There are several ways to create walls, depending on what you are starting with. You saw in Chapter 6 how space boundaries were used to generate generic walls. You won't have to create walls in this situation but you'll probably need to edit them. Otherwise, you can create walls directly by drawing them or by converting existing linework into walls. Another approach is to create a wall by converting a Mass Element or 3D Solid.

CREATING WALLS DIRECTLY

If you chose not to build a conceptual model, you'll have to create walls from scratch, drawing them as you might draw lines. You'll also have to pay attention to justification and direction as you are drawing walls.

1. Start a new blank drawing with the default template.

2. Select the Walls tool palette. Click the CMU-8 Rigid-1.5 Air-2 Brick-4 Furring-2 tool.

3. In the Properties palette, change Justify to Left.

4. Click the start point in the upper-left corner of the drawing window. Move the mouse horizontally an arbitrary distance and click along the zero degree polar tracking line to set the endpoint.

5. Notice that a wall segment is attached to your cursor. Just like the Line command, the WallAdd command assumes that you might like to continue adding wall segments. The start point of the second segment is the same as the endpoint of the first segment. Click the endpoint of the second segment some distance down 90 degrees using polar tracking.

6. Right-click and choose Ortho Close from the shortcut menu. Read the command line:

   ```
   Point on wall in direction of close:
   ```

   Click to the left at an angle of 180 degrees to the point you clicked previously. Two additional wall segments are added, closing the walls orthogonally. The placement of start points and endpoints determine which direction the walls face. As you can see from Figure 8.8, Left and Right justifications are relative to where each segment's start point and endpoint is located.

TIP Draw walls in a clockwise fashion to make their exterior sides face outward. Draw walls counterclockwise to make their interior sides face outward. All the wall styles that ship with ADT were designed so that the exterior surface is on the left. Although ADT doesn't force you to design wall styles this way, it is a good idea to do so for consistency.

CREATING WALLS FROM LINEWORK, MASS ELEMENTS, AND 3D SOLIDS

You can convert existing linework such as lines, arcs, circles, and polylines into walls. This is the approach to take if you need to convert a legacy AutoCAD drawing's 2D linework into walls. Be aware that you'll probably have to trace single-line polylines over double-line representations of walls, however; you can't just convert a whole AutoCAD drawing to walls, unfortunately.

FIGURE 8.8
Using Ortho Close

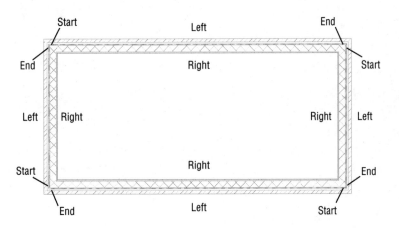

It is usually only appropriate to create walls from mass elements and/or 3D solids for unusual forms because you'll have to 3D model them first. However, this method might save you a lot of time if you have a particularly complex wall segment that you want to create.

1. Press I↵ and click the Browse button in the Insert dialog box. Choose the file Polyline.dwg from the companion DVD. Check Specify On-Screen in the Insertion Point group, check Explode, and click OK. Click to insert the polyline in your drawing.

2. Right-click the same wall tool and choose Apply Tool Properties To ➢ Linework. Select the polyline and press Enter. Type Y↵ to erase the polyline. Wall segments replace the polyline. ADT is smart enough to automatically locate the exterior side of the walls on the outside of the closed polyline. Press Esc and then click the arc wall segment shown in Figure 8.9.

NOTE   You can also draw arc wall segments directly by changing Segment Type to Arc in the Properties palette. Note that you cannot create walls from complexly curving spline objects: Only arcs, circles, or polylines with circular curvature can be converted.

3. Play with the arc segment grips; they behave as you probably expect. The differences stem from the wall segment being an arc rather than a line. Look at the Dimensions group in the Properties palette; the design illustration shows the additional parameter D - Radius that isn't present in a straight-line wall. Notice also that walls converted from linework use Baseline justification.

FIGURE 8.9
Arc wall segments after
conversion from polyline

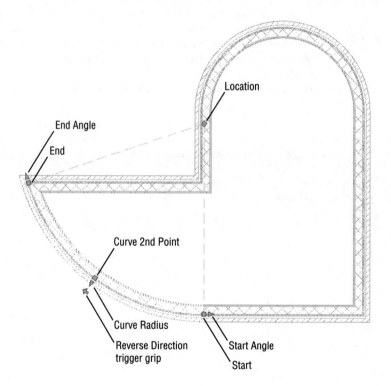

CONVERTING OBJECTS TO 3D SOLIDS

It's possible to convert walls and other objects into 3D Solids, so you can export them into programs that do not support architecture, engineering, and construction (AEC) objects (such as Maya, for example). Open the Content Browser and drag the following tool to the Tool Palettes in ADT:

```
Stock Catalog > Modeling Tools > 3D Solids > Convert to 3D Solids Tool
```

Before using this tool, switch into an isometric viewpoint. Most objects yield only 2D linework when this tool is applied in a plan view.

1. Switch into an isometric viewpoint if you're not already there.

2. Click the Convert to 3D Solids Tool.

3. Select the wall object you converted from a mass element earlier and press Enter. ADT will pause a moment while the Modeler code loads.

4. Type **Y**↵ to erase the original object. The 3D Solid turns green as it gets converted.

5. Select the entity and verify that it appears as 3D Solid in the Properties palette. Its grips are blue, which indicates that it is now an entity and no longer an object.

6. Choose File ➢ Export and choose a file format that works with your other software.

7. Close the file in ADT without saving.

If you are using custom display blocks in any of your objects, convert them first to free form mass elements and then into 3D Solids (otherwise, they won't convert).

Editing Walls

In addition to grip editing, there are several additional ways to edit walls. Some of the AutoCAD Modify commands are useful when working with walls. There is also a number of specialized editing tools we'll be looking at.

SETTING DRAWING DEFAULT OPTIONS FOR WALLS

Before editing walls, the first things to check are the wall settings in the Options dialog box. These settings are stored individually in each drawing file.

1. Start a new blank drawing with the default template.

2. Right-click in the Command Window and choose Options from the shortcut menu.

3. Click the right tab navigation arrow several times and then click the AEC Object Settings tab. In the Wall Settings group you'll find a number of important defaults that pertain to this object type. There are essentially three categories of options here that pertain to dimensions, auto-snap, and opening endcap styles (see Figure 8.10).

4. You can choose whether to dimension walls to the center or outer frame of openings such as doors, windows, and true openings (see Chapter 9, "Doors, Windows, and Openings") by clicking the appropriate radio button. Verify that Dimension To Center of Opening is selected.

FIGURE 8.10
Verifying Wall Settings

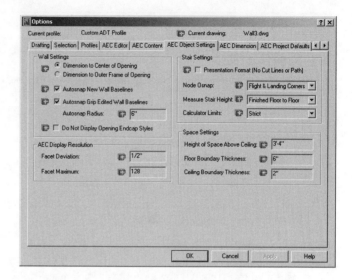

5. Autosnap affects how close the walls have to be to automatically join together. Autosnap radius controls the distance from a wall's graphline (see the section "Cleaning Up Walls") within which walls will be automatically joined. Verify that both Autosnap New Wall Baselines and Autosnap Grip Edited Wall Baselines are checked. That way, you can use autosnap when making new walls and when grip editing existing wall objects.

WARNING Autosnap actually works with wall graphlines, not baselines. The text in the AEC Object Settings tab in the Options dialog box is incorrect. Often the graphline is equal to the baseline, but it doesn't have to be (see the section "Cleaning Up Walls").

6. As you'll learn in "Working with Wall Styles," walls have two possible kinds of endcaps, or termination conditions: endcaps proper (at start and endpoints), and opening endcaps. Opening endcaps appear—you guessed it—in openings in the wall. You can elect not to display such endcaps by checking the box: this would be appropriate if you will not be displaying individual components, such as in the Low Detail display configuration. You will get a very slight performance improvement by checking Do Not Display Opening Endcap Styles. It's important at least to be aware this option exists to avoid pulling out your hair later if you are trying to display opening endcaps and wondering why they do not show.

7. Click OK to close the Options dialog box.

Let's see how Autosnap works with new walls and with walls you edit with grips.

1. Click the CMU-8 Rigid-1.5 Air-2 Brick-4 Furring-2 tool on the Walls palette. Draw a **10′** horizontal wall from left to right using Baseline justification. The interior gypsum wallboard (GWB) side of the wall is on the lower edge.

2. Click the Stud-4 GWB-0.625 Each Side tool and choose Justify Left in the Properties palette. Draw a short vertical segment that perpendicularly intersects the GWB of the CMU wall you drew previously. Autosnap was not triggered in this case (read on to find out why).

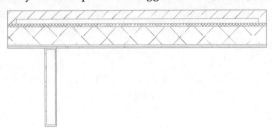

3. Draw another vertical stud wall, but this time click its endpoint inside the CMU wall near its baseline: the intersection of the rigid insulation and the CMU (see Figure 8.11). If you click within 6″ of the baseline (the autosnap radius), autosnap is triggered and the walls components will merge according to design rules and priorities stored in the wall styles (see "Working with Wall Styles").

4. Draw another stud wall, but this time make a horizontal segment under the CMU wall that isn't touching any other segments.

5. Click the horizontal stud wall and click its Lengthen grip on the left side. Move the cursor to the right edge of the vertical stud wall and click to grip edit the horizontal stud wall. The wall components merge because autosnap was triggered. The stud wall is less than 6″ wide (within the Autosnap threshold), so grip editing to the right side of the vertical stud wall triggered autosnap (see Figure 8.12). Autosnap moved the grip over to the baseline of the wall it snapped to.

FIGURE 8.11
Drawing with Autosnap

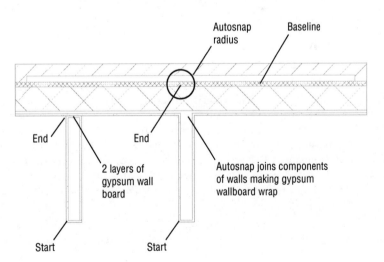

AUTOCAD EDITING COMMANDS

AutoCAD's MOVE, COPY, TRIM, EXTEND, BREAK, FILLET, and CHAMFER commands work equally well on wall objects. In particular, using FILLET with a radius of zero is a time-tested way to join lines (and walls) at their endpoints. Note that walls are defined along their graphlines for the purposes of editing commands (see the section "Cleaning Up Walls").

You can edit walls in many of the same ways by using grips instead of, or in addition to, the explicit AutoCAD commands. One of the best things about ADT is the fact that it is based on AutoCAD, so you can leverage many of the drafting habits and instincts you might have built up over many years to edit walls.

FIGURE 8.12
Grip editing with
Autosnap

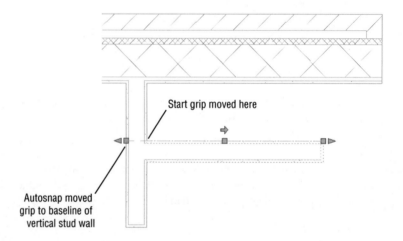

Start grip moved here

Autosnap moved
grip to baseline of
vertical stud wall

SPECIALIZED EDITING COMMANDS

There are a few specialized editing commands that were designed to make it easier to work with walls. You might have been accustomed to using OFFSET to lay out linework in AutoCAD. Now there is a better tool for the job that relates specifically to wall components: it's called WallOffsetCopy.

   This command, which can be more easily accessed from the object shortcut menu, allows you to offset from the face or center of any component within the wall. It will be your primary wall layout command. Use it when you know the clear dimension you want inside a room, but don't necessarily know the distance from wall center to wall center. It is usually much more convenient to say you want a 12′ room, rather than having to calculate how thick the walls are so you can figure out how far to offset a wall from its baseline.

1. Click the horizontal stud wall if it's not already selected. Right-click and choose Offset ≻ Copy from the shortcut menu. Toggle off OSNAP and POLAR on the application status bar.

2. Move the mouse and notice that there is a red line that allows you to select the component to offset from. Hold the mouse along the lower edge: the ToolTip says Face of GWB - CTRL for Center. You can offset from the finished face of the GWB, or even from its center. Click the lower face of the GWB.

3. Move the cursor down and observe the dynamic dimension (see Figure 8.13). Type **8´** and press Enter twice to complete the command. The new wall was precisely offset 8´ from the lower face of the GWB.

4. Use the `DISTANCE` command and verify the clear dimension—it is 8´. This is not something you can do with the AutoCAD `OFFSET` command without first having to calculate and add half the width of the wall to the distance you are offsetting. The specialized command makes accurate wall layout easy without burdening you with math (which can be especially irksome in Imperial units).

There are two very similar commands (`WallOffsetMove` and `WallOffsetSet`) that work identically to the `MOVE` and `RepositionFrom` commands with the addition of being able to select the edge of the component to start from. These commands can be more easily accessed from the Offset submenu in the shortcut menu (which has Copy, Move, and Set From).

Join works like the opposite of AutoCAD's `BREAK` command. Join reunites wall segments into a single segment. Join is accessed from the shortcut menu and has no options. Join actually reconnects baselines, so segments that can be joined must share the same justification, style, and widths. In addition, segments to be joined must also have collinear baselines in the same XY plane and belong to the same cleanup group. Essentially, you can only join walls that look like they might have just been broken apart. Subsequent edits to the segments often make them unjoinable.

FIGURE 8.13
Using WallOffsetCopy

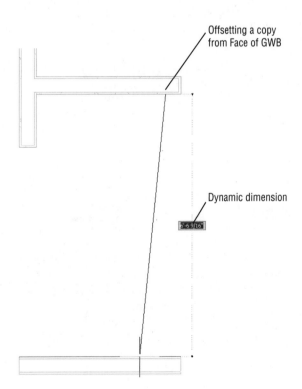

Offsetting a copy
from Face of GWB

Dynamic dimension

8´-6 9/16˝

TIP You can always erase both segments and create a new single segment wall if you are having problems joining. However, joining might be faster if the walls have a lot of children.

As you might expect, the new joined segment inherits all the children and anchored objects from the joining segments. In this context, a wall's children might be its roofline, floor line, anchors (doors, windows, openings), wall modifiers, wall style overrides, and interference conditions.

Cleaning Up Walls

Wall objects are great, but ADT's dirty little secret is that walls often have problems when they come together. You'll need to learn cleanup skills so that your walls and their components appear exactly as you intend. The dreaded defect marker indicates a problem that needs your attention.

Cleaning up walls can be very frustrating, to say the least, until you understand how walls work and what cleanup procedures to follow. Once you learn cleanup basics, fixing defects will be easy. The first step is to toggle on wall graph display. I like to leave this on whenever I'm cleaning up walls. Wall objects all have a graph display representation that can be toggled on miraculously without needing to change display configurations (refer to Chapter 2, "Object Display").

1. Open the file `ProblemWalls.dwg` from the companion DVD.

2. Select any wall, right-click, and choose Cleanups ➤ Toggle Wall Graph Display. You will see a nonplotting dashed blue line appear on top of your walls that represents each segment's *graphline* (see Figure 8.14). The graphline position determines when automatic cleanup occurs.

3. Select all the wall objects and look at the Advanced group in the Properties palette. Toggle the illustration on in the Cleanups subcategory. Blue lines on each wall segment are labeled A in the illustration. Click the value for A - Graphline Position. Notice that there are two possible choices: Wall Justification Line or Wall Center Line. Choose Wall Justification Line. This means the graphline will appear wherever the segment is justified: left, center, right, or baseline. Now cleanup is in line with justification. Press Esc.

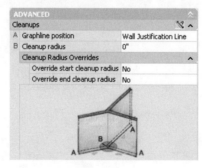

WARNING I strongly urge you to choose Wall Justification Line as your graphline position. Early versions of ADT used Wall Center Line, and that's why this choice lingers around today: for compatibility with legacy drawings. You'll have more cleanup problems with walls that are not center-justified if you set the graphline position to Wall Center Line

4. The sample file contains several labeled cleanup problems that you'll learn how to fix in this section. Zoom in on Problem A (see Figure 8.15). Look closely at the graphline; the vertical wall overshoots the horizontal one. If these walls were drawn with clean drafting practices—where the graphlines meet at their endpoints—we would not have a problem. We can fix it with an AutoCAD modify command.

FIGURE 8.14

Defect marker
means trouble

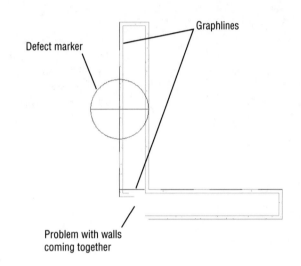

FIGURE 8.15

Cleanup problems

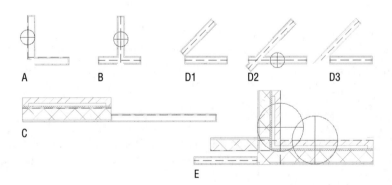

5. Type **F⏎** and click each of the segments in Problem A. They are filleted together with a zero radius. The walls clean up because their graphlines meet precisely at their endpoints.

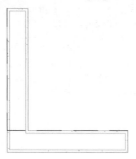

6. Navigate to Problem B. Recognize this as a situation in which segments meet like the letter T. Select the vertical segment, right-click and choose Cleanups ➤ Apply 'T' Cleanup. Select the other segment, and the intersection is cleaned up. The T Cleanup command trims or extends one graphline as needed forming a perfect 'T'. You always need to select the stem of the 'T' first for proper cleanup.

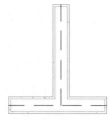

7. Navigate to Problem C. Zoom in on the intersection of the two segments. Here the walls are snapped correctly together, but their components do not merge. Notice how the gypsum board appears to have a division where the walls meet. Select both segments to reveal their grips (see Figure 8.16). Grips appear on the segments' graphlines. The reason these segments have not cleaned up is because their graphlines do not meet, due to the fact that Segment 1 is so much wider than Segment 2.

When wall graph display is toggled on, you will see cleanup grips appear on the walls. These angled arrows can be used to override the cleanup radius. Before we get into that, you need to understand what the cleanup radius does first. Segments have the potential to have cleanup circles at their start points and endpoints. The Cleanup Radius controls how large both cleanup circles are. Right now it is set to zero, so you don't see cleanup circles in the drawing window.

The Cleanup Radius is set for each segment in the Advanced group of the Properties palette. It is labeled B - Cleanup Radius in the illustration.

Automatic cleanup is triggered whenever the cleanup circle of one segment overlaps the graphline of another segment. Let's see how this works by fixing Problem C.

FIGURE 8.16

Cleanup radius grips appear when wall graph display is on

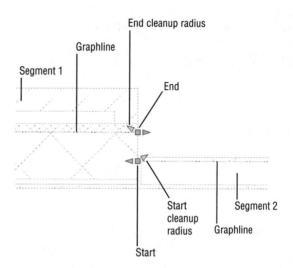

Type **6″** for the Cleanup Radius value under the Advanced > Cleanups subcategory in the Properties palette. Press Enter. Cleanup circles appear at each selected segment's start points and endpoints. Press Esc to deselect. Notice that one cleanup circle appears midway between the end cleanup circle for Segment 1 and the Start cleanup circle for Segment 2. The GWB components in the two segments merge together now that these segments have been cleaned up.

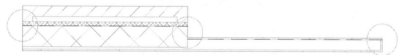

If the cleanup radius fixes cleanup problems, you might think that setting a large cleanup radius on all segments would be smart. However, this is completely wrong—large cleanup radii end up interfering with nearby wall segments where you don't want to trigger cleanup. You'll often have wall segments of different types adjacent to one another that you do not intend to merge together. Therefore, the rule is: Leave a zero cleanup radius whenever possible. It would be better to set just one of the two walls to have a 6″ cleanup radius at the end where the walls meet.

Cleanup will not occur when cleanup circles overlap each other but do not overlap their segments' graphlines, nor if wall segments graphlines are in different XY planes. Cleanup will not occur when segments belong to different cleanup groups; this fact can be used intentionally to deny cleanup where appropriate.

Sometimes you cannot fix cleanup problems without using a cleanup circle. Fortunately, you can be more selective by overriding one cleanup radius at a time. You can choose to override only the start or end cleanup radius on the affected segment. Let's see how this works with Problem D.

1. Navigate to Problem D1. Select the horizontal segment. Toggle off object snap by pressing F3. Click its Start Cleanup Radius grip and drag it outward; click when it overlaps the graphline of the other segment (see Figure 8.17).

FIGURE 8.17
Before (left) and after
(right) overriding a
cleanup radius

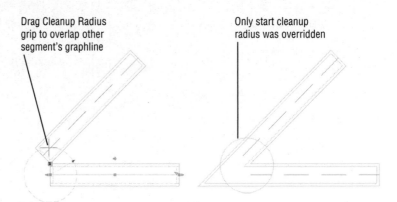

Drag Cleanup Radius
grip to overlap other
segment's graphline

Only start cleanup
radius was overridden

2. Look in the Properties palette under the Cleanup Radius Overrides subcategory and notice that the distance you dragged the grip is shown and editable there. You can also toggle the override on and off by choosing Yes or No.

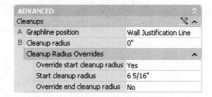

3. Using cleanup circles is not the only way to trigger automatic cleanup. It is preferable to use AutoCAD modify commands, do grip editing, or use 'T' or 'L' cleanups before resorting to using cleanup circles. Navigate to Problem D2. The reason these segments show a defect marker is that their graphlines intersect but do not meet. You can fix this easily: Select one of the segments, right-click, and choose Cleanups ➤ Apply 'L' Cleanup. Select the other segment, and cleanup is triggered. The result shows both segments' graphlines touching at their endpoints. Compare that with Figure 8.17, in which a cleanup circle was used to achieve the same effect.

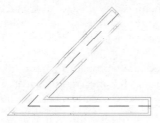

4. Navigate to Problem D3. Press F3 to toggle object snap back on. Select the horizontal segment. Click its start grip and snap it on the endpoint of the angled segment. Cleanup

does not occur, even if the graphlines of two segments are snapped precisely together (see Figure 8.18).

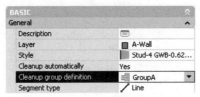

5. Look in the Properties palette in the Basic ➢ General subcategory. Cleanup Group Definition is set to GroupA. The other segment uses Standard. Change the Cleanup Group Definition to Standard. The walls immediately clean up.

Cleanup Group Definitions are made and edited in the Style Manager. Choose Format ➢ Style Manager. Expand ProblemWalls.dwg ➢ Architectural Objects ➢ Wall Cleanup Group Definitions. Click the Standard node. Select the Design Rules tab in the content pane. It is very simple—there are two check boxes. Each cleanup group holds two options:

◆ Allow wall cleanup between host and XRef drawings

◆ Allow objects anchored to walls in other cleanup groups to be moved or copied to walls in this cleanup group.

By default, the latter option is checked—allowing the transference of children such as doors, windows, and openings. Uncheck this setting for cleanup groups you assign to walls, such as toilet or cubicle partitions that are not meant to accept anchored objects. Toilet partitions often have doors – but perhaps in a style that should not be used elsewhere, nor should "regular" doors be used in toilet partition walls.

Check the first setting, Allow Wall Cleanup Between Host And XRef Drawings, when you want to allow automatic cleanup to occur through XRefs, as in elements and constructs. You might want to make an XRef Wall Cleanup Group Definition and check the first setting. Then assign the XRef cleanup group to wall objects in the host drawing you want to have cleaned up with the walls in an XRef drawing.

WARNING Avoid making duplicate wall objects that occupy the same position. Overlapping wall objects show defect markers. Overlapping walls can also occur through the use of XRefs.

FIGURE 8.18
No cleanup occurs with this grip edit, because the cleanup group definitions don't match.

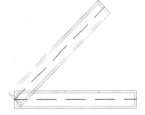

You can avoid making duplicate walls in XRefs by not using the Refedit feature. Instead, use the older procedure that was used before the Refedit feature was introduced. It goes as follows: Open an XRef drawing itself and make changes to it in the source file. When you are done, save the XRef, go back to the host drawing, and reload its XRefs. You'll save a lot of grief this way.

The last and most powerful cleanup tool is called Adding A Wall Merge Condition. Reserve this technique for seemingly impossible situations in which all the other automatic cleanup techniques you have learned do not work. Wall merge conditions are the way to manually force cleanup between two or more segments.

1. Navigate to Problem E. There are several issues here, and not all of them have to be solved with wall merge conditions. Try to get as far as possible without adding wall merge conditions. Select the vertical CMU wall segment, right-click, choose Cleanups ➤ Apply 'L' Cleanup, and select the horizontal CMU wall. The defect markers disappear as two segments form an 'L' intersection.

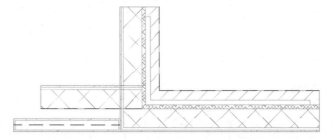

2. Notice that the stud wall segment on the lower left doesn't merge with the lower CMU segment. Changing the graph line isn't feasible here because we want the finished surfaces to remain flush. Let's try overriding a cleanup radius. Click the Cleanup Radius grip at the start point of the stud wall. Move this radius out and click when it overlaps the graphline of the horizontal CMU wall. Instead of fixing the problem, you have made it much worse; look at all the defect markers that appear!

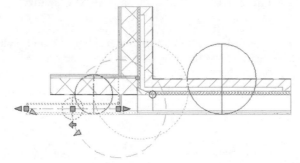

3. Press Esc to deselect and then click the Undo button. Now you know you'll have to use a wall merge condition. Select the stud wall, right-click, and choose Cleanups ➤ Add Wall Merge Condition. Select the vertical CMU wall and press Enter; the walls merge and the GWB connects. Select the stud wall again; notice that it has an arc connecting it to the wall that is merged

with it (see Figure 8.19). You can click the trigger grip at any time to remove the wall merge condition; there is no equivalent to this in the Properties palette.

4. Press Esc and then select the smaller horizontal CMU wall above the stud wall. Right-click and choose Cleanups ➤ Add Wall Merge Condition. Select the vertical CMU wall and press Enter; the walls merge and the CMU connects.

5. Apply a second wall merge to the stud wall, this time with the horizontal CMU wall, then using the lengthen grip to stretch the right end of the stud wall so that its end is at least ⁵/₈″ to the right of the inside face of the GWB of the vertical CMU wall.

6. Close the file without saving.

NOTE The way components clean up is controlled by priority in the wall style. You'll learn about this in the next section.

FIGURE 8.19
Merging walls

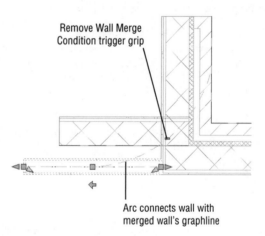

Remove Wall Merge
Condition trigger grip

Arc connects wall with
merged wall's graphline

Working with Wall Styles

Wall styles are where you define and control wall components, set their priorities, choose endcaps, choose materials, display properties, and more. Understanding how to work with wall styles is critical to achieving success with ADT because walls are perhaps the most important and fundamental aspects of any design.

Editing Components and Priorities

Walls are sandwiches made from their components. Remember from your experiences in the last section that a wall's baseline is the zero point around which components are offset in both directions. The baseline usually represents the outer edge of structural load-bearing components. This makes it possible to redefine cladding components and their widths without disturbing the building envelope as defined by exterior walls' baselines.

MAKING VARIABLE WIDTH COMPONENTS

Components are essentially parallel edges that are each given a width corresponding to a real-world material and offset some distance from the wall's baseline. Components offset away from the baseline toward the exterior of a wall have a positive edge offset. Components offset toward the interior use negative offset values. Let's take a look at an example.

1. Open the file WallStyles.dwg from the companion DVD.

2. Select the CMU wall, right-click, and choose Copy Wall Style and Assign from the shortcut menu. The Wall Style Properties dialog box appears. On the General tab, rename the style to CMU-8 Rigid-1.5 Air-X Brick-4 Furring. We will be creating a variable-width air gap in this style instead of the 2″ air gap it started with. Click the Components tab. Click each component in the list and observe it highlighted in green in the preview pane (see Figure 8.20).

TIP   You can navigate in the preview pane just as you are using the 3D Orbit command. Right-click in the preview pane to access its shortcut menu.

3. Select the Rigid Insulation component Index number 3. Notice that its Edge Offset value is zero. This means that this component starts on the baseline; usually the first thing you'll want to identify in any wall style. Remembering your experience earlier in this chapter, this makes sense: You have worked with the graphline located at the junction between the Rigid Insulation and the CMU. The Width values always correspond to real-world thickness.

4. Click the Air Gap component with index number 2. Its Edge Offset value starts at $1\,1/2″$, which is the same value as the Rigid Insulation's Width. In other words, the Air Gap component starts where the Rigid Insulation leaves off. This must be the case so there are no gaps between components.

FIGURE 8.20
Editing Components

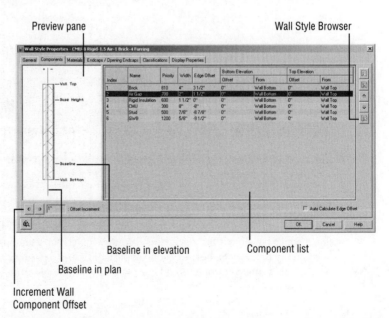

WARNING Do not overlap components or leave any gaps between components. If you want a gap, make it explicit by creating an Air Gap component. Otherwise, you will have problems with walls, areas, cleanup, and so on.

5. Click the Width value for the Air Gap component; a drop-down arrow appears. Click this arrow and enter 0″ in the first text box. Click the next drop-down arrow and choose Base Width. You can even make more complex formulas by using the last two controls that let you add, subtract, multiply, or divide by some value you enter in the last text box. Click outside the entire drop-down list to close it. In the end, the variable BW should appear as the Width value of the Air Gap. You'll be able to enter any Width value you like in the Properties palette later on, and it will control the Air Gap width through the BW variable.

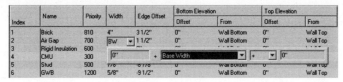

6. Now the next component must abut the Air Gap. Click the Brick's Edge Offset value to open its drop-down list. Type **1 ¹/₂″** and choose Base Width. Make sure that the entire formula reads 1 ¹/₂″ + Base Width + 0″ before closing the drop-down list. Click OK to close the Wall Style Properties dialog box.

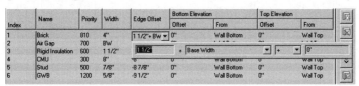

7. The shortcomings of endcaps with variable width walls are now quite apparent, as the brick returns are 2″ (as designed for the original wall style), leaving a 4″ gap to the insulation. In the Properties palette, notice that the Width parameter is editable and has a value of 6″. Change it to 0″ and hit Esc. The Air Gap has completely disappeared in the wall object because the Width value now controls it.

8. Select the same wall again and change its width value to **1″**. The Air Gap reappears, but this time it is an inch smaller that it was before you copied and assigned the new wall style.

SETTING COMPONENT PRIORITY VALUES

The order in which you create wall objects does not matter. Instead, priority values control which components overlap other components when walls merge or are cleaned up. Lower priority values take precedence over higher values. Let's see an example.

1. Select the CMU wall and lengthen it 5′ on the left.

2. Select one of the stud walls, right-click, and choose Add Selected. This is a quick way to add an object of matching style without having to hunt for the correct tool. Start the new wall some distance to the left of the existing stud walls below the CMU wall. Click its endpoint perpendicular

to the CMU wall near its baseline. By using Autosnap (set in Options) you just have to click with 6″ of the CMU's baseline to get it to snap precisely (see Figure 8.21).

3. Select the new stud wall, right-click, and choose Edit Wall Style. Click the Components tab and change the Stud component's Priority value from 500 to 250. Click OK to close the Wall Style Properties dialog box. All the stud walls sharing this style immediately penetrate through the CMU. Although this is not very realistic in terms of construction, you can see how priorities control the way components interact.

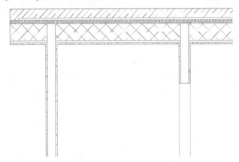

4. Select the CMU wall, right-click, and choose Edit Wall Style. Check the priority of the CMU component; it has a value of 300. When you previously set the Stud component's priority value to 250, it "beats" the value of 300—that's why the stud component interrupts the CMU. Click Cancel.

FIGURE 8.21
Drawing another
Stud Wall

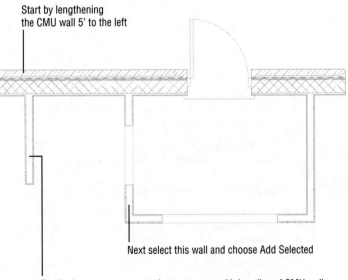

Start by lengthening
the CMU wall 5' to the left

Next select this wall and choose Add Selected

Finally draw a new segment that autosnaps with baseline of CMU wall

5. Click the Undo button twice to undo the change to the Stud component's priority. You don't have to change the priority of an entire style; in fact, I caution you against it. It is safer to create priority overrides only where you need them. Select the stud wall you created in step 2. In the Properties palette, locate the Advanced ➢ Style Overrides subcategory. Click the Priority Overrides worksheet icon. Click the Add Priority Override button and then choose (2) Stud from the Component drop-down list. Choose At End Of Wall from the Override drop-down list, type a Priority of **250** in the Priority Overrides worksheet, and click OK (see Figure 8.22). Now only one stud wall segment penetrates through the CMU; the other stud walls sharing the same style do not. Priority overrides give you specific control where you need it in exceptional circumstances.

A lot of thought has gone into developing priority values for various wall components stored in the styles that ship with ADT. You would be wise to follow these standards yourself (see the section "Creating a New Wall Style"). In general, the numerical values mirror the sequence of construction. For example, Concrete has a priority of 200 because it is one of the first building components to be constructed, and so on: CMU=300, Studs=500, Bricks=800, Siding=900, and Glass=1200. Components farther from the baseline of a wall usually have higher priority values because they are added later.

If you need to add a new component that you can't find in any of the preset wall styles, it is wise to leave space between priority integer values; make a new priority 150 rather than 199 if you want it to pass through concrete. That way, you'll have numerical wiggle room to add another priority in-between values that have already been spoken for in the future (say 175).

FIGURE 8.22
Making Priority
Overrides

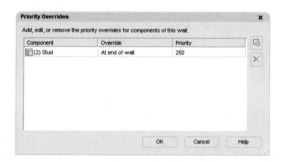

Creating a New Wall Style

You can create a new wall style completely from scratch or get a jump start by using the wall style browser to scavenge existing components from other styles. Let's gain experience with both methods by making both simple and fairly complex wall styles.

CREATING WALL STYLES FROM SCRATCH

Let's create a simple wall style completely from scratch. It will ultimately consist of three components: concrete, metal furring, and gypsum board. I provided a sample file containing a generic wall penetrated by an opening fenestration (you'll learn about openings in Chapter 9). It is helpful to have an opening when designing a wall style because you'll eventually address how the wall meets fenestrations in the next section.

1. Open the file `SimpleWallStyle.dwg` from the companion DVD. It contains a generic wall with an opening.

2. Choose Format ➢ Style Manager. Expand SimpleWallStyle.dwg ➢ Architectural Objects. Right-click the Wall Styles node and choose New from the context menu. Give the new style the name **SimpleWall**.

3. Click the Components tab in the content pane. Change Name to **Concrete**, Priority to **200**, Width to **8″**, and Edge Offset to **-8″**. Leave the Elevation values at their defaults. By setting the edge offset equal to the width, but with a negative value, this component's left edge rests on the baseline. Zoom into the preview pane and verify this relationship.

4. Click the Add Component button on the right edge of the content pane. Select component 2 and change Name to **Metal Stud**, Priority to **500**, and Width to **⁷/₈″**. Type ⁷/₈″ in the Offset Increment text box at the bottom edge of the preview pane. Click the Decrement Wall Component Offset button. Notice that the Edge Offset for the Metal Stud has changed: The two components abut edge to edge.

Index	Name	Priority	Width	Edge Offset	Bottom Elevation		Top Elevation	
					Offset	From	Offset	From
1	Concrete	200	8″	-8″	0″	Wall Bottom	0″	Wall Top
2	Metal Stud	500	7/8″	-8 7/8″	0″	Wall Bottom	0″	Wall Top

5. Add the final component and call it **GWB**. Set its Priority to **1200**, and Width to **⁵/₈″**. Type ⁵/₈″ in the Offset Increment text box and click the Decrement Wall Component Offset button. All three components exist edge to edge without any gaps (see Figure 8.23). The components extend all the way from the Wall Bottom to the Wall Top. Click Apply.

TIP Check Auto Calculate Edge Offset to have ADT calculate values for you.

6. Click the Materials tab. All three components are listed here plus *Shrink-wrap*. Shrink-wrap is an outline that wraps around the wall when its components are cut in section (see Chapter 16). Click the Standard Material Definition for Concrete and notice that the drop-down list doesn't have any other choices yet. Because we are creating this style from scratch, we have to manually load material definitions before they'll be available here.

7. In the Style Manager menu bar, choose File ➢ Open Drawing. In the Open Drawing dialog box, click the Content folder in the Favorites pane. Double-click Styles and then Imperial. Choose the `Material Definitions (Imperial).dwg` file and click Open.

8. Scroll up in the tree pane in the Style Manager and expand Material Definitions (Imperial).dwg ➢ Multi-Purpose Objects. Click the Material Definitions node. Ctrl+click the following materials in the content pane (to select them simultaneously):

   ◆ Concrete.Cast-in-Place.Flat.Grey

   ◆ Finishes.Metal Framing Systems.Furring

   ◆ Finishes.Plaster and Gypsum Board.Gypsum Wallboard.Painted.White

FIGURE 8.23
Configuring Simple
Wall components
from scratch

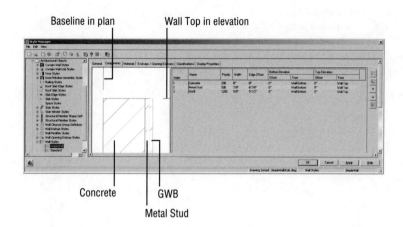

Baseline in plan   Wall Top in elevation

Concrete   GWB

Metal Stud

Scroll down in the tree pane and locate the SimpleWallStyle.dwg node. Drag the selected nodes from the content pane and drop them on the SimpleWallStyle.dwg node. Expand SimpleWall-Style.dwg ➢ Multi-Purpose Objects ➢ Material Definitions and verify that the three copied materials are in there.

9. Select the SimpleWall node under Architectural Objects for this drawing. Assign the appropriate material to each component. Leave Shrinkwrap assigned the Standard material. Click OK to close the Style Manager.

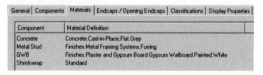

10. Select the generic wall and assign SimpleWall style using the Properties palette. Go into Flat shaded view and an isometric viewpoint. Change viewpoints to get a look at both sides of your new wall style (see Figure 8.24).

11. Save your work as **SimpleWallStyle2.dwg**. You can leave this file open—you'll be using it again in the Editing Endcaps section.

USING THE WALL STYLE BROWSER

The wall style browser can be quite helpful when making wall styles that use common components present in other styles. Let's create a much more complicated wall style to gain some valuable experience designing wall components.

1. Open the file `ComplexWallStyle.dwg` from the companion DVD. Like the previous tutorial, this file contains a generic wall with an opening, but this time the wall has a taller Base Height at 12′, plus its floor line has been extended downward 4′, making the height 16′ overall. You'll learn about floor lines in the "Altering Wall Form" section.

FIGURE 8.24
Completed SimpleWall
style applied to object

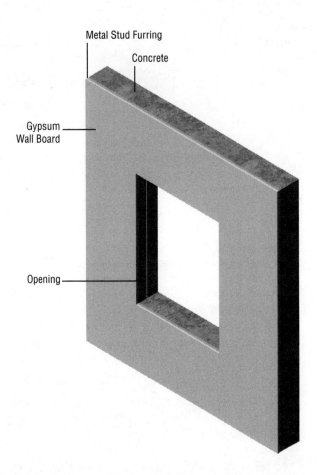

2. Before we dive into designing the components for the new wall style, we need to insert wall styles that have components we think we might need. The easiest way to do that is to right-click a tool and choose Import from its shortcut menu. Click the Walls palette and import both the CMU-8 Rigid-1.5 Air-2 Brick-4 Furring-2 and Concrete-8 styles.

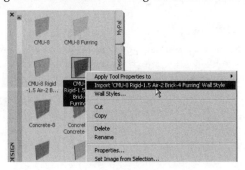

TIP You can also open files within the Wall Style Browser to "steal" components from their wall styles, just like you can "steal" styles from other files in Style Manager.

3. Choose Format ➤ Style Manager. Expand ComplexWallStyle.dwg ➤ Architectural Objects. Right-click the Wall Styles node and choose New from the context menu. Give the new style the name **ComplexWall**. Click the ComplexWall node.

4. Select the Components tab. Click the Wall Style Browser button on the right edge of the content pane. Expand the nodes for both the CMU and Concrete styles. Drag each component from these styles into the content pane of the Style Manager (see Figure 8.25).

5. Click a blank area of the Style Manager to restore focus to it. Click the Materials tab in the content pane and notice that each component already has the proper material assigned. Click the Components tab. Now you have "building blocks" from which you can fashion the Complex-Wall style. You don't have to hassle with loading and assigning materials because the components you dragged over already have the proper materials assigned. Each component also has the correct priority value assigned.

6. This time, I assume that you know how to input values in the Style Manager. Enter the values given in Table 8.1. Edit, rename, move, copy, and paste styles as needed. Avoid creating components from scratch, as they will have the Standard material assigned. The sample file `ComplexWallStyle2.dwg` provided on the companion DVD contains this style with all the values entered if you don't want to enter them yourself.

7. Right-click the sample styles you imported in step 2 and choose Purge. Click the ComplexWall node and go to its Component tab. Click each component in turn and watch each highlight in green in the preview area on screen (see Figure 8.26). Think about how you could separate components from left to right (in plan) and top to bottom (in elevation) by using the values you input in the previous step. This will teach you a lot about how components work. Click OK to close the Style Manager.

FIGURE 8.25

Dragging and Dropping from the Wall Style Components Browser

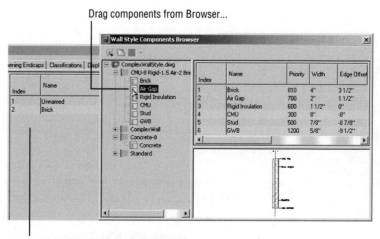

FIGURE 8.26
ComplexWall
components

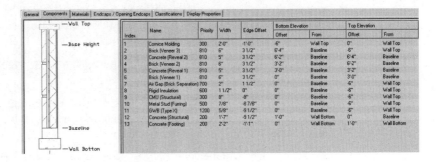

FIGURE 8.27
Completed Complex-
Wall style applied to
object

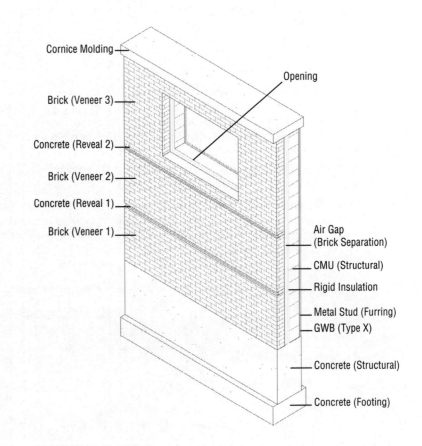

8. Select the generic wall and assign ComplexWall as its Style in the Properties palette. Change to Hidden line shading mode. Check out the wall object from different vantage points (see Figure 8.27). You should be able to build just about any wall style you can imagine now.

9. Save your work as **ComplexWallStyle2.dwg**. You can leave this file open.

TABLE 8.1:   Component Values for ComplexWall Style

Index	Name	Priority	Width	Edge Offset	Bottom Elevation Offset	From	Top Elevation Offset	From
1	Cornice Molding	300	2´-0″	1´-0″	6″	Wall Top	0″	Wall Top
2	Brick (Veneer 3)	810	6″	3 1/2″	6´-4″	Baseline	6″	Wall Top
3	Concrete (Reveal 2)	810	5″	3 1/2″	6´-2″	Baseline	6´-4″	Baseline
4	Brick (Veneer 2)	810	6″	3 1/2″	3´-2″	Baseline	6´-2″	Baseline
5	Concrete (Reveal 1)	810	5″	3 1/2″	3´-0″	Baseline	3´-2″	Baseline
6	Brick (Veneer 1)	810	6″	3 1/2″	0″	Baseline	3´-0″	Baseline
7	Air Gap (Brick Separation)	700	2″	1 1/2″	0″	Baseline	6″	Wall Top
8	Rigid Insulation	600	1 1/2″	0″	0″	Baseline	6″	Wall Top
9	CMU (Structural)	300	8″	8″	0″	Baseline	6″	Wall Top
10	Metal Stud (Furring)	500	7/8″	8 7/8″	0″	Baseline	6″	Wall Top
11	GWB (Type X)	1200	5/8″	9 1/2″	0″	Baseline	6″	Wall Top
12	Concrete (Structural)	200	1´-7″	9 1/2″	1´-0″	Wall Bottom	0″	Baseline
13	Concrete (Footing)	200	2´-2″	1´-1″	0″	Wall Bottom	1´-0″	Wall Bottom

Editing Endcaps

Endcaps terminate components. Think of a wall object in plan: Endcaps are what you see at either end of the wall object. One wall endcap style is assigned to it, but you can override it at either or both ends of a wall object, so each end has the potential to be different. The preset CMU style we have been using so often in this chapter has turned-in brick endcaps (see Figure 8.28). The Standard wall endcap style is a straight line. Endcap Styles are based on open polylines, so you can draw your own polylines and have ADT auto-calculate a new wall endcap style for you.

Fenestrations in ADT include Openings, Doors, Windows, and Door/Window Assembly objects (see Chapter 9 and Chapter 10, "Curtain Walls and Assemblies"). Each of these objects can have its own endcap treatment called a Wall Opening Endcap Style. You'll learn how to assign endcaps to the jambs, heads, and sills of any fenestration object. After endcaps styles are defined, they can be edited in place for easy modification. Let's start this exploration by auto-calculating wall endcap styles.

FIGURE 8.28
CMU-8 Rigid-1.5 Air-
2 Brick-4 Furring (End 1)
Wall Endcap Style

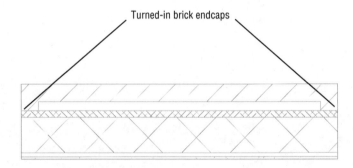

Turned-in brick endcaps

CALCULATING ENDCAPS AUTOMATICALLY FROM POLYLINES

You will draw termination conditions for each component in the SimpleWall style using polylines. Then we'll have ADT create a Wall Endcap Style and assign it to the Wall Style.

1. Switch to the `SimpleWallStyle2.dwg` if it is still open. Otherwise, open this file from the companion DVD. Go to the Top viewpoint and zoom into the right edge of the wall object.

TIP If you want to create a new Wall Endcap Style for a wall in your design, add the selected wall object off to the side of your drawing. Draw a short horizontal wall segment as a temporary helper. After you have assigned the endcap to the style, delete the helper. The process is much like redefining an AutoCAD block.

2. Draw a chamfered polyline using POLAR and OTRACK tracking modes. Start the polyline at the end of the lower edge of the concrete component. Move the cursor at a 45-degree angle, type 2″ in the dynamic dimension, and press Enter. Move the cursor up and acquire the endpoint as a tracking target. Move the cursor back at a negative 45-degree angle and click where it intersects with the vertical tracking line. Finally, click the endpoint and press Enter to finish the polyline (see Figure 8.29).

NOTE You do not have to draw every component when auto-calculating endcaps. Any components you skip will have straight edges that align with the start points of any polylines that you do draw.

FIGURE 8.29
Drawing concrete
endcap polyline

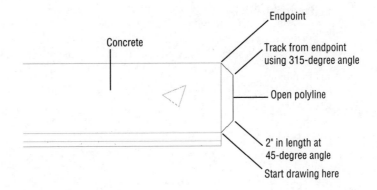

Endpoint

Concrete

Track from endpoint
using 315-degree angle

Open polyline

2" in length at
45-degree angle

Start drawing here

3. Draw another open polyline to terminate the GWB. This time make it a square profile that aligns with the right edge of the concrete endcap polyline. Be consistent and start this polyline along the lower edge of the GWB component (see Figure 8.30). Click four points and press Enter, leaving this an open polyline. Draw a vertical construction line on the right edge of the wall object: this will help you maintain the outer edge of the object.

TIP Polyline segments with non-zero widths are invisible in endcaps. Use the PEDIT command to change widths of individual polyline segments. Use this fact to make components appear open at their endcaps; that is, GWB wrapping around a stud.

4. Move both polylines to the left so their right edges align with the construction line.

5. Select the wall object, right-click, and choose Endcaps ➢ Calculate Automatically. Select both polylines and press Enter. Type **Y↵** to erase the polylines. The command line reads as follows:

```
Apply the new wall endcap style to this end as [Wallstyledefault/Override]
<Wallstyledefault>:
```

Press Enter to accept the default. You will be altering the wall style. Type **Chamfered Edge** in the New Endcap Style worksheet that appears and click OK. Endcaps appear on both ends of the wall object.

FIGURE 8.30
Drawing GWB
endcap polyline

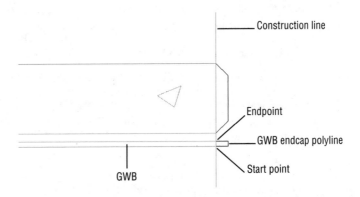

Construction line

Endpoint

GWB endcap polyline

Start point

GWB

6. Notice that the right edge is still flush with the construction line. Open the Style Manager and select the Chamfered Edge wall endcap style. Click the Dimensions tab in the content pane. There is only one editable parameter in wall endcap styles: A- Return Offset. Entering a value here pushes the edge of the wall back from the wall end grip point. This can be used, for example, to get the GWB component to wrap the wall end and into a window frame, while keeping the other components adjacent to the frame.

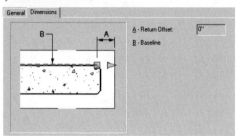

7. Expand the Wall Styles node and select SimpleWall. Click the Endcaps/Opening Endcaps tab in the content pane. Verify that the Wall Endcap Style now is assigned Chamfered Edge. This is what Calculate Automatically did for you. Change the Wall Endcap Style back to Standard for now; we need it looking generic for the next section.

WARNING Endcaps cannot introduce new components or materials. Endcaps simply terminate existing components.

8. Leave the file open.

MAKING OPENING ENDCAP STYLES

Openings have four possible positions for wall endcap styles: Jamb Start, Jamb End, Head, and Sill. We will create a new wall endcap and assign it within a Wall Opening Endcap Style. In this tutorial you will make an opening endcap that overhangs the outer edges of the wall.

1. Draw a new polyline starting at the lower edge of the concrete component. Continue adding segments according to Figure 8.31.

2. Move the polyline over 4″ to the left so that its right edge aligns with the construction line.

3. Select the wall object, right-click, and choose Endcaps ➢ Calculate Automatically. Select the polyline and press Enter. Type **Y**↵ to erase the polyline. At the next prompt, right-click and choose Override. Type the name **Chamfered Overhang** in the New Endcap Style worksheet that appears and click OK.

4. Notice that only the right end of the wall object is affected. Select the wall object and check out the Style Overrides subcategory, under Advanced in the Properties palette. The Ending Endcap is currently assigned Chamfered Overhang. This is what Calculate Automatically did for us when we chose Override. Change the Ending Endcap back to *BYSTYLE*. We never intended this to be an endcap!

5. Right-click and choose Edit Wall Style. Click the Endcaps/Opening Endcaps tab. At the bottom of the left pane there are two buttons. Click Add a New Opening Endcap Style.

6. The Opening Endcap Style dialog box appears. Click its General tab and type the name **Chamfered Overhang Opening**. Click the Design Rules tab. Change the Sill Endcap Style to Chamfered Overhang (see Figure 8.32). Click OK to close the dialog box.

7. In the Style Manager, the Opening Endcap Style you just created still has not been assigned. Assign **Chamfered Overhang Opening** as the Opening's Opening Endcap Style. That's a tongue twister—it will probably make more sense to you than it sounds. ADT suffers from much confusing jargon (take a look at Figure 8.33 to keep terms straight). Select Chamfered Edge as the Wall Endcap style and click OK.

FIGURE 8.31
Drawing Chamfered Overhang endcap polyline

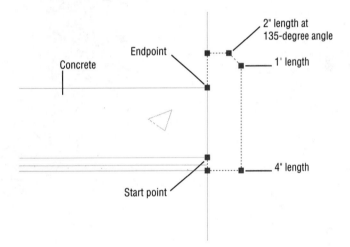

FIGURE 8.32
Creating an Opening Endcap Style and assigning an Endcap Style to the Sill

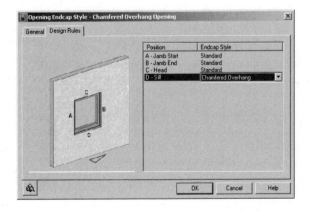

FIGURE 8.33
Completed Opening
Endcap Style

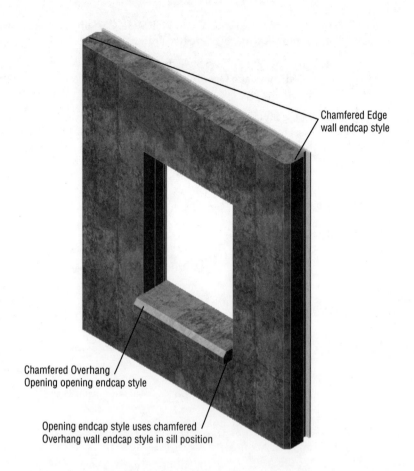

Chamfered Edge
wall endcap style

Chamfered Overhang
Opening opening endcap style

Opening endcap style uses chamfered
Overhang wall endcap style in sill position

8. You still can't see the effect. Opening endcaps are visible only in High Detail in 3D. Switch to the High Detail display configuration and a NW isometric view. Choose View ➢ Regen Model, select the wall object, and press Enter. The concrete sill finally appears—congratulations!

9. Save your work as **SimpleWallStyle3.dwg**; the style is not so simple after all! Leave the file open.

EDITING ENDCAPS IN PLACE

After you've gone to the trouble of defining endcap and opening endcap styles, you can easily edit their profiles without having to redefine them entirely. Let's give it a try by altering the shape of the concrete sill.

1. Open SimpleWallStyle3.dwg if it is not already open. Switch to Hidden shading mode for better display performance. Look at the model from the NW Isometric viewpoint.

2. Select the wall object, right-click, and choose Endcaps ➢ Edit In Place. Click the midpoint of the sill. The profile highlights, and the familiar Edit In Place toolbar appears (refer to Chapter 1, "The Basics," and Chapter 4, "Mass Modeling"). Notice that the profile shown is the union of wall and sill (see Figure 8.34).

FIGURE 8.34
Editing the sill profile
in place

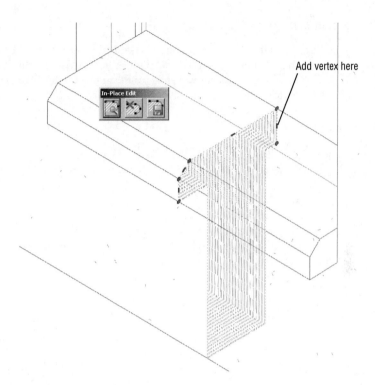

Add vertex here

3. Right-click and choose Add Vertex from the shortcut menu. Snap to the midpoint of the vertical edge and then press Enter to exit the command.

4. Select the profile. Move the corner vertex forward toward the exterior side. Move the new vertex up to approximate a 45-degree chamfer on the interior edge. You might need to use 3D Orbit to see the chamfer more clearly (see Figure 8.35). Click the Save All Changes button on the In-Place Edit toolbar.

FIGURE 8.35
Vertices edited in place

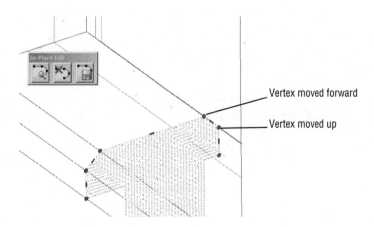

Vertex moved forward

Vertex moved up

TIP You can replace a profile you are in-place editing with another polyline drawn previously.

5. Select the wall object, right-click, and choose Endcaps ➤ Edit In Place. Click the midpoint along the wall object's start edge in plan. Select both profiles and note that you can also edit the Chamfered Edge wall endcap style profile in this mode. This is an alternative to overriding the wall endcap style at this end. Click the Discard All Changes button on the In-Place Edit toolbar.

6. Close the file without saving.

Understanding Wall Display Properties

Walls have some of the most complicated display properties of any objects. This is partly due to the fact that walls can have up to 20 components, each of which has boundary and hatch display components. Let's take a look at wall display properties.

Reopen the file ComplexWallStyle2.dwg from your hard drive or the companion DVD.

Switch into the Top viewpoint. Verify that Medium Detail is the current display configuration. Notice that the Cornice Molding component at the top of the wall is visible in plan. Toggle LWT on in the application status bar (see Figure 8.36).

FIGURE 8.36

Viewing plan with lineweight display turned on

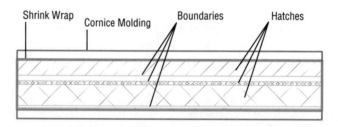

Select the wall object, right-click, and choose Edit Wall Style from the shortcut menu. Click the Display Properties tab of the Wall Style Properties dialog box.

Place a check in the Style Override column for the Plan display representation. The Display Properties dialog box appears; click its Layer/Color/Linetype tab if it isn't already selected (see Figure 8.37). Basically the display components break down into five categories: Cut Plane, Shrink Wrap, Defect Warning, Boundaries, and Hatches (as discussed in the following sections).

Cut Plane In any plan representation, you are looking at geometry below the cut plane: Below Cut Plane is on and Above Cut Plane is off. The Reflected representations are the opposite because then you are looking up.

Shrink Wrap Shrink wrap is a border surrounding geometry that is cut by the cut plane and is normally shown in plans. Shrink wrap hatch is shown in the Presentation display configuration. The shrink wrap hatch pattern is controlled on the Hatching tab.

Defect Warning It's a good idea to always leave this on because it alerts you to cleanup problems that need your attention. The defect marker will never plot because it is on a nonplotting layer by default. I recommend reserving the color red for defect markers so you'll know something is wrong when you see red.

Boundaries   Each component has a boundary that shows up as parallel edges in plan. Notice that there are 13 boundaries in the example because ComplexWall style has 13 components. They are all conveniently labeled in an override, but not so when you edit the drawing default display properties.

Hatches   Each component has its own hatch component whose layer/color/linetype/etc. are controlled here. The patterns are controlled from the Hatching tab.

Click the Hatching tab (see Figure 8.38). Here you can set the patterns for the Hatch components plus the Shrink Wrap Hatch. By default, all the Hatch display component patterns are grayed-out, but they don't have to be. The surface hatching of materials supersedes the patterns found here. To enable these controls, uncheck By Material on the Layer/Color/Linetype tab.

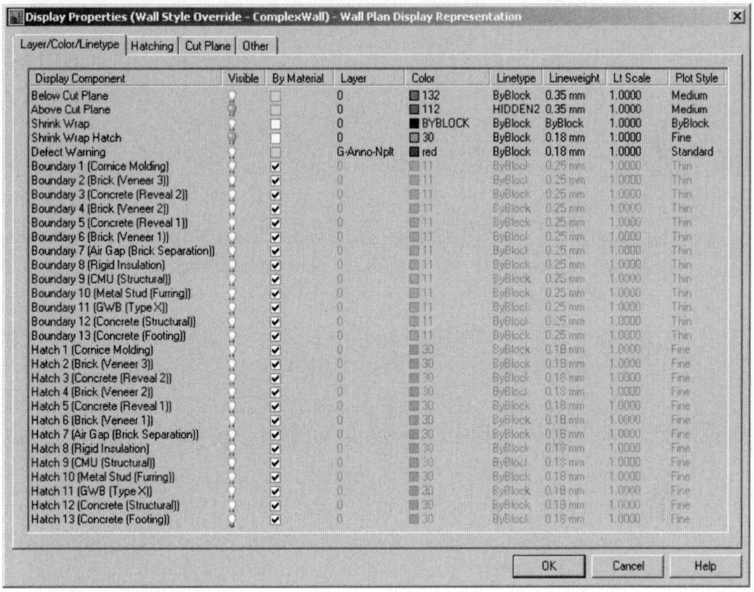

FIGURE 8.37

Wall Style Override—
Display Properties—
Layer/Color/
Linetype tab

FIGURE 8.38

Wall Style Override—
Display Properties—
Hatching tab

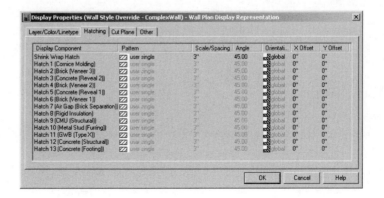

Click the Cut Plane tab. By default, Automatically Choose Above and Below Cut Plane Heights is selected; uncheck it now. This hides the Cornice Molding component. Normally cut plane height is globally set in the display configuration (refer to Chapter 2, "Object Display"). You can override it at the style or object levels: check Override Display Configuration Cut Plane. Leave the Cut Plane Height set to 3´-6″. Check Manual Above and Below Cut Plane Heights. Click the Add button and edit the Cut Plane height from zero to 3´-0″ (see Figure 3.39).

Click the Other tab. Check Component 4 in the Draw Miter For Components list. Component 4 in this style is Brick (Veneer 2), which happens to be cut by the cut plane at 3´-6″. Miters are diagonal lines that appear in plan where wall components come together. There are many other options here for you to familiarize yourself with (see Figure 8.40): Read through them and click OK.

Display Inner Lines   You can choose whether to display dashed inner lines from components that are above or below the cut plane, for example through a window or door in a wall. This might be good for some details.

Hide Lines Below Openings   You can hide lines above or below a window, door, or opening at the cut plane.

Display Endcaps   Unchecking this setting displays straight-lined endcaps no matter which endcaps style is defined. Consider using this option in the Plan Low Detail representation.

Cut Door and Window Frames   When checked, these settings cut the wall at the outer edge of door and window frames. When unchecked, the wall is cut at the inner edges of the frames.

Draw Order or Priority   When checked, this setting ignores priority values and draws components by their index number (the order they were created). Do not check this unless you have a very good reason because it disables the priority system.

Do True Cut   Check to perform a more accurate 3D slice that includes wall sweeps and body modifiers. Leave unchecked for better performance and less 3D accuracy.

Draw another wall segment of the same style and connect it to the existing wall object, cleaning up its intersection if necessary. Take a look at the mitered bricks and notice that the Cornice Molding component is hidden (you did that in step 6). Toggle off LWT on the application status bar. Close the file without saving.

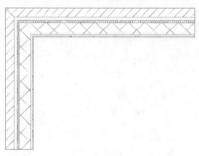

FIGURE 8.39
Wall Style Override—
Display Properties—
Cut Plane tab

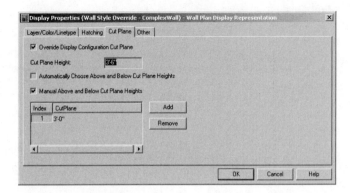

FIGURE 8.40
Wall Style Override—
Display Properties—
Other tab

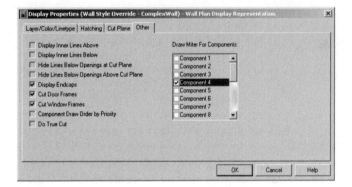

Altering Wall Form

Walls' three-dimensional forms can be altered in several ways. We'll start by editing roof and floor lines to take the wall beyond a monolithic slab. Walls can be further tweaked with plan (2D) and body (3D) modifiers that can alter them in just about any way you can imagine. In addition 2D profiles can be swept along the length of any component to create attractive moldings. Finally, this chapter concludes with sections on managing interference conditions and surface hatch overrides.

Editing Roof and Floor Lines

A generic wall object starts out being represented as a slab-like extrusion in three dimensions—extending from the baseline on the ground up to the value of its base height. All walls have the potential to extend below the baseline—down to the wall bottom and above the base height—up to the wall top. These potential extensions have profiles called floor and roof lines (see Figure 8.41).

You cannot draw the floor or roof lines directly in the drawing window. Instead, the vertices of the floor and roof lines are edited through a worksheet interface, or are projected to a polyline or other ADT objects. Let's take a look.

1. Create a new blank drawing with the default template.

FIGURE 8.41
Roof and floor
line diagram

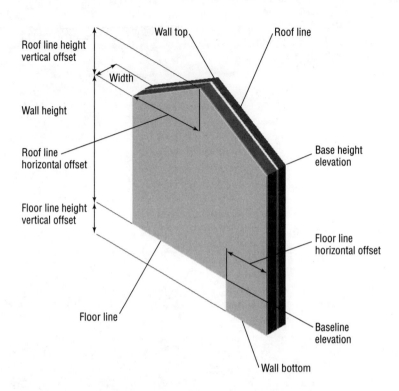

2. Select the Walls palette and click the CMU-8 Rigid-1.5 Air-2 Brick-4 Furring-2 tool. Draw a **10′** horizontal wall segment from left to right.

3. Select the wall object you just drew. In the Properties palette, click the Roof/Floor Line worksheet icon at the extreme bottom of the Advanced category. The Roof and Floor line worksheet that appears shows a diagram of the wall in elevation. Right now, both the roof and floor line are straight lines connecting two vertices at the start and endpoints of the wall segment. You can edit either the roof line or the floor line by choosing the appropriate radio button. Verify that Edit Roof Line is selected and click the Add Gable button. Select the new vertex and click the Edit Vertex button. In the Wall Roof/Floor Line Vertex worksheet that appears, type **3′** in the Distance text box in the Vertical Offset group. Click OK twice to close both worksheets.

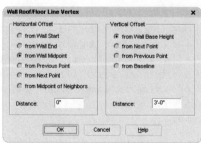

4. Switch to NW Isometric viewpoint in Hidden line shading mode. There is your perfect gable.

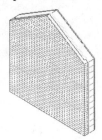

5. Reopen the Roof and Floor line worksheet. Click the Edit Floor Line radio button and then click Add Step. Select the second vertex in the elevation diagram and click Edit Vertex to open the Wall Roof/Floor Line Vertex worksheet. Verify that the From Wall Midpoint radio button is selected and type **2′** in the Distance text box in the Horizontal Offset group. Notice all the radio buttons that let you make offsets accurately from many different wall features. Click OK.

6. Select the third vertex in the elevation diagram at the bottom of the step. Click Edit Vertex and type **2′** as the horizontal offset distance from Wall Midpoint and **-2′** as the vertical offset distance from Wall Base Height. Click OK.

7. Select the fourth and final vertex on the right side of the elevation diagram. Click Edit Vertex and type **-2′** as the vertical offset distance from Wall Base Height. The horizontal offset controls are grayed-out because you are editing the end vertex—its position is controlled by the endpoint of the wall object. Click OK. The completed elevation sketch shows the modifications you made to the roof and floor lines (see Figure 8.42). Click OK.

8. Save your work as **RoofFloorLine.dwg**. Leave the file open.

Adding Plan and Body Modifiers

Plan modifiers alter the 3D form of a wall using a 2D polyline. The process starts by drawing the shape of the modification you want to make in the top viewpoint with an open polyline. Then add it as a plan modifier to vertically extrude a 3D form. Plan modifiers have numerous controls to ensure that you get exactly the form you envision.

FIGURE 8.42
Roof and Floor Line
worksheet

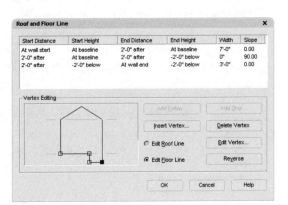

Body modifiers let you alter the 3D form of a wall using 3D mass elements or mass groups. A body modifier applies to specific components. You can even entirely replace components by explicitly modeling them as body modifiers. Figure 8.43 illustrates both types of modifiers.

1. Open RoofFloorLine.dwg if it isn't already open.

2. Switch to the Top viewpoint. Draw a chamfered polyline along the interior face of the wall. Its dimensions aren't important for this example. Make sure that the polyline starts and ends somewhere along the interior wall face.

3. Select the wall, right-click, and choose Plan Modifiers ➢ Convert Polyline To Wall Modifier from the shortcut menu. The Add option allows you to draw a plan modifier directly without using a polyline. In this case, select the polyline you drew previously and press Enter. Type **Y**↵ to erase the polyline. Type **Interior Build Out** as the New Wall Modifier Style Name and click OK: the Add Wall Modifier worksheet appears. Verify the Wall Component you are applying the plan modifier to GWB. Set the Start Elevation Offset at zero from the Wall Baseline. Set the End Elevation Offset at **3′** from the Wall Baseline and click OK.

NOTE   A wall can have more than one plan modifier attached to it.

4. Switch into the SW Isometric viewpoint and admire your plan modifier. It appears to be made entirely of GWB—even if this component is only $5/8″$ wide in the wall style.

5. Switch to the NW Isometric viewpoint so you can see the exterior face of the wall. Select the Massing palette and create a Cone mass element off to the side. Create a Box mass element that is at least as tall as the cone. Move the box so it overlaps half the cone. Set FACETDEV to $1/16″$ so you can see curves more smoothly. Select the cone, right-click, and choose Boolean ➢ Subtract and click the box. Type **Y**↵ to erase the box. Move the cone flush with the exterior face of the wall (you might need to go back to the Top viewpoint if it helps).

6. Select the wall, right-click, and choose Body Modifiers ➢ Add. Select the cone and press Enter; the Add Body Modifier worksheet appears. Set the Wall Component to **Brick**, set Operation to **Additive**, type **Cone form** as the Description, check **Erase Selected Objects**, and click OK. The cone becomes part of the wall and appears with the brick component's material. Although this is not very realistic in terms of construction, it demonstrates this concept clearly: You can model anything at all and add it as a body modifier.

FIGURE 8.43
Plan and body modifiers

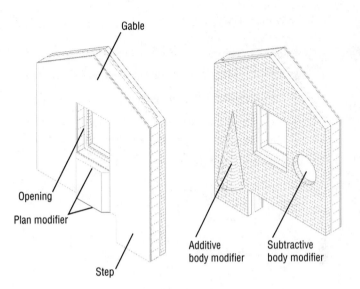

WARNING   After you add a mass as a body modifier, you can no longer edit the form. For this reason, consider storing any masses used to create body modifiers on a separate nonplotting layer in case you ever want to change the form.

7. You can also use body modifiers to subtract forms from wall components. Create a sphere mass element and move its center flush with the wall's exterior edge as you did before with the cone. Move the sphere up in the Z direction. Add it as a body modifier, but this time choose the Subtractive operation in the Add Body Modifier worksheet. You have cut a round hole in the brick component only (see Chapter 9, "Doors, Windows, and Openings" to learn how to make openings that go all the way through a wall). Figure 8.43 shows an opening that penetrates all the way through the wall.

8. Select the wall and click the Body Modifiers worksheet icon at the bottom of the Properties palette. Use this worksheet to manage modifiers, change the components affected, or alter the operations performed. Click Cancel.

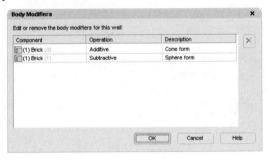

9. Save the file as **RoofFloorLine2.dwg** if you want, although we won't be using it again. This file is provided on the DVD. Close the file.

Sweeping Profiles

Sweeps are extrusions along the length of a component that are commonly used to make moldings. You can very easily add a profile and edit it in-place to define a sweep.

1. Open the file ComplexWallStyle3.dwg from the companion DVD.

2. Set FACETDEV to ¹/₃₂″ to make curves appear very smooth.

3. Select the wall segment with the opening, right-click, and choose Sweeps ➤ Add. In the Add Sweep worksheet, set Wall Component to Cornice Molding, set Profile Definition to Start from Scratch, type **Cornice Profile** as the name, leave the other settings checked, and click OK.

TIP Polylines can be used to create profiles that can be swept. Draw a polyline, right-click, and choose Convert To ➤ Profile Definition. Profile definitions are editable in the Style Manager under Multi-Purpose Objects.

4. Zoom into the top edge at the end of the wall and click a point on the cornice molding near the corner. The In-Place Edit toolbar appears, and the profile is highlighted. Click the front edge grip, press Ctrl twice, and move the cursor away from the wall. Type **2″** and press Enter to give the front a bullnose edge.

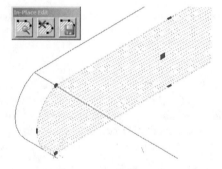

5. Continue adding and moving vertices in the profile as you see fit to define the cornice profile. Click the Save All Changes button in the In-Place Edit toolbar when done.

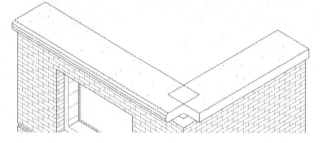

NOTE The profile you create is not scaled when it is swept along the wall; the profile's height and width are completely up to you and might exceed the boundary defined in the wall style.

6. The second wall segment does not have the sweep you applied previously (it would have if you selected both objects before adding the sweep). Instead, you'll add the profile you already defined to the other wall segment. Select the wall on the right. Right-click and choose Sweeps ➤ Add. In the Add Wall Sweep worksheet, choose Cornice Profile from the Profile Definition drop-down list and click OK. The sweep now appears on this wall.

7. Select both wall segments, right-click, and choose Sweeps ➤ Miter. They are joined as shown in Figure 8.44.

8. Close the file without saving.

One of the limitations that sweeps have is that they must follow the length of wall components. Consider the condition that occurs at an opening within a wall; sweeps cannot turn the corner into the opening because the component does not turn—it is interrupted instead. This can be a problem if you have molding that is mitered into an opening.

Using a structural member as a multinode beam that uses the profile definition of a molding is one creative solution to this problem. There are numerous examples where ADT users have created novel structures using AEC objects not as they were originally envisioned by the programmers. Don't let the fact that an object is called a structural member stop you from using it to build a lightweight molding; be creative with all the tools at your disposal.

FIGURE 8.44

Sweeping profile along Cornice Molding component

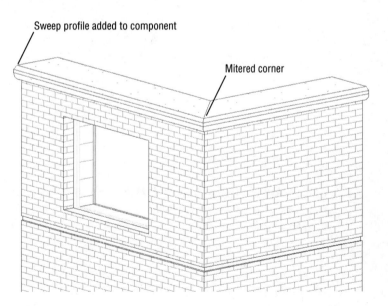

Sweep profile added to component

Mitered corner

Managing Interference Conditions

Walls can be assigned interference conditions just like Mass Elements interfering with Spaces (refer to Chapter 6, "Space Planning"). In addition, you can choose how you want to manage the condition: additive, subtractive, or ignore. The choice you make affects the way the Shrink Wrap display component appears in plan. Interference conditions affect all components that the interfering object touches.

1. Open the file `Interference.dwg` from the companion DVD. It contains a wall and column placed so they are overlapping.

2. Select the wall, right-click, and choose Interference Condition ➤ Add. Select the structural member and press Enter.

3. Right-click and choose Additive. Toggle LWT on in the application status bar so you can clearly see the Shrink Wrap component. In additive mode, the shrink wrap extends around the column. Select the wall and click the Interference worksheet in the Properties palette. Change the Shrinkwrap Effect to Subtract and click OK. Figure 8.45 shows what happens at an interference condition.

4. Move the column to a new position relative to the wall, but keep it overlapping. The shrink wrap immediately updates because the interference condition is maintained.

5. Switch into an isometric viewpoint and shaded mode. In 3D viewpoints, the interference condition always appears subtractive.

6. Leave the file open.

Assigning Material Surface Hatch Overrides

Materials control the surface hatching visible in wireframe and hidden line display modes (refer to Chapter 3). You can override any surface hatch origin point.

1. Zoom in on the brick pattern on the exterior face of the wall in an isometric viewpoint. Change to Hidden display mode. Depending upon where you placed the column in the last section, there might be less than a whole brick at the column interface. Select the wall, right-click, and choose Materials ➤ Add Surface Hatch Override. Select the face to override, as prompted. The Surface Hatch Override worksheet appears. Click the pick button adjacent to the X Offset and Y Offset text boxes. Click two points on the screen to set both offset values (see Figure 8.46) and then select OK.

FIGURE 8.45
Top, with no interference condition; middle, with an additive condition; bottom, with a subtractive condition

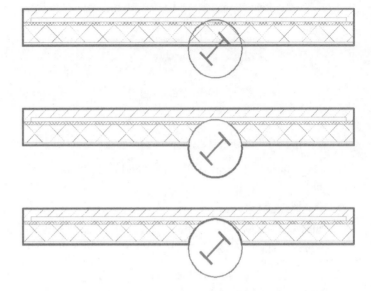

FIGURE 8.46
Applying a Surface Hatch Override

2. The surface pattern on the brick moves. Select the wall again, right-click, and choose Materials ➤ Edit Surface Hatch Override. You are brought into an In-Place Edit mode. Click the surface of the brick wall. Move the pattern again and click the Save All Changes button on the In-Place Edit toolbar.

3. If you want to change the surface hatch pattern globally instead of on a single object, you can edit the material. Select the wall, right-click, and choose Edit Wall Style. Click the Materials tab. Select the Brick component. Click the Edit Material button on the right edge of the Wall Style Properties dialog box. Double-click the currently overridden display rep (General Medium Detail) to open the Display Properties dialog box. Here is where you can edit the

display properties for the surface hatch component. You can change its pattern, scale, angle, orientation, rotation, and X and Y offsets.

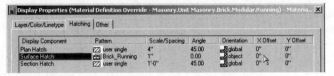

WARNING Changing display properties of a material affects all styles that reference it.

4. Cancel out of all dialog boxes and close all files. That's it!

Summary

This chapter covered everything you ever wanted to know about walls. Walls are one of the most complex objects for good reason—you work with walls every day, and the intelligent object standing in for them must be able to represent every conceivable situation. You studied wall components and learned how to lay out wall objects efficiently. You learned a few simple techniques that will allow you to clean up wall intersections perfectly when problems arise. Finally, you delved deeply into wall styles and hopefully kept your head above water when you learned the complexities of endcaps and all the ways you can alter wall form. The next chapter promises to be a bit lighter—you'll learn how to make holes in walls with openings, doors, and windows.

Chapter 9

Doors, Windows, and Openings

Doors, windows, and openings are related intelligent objects that I will refer to as *fenestrations*, a term whose etymology comes from the Latin *fenestra* (meaning "openings in wall"). Fenestrations are typically anchored to wall objects, although they can also exist in freestanding form. Wall objects automatically make appropriately shaped voids that perfectly fit any fenestration anchored to them.

Doors, windows, and openings have a lot in common, although there are many important differences between them that you'll learn in this chapter. You'll learn to create and edit these objects within walls. You'll edit object display and style and learn the intricacies of their display properties. Unlike most of the other chapters, you'll learn simply by experimenting in this chapter, rather than by building a project. In the end, you'll be able to create any custom fenestration you can imagine. After you master these objects, you'll design them into Door/Window Assemblies and Curtain Walls in Chapter 10, "Curtain Walls and Assemblies." This chapter's topics include the following:

- ◆ Creating Fenestrations
- ◆ Editing Fenestrations
- ◆ Editing Door and Window Styles
- ◆ Customizing Profiles
- ◆ Controlling Object Display
- ◆ Adding Display Blocks

Creating Fenestrations

Early in the design process, it helps to formulate spatial ideas by creating generic fenestrations. As you continue to think about the design, you will progressively refine ideas by editing and assigning styles to the generic objects. Although fenestrations can stand on their own, they are almost always anchored to walls, space boundaries, or door/window assembly grids.

Creating Generic Fenestrations from Scratch

Doors, windows, and opening objects share a common creation parameter called Position Along Wall—shown with a starburst icon in the Properties palette. This parameter has two choices: Offset/Center and Unconstrained. Unconstrained lets you place the object anywhere along the length of a wall. Offset/Center is a very handy setting that lets you quickly create a fenestration centered on a wall segment, or offset a given distance from either end of the wall or from other fenestrations. Let's anchor some generic fenestrations in a wall by using the Standard style.

1. Start a new blank drawing with the default template.

2. Select the Design palette and create a generic horizontal wall 20′ in length from left to right.

3. Click the Door tool. In the Properties palette, take a look at the Location subcategory. Set Position Along Wall to Unconstrained. Verify that Vertical Alignment is set to Threshold and that Threshold Height is zero, meaning the door will be placed at ground elevation. Set Measure To Inside Of Frame in the Dimensions subcategory, if it's not already selected (see Figure 9.1).

4. Select the wall and move the cursor around along the length of the wall. You can place it anywhere—but don't click yet. Move the cursor below and then above the wall; the ghosted door's swing flips sides. The position of the cursor determines the door's initial swing direction. With the cursor above the wall, type **1′-6″** to locate the door this distance from the start point of the wall by using the dynamic dimension. Press Enter to end the command. The door is automatically anchored to the wall.

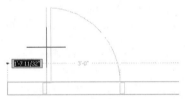

NOTE Doors typically are measured to inside of frame so that the door panel equals the Width parameter and the opening for the door frame exceeds that dimension. Windows are typically measured to the outside of frame so that the entire opening equals the Width parameter and the window frame fits inside.

FIGURE 9.1
Door Properties

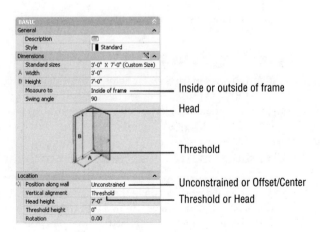

5. Click the Window tool. Set Position Along Wall to Offset/Center. Verify that Head is selected as the Vertical Alignment and set the Head Height to 7'-0" (see Figure 9.2). Set Measure To to Outside Of Frame, if it's not already selected.

6. Select the wall and move the cursor along the wall; the window magnetically stops in the center. Notice that the dynamic dimensions extend to the inside of the door frame, which is where you measured the door frame to previously. Click near the center to locate the window there. Press Enter or Esc to end the command.

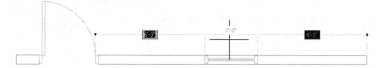

TIP   You can create freestanding fenestrations while using a door, window, or opening tool by pressing Enter instead of selecting a wall, space boundary, or assembly grid to anchor to.

7. Select the wall, right-click, and choose Insert ➢ Opening—this method of creating fenestrations is an alternative to using tools in the Tool palettes. Verify that Shape is set to Rectangular. Set the Width to **3'** and Height to **4'**. Set Position Along Wall to Offset/Center and type **6"** as the Automatic Offset value. Set Vertical Alignment to Sill and type **3'** as the Sill Height (see Figure 9.3).

NOTE   Openings can represent pass-through doors or windows, depending upon how large you make them. Set Sill Height to zero and Head Height to a typical door height to make a door-like pass-through opening.

FIGURE 9.2
Window Properties

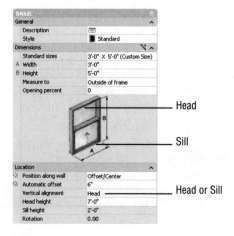

FIGURE 9.3
Opening Properties

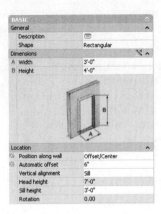

8. Select the wall and move the cursor between the door and window. There are three magnetic stops: 6″ from the right edge of the door, the center, and 6″ from the left edge of the window. Notice that the offset value isn't the focal dynamic dimension; click when the opening is 6″ from the left edge of the window.

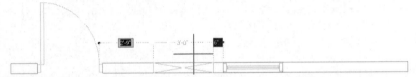

9. Save your work as **Fenestrations.dwg**. Leave the file open.

Assigning Preset Styles to Generic Doors and Windows

Numerous preset fenestration styles are part of ADT. Many are accessible from the Doors and Windows palettes, but the real storehouse is in the Content Browser. You can assign any of these styles to generic door and window objects. Openings do not have styles because they are merely voids in the substance of a wall, space boundary, or door/window assembly grid.

You can convert object types between doors, windows, openings, and door/window assemblies by applying tool properties of your chosen object to an object of another type. The resulting object takes the shape of its previous incarnation. This almost mystical feature is new in ADT 2006, and is very convenient—saving you from having to erase and re-create the shape of the fenestration.

1. Open the file Fenestrations.dwg from your hard drive or from the Chapter 9 folder on the companion DVD, if it's not already open. Switch into an isometric viewpoint and shaded display mode. Generic objects appear in gray because all their components are assigned the Standard material. Openings always cut through all the components of the wall they are anchored to. Notice the line at the center of the opening (blue on screen); this is how you can select it in the Model representation (see Figure 9.4).

2. Select the Doors tool palette. Right-click the Hinged - Single - Full Lite tool and choose Apply Tool Properties To ➤ Door. Click the generic door and press Enter. Check the Properties palette and verify that the Hinged - Single - Full Lite style was loaded and assigned to the generic object in this step. Press Esc to deselect.

FIGURE 9.4
Generic objects have
gray appearance

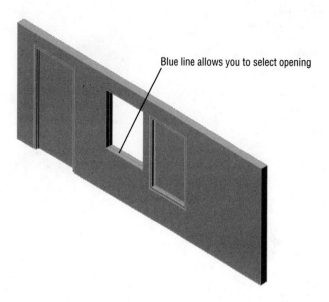

Blue line allows you to select opening

NOTE "Lite" is a term referring to the glazing inside a door. A "sidelite" is glazing immediately adjacent to a door, most often represented by door/window assemblies (see Chapter 10).

3. Open the Content Browser by clicking its button on the Navigation toolbar. Open the Design Tool catalog and navigate to Doors and Windows ➤ Windows. Advance to Page 2 and locate the Bay Window Set tool. Drag its i-drop icon into the ADT drawing window to load its style. Press Esc to cancel the WindowAdd command. The style has been loaded into the drawing. Close the Content Browser.

Design Tool Catalog - Imperial
Catalog Top < Doors and Windows < Windows

Page (2 of 8) 1 2 3 4 5 6 7 8

Bay
Bay Window Set

4. Select the generic window object. In the Properties palettes, change Style to Bay. The generic objects transforms into a styled one (see Figure 9.5). Don't worry about the gap that appears between the top of the bay "roof" and the wall; this is an interesting example of a "roof" defined within a window style.

5. Click on the Doors palette. Right-click the Cased Opening tool and choose Apply Tool Properties to ➤ Door. Click the styled door object in the drawing window and press Enter. It appears as a framed opening, but notice that it is identified as a Door in the Properties palette. The "cased opening" is not truly an opening—it is actually a pass-through door!

FIGURE 9.5
Styled doors and
windows show
materials

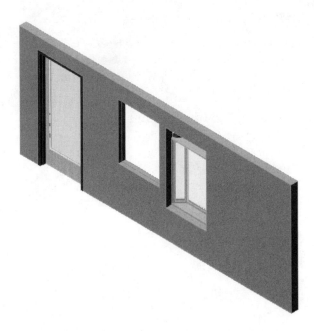

6. Click the Style drop-down list in the Properties palette. The Hinged - Single - Full Lite style is still available, even if it is not currently assigned to any objects in the drawing. Any styles you import through tool palettes or from the Content Browser become part of the current drawing. Press Esc.

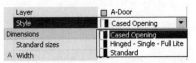

TIP To make your drawing files smaller, purge unused styles in the Style Manager.

7. Right-click the Cased Opening tool in the Doors palette and choose Apply Tool Properties to ➢ Door/Window Assembly, Opening, Window. Select the opening object and press Enter; it converts to a cased opening with casing showing up on three edges but not the bottom edge (it is a door, after all). You would be better off using a pass-through window that has casing on the bottom edge.

8. Select the Design palette. Right-click the Opening tool and choose Apply Tool Properties To ➢ Door, Door/Window Assembly, Window. Select the original door object and press Enter. The casing disappears as the object is converted to an opening.

9. Close the file without saving.

Editing Fenestrations

In this section you'll learn how to change the shape of openings to any of a large number of preset forms. The shapes of doors and windows are controlled by their styles, which are covered in the next section. In addition, you'll learn tricks for manipulating anchored objects, learn how to reposition fenestration relative to their container, and learn how to edit and flip fenestration using grips.

Changing Opening Shapes

Openings lack style, so they are controlled entirely at the object level. There are 13 different preset shapes for openings. Four of these shapes have an additional parameter called Rise, which can be used to further tweak the opening shape parametrically. In addition, it is possible to create a custom profile and assign it to an opening—you'll learn how to do that later in the "Customizing Profiles" section.

1. Start a new blank drawing with the default template.

2. Create a generic wall and insert an opening.

3. Select the opening and click its Shape parameter. A long list of preset shapes appears in the drop-down list. Select Round.

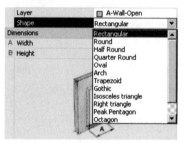

4. Create additional openings and try out a few of the other opening shapes (see Figure 9.6).

5. Change one of the opening's shapes to Arch. Notice that an additional parameter, Rise, appears in the Properties palette. Change the value of the opening's Width to 4' and then set Rise to 2', making a Roman arch. The Rise value cannot exceed half the Width of an opening.

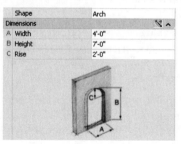

NOTE The Gothic, Arch, Trapezoid, and Peak Pentagon preset shapes have a Rise parameter. Rise is measured from the top of the rectangular portion of an opening to its peak.

6. Close the file without saving.

FIGURE 9.6
Opening Shapes

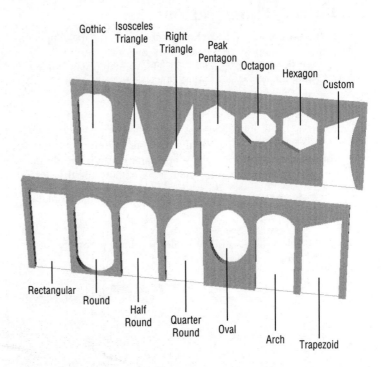

Manipulating Anchored Objects

Anchored fenestrations are manipulated differently from normal objects. On the most basic level, a fenestration cannot move freely in space when it is anchored. Instead, it can normally be moved only along the length of its container. However, you'll learn a few special commands that let you reposition fenestrations both along and within their containers, allowing greater freedom of movement. In addition, you'll pick up a few tips on selecting styled objects.

SELECTING STYLED OBJECTS

In addition to clicking, and making enclosing and crossing windows to select objects, there are several tips I want to share with you that make selecting styled objects far easier in complex drawings.

In no particular order, here are a few selection features that are worth understanding not just for fenestrations, but for all objects:

PICKADD is a system variable that has two possible values: 0 and 1 turn it off and on, respectively. When off, the most recently selected objects replace the previous selection set. When on, the most recently selected objects are added to the selection set.

Add Selected is an option in every object shortcut menu. When chosen, this command adds a new object identical to the selected one (matching in style and all other properties). This is great when you want to add another one of "those" doors, but don't want to bother with the entire sequence of steps: selecting the existing door, determining what style it is, clicking the generic door tool, assigning the style you determined earlier, and finally creating the door.

Select Similar selects all objects sharing the same type and style. This is helpful when you want to change a parameter that all objects sharing the same style have in common.

Quick Select is another way to select objects. You can select all objects of a specific type, or use more complicated criteria with this powerful command.

Here's some practice with these selection methods:

1. Open the file Selecting.dwg from the companion DVD.

2. Click the PickAdd button at the top of the Properties palette. It changes to a 1 icon (paradoxically changing PICKADD to zero). Click the wall object with the fenestrations to select it.

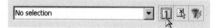

3. Click one of the door objects to select it. Notice that the wall was automatically deselected. Select the window; again the previous selection set (the door) was deselected. This mode is handy when you want to adjust the properties of one object at a time. Press Esc to deselect.

4. Click the PickAdd button again to toggle it. The button looks like two objects connected with a plus symbol (setting PICKADD to 1). Select one door object.

5. Select another door object. Both objects are now selected, so you can edit their shared properties. This mode is most useful when you want to alter the properties of more than one object at a time. This is the normal selection behavior. Press Esc.

6. Select the window object, right-click, and choose Add Selected. Add the window to the center of the wall on the right. The new window on the right matches the style of the original window on the top (Glider).

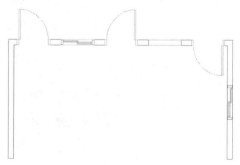

7. Select the door object on the upper-left, right-click, and choose Select Similar. The door on the right is selected, but not the door in the middle. Only doors sharing the same style (in this case Hinged - Single) are selected. Press Esc.

8. Click the Quick Select button at the top-right corner of the Properties palette; the Quick Select dialog box appears. Change Object Type to Doors and click OK. All three door objects are selected. Press Esc.

9. Click Quick Select again. Change Object Type to Opening. In the Properties list, scroll down and click Height: only the properties for openings appear in the list. Leave Operator set to Equals and type a Value of **3′**. (See Figure 9.7.) Click OK; a previously hidden opening meeting the criteria appears. Press Esc.

NOTE Fenestrations above the cut plane do not appear by default in plan. You'll learn to override this behavior later in the "Controlling Object Display" section of this chapter.

10. Leave the file open.

FIGURE 9.7
Quick Select

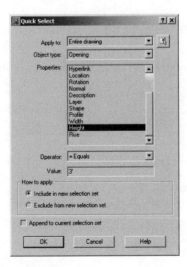

EDITING ANCHORS

ADT automatically assigns anchors to fenestrations when you place them within walls, space boundaries, and door/window assembly grids. You can edit these anchors by using the object shortcut menu and/or the Properties palette.

1. Select the middle door, right-click, and choose Wall Anchor ➤ Set Wall. Click the concrete masonry unit (CMU) wall above. At the location you click, the door appears. The door's anchor was transferred from the generic wall to the CMU wall.

2. Select the door in the CMU wall, right-click and choose Wall Anchor ➤ Flip X: the hinge is flipped to the other jamb. Right-click again and choose Wall Anchor ➤ Flip Y: the swing is flipped to the other side of the wall. Choose Wall Anchor ➤ Release: the door becomes freestanding and its rough opening no longer penetrates the wall.

3. Click the Undo button to reanchor the door to the wall.

4. Select the same door and click the Anchor worksheet icon in the Properties palette. The anchor has three axes of control: Position Along (X), Position Within (Y), and Position Vertical (Z). The Anchor worksheet provides the greatest control of anchoring details, including the ability to change the distances in all three axes, orientation controls, and flip check boxes (see Figure 9.8).

5. In the Position Within (Y) group, change the To drop-down to Back of Object and type **6″** in its Distance text box. Click OK and observe the door move relative to the transverse dimension (width) of the wall. The center of the door is 6″ from the interior (back) side of the wall.

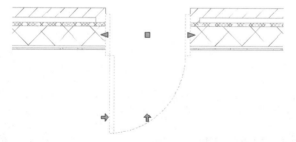

NOTE   You'll learn how to adjust the door frame dimensions in the section "Editing Door and Window Styles."

6. Leave the file open.

FIGURE 9.8

Adjusting the Anchor

Anchor ? ✕

Change the position of this door relative to the wall it is anchored to:

Position Along (X)
From: Start of wall
Distance: 8'-1 9/16"
To: Center of object

Position Vertical (Z)
From: Bottom of wall height
Distance: 0"
To: Threshold of object

Position Within (Y)
From: Center of wall width
Distance: 6"
To: Back of object

Orientation
X Rotation: 0.00
Z Rotation: 0.00
☐ Flip X ☑ Flip Y ☐ Flip Z

OK   Cancel   Help

REPOSITIONING FENESTRATION

If the Anchor worksheet seems overly intimidating with all its controls, there are two commands you'll like that are easier to understand: Reposition Along Wall and Reposition Within Wall. These tools move the fenestration's anchor in the Position Along (X) and Position Within (Y) directions, respectively to their container.

1. Select the door in the CMU wall, right-click, and select Reposition Within Wall. Move the cursor over the door and observe there are three red lines that appear as you move the cursor over the top, center, and bottom edges of the door.

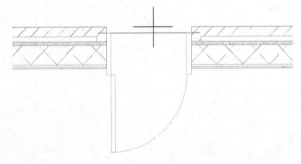

2. Click when the cursor highlights the red edge closest to the exterior face of the wall. The command line reads as follows:

```
Select a reference point:
```

Click the top-left corner of the opening the door is making in the wall.

3. Type **8″** and press Enter to set the distance between the edge you selected in step 1 and the point you clicked previously. There is now a gap of 8″ between the exterior face of the wall and the edge of the door frame.

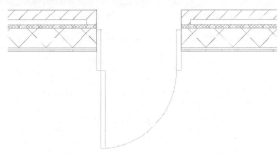

4. Draw a vertical construction line some arbitrary distance to the right of the door you have been working with.

5. Select the door, right-click, and choose Reposition Along Wall. Move your cursor over the door and again notice that there are three red edges that highlight as you pass over the door: left, center, and right. Click when the right edge highlights.

6. Shift+right-click and choose Perpendicular. Click the construction line to select the reference point (see Figure 9.9). The command line reads as follows:

```
Enter the new distance between the selected points <8">:
```

Type **0** and press Enter so there is no gap between the position on the opening and the reference point. The door jumps over so its right edge is flush with the construction line.

TIP You can also reposition fenestration using grips (see the next section).

FIGURE 9.9
Repositioning
fenestration along
a wall

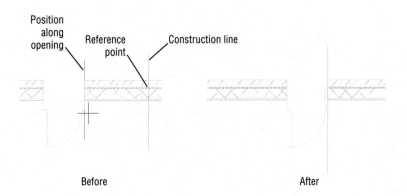

Before   After

Editing with Grips

Grips allow more visual and intuitive editing than other methods that offer similar functionality. Fenestration objects share similar grips. Let's take a look at a window object to understand which grips are available in a typical fenestration.

1. Create a new blank drawing with the default template.

2. Select the Windows palette and click the Glider tool. Press Enter to create a freestanding window and then locate Standard Sizes in the Properties palette. Choose 5'-0" X 5'-0" from the Standard Sizes drop-down list. Notice the extensive list of sizes.

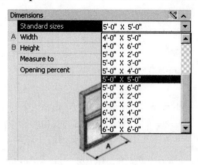

NOTE   Door and window objects come in standard sizes just like real manufacturer's offerings. You can create a custom sized window object by entering values in the Width and Height parameters.

3. Click a point in the drawing window to locate the window; then press Enter twice to orient the object and end the command. Switch to an isometric viewpoint and shaded display mode. Select the window and hover the cursor over each grip (see Figure 9.10).

4. Click the Width grip on the right; a series of marks appears. All the marks represent standard sizes, and you can click any mark to instantly resize the width to a standard size. The long gray marks indicate a standard width where the current height is also standard. Short red marks show standard widths where the current height is non-standard (see Figure 9.11). If you press Ctrl in this mode, you switch to non-standard mode and the marks disappear. Click the second red mark from the left to resize the width to this standard size.

5. Click the Height grip; a new series of marks appear. In a similar fashion, these grips indicate standard heights. Long gray marks reveal the standard sizes that are available for the given Width (see Figure 9.11). Click the second long gray mark. The window ends up being 3' square in the Properties palette—still a standard size.

FIGURE 9.10
Fenestration grips

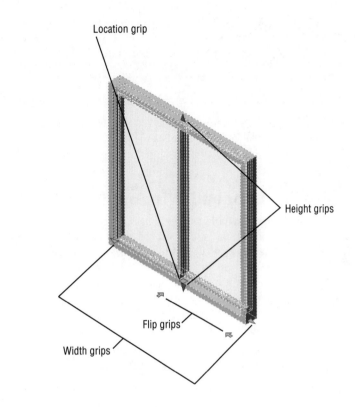

FIGURE 9.11
Using marks to snap to
standard sizes

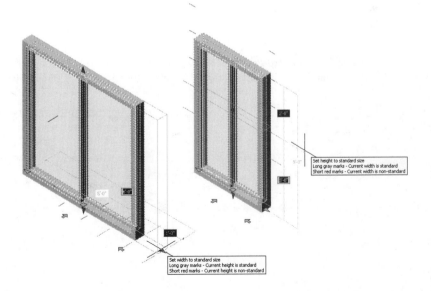

6. Click the right Width grip again. Press the Ctrl key once; the marks disappear. Move the cursor a short distance to the right and click to set a custom width. The Properties palette reveals that this is a (Custom Size) in the Standard Sizes parameter.

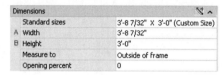

7. Close the file without saving.

Editing Door and Window Styles

Editing door and window styles is the key to controlling fenestration forms both in 2D and 3D. The Style Properties dialog boxes for these objects have the same tabs and offer similar functionality. The Dimensions tabs contain illustrations that control all the relevant parameters that can be set for doors and windows. Remember, openings do not have styles and are therefore controlled entirely by their object-level properties.

1. Start a new blank drawing with the default template.

2. Draw a generic horizontal wall 10′ in length.

3. Select the Doors palette. Click the Hinged - Single - Exterior tool and anchor a door in the wall. Select the Windows palette. Click the Glider tool and anchor a window in the wall.

4. Select the door, right-click, and choose Edit Door Style. Click the Dimensions tab of the Style Properties dialog box (see Figure 9.12). Study the illustration: Notice the blowup of the stop and the corresponding labeled parameters. Parameters A–E can be set here, F, G, H, and J are set in the Standard Sizes tab. Note also the unlabeled Glass Thickness parameter that applies only when there is glazing in the door panel. Press Esc.

NOTE The door stop is visible in Model and Elevation but turned off in all Plan representations by default. You'll learn how to change this in the "Controlling Object Display" section.

FIGURE 9.12
Door style
Dimensions tab

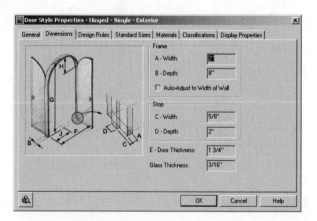

5. Select the window, right-click, and choose Edit Window Style. Click the Dimensions tab (see Figure 9.13). Again, study the illustration: parameters A–E can be set here, but parameters F–H are set in the Standard Sizes tab. Press Esc. Parameters set in the Dimensions tab of the Style Properties dialog box are common to all objects sharing the style. Parameters in the Properties palette are specific to the object.

There are two "design rules" for fenestrations: shape and type. The Design Rules tab is where you set the rules you want to use for each style. You already explored shape through opening objects (refer to the previous section "Changing Opening Shapes"). The shapes available for doors and windows are a subset of what is available for openings. Doors and windows each have their own lists of types to choose from in the Design Rules tab.

1. Create a freestanding Hinged - Single - Exterior door.

2. Select this door, right-click, and choose Edit Door Style. Click the Design Rules tab.

3. Click the Predefined shape drop-down list. You will recognize the available shapes from studying openings: choose Arch (see Figure 9.14).

FIGURE 9.13
Window style
dimensions

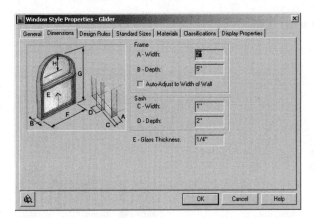

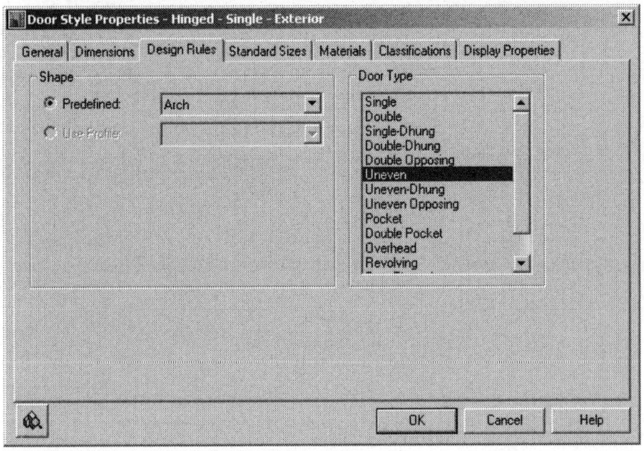

FIGURE 9.14
Door style Design
Rules tab

4. In the Door Type group, choose Uneven and click OK. Figure 9.15 shows all the rectangular shaped door types. The abbreviation *Dhung* stands for double-hung, meaning doors that can pivot 180 degrees on their hinges. Dhung doors do not have stops in their frames. The Pass Through type is what creates a cased opening. Uneven doors have two panels with uneven sizes. The *leaf* parameter measures the size of the uneven second panel in Uneven, Uneven-Dhung, and Uneven Opposing door types.

5. You'll see a message appear: Invalid standard sizes were automatically adjusted. Click OK.

6. Reselect the door, right-click and choose Edit Door Style from the shortcut menu. Click the Standard Sizes tab. Here you'll find a spreadsheet-like interface in which standard sizes for this type of door are entered (see Figure 9.16).

FIGURE 9.15
Door types

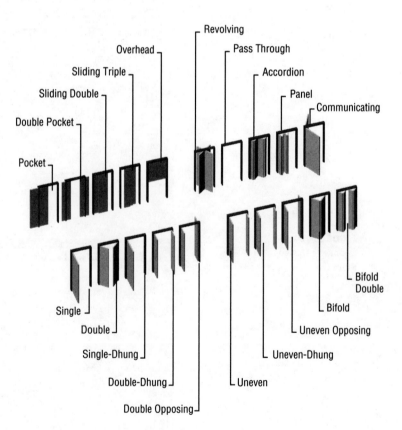

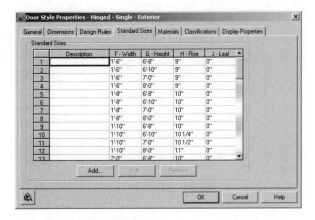

FIGURE 9.16

Door style Standard Sizes tab

7. Scroll down to the bottom of the Standard Sizes list. Select the spreadsheet cell in the J-Leaf column for item number 49. Click the Edit button. Type **1'-6"** in the Leaf text box and click OK.

8. Double-click the Description cell for the item you edited previously. Type **Preferred** in the Description text box and click OK. Click OK to close the Style Properties dialog box.

9. Switch to the NE Isometric viewpoint and Hidden line display mode. Select the door and locate the Standard Size parameter in the Properties palette. Click its drop-down list and select **4'-0" X 6'-8" Rise: 10" Leaf 1'-6"**. You have Rise and Leaf Width parameters because they are called for by the shape and type chosen by this style's design rules. Press Esc.

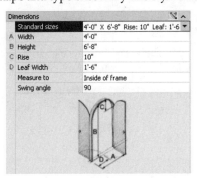

FIGURE 9.17
Window types

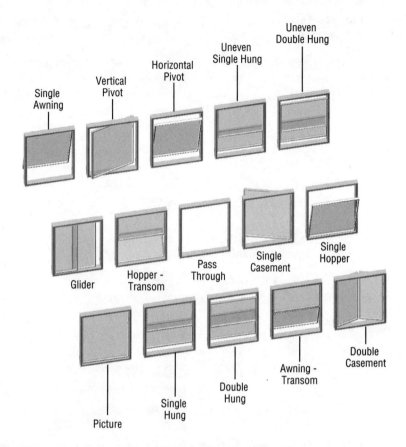

Windows also have a set of unique types governed by design rules. Windows function exactly like doors in this regard. Figure 9.17 shows rectangular shaped windows of every available type. They are shown slightly open for clarity.

TIP   Try using the Edit In Section command (refer to Chapter 2, "Object Display") when designing windows; it helps to see the frame in this way.

Customizing Profiles

For the ultimate in control, you can customize the elevation profiles of openings, doors, and windows. Start from scratch by defining a profile or tweak an existing profile by editing it in place.

1. Open `Profiles.dwg` from the Chapter 9 folder on the companion DVD (Figure 9.18). It contains a generic wall, glider window, full lite door, and a polyline drawn in plan.

FIGURE 9.18
The DVD file Profiles.dwg provides some generic contents to work with.

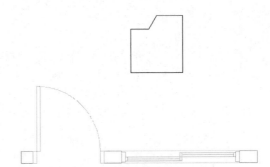

2. Select the polyline, right-click, and choose Convert To ➤ Profile Definition. The command line reads as follows:

   ```
   Insertion point or [Add ring/Centroid]:
   ```

   Press C for *centroid* (center of profile area) and then press Enter.

3. Press Enter again to accept the default and create a new profile. Type **Angled Step** in the New Profile Definition worksheet and click OK. Delete the polyline now that it is a profile definition.

4. Switch into an isometric viewpoint and hidden line display mode. Select the window, right-click, and choose Add Profile. Change Profile Definition to Angled Step in the Add Window Profile worksheet and click OK. The window assumes the new profile.

5. You can edit the shape of any fenestration in place that is based on a custom profile. Select the door, right-click, and choose Edit Door Style. Click the Design Rules tab. Note that the shape is based on a profile called Hinged - Single - Full Lite. Click Cancel.

6. Select the door, right-click, and choose Edit Profile In Place. Click Yes in the small dialog box that appears, warning you that the profile will be scaled to actual size. Click the lower-edge grip of the lite area. Move the cursor upward, type **2′**, and press Enter (see Figure 9.19). Click the Save All Changes button on the In Place Edit toolbar.

WARNING   You can edit a fenestration's profile in place only after a profile has been added to the style. Preset shapes cannot be edited.

FIGURE 9.19
Editing a door
profile in place

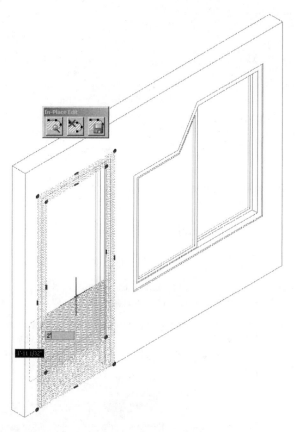

 It is possible to create profiles that have multiple rings inside them and then use them to shape fenestrations.

1. Open ProfileRings.dwg from the companion DVD. This file contains a concrete wall and three polylines.

2. Select one of the three polylines, right-click, and choose Convert To ➢ Profile Definition. The command line again reads as follows:

```
Insertion point or [Add ring/Centroid]:
```

Press A to add another ring and press Enter; click the second polyline. Press A↵ again and click the last polyline. Press C↵ to set the insertion point at the centroid of all three rings. Type **Tree** in the New Profile Definition dialog box. Delete the polylines.

3. Click the Opening tool on the Design palette. In the Properties palette, set Shape to Custom, Profile to Tree, Width to 3′, Height to 3′, Position Along Wall to Offset/Center, Automatic Offset to 1′, Vertical Alignment to Sill, and Sill Height to 4′.

4. Add three adjacent custom profile openings to the concrete wall. Curvilinear voids open up in the concrete.

5. Your imagination is the only limit to what you can do with fenestrations. Select the Windows palette. Right-click the Picture tool and choose Apply Tool Properties To ➢ Door, Door/Window Assembly, Opening. Select all three openings and press Enter.

6. Select one of the picture windows, right-click, and choose Edit Window Style. Click the Dimensions tab, change A - Width to **1″,** and B - Depth parameter to **2″.** Click the Design Rules tab. In the Shape group, click the Use Profile radio button and select Tree from the drop-down list. Click OK. All three windows appear, using your custom profile (see Figure 9.20).

TIP You can use Style Manager to add voids inside profiles; this is how you make lites inside door panels (see the ADT Help).

Controlling Object Display

Fenestration objects have display components that are controlled at the drawing default, style, and object levels (refer to Chapter 3, "Object Styles"). Understanding these components is the key to being able to successfully show fenestrations the way you intend.

FIGURE 9.20
Custom-profiled
windows

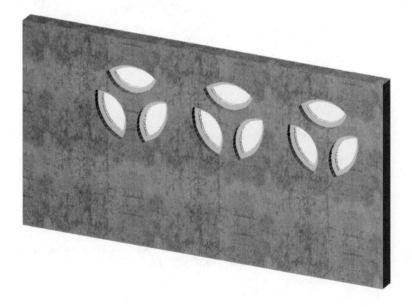

Overriding the Wall Opening Endcap Style with Fenestrations

In Chapter 8, "Walls," you learned how to define endcaps and opening endcap styles and assign them to the ends of the wall. In addition, you learned how to assign opening endcaps to fenestration objects that appear as openings within a wall. In this chapter you will learn to override these definitions using an object property belonging to fenestrations.

1. Open OpeningEndcap.dwg from the companion DVD. This file contains a two-layer gypsum board wall and an opening fenestration. The gypsum board does not wrap into the opening.

2. Let's start by investigating the wall. Select the wall, right-click, and choose Edit Wall Style from the shortcut menu. Click the Endcaps/Opening Endcaps tab. An endcap style is assigned to the wall and an opening endcap style is assigned to Door/Window Assembly objects. Note that the Standard opening endcap style is assigned to Opening objects (see Figure 9.21). You could cause the gypsum board to wrap around Opening objects by assigning them an opening endcap style, but that would affect all objects of this style. Click Cancel.

3. A more specific approach is to override the opening endcap style in the fenestration object itself instead of in the wall style. Select the Opening object. Locate the Endcaps subcategory at the bottom of the Properties palette. Click the Opening Endcap drop-down list and select Stud-4 GWB-0.625 2 Layers Each Side (End 1)(2-Sided). This is the same wall opening endcap style you saw assigned to Door/Window Assemblies previously.

WARNING   You cannot override an opening endcap style in fenestration objects unless the style is already defined in the drawing.

4. Take a look at the condition at the opening: Gypsum board wraps into the opening because you overrode the opening endcap style at the object level.

5. Close the file without saving.

TIP   Change to the High Detail display configuration and then choose View ➤ Regen Model and press Enter to see opening endcaps in 3D viewpoints.

FIGURE 9.21
Wall opening endcap
style assignments

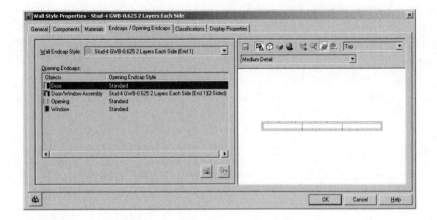

FIGURE 9.21
Wall opening endcap
style assignments

Understanding Display Properties

In Chapter 2 you learned how object display is controlled ultimately through components in display representations. Representations are organized into sets, and sets into configurations. Figure 9.22 shows object display matrices for each fenestration object accessible in the Display Manager. Studying these matrices reveals which display representations are being used in each set (that is, the Plan and Threshold Plan reps are both used in the door's Plan set).

This section summarizes the most important fenestration display components in several categories of representation: elevation and model, plan, plus threshold and sill plan.

ELEVATION AND MODEL DISPLAY REPRESENTATIONS

Elevation and model display representations have many of the same components. Figure 9.23 shows these components for fenestrations.

Let's explore some of these display components with a sample file.

1. Open DisplayComponents.dwg from the companion DVD. The file opens in an isometric viewpoint.

2. Select the door object, right-click, and choose Edit Door Style from the shortcut menu. Click the Display Properties tab.

3. Place a check in the Style Override column for the Model display representation (shown in bold because it is current). The Display Properties dialog box appears; click the Other tab.

4. Notice that by default, Override Open Percent is checked and uses a value of zero (meaning that the door is shut). Uncheck Override Open Percent. Click OK to close each open dialog box. The door opens.

FIGURE 9.22
Fenestration object display matrices: top, for a door object; center, for an opening object; bottom, for a window object

	Sets												
Display Representations	Model	Model High Detail	Model Low Detail	Model Presentation	**Plan**	Plan Diagnostic	Plan High Detail	Plan Low Detail	Plan Presentation	Plan Screened	Reflected	Reflected Screened	Section_Elev
Elevation													✓
Model	✓												
Model High Detail		✓		✓									
Model Low Detail			✓										
Nominal						✓							
Plan					✓				✓				
Plan High Detail							✓						
Plan Low Detail								✓					
Plan Screened										✓			
Reflected											✓		
Reflected Screened												✓	
Threshold Plan					✓		✓		✓				
Threshold Plan Screened										✓			
Threshold Symbol Plan													

	Sets												
Display Representations	Model	Model High Detail	Model Low Detail	Model Presentation	**Plan**	Plan Diagnostic	Plan High Detail	Plan Low Detail	Plan Presentation	Plan Screened	Reflected	Reflected Screened	Section_Elev
Model	✓	✓	✓	✓									✓
Plan					✓				✓				
Plan High Detail						✓	✓						
Plan Low Detail								✓					
Plan Screened										✓			
Reflected											✓		
Reflected Screened												✓	
Sill Plan					✓		✓		✓				
Sill Plan Screened										✓			

	Sets												
Display Representations	Model	Model High Detail	Model Low Detail	Model Presentation	**Plan**	Plan Diagnostic	Plan High Detail	Plan Low Detail	Plan Presentation	Plan Screened	Reflected	Reflected Screened	Section_Elev
Elevation													✓
Model	✓												
Model High Detail		✓		✓									
Model Low Detail			✓										
Nominal						✓		✓					
Plan					✓				✓				
Plan High Detail							✓						
Plan Low Detail													
Plan Screened										✓			
Reflected											✓		
Reflected Screened												✓	
Sill Plan					✓		✓		✓				
Sill Plan Screened										✓			

FIGURE 9.23
Fenestration display
components in
(top) Model and
(bottom) Elevation
representations

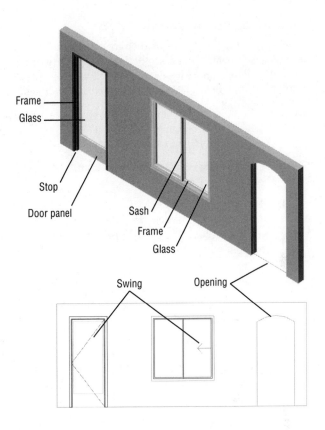

5. Select the door and look at the Properties palette; the Swing Angle parameter shows 90 degrees in the Dimensions subcategory. Quite confusingly, the object properties use degrees and the style uses a percentage. Change Swing Angle to 45. The door opens halfway.

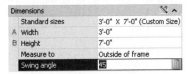

6. Switch to the Front viewpoint. In the Medium Detail configuration, this viewpoint triggers the Section_Elev set and through it, the Elevation display representations for door and window objects.

7. Select the door again and edit its style. Create a style override for the Elevation representation. In the Display Properties dialog box, click the Other tab. Check Reverse Chevrons. Notice that each representations stores different display properties, and many have unique options. Click OK in both open dialog boxes. The door swing reverses direction. Leave the file open.

PLAN DISPLAY REPRESENTATIONS

Fenestrations have numerous display components in their several plan display representations. Figure 9.24 reveals these components and illustrates some of the available options.

As you know, openings do not have styles. The display properties of openings must therefore be edited at the object level. You'll edit doors and windows at their style levels, although object overrides are also possible.

1. Switch to the Top viewpoint and 2D Wireframe display mode. Change the current display configuration to High Detail.

2. Select the opening object, right-click, and choose Edit Object Display. In the Object Display dialog box, click the Display Properties tab.

3. Place a check in the Object Override column for the Plan High Detail display representation. The Display Properties dialog box appears. Click the Layer/Color/Linetype tab if it's not already selected. Toggle the visibility of all five display components on. Change the Hatch component to color 255 (light gray).

Display Component	Visible	By Material	Layer	Color	Linetype	Lineweight	Lt Scale	Plot Style
Length Lines			0	■ BYBLOCK	HIDDEN2	ByBlock	1.0000	ByBlock
Width Lines			0	■ BYBLOCK	HIDDEN2	ByBlock	1.0000	ByBlock
Cross Line A			0	■ BYBLOCK	HIDDEN2	ByBlock	1.0000	ByBlock
Cross Line B			0	■ BYBLOCK	HIDDEN2	ByBlock	1.0000	ByBlock
Hatch			0	□ 255	ByBlock	0.18 mm	1.0000	Fine

4. Click the Hatching tab; note that the Hatch component will be filled with a solid hatch pattern (you can optionally change the pattern). Click the Fill Type tab. Cycle through the five radio buttons in the Hatch Type group to see the effect of each; choose Cross A. Click OK in both open dialog boxes. The opening appears as shown in Figure 9.24.

5. Select the window object, right-click, and choose Edit Window Style from the shortcut menu. Make a style override for the Plan High Detail display representation. In the Display Properties dialog box, click the Frame Display tab. Type **2"** in the A - Extension field. Click OK in both open dialog boxes. The window frames are offset inward, as shown in Figure 9.24. This kind of offset is entirely optional and can help make windows more readable in plan by disengaging them from the wall. Be aware that the offset makes the windows appear smaller than their Width parameter actually reads.

FIGURE 9.24

Plan display components for (left) door, (middle) window, and (right) opening fenestrations

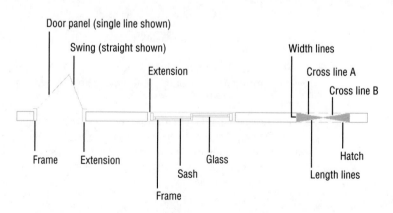

6. Click the Undo button. Select the door object, right-click and choose Edit Door Style from the shortcut menu. In the Door Style Properties dialog box, click the Display Properties tab. Make a style override for the Plan High Detail display representation. In the Display Properties dialog box, click the Other tab. Check both Straight Swing and Draw Panel As A Single Line. Click the Frame Display tab. Cycle through all three radio buttons in the Type group: choose L-Shaped. Type **2″** in the B - Extension text box. Click OK in both open dialog boxes. The door appears as shown in Figure 9.24.

In Chapter 2 you learned that the global cut plane level is set in the current display configuration. In Chapter 8 you learned how to override the global cut plane in the display properties of wall objects. In this chapter we are examining the last level of the cut plane hierarchy—at the level of anchored objects. Fenestration objects respect the cut plane of their container by default; let's see how we can override this using display properties, and learn why this is important.

1. Select the window object. In the Properties palette, change the Standard Sizes drop-down list to 5′-0″ X 2′-0″. The window disappears from the plan! The reason you can no longer see the window is because now that it is smaller, its sill height is above the cut plane (the default is 3′-6″ as defined in the High Detail display configuration).

TIP   Use Quick Select to select windows that you cannot see in plan.

2. Right-click and choose Edit Window Style. Make a style override for the Plan High Detail display representation.

3. In the Display Properties dialog box, click the Other tab. Uncheck Respect Cut Plane Of Container Object When Anchored. Click OK in both open dialog boxes. The window reappears— this is how you can force the display of clerestory windows in plan.

4. Close the file without saving.

THRESHOLD, SYMBOL, AND SILL PLAN DISPLAY REPRESENTATIONS

You may remember from studying Figure 9.1 that by default, doors and windows use Threshold Plan and Sill Plan display representations in plan. Displaying these representations' components is optional—they allow you to show thresholds and sills on either side of a wall. Figure 9.25 shows the display components for these representations.

Let's explore these display components with a sample file.

1. Open `ThresholdSill.dwg` from the companion DVD.

2. Threshold B is currently displayed for the door object. Let's turn on Threshold A and adjust its design rules. Select the door, right-click, and choose Edit Door Style from the shortcut menu. Click the Display Properties tab of the Door Style Properties dialog box. Notice that the Threshold Plan representation already has a style override, which is why Threshold A is visible. Double-click Threshold Plan's icon; the Display Properties dialog box appears. Click the Layer/Color/Linetype tab and toggle the visibility of the Threshold A component on.

3. Click the Other tab of the Display Properties dialog box. Type **1″** for A - Extension and **4″** for B - Depth (see Figure 9.26). Click OK in both open dialog boxes. Threshold A appears with the extension and depth as shown in Figure 9.25.

FIGURE 9.25
Threshold, symbol,
and sill plan

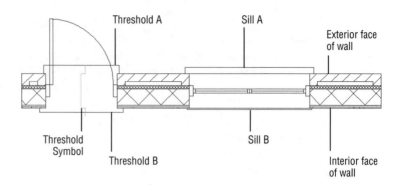

FIGURE 9.26
Other tab of Threshold
Plan Display Properties

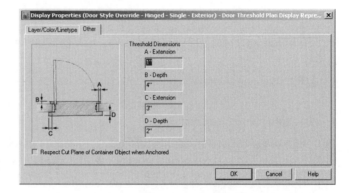

4. Select the window, right-click, and choose Edit Window Style from the shortcut menu. Click the Display Properties tab of the Window Style Properties dialog box. Place a check in the Style Override column for the Sill Plan representation; the Display Properties dialog box appears. Click the Layer/Color/Linetype tab and note that both Sill A and Sill B are visible by default. You have the option to turn one on and not the other.

5. Click the Other tab of the Display Properties dialog box. Type **2"** for A - Extension, **3"** for B - Depth, **1"** for C - Extension, and ¹/₂" for D - Depth (see Figure 9.27). Click OK in both open dialog boxes. The sills appear with the extensions and depths as shown in Figure 9.25.

TIP Hide the wall's cut plane lines below the opening on the Other tab of its display properties.

6. Select the door, right-click, and choose Edit Door Style from the shortcut menu. Click the Display Properties tab of the Door Style Properties dialog box. Place a check in the Style Override column for the Threshold Symbol Plan representation; the Display Properties dialog box appears. Click the Layer/Color/Linetype tab and toggle the visibility of the Threshold Symbol display component on.

7. Click the Other tab of the Display Properties dialog box. Cycle through each radio button in the Symbol group (Heel, Threshold, Pass Through, and No Symbol). Choose Threshold and click OK in both open dialog boxes.

FIGURE 9.27
Other tab of Sill Plan
Display Properties

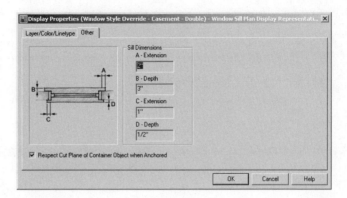

FIGURE 9.27
Other tab of Sill Plan
Display Properties

8. Choose Format ➢ Display Manager. Expand the Configurations and Medium Detail and click on the Plan node. Click the Display Representation Control tab in the content pane; the object matrix appears. Click the Door object to highlight its row. Scroll over and place a check in the Threshold Symbol Plan column. Click OK to close the Display Manager. Choose View ➢ Regen Model and select the door. Press Enter, and the threshold symbol finally appears, as shown in Figure 9.25.

9. Close the file without saving.

Adding Display Blocks

Display blocks offer the potential to go beyond what the default display components offer: You can model anything as a custom display block and make it appear as a display component. Examples include door hardware such as handle sets and lock sets, and shutters on windows. In this section, you'll also learn how to add *muntins*, or custom divisions that appear in window glazing. Muntins are a specialized kind of display block.

Let's get started by adding a handle set to a door. The sample file has a wall that already contains a door. Not visible in the file is a block of a doorknob stored in the drawing database. The block was modeled with mass elements and given a material using a mass element style (refer to Chapter 4, "Mass Modeling").

1. Open DisplayBlocks.dwg from the companion DVD.

2. You can assign display blocks to any representation. Switch into the NW Isometric viewpoint and Hidden display mode. Our first goal is to add the handle set to the interior face of the door.

3. Select the door, right-click, and choose Edit Door Style. Place a check in the Style Override column for the Model representation; the Display Properties dialog box appears. Click the Other tab. Click the Add button in the Custom Block Display group; the Custom Block dialog box appears.

4. Click the Select Block button; the Select A Block dialog box appears. Click Handleset and click OK, closing the dialog box. The handle set appears in the lower-left corner of the door in the object viewer on the right side of the Custom Block dialog box. Next we have to get the handle set into the correct position relative to the door.

5. Change the insertion points as follows: X to Right, Y to Back, and Z to Bottom. For the insertion offsets, type **-6"** for X, **0"** for Y, and **3'** for Z. Leave the Frame Component set to be measured from the Outside. The handle set looks like it's in the correct position in the object viewer. Click OK in all three open dialog boxes. The doorknob appears correctly on the outside of the door.

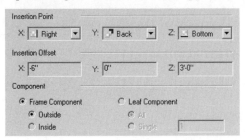

6. Switch to the SW Isometric view; no doorknob appears on the inside of the door. Edit the door style and open the Model style override display properties again. You'll have to add a second custom block for the interior handle set. Click the Add button to open the Custom Block dialog box. Select the Handleset block again. This time, check Mirror Y to flip the handle set. Change the insertion points as follows: X to Right, Y to Front, and Z to Bottom. For the insertion offsets, type **-6"** for X, **0"** for Y, and **3'** for Z. Click OK in all three open dialog boxes. The doorknob appears correctly on the inside of the door.

7. Go back to the Other tab of the Display Properties dialog box you edited previously. Uncheck Override Open Percent and click OK in both open dialog boxes. The door opens, but the doorknobs stay in their original "closed" position. Unfortunately, ADT is not yet smart enough to anchor custom blocks to door swings.

WARNING   Add custom blocks to doors only after you decide to leave them open or closed.

8. There is a nicely designed window tool in the Content Browser that already uses custom blocks to represent exterior shutters. Open the Content Browser and navigate to Design Tool Catalog ➢ Doors and Windows ➢ Windows ➢ Page 8. Drag the Shutters - Dynamic tool into the Windows palette in ADT. Close the Content Browser.

9. Click the Shutters - Dynamic tool and place a window centered in the remaining space in the wall.

10. Select the window, right-click, and choose Edit Window Style. Click the Display Properties tab. Open the Model windows style override's Display Properties dialog box and click the Muntins tab. The interface here looks very much like the Other tab. Click the Add button in the Muntins Block Display group; the Muntins Block dialog box appears.

11. The Muntins_block is a built-in feature of ADT. In the Lights group, click the Pattern drop-down list and cycle through each option; choose Prairie - 9 Lights (see Figure 9.28). Verify that Convert To Body is selected; this generates 3D geometry—otherwise, linework is used.

TIP Uncheck Convert To Body in the Muntins Block dialog box if you want to make an elevation only. Displaying linework is much more efficient than 3D geometry.

12. Click OK in all three open dialog boxes. Switch to the NW Isometric viewpoint and use a shaded display mode. Figure 9.29 shows the completed muntins, shutters, and handle set. This level of detail is usually necessary only to prepare for 3D renderings (see Chapter 18, "Using VIZ Render").

13. Select the door object and edit its style. Open the Model display representation style override. In the Display Properties dialog box, click the Layer/Color/Linetype tab. Notice that there are now two Handleset display components. Toggle their visibility off and click OK in both dialog boxes. They disappear only because the display block was defined with all its properties set to ByBlock.

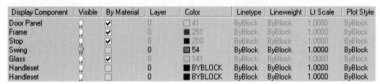

Display Component	Visible	By Material	Layer	Color	Linetype	Lineweight	Lt Scale	Plot Style
Door Panel		✔	0	☐ 41	ByBlock	ByBlock	1.0000	ByBlock
Frame		✔	0	■ 251	ByBlock	ByBlock	1.0000	ByBlock
Stop		✔	0	■ 250	ByBlock	ByBlock	1.0000	ByBlock
Swing		☐	0	■ 54	ByBlock	ByBlock	1.0000	ByBlock
Glass		✔	0	☐ 141	ByBlock	ByBlock	1.0000	ByBlock
Handleset		☐	0	■ BYBLOCK	ByBlock	ByBlock	1.0000	ByBlock
Handleset		☐	0	■ BYBLOCK	ByBlock	ByBlock	1.0000	ByBlock

NOTE Always set object properties to ByBlock when you are designing geometry destined to be added as a custom display block.

14. Close the file without saving. Congratulations—you have finished this chapter!

FIGURE 9.28
Configuring Muntins

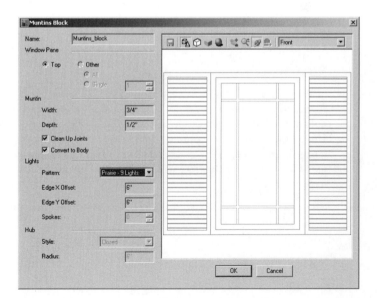

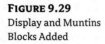

FIGURE 9.29
Display and Muntins
Blocks Added

Summary

In this chapter you learned everything there is to know about fenestrations in ADT. You created and edited doors, windows, and openings in almost every possible way. You worked extensively with door and window styles; hopefully the more energy you put into studying, the easier it becomes. Things should really be coming together for you by now, as you get into the "mind of ADT." ADT forces us to think in very structured ways, but after you master these thought forms through practice, the easier working with ADT will become, and the faster you'll be able to absorb the material in subsequent chapters.

Chapter 10

Curtain Walls and Assemblies

Curtain walls are portions of the building envelope that hold glazing and exterior cladding. Curtain walls are lightweight, are non-load-bearing, and typically hang—like a curtain—from the building's structural frame. Most curtain walls use modular panels and frames that fit into grid cells—making them much more flexible than conventional walls and punched fenestrations.

Curtain walls are the most complicated object in Architectural Desktop. In fact, I'd advise you to not make a curtain wall object directly unless its design is very simple, indeed. Instead, the process of making curtain walls is best approached by reducing the overarching design into a series of modules acting as *infill*—to be inserted into the framework of a curtain wall. This chapter takes a tutorial approach; you'll proceed by designing many types of infill styles that will ultimately replace or override cells in a complex curtain wall's grids.

Before you dive into the specifics of making infill, it is important to first sketch the curtain wall you have in mind, so you'll know what infill is needed and how it fits into the big picture. We will start this chapter by developing a conceptual sketch for a particular curtain wall. Then we'll use the rest of the chapter to develop the sketch into a curtain wall model. This chapter's topics include:

- ◆ Sketching a Curtain Wall
- ◆ Working with AEC Polygon Styles
- ◆ Designing Curtain Wall Units
- ◆ Creating Door/Window Assemblies
- ◆ Working with Curtain Walls

Sketching a Curtain Wall

Many building projects use curtain walls to enclose previously designed structures. In this chapter we will instead make the curtain wall the central design feature—basing the design of a building on its facade. This gives us complete freedom to play with proportion to come up with a pleasing curtain wall. You'll start by designing the overall curtain wall by studying and playing with proportion. Then you'll plan infill styles that will plug into the curtain wall that you'll create in subsequent sections of this chapter.

Designing with a Sketch

Before trying to build a curtain wall, it is essential that you make a sketch on paper or by drawing linework on screen. The more thinking and organization you can do up front the easier it will be to input the curtain wall you imagine into ADT. We will work with proportion to generate a curtain wall sketch.

Perhaps the most famous and psychologically pleasing proportion ever known is called the *golden section* or *golden ratio*. This proportion is 1:1.6180339887… (much like pi, the decimals go on forever). This mysterious mathematical relationship is known by the Greek letter *phi* (ϑ), as defined by Euclid some 2000 years ago. Phi (pronounced "fee") governs the natural proportions found in seashells, sunflowers, crystals, and the human body, to the shape of galaxies. Artists and architects since antiquity have used phi in their works—and so will we to design a curtain wall. Figure 10.1 shows how to graphically derive the golden rectangle, whose proportion is based upon phi.

NOTE A good introduction to phi can be found in Mario Livio's book *The Golden Ratio* (Broadway Books, 2002).

You'll use the golden rectangle to design the curtain wall. Although this book isn't about architectural design, I'll quickly show you how I derived the facade design we'll be using in this chapter—it all comes from the golden rectangle. Open `GoldenRectangleForms.dwg` from the companion DVD. The rectangles in this file have been scaled up and rounded off to even dimensions that approximate the phi proportion.

The top-left shape in Figure 10.2 is a golden rectangle and has a nice aspect ratio for a storefront—longer than it is tall. At 10′ in height, it frames the human scale. The overall facade should respect human scale at least near street level, and the building will transition through square proportions before soaring to tall aspect ratio of the golden rectangle on higher floors. Figure 10.3 shows the overall facade layout.

To develop infill for the bays, I played with variations upon a theme by starting with the four basic shapes: two squares and two golden rectangles. I inserted the smaller square inside the other shapes and began exploring the possibilities of form (see Figure 10.4). Feel free to experiment by making your own variations on the geometrical theme that is being developed. Close `GoldenRectangleForms.dwg` when you are satisfied.

FIGURE 10.1
Deriving phi graphically (ϑ = 1.6180339887…) by drafting a golden rectangle

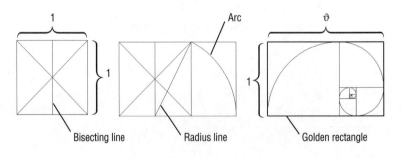

FIGURE 10.2
Design elements based on the golden rectangle

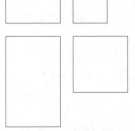

FIGURE 10.3
Overall facade layout
using variations of the
golden rectangle and
the square

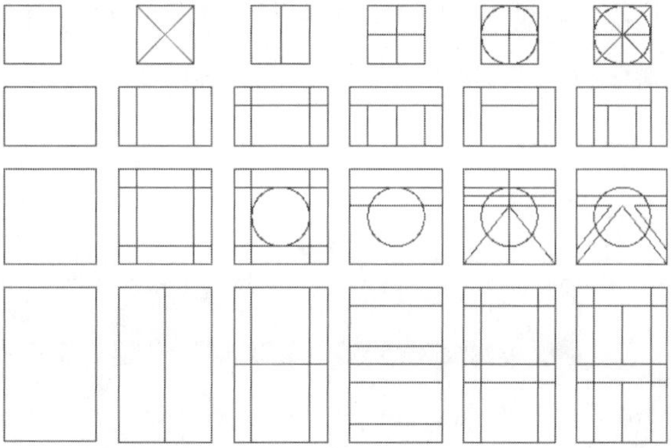

FIGURE 10.4
Variations upon a theme

Planning Infill

Curtain walls are formed from grids whose cells can be infilled with additional content. The types of infill that can be used in curtain walls (CW) include: AEC Polygons, curtain wall units (CWU), door/window assemblies (DWA), doors, windows, and custom blocks. AEC Polygon styles offer hatch patterns and fill colors that act as a basic type of infill.

CW, CWU, and DWA all share similar Design Rule interfaces. However, door/window assemblies and curtain wall units are different from curtain walls—the former two can act as infill to the latter. You'll learn the basic structure of curtain walls by designing several CWU and DWA.

DWA are more complex than CWU because they can accommodate CWU, door, and window styles acting as infill, and they use shaped profiles. DWA can also be used as independent objects in the drawing file whereas CWU cannot. DWA can be anchored to a wall and cut into the wall, just like doors, windows and openings (see Chapter 9). Still, DWA are simpler than CW, which include wall-like qualities such as roof/floor line, interferences, and overrides. You'll use all the styles you design to act as infill to the final curtain wall style you'll make at the end of this chapter.

Open the file FacadeDesign.dwg, which we'll be using in the following section. It contains the overall facade bay layout, as shown in Figure 10.3, plus some of the variations that were developed in Figure 10.4. Figure 10.5 shows the elevation sketches that were chosen to act as infill.

You will be turning each one of the sketches in Figure 10.5 into styles that can be used in the curtain wall. The curtain wall will look like Figure 10.6 by the time we reach the end of this chapter. Refer to it for inspiration and clarification from time to time as you progress through the sections.

Working with AEC Polygon Styles

AEC Polygons are useful in many ways—they use the same edge and vertex grips as extruded mass elements (see Chapter 4, "Mass Modeling") and spaces (see Chapter 6, "Space Planning"), and can be used to represent floor patterns.

AEC Polygons styles can also act as infill for CW and DWA. You might use AEC Polygons in situations in which a simple hatch pattern or color is enough to represent infill. AEC Polygons are 2D, so their use is best limited to depicting objects having planar geometry, such as metal or masonry panels.

1. Open FacadeDesign.dwg if it's not already open.

2. Open the Content Browser by clicking its button on the Navigation toolbar.

3. Open the Stock Tool Catalog and click the Helper Tools category. Drag the AEC Polygon tool's i-drop icon and drop it on one of the Tool palettes—I suggest placing it on MyPal if it is still present from Chapter 7, "Parametric Layouts, Anchors, and Structural Members."

4. Click the AEC Polygon tool and draw a 10' square using object tracking and dynamic dimensions.

5. Select the AEC Polygon and notice its familiar edge and vertex grips.

We don't need to alter the form of the AEC Polygon in any way because we are concerned here only with its style, not this particular object's shape. The AEC Polygon style is what will ultimately be used as infill within DWA and CW styles.

1. Right-click and choose Copy AEC Polygon Style And Assign. Click the General tab in the AEC Polygon Style Properties dialog box and give it the name **StoneClad**.

2. Click the Display Properties tab and place a check in the Style Override column for the Model display representation. In the Display Properties dialog box, click the Layer/Color/Linetype tab if it's not already selected. Toggle the visibility of the Interior Hatch component on (see Figure 10.7).

FIGURE 10.5
Infill elevation sketches

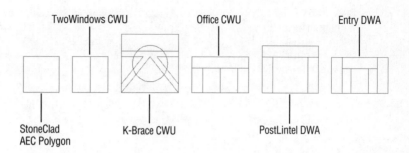

FIGURE 10.6
Completed curtain wall

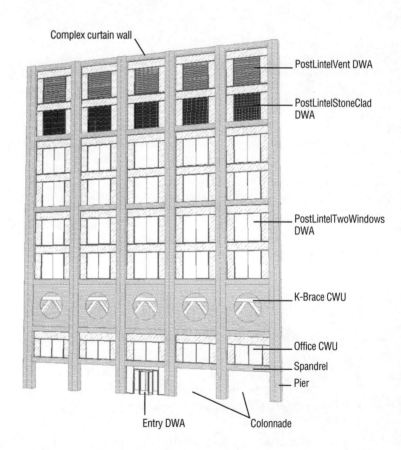

3. Click the Hatching tab and then click the pattern swatch for the Interior Hatch display component. A small Hatch Pattern dialog box appears. Change the Type drop-down list to Predefined and then click the Browse button.

4. When the Hatch Pattern Palette dialog box appears, click the Other Predefined tab and scroll down until you locate the NET pattern (see Figure 10.8). Select NET and click OK twice to close two dialog boxes.

FIGURE 10.7
Turning on the
Interior Hatch display
component in an AEC
Polygon style override

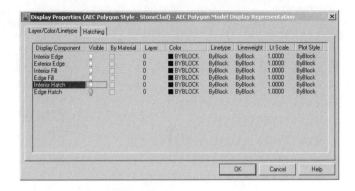

FIGURE 10.8
Choosing a predefined
hatch pattern for the
Interior Hatch display
component

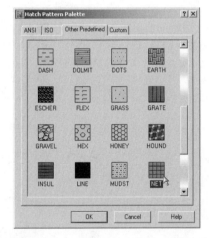

5. On the Hatching tab of the Display Properties dialog box, change the Scale/Spacing of the NET pattern to 3'-0". Then change the Angle value to zero and click OK twice more to close all remaining dialog boxes. The AEC Polygon object you drew in Step 4 shows the selected hatch pattern.

AEC Polygons also have an interesting display representation called True Color, which allows you to fill AEC Polygons with color instead of hatch patterns. If you wanted to make a colorful conceptual rendering of a CW or DWA, this might be just the ticket. Let's see what steps are necessary to set up this alterative.

1. Select the AEC Polygon, right-click, and choose Copy AEC Polygon Style And Assign. Click the General tab in the AEC Polygon Style Properties dialog box and give it the name **StoneFilled**.

2. Click the Other tab and check Use Background Mask. This feature completely obscures whatever is behind the AEC Polygon.

3. Click the Display Properties tab and place a check in the Style Override column for the True Color display representation. In the Display Properties dialog box that appears, check Interior Fill and then click the Interior Color swatch drop-down list (see Figure 10.9). Click on one of

the swatches. Note that you can also pick a custom color, if desired, by clicking Other. Click OK in every open dialog box.

4. You still can't see any fill inside the AEC Polygon because the True Color representation is not used by default. Choose Format ➤ Display Manager. Expand the current drawing, Configurations, and Medium Detail nodes. Click the Plan set node in the tree pane and click the Display Representation Control tab in the content pane; the object matrix appears. Place a check in the True Color column of the AEC Polygon row. Notice that the AEC Polygon is the only object using this representation. Click OK to close the Display Manager.

5. You still can't see the fill! The final step is to regenerate the objects in the drawing. Choose View ➤ Regen Model and press Enter. The AEC Polygon finally displays filled with the color you chose in Step 3.

6. Select the AEC Polygon object. Copy it some arbitrary distance to the side. In the Properties panel, change the Style from StoneFilled back to StoneClad. Notice that the outer edge remains hidden, now that the True Color representation is on.

7. Switch to Hidden display mode: the StoneFilled AEC Polygon disappears. Switch back to 2D Wireframe.

WARNING   AEC Polygons using the True Color display representation appear only when using 2D Wireframe display mode.

8. Save the file as **AECPolygonStyles.dwg**. Plan on always leaving files open in this chapter if you plan on continuing to subsequent sections.

FIGURE 10.9
Display Properties

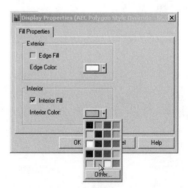

Designing Curtain Wall Units

The role of a curtain wall unit is to act as infill to a curtain wall. The way you go about designing both types of objects is very similar. Strictly speaking, you do not need to use curtain wall units to make a curtain wall. In fact, one could design an entire facade and all its infill as a single curtain wall.

By this logic, you might wonder why we bother with curtain wall units at all. The answer is that by modularizing a complex curtain wall into curtain wall units—and door/window assemblies—you can keep the design rules as simple as possible.

Design rules for CW, CWU, and DWA can easily get out of hand and become so complicated that they become a nightmare. When working with these objects, keep in mind that your goal should be to strive for simplicity wherever possible. Not only will a modular curtain wall be easier to design and maintain, but your colleagues will thank you should they have to edit your creations.

Designing a Basic Curtain Wall Unit

We'll begin designing the TwoWindows CWU style (refer to Figure 10.5 for its elevation sketch). It is very basic indeed—having just two windows, as its name suggests. A notable fact about the curtain wall unit is that no tool of this name appears on the Design palette by default. There is a CWU tool in the Stock Tool Catalog, however.

1. Open AECPolygonStyles.dwg from your hard drive or the companion DVD if it's not already open.

2. Open the Content Browser by clicking its button in the Navigation toolbar. Open the Stock Tool Catalog and click on the Architectural Object Tools category.

3. Drag and drop the Curtain Wall Unit tool into the Design palette in ADT. Close the Content Browser.

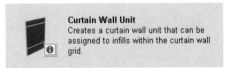

4. Reorganize the tools on the Design palette by dragging their icons within the palette according to Figure 10.10.

FIGURE 10.10
Reorganizing the Design palette

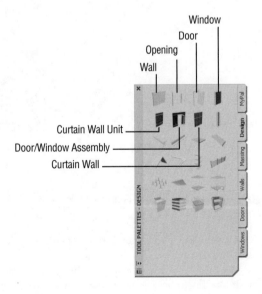

5. Switch to the SW Isometric viewpoint and zoom into the area where the TwoWindows elevation sketch (drawn in plan) is located. Select the rectangle and line that make up the TwoWindows sketch and click the Isolate Objects lightbulb icon in the drawing tray. Choose Isolate Objects from the shortcut menu.

6. Click the CWU tool in the Design palette. Click the start point at the low corner and endpoint at the middle right corner of the sketch. The command line asks for a Height; type **10′**↵. The Curtain Wall Unit Styles dialog box appears, listing Standard as the only CWU style yet defined in this drawing. Click OK. The CWU object appears and stands up vertically in elevation.

7. Select the CWU and look at the Properties palette (see Figure 10.11). There are four labeled properties that correspond with the illustration. The Start and End Miter properties affect the intersections of CWU segments. Note that this object is currently assigned the Standard style, and I recommend leaving the Standard style unaltered.

8. Right-click the CWU and choose Copy Curtain Wall Unit Style And Assign from the shortcut menu; the Curtain Wall Unit Style Properties dialog box appears. Click the General tab and rename the style **TwoWindows** (no space).

9. Click the Design Rules tab (see Figure 10.12). You will be spending a lot of time working with design rules in this chapter. Vertical and horizontal dividers meet in a T shape, splitting the interface into three panes. The tree pane is on the left, the selection pane is on the top right, and the content pane is located at the right bottom. Drag the dividers to see how you can resize the panes. Resize the dialog box and the panes until you do not see any scroll bars.

Design rules can be understood by analyzing the tree pane. *Grids* and the *cells* they contain form the basic structure of design rules. Figure 10.12 shows only one grid—called the Primary Grid—at the top of the hierarchy. Grids can be nested, and all the grids (with their assignments) taken together comprise the design rules.

FIGURE 10.11
Curtain Wall
Unit Properties

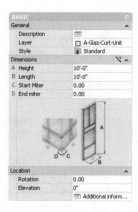

FIGURE 10.12
The Design Rules tab has a tree pane on the left, a selection pane at the top right, and a content pane at the bottom right.

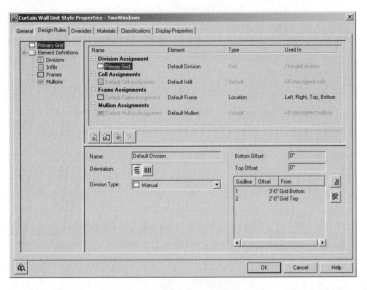

Notice the dotted line connecting the Primary Grid to the Element Definitions folder below. Element definitions function like tools that can be assigned to any number of grids. Think of the Element Definitions folder as your design rule toolbox. Element definitions include the following:

Divisions Abstract entities that determine the orientation and spacing of cells.

Infills Determine what each cell contains.

Frames Form the four outer edges of a grid. Each edge can be toggled on and off.

Mullions Form internal separations between cells of a grid.

To understand the way element definitions interact with grids, let's continue designing the TwoWindows CWU.

1. Click the Divisions node in the tree pane. The selection pane lists the Default Division. For clarity, I recommend always giving element definitions descriptive names. If you edit any default element without renaming it, you might be confused in the future about what its purpose is within the overall design rules. Click the New Division button on the lower edge of the selection pane. Give this new division the name **Vertical Division** and press Enter.

2. In the content pane, click the vertical orientation button. Each division is either horizontal or vertical; there are no other orientation choices. Verify that the Division Type drop-down list is set to Fixed Cell Dimension. The choice of division type affects which controls appear on the right side of the content pane.

    Cells are organized into three designations within every division: Start, Middle, and End for vertical divisions—and Bottom, Middle, and Top for horizontal divisions. When there are more than three cells in a division, all additional cells are categorized as fitting the Middle designation.

3. On the right side of the content pane, verify that Start and End offsets are set to zero. You might use offsets to push cells over at Start, End, Bottom, and/or Top, depending upon the orientation of the division. Verify that the Cell Dimension is set to 5'-0".

4. Check Auto-Adjust Cells. This powerful feature automatically adjusts cell spacing when dividing the length or height of the object by the specified cell dimension does not yield a whole number. When there is a remainder, Auto-Adjust can spread it out by shrinking or growing specific cells that you choose. In this case, choose Grow from the Cell Adjustment drop-down list. Click the Start and End Specific Cell buttons.

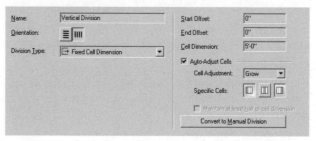

5. Click the Infill node under Element Definitions in the tree pane. Click the New Infill button on the lower edge of the selection pane. Name the new infill **Glass Infill** and press Enter. In the content pane, notice that the Infill Type is set to Simple Panel; this is the only option for CWU. DWA and CW have the option of choosing a Style here, as we shall see in later sections. Type **5/8″** in the Panel Thickness text box. Leave Alignment set to Center and Offset to zero. Alignment and Offset control the placement of the infill within the CWU.

6. Click the Frames node under Element Definitions in the tree pane. Click the New Frame button on the lower edge of the selection pane. Name the new frame **Window Frame** and press Enter. In the content pane, change the Width to **1″** and Depth to **2″**.

7. Click the Mullions node under Element Definitions in the tree pane. Click the New Mullion button on the lower edge of the selection pane. Name the new mullion **Window Mullion** and press Enter. In the content pane, change the Width to **¹/₂″** and Depth to **1″**.

You have made all the element definitions necessary to construct the TwoWindows curtain wall unit style. Now you'll assign these elements to the grid.

1. Click the Primary Grid node in the tree pane. In the selection pane's Element column, assign Vertical Division to the Primary Grid, Glass Infill as the Default Cell Assignment, Window Frame as the Default Frame Assignment, and Window Mullion as the Default Mullion Assignment. Whatever appears in light gray cannot be edited.

2. The last step in working with design rules is to delete any element definitions that you are not using. Click the Divisions node in the tree pane; then right-click Default Division in the selection pane and choose Remove from the shortcut menu. Click the Infills node in the tree pane; then right-click Default Infill in the selection pane and choose Remove from the shortcut menu. Repeat this process twice more, removing the Default Frame and Default Mullion element definitions. Click OK to close the dialog box. The CWU appears with two windows.

Like most objects, CWU, DWA, and CW all have components that can accept material assignments. The final task left in designing the TwoWindows CWU style is to assign some materials to its components.

1. Click the Materials tool in the Design palette and click the CWU in the drawing window. In the Apply Materials To Components worksheet, select the following material definition from the drop-down list:

```
Doors & Windows.Glazing.Glass.Clear
```

Click Leave As Is in the Apply To column corresponding to the Glass Infill component and select Style from the drop-down list that appears (see Figure 10.13). Click OK to close the worksheet. Switch to the SE Isometric viewpoint. In a few moments, the wireframe display of the glass infill changes color in the drawing window after the material is assigned.

2. Press the spacebar to repeat the MaterialApply command and click the CWU again. Choose the following material definition from the drop-down list:

```
Doors & Windows.Metal Doors & Frames.Aluminum Windows.Painted.White
```

Apply this material to both the Window Frame and Window Mullion components by changing the Apply To column to Style for both rows. Click OK and the CWU style is done (see Figure 10.14).

3. Save your work as **TwoWindows.dwg**.

FIGURE 10.13

Applying a material to a CWU component

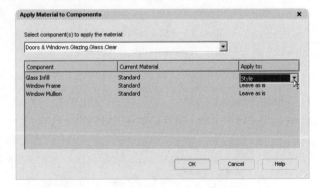

FIGURE 10.14
Two Windows CWU
components

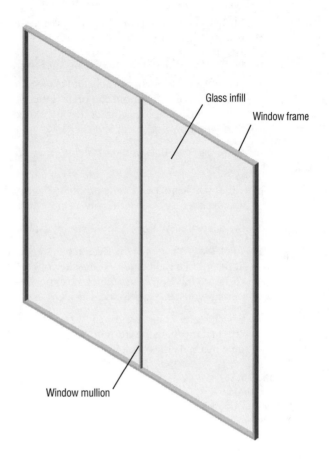

FIGURE 10.14
Two Windows CWU
components

Glass infill

Window frame

Window mullion

Using Profiles in Frames and Mullions

Instead of the Width and Depth parameters, which result in square or rectangular forms, you have the option of using profiles in frames and mullion element definitions. Profiles are extruded along the length of the frame or mullion and are great for modeling complex cross-sections.

Be aware that you might not need true-to-life detail in a curtain wall unit, so think twice before drawing a complex aluminum frame as a profile when a simpler rectangle might do. You can always cover minutiae in detail drawings and not have to worry about modeling it into your overall curtain wall.

We will design the Vent CWU style to contain a metal frame and horizontal louvers for the ventilation system. You'll make the louvers by drawing a closed polyline and converting it to a profile definition. Then the profile can be assigned to the mullions of the Vent CWU style you'll design in this section.

1. Open TwoWindows.dwg from your hard drive or the companion DVD if it's not already open.

2. Click the red lightbulb icon in the drawing tray and choose End Object Isolation from the short-cut menu. Switch into the Top viewpoint.

3. Make layer zero current and draw a vertical 6″ line. Zoom in closely on the line. Offset it twice using a $^1/_2$″ offset distance.

4. Draw a closed polyline connecting the points shown in Figure 10.15.

5. Select the polyline, right-click, and choose Convert To ➢ Profile Definition from the shortcut menu. Type **C** for centroid and press Enter. This sets the insertion point of the profile definition at the center of the area bounded by the closed polyline. Type the name **Louver** in the New Profile Definition worksheet and click OK.

6. Erase the three lines and the polyline; they are not needed any longer after the profile has been defined.

Now that you have defined the profile to be used in the CWU, you can begin designing its style. This CWU is also very basic with only a frame and many horizontal louvers acting as mullions.

1. Switch to the SW Isometric viewpoint. Isolate the square to the left of the TwoWindows CWU.

2. Click the CWU tool in the Design palette. Click the start point at the low corner and endpoint at the middle right corner of the sketch. The command line asks for a Height; type **10′**↵. The Curtain Wall Unit Styles dialog box appears, listing Standard and TwoWindows. It does not matter which one is selected. Click OK and the new CWU object appears.

3. Select the new object, right-click, and choose Copy Curtain Wall Style And Assign from the shortcut menu. In the Curtain Wall Unit Style Properties dialog box, click the General tab and give this style the name **Vent**.

FIGURE 10.15
Drawing the louver profile with a closed polyline

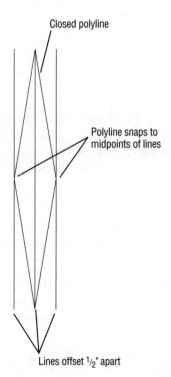

Closed polyline

Polyline snaps to midpoints of lines

Lines offset $^1/_2$″ apart

4. Click the Design Rules tab. This time we will make changes to the element definitions directly from the Primary Grid node in the tree view. The Primary Grid is currently assigned the Default Division in the selection pane. Change the Name in the content pane to **Horizontal Division**. Verify that the Horizontal orientation button is selected.

5. Open the Division Type drop-down list and choose Fixed Cell Dimension. On the right side of the content pane, enter **8″** as the Cell Dimension.

6. In the selection pane, click the Default Cell Assignment node; Default Infill properties appear in the content pane. Change the name to **Void** and change the panel thickness on the right of the content pane to zero. Elements with zero dimensions do not appear. This style will not use infill.

7. Click the Default Frame Assignment node in the selection pane. In the content pane, rename it to **Metal Frame**. Give it a Width of **1″** and a Depth of **3″**.

8. Click the Default Mullion Assignment in the selection pane. Rename it in the content pane to **Blade**. Set both its Width and Depth parameters to zero because it would be confusing to use different values as compared to the dimensions of the profile, which are automatically determined. Check Use Profile; Louver automatically appears in the Profile drop-down list because it is the only profile definition in the drawing. Type **60** in the Rotation text box.

The design rules for this CWU were specified entirely from the Primary Grid node. Perhaps it is a more convenient way to work with element definitions, but might be less clear as compared with editing within the Element Definitions folder.

The next thing to consider is what materials are assigned to the components of this style. Because we will be assigning materials that are already part of this drawing, let's use the Materials tab of the Curtain Wall Unit Style Properties dialog box instead of the Material tool as we did before.

9. Click the Materials tab. Notice that there are three components listed: Void, Metal Frame, and Blade. Because the Void component doesn't really even exist, it doesn't matter what material is assigned to it. Choose Doors & Windows.Metal.Doors & Frames.Aluminum Windows.Painted .White in the Material Definition drop-down lists for the Metal Frame and Blade components.

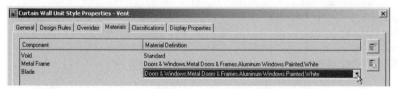

10. Click OK to close the dialog box. Switch to Flat shaded display mode and 3D Orbit a bit to better visualize what you have built (see Figure 10.16). Save your work as **Vent.dwg**.

FIGURE 10.16
Vent CWU components

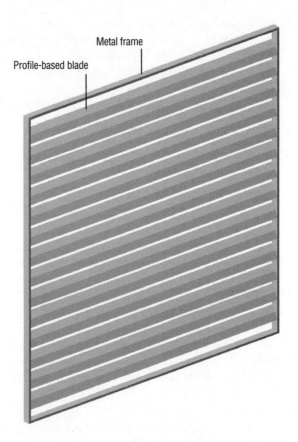

Metal frame

Profile-based blade

Replacing Display Components with Custom Graphics

The design of the K-Brace CWU (refer to Figure 10.6) calls for more geometry than the default element definitions can deliver. We will design custom graphics to replace the Simple Panel infill that is part of a typical CWU style. *Custom graphics* can be anything that you define as a block (see Chapter 11, "Roofs and Slabs," for more on blocks). This really opens the door to your creativity because it means that you can replace any element in a curtain wall unit with whatever geometry you care to imagine.

NOTE   Many advanced ADT users push the envelope by designing CW, CWU, and DWA styles having custom graphics that may not have anything to do with actual curtain walls. For example, some users have made theatre seating, parking spaces, residential cornices, casework, stud walls, and wrought iron fences with these styles. Autodesk has some interesting styles that users have contributed: browse to Autodesk.com ➤ Products ➤ ADT ➤ Data & Downloads ➤ Styles ➤ Curtain Walls.

In this section we will model a K-brace with structural members and panels with wall objects. This will be an opportunity to practice some of the concepts you learned in Chapter 7, "Parametric Layouts, Anchors, and Structural Members," and Chapter 8, "Walls." We'll turn our custom model of infill into a block and then design a CWU style that can accommodate our custom graphics. Let's begin by adding structural steel to an elevation sketch.

1. Open Vent.dwg from your hard drive or the companion DVD if it's not already open.

2. Click the red lightbulb icon in the drawing tray and choose End Object Isolation from the shortcut menu.

3. Switch to the SW Isometric viewpoint and use 2D Wireframe display mode. Zoom in on the K-Brace CWU sketch (refer to Figure 10.5). Select the sketch geometry and isolate it.

4. The K-Brace sketch was drawn in plan, so it looks as if it is flat on the ground. For this style it will be helpful to refer to the sketch in elevation, so we need to rotate it up. On the command line, type **ROTATE3D** and press Enter. Select all the lines, polylines, and circle in the sketch and press Enter. Type **O**↵ for the Object option and click the line at the base of the sketch. Type **90**↵ to tilt up the sketch. Notice that it appears to be the letter "K" turned on its side—this is the origin of the name *K-Brace*.

5. Measure the distance between the top midpoint of the "K" and the point where the diagonal lines come together; it is 1'-6-$^1/_2$". This is the dimension of the structural steel that we need.

6. Choose Format ➤ Structural Members ➤ Wizard. In the Structural Member Style Wizard dialog box, expand the Steel node and select Wide Flange (I) on page 1 of the wizard. Click Next.

7. On page 2 of the wizard, input the value of **1'-6 1/2"** for both the A - Section Depth and B - Section Width parameters (see Figure 10.17). Click Next.

FIGURE 10.17

Entering dimensions in the Structural Member Style Wizard

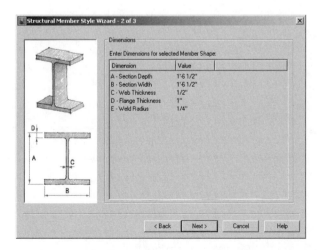

8. On page 3 of the wizard, type the name **WideFlange** as the style name and click Finish.

9. Click the Structural Beam tool on the Design palette. In the Properties palette, verify that Wide-Flange is assigned as the style. Change Justify in the Dimensions subcategory to Top Left. Snap the start point at the lower left and the endpoint of the beam to the upper right of the elevation sketch (see Figure 10.18).

10. Switch to the Front viewpoint. Click the Structural Brace tool and verify that WideFlange is assigned as the Style in the Properties palette. Change Justify to Bottom Right in this case. Click the start points and endpoints according to Figure 10.19.

11. Select the structural brace, right-click, and choose Trim Planes ➢ Add Trim Plane. Press Enter to specify trim line points. Click the first point of the trim line at the brace's start point. Click the second point horizontally to the left, snapping to the start of the structural beam (snap to endpoint). The penetrating steel is trimmed away.

12. Again, select the structural brace, right-click, and choose Trim Planes ➢ Add Trim Plane. Click the first point of the trim line at the brace's endpoint. Click the second point vertically up, snapping again to the start of the structural beam. Mirror the brace about the midpoint of the beam.

13. Click the Material tool and click the structural beam. Assign the Metals.Metal.Joists.Steel material to the style. The braces receive this material automatically because they have the same structural member style. Switch to the SE Isometric viewpoint and flat shaded display mode (see Figure 10.20).

FIGURE 10.18
Snapping a structural
beam to the elevation
sketch

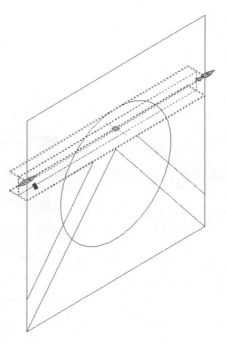

FIGURE 10.19
Snapping a structural
brace to the elevation
sketch

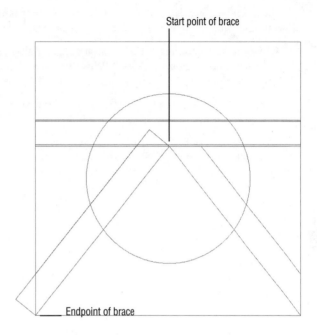

Start point of brace

Endpoint of brace

FIGURE 10.20
Completed structural
steel

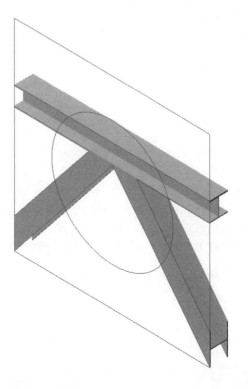

The next objects to add are wall panels that sandwich the steel. The panel in front will get a circular cutout, revealing the K-Brace, and the panel in back will remain solid.

1. Select the Walls palette and right-click the Brick-4 Brick-4 tool; this style contains two layers of brick. Choose Import 'Brick-4 Brick-4' Wall Style from the shortcut menu. No wall object has been created; only the style as imported into our drawing.

2. Choose Format ➢ Style Manager. Expand the current drawing, Architectural Objects, and Wall Styles nodes. Click Brick-4 Brick 4 in the tree pane.

3. In the content pane of the Style Manager, click the General tab. Rename the style **BrickPanel** and type **4" Brick Panel** as a description. Click the Components tab. Select component 2 Brick Veneer (Structural). Click the Remove Component button on the right edge of the content pane and click OK, closing the Style Manager.

4. Type **UCS↵W↵** to revert to the world coordinate system (WCS). Select the Design palette and click the generic Wall tool. Draw a segment flush with the elevation sketch, choosing Left justification. In the Properties palette, change Style to BrickPanel.

5. Select the wall object and snap its Base Height grip to the top of the elevation sketch. Mirror the wall about the midpoint of the structural beam, making a brick-and-steel sandwich— mmm, good!

The final thing to do modeling-wise is to cut a round hole out of the front brick panel. You'll do this by making a cylindrical mass element and adding it as a body modifier to the wall.

1. Switch into 2D Wireframe shading mode. So you can see through the brick, click the Surface Hatch Toggle icon in the drawing tray.

2. To be able to draw a cylinder on the side of the wall, you will have to adjust the user coordinate system (UCS). Hold down the UCS flyout on the Navigation toolbar and choose the X option. Type **90** and press Enter. The UCS icon shows the XY plane along the face of the front brick panel.

3. Select the Massing palette and click the Cylinder tool. Verify that Specify On Screen is set to Yes on the Properties palette. Snap its center to the center of the circle in the elevation sketch. Snap its radius to any quadrant of the circle. Click another point to set any height that is larger than the wall panel's width.

4. Select the cylindrical mass element and adjust its height grip so it clearly penetrates through the front panel. Make sure that you do not move the cylinder (see Figure 10.21).

5. Select the front wall object, right-click and choose Body Modifiers ➢ Add. Click the cylinder, and the Add Body Modifier worksheet appears. Change the Operation drop-down list to

Subtractive, type **Round Hole** as a description, and check Erase Selected Object(s). Click OK, and the cylinder disappears, leaving a circular hole in the brick panel.

FIGURE 10.21
Using a cylindrical mass element to cut a hole in the front panel

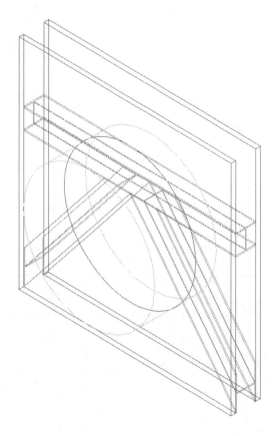

6. Type **UCS↵W↵** to revert to the WCS. Turn off the Layout layer. Select all three structural members and the two wall panels. Press **B** to open the Block Definition dialog box. Type the name **BracePanel** and click the Pick Point button in the Base Point group. Click the lower-left corner of the outer face of the brick panel with the hole in it. Click the Delete radio button in the Objects group and click OK (see Figure 10.22). The objects disappear from the drawing window but are defined as a block in the drawing database.

7. Save your work as K-Brace.dwg.

FIGURE 10.22

Defining a block from
the custom graphics

DESIGNING SINGLE CELL CWU STYLE

Now that we have defined the block we plan to use as custom graphics, we can concentrate on making the CWU style. The design rules for this style couldn't be any simpler because we want only one cell. Replacing the display components with custom graphics happens in display properties, not design rules.

1. Turn the Layout layer back on. Click the Curtain Wall Unit tool in the Design palette. Click the start points and endpoints along the lower edge of the elevation sketch. Type a height value of **16′-2″** on the command line and press Enter. Select Standard from the Curtain Wall Unit Styles dialog box and click OK. The CWU object appears.

2. Select the new CWU object, right-click, and choose Copy Curtain Wall Unit Style from the shortcut menu. Click General tab and rename the style **K-Brace**.

3. Click the Design Rules tab. Change the name of the Default Division in the content pane to **One Division**. Click the Division Type drop-down list and select Fixed Number Of Cells. Set the Number Of Cells on the right side of the content pane to 1.

4. In the selection pane, click the Default Cell Assignment node. In the content pane, change the name to Custom Infill and set the Panel Thickness to 2′-2″.

5. We don't want any frames to appear in this style. You can either assign a null frame with zero width and depth, or turn off all the places in which the frames are used; we'll take the latter

approach here. Click the Default Frame Assignment node and notice the Used In column says Left, Right, Top, and Bottom. Click in this area, and an ellipsis button appears; click it.

Name	Element	Type	Used In	
Division Assignment				
Primary Grid	One Division	Grid	This grid division	
Cell Assignments				
Default Cell Assignment	Custom Infill	Default	All unassigned cells	
Frame Assignments				
Default Frame Assignment	Default Frame	Location	Left, Right, Top, Bottom	...
Mullion Assignments				
Default Mullion Assignment	Default Mullion	Default	All unassigned mullions	

6. A small Frame Assignment dialog box appears. Uncheck Left, Right, Top, and Bottom, and click OK. The small dialog closes, and the selection pane shows Used in *NONE*.

7. Likewise, we do not want any mullions to appear in this style, and none will appear because we have only one cell after all—so no worries. If you really want to be explicit, rename the Default Mullion to **Null Mullion** and changes its Width and Depth parameters to zero. Click OK to close the dialog box. A 2'-2" by 16'-2" monolith appears—not the most complex curtain wall unit style to be sure!

ASSIGNING CUSTOM GRAPHICS TO DISPLAY PROPERTIES

The final procedure involves making a style override and adding custom model components through the display properties. This procedure will be the most satisfying part of designing this style because you'll see all your work designing the block pay off.

1. Select the CWU object, right-click, and choose Edit Curtain Wall Unit Style from the shortcut menu. Click the Display Properties tab. Place a check in the Style Override column for the Model display representation.

2. In the Display Properties dialog box that appears, click the Other tab. Click the Add button in the Custom Model Components group.

3. In the Custom Display Components dialog box that appears, click the Component Type drop-down list and note that you can create Infill, Frame, or Panel custom components. Choose Infill in this case. Click the Select Element button. The small Select Element Definition dialog box appears. Choose Custom Infill from the K-Brace CWU style node and click OK, closing the small dialog box.

4. Back in the Custom Display Component dialog box, check Draw Custom Graphics. Click the Select Block button, and the small Select A Block dialog box appears. Choose BracePanel and click OK, closing the small dialog box.

5. Once more in the Custom Display Component dialog box, check Replace Graphics (see Figure 10.23). (When unchecked, the custom graphics you are making work in addition to the default component.) In our case, we need to replace the graphics because we do not want the monolithic Custom Infill component to appear at all.

NOTE There is no need to assign a material to the Custom Infill component because it has been replaced by custom graphics, which carry their own materials.

6. Click OK three times to close the three open dialog boxes. The curtain wall unit appears centered on the elevation sketch (see Figure 10.24). Save your work as **K-Brace.dwg**.

Converting an Elevation Sketch into a Curtain Wall Unit

Divisions can have either a horizontal or vertical orientation; not both. To specify design rules having both horizontal and vertical divisions, nested grids are normally used. We will hold off until the next section to talk about nested grids.

Instead, in this section you will learn another way of integrating both horizontal and vertical cells in the same grid: making a *custom grid division* by converting an elevation sketch into a CWU. In fact, custom grid divisions can even accommodate angled grid lines. Unfortunately, you cannot edit a custom grid division after it has been created—this is this technique's main limitation.

We will rotate the Office elevation sketch up and convert the sketch directly to a custom grid division within a CWU object. Design rules made in this way are attached at the object level. Later, you'll save the object-based design rules to a style—so the style can ultimately be used as infill in a curtain wall.

1. Open K-Brace.dwg from your hard drive or the companion DVD if it's not already open.

2. Click the red lightbulb icon in the drawing tray and choose End Object Isolation from the shortcut menu.

FIGURE 10.23
Custom Display
Component dialog box

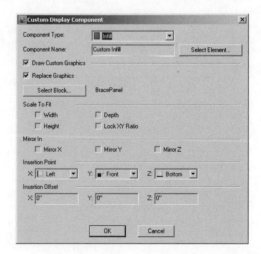

FIGURE 10.24
Completed K-Brace CWU

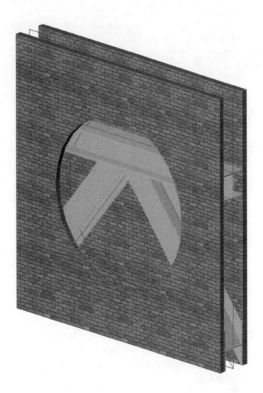

3. Switch to the SE Isometric viewpoint and use 2D Wireframe display mode. Zoom in on the Office CWU sketch (refer to Figure 10.5). Select the sketch geometry and isolate it.

4. The Office sketch was drawn in plan. We need to tilt up the sketch into elevation. On the command line, type **ROTATE3D** and press Enter. Select all the lines in the sketch and press Enter. Type **O**↵ for the Object option and click the line at the base of the sketch. Type **90**↵.

5. In the Design palette, right-click the Curtain Wall Unit tool and choose Apply Tool Properties To ➢ Elevation Sketch. Select all the linework in the Office sketch and press Enter. The command line reads as follows:

```
Select baseline or RETURN for default:
```

Press Enter. Type **Y**↵ to erase the layout geometry (the sketch). A CWU object appears, having both horizontal and vertical cells matching the elevation sketch layout.

6. In the Properties palette, notice that an Advanced category has appeared for the first time. Click the Design Rule worksheet icon. The Design Rules dialog box appears, breaking the convention that a worksheet icon normally opens a worksheet. Most significantly, you are looking at design rules separate from the rest of the tabs in the Style Properties dialog box (refer to Figure 10.12). The reason is simple: These design rules are applied at the object level, so they are not part of a style. Rename the grid **Elevation Sketch** (see Figure 10.25).

FIGURE 10.25
Object-level Design
Rules use Custom
Grid division

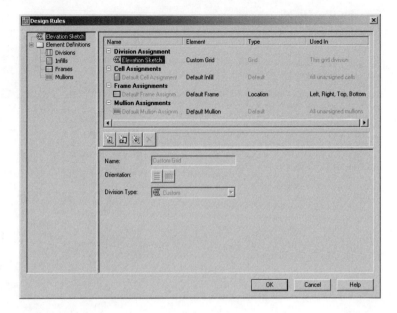

7. In the tree pane, click the Divisions node. Only the Default Division is listed here; the Custom Grid division does not appear because it is not editable. If you need to edit it, you'll have to undo and edit the elevation sketch prior to conversion. Rename the Default Division to **Not Used** in the content pane.

8. Click the Infills node in the tree pane. Rename the Default Infill to **Panel**.

9. Click the Frames node in the tree pane. In the Content pane, rename Default Frame to **Window Frame** and give it a Width of **2″** and a Depth of **4″**.

10. Click the Mullions node in the tree pane. In the Content pane, rename Default Mullion to **Window Mullion** and give it a Width of **2″** and a Depth of **4″**.

11. Click the Elevation Sketch node at the top of the tree view. Examine the selection pane and verify the assignments. The division is assigned a custom grid. Cell, Frame, and Mullion elements have Panel, Window Frame, and Window Mullion in their default assignments, respectively. Click OK to close the Design Rules dialog box.

WARNING   You cannot nest additional grids inside a custom grid. The custom grid is solely responsible for determining the structure of cellular division in the design rules.

The next procedure is to transfer the object-based design rules to a new style. We'll assign materials and learn how to create additional assignments. We'll need multiple cell assignments to be able to have glass in two of the cells and solid panels in the rest.

1. Select the CWU object, right-click, and choose Design Rules ➤ Save to Style. The Save Changes worksheet appears. Click the New button, type the name **Office** in the small New Curtain Wall Unit Style worksheet, and click OK. Office CWU style appears in the Save Changes worksheet. None of the check boxes are enabled because we haven't overridden anything in the object. Click OK to close the Save Changes worksheet.

2. Click the Material tool in the Design palette and then select the CWU object; the Apply Materials To Components worksheet appears. Select the following material from the drop-down list:

   ```
   Doors & Windows.Glazed.Curtain Walls.Stainless Steel.Curtain Wall
   ```

   Apply the material to the Style of the Panel component. Click OK to close the worksheet. The wireframe depiction of the panels changes color in the drawing window.

3. Select the CWU object again and notice that the Advanced category has disappeared from the Properties palette, now that the design rules have been transferred to the new CWU style. Right-click and choose Edit Curtain Wall Unit Style from the shortcut menu; the Curtain Wall Unit Style Properties dialog box appears. Click the Design Rules tab and notice that the custom grid design rules appear there.

4. Click the Materials tab and assign the following material to both the Window Frame and Window Mullion components:

   ```
   Doors & Windows.Metal Doors & Frames.Aluminum Windows.Painted.White
   ```

   Click OK to close the Curtain Wall Unit Style Properties dialog box. Switch to Flat Shaded, Edges On display mode (see Figure 10.26). The CWU style shows painted metal frames and mullions with solid stainless steel panels in every cell.

TIP   You can also transfer design rules from a style to an object. Select a styled CMU, DWA, or CW; right-click; and choose Design Rules ➤ Transfer To Object. This is useful when you have multiple segments and want to make changes to one exceptional object where the overhead of creating a new style isn't warranted.

5. Select the CWU object, right-click, and choose Edit Curtain Wall Units Style from the shortcut menu. Click the Design Rules tab. There are buttons on the lower edge of the selection pane; click the New Cell Assignment button. A new node appears in the selection pane: rename it to

Glazing A. Click the Panel element in the same row to open its drop-down list. Select New Infill from the drop-down list.

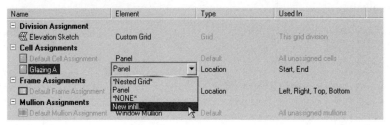

6. In the content pane, rename the new infill to **Glass** and give it a Panel Thickness of **5/8″**.

7. In the selection pane, click the word Location in the Type column and Glazing A row. Choose Index from the drop-down list that appears.

8. Click the word *NONE* in the Used In column and Glazing A row. Type **2** and press Enter. Glass will appear in the second cell in the Custom Grid.

9. Click the Materials tab and assign the Doors & Windows.Glazing.Glass.Clear material to the Glass component. Click OK to close the dialog box. Glass appears in the lower-left cell of the CWU object. The top cell is likely to be index number 1, and the central cells probably are indexes 3 and 4. With complex custom grids, guessing the index numbers can be a trial-and-error situation.

FIGURE 10.26
Shaded view of Office
CWU style with stainless
steel panels in every cell

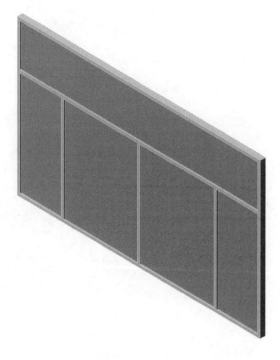

10. Edit the style again and change the index number of Glazing A to **3**. Add another cell assignment called **Glazing B** and give it index number **4**. Using index numbers, you could theoretically have a different cell assignment for each and every cell if you wanted.

Name	Element	Type	Used In
⊟ **Division Assignment**			
⛃ Elevation Sketch	Custom Grid	Grid	This grid division
⊟ **Cell Assignments**			
☐ Default Cell Assignment	Panel	Default	All unassigned cells
☐ Glazing A	Glass	Index	3
☐ Glazing B	Glass	Index	4
⊟ **Frame Assignments**			
▦ Default Frame Assignment	Window Frame	Location	Left, Right, Top, Bottom
⊟ **Mullion Assignments**			
▥ Default Mullion Assignment	Window Mullion	Default	All unassigned mullions

NOTE You could create a single cell assignment called Glazing that is used in indices 3 and 4, instead of maintaining two separate cell assignments. Separate index numbers with commas to assign multiple indices to one cell.

11. Click OK to close the Curtain Wall Unit Style Properties dialog box. Figure 10.27 shows the completed style. Save your work as **Office.dwg**.

FIGURE 10.27
Completed Office CWU

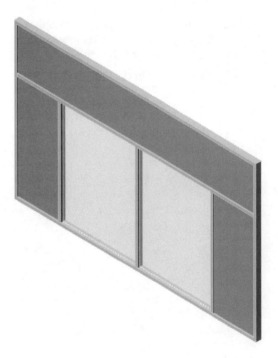

Creating Door/Window Assemblies

Door/window assemblies also are reminiscent of—you guessed it—doors and windows. DWA can have shaped profiles just like their less-complicated relatives. In this tutorial, we will be using only the predefined rectangular shape to fit the DWA into the golden rectangles of the overall curtain wall design. Refer to Chapter 9, "Doors, Windows, and Openings," to review shapes if you need to use anything other than predefined rectangular in your own work.

In addition, DWA have design rules much like curtain wall units, but with a twist. Instead of having just the Simple Panel infill type, DWA also have the capability to assign a style as a type of infill. Types of styles that can act as infill include AEC Polygons, curtain wall units, doors, and windows.

Creating the PostLintel Door/Window Assembly Style

In this section we will design the PostLintel DWA style that will act as a sort of "template" to infill other styles. The style gets its name—PostLintel—from the post-and-lintel construction archetype that the sketch is reminiscent of. The central void is where we will ultimately infill other styles in the next section.

1. Open Office.dwg from your hard drive or the companion DVD if it's not already open.

2. Click the red lightbulb icon in the drawing tray and choose End Object Isolation from the short-cut menu.

3. Switch to the Top viewpoint and use 2D Wireframe display mode. Zoom in on the PostLintel DWA sketch (refer to Figure 10.5). Select the sketch geometry and isolate it. Figure 10.28 details the design intent of the sketch.

FIGURE 10.28
PostLintel DWA elevation sketch and its cells

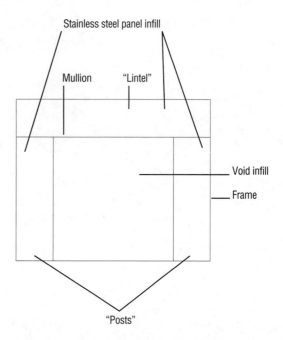

4. Measure the distances in the sketch. For your reference, the posts and lintel are 3'-1" wide, and the overall dimensions are 16'-2" by 13'-1". Now we are ready to begin designing the DWA style. This time we won't rotate the sketch up from plan.

5. Switch back into the SE Isometric viewpoint. Click the Door/Window Assembly tool on the Design palette. The command line says the following:

```
Select wall, grid assembly, or RETURN:
```

Press Enter because we will be creating a freestanding object. Just as with doors and windows, DWA are often anchored to walls or curtain wall units. Click the insert point at the lower-left corner of the elevation sketch and press Enter twice to complete the command.

6. The DWA object does not yet fit the sketch. Select the object, and in the Properties palette, change its Width to **16'-2"** and Height to **13'-1"**. Notice that the style is Standard.

7. Right-click and select Copy And Assign Door/Window Assembly Style from the shortcut menu. Click the General tab and rename the style to **PostLintel**.

There are both vertical and horizontal cells in the sketch. Instead of making a custom grid as we did before, this time we'll nest two grids to achieve the desired pattern. The benefit of nesting is that the divisions remain editable, unlike a custom grid. This relatively simple design calls for two grids. The first grid will be horizontal, creating the "lintel" and entire bottom area. The second grid will nest inside the bottom area, forming three vertical cells that define the "posts" and the void infill in-between.

1. Click the Design Rules tab. Click the Divisions node in the tree pane. In the content pane, rename Default Division to **Horizontal Division**. Click the Horizontal orientation button. Verify that Division Type is set to Fixed Cell Dimension. Input a **10'-0"** cell dimension value and uncheck Auto-Adjust Cells.

2. In the selection pane, click the New Division button. Give the new division the name **Vertical Division**. In the content pane, click the Vertical orientation button. Change Division Type to Manual. On the right side of the content pane, click the Add Gridline button. Gridline 1 appears in the spreadsheet immediately to the left of the Add Gridline button. Click the Offset value for Gridline 1 and change its value to **3'-1"**. Click the From cell for Gridline 1 and change it to Grid Start with the drop-down list that appears.

3. Click the Add Gridline button again and add Gridline 2. Change its From setting to Grid End.

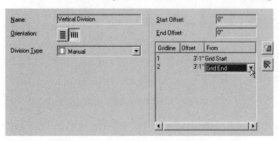

4. Click the Infills node in the tree pane. In the content pane, rename Default Infill to **Panel.**

5. In the selection pane, click the New Infill button. Rename the new infill to **Void Infill**. In the content pane, change Panel Thickness to **0".**

6. Click the Frames node in the tree pane. In the content pane, rename Default Frame to **Metal Frame** and give it a width of **2″** and height of **4″**.

7. In the selection pane, click the New Frame button. Rename the new frame to **Null Frame**. In the content pane, change both Width and Depth to **0″**.

8. Click the Mullions node in the tree pane. In the content pane, rename Default Mullion to **Metal Mullion** and give it a width of **2″** and height of **4″**.

You have added all the element definitions needed to complete this style. Now you'll create a nested grid and assign elements appropriately to both grids.

1. Click the Primary Grid node in the tree pane. In the selection pane, click the New Cell Assignment button. Change its Element assignment to *Nested Grid*. A New Nested Grid node immediately appears indented under Primary Grid in the tree pane.

2. Select and rename New Nested Grid to **Secondary Grid** in the tree pane. Click on the Primary Grid node again.

3. In the selection pane, click the Used In column for the Secondary Grid row and click the ellipsis button. The small Cell Location Assignment dialog box appears. Check Bottom only and click OK, closing the small dialog box. Now the secondary grid will appear nested within the bottom cell of the primary grid.

4. Click the Secondary Grid node in the tree pane. The entire selection pane is replaced with the assignments of the secondary grid. Change its division assignment to Vertical Division.

5. In the selection pane, click the New Cell Assignment button and name the new node **Infill**. Assign the Void Infill element. Click the Used In column for the Secondary Grid row and click the ellipsis button; select Middle only. Click OK to close the Cell Location Assignment dialog box.

6. Assign Null Frame to the Default Frame Assignment node. Leave Metal Mullion as the default mullion assignment. Double-check your work against Figure 10.29, which shows the completed selection panes for both the primary and secondary grids.

7. Click the Materials tab. Assign Doors & Windows.Glazed.Curtain Walls.Stainless Steel.Curtain Wall to the Panel component, and Doors & Windows.Metal Doors & Frames.Aluminum Windows.Painted.White to both the Metal Frame and Metal Mullion components. Click OK to close the Door/Window Assembly Style Properties dialog box.

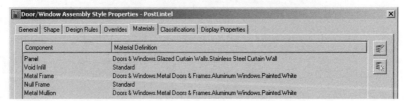

8. Right-click the red lightbulb icon in the drawing tray. Click Isolate Additional Objects from the shortcut menu. Select the DWA and press Enter. The completed style has three stainless steel panels and one open panel that you will infill with other styles (see Figure 10.30). Save your work as **PostLintel.dwg**.

FIGURE 10.29
Assigning elements
to the primary grid
(top) and secondary
grid (bottom)

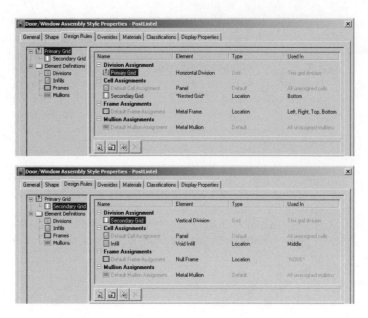

FIGURE 10.29
Assigning elements
to the primary grid
(top) and secondary
grid (bottom)

FIGURE 10.30
Completed
PostLintel DWA

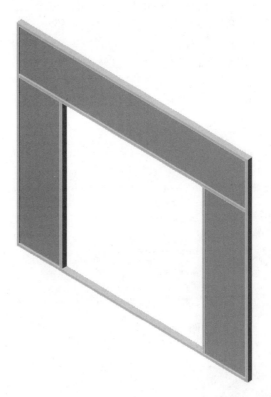

Infilling Styles Within a Door/Window Assembly

You will infill some of the other styles you have already made in this chapter into the PostLintel DWA that was just completed in the last section. In this section we will make three DWA styles: PostLintel-StoneClad, PostLintelTwoWindows, and PostLintelVent. The naming convention I use clearly identifies the DWA style concatenated with its infill style (that is, PostLintel DWA + StoneClad AEC Polygon = PostLintelStoneClad DWA). I suggest following this naming convention in your own projects so you'll know at a glance where to turn when you want to make changes. Alterations made to AEC Polygon, CWU, Door, and/or Window styles that are used as infill in DWA styles immediately propagate to DWA objects.

Creating the PostLintelStoneClad Door/Window Assembly Style

PostLintelStoneClad has an AEC Polygon style acting as infill within a Door/Window Assembly style. In this first example, we will edit the DWA style's design rules and explicitly define a new infill element that references an AEC Polygon style. Then we will replace the existing Void Infill element with the new infill. It is much easier than it sounds.

1. Open `PostLintel.dwg` from your hard drive or the companion DVD if it's not already open.

2. Select the DWA object, right-click, and choose Copy And Assign Door/Window Assembly Style. Click the General tab and rename the style to **PostLintelStoneClad**.

3. Click the Design Rules tab. In the tree pane, click the Infills node. Click the New Infill button in the selection pane and name the new infill **Stone Infill**.

4. In the content pane, click the Infill Type drop-down list and select Style. On the right side of the content pane, scroll up and select the StoneClad AEC Polygon Style.

5. Click the Secondary Grid node in the tree pane. In the selection pane, change the Infill cell assignment to use the Stone Infill element. Click OK to close the Door/Window Assembly Style Properties dialog box.

6. Save your work as **PostLintelStoneClad.dwg** (see Figure 10.31).

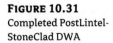

FIGURE 10.31
Completed PostLintel-
StoneClad DWA

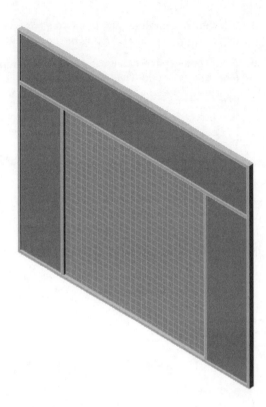

7. Click the AEC Polygon inside the DWA object. Note that the AEC Polygon is selected by itself. Take a look at the Properties palette and you'll see AEC Polygon's properties, even if it is anchored to a cell within the DWA object. Press Esc to deselect.

CREATING THE POSTLINTELTWOWINDOWS DOOR/WINDOW ASSEMBLY STYLE

In the last section you replaced the Void Infill element with the StoneClad style. In some situations you might not want to replace an existing element. What if you aren't replacing Void Infill (because there is nothing there anyway), but some other infill element that you want to keep?

Fortunately, it is possible to create a new cell assignment that can be displayed concurrently with existing elements. You'll learn how to display the TwoWindows style concurrently with Void Infill. The utility of this technique goes beyond this example in which Void Infill isn't displaying anything in the first place. It's important to understand how to display elements concurrently to be able to make sense of the more complex styles that you'll see in subsequent sections.

1. If it's not already, open PostLintelStoneClad.dwg from your hard drive or the companion DVD.

2. You will start with the "template" style as the basis of the new style. Select the DWA object and change its style assignment to PostLintel in the Properties palette.

3. Right-click and choose Copy And Assign Door/Window Assembly Style. Click the General tab and rename the style to **PostLintelTwoWindows**.

4. Click the Design Rules tab. In the tree pane, click the Infills node. Click the New Infill button in the selection pane and name the new infill **TwoWindows**.

5. In the content pane, change the Infill Type drop-down list to Style. On the right side of the content pane, select the TwoWindows CWU style.

6. In the tree pane, click the Secondary Grid node. Click the New Cell Assignment button in the selection pane. Rename the new cell assignment to **Infill Style**. Change Element to TwoWindows, Type to Index, and Used In to 2. Index number 2 is the middle of three vertically oriented cells. This arrangement means that both the Void Infill and TwoWindows will be displayed concurrently in the same middle cell. In this case, Void Infill has a panel thickness of zero, so it is invisible. Click OK to close the dialog box.

7. Click on either of the two windows that now appear as infill with the DWA (see Figure 10.32). The Properties palette reveals access to the anchored CWU object. Press Esc and click the edge of one of the stainless steel panels: the DWA properties appear.

8. Save your work as **PostLintelTwoWindows.dwg**.

9. For the last PostLintel-based DWA style, manually add the Vent infill style to the secondary grid, as we did for the other PostLintel-based styles. Save your work as as **PostLintelVent.dwg**.

FIGURE 10.32
Completed PostLintel_
TwoWindows DWA

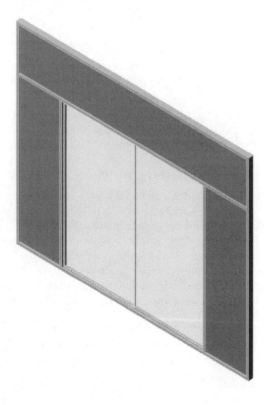

IN-PLACE GRIP EDITING

There is a new feature in ADT 2006 called in-place grid editing. You can edit cells and divisions in place and modify frame and mullion assignments interactively. In-place grid editing is quick and convenient and doesn't require that you really understand the style you are editing.

Although this may sound good at first, I recommend avoiding in-place grid editing if clarity of style is important to you—and it should be, if you plan to elaborate your styles with additional infills in the future. On the other hand, if you are making final modifications to design rules and don't especially need absolute clarity of style, editing a grid in-place is the most expedient solution.

Editing the grid in-place will leave you with messy design rules. Additional grids and cell assignments will be created automatically that have generic names, such as New Nested Grid and New Cell Assignment (5)—not exactly descriptive names. That might be hard to figure out a month from now when you might need to redesign—and therefore understand—the style.

Creating the Entry Door/Window Assembly Style

The last DWA style that we are going to design is called Entry. It will use different door styles as infill: two hinged doors and one revolving door. In addition, the DWA will have two *sidelights*, or vertical glazed cells, on either side of the hinged doors. One continuous glazed *transom* will extend horizontally across the top of all the door cells. We will explicitly specify all aspects of this style for maximum clarity. The Entry DWA style's design rules will use three nested grid levels. I assume that you understand how design rules work by now, so this tutorial is at a slightly higher level than previous ones.

1. Open `PostLintelVent.dwg` from your hard drive or the companion DVD if it's not already open.

2. Click the red lightbulb icon in the drawing tray and choose End Object Isolation from the shortcut menu.

3. Switch to the Top viewpoint and 2D Wireframe display mode. Zoom in on the Entry DWA sketch (refer to Figure 10.5). Select the sketch geometry and isolate it. Figure 10.33 details the design intent of the sketch. The overall dimensions of the sketch are 16′-2″ in length by 10′-0″ in height.

4. Switch to the SE viewpoint and zoom out a bit. Click the Door/Window Assembly tool in the Design palette, press Enter to create a freestanding DWA object, and click the insertion point in the lower-left corner of the sketch. Press Enter twice more to complete the command.

5. Select the DWA object and in the Properties palette, enter 16′-2″ for Length and 10′-0″ for Height.

6. Right-click and choose Copy and Assign Door/Window Assembly Style from the shortcut menu. Give the style the name **Entry**. Click the Design Rules tab of the Door/Window Assembly Style Properties dialog box. Create the following element definitions:

Vertical Division	Manual with 2 gridlines 3′ from both Grid Start and Grid End.
Horizontal Division	Manual with 1 gridline 3′ from Grid Top.

Smaller Vertical Division	Manual with 2 gridlines 2'-6" from both Grid Start and Grid End.
Glass Infill	Simple panel with thickness of $5/8$".
Hinged Door Infill	Simple panel with thickness of 0". We will assign a style later.
Revolving Door Infill	Simple panel with thickness of 0". We will assign a style later.
Metal Frame	Set width to 2" and depth to 4".
Null Frame	Set both width and depth to zero.
Metal Mullion	Set width to 2" and depth to 4".
Null Mullion	Set both width and depth to zero.

7. In the tree pane, click the Primary Grid node. Set Primary Grid to Vertical Division. In the selection pane, click the New Cell Assignment button. To the new cell assignment, assign *Nested Grid* with Location type. Set Used In to Middle. Click the New Nested Grid node in the tree pane and rename it to Secondary Grid.

8. In the tree pane, click the Secondary Grid node. Set Secondary Grid to Horizontal. In the selection pane, click the New Cell Assignment button. To the new cell assignment, assign *Nested Grid* with Location type. Set Used In to Bottom. Change Default Frame Assignment to Null Frame. Double-click the New Nested Grid node in the tree pane and rename it to **Tertiary Grid**.

FIGURE 10.33
Entry DWA elevation sketch and its cells

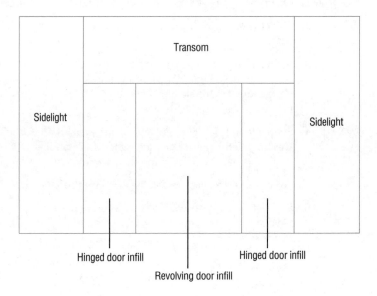

9. In the tree pane, click the Tertiary Grid node. In the selection pane, change Default Cell Assignment to Hinged Door. Click the New Cell Assignment button and give it the name Center Door. To the new cell assignment, assign Revolving Door with Location type. Set Used In to Middle. Change Default Frame Assignment to Null Frame. Change Default Mullion Assignment to Null Mullion (see Figure 10.34).

10. Click OK to close the dialog box. Switch to Flat Shaded, Edges On display mode.

There are actually three cells occupying the void within the Entry DWA style. You can't see them yet because they have zero thickness and do not display frames or mullions. We will now import the styles we want to use as infill to fill this void. Completing the design for this style is then just a question of assigning styles to the Hinged Door and Revolving Door infill elements. Also, the bottom frame of the Primary Grid extends below the door cells; we need to turn this off.

1. Click the Doors palette and scroll down. Right-click the Hinged - Single - Full Lite tool and choose Import Style from the tool menu.

FIGURE 10.34
Entry DWA design rules: primary grid (top), secondary grid (middle), and tertiary grid (bottom)

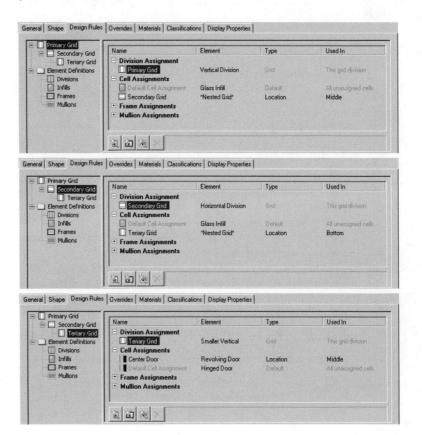

2. For the revolving door, you'll need to import a style from the Content Browser. Press Ctrl+4 to open it. Open the Design Tool Catalog and navigate to the Doors subcategory. Click the link to page 5. Drag the i-drop icon of the Revolving - Custom tool into ADT's drawing window. Press Esc to cancel creating an object; the style has already been imported. Close the Content Browser.

3. Select the DWA object, right-click and choose Edit Door/Window Assembly Style from the shortcut menu. Click on the Infills node in the tree pane. Select Hinged Door in the selection pane. Change the Infill Type from Panel to Style in the content pane. On the right side of the content pane, select the Hinged - Single - Full Lite door style.

4. Repeat step 3 but assign the Revolving - Custom style to the Revolving Door infill.

5. Click the Materials tab and assign the following materials to components:

Doors & Windows.Metal Doors & Frames.Aluminum Windows.Painted.White	To both the Metal Frame and Metal Mullion components
Doors & Windows.Glazing.Clear	To the Glass Infill component

Click OK to close the dialog box.

We still have a problem: the bottom frame of the primary grid cuts through the doors. If you don't use the frame on the bottom, it will not appear at the bottom of the sidelights where it is needed.

To solve this problem, you will create infill overrides the for the middle (door) cells, so the frames disappear there but remain at the bottom of the sidelights. However, cell overrides normally affect objects, not the style itself.

In the end, we need the infill overrides to affect the DWA style so that it can be used as infill within a curtain wall. To accomplish this, you will transfer design rules to the object, make the infill overrides, and then save the changes back to the style. This convoluted path will result in the style we are looking for, complete with overrides stored forever in the style.

1. Select the Entry DWA object, right-click and choose Design Rules ➢ Transfer To Object.

2. Select the Entry DWA object, right-click and choose Infill ➢ Show Markers.

3. Reselect the same object, right-click and choose Infill ➢ Override Assignment. Select the infill marker in the right door's cell. The Infill Override Assignment dialog box appears.

Make sure the Modify Infill radio button is chosen and check Bottom in the Frame Removal group (see Figure 10.35). Click OK and the frame under the door disappears

4. Repeat the previous step twice more and remove the bottom frames from the other two door cells by making infill assignment overrides.

5. Select the Entry DWA object, right-click and choose Design Rules ➢ Save to Style. Check Transfer Infill Overrides To Style in the Save Changes dialog box that appears (see Figure 10.36). Make sure Entry is the selected style and click OK.

TIP Check the Overrides tab in the Entry DWA style properties to manage overrides that have been reintegrated into a style.

6. Hide the elevation sketch lines and save your work as **Entry.dwg**. Figure 10.37 shows the completed style.

FIGURE 10.35
Removing one frame by making an infill assignment override

FIGURE 10.36
Transferring infill overrides back to style

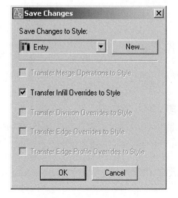

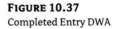

FIGURE 10.37
Completed Entry DWA

Working with Curtain Walls

Curtain walls provide a framework for inserting infill styles including DWA, CWU, AEC Polygons, doors, and windows. Acting more like walls, curtain walls stand on their own and have wall-like features such as a baseline and roof and floor lines, and they can handle interferences.

The Complex CW style we will be designing in this tutorial is the culmination of all your hard work in this chapter. We will construct the complex style element by element, and eventually be in a position to plug in all the styles you have made in this chapter.

Creating the Complex Curtain Wall Style

In sketching the curtain wall, we designed the facade layout using the golden rectangle and the square. We will be referring to this original sketch when designing the complex curtain wall style. Instead of trying to get all the design rules for the complex curtain wall correct the first time they are entered (because we probably won't get it), it is much better to start as simply as possible, and add complexity as we go. That way, we'll avoid having to debug too many errors by using an incremental approach to specifying design rules.

SETTING UP THE ELEVATION SKETCH AND PRIMARY GRID

Let's start by drawing a polyline and from it define a profile that will be used in the CW style. Then we'll create a few element definitions and work on making the Primary Grid perfect. When we are satisfied that the Primary Grid is correct, then we'll go on to add secondary and tertiary nested grids.

1. Open `Entry.dwg` from your hard drive or the companion DVD if it's not already open.

2. Click the red lightbulb icon in the drawing tray and choose End Object Isolation from the short-cut menu.

3. Switch to the Top viewpoint and 2D Wireframe display mode. Zoom in on the facade layout sketch (refer to Figure 10.3). The sketch depicts the bays for which we have already modeled a number of infill styles. The layout and spacing between these bays is how we want the curtain wall to eventually appear. Measure the distance between bays—there are 3'-10" horizontal gaps and 1'-10" vertical gaps. Verify this yourself.

4. To help you visualize where the columns will fit into layout, we'll draw a few alignment lines that we'll delete later on. Make layer zero current and draw a short vertical line 10' down from the bottom left corner of the sketch. Copy this line to every vertex along the bottom of the sketch. Offset the outer lines one column thickness, which is 3'-10", on either side.

5. Switch into the SE Isometric viewpoint. Using the ROTATE3D command and flip up the entire facade sketch 90 degrees from plan to elevation (see Figure 10.38).

FIGURE 10.38
Alignment lines (bottom) on the facade layout sketch

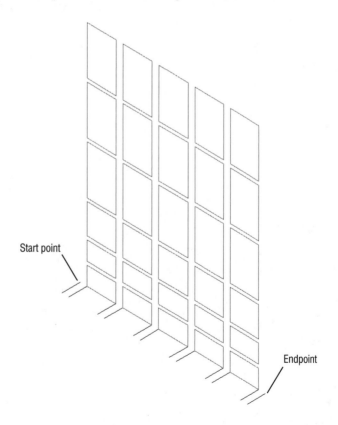

6. Switch back to the Top viewpoint to define the profile you'll use for the columns, which we'll call *piers* in this style. Make the red Layout layer current. Off to the side, draw a rectangle measuring 3'-10" wide by 2'-10" high. Draw a short vertical line measuring 6" down from the midpoint of the rectangle's lower edge, as shown on the left in Figure 10.39.

7. Make Layer zero current. Draw a closed polyline with five vertices around the rectangle and tip of the line, as shown on the right in Figure 10.39.

8. Select the polyline, right-click, and choose Convert To ➤ Profile Definition. Using endpoint object snap, click the insertion point shown in Figure 10.39. Press Enter to create a new profile. Type **Pier** in the New Profile Definition worksheet that appears and click OK. Erase the linework you used to define this profile.

9. Switch back to the SE Isometric viewpoint and change to the Hidden display mode.

Now we are prepared to create the curtain wall object and begin editing its design rules in a new style. The profile definition you just made will be used for some of the element definitions in the primary grid.

1. On the Design palette, click the Curtain Wall tool and click the start points and endpoints, as shown in Figure 10.38. Notice that like the Wall tool, after you draw the first segment, an additional curtain wall segment is attached to the cursor. Because we only want to create one segment, press Enter to end the command.

FIGURE 10.39
Drawing a polyline to
define the Pier profile

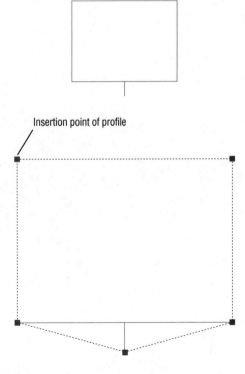

Insertion point of profile

TIP   Change Segment Type to Arc in the Properties palette when you want to draw curtain walls with circular curvature.

2. Select the CW object, right-click, and choose Copy And Assign Curtain Wall Style from the shortcut menu. Click the General tab and rename the style **Complex**.

3. Click the Design rules tab and notice that by default, curtain wall styles have primary and secondary grids. As mentioned before, we want to start as simply as possible, so change the Secondary Grid assignment from *Nested Grid* to Default Infill. The Secondary Grid node disappears from the tree pane. Let's get the Primary Grid perfect before nesting grids.

4. Click the Divisions node in the tree pane. Right-click the Vertical Division in the selection pane and choose Remove from the shortcut menu. In the content pane, rename Horizontal Division to **Vertical Bay**. Click the vertical orientation button. Set Cell Dimension to **20'-0"** and uncheck Auto-Adjust Cells.

5. Click the Infills node in the tree pane. Rename Default Infill to **Null Infill** and change Panel Thickness to **0"**.

6. Click the Frames node in the tree pane. Rename Default Frame to **Pier Frame** and change both Width and Height to **0"** because we want dimensions to come from a profile instead. Check Use Profile and select the **Pier** profile from the Profile drop-down list.

7. Click the Mullions node in the tree pane. Rename Default Mullion to **Pier Mullion** and change both Width and Height to **0"** because we again want dimensions to come from a profile instead. Check Use Profile and select the **Pier** profile again.

8. In the tree pane, click the Primary Grid node. The Pier profile is used in both frame and mullion elements. We don't want piers running horizontally, so change the default frame assignment to be used in Left and Right only. Click OK to close the dialog box.

9. The first pier is offset from the alignment lines you drew earlier by one whole pier width. Select the CW object, right-click, and choose Edit Curtain Wall Style from the shortcut menu. In the tree pane, click the Frames node. On the right side of the content pane, type **-3'-10"** in the X text box in the Offsets group. Using a negative value will move the frame inward. Click OK to close the dialog box. All the piers align properly (see Figure 10.40). Erase all the alignment lines, now that their purpose has been fulfilled.

TROUBLESHOOTING GRIDS

At first glance, the primary grid looks good because we have succeeded in aligning piers along the curtain wall (X direction). However, as you will soon see, there are two more issues to resolve before the primary grid will be complete.

All the infill styles you made earlier in the chapter were centered on their baselines. To simplify infill alignment, we need to move the pier profiles back within the curtain wall (Y direction) approximately half their depth, which is 1'-5".

Edit the Complex CW style and enter a **1'-5"** Y offset for both the Pier Frame and Pier Mullion elements. Closing the Style Properties dialog box shows that the piers have moved back relatively so that the infill is centered within the piers (see Figure 10.41).

FIGURE 10.40
Offsetting profiles to
align piers with sketch

FIGURE 10.41
Offsetting piers within
the curtain wall

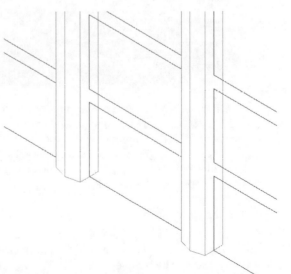

When analyzing any curtain wall, it is helpful to turn on infill markers, which appear in the center of each grid cell and provide a means to visually check the grids you are designing. Select the curtain wall, right-click, and choose Infill ➢ Show Markers. Switch into the Front viewpoint (see Figure 10.42).

The profiles used in the frame and mullion definitions do not delineate cell boundaries by themselves, which will be a problem when we replace the Null Infill with the CWU and DWA styles made earlier. Therefore, you must come up with a solution that ends the cell boundaries exactly at the pier edges, so that the infill styles will fit into the curtain wall without being buried in the piers. The infill markers should appear centered within the bays of the elevation sketch.

The solution to this problem is to nest a secondary vertical grid within the primary grid. The secondary grid will use a division whose spacing matches the width of the columns. Only then will we get cell boundaries exactly where we want them. This is typical of the type of problem solving you have to do when designing curtain walls.

1. Select the CW object, right-click, and choose Edit Curtain Wall Style from the shortcut menu. In the tree pane, click the Divisions node. Click the New Division button in the selection pane. Rename the new division to **Vertical Pier Bay**. Change orientation to Vertical. Change Division Type to Manual. On the right side of the content pane, click the Add Gridline button and give it a **3'-10"** offset value from **Grid Start.**

2. In the tree pane, click the Primary Grid Node. In the selection pane, change the grid's cell assignment to use the *Nested Grid* element. Rename New Nested Grid to Secondary Grid in the tree pane.

FIGURE 10.42
Using infill markers to analyze cell boundaries

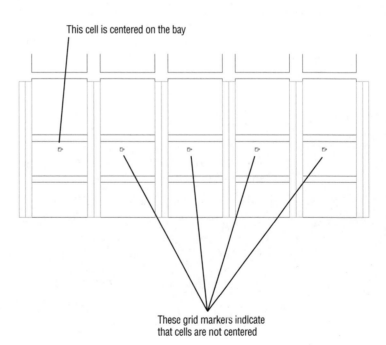

This cell is centered on the bay

These grid markers indicate that cells are not centered

3. Create a Null Mullion element definition and assign it to the secondary grid. Make sure that Null Mullion does not use the Pier profile, and has zero for all other values. Assign the Vertical Pier Bay as the secondary grid element. Click OK to close the Style Properties dialog box. The cell markers are all centered on their bays now (see Figure 10.43). You have succeeded in perfecting the *colonnade* (row of columns or piers) that forms the base of the curtain wall using the frames and mullions of the curtain wall style.

FIGURE 10.43
Secondary grid
centers infill markers
within bays

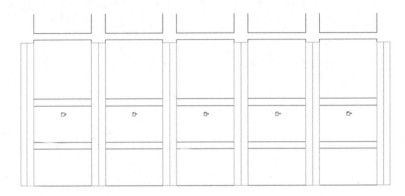

ADDING SPANDRELS

Now we turn our attention to designing *spandrels* (refer to Figure 10.6). The first definition of the term spandrel is *the space in a wall bounded between adjacent arches in an arcade and the stringcourse above them*—as such it is a leftover space. The second definition defines this more abstractly as *any gap between other features that often has a use of its own*. We will bridge the horizontal gap between piers with spandrels. The spandrels will act as mullions within a tertiary grid.

1. Edit the Complex CW style. Add a new mullion element definition called **Spandrel Mullion**. Give it a width of **1'-10"** to match the vertical distance between bays in the elevation sketch. Enter a Depth of **2'-10"** to match the depth of the pier edge defined in the profile. Set the Y offset to 0, if necessary.

2. Click the Secondary Grid node in the tree pane. Change the default cell assignment to *Nested Grid*, and rename the new grid **Tertiary Grid**.

3. Assign Spandrel Mullion to the Tertiary Grid.

4. Assign a new division to the Tertiary Grid and name it **Horizontal Divisions**. Change orientation to Horizontal, change Division type to Manual, and add the first gridline with a **10'-11"** offset from **Grid Bottom.** This is the distance from the baseline to the center of the spandrel between the first and second levels. We will approach this division stepwise to make sure that we are designing it correctly as we go. Click OK to close the Style Properties dialog box.

5. In the Front viewpoint, switch to 2D Wireframe display mode. The spandrels appear correctly superimposed over the elevation sketch.

6. Select the CW object and adjust its Height in the Properties palette to 130′ so it extends some distance above the elevation sketch. Make some measurements to determine how far it is from the baseline of the curtain wall to the upper edge of each spandrel. Note these distances down on paper.

7. We are now in a position to add additional gridlines to Horizontal Divisions. Edit the style yet again and add the following gridlines all measured from Grid Bottom: 23′-8″, 41′-8″, 69′-8″, 97′-8″, and 125′-8″.

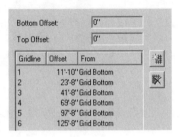

8. Click the Mullions node in the tree pane and select Spandrel Mullion in the selection pane. Give it an 11″ X offset to move the spandrels down half their width. Click OK to close the dialog box.

WARNING Style-based infills start at the grid line and do not respect the mullion thickness, even when it is a "proper" mullion set with explicit sizes and not a 0″ mullion with a profile assigned. For this reason you must offset spandrels so that the infill cell edges match the elevation sketch.

TIP You may have to edit the first gridline to accommodate the spandrel offset. Always compare the evolving curtain wall with the elevation sketch to stay on track.

9. Select the curtain wall and snap its Base Height grip to the top edge of the uppermost spandrel. In the Properties palette, give the curtain wall a height of 125′-9″ to force the top spandrel to appear. Switch to the SE Isometric viewpoint and use Flat Shaded, Edges On display mode.

10. Use the Material tool to assign Masonry.Unit Masonry.Brick.Modular.Running to the following components at the style level: Pier Frame, Pier Mullion, Spandrel Mullion. Congratulations, the curtain wall style is complete (see Figure 10.44). Type **UCS⏎W⏎** to revert to the WCS. Save your work as **Complex.dwg**.

Adding Infill to the Complex Curtain Wall

The last procedure in this chapter—adding infill to the complex curtain wall—is perhaps the most satisfying one because it brings together everything you learned in this chapter. You will define infill elements in the Complex CW style for each infill style that you plan on fitting into its bays. Then you'll override the infill assignment in each cell you want to fill. In addition, some of the cells in the upper courses of the curtain wall need to be subdivided before their infill is overridden; you'll do that with in-place grid editing.

1. Open Complex.dwg from your hard drive or the companion DVD, if it's not already open.

FIGURE 10.44
Completed Complex CW
style

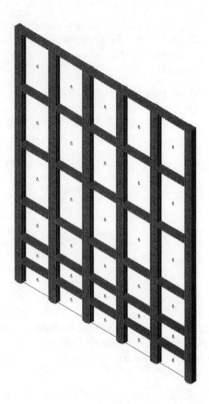

2. Delete all the objects except for the curtain wall. You can use Quick Select to select the elevation sketch linework for deletion (select Line entities).

3. Switch to 2D Wireframe display mode and change to the Front viewpoint. Verify that the Surface Hatch Toggle is off. Hiding the brick surface hatch will speed up display of the curtain wall.

4. Select the CW object, right-click, and choose Edit Curtain Wall Style from the shortcut menu. Click the Design Rules tab and select the Infills node in the tree pane. Add the following infill definitions and match them to their corresponding CWU or DWA style: K-Brace, Office, PostLintelStoneClad, PostLintelTwoWindows, PostLintelVent, and Entry. Click OK to close the dialog box.

5. Select the curtain wall, right-click, and choose Infill ➤ Override Assignment. Click the infill marker in the middle cell of the bottom row and press Enter; the Infill Assignment Override worksheet appears.

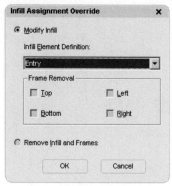

6. Select Entry from the drop-down list and click OK to close the worksheet. Switch to the SE Isometric viewpoint and Hidden display mode. The Entry DWA appears inside the curtain wall (see Figure 10.45).

7. Select the curtain wall. In the Properties palette, click the Overrides worksheet icon in the Advanced category. The Overrides worksheet appears, showing one infill assignment called Primary Grid(3).Secondary Grid(2).Tertiary Grid(1) that is overridden with the Entry infill element. The infill assignment's naming convention is a kind of cellular coordinate system defined in reference to the three grid levels. You might use this worksheet to change the assignment or delete a particular override.

FIGURE 10.45
Overriding infill assignment in curtain wall

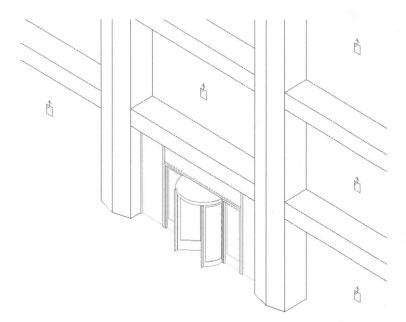

FIGURE 10.46
Overriding infill assignments on the second and third floors

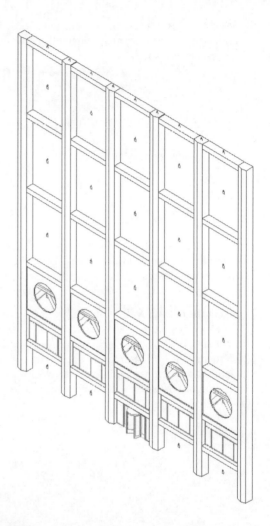

8. You can override infill assignments within multiple cells at the same time. Let's override the entire second level's open bays with Office infill, and the third level's bays with K-Braces. Switch into the Front viewpoint in Hidden display mode.

9. Select the CW object, right-click, and choose Infill ➢ Override assignment. Click each of the five infill markers in the center of each bay on the second level. Press Enter, and the Infill Assignment Override worksheet appears. Choose Office from its drop-down list and click OK. Office CWUs appear as infill.

10. Repeat the previous step, overriding K-Braces in all the bays of the second level. Switch to the SE Isometric viewpoint (see Figure 10.46).

11. Save your work as **ComplexInfill.dwg**.

If you remember from the Creating Door/Window Assemblies section, the PostLintel-based styles are 13'-1" in height. The bays in the curtain wall are exactly double that, measuring 26'-2" in height. Therefore, we must subdivide the remaining bays into upper and lower parts to accommodate the infill. To solve this problem, we could either rethink the design of the entire grid structure or do in-place grid subdivision. We'll take the latter approach because it is a quick way of solving the problem, although it will make a mess of our design rules.

1. Switch to the Front viewpoint in Hidden display mode and select the curtain wall. Zoom out slightly.

2. Click the Edit Grid trigger grip just below the baseline. Press **C** for cell and press Enter. Hold down the Ctrl key first and then click each one of the five bay infill markers on the next course; then press Enter (see Figure 10.47).

3. The Edit Cells worksheet appears. Verify that the Subdivide radio button is selected. To split these cells in half, we need to define a new division. Click the New Division button. The Design Rules dialog box appears, showing only element definitions. Rename the new division to **Half Horizontal**. Verify that orientation is set to Horizontal. Change Division Type to Fixed Cell Dimension. Give the division a 13'-1" cell dimension and click OK to close the Design Rules dialog box.

4. Back in the Edit Cells worksheet, Half Horizontal is selected in the Division drop-down list. Change Mullion to Null Mullion and check Replace Cell (see Figure 10.48). Click OK, and the cells subdivide in half. Press Enter to end the command.

5. Select the curtain wall, right-click, and choose Infill ➢ Override Assignment. Select all the infill markers in the subdivided row (there are 10) and press Enter; the Infill Assignment Override worksheet appears. Choose PostLintelTwoWindows from the drop-down list and click OK.

6. Repeat steps 2–5 for the next two levels. Subdivide the cells using the existing Half Horizontal division Override the second level infill assignments with more PostLintelTwoWindows infill.

7. Override the lower cell of each bay in the top level with PostLintelStoneClad infill.

8. Override the upper cell of each bay in the top level with PostLintelVent infill. Select the curtain wall, right-click, and choose Infill ➢ Hide Markers. Figure 10.49 shows the final result.

FIGURE 10.47
Selecting cells in In-Place Edit mode

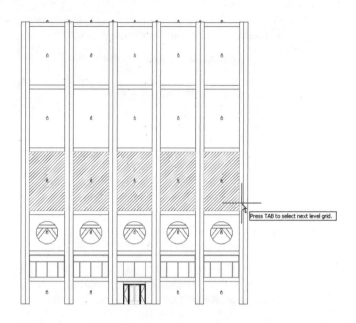

Press TAB to select next level grid.

9. Edit the Complex CW style and take a look at the design rules: they have many more nodes because of the in-place subdivision (see Figure 10.50). You can manage the infill through the Overrides worksheet on the Properties palette. Click Cancel.

TIP If you transfer design rules to object prior to making infill overrides, you have the opportunity to save the overrides back to the style. Use this approach when you want to integrate overrides into a style so that the overrides can be used on multiple curtain wall objects, for example.

10. Save your work as **ComplexInfillComplete.dwg**. This file is provided on the companion DVD for comparison with your own work.

FIGURE 10.48
Subdividing cells

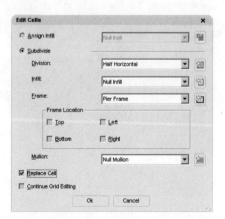

FIGURE 10.49
Completed Complex CW
with infill

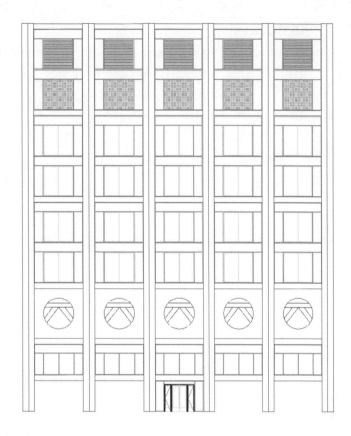

FIGURE 10.50
Complex CW
design rules

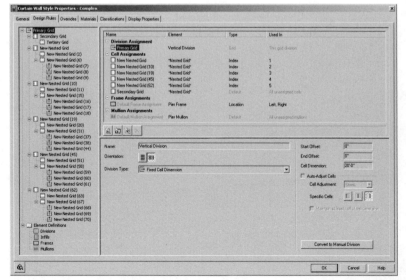

Summary

This chapter has been an in-depth exploration of curtain walls, curtain wall units, door/window assemblies, and AEC Polygon styles. You have seen how all these styles work in similar ways and how each can act as infill in an overall curtain wall. If you could handle the level of complexity found in curtain walls, learning the rest of Architectural Desktop will be a downhill journey. In the next chapter, we'll look at two more object types—slabs and roofs—and explore blocks and related structures.

Chapter 11

Roofs and Slabs

In this chapter we will explore nonvertical building surfaces, including roofs and slabs. In Architectural Desktop, roofs are typically made in three stages. In the first stage, you'll make the overall roof structure by using the Roof tool. Not being style-based, the Roof tool has a limited set of properties that are used to design an integrated set of roof surfaces as a single object.

The second stage of roof design begins after you have gone as far as possible with the Roof object—then you'll convert its roof surfaces into individual roof slabs. Roof slabs are style-based objects that offer you greater control and thus allow you to design the roof, surface by surface. You'll create a variety of roof types, add dormers, and extend the roof, all using roof slabs. In addition, you'll learn how to work with slabs, which are similar to but different from roof slabs. Slabs are style-based objects that can be used for interior horizontal surfaces such as floors, stair landings, and basements.

The final stage of roof design deals with customizing roof slab edges. You'll add profile-based fascia and soffits to individual roof slab edges to further articulate the roof design. Slab edges and roof slab edges work in very similar ways and are based on styles. This chapter's topics include:

◆ Making Roofs

◆ Working with Slabs and Roof Slabs

◆ Customizing Roof Slab Edges

Making Roofs

The simplest roof form is the flat roof. In reality, flat roofs are not perfectly flat; they have a slight *pitch* (degree of deviation from a horizontal plane) to allow for drainage. Although it is technically possible to simulate very slight pitches in ADT, I do not recommend it. It is not worth the effort because slight pitches would hardly be perceived in the 3D model. Instead, slight pitches should be covered in detail drawings or with keynotes. Therefore, flat roofs can be perfectly flat in ADT and are thus easily made directly with roof slabs, which you will learn about later in "Working with Slabs and Roof Slabs."

All other types of roofs are made with the Roof tool as single objects. Before we start making roof objects, it is important to understand some common architectural terms for traditional roof forms. Figure 11.1 shows four such roof types: gable, hip, gambrel, and mansard.

The Gable roof—also known as a saddle roof—is perhaps the most common form. It is composed of two pitched surfaces meeting along a ridge line at the top. The top outer edge of a load-bearing wall is called the *plate line*—whose plate height is equal to the wall's base height. If the walls form a rectangle, the pitches typically spring from the longer sides to minimize the spanned space. The shorter plate edges form *gables*, which are end walls forming an inverted V. The angle of a pitched surface is called its *slope*.

FIGURE 11.1
Architectural roof types

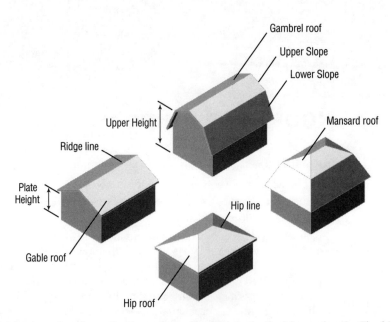

Hip roofs are formed from roof surfaces that have the same pitch on both sides and ends. The *hip line* is the exterior edge where two intersecting pitched roof surfaces meet. Hip roofs can also have a ridge line at the top if the surfaces spring from a rectangle. The ridge line is absent in square hip roofs, whose hip lines all meet in a point at the top of the roof.

Gambrel roofs are gable roofs with two different pitches on either side (with the lower slope being steeper). The upper slope is flatter, and the gable ends have a constant cross-section along the long axis of the structure. Gambrel roofs are typically built from trusses that leave a large portion of the interior open. In barn structures the level that fits within the lower portion of the Gambrel roof is called a *hayloft*.

Mansard roofs—also known as French roofs—have the same Gambrel double pitches on both sides and ends. Think of Mansard roofs as a combination of Gambrel and Hip roof designs. A bit of trivia: An upper floor fitting entirely within the lower roof slopes is called a *garret*. Now that you have reviewed the traditional architectural terminology, let's go ahead and make each of these roof types using the Roof tool.

Creating Roofs Interactively

The Roof tool allows you to create a roof structure composed of multiple faces all in a single object. The Roof tool is somewhat unusual in ADT because it requires that you keep going back to the Properties palette to change the parameters before you create each edge of the roof. In addition, roof objects are normally made by clicking vertices along the exterior base of the walls, rather than on the top of the wall plate.

CREATING A GABLE ROOF

Let's create Gable, Hip, Gambrel, and Mansard roofs in a sample file. In a later section, you'll discover an easier way to create some types of roofs using polylines.

1. Open House.dwg from this chapter's folder on the companion DVD. It contains four sets of rectangular walls. Switch to the SE Isometric viewpoint. Zoom in on the upper-left set of four walls.

2. Click the Design palette and click the Roof tool (see Figure 11.2).

NOTE The Design palette was reorganized in Chapter 10, "Curtain Walls and Assemblies," where the Curtain Wall Unit tool was added to the palette.

3. We'll begin by making a Gable roof. In the Properties palette, change Thickness to 8" and Edge Cut to Square in the Dimensions category. In the Next Edge category, change Shape to Single Slope, Overhang to 1'-0". In the Lower Slope subcategory, change Plate height to 13'-0" to match the base height of the walls. Change Rise to 6" (see Figure 11.3). Notice that Run is grayed-out, meaning that it is not editable. The ratio of rise to run is always some rise distance relative to 12" of horizontal run. If you want, you can enter a Slope angle and then the Rise value will be calculated.

TIP A rise-to-run value of 6:12 is pronounced "six in twelve," meaning that the roof pitch rises 6" vertically for every 12" of horizontal run. This very common pitch has a 26.57 degree slope—you can see why people prefer to speak in terms of rise to run.

4. Click the first and second points shown in Figure 11.4. This sets the first edge with a 6:12 slope.

FIGURE 11.2
Roof and slab tools

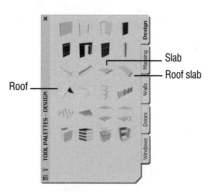

Roof

Slab

Roof slab

FIGURE 11.3
Single slope roof
creation properties

FIGURE 11.4
Sequence of creation
for roof object

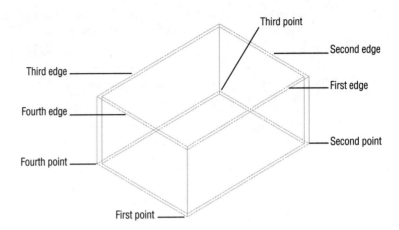

5. In the Properties palette, change Shape to Gable. Click the third point, setting the second edge as a gable end.

6. Change Shape back to Single Slope and click the fourth point. This sets the third edge with a 6:12 slope.

7. Change Shape to Gable again and click the first point once more, setting the fourth edge as a gable end. Press Enter to end the command. The Gable roof appears on top of the wall plate.

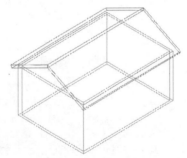

8. There is a gap between the gable end walls and the roof itself. You can easily fill in this gap by projecting the roof line of the walls up to meet the roof. Select both end wall segments, right-click, and choose Roof/Floor Line ➤ Modify Roof Line. The command line says:

```
RoofLine [Offset/Project to polyline/Generate polyline/Auto project/Reset]:
```

Type **A** for Auto Project and press Enter. Select the roof object and press Enter twice more to end the command. The gap is filled by the end walls.

9. Switch into the Top viewpoint. Select the roof object and change Overhang to 1'-6" in the Properties palette. The outer edge of the roof extends farther away from the plate line equally in all directions (see Figure 11.5).

10. Switch into the Front viewport. Zoom in on the Gable roof. Select the roof object and change Edge Cut to Plumb in the Properties palette (see Figure 11.6). Square edge cuts are square with respect to the roof surface itself. Plumb edge cuts have an outer vertical edge perpendicular to the ground plane.

NOTE Actual roof thickness depends on whether you choose square edge cut or plumb cut. In the tutorial, the square cut roof has a thickness of 8" while the plumb cut roof is thinner; with an approximately thickness of 7-5/32", it measures 8" vertically along the vertical plumb edge.

FIGURE 11.5
Roof in plan

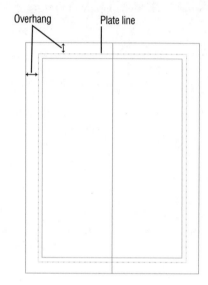

FIGURE 11.6
Roof in elevation

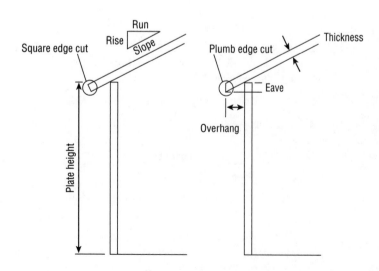

CREATING A HIP ROOF

Let's create a really cool—I mean Hip—roof to be adjacent to the Gable roof you made previously. Instead of switching Shape to Gable on each end, we will leave it set to Single Slope for all four edges.

1. Switch into the SE Isometric viewpoint. Zoom into the set of rectangular walls second from the left. Change the UCS to World.

2. Click the Roof tool. In the Properties palette, change Edge Cut to Plumb, Overhang to 1'-6".

3. Click the first through fourth points (refer to Figure 11.4). Press Enter, and the Hip roof is created. Switch to Hidden display mode.

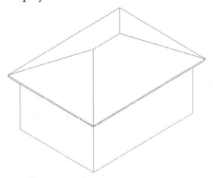

CREATING A GAMBREL ROOF

The Gambrel roof has two different slopes that carry all the way through its long axis. To control where the two pitches intersect, you'll specify the Upper Height parameter (refer to Figure 11.1). I'll give you a value in this tutorial, but you might want to make an elevation sketch to determine the Upper Height value in your own projects.

1. Pan over to the third set of rectangular walls, adjacent to the Hip roof you have already created. Switch to 2D Wireframe display mode.

2. Click the Roof tool. In the Properties palette, change Edge Cut to Square, Shape to Double Slope, Overhang to 1'-0", Lower Slope Rise to 2' 2-1/2", Upper Height to 20'-8", and Upper Slope Rise to 6" (see Figure 11.7).

3. Click the first two points (refer to Figure 11.4) to set the first edge with double slopes.

4. In the Properties palette, change Shape to Gable. Click the third point, setting the second edge as a gable end.

5. Change Shape back to Double Slope and click the fourth point. This sets the third edge with double slopes.

6. Change Shape to Gable again and click the first point once more, setting the fourth edge as a gable end. Press Enter to end the command. The Gambrel roof appears on top of the wall plate.

7. Fill the wall gap by selecting both end wall segments, right-click, and choose Roof/Floor Line ➢ Modify Roof Line. Type **A** for Auto Project and press Enter. Select the roof object and press Enter twice more to end the command.

FIGURE 11.7
Gambrel roof
creation properties

CREATING A MANSARD ROOF

The Mansard roof is easily made by setting double slopes on all four edges.

1. Pan over to the last set of rectangular walls.

2. Click the Roof tool. In the Properties palette, change Shape to Double Slope. All the parameters retain their values from making the Gambrel roof, so you don't have to change anything else.

3. Click the first through fourth points (refer to Figure 11.4). Press Enter, and the Mansard roof is created. Switch to Flat Shaded, Edges On display mode. Figure 11.1 shows similar results.

4. Save your work as **RoofTypes.dwg**. Unless otherwise noted, always leave sample files open in this chapter.

TIP Files are provided on the companion DVD at the end of each section in case you decide to jump in anywhere.

Creating Roofs from Polylines

An alternative to interactively creating roofs edge-by-edge is to create roofs from polylines. This is a faster way to generate Hip and Mansard roofs. The beauty of the Roof tool is how it can calculate complex ridge and hip line intersections in a fraction of a second. This is surely an example of ADT's power to solve complex problems quickly compared with traditional CAD or manual drafting projection techniques.

1. Open the file RoofTypes.dwg if it is not already open.

2. Thaw the Layout layer. Two polylines appear: one with a curve and the other with all rectangular edges.

3. Right-click the Roof tool in the Design palette. Choose Apply Tool Properties To ➤ Linework and Walls. Click the exclusively rectangular-edged polyline and press Enter. The command line says:

```
Erase layout geometry? [Yes/No] <No>:
```

Press Enter twice to complete the command and leave the original polyline intact. A Mansard roof appears directly on the ground. The reason for this is that a double-sloped roof was the last roof shape you made in the previous section; parameters persist in the Roof tool until you change them.

NOTE You'll create a roof from walls in the "Making a Lantern" section later in this chapter.

4. In the Properties palette, change Shape to Single Slope. An enormously tall roof appears. For the moment the new roof is as tall as the Mansard roof created previously.

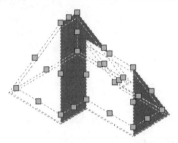

5. Change Rise to 6″, and the roof's overall height gets recalculated so that it assumes a more compact size. Change Plate Height to 13′, and the roof object almost magically floats over non-existent walls. ADT has calculated precisely where the ridge and hip lines need to be given the slope of the individual roof surfaces (see Figure 11.8).

6. Right-click the Wall tool in the Design palette and choose Apply Tool Properties To ➢ Linework. Select the polyline and press Enter twice. On the Properties palette, set the wall's base height to 13′, if necessary. Generic walls appear supporting the complex hip roof.

Let's make a curved roof from the remaining polyline. Although ADT does not make true curved roof surfaces, it approximates curves with faceted surfaces. The most efficient way to create a curved roof surface is to convert an existing polyline into a roof. You'll see in the next section how you can control the number of faceted segments comprising a roof object (not with the FACETDEV system variable as you might suspect).

1. Right-click the Roof tool in the Design palette. Choose Apply Tool Properties To ➢ Linework and Walls. Select the remaining polyline and press Enter twice.

2. In the Properties palette, change Shape to Single Slope, Rise to 9″, Plate Height to 13′-0″, and Edge Cut to Plumb. Press Esc to deselect.

3. Right-click the Wall tool in the Design palette and choose Apply Tool Properties To ➢ Linework. Select the polyline and press Enter twice. On the Properties palette, set the wall's base height to 13′, if necessary. Generic walls appear supporting the curved roof. The curved hip roof is made of straight-line faceted edges that each joins the ridge line with individual hip lines (see Figure 11.9).

4. Save your work as **PolylineRoofs.dwg**.

FIGURE 11.8
Complex Hip roof
created from polyline

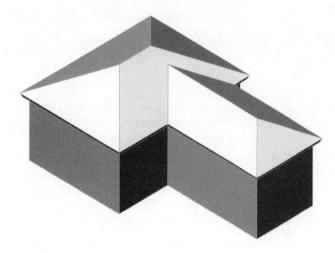

FIGURE 11.9
Curved roof created
from polyline

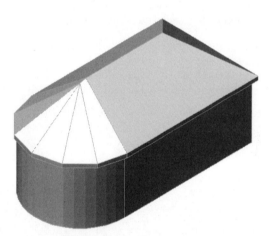

Editing Roofs

Roofs have limited editability as roof objects. You can edit roofs with grips, and it is also possible to edit a roof's individual edges and faces. Changes you make to one portion of the roof object are coordinated with respect to all the other surfaces in the roof. The roof object ensures that you always get clean surface intersections in ridge and hip lines. In general, take roof editing as far as possible before converting the one-piece roof into separate roof slabs.

EDITING WITH GRIPS

The most obvious way to edit a roof object is by using its grips. We will extend a roof beyond its plate line by strategically moving grips. In addition, you'll convert a Hip end into a Gable end by moving one grip. This will produce a roof structure that is a hybrid Gable/Hip type.

1. Open PolylineRoofs.dwg if it's not already open.

2. Switch to the Top viewpoint in 2D Wireframe display mode. Zoom in on the Gambrel roof.

3. Select the Gambrel roof to turn on its grips. Click the upper grip and move it vertically upward a distance of 2' using polar tracking (you might need to turn off dynamic dimensions if they interfere with polar tracking). Click the lower grip and move it down 2' (see Figure 11.10). Press Esc to deselect.

4. Switch back to the SE Isometric viewpoint. Change to Hidden display mode and zoom in on the Gambrel roof. Notice the eave line poking out beyond the wall plate—this indicates that the eaves have been deepened (see Figure 11.11).

5. Pan over to the Hip roof and select it. There are three grips along the ridge line: one in the middle and two where the ridge line meets the two hip lines on either side. Click the leftmost ridge line grip and move it along a line parallel to the long axis of the roof. Click a point some arbitrary distance in front of the building, being sure to be at least beyond the edge of the roof itself (see Figure 11.12). The front hip becomes a gable.

6. Fill the wall gap by selecting the front wall segment, right-click, and choose Roof/Floor Line ≻ Modify Roof Line. Type **A** for Auto Project and press Enter. Select the roof object and press Enter twice more to end the command. Switch to Flat Shaded, Edges On display mode (see Figure 11.13).

FIGURE 11.10
Making deeper eaves by grip editing the Gambrel roof

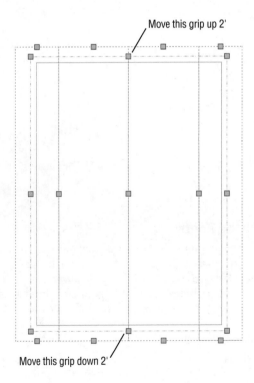

Move this grip up 2'

Move this grip down 2'

FIGURE 11.11
Eave line shows evidence of roof extending beyond wall plate.

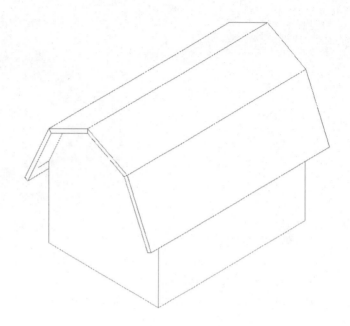

FIGURE 11.12
Converting a hip end to gable end by moving a grip

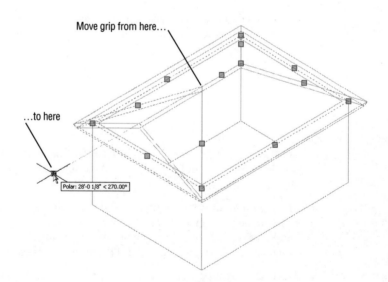

Move grip from here…

…to here

Polar: 28'-0 1/8" < 270.00°

FIGURE 11.13
Hybrid roof with gable
(left) and hip (right) ends

EDITING ROOF EDGES AND FACES

There are two ways to edit roof edges and faces: all at once or one at a time. Access to the all-at-once method is provided from a worksheet in the Properties palette. The one-at-a-time method is accessed through the roof object's right-click menu. Let's try both methods.

1. Zoom into the curved roof and select it. Starting with the all-at-once method, click the Edges/ Faces worksheet icon in the Dimensions category of the Properties palette. The Roof Edges and Faces worksheet is organized into two parts: Roof Edges and Roof Faces (by Edge). There are illustrations in the worksheet that identify the labeled parameters of Height, Overhang, and Eave. In addition, for curved edges you can adjust the number of straight-line Segments that approximate the curve and the Radius of the curve itself. The edges are numbered sequentially starting at zero.

2. In the Roof Edge group, change Edge 2's Radius to 12′-0″ and Segments to 12.

3. The Face information that appears in the Roof Faces (by Edge) group depends on which Edge is selected in the Roof Edges group. Make sure that Edge 2 is selected, and change Slope to 45.00 degrees (see Figure 11.14). Click OK to close the worksheet.

4. Moving on to the one-at-a-time method, right-click and select Edit Edges/Faces from the shortcut menu. Click the rear edge of the curved roof object and press Enter. The Roof Edges and Faces worksheet reappears, but this time only one edge (and face) is listed. Change the face's slope to 90 degrees and click OK; the back edge becomes a gable end (see Figure 11.15).

5. The walls that support the curved roof no longer line up with it because of the changes that were made to the roof object's edges and faces. We won't pursue this issue further in this chapter, but of course you would alter the curved wall to fit properly under the curved roof in a real project. Delete all objects except for the Gambrel roof and its walls: we will focus on this structure for the rest of this chapter. Save your work as **EditedRoof.dwg**.

FIGURE 11.14
Editing roof edges and
faces in the curved roof

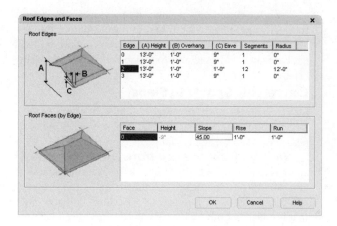

FIGURE 11.15
Edited curved roof

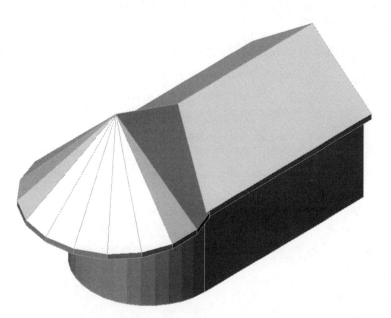

Working with Slabs and Roof Slabs

Slabs and roof slabs have much in common, although they are controlled through different styles. Use slabs for floors, stair landings, and any other flat or sloping planar surface. The obvious distinction is to use roof slabs for roofs; roof slabs do everything slabs do and more.

You can create roof slabs from scratch or convert the surfaces of a roof object into individual roof slabs. Either way, roof slabs give you much greater control over the way roof surfaces meet, including the ability to cut holes, add or subtract volumes, and add dormers.

The edge conditions of slabs and roof slabs are controlled by separate styles called slab edge and roof slab edge styles, which are responsible for overhang length, edge cut orientation, and more. You'll learn how to control edge conditions later in this chapter. In this section, you will build several different kinds of slab-based and roof slab-based structures during the course of the tutorials that follow.

Converting Spaces to Slabs

New!

Slabs are pretty straightforward because they are, well—slabs. Not too much going on there, if you ask me. You can create slabs from scratch by clicking vertices, or (now in ADT 2006) convert existing space or area objects into slabs.

Whether you choose to use spaces, areas, or slabs depends upon the purpose of your model. Both space and area objects can calculate floor areas. Spaces are often used to accept property data and annotation (see Chapter 13, "Annotating, Tagging, and Dimensioning"). Areas have complex calculation features (see Chapter 14, "Schedules, Display Themes, and Areas"). Slabs possess volumes that are visible both in 3D viewpoints and in renderings (see Chapter 18, "Using VIZ Render"). So choosing which object to represent a floor depends upon what your needs are. You can also use some combination or use slabs, spaces, and areas concurrently.

The sample file contains a couple of hidden spaces that you'll convert to slabs. Then you'll take a look at the simple design rules of slab styles.

1. Open EditedRoof.dwg if it's not already open. Switch to the 2D Wireframe display mode.

2. Click the red light bulb icon in the drawing tray and choose End Object Isolation from the shortcut menu. Two spaces appear within the structure.

3. Select the roof object and all four walls. Click the yellow light bulb icon in the drawing tray and choose Hide Objects from the shortcut menu.

4. Switch to Flat Shaded, Edges On display mode. The space objects have materials assigned to their Floor and Ceiling components (see Figure 11.16).

5. Right-click the Slab tool in the Design palette and choose Assign Tool Properties To ➢ Spaces. Select both space objects and press Enter.

6. In the Convert Space to Slab worksheet that appears, check Erase Layout Geometry to delete the spaces. Note that you have the option of creating slabs for ceilings as well. Click OK. The ceilings from the spaces disappear, and gray slabs replace the floors.

FIGURE 11.16
Spaces with floors and
ceilings appear within
building.

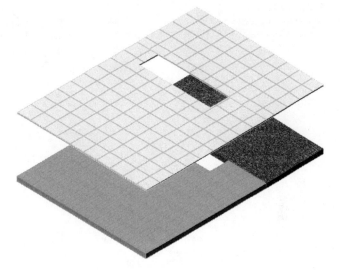

FIGURE 11.16
Spaces with floors and
ceilings appear within
building.

7. Select the new slabs, right-click, and choose Edit Slab Style from the shortcut menu. Click the Design Rules tab and notice the very simple interface. Check Has Fixed Thickness and type **1'-0"** in the Thickness text box (see Figure 11.17). Thickness Offset is often used with a negative value equal to the Thickness value if you want the slab to extend downward from its baseline. In this case, leave Thickness Offset at zero and click OK.

8. Select the slab objects, right-click, and look in the Properties palette. Notice that the Thickness property is grayed-out, meaning that it is not editable. This property was editable before you checked Has Fixed Thickness in the slab style—now the style controls thickness. Note that there is a Slope subcategory so you can have angled slabs (see Figure 11.18). We will explore this functionality in the context of roof slabs instead.

9. Save your work as **Slabs.dwg**.

FIGURE 11.17
Slab style design rules

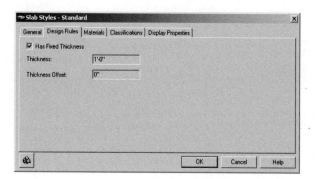

FIGURE 11.18
Slab object properties

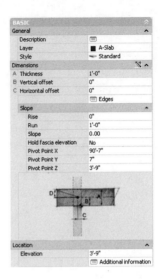

Creating Roof Slabs from Scratch

Creating a roof slab from scratch is a good introduction to this complex object type. Although roof slabs are usually made by converting roof objects, it is instructive to understand the roof slab object by itself. You'll first need to understand how roof slabs work to make all the interesting roof structures in the following sections (see Figure 11.19).

To get started creating roof slabs from scratch, let's create a wall off to the side and project a roof slab on top of its plate line.

1. Open Slabs.dwg if it's not already open. Switch to 2D Wireframe display mode.

2. Create a 15′ generic wall object off to the side and parallel to the long axis of the building (in the Y direction). Set the generic walls to have an 8′ base height; we will have to match this height in the roof slab we will create next.

FIGURE 11.19
Structures made with roof slabs

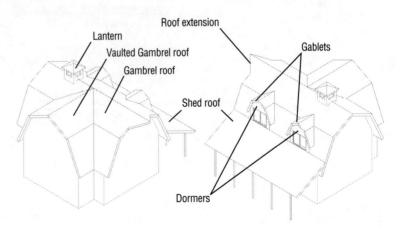

3. Click the Roof Slab tool in the Design palette. In the Properties palette, set Mode to Projected if it is not already set. In the Dimensions category, change Thickness to 1', Justify to Slopeline, Base Height to 8', and Overhang to 2'. In the Slope subcategory, change Rise to 4".

4. Click the first and second points of the roof slab at the wall's start and end points. Move the cursor in the 180-degree direction (perpendicular to the first two points) and type **10'**. The command line says:

```
Specify next point or [Style/Mode/Height/Thickness.Slope/Overhang/
Justify/Match/Undo/Ortho close/Close]:
```

Type **O** for Ortho close and press Enter twice to end the command. The roof slab appears atop the wall.

5. Select the roof slab object and look at the Properties palette; all the starburst icons are gone—they only appear prior to object creation. Change Vertical Offset to 6" and Horizontal Offset to 24" (see Figure 11.20).

WARNING   You cannot change the Justify property for roof slabs after object creation: it must be set prior.

6. Switch into the Top viewpoint. The dashed blue line is the baseline; the lower edge of the roof slab might overhang the baseline, and it does in this example. Each edge has a grip defining the perimeter and also an edge overhang grip that allows you to extend any edge beyond the perimeter of the roof slab you drew in step 4. In this example, the horizontal offset distance transformed the baseline outward 2' relative to the plate line.

FIGURE 11.20
Roof slab properties prior to object creation (left) and after (right)

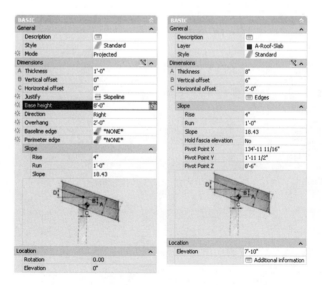

7. Switch to the Front view. You'll find a Pivot Point grip in this viewpoint that controls the center of rotation for the slab. The Angle grip can be used to rotate the slab. Switch back to SE Isometric view, study Figure 11.21, and correlate it with what you see in the drawing window. Reset the UCS to World.

8. Save your work as **RoofSlab.dwg**.

FIGURE 11.21
Critical roof slab
dimensions and grips

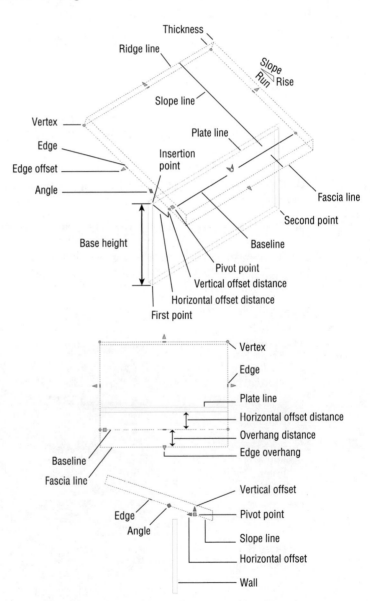

To understand the roof slab object, think through its creation process. You first clicked two points along the base of the wall. This initially determined the roof slab baseline, but the baseline was immediately offset upward by the Base Height creation property to match the height of the wall. So the roof slab's insertion point became the top of the wall directly above the first point you clicked. So far so good: The wall's plate line matches the roof slab baseline.

In step 5 you offset the baseline both vertically and horizontally from its original position, which might be helpful in situations where you are aligning with other geometry such as structural members or other roof slabs.

The pivot point is always at the end of the baseline. What makes matters slightly confusing is there is also a vertex grip coincident where the pivot point resides, so ADT bumps the pivot point slightly over along the baseline or toward the eave so you can still access the vertex grip.

The *slopeline* is an imaginary line that runs perpendicular to the baseline in section along the slope of the roof slab. The slopeline is the position of the slab baseline relative to its bottom face. The value you enter for the thickness offset in the roof slab style determines the distance between the baseline and the bottom face of the roof slab. In our example, the slopeline is flush with the bottom face of the roof slab, but it doesn't have to be. The Justify creation property also affects the placement of the roof slab relative to its baseline.

Study the placement of the baseline, fascia line, ridge line, and slopeline to familiarize yourself with these concepts. What you might have initially considered to be an inert slab actually contains a great deal of complexity. It is this complexity that gives the roof slab enough flexibility to fit into almost any architectural situation.

Making a Vaulted Gambrel Roof

A vaulted roof is one that forms a perfect intersection between two perpendicular roof structures the way a medieval groin vault is the intersection of two barrel vaults. To make a vaulted Gambrel roof, we will copy the existing roof in-place and rotate it 90 degrees from the midpoints of both roof ridge lines.

1. Open RoofSlab.dwg if it's not already open.

2. Click the red light bulb icon in the drawing tray and choose End Object Isolation from the shortcut menu. The Gambrel roof, its walls, and the slabs within reappear.

3. Select the freestanding roof slab object and its single wall segment. Click the yellow light bulb icon in the drawing tray and choose Hide Objects from the shortcut menu.

4. Select the roof object, right-click, and choose Basic Modify Tools ➢ Copy. The command line asks you to specify a base point. Instead of actually clicking in the drawing window, press @ and Enter. This means that the base point is relative to the roof's existing base point. The command line now says:

   ```
   Specify second point or [Exit/Undo] <Exit>:
   ```

   Press @ and Enter again to indicate that the second point is also equal to the original base point. Press Enter once more to end the command. This little trick copies the object in-place.

5. To rotate only one roof object, we'll use another lesser-known AutoCAD feature called Last Object Selection mode. The "last" object is defined as the last object or entity that was created

of those on the screen at the time "last" is specified. Type **RO** and press Enter to execute the Rotate command. Press **L** and Enter to select the roof created in the previous step. Press Enter once more to exit selection mode. Snap to the midpoint of the ridge for the base point. Type **90** and press Enter to rotate the second roof perpendicular to the original roof (see Figure 11.22).

6. Convert the roof objects to a collection of roof slabs; select both roofs, right-click, and choose Convert To Roof Slabs from the shortcut menu. Check Erase Layout Geometry in the Convert To Roof Slabs worksheet that appears. We'll use the Standard roof slab style at this point; click OK to close the worksheet. Eight roof slab objects replace the two roofs. Press Esc to deselect.

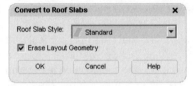

7. To differentiate the two roofs, you will assign a material to the original roof structure, which has become four roof slabs. Select these four slabs, right-click and choose Copy Roof Slab Style And Assign. Click the General tab, rename the style **GambrelRoof**, and click OK. Click the Material tool in the Design palette and select one of the original roof slabs; the Apply Materials To Components worksheet appears. Assign following material to the Style:

```
Thermal & Moisture.Shingles.Asphalt Shingles.3-Tab.Black
```

Click OK to close the worksheet.

FIGURE 11.22
Rotating a copy
perpendicular to
the original roof

8. Select the nearest lower slope shingled roof slab that overhangs the walls. Right-click and choose Miter from the shortcut menu. The command line says:

```
Miter by [Intersection/Edges] <Intersection>:
```

Press Enter to accept Intersection as the method and then click the two overhanging eaves shown in Figure 11.23. Mitering is the roof slab equivalent of filleting linework.

9. Miter the upper slopes in much the same way. Click the upper slope roof slab of the shingled roof, right-click, and choose Miter and press Enter for Intersection. Select both upper sloped roof slabs on this side of the ridgeline of the shingled roof and press Enter. You will eventually mirror the beautifully mitered slabs about the midpoint of the ridge line to complete the vaulted Gambrel. Half of the vaulted roof is now redundant; delete both these roof slabs (see Figure 11.24).

10. Select both vaulted roof slabs and change their Style to GambrelRoof in the Properties palette. Mirror all four roof slabs on this side of the ridge line about the center of the vault to complete the roof structure. Switch to Hidden display mode (see Figure 11.25).

11. The walls need to be addressed at this point so that they support the vaulted roof. Switch to the Top viewpoint and use 2D Wireframe display mode. So you can see through the roof, toggle surface hatch off in the drawing tray. In the Design palette, click the Wall tool and change Justify to Right in the Properties palette. Click the four points indicated in Figure 11.26 along roof slab baselines. Press Enter to complete the AddWall command.

FIGURE 11.23
Mitering roof slabs where they intersect

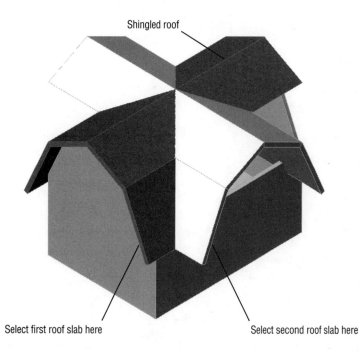

Shingled roof

Select first roof slab here

Select second roof slab here

FIGURE 11.24
Mitering upper-sloped
roof slabs and deleting
redundant roof slabs

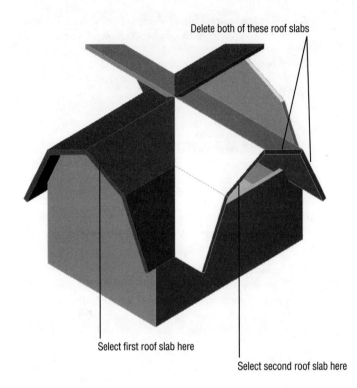

Delete both of these roof slabs

Select first roof slab here

Select second roof slab here

FIGURE 11.25
Completed vaulted
Gambrel roof

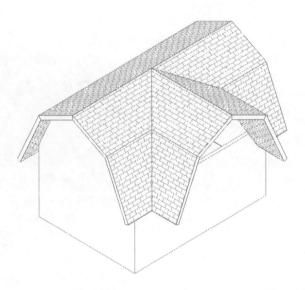

FIGURE 11.26
Creating walls to support
the roof structure

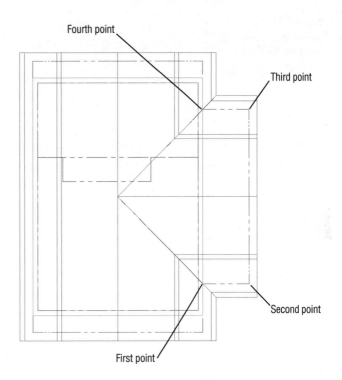

Fourth point

Third point

Second point

First point

12. Switch back to the SE Isometric viewpoint and use Hidden display mode. The walls you created previously are at the elevation of the roof baseline. Select all three wall segments and change Elevation to zero and Base Height to 13′ in the Properties palette.

13. Type **TR** and press Enter to execute the Trim command. Select both of the shorter wall segments as the cutting edges and press Enter. Click the middle of the existing wall to trim it away. Press Enter again to complete the command.

14. Select all three wall segments again. Right-click and choose Roof/Floor Line ➢ Modify Roof Line. Press **A** and then Enter for the Auto-Project option. Select all four vaulted roof slabs and press Enter. The walls reach the roof that overhangs them (see Figure 11.27).

15. Save your work as **VaultedGambrel.dwg**.

FIGURE 11.27
Adjusting walls to
complete building
envelope

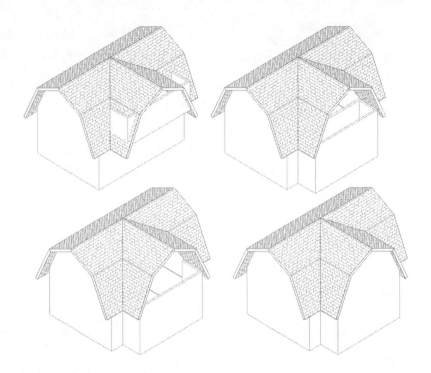

Making a Shed Roof

A *shed roof* is one that has a single slope and roof slab. We will hang a shed roof off the side of our Gambrel roof—traditionally a very common variant and complement to the Gambrel.

1. Open VaultedGambrel.dwg if it's not already open.

2. Switch to the Front viewpoint. We will make shed roof on the left side of the structure, opposite the vaulted Gambrel structure you made in the previous section. I want to match the shed roof's slope to the upper slope of the Gambrel roof. The easiest way to do this is to copy the upper roof slab and then adjust it to become the new shed roof.

3. To properly align the shed roof with the structure make some construction lines; click the Construction Line tool in the Shapes toolbar (this executes the AecConstructionLine command, not the old XLINE command from AutoCAD). Click the outer edge of the building wall and press Enter to avoid inputting an offset value. Click the outer edge of the lower Gambrel roof slab and press Enter and then Esc to end the command. Copy the upper roof slab from the ridge line to the intersection of the two construction lines (see Figure 11.28).

WARNING Construction lines must intersect in 3D to snap an object to their intersection point. You may need to look at the model from different viewpoints to understand exactly where the construction lines are in three dimensions.

FIGURE 11.28
Copying the upper
roof slab

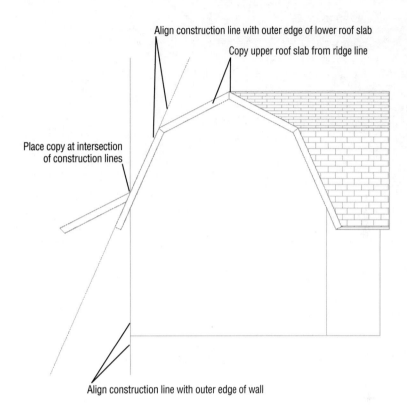

Align construction line with outer edge of lower roof slab

Copy upper roof slab from ridge line

Place copy at intersection
of construction lines

Align construction line with outer edge of wall

4. Switch into the NW Isometric viewpoint. Your shed roof might not be snapped correctly in all three dimensions because you copied it in the Front elevation. Type **ALIGN** on the command line and press Enter. Click the first source point at the endpoint of the shed roof. Snap the first destination point perpendicular to the edge of the roof slab you want to align with and press Enter (see Figure 11.29). The shed roof should line up perfectly. Delete the construction lines.

5. Select the shed roof, right-click, and choose Cut. The shortcut menu also lists Trim and Extend, which are to roof slab objects as the AutoCAD TRIM and EXTEND commands are to entities.

FIGURE 11.29
Aligning shed roof
with structure

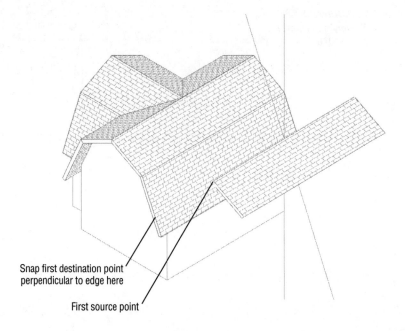

Snap first destination point
perpendicular to edge here

First source point

6. Select the lower slope roof slab as the cutting object and press Enter. The intersecting volume of the shed roof is cut away.

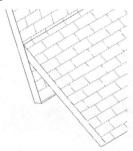

7. Select the shed roof and click its middle edge grip. Move the cursor down using Polar object tracking, type **4′**, and press Enter. You might need to turn off dynamic dimensions if they interfere with polar tracking. The shed roof extends outward, maintaining its slope of 6:12 (see Figure 11.30). A temporary UCS is used as you extend the roof, and then the UCS reverts back to what it was before.

8. Create five equally spaced 4x4 wooden posts to support the shed roof's outer edge. Figure 11.31 shows the result. Don't worry about creating the posts now if you haven't yet read Chapter 7, "Parametric Layouts, Anchors, and Structural Members."

9. Save your work as **ShedRoof.dwg**.

FIGURE 11.30
Extending Shed roof
with edge grip

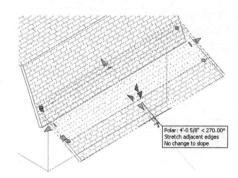

FIGURE 11.31
Completed Shed roof
with supporting posts

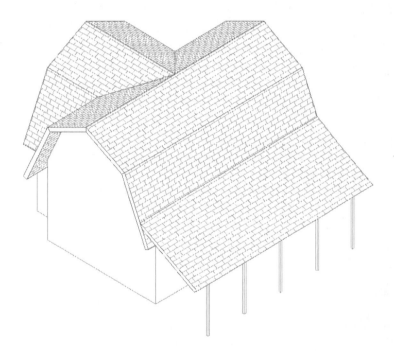

Making a Lantern

The architectural definition of the term *lantern* is a light covered structure set upon a roof to bring light and air into the interior. The term *cupola* refers to a similar ancillary structure, although cupolas typically sit upon domes. Lanterns are sometimes seen sitting upon cupolas, as in the case of the Florence cathedral, for example. We will make a lantern to sit upon the ridge line of the Gambrel roof.

1. Open ShedRoof.dwg if it's not already open.

2. Switch to the Top viewpoint and use 2D Wireframe display mode.

3. Draw a few construction lines, as shown in Figure 11.32. Select all three construction lines and change Basepoint Z to zero in the Properties palette—moving all the construction lines to the ground plane.

4. Off to the side, draw a polyline in the shape of a square with a 2'-6" edge length.

5. Right-click the Wall tool in the Design palette and choose Assign Tool Properties To ➤ Line-work. Select the square polyline and choose to erase the layout geometry. Four generic walls appear with a Base Height of 8'. In the Properties palette, change Justify to Left so that the walls are offset outside the square.

6. Switch to the SE Isometric viewpoint in Hidden display mode. Add four openings measuring 2'x1'-6" centered on each edge. Select all four openings and change the Sill Height to 6' in the Properties palette. Air and light will enter the interior through these openings in the lantern.

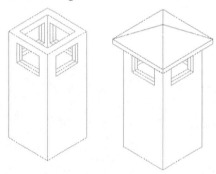

FIGURE 11.32
Aligning construction lines with salient geometry

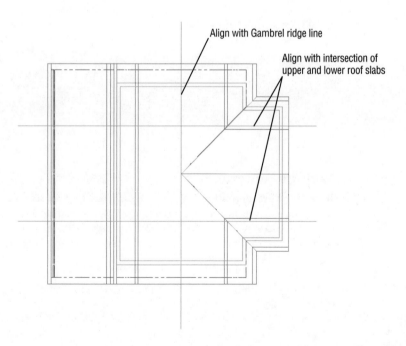

Align with Gambrel ridge line

Align with intersection of upper and lower roof slabs

7. To make the hip rooflet sitting atop the lantern, right-click the Roof tool in the Design palette, and choose Apply Tool Properties To ➤ Walls. Select all four walls of the lantern and press Enter. Do not erase the layout geometry because you'll need the walls to form the lantern's enclosure. In the Properties palette, set Thickness to 4", Edge Cut to Plumb, Shape to Single Slope, Overhang to 6", Plate Height to 8', and Rise to 6". There is no need to convert the rooflet to roof slabs because it is perfect as it is.

8. Switch to the Top viewpoint and use 2D Wireframe display mode. Move all the parts of the lantern from the center of the rooflet to the intersection of the construction lines at the point shown in Figure 11.33. Switch to the Front viewpoint. Move the previous selection set up 29' above the ground plane.

9. Switch to the NW Isometric viewpoint and toggle surface hatch off. Zoom in on the lantern and set the UCS to World. Select all four lantern walls, right-click, and choose Modify Roof/Floor Line ➤ Modify Floor Line. Type **A** for auto-project, select both upper roof slabs, and press Enter twice to end the command. The lantern walls are truncated where they penetrate the roof slabs—switch to Hidden display mode (see Figure 11.34).

10. Save your work as **Lantern.dwg**.

FIGURE 11.33
Positioning the Lantern

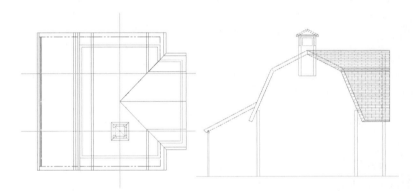

FIGURE 11.34
Completed Lantern

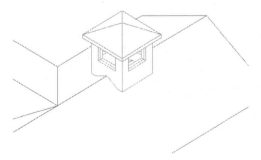

Making a Roof Extension

Many historic barns have roof extensions to accommodate a block-and-tackle or pulley system to hoist goods up to the hayloft. We will make just such a roof extension to the Gambrel roof in decorative homage to this practical architectural tradition. The technique shown can suit any situation in which you want to alter the form of a roof in a completely ad-hoc fashion.

1. Open Lantern.dwg if it's not already open.

2. Before we can extend the roof, we need to create the *topology*—or wireframe structure—to support our ideas. We'll start by adding new vertices to the roof slabs where we plan to sprout an extension. Select the upper-slope roof slab on the far side of the ridge line. Right-click and choose Add Vertex from the shortcut menu. Click the midpoint of the overhanging edge (see Figure 11.35). A new edge appears.

TIP   Add vertices anywhere you want to be able to fold roof slab topology.

3. Repeat the previous step, adding a new vertex and edge to the opposite upper-slope roof slab at its overhanging edge's midpoint.

4. Select both roof slabs to which you added vertices. Click the Vertex grip on the ridge line that overhangs the eave. Toggle off DYN in the application status bar and move the cursor outward along the zero degree line, type **3'-6"** and press Esc to deselect. Switch to Flat Shaded, Edges On display mode (see Figure 11.36).

5. Save your work as **RoofExtension.dwg**.

FIGURE 11.35
Adding a vertex to
a roof slab

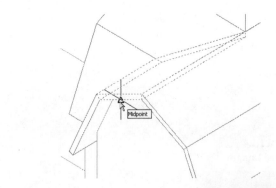

FIGURE 11.36
Creating a roof extension
by moving new vertices

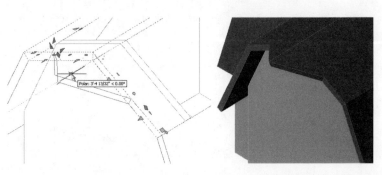

Making Dormers

A *dormer* is a house-like extension accommodating a vertical window set within a sloping roof. We will add two dormers to the Gambrel roof, which themselves will have Gambrel *gablets*—roofs covering the dormers. This way, the gablets will repeat the same architectural vocabulary as the main roof structure at a smaller scale (refer to Figure 11.19).

You will start by building dormers off to the side as fully enclosed and roofed "rooms" with dormer windows. Then the dormers will be carefully positioned with respect to the main roof and integrated therein by using a special tool. Afterward, you'll delete the back enclosing walls that will be left floating in space.

1. Open RoofExtension.dwg if it's not already open. Switch to 2D Wireframe display mode.

2. Make the Layout layer current. Off to the side draw a rectangle (closed polyline) on the ground measuring 14'x7'.

3. Right-click the Wall tool in the Design palette and choose Apply Tool Properties To ➤ Linework. Select the rectangle, choose to erase the layout geometry, and change Justify to Right in the Properties palette so the walls will be inset within the original rectangular boundary. Generic walls appear, forming an enclosed boundary for the dormer "room."

4. Click the Roof tool in the Design palette to begin the process of making the Gambrel gablet. In the Properties palette, set Thickness to 6", Edge Cut to Square, Shape to Double Slope, Overhang to 6", Plate Height to 8', Lower Slope Rise to 2'- 2-1/2", Upper Height to 11', and Upper Slope Rise to 6". Click first and second points at the corners along the nearest long edge of the dormer walls.

5. Change Shape to Gable and click the third point. Change Shape to Double Slope and click the fourth point. Change Shape to Gable and click the first point again. Press Enter, and the Gambrel gablet appears (see Figure 11.37).

FIGURE 11.37
Making a Gambrel gablet

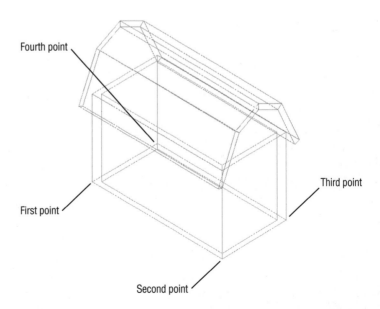

Fourth point

Third point

First point

Second point

6. Select all four dormer walls, right-click, and choose Roof/Floor Line ➤ Modify Roof Line. Type **A** for auto-project and press Enter. Select the gablet and press Enter. The walls stop where they meet the roof object.

7. Select the Windows palette and click the Glider tool. In the Properties palette, change Width to 5′, Height to 4′, Position Along Wall to Offset/Center, and Head Height to 9′. Click the midpoint of the nearest short wall in the dormer to place the window.

8. Select the gablet, right-click, and choose Convert To Roof Slabs from the shortcut menu. Check Erase Layout Geometry in the Convert To Roof Slabs worksheet. Verify that GambrelRoof is the Roof Slab Style and click OK to close the worksheet. Switch to Hidden display mode. The dormer "room" is complete.

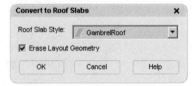

WARNING Roof dormers must form enclosed "rooms" or they will not intersect properly with the roof they are inserted into.

Now that you have succeeded in creating an enclosed dormer room, you can move it into position with respect to the main structure's Gambrel roof. You will center two dormers on the construction lines and line up the dormers in elevation.

1. Move the entire dormer from its lower corner to the top endpoint of the shed roof, as shown in Figure 11.38.

FIGURE 11.38
Moving dormer "room"

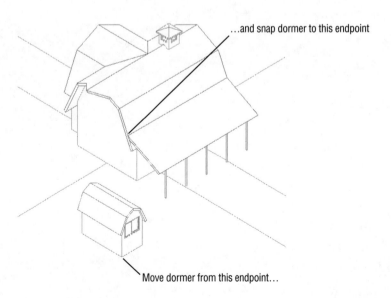

2. Switch into the Top viewpoint and use 2D Wireframe display mode. Type **M** and press Enter to execute the MOVE command. Press P and then Enter twice to use the previous selection set. Type **.xy** (dot-x-y) and press Enter to use a point filter. Snap to the endpoint of the gablet ridge line, as shown in Figure 11.39. The command line says:

```
Specify base point or [Displacement] <Displacement>: .xy of (need Z):
```

Type **0** (zero) and press Enter. This point filter used the XY coordinates of the point you previously clicked when moving the dormer, but you had to type the Z coordinate. This is a way of being absolutely certain of the 3D coordinates you are specifying; otherwise, the point you click wouldn't be snapping on the ground plane.

NOTE Refer to the AutoCAD's *User Guide* to review the use of point filters. They are useful tools for working with 3D models.

3. Move the cursor down and snap perpendicularly to the horizontal construction line (refer to Figure 11.39). Because the construction line is already on the ground, the move operation merely slid the dormer without disturbing its world Z position.

4. Switch to the Front viewpoint in Hidden display mode. Type **DI**⏎ and click the two points shown in Figure 11.40. The command line lists the Delta Y distance between these points as 4′ 9-15/16″. Type **M**⏎**P**⏎⏎ to move the previous selection; then click an arbitrary point off to the side and move the cursor vertically down using polar tracking. Type **4′-10″** and press Enter to move the dormer down so the seam between the slopes of the gablet approximately meet the corresponding seam between the slopes of the Gambrel roof (see Figure 11.40).

FIGURE 11.39
Moving dormer
using point filter.⏎

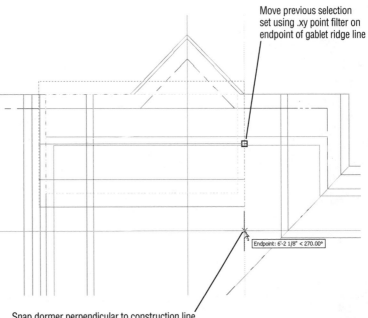

Move previous selection
set using .xy point filter on
endpoint of gablet ridge line

Endpoint: 6′-2 1/8″ < 270.00°

Snap dormer perpendicular to construction line

5. Switch into the NW Isometric viewpoint and use 2D Wireframe display mode. Set UCS to World. To copy a second dormer, you will use the previous selection set yet again. Type **CO↵P↵↵** to copy the previous selection. Type **NEA**, press Enter, and click an arbitrary (nearest) point on the construction line under the first dormer. Click a point perpendicular to the second construction line to make the copy symmetrically along the structure and press Enter to end the command (see Figure 11.41). Delete all three construction lines.

FIGURE 11.40
Measuring and moving the dormer down in elevation

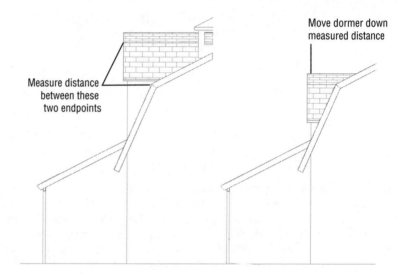

FIGURE 11.41
Copying a second dormer

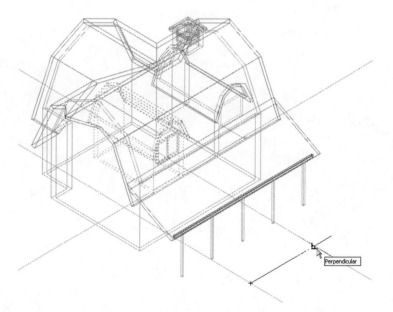

6. And now the moment of truth: Zoom in closer to the first dormer. Select the lower roof slab in the Gambrel roof, right-click, and choose Roof Dormer from the shortcut menu. Carefully select every piece of the first dormer including the four gablet roof slabs, the four "room" walls, and the dormer window. Press Enter and the command line says:

```
Slice wall with roof slab [Yes/No] <Yes>:
```

Press Enter to accept Yes as the default. The roof slab is sliced by the "room," and the walls are also sliced by the roof slab. The dormer has been created. Delete the back wall that floats in space: it is no longer needed (see Figure 11.42).

WARNING Dormers will fail to form if the objects you select do not form a complete enclosure or if the objects do not fully penetrate the roof slab you are cutting through.

7. Repeat step 6 for the second dormer.

8. Switch into the Front viewpoint in Hidden display mode. Notice that the upper slopes of the gablets do not meet the upper slope of the main roof because the Roof Dormer tool affected only the lower slab of the main roof. You will have to manually extend and trim the upper gablet roof slabs. Select a roof slab you want to extend. Drag its edge grip over some arbitrary distance. Right-click and choose Trim from the shortcut menu. Click the upper roof slab of the main roof as the trimming object and click on the side of the gablet roof slab you want to trim away.

FIGURE 11.42
Deleting back wall after dormer has been cut

Delete the back wall

9. Switch into the NW Isometric view and repeat step 8 three more times for each of the remaining gablet roof slabs that need to be extended. Notice that the gablet roof slabs are now perfectly edged in Hidden display mode—that is a sign you have made the dormers correctly (see Figure 11.44).

10. Save your work as **Dormers.dwg**.

FIGURE 11.43
Gablet roof slabs do not reach main roof (left), extending them with edge grips (middle), and trimming off excess (right)

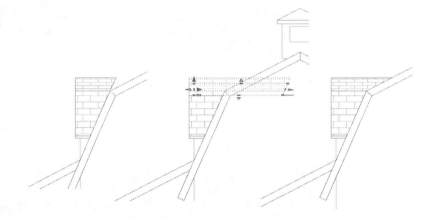

FIGURE 11.44
Completed dormers

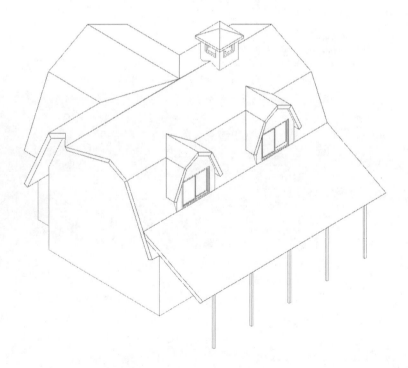

Customizing Roof Slab Edges

Just as slabs and roof slabs have different styles, slab edges and roof slab edges are also maintained as separate styles to better manage the edge conditions. The functionality is virtually identical for both slab edges and roof slab edges, so I will focus here on roof slab edges in the context of this chapter's continuing tutorials.

During the final stage of roof design, we turn our attention to the edge conditions of the roof slabs that we modeled in the last section. Each roof slab might have multiple exposed edges that can each have a fascia and soffit attached.

Fascia is a form of architectural trim attached to the outside face of a roof slab edge. Fascia often have a *gutter* attached that funnels rainwater away from the structure. *Soffits* are horizontal trim members that span the gap between the exterior wall and the fascia. You'll typically see soffits covering rafters under the eaves, often acting as porch ceilings. In addition, a soffit can occasionally have a *frieze* attached underneath, which is a kind of decorative molding. Figure 11.45 shows the components found at the edge of a roof slab.

Defining Profiles

Before you can work effectively with edge conditions, you must first define a few profiles that can be used for fascia and soffits. We'll insert a sample file that has predrawn sketches of some common components you might use at roof slab edges.

1. Open Dormers.dwg if it's not already open. Switch to the Top viewpoint in 2D Wireframe display mode.

FIGURE 11.45
Roof slab edge
conditions

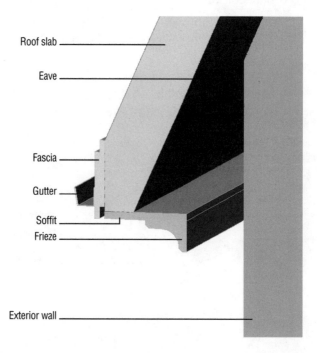

Roof slab

Eave

Fascia

Gutter

Soffit

Frieze

Exterior wall

2. Choose Insert ➤ Block and click the Browse button in the Insert dialog box. Navigate to this chapter's folder on the companion DVD and open the file `ProfileSketches.dwg`. In the Insert dialog box, check Specify-On-Screen in the Insertion point group and check Explode. Click OK and click a point off to the left side of the building. Three sketches appear (see Figure 11.46).

3. Architectural Desktop supports only two kinds of edge profile: fascia and soffit. These profiles can take any shape you want as long as they are made with nonself-intersecting closed polylines. Delete the two lines shown in Figure 11.46 to reveal continuous boundaries between the soffit and frieze, and the fascia and gutter. Make Layer 0 (zero) the current layer.

4. Type **BO** and press Enter to execute the BOUNDARY command. Click a point inside each of the three shapes to create three new closed polylines. Press Esc to end the command. Freeze the Layout layer.

TIP Haunches, cants, and curbs can be defined as profiles and used as fascia and soffits in slab edge styles commonly used with concrete slabs.

5. Select the first profile on the left, right-click, and choose Convert To ➤ Profile Definition. Click the insertion point in the upper-right corner (refer to Figure 11.46 for placement). Type **Soffit + Frieze** in the New Profile Definition worksheet and click OK.

6. Select the second profile from the left, right-click, and choose Convert To ➤ Profile Definition. Click the insertion point in the upper-left corner (refer to Figure 11.46 for placement) and press Enter to choose New profile. Type **Fascia + Gutter** in the New Profile Definition worksheet and click OK.

7. Select the profile on the right, right-click and choose Convert To ➤ Profile Definition. Click the insertion point in the upper-left corner (refer to Figure 11.46 for placement) and press Enter to choose New profile. Type **Fascia** in the New Profile Definition worksheet and click OK.

8. Delete the closed polyline sketches. You won't need these any more now that profiles have been defined as styles.

9. Save your work as **Profiles.dwg**.

FIGURE 11.46
Fascia and soffit sketches

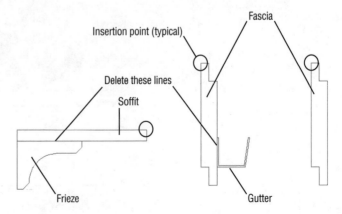

Designing Roof Slab Edge Styles

After defining profiles, the next step is to design roof slab edge styles. It is really just a question of creating a few well-named styles and assigning them the profiles you made previously.

1. Open Profiles.dwg if it's not already open. Switch to the SW Isometric viewpoint in Hidden display mode.

2. Choose Format ➢ Style Manager. In the tree pane, expand the current drawing, Architectural Objects, and Roof Slab Edge Styles nodes.

3. Right-click Roof Slab Edge Styles and choose New from the shortcut menu. Give the new style the name **Fascia Edge**.

4. In the content pane, click the Design Rules tab (see Figure 11.47) and study the illustration: The fascia is attached to the end of roof slab, and the soffit floats underneath. Check Fascia to enable this feature and choose the Fascia profile in the drop-down list. Uncheck A - Auto-Adjust to Edge Height.

NOTE A fascia follows the orientation of the roof slab edge: plumb or square edge cut. Soffits, however, are normally oriented horizontally, although it is possible to angle either component.

5. Right-click Roof Slab Edge Styles in the tree pane and choose New from the shortcut menu. Give the new style the name **Fascia + Gutter Edge**. Check Fascia and choose the Fascia + Gutter profile in the drop-down list. Leave A - Auto-Adjust to Edge Height checked.

6. Right-click Roof Slab Edge Styles in the tree pane and choose New from the shortcut menu. Give the new style the name **Fascia + Soffit + Frieze Edge**. Check Fascia and choose the Fascia profile in the drop-down list. Uncheck A - Auto-Adjust to Edge Height. Check Soffit to enable this feature and choose the Soffit + Frieze profile from the Soffit drop-down list. Leave B - Auto-Adjust to Overhang Depth unchecked. Click OK to close the Style Manager.

7. Save your work as **RoofSlabEdgeStyles.dwg**.

FIGURE 11.47
Roof slab edge style
design rules

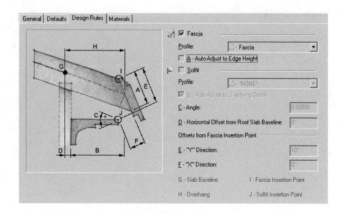

Altering Edges

You are prepared to alter the edges of slabs and roof slabs only after you have created some slab edge styles and/or roof slab edge styles. I know it is a lot of prep work, but your efforts will pay off in the end. First we'll add fascia and soffits to selected roof slab edges.

TIP A novel use of roof slabs is to make a skylight with a transparent roof slab. You can fashion a frame with roof slab edges. Windows do not display correctly when they aren't vertical, so making a skylight out of a roof slab is the perfect solution to this common problem.

ADDING FASCIA AND SOFFITS TO SLABS AND ROOF SLABS

Adding fascia and soffits to roof slab edges can be a tedious process because you must assign edge styles to one edge at a time. Therefore, consider the possibility of leaving off edge styles entirely and documenting these conditions in detail drawings—a workable compromise between 3D realism and practicality. However, if you've made it this far, you'll want to add this detail directly to the single building model—so let's get to it!

1. Open RoofSlabEdgeStyles.dwg if it's not already open.

2. Select the shed roof, right-click, and choose Edit Roof Slab Edges from the shortcut menu.

3. Click the lower outer edge of the shed roof and press Enter; the Edit Roof Slab Edge worksheet appears. Change Edge Cut to Plumb, Angle to 0 (zero), and Edge Style to Fascia + Gutter Edge. The right half of the worksheet contains an object viewer that is a handy way to visualize the edge condition; zoom in on the selected edge and click the Hidden button in the object viewer toolbar (see Figure 11.48). Click OK to close the worksheet. The shed roof has a fascia and gutter.

4. Select the lower slope roof slab of the Gambrel roof that is connected with the shed roof. Right-click and choose Edit Roof Slab Edges from the shortcut menu. Click the selected roof slab's lower edge and press Enter. Change Edge Style to Fascia + Soffit + Frieze Edge, Edge Cut to Plumb, and Angle to 0 (zero) in the Edit Roof Slab Edge worksheet and click OK. Switch to the Front viewpoint (see Figure 11.49).

FIGURE 11.48
Edit Roof Slab Edges worksheet

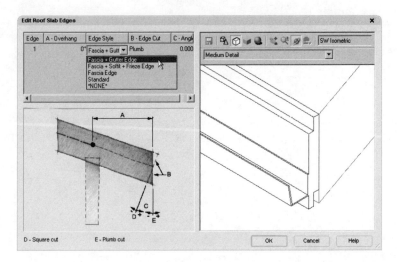

FIGURE 11.49
Assigning edge
conditions to roof
slabs

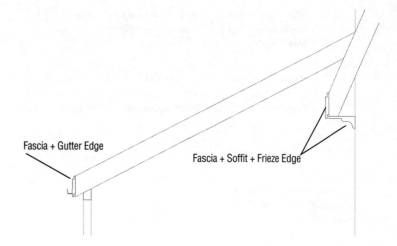

Fascia + Gutter Edge

Fascia + Soffit + Frieze Edge

5. Edit the edges of all the overhanging roofs on the western side of the building. Change Edge Style to Fascia Edge, Edge Cut to Square, and Angle to 0 (zero) in the Edit Roof Slab Edge worksheet for each of these five edges. You'll have to repeat this step five times to accomplish it (see Figure 11.50).

6. The descending fascia on the lower slope has a very sharp edge that is unacceptable. Unfortunately, there is no provision within the edge style to control this condition. You can solve the problem by cutting off the sharp edge with a Boolean subtraction. Select the Massing palette and click the Box tool. Create a box and position it below the sharp end of the fascia jutting out from the lower roof slab of the Gambrel roof. You might need to change viewpoints and use point filters to position the mass so it intersects only with the portion of the fascia you want to cut away.

FIGURE 11.50
Fascia bound to over-
hanging edges

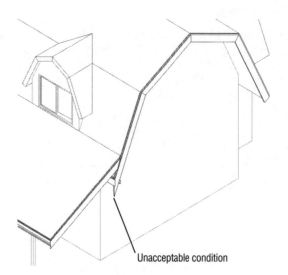

Unacceptable condition

7. Select the roof slab, right-click, and choose Boolean ➢ Subtract. Select the mass element and press Enter. The mass element is still there; hide it using the red light bulb icon in the drawing tray (see Figure 11.51). Even after the subtraction, you have a less-than-perfect intersection.

WARNING I suggest that you really think hard about editing edges and consider whether it is worth your time. Edge styles are great in simple cases, but the amount of 3D modeling effort required to fix problems with complex intersections goes up exponentially.

8. If you want to study this file again, save your work as **EditedEdges.dwg**. Congratulations on completing all the tutorials!

FIGURE 11.51
Cleaning up fascia inter-
section by positioning
mass element (left),
performing a Boolean
subtraction, and hiding
the mass element (right)

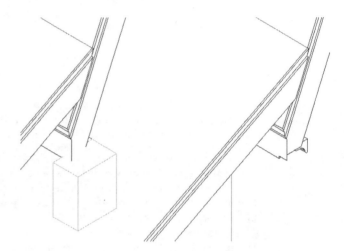

Summary

This chapter explored all aspects of roof objects, roof slabs, roof slab edges—and, by extension, slabs and slab edge styles. By following the three-stage process for creating roofs, you learned everything necessary to roof your own structures, at least as far as Architectural Desktop is concerned. In the next chapter we will look at the last objects needed to complete your design development skill set: stairs, railings, and stair towers.

Chapter 12

Stairs, Ramps, and Railings

This chapter explores all facets of vertical circulation in a building. You'll start with stairs because they are the most common way of moving vertically between levels. As you delve into the complexities of stair objects, you'll learn how to make straight, spiral, multi-landing, and U-shaped flights using a stair training structure that has been designed to facilitate your experiments. You'll also learn how to tweak stair objects to fit into almost any existing situation, and create new stairs that automatically adhere to building code requirements.

You'll style stairs to represent a wide variety of real world types, including flights made from wood, concrete, and steel—as well as gradually sloping concrete ramps. You'll attach railings to the stairs you have made and learn to create freestanding railings. In addition, you'll design a wide array of railing styles by locating their rails, posts, and balusters—and using profiles and custom blocks where appropriate.

At the end of the chapter, you'll open a sample project and generate a *stair tower*—a stack of interconnected stairs spanning multiple levels—typically found in modern commercial buildings. Stair towers can include stairs, railings, and slabs. This chapter's topics include:

◆   Creating Stairs

◆   Editing Stairs

◆   Working with Stair and Ramp Styles

◆   Adding Railings

◆   Generating a Stair Tower

Creating Stairs

In Architectural Desktop, ramps (inclined planes) are not defined as architecture, engineering, and construction (AEC) objects in their own right. Instead, a ramp is considered to be a special case of the general-purpose stair object. Later, in "Working with Stair and Ramp Styles," you'll learn how create ramp styles that you'll assign to stair objects.

FIGURE 12.1

Basic stair components

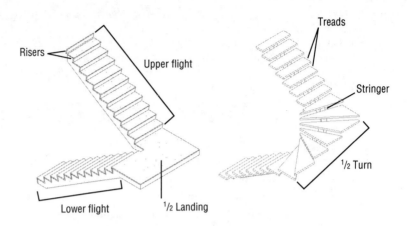

Therefore, we turn our attention to the stair object. A stair can have multiple *flights*—continuous runs of steps. Long flights might be difficult for some to handle without resting, so flights often come to a *landing*—a short horizontal surface between flights. When less horizontal area is available, steps might turn between flights without landing (see Figure 12.1).

The fractions in Figure 12.1 refer to the placement of the turn—or landing—roughly halfway between the floors that the stairs connect. Later on, you'll make stairs that have two landings and turns appearing between floors; they are referred to as quarter turns because they turn 90 degrees, or one quarter of a circle.

When working in a project, you'll normally add stairs to one construct at a time; each construct you add stairs to is associated with one specific level (see Chapter 5, "Project Management"). Because of this, you won't normally see stairs in conjunction with the upper floors they connect to in isometric viewpoints. Instead, you can overlay constructs to verify and adjust stair alignment with respect to the walls on each level.

To make it easier to understand and visualize stairs, I created a 3D training structure that you'll use to experiment with stairs in this chapter (TrainingStructure.dwg on the companion DVD; see Figure 12.2). The training structure contains an upper-level slab that you will reach by adding a variety of different stairs from ground level. Each stair you'll build will have a different geometry and spatial requirements. You can use the stairs and styles we'll build in this chapter as prototypes for your own projects.

NOTE Many of the styles we will create in this chapter come from content drawings that ship with ADT. We are building styles from scratch in this chapter to better understand the styles themselves and their creation process.

In the next sections, you'll learn how to create straight, spiral, multi-landing, and U-shaped stairs (see Figure 12.3). Each type of stair is made in a slightly different way, with different constraints and possibilities. Like many other objects in ADT, you'll set up object properties prior to creating the stairs themselves. We'll start by making generic stairs that all use the Standard style.

FIGURE 12.2

Training structure
for building stairs: NE
Isometric (top) and SW
Isometric (bottom)
viewpoints

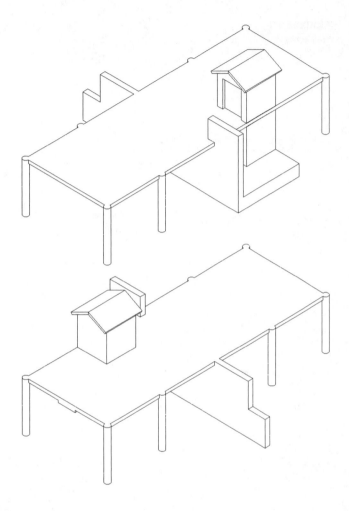

Making a Straight Stair

The straight stair is the simplest and most common type. Straight stairs can actually have landings
that appear inline automatically if you set flight height limits (see "Editing Advanced Properties"
later in this chapter). If you want more control over landings in a straight stair, use the multi-landing
type instead. We'll create a straight stair without any landings at first.

1. Open TrainingStructure.dwg from this chapter's folder on the companion DVD. Visualize
   the file using the 3D Orbit command. Switch to the Top viewpoint when done.

2. In the Design palette, click the Stair tool (see Figure 12.4).

FIGURE 12.3
Stair types

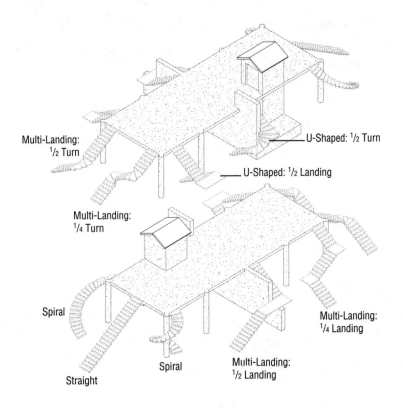

FIGURE 12.4
Stair, Stair Tower, and
Railing tools

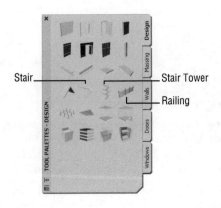

3. Open the Properties palette. In the General section, set Shape to Straight and Vertical Orientation to Up, meaning that the stair will start on the ground plane at zero in the Z direction and step upward toward the level above. On the one hand, choosing Down would be appropriate if you want to create a stair going down to a basement from the first level, for example. On the other hand, you might create an Up oriented stair in the basement level instead.

4. In the Dimensions subcategory, verify that Width is set to 3'-8". Change Height to 13'. Verify the following and change them if necessary: Justify Center, Terminate With Riser, Flight Length is Tread Length, and Calculation Rules are set to Tread. Set Tread to 11" if it is not already. Study the illustration in the Dimensions subcategory and its labeled parameters (see Figure 12.5).

NOTE   A *tread* is the depth of an individual step; typical treads measure 10–12" deep. A *riser* is the height of an individual step; typical risers usually are between 6–8" in height.

5. Click the flight start point way off to the left side of the training structure—don't try to connect the stair with the structure yet. Riser numbers $2/23$ appear above an outline of the stair, meaning that you are currently seeing the *nosing*—or front edge of—the second riser out of a total flight of 23 risers. Move the cursor horizontally to the right using polar tracking. After the riser numbers read 23/23, click to set the flight endpoint. You can click way off to the right side, and the flight endpoint will automatically jump to the calculated end of the flight length (see Figure 12.6).

In this example, the flight's length (Straight Length) was ultimately calculated by multiplying the number of treads times the tread distance. Because the stair is terminated with a riser, the number of treads equals the number of risers minus one. Therefore, in just this one case, Straight Length = (Riser Count – 1) × Tread.

FIGURE 12.5

Setting straight stair dimensions

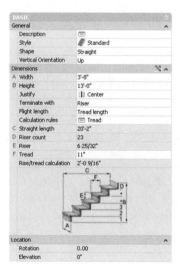

FIGURE 12.6
Clicking flight start (top), and flight endpoints (bottom)

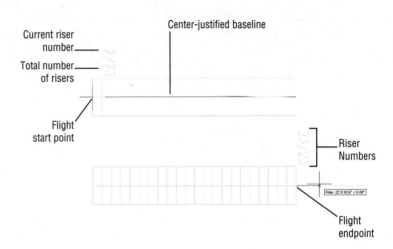

Thankfully, you don't need to do the math to make a stair. However, you do have to be aware of how stairs are calculated in case you want to change the calculation rules. This becomes necessary if you want to specify the number of risers or the typical riser distance, instead of the typical tread length to determine the flight's length. Another option is to directly specify Straight Length and have ADT calculate the other variables for you. Let's take a look at Calculation Rules.

1. Select the straight stair object you made previously.

2. In the Properties palette, click the Calculation Rules worksheet icon in the Dimensions subcategory. The Calculation Rules worksheet contains four variables that can be frozen, automatically calculated, or edited by you (see Figure 12.7).

NOTE The rule-based calculator keeps calculation rules compliant with building codes, so your stairs rise at the proper slope. You'll see how to enter rules into the calculator to comply with your local building codes later on. Many existing stairs do not comply with current codes, so you'll have to turn off the rule-based calculator to simulate them (see "Making Design Rules" in the section "Working with Stair and Ramp Styles").

3. Click the Editable button ▣ and observe that all the buttons in the Calculation Rules worksheet turn to Automatic buttons ▣ . Click the Automatic button next to Straight Length; it turns to an Editable button. Now the other variables will be calculated from Straight Length. Type **18′** in the Straight Length text box and click OK to close the worksheet. The stair appears with a large red defect symbol, warning you that it is no longer code-compliant.

4. Look in the Properties palette again and notice that Calculation Rules says Straight Length next to the worksheet icon, and the Straight Length parameter is editable. Obviously, the calculation rules control which parameters are editable and which are calculated. Click the worksheet and click the

Editable button next to Straight Length. Click the Automatic button next to Tread and click OK. The defect warning disappears as the stair's slope returns to the way it was before.

5. Move the straight stair from the midpoint of its top edge to the midpoint on the left edge of the training structure. In the Properties palette's Location subcategory, set Elevation to 0 (zero). This is necessary because when you snapped to the midpoint of the training structure, it snapped to the top of the slab. Switch to the SW Isometric viewpoint and check out your work (see Figure 12.8).

FIGURE 12.7
Calculation Rules
worksheet

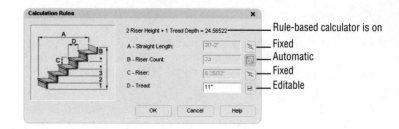

FIGURE 12.8
Snapping the straight
stair to training struc-
ture in plan (top) and
SW Isometric (bottom)
viewpoints

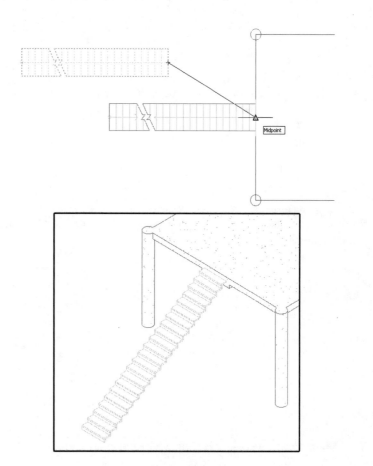

If you'll be working all the way through this chapter, leave the sample file open throughout, and I'll give you a few Save As points along the way.

Making Spiral Stairs

Spirals are some of the most dramatic forms stairs can take. You can make anything from tight spirals that are supported by steel poles, to larger spirals that gracefully turn around a central void, to anything inbetween. Spiral stair objects in ADT revolve about a circular radius.

WARNING   ADT cannot make stairs with elliptical spirals or spirals with ever-changing curvature—but in all likelihood, neither can your budget.

1. Switch back to the Top viewpoint. Click the Stair tool in the Design palette. In the Properties palette, change Shape to Spiral, Horizontal Orientation to Counterclockwise, and Vertical Orientation to Up.

2. In the Dimension subcategory, change Width to 3', Height to 13', Justify to Center, Terminate With Riser, Specify On Screen to No, Radius to 3', and Arc Constraint to Free. We're choosing not to specify on-screen because you will set values in the Properties palette instead. Setting the Arc Constraint to Free means that Arc Angle will be calculated. Verify that Calculation Rules are set to Tread, and Tread is set to 11" (see Figure 12.9). The tread depth is measured through the center of the steps.

3. Using Center object snap, click the center of the spiral stair at the center of the lower-left column of the training structure. You won't need to adjust the elevation value of this stair because the center of the column snaps to the ground plane. The command line says the following:

```
Start point or [SHape/STyle/Tread/Height/Width/Justify/Radius/Match/Undo]:
```

Using polar object tracking, move the cursor horizontally to the right and click a point. Press Esc to end the command; the spiral stair object appears (see Figure 12.10).

FIGURE 12.9
Spiral stair object properties

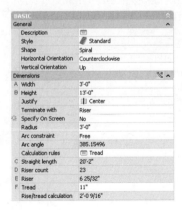

FIGURE 12.10

Snapping a spiral stair to the center of a column

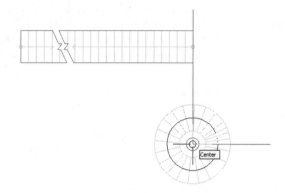

4. Although the bottom stair edge is flush with the horizontal edge of the slab, this is not what we want. This spiral stair's total arc angle was calculated based on tread length in the calculation rules. Therefore, we could not predict where the top edge would be before we created the stair. The stair must be rotated so that the top riser aligns with the slab above. Select the spiral stair, right-click, and choose Basic Modify Tools ➤ Rotate.

5. Snap the base point to the center of the spiral stair. The command line says the following:

```
Specify rotation angle or [Copy/Reference] <0.00>:
```

Type **R** for the Reference option and press Enter. Type **@** to use the base point as the first point of the reference angle and press Enter. Click the second point of the reference angle at the endpoint of the darker radial line. Click the new angle point along the horizontal edge of the slab using polar object tracking. Switch to the SW Isometric viewpoint. Notice that the spiral stair has been rotated the precise amount so that its top edge is flush with the slab (see Figure 12.11).

NOTE If you switch to 2D Wireframe display mode, you'll notice that the top riser is embedded in the slab above—that is normal for any stair terminated with a riser.

FIGURE 12.11

Rotating the spiral stair using a reference angle (left and middle) and the result in SW Isometric (right)

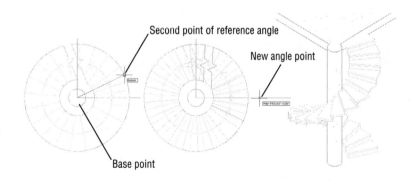

To demonstrate another common method of making spiral stairs, let's make a stair that has a fixed arc angle. When you specify an exact arc angle, the radius of the stair will be calculated automatically. As is typical with constraints, you can't specify every parameter and end up with a code-compliant stair. When you choose to specify one parameter, others must be calculated.

1. Switch back to the Top viewpoint. Click the Stair tool in the Design palette. In the Properties palette, change Horizontal Orientation to Clockwise.

2. In the Dimension subcategory, change Width to 3', Height to 13', Justify to Center, Terminate With Riser, Specify On Screen to No, and Arc Constraint to Total Degrees. Type **180** in the Arc Angle text box. Notice that the Radius parameter is grayed-out and now reads the calculated 6'-5 1/32".

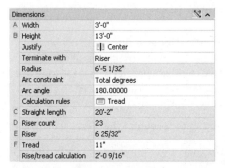

Dimensions	
A Width	3'-0"
B Height	13'-0"
Justify	Center
Terminate with	Riser
Radius	6'-5 1/32"
Arc constraint	Total degrees
Arc angle	180.00000
Calculation rules	Tread
C Straight length	20'-2"
D Riser count	23
E Riser	6 25/32"
F Tread	11"
Rise/tread calculation	2'-0 9/16"

3. Click the center of the spiral stair away from the training structure, off to the left side. It won't be possible to snap the stair where we want it yet because the cursor is attached to the center of the spiral, and the stair is rotated 180 degrees from where we want it. Click a point to the left of the first point to set the rotation.

4. Move the stair's inner top endpoint to the center of the upper-left column in the training structure (see Figure 12.12). Finally, move the stair over 1'-6" horizontally to the right in order to clear the column.

5. Switch to the NW Isometric viewpoint to check your work. Save your work as Stairs.dwg.

FIGURE 12.12
Orienting and positioning the 180 degree spiral stair

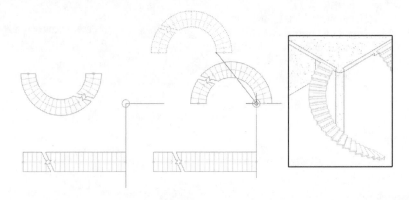

Making Multi-Landing Stairs

Multi-landing stairs give you a great deal of flexibility. With multiple flights and turns, you can make a huge variety of multi-landing stairs. The two most significant decisions to make regarding multi-landing stairs must be made prior to creating the stair: whether you want landings or steps that continue through turns, and whether you want flights divided in half or in quarter increments of the total height. These two decisions together yield the four turn types that we'll be exploring in this section: 1/2 Landing, 1/4 Landing, 1/2 Turn, and 1/4 Turn.

TURN TYPE: 1/2 LANDING

The 1/2 Landing turn type creates a stair that has one landing located roughly midway between the top and bottom of the stair. Multi-landing stairs can have straight, acute, right, or obtuse angles between flights.

1. If you are jumping in here, we've been using Stairs.dwg from the companion DVD. Switch to the SW Isometric viewpoint and draw a short line angled segment that snaps to the intersection point shown in Figure 12.13. It doesn't matter how long this line is because you will erase it shortly. You will snap the new stair to this temporary line segment in plan.

2. Switch to the Top viewpoint. Click the Stair tool in the Design palette.

3. In the Properties palette, set Shape to Multi-Landing, Turn Type to 1/2 Landing, and Vertical Orientation to Down, meaning that we will draw the stair from the top down.

4. In the Dimensions subcategory, change Width to 3'-8". Change Justify to Right so the stair will exist on the right side of the wall as we draw it from the top down.

5. Click the flight start point at the endpoint of the temporary line, where it intersects with the training structure. Move the cursor down vertically using polar object tracking until the riser numbers read $^{11}/_{23}$; click to create the upper flight.

FIGURE 12.13
Drawing a temporary
line to snap the stair to

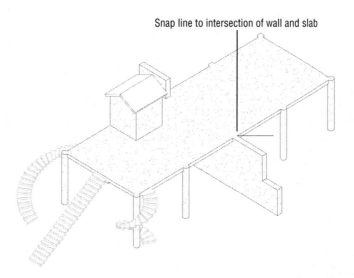

Snap line to intersection of wall and slab

   6. Now you specify the length of the landing; this can be as short or long as you want. Move the cursor horizontally to the left, type **6'**, and press Enter.

   7. To create the lower flight, continue moving the cursor horizontally to the left until the riser numbers read $^{23}/_{23}$; click to complete the stair. Press Esc to end the command. Figure 12.14 illustrates the last three steps.

   8. Switch back to the SW Isometric viewpoint. Erase the temporary line. Figure 12.15 shows the result.

   9. Select the stair and examine the Properties palette. Notice that Shape and Turn Type are both grayed-out. You cannot change these properties after the stair has been created; they are available as creation properties but—unlike properties with starburst icons—remain in the palette for your information.

FIGURE 12.14
Creating the upper flight (left), 1/2 landing (middle), and lower flight (right)

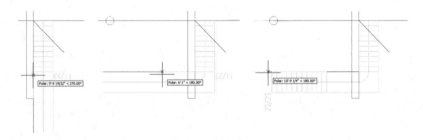

FIGURE 12.15
Completed Multi-Landing—1/2 Landing stair

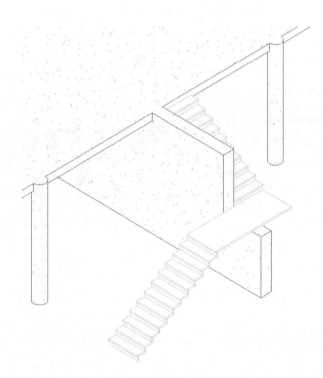

TURN TYPE: 1/4 LANDING

The 1/4 Landing option offers the possibility of creating two landings located in roughly one-quarter and three-quarter positions with respect to the total height of the stair. Quarter landings automatically have a length equal to the width of the stair. Each corner may turn in the same or in opposite directions.

1. Switch to the Top viewpoint. Click the Stair tool in the Design palette.

2. In the Properties palette, set Turn Type to 1/4 Landing and Vertical Orientation to Up. This time you will draw the stair off to the side and attach it to the training structure later on.

3. In the Dimensions subcategory, change Justify to Center because you are not trying to snap the stair to specific geometry on either of its edges. Verify that Flight Length is set to Tread Length.

4. Well below the training structure, click the flight start point. Move the cursor up vertically by using polar object tracking until the riser numbers read $8/23$; click to create the lower flight.

5. A quarter landing will automatically be inserted between flights. Move the cursor horizontally to the right until the riser numbers read $16/23$; click to create the middle flight.

6. To create the second landing and upper flight move the cursor up vertically until the cursor numbers read $23/23$; click to complete the stair. Press Esc to end the command. Figure 12.16 illustrates the last three steps.

7. Move the stair from its upper-right endpoint and snap it to the center of the lower-right column of the training structure. So the stair clears the column, move it horizontally to the left a distance of 1'-6" (see Figure 12.17). Verify that Elevation is set to 0 (zero) in the Properties palette.

8. Switch to the SW Isometric viewpoint and examine your new stair (see Figure 12.18).

FIGURE 12.16
Creating the lower flight (left), lower landing / middle flight (middle), and upper landing / upper flight (right)

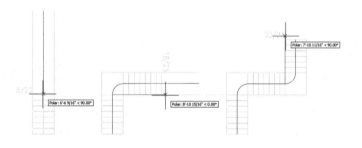

FIGURE 12.17
Snapping the stair to the structure (left) and then moving it over (right)

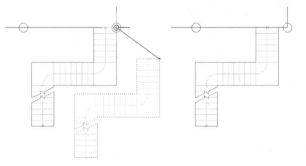

FIGURE 12.18
Completed Multi-
Landing—1/4 Landing
stair

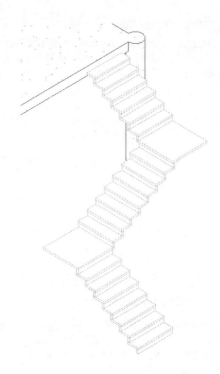

TURN TYPE: 1/2 TURN

Both "Turn" options allow stairs to fit within small areas because steps continue through corners without a rest. The 1/2 Turn option allows for a single turn zone midway in the stair's height. Think of the 1/2 Turn like the 1/2 Landing except that there are steps in the turn instead of a flat surface. Both turn options use winder styles that control the angle of the steps in plan—you'll learn more about winder styles after creating both multi-landing turn type stairs. The 1/2 Turn option requires that both turns be made in the same direction.

1. Switch to the Top viewpoint. Click the Stair tool in the Design palette.

2. In the Properties palette, set Turn Type to 1/2 Turn. Notice that Winder Style appears and is set to Balanced. Leave it as it is for now.

3. Off to the right side of the training structure, click the flight start point. Move the cursor up vertically using polar object tracking until the riser numbers read $^9/_{23}$; click to create the lower flight.

4. Move the cursor up and to the left using polar object tracking until the ToolTip shows that you are working at a 135-degree angle. When the riser numbers read $^{11}/_{23}$, click to create the beginning of the turn.

5. Move the cursor horizontally to the left (angle of 180 degrees) until the cursor numbers read $^{23}/_{23}$; click to complete the stair. Press Esc to end the command. Figure 12.19 illustrates the last three steps.

6. Move the stair from its endpoint shown in Figure 12.20 and snap it to the center of the lower-right column of the training structure. So the stair clears the column, move it up vertically a distance of 1'-6".

7. Switch to the SE Isometric viewpoint and examine your new stair (see Figure 12.21).

FIGURE 12.19

Creating the lower flight (left), turn (middle), and upper flight (right)

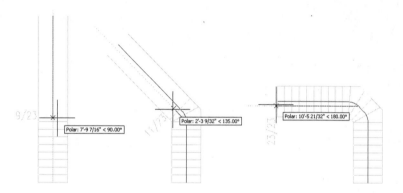

FIGURE 12.20

Snapping the stair to the structure (left) and then moving it up (right)

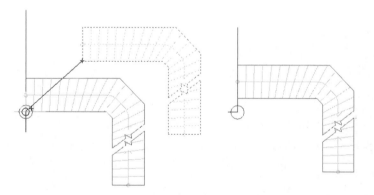

FIGURE 12.21
Completed Multi-
Landing 1/2 Turn stair

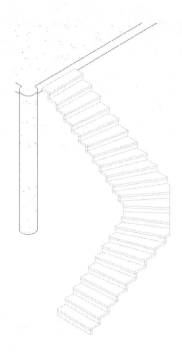

TURN TYPE: 1/4 TURN

The 1/4 Turn option is analogous to the 1/4 Landing option, except that steps continue through the turns instead of having flat surfaces on which to rest. This option can accommodate turns in either direction.

1. Switch to the Top viewpoint. Click the Stair tool in the Design palette.

2. In the Properties palette, set Turn Type to 1/4 Turn.

3. Off to the right side of the training structure, click the flight start point. Move the cursor horizontally to the left by using polar object tracking until the riser numbers read $7/23$; click to create the lower flight.

4. Move the cursor up vertically until the riser numbers read $14/23$; click to create the middle flight.

5. Move the cursor horizontally to the left until the cursor numbers read $23/23$; click to complete the stair. Press Esc to end the command. Figure 12.22 illustrates the last three steps.

6. Move the stair from its endpoint shown in Figure 12.23 and snap it to the endpoint of the slab of the training structure. So the stair clears the column, move it down vertically a distance of 1'-6".

7. Change Elevation to 0 (zero) in the Properties palette. This step was necessary this time because you snapped to the endpoint of the slab, which is on the upper level. We want the stair to exist on the ground plane because its Vertical Orientation is set to Up.

8. Switch to the SE Isometric viewpoint and examine the latest stair (see Figure 12.24).

FIGURE 12.22
Creating the lower flight (left), middle flight (middle), and upper flight (right)

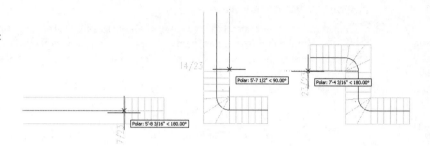

FIGURE 12.23
Snapping the stair to the structure (left) and then moving it down (right)

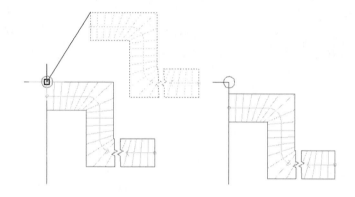

FIGURE 12.24
Completed Multi-Landing 1/4 Turn stair

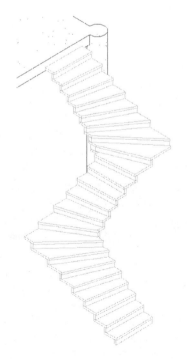

WORKING WITH STAIR WINDER STYLES

Stair Winder Styles control the way stairs behave through turns. The turn type stairs you already made use the Balanced winder style by default. Balanced winders get tighter up to the middle of the turn, and then they get wider. This was the only behavior for turn type stairs back in ADT 3. Now we have more choices.

We will create two additional winder styles to use with the turn type stairs.

1. Choose Format ➤ Style Manager.

2. Expand the current drawing, Architectural Objects, and Stair Winder Styles nodes. Click Balanced in the tree pane.

3. Right-click the Balanced node in the tree pane and choose New from the shortcut menu.

4. Type the name **SinglePoint** as the new stair winder style name. Select the Settings tab in the content pane. Choose SinglePoint from the Winder Type drop-down list. Uncheck Riser Line so the winder style will show nosing on the treads instead.

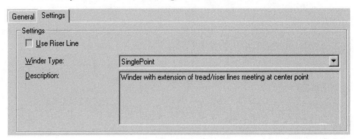

5. Create another stair winder style called **Manual**. Choose Manual from its Winder Type drop-down list. Leave Riser Line checked. Click OK to close the Style Manager.

Next, let's assign the winder styles you made to the stair objects and observe their effects. Then we'll straighten treads with manual grip editing to end up with custom stairs.

1. Select both the Multi-Landing 1/2 Turn and Multi-Landing 1/4 Turn stair objects. In the Properties palette, change Winder Style to SinglePoint. The stairs change so the risers merge into single points in the turns. Defect warnings might appear on several risers because the winder style forces the stair out of code compliance (see Figure 12.25). On the plus side, the risers have been straightened out in the flights.

2. While both stairs are still selected, change Winder Style to Manual. None of the risers change position, even though you changed winder styles. Changing winder styles from Balanced to SinglePoint and then to Manual yields a different topology than changing directly from Balanced to Manual. Press Esc to deselect.

3. Select the Multi-Landing 1/2 Turn stair. Click its Edit Turns trigger grip, which is located at the single point the risers currently radiate from. Click three Straighten Tread grips shown in Figure 12.26. Press Esc to deselect. If you saw defect warnings, they will disappear, and

you are left with a better and more practical stair that confines the winding as nearly as possible to the turns while maintaining the proper slope throughout.

4. Switch to the SE Isometric viewpoint and admire your turn type stairs (see Figure 12.27). Instead of having every stair be angled, winding is confined closer to each turn.

5. Save your work as Stairs.dwg.

FIGURE 12.25
Defects appear on many risers when changing winder style.

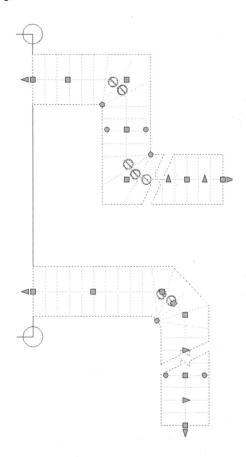

FIGURE 12.26
Entering Edit Turns mode (left), straightening treads (middle), and exiting Edit Turns mode (right)

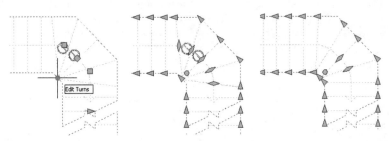

FIGURE 12.27
Completed alterations to winders

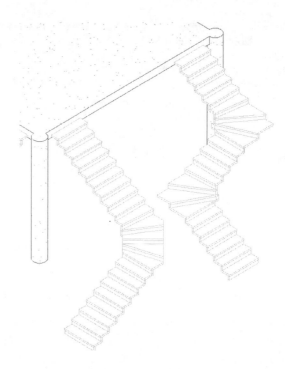

Making U-Shaped Stairs

U-shaped stairs are found in most modern buildings, especially in stair towers because they fit into compact rectangles that lend themselves to repetition on multiple levels. There are two Turn Types for U-shaped stairs: 1/2 Landing and 1/2 Turn. Let's build both types.

TURN TYPE: 1/2 LANDING

The U-shaped 1/2 Landing stair is the most common variant, having a large landing midway between levels.

TIP U-shaped stairs use constraints that you'll learn about later in "Editing Advanced Properties."

1. Switch to the Top viewpoint. Click the Stair tool in the Design palette.

2. In the Properties palette, set Shape to U-Shaped and Turn Type to 1/2 Landing.

3. Some distance above the training structure in plan, click the flight start point. Move the cursor horizontally to the left using polar object tracking, type **4'** and press Enter. The U-shaped stair appears and is oriented so the top and bottom edges are on the lower edge (see Figure 12.28). Press Esc to end the command.

4. Move the stair from its lower-left endpoint and snap it to the center of the second column from the right along the top edge of the training structure. So the stair clears the column, move it horizontally to the right a distance of 3'-6" (see Figure 12.29).

5. Select the U-shaped stair and click the flip grip at the top of the stair to flip it to the other side. Clicking the other flip grip would mirror the stair horizontally. Switch to the NE Isometric viewpoint and examine the stair (see Figure 12.30).

FIGURE 12.28
Clicking the flight start point (left) and determining the orientation and flight endpoint (right)

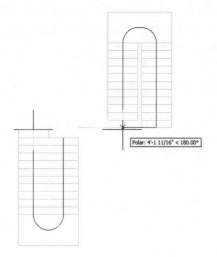

FIGURE 12.29
Snapping the U-shaped stair to the structure (left) and then moving it horizontally (right)

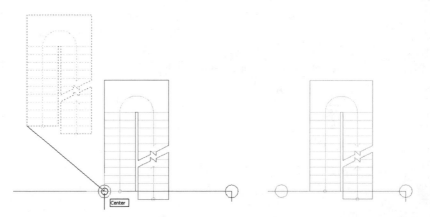

FIGURE 12.30
Mirroring using a flip grip (left) and viewing the completed U-shaped 1/2 Landing stair (right)

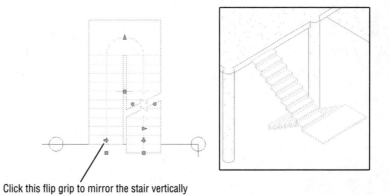

Click this flip grip to mirror the stair vertically

TURN TYPE: 1/2 TURN

The U-shaped 1/2 Turn stair takes up less area because it has steps that continue though the turn. Use this type in situations where area is at a premium and building codes do not require a landing. We will wrap this stair around a wall that projects out from the training structure.

WARNING   1/4 Landing and 1/4 Turn variants are not available for U-shaped stairs.

1. Switch to the NE viewpoint. Draw a temporary line, as shown in Figure 12.31. Don't worry about the length of this line because we will be deleting it after the stair is created.

2. Switch to the Top viewpoint. Click the Stair tool in the Design palette. In the Properties palette, set Turn Type to 1/2 Turn and Winder Style to SinglePoint.

3. In the Dimensions category, change Justify to Inside because we will be wrapping the inside of the stair around a wall.

4. Click the flight stair point at the endpoint of the temporary line you drew earlier. Move the mouse horizontally to the left using polar object tracking, type **1'-4"** (to match the width of the wall), and press Enter. The stair appears; press Esc to end the command.

5. Switch to the NE Isometric viewpoint again to check out the stair. Select the stair and change its elevation to 0 (zero) in the Properties palette. Delete the temporary line. Switch to the NW Isometric viewpoint to see the top of the stair (see Figure 12.32).

6. Save your work as **Stairs.dwg**.

NOTE   We will hold off on making ramps until you learn how to adjust code limits in stair styles. See "Making Ramps" later in this chapter.

FIGURE 12.31
Snapping temporary line to training structure

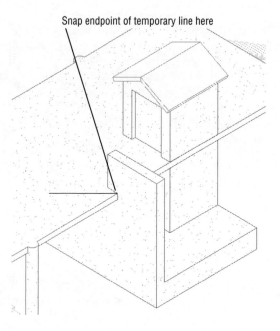

Snap endpoint of temporary line here

FIGURE 12.32
Completed U-shaped
1/2 Turn stair in NE
Isometric (left) and
NW Isometric view-
points (right)

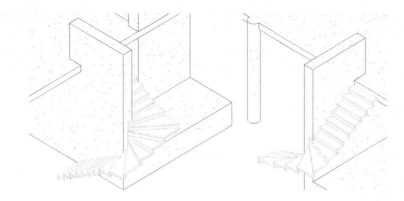

Editing Stairs

Stairs are complex structures having numerous subtleties that you must pay attention to as your design gets more refined. One strategy is to ignore the finer points in early design stages and just create the stair types that are necessary to rough-in the design—similar to what we have done up to this point in this chapter. Later on, you can refine each stair to suit its particular environment and context. After you have created stair objects, you can edit their edges and advanced properties to get exactly the geometry you are looking for.

Customizing Edges

Customize stair edges by editing them directly with grips to widen or taper individual flights. You can also project edges to meet a complex boundary shape that you draw with a polyline.

EDITING WITH GRIPS

Stairs have two levels of grips: object grips and edge grips. Object grips are what you see when selecting a stair object; they allow direct manipulation similar to the way you have been editing most objects in ADT. Edge grips are activated by clicking a trigger grip that takes you into a mode for editing. Edge grips allow stairs to be widened or tapered; they are available at the top and bottom of every flight on both left and right edges.

1. Open Stairs.dwg from your hard drive or the companion DVD if it is not already open.

2. Switch to the Top viewpoint, zoom in on the straight stair, and select it. Its object grips appear (see Figure 12.33). The graphics path is the line with an arrow at its tip that indicates flight direction. The Construction Line Location grip controls the position of baseline that the grips reside on.

NOTE The Lengthen Stair grip moves a straight stair unless it ends with a landing. Each stair type shows its own set of object grips appropriate to its form. Hold the cursor over any grip to read what it does in its ToolTip.

3. Click either one of the Edit Edges trigger grips. Edge grips replace the object grips while you are in Edit Edges mode. Click the Flight Width edge grip along the lower edge in plan. Move the cursor down and type **2′-6″** into the dynamic dimension.

4. Click the upper Flight Width edge grip. Move the cursor up and type **2′-6″** into its dynamic dimension.

5. Click the lower-left Flight Taper grip. Move the cursor down and type **4′** into the dynamic dimension. Click the upper-left Flight Taper grip, move it up, and type **4′** into its dynamic dimension. Switch to the SW Isometric viewpoint (see Figure 12.34).

FIGURE 12.33
Object grips on straight stair

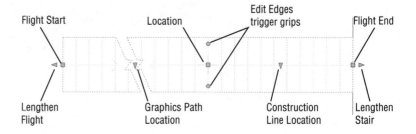

FIGURE 12.34
Widening (upper left), tapering (lower left), and editing stair (right)

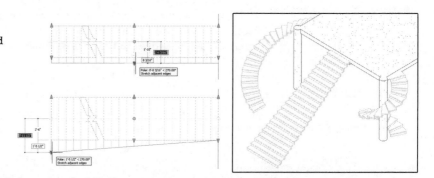

PROJECTING EDGES

You can project the edges of any stair to meet a complex boundary that you draw as a polyline. This is especially useful to get stairs to fit into unusual plan shapes defined by the surrounding walls. In most cases you would trace the boundary of the walls surrounding a stair with a polyline, but in this tutorial we will simply draw a polyline or arbitrary shape to demonstrate this concept.

1. Switch to the Top viewpoint and zoom in on the spiral stair that spans a total of 180 degrees.

2. Type **PL** and press Enter to draw a polyline. Snap the start point to the top outer edge of the spiral stair. Press **A** and then Enter for the Arc option; press **S** and then Enter for the Second Pt option. Click the second point well above and to the left of the top of the spiral arc. Click the third and last point well to the left of the spiral stair's lower-left corner (see left side of Figure 12.35). Press Esc to end the command.

3. Select the spiral stair, right-click, and choose Customize Edge ➤ Project. Click the spiral stair's outer edge, click the polyline, and press Enter. The stair's outer edge projects outward in plan to meet the edge you drew previously (see right side of Figure 12.35).

4. Switch to the SW Isometric viewpoint to check out the widening spiral and delete the polyline arc.

FIGURE 12.35
Drawing a polyline (left) and projecting the outer stair edge to meet it (right)

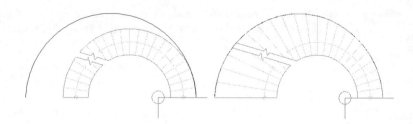

Editing Advanced Properties

The Properties palette contains additional stair controls in the Advanced category including constraints, floor settings, flight height limits, and interference clearances.

ADJUSTING CONSTRAINTS

Constraints are available only for U-shaped stairs. Use constraints for very fine control over the way treads and risers align. You'll draw a temporary line to help you perceive subtle alignment changes.

1. Select the U-shaped 1/2 Landing stair and the training structure. Click the yellow lightbulb icon in the drawing tray and choose Isolate Objects from the shortcut menu.

2. Switch to the Right viewpoint and use 2D Wireframe shading mode. Zoom into the landing area.

3. Draw a short vertical line connecting the lower corner of the top tread in the lower flight with the top corner of the second tread in the upper flight (see Figure 12.36). At this point the nosing of both treads should line up perfectly.

4. Select the stair. In the Properties palette, expand the Advanced category if necessary and locate the Constraints subcategory: Alignment Type is currently set to Tread To Tread—that is why the treads line up. Verify that Extend Alignment is set to Lower Flight, which affects which flight moves in plan when alignment is changed. Then change Alignment Type to Tread To Riser. The upper flight jogs over slightly to maintain the new alignment constraint.

5. Set Alignment Type to Riser To Riser: the upper flight moves a bit more to the right so the risers line up vertically. Move the short line segment over so its lower end snaps to the corner of the riser in the lower flight. Now you can see that the upper flight risers are in line with the lower-flight risers. Figure 12.36 illustrates the last three steps.

TIP The Alignment Offset property allows you to intentionally shift the alignment relationship between treads and risers by a short distance. Positive values shift the lower-flight treads closer to the landing relative to the upper-flight treads.

FIGURE 12.36
Adjusting constraints of U-shaped stair: Tread To Tread (left), Tread To Riser (middle), and Riser To Riser (right)

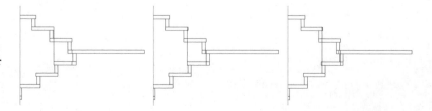

6. Switch the Alignment Type to Free: this places treads and risers wherever necessary to complete the stair—in this case it is the same as Tread To Tread. Delete the temporary vertical line you used to perceive alignment.

7. Switch to the Top viewpoint and zoom in on the stair. Set Uneven Tread to Upper Flight. As the distribution of treads changes, the extra tread appears on the right side in plan, which is the upper flight in this example. This setting affects only U-shaped stairs that have an uneven number of treads. Change Uneven Treads back to Lower Flight to set the stair back the way it was before and press Esc to deselect.

CHOOSING FLOOR SETTINGS

You can tweak floor settings to adjust the location of a stair's risers in relation to top and bottom finished floor surfaces. By default, stairs align perfectly with both floor surfaces, assuming that the finished floor is at zero elevation in each construct. Although that's a safe bet, it's not always the case. There are probably times when you'll add a thin slab representing flooring material to a slab surface, so the top of the finished floor will effectively float above elevation zero. In cases like these, you'll need to offset floor settings in stairs so the tread-to-tread distance will be the same from the top step to the top floor, as it is in the rest of the stair.

1. Switch to the Right viewpoint. Pan over to the top of the U-shaped 1/2 Landing stair where it meets the top level of the training structure. Notice that there is a gap between the last riser and the top of the slab. The distance between the top of slab and top tread is the same as all the other tread-to-tread distances.

2. In the Properties palette, under Advanced ➤ Floor Settings, change Top Offset to **2"** (this is equal to the tread thickness). Study the illustration under the Floor Settings subcategory.

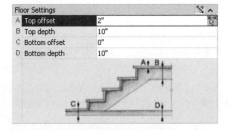

The entire flight shifted upward so that the top edge of the top riser is flush with the top of the slab. The overall height of the stair was increased by 2" and the Riser dimension increased to distribute the additional 2" over all the risers. The top of the top riser aligns with the top of the slab because the treads are 2" in the Standard stair style. Note, however, that the top of slab to top tread dimension is no longer equal to the tread-to-tread dimension in the rest of the stair. In other words, the top step is shorter than all the rest (see Figure 12.37). This would be desirable if you planned on placing a 2" floor slab on top of the training structure—to simulate a hard wood floor, for example. Then a person ascending the stair would step off the top tread and land on the top floor after going up one last rise equal to the riser distance of the stair.

3. We won't need to make another slab in this continuing tutorial, so change Top Offset back to 0 (zero). Note that you can also add a bottom offset to simulate a finished floor below.

FIGURE 12.37
Adjusting Top Offset

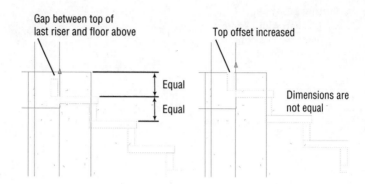

NOTE   The Top Depth and Bottom Depth properties in the Floor Settings subcategory affect how stringers meet floor slabs. You'll learn more about stringers in "Creating Stringers" in the "Working with Stair and Ramp Styles" section later in this chapter.

4. Switch to the SW Isometric viewpoint and Hidden display mode. Click the red lightbulb icon in the drawing tray and choose End Object Isolation from the shortcut menu.

SETTING FLIGHT HEIGHT LIMITS

Setting flight height limits is entirely optional. You can set maximum and/or minimum limits to comply with relevant building codes or just to ensure that flights have reasonable sizes and numbers of risers.

1. Switch to the Top viewpoint, zoom in on the straight stair, and select it.

2. In the Properties palette notice that by default the stair has no flight height limits. Under Advanced ➤ Flight Height change Maximum Limit Type to Risers. Verify that the Maximum Risers property that appears below is set to 15 risers. A landing appears in the middle of the straight stair because the stair has 23 risers, thus exceeding the limit.

TIP   If you want control over landing size or placement in a straight stair using flight height limits, create a Multi-Landing 1/2 Landing stair instead.

3. The new landing offset the top edge of the stair to the right. Move the straight stair back to the left, making it flush with the left edge of the training structure. In the Properties palette, set Elevation to 0 (zero).

4. Switch to the SW Isometric viewpoint in Hidden display mode and examine the straight stair's landing that was created automatically by setting the maximum flight height limit (see Figure 12.38).

Setting a minimum flight height limit applies to stairs with multiple flights where you want to avoid very short flights. Landings will be generated whenever a stair doesn't fit within the flight height limits you specify.

FIGURE 12.38
Straight stair with land-
ing generated by setting
flight height limits

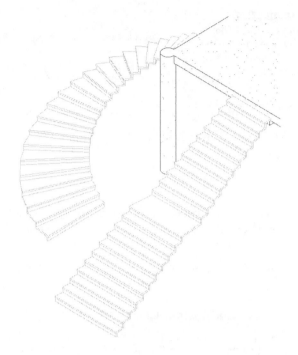

CONTROLLING INTERFERENCE

Stairs can interfere with slabs, walls, spaces, curtain walls, and door/window assemblies. You can set two properties in the stair that define a volume that determines the interference boundary between the stair and other objects. After the stair's interference properties are set, perform a Boolean subtraction using the stair itself to cut other objects. This feature is a very convenient way to cut holes in slabs that are perfectly fitted to the stairs that penetrate them.

1. Move the straight stair horizontally to the right (angle zero) a distance of 5' so that the top of the stair is deeply embedded in the slab of the training structure.

2. Select the straight stair, and in the Properties palette under Advanced > Interference, set Headroom Height to 8' and Side Clearance to 1'. Press Esc to deselect.

3. Select the training structure, which is a complex slab-based object. Right-click and choose Boolean ➤ Subtract. Select the straight stair and press Enter. The training structure is cut away where it intersects the interference boundary of the stair (see Figure 12.39). There are side clearances of 1' on either side. If the stair were completely surrounded by a slab, the cut hole would allow enough room to provide 8' of clear space between the stairs and slab above.

NOTE The slab is also cut for the embedded riser, leaving a void above the stair where the next tread would be if the stair did not end in a riser. Rather than a "defect," this provides an oportunity to add an object (such as a slab or mass element) to simulate a top nosing.

4. Save your work as **EditedStairs.dwg**.

FIGURE 12.39
Subtracting straight stair from slab after interference conditions were set in the stair

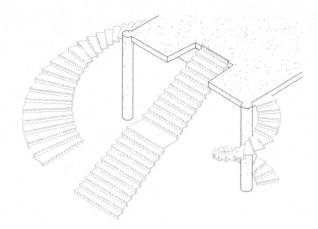

Working with Stair and Ramp Styles

Stairs and ramps are both governed by stair styles. Stair styles contain design rules that maintain the riser height to tread depth ratio within limits that you can set. Stairs can optionally use a rule-based calculator, which works like a formula, to keep the stair as close as possible to the optimum slope as determined by the building code.

Stair styles provide the option to have *stringers*—members running along the length of the stair—that structurally support the stair. You'll use stair styles to determine whether risers and/or treads are to be displayed in the style. Flight and landing dimensions are also set for each component, and stair styles are also where landing extension options are set. In this section, you will create all the stair styles shown in Figure 12.40.

Let's create all the styles first and then assign them to the stair objects afterward. You'll create a ramp later on using a premade style. Finally, we'll examine the display properties that all stair styles have in common.

Making Design Rules

Stair design rules control what slopes are possible for the style. Defect warning symbols appear on stairs that do not adhere to the design rules set in their styles. We'll use the Style Manager to create a series of stair styles that we will continue to customize as we go along.

1. Open EditedStairs.dwg from your hard drive or the companion DVD if it's not already open.

2. Choose Format ➤ Style Manager. Expand the current drawing, Architectural Objects, and Stair Styles nodes. Right-click the Standard node in the tree pane and choose New from the context menu. Give the new style the name **Existing**.

3. Repeat the previous step, creating the following new stair styles: **Cantilever**, **WoodSaddle**, **Steel**, **WoodHoused**, **HalfRailWall**, **Concrete**, and **RampCurb**.

4. Select Existing in the tree pane. In the content pane, click the Design Rules tab. The Existing style is designed to accommodate stairs as they have been built, even if they do not come close to modern building codes. Therefore, create broad code limits for this style. Change Maximum Slope Riser Height to 11″ and Tread Depth to 7″. Uncheck Use Rule Based Calculator (see Figure 12.41).

FIGURE 12.40
Stair styles

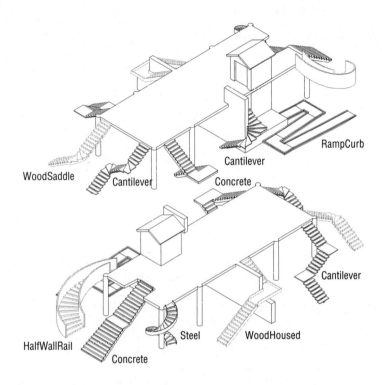

FIGURE 12.41
Making design rules for
stair style

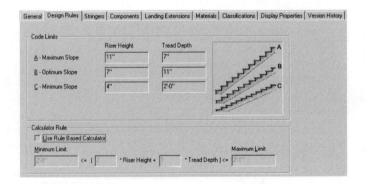

WARNING The values used in this book do not necessarily comply with local building codes.

5. In the tree pane, click the RampCurb node. Ramps obviously slope very slowly compared with stairs—you'll need to adjust code limits accordingly. In the content pane, change Maximum Slope Riser Height to $^{11}/_{16}$" and Tread Depth to 1'. Change Optimum Slope Riser Height to 1"

and Tread Depth to 1'-3". Change Minimum Slope Riser Height to $^{15}/_{16}"$ and Tread Depth to 1'-8". Uncheck Use Rule Based Calculator. Click OK to close the Style Manager.

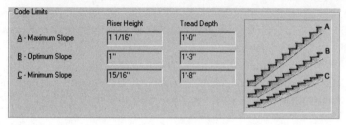

NOTE All the other stair styles use the Rule Based Calculator, which constrains the slope of stairs as they are created. The rule is expressed as $MIN \leq ([X \times \text{Riser Height}] + [Y \times \text{Tread Depth}]) \leq MAX$, where X and Y are integers, and MIN and MAX are limit distances. Check your local building codes to verify the formula you must use (if any) in your projects.

6. Right-click the command line and choose Options from the shortcut menu. In the Options dialog box, select the AEC Object Settings tab. Calculator Limits can be set either to Strict or Relaxed. Strict, which is the default, means that a defect marker will appear on any stair that violates the rule-based calculator's limits set in the Design Rules tab of the stair style. It is a good idea to leave this set to Strict so you'll know if there is a violation (Relaxed never shows defect markers). You might encounter drawings made in ADT 3 or earlier that have this option set to Relaxed—now you know where to change this option if necessary. Click Cancel to close the Options dialog box.

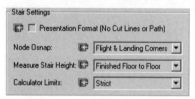

7. Leave the sample file open throughout this section as you continue to add to its stair styles.

Creating Stringers

As mentioned earlier, stringers form the actual structure of stairs and they carry loads from the treads to the building. There are four types of stringers available in ADT. *Saddled stringers* support treads from underneath, and *housed stringers* supports treads from their sides. *Slab stringers* fuse treads and risers into a monolithic structure, as found in concrete stairs. *Ramp stringers* are slabs that slope gently in an inclined plane.

ADDING SADDLED STRINGERS

You create saddled stringers for two stair styles: Cantilever and WoodSaddle. The Cantilever style has one thick concrete stringer in the center that metal treads on top are cantilevered off of. Wood-Saddle has two separate stringers offset inward slightly from the sides that support treads and risers above.

1. Choose Format ➤ Style Manager. Expand the current drawing, Architectural Objects, and Stair Styles nodes. Click the Cantilever node in the tree pane. In the content pane, click the Stringer tab. Study the illustration and its labeled parameters.

2. Click the Add button and change the new component's name from Unnamed to **Stringer**. Set Type to Saddled, Alignment to Center, A - Width to 6″, B - Offset to 0″, C - Waist to 6″, E - Waist to 6″, and Cleanup to Truncate (see Figure 12.42).

3. Click the WoodSaddle node in the tree pane. In the content pane, click the Add button. Rename the component **Left**. Set Type to Saddled, Alignment to Align Left, A - Width to 1 1/2″, B - Offset to 2″, C - Waist to 6″, and E - Waist to 6″.

4. Select the Left component and then click the Add button. Rename the new component **Right**. Change Alignment to Align Right, if necessary.

FIGURE 12.42

Adding a stringer

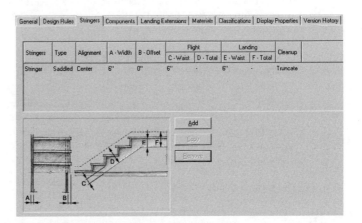

ADDING HOUSED STRINGERS

You'll add three sets of housed stringers to the following styles: Steel, WoodHoused, and HalfWall-Rail. Housed stringers carry loads by attaching to the outer edges of treads and risers. Unlike the saddled stringers, housed stringers use D and F parameters to carry the stringers above the treads and risers. HalfRailWall is a unique style that extends the concept of housed stringers to the point at which the stringers themselves become half walls—like railings that are part of the stair itself.

1. Select the Steel style in the tree pane. In the content pane, click the Add button and change the new component's name to **LeftEdge**. Set Type to Housed, Alignment to Align Left, A - Width to 1 1/2″, C - Waist to 2″, D - Total to 1′, E - Waist to 2″, and F - Total to 1′.

2. Select LeftEdge and then click the Add button. Rename the new component **RightEdge**.

3. Click the WoodHoused style in the tree pane. In the content pane, click the Add button and name the component **LeftEdge**. Set C - Waist to 1 1/2″, D - Total to 11 1/2″, E - Waist to 1 1/2″, and F - Total to 11 1/2″.

4. Select LeftEdge and then click the Add button. Rename the new component **RightEdge**.

5. Click the HalfWallRail style in the tree pane. In the content pane, click the Add button and name the component **LeftWall**. Set A - Width to 4", C - Waist to 4", D - Total to 4', E - Waist to 4", and F - Total to 4'.

6. Select LeftWall and then click the Add button. Rename the new component **RightWall**.

ADDING SLAB STRINGERS

Slab stringers are really found only in concrete stairs formed from a monolithic slab that spans across the full width of the flight. Select the Concrete style in the tree pane. In the content pane, click the Add button and change the new component's name to **Slab**. Set Type to Slab, Alignment to Full Width, C - Waist to 6", E - Waist to 6".

ADDING RAMP STRINGERS

One of the components of creating a successful ramp involves setting its style's stringer type to ramp. You'll make the RampCurb style that is both a ramp and has housed stringers along the edges forming integral curbs.

1. Select the RampCurb style in the tree pane. In the content pane, click the Add button and change the new component's name to **Ramp**. Set Type to Ramp, Alignment to Full Width, C - Waist to 4", D - Total to 4", E - Waist to 4", and F - Total to 4".

2. Click the Add button and rename the new component **LeftCurb**. Set Type to Housed, Alignment to Align Left, A - Width to 4", C - Waist to 4", D - Total to 6", E - Waist to 4", and F - Total to 6".

3. Select LeftCurb and then click the Add button. Rename the new component **RightCurb**.

Controlling Components

The thickness dimensions of treads, risers, and landings are set on the Components tab in the stair style. In addition, the length of the *nosing*—or projection of treads that overhangs risers—is set as a flight dimension component. Landings can have additional width as an option set as a style component. Now you'll set up all the stair styles' components with appropriate dimensions.

1. Select the Cantilever style and click the Components tab in the content pane of the Style Manager dialog box. Study the illustration and its labeled parameters.

2. Cantilever stairs have only treads, not risers. Uncheck Riser in the Flight Dimensions group (see Figure 12.43).

3. Select the Concrete style. Set A - Tread Thickness to 1", B - Riser Thickness to 1", C - Nosing Length to 1 1/2", and D - Landing Thickness to 1". Check Sloping Riser to force the risers to slope backward slightly, providing additional toe room on each tread.

4. Select the Existing style. Check Allow Each Stair To Vary. Normally components are set exclusively in the style. By allowing each stair to vary, you are essentially converting all the component properties to the object level. After we finish setting components for the rest of the styles, we'll open worksheets from the object level.

5. Select the HalfWallRail style. Set A - Tread Thickness to 1", B - Riser Thickness to 1", C - Nosing Length to 1 1/2", and D - Landing Thickness to 1".

FIGURE 12.43

Setting stair style
component properties

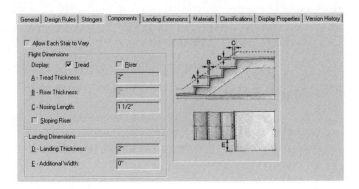

6. Select the RampCurb style. Ramps do not have treads or risers. Uncheck both of these display settings.

7. Select the Steel style. It is optional to have risers on housed steel stairs. Uncheck Riser in this example. Set A - Tread Thickness to 1", C - Nosing Length to 1 1/2", and D - Landing Thickness to 1".

8. Select the WoodHoused style. Set A - Tread Thickness to 1", B - Riser Thickness to 1", C - Nosing Length to 1 1/2", and D - Landing Thickness to 1".

9. Repeat the previous step, using the same settings for the WoodSaddle style. Click OK to close the Style Manager.

WARNING Be especially careful not to click the Cancel button or close the box in the upper-right corner of the Style Manager dialog box after making a long series of changes. If you cancel, everything you have changed since opening the dialog box will be lost. It is a good idea to click the Apply button after making a series of changes. Clicking Apply periodically can reduce loss from unintentional closure of the Style Manager.

In step 4 you chose to allow the Existing style's components to vary with each stair. This is another way of saying that you transferred components from the style to each object assigned that particular style. Let's create a new stair using the Existing style to demonstrate an object level worksheet.

1. Create a stair using the Existing style off to the side and not attached to the training structure. Make the stair the type of your choosing—we will delete it shortly.

2. Select the new stair object and click the Components worksheet icon in the Properties palette under Advanced > Worksheets. The Stair Components worksheet appears (see Figure 12.44). It contains the same properties as are found on the Components tab of the stair style. The difference here is that the worksheet properties are specific to this particular stair object—and not all the stairs share the same style. Notice that there is a Reset To Style Values button that you can use to drop any object-level modifications that may have been made. Click Cancel to close the worksheet. Delete the stair you made previously.

3. Select any one of the other stair objects. Click the Components worksheet icon in the Properties palette. This time all the properties on the worksheet are grayed-out and are not editable. A note at the top of the worksheet says, "Properties are fixed by the style and may not vary." Click Cancel.

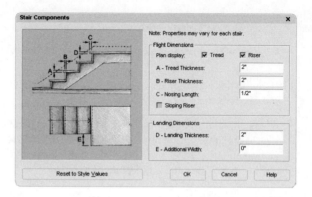

FIGURE 12.44
Stair Components
worksheet

Making Landing Extensions

Some of the finer points relating to stairs are landing extensions. These optional extensions of landing surfaces affect only stairs using the 1/2 Landing or 1/4 Landing turn types. There are two landing extensions that can be made on the up and/or down sides of the landing. You can extend the landing a distance equal to the tread depth or add an additional offset to get the edge of the landing exactly where you want it. Let's set landing extension options for each of the stair styles.

1. Choose Format ➤ Style Manager. Expand the current drawing, Architectural Objects, and Stair Styles nodes. Select the Cantilever style in the tree pane. In the content pane, select the Landing Extensions tab. Check Add Tread Depth under B - Distance To First Tread UP. This will add one tread depth to the landing on the upper flight side. Study the illustration and its labeled parameters (see Figure 12.45).

2. Select the Concrete style. Check Add Tread Depth under B - Distance To First Tread UP.

3. Select the RampCurb style. In the Stringer Resolution group, check Extend Landing To Merge Flight Stringers With Landing Stringers. This option is appropriate for all ramps.

4. Select the Steel style. Type **1 ½"** in the B - Distance To First Tread UP text box and check Add Tread Depth. This formula extends the landing by ($1\,^1/_2$" + T), where T is the tread depth.

FIGURE 12.45
Setting Landing
Extension properties
in style

5. Select the WoodHoused style. Type **2 ½"** in the B - Distance To First Tread UP text box and check Add Tread Depth.

6. Repeat the previous step for the WoodSaddle style.

TIP Adjusting extension distances usually involves testing, measurement, and readjustment until you get the stair style exactly as you envision it.

Notice that there is an Allow Each Stair To Vary check box at the top of the Landing Extensions tab. Similar to the same setting on the Components tab, this feature converts the style-based properties on this tab to an object level worksheet of the same name. Use this option when you want finer control of landing extensions at the object level.

Adding Materials

Materials are assigned to stair components in much the same way as other style-based AEC objects. The material definitions must first exist within the drawing file before they can be assigned to components. We will open a content drawing within the Style Manager to efficiently load all the materials needed to represent the stair components into the drawing. Then you can assign materials as appropriate to each style and component.

1. In the Style Manager dialog box's menu bar, choose File ➤ Open Drawing. In the Open Drawing dialog box that appears, click the Content button in the Favorites pane. In the navigation pane, double-click Styles and then Imperial. Select `Material Definitions (Imperial).dwg` and click Open. The Open Drawing dialog box disappears and the Material Definitions (Imperial).dwg node appears in the Style Manager's tree pane.

2. In the tree pane, expand the Material Definitions (Imperial).dwg, Multi-Purpose Objects nodes. In the content pane, hold down Ctrl and select the following material definitions:

```
Metals.Metal Fabrications.Metal Stairs.Galvinized
Concrete.Cast-in-Place.Flat.Grey
Wood.Architectural Woodwork.Wood Stairs and Railings.Ash
Finishes.Plaster and Gypsum Board.Gypsum Wallboard.Painted.White
```

Drag the selected nodes into the EditedStairs.dwg node in the tree pane and release the mouse button. I will refer to these materials more succinctly as Metal, Concrete, Wood, and Paint for the rest of this section.

3. In the tree pane, expand the EditedStairs.dwg, Architectural Objects, and Stair Styles nodes. Select the Cantilever style. In the content pane, select the Materials tab. Assign Metal to Tread and Landing components, and Concrete to Stringer (see Figure 12.46).

4. Select the Concrete style. Assign Concrete to all of its components.

5. Select the HalfWallRail style. Assign Wood to Tread, Riser, and Landing components. Assign Paint to LeftWall and RightWall.

6. Select the RampCurb style. Assign Concrete to all its components.

7. Select the Steel style. Assign Metal to all its components.

8. Select the WoodHoused style. Assign Wood to all its components.

9. Select the WoodSaddle style. Assign Wood to all its components. Click OK to close the Style Manager.

10. Switch to the Top viewpoint. Assign styles to each stair object according to Figure 12.47.

11. Landing Extension properties often cause stair objects to resize. Move any stairs that change size after being assigned a style back into position so that their top edges are flush with the training structure.

FIGURE 12.46
Assigning material definitions to stair components

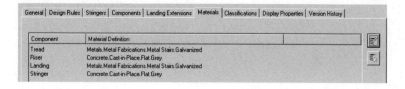

FIGURE 12.47
Assigning styles to stair objects

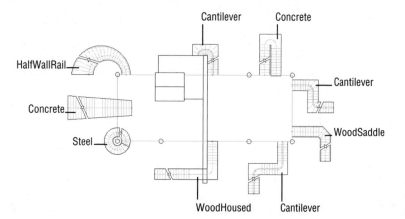

Making Ramps

Now that we have a stair style that defines a gently sloping ramp, we will go ahead and create it. Unlike most stairs, ramps are more easily made after you define their styles.

1. Click the Stair tool in the Design palette. In the Properties palette, set Style to RampCurb, Shape to Multi-Landing, Turn Type to 1/4 Landing, and Vertical Orientation to Down.

2. In the Dimensions subcategory, set Height to 3' and Justify to Right. Click the Calculation rules worksheet icon. Change all the buttons to Automatic in the Calculation Rules worksheet and click OK. This sets the rules to create the slope based on Height alone.

3. Click the flight start point at the corner of the low concrete slab (see A in Figure 12.48). Move the cursor horizontally to the left using polar object tracking. Click when the riser numbers read $^6/_{36}$.

FIGURE 12.48
Creating a ramp in stages
A through E

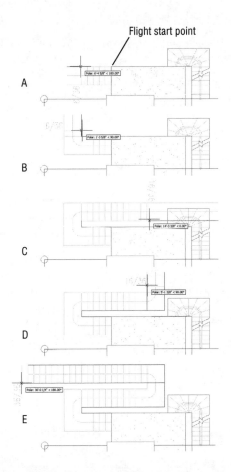

Flight start point

A

B

C

D

E

4. Move the cursor vertically up and click again when the riser numbers read $5/36$ (see B in Figure 12.48).

5. Move the cursor horizontally to the right and click when the riser numbers read $15/36$. You need to stop short of the adjacent stair to allow room for another landing (see C in Figure 12.48).

6. Move the cursor vertically up and click when the riser numbers read $15/36$. Once again you are making a landing (see D in Figure 12.48).

7. Finally, move the mouse horizontally to the left and click when the riser numbers read $36/36$ (see E in Figure 12.48). The ramp appears; press Esc to end the command.

8. Select the ramp and set its Elevation property to 3' to match the height of the low slab.

TIP Try increasing the ramp height to 3'-1" to get it to actually run from elevation zero to 3'-0". Ramps can be a bit finicky.

Setting Display Properties

Stairs have some specialized display properties that you should be aware of. Aside from controlling display components, you can position the cut plane and stair line, choose an arrow and break mark, and set the style and location of riser numbering. Let's alter one of the styles to see which display properties are available for stairs.

1. Switch to the Top viewpoint, zoom in on the WoodSaddle styled stair object, and select it.

2. Right-click and choose Edit Stair Style from the shortcut menu. In the Stair Styles dialog box, choose the Display Properties tab. Put a check in the Style Override column for the Plan display representation.

3. The Display Properties dialog box appears. Click the Layer/Color/Linetype tab if it is not already selected. There are essentially two sets of display components: those above the cut plane and those below it. Toggle all the display components with "down" in their names to toggle the components above the cut plane off (see Figure 12.49). Toggle Riser Numbers Up on.

4. Click the Other tab in the Display Properties dialog box. Change the Elevation value to 5' so that the cut plane override will be a bit higher—this will show more steps going up. Change Type to Curved in the Break Mark group. Study the options available in the dialog box (see Figure 12.50). The Stair Line is the line the arrowhead is on.

5. Click the Riser Numbering tab. This tab controls the Riser Numbers Up and Riser Numbers Down display components. Change Style to RomanS for smooth and simple text. Change Text Height to 6". In the Location group, set Y Offset to -6" (see Figure 12.51). Negative values move the riser numbers to the right relative to the lower edge of the stair. Uncheck Number Final Riser.

6. Click OK to close the Display Properties dialog box. Click OK again to close the Stair Styles dialog box. Now only the flight going up shows in the drawing window. Figure 12.52 shows the relevant display components of the plan display representation.

FIGURE 12.49
Stair display components in the plan display representation

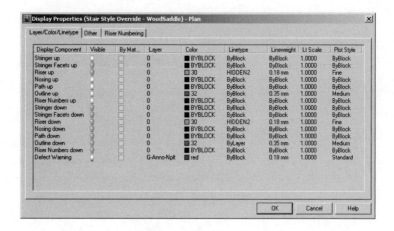

7. Switch to the NE Isometric viewpoint in Hidden display mode and select the U-shaped 1/2 Landing Concrete stair object. Right-click and choose Edit Stair Style from the shortcut menu. In the Stair Styles dialog box, choose the Display Properties tab. Put a check in the Style Override column for the Model display representation.

8. The Display Properties dialog box appears. Turn on the Clearance display component. Notice that there is only one set of display components in the model display representation because you see the entire stair (unlike in the plan display representations).

Display Component	Visible	By Mat...	Layer	Color	Linetype	Lineweight	Lt Scale
Defect Warning		☐	G-Anno-Nplt	■ red	ByBlock	0.18 mm	1.0000
Stringer		☑	0	■ 225	ByBlock	ByBlock	1.0000
Tread		☑	0	■ 235	ByBlock	ByBlock	1.0000
Landing		☑	0	■ 235	ByBlock	ByBlock	1.0000
Riser		☑	0	■ 245	ByBlock	ByBlock	1.0000
Clearance		☐	0	■ BYBLOCK	ByBlock	ByBlock	1.0000

9. Click OK in each open dialog box. Figure 12.53 shows the result. The Clearance component is helpful in planning interferences.

FIGURE 12.50
Other tab of Display Properties dialog box

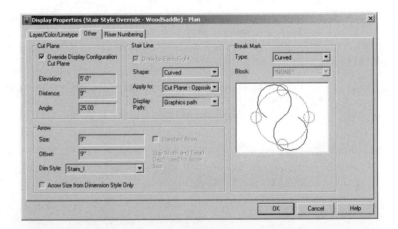

FIGURE 12.51
Controlling riser numbering

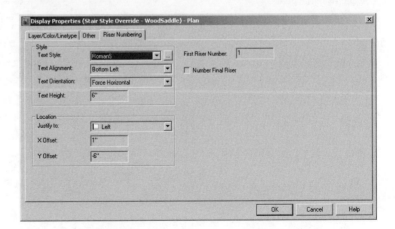

10. Select the U-shaped 1/2 Landing Concrete stair object again. Right-click and choose Edit Stair Style from the shortcut menu. In the Stair Styles dialog box, remove the style override in the model display representation; you don't need to keep it for the purposes of the continuing tutorial.

11. Save your work as **StairStyles.dwg**.

FIGURE 12.52
Resulting appearance
of stair

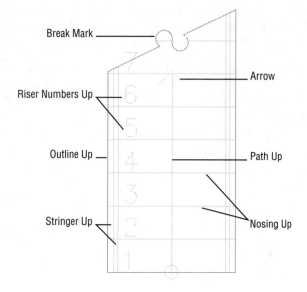

FIGURE 12.53
Stair showing Clearance
component of Model
display representation

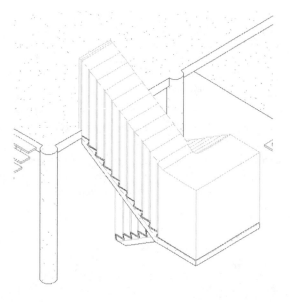

Adding Railings

Railings can be added as freestanding objects or they can be attached to stairs. When attached, the railing's shape is controlled by the stair, so when the stair changes the railing automatically updates. Railings are styled objects that—like stairs—can transfer some of their properties to the object level if desired. You might transfer properties to the object level when the overhead of creating a new style isn't warranted.

In this section you'll create a freestanding railing on top of the training structure and attach railings to every stair object made in this chapter. Then you'll design some railing styles that you can use as railing prototypes for your own projects.

TIP   Consider making extremely complex railings or gates as curtain wall styles instead (see Chapter 10, "Curtain Walls and Assemblies"). You are better off sticking with railings if you plan to attach them to stairs because railings are the only objects that automatically conform to stair shape.

Creating Railings

Railings protect people from falling over exposed floor edges. Drawing freestanding railings is much like drawing straight segmented polylines: simply by clicking vertex points. You can incorporate curved segments into freestanding railings by first drawing a polyline that includes arc segments and then applying railing tool properties to the polyline. We will take the latter approach in this tutorial.

Figure 12.54 illustrates typical railing components. Fixed posts are at its start and endpoints, and appear at railing vertices. Dynamic posts can appear at intervals between fixed posts. The term *baluster* refers to a vertical protective component within the railing that keeps people (especially children) from falling through. The Bottomrail—also known as the *Toe*—is a horizontal component that can be repeated multiple times within the overall railing; Bottomrails also provide a protective function. The Guardrail is the upper horizontal component that sometimes serves to cap railings. The Handrail is an obvious safety aid that is usually placed at hand height between 2'-10" and 3'. The Return component extends beyond the start or endpoint of a railing and must be added as a custom display block if it is to be included in a railing style. The term *escutcheon* refers to a protective covering that, in the case of a railing, shields and terminates the Handrail at a wall surface.

Let's begin by drawing a polyline and then converting it to a railing object. Then we'll attach railings to all the stair objects in the sample file.

1. Open `StairStyles.dwg` from your hard drive or the companion DVD if it is not already open. Switch to the Top viewpoint. Turn off the A-Roof layer.

WARNING   The Top viewpoint is the ideal place to attach railings to stairs because you can easily see both sides of the stair and can attach railings appropriately. You might run into trouble attaching railings to stairs in isometric viewpoints. Be careful not to attach more than one railing per side to a stair.

2. Draw a polyline that roughly matches the one shown in Figure 12.55. Snap its first point to the corner of the elevator structure and draw a straight segment vertically down. Draw two arc segments with opposite curvature to complete the polyline. Do not worry about trying to perfectly match the illustration—any polyline will do.

FIGURE 12.54
Railing components

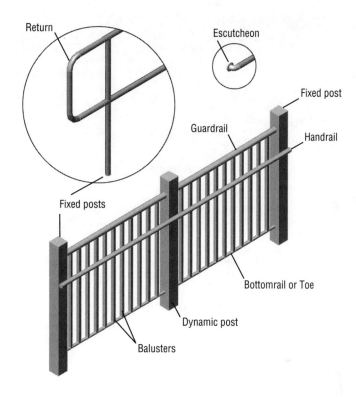

FIGURE 12.55
Drawing a polyline
with straight and arc
segments

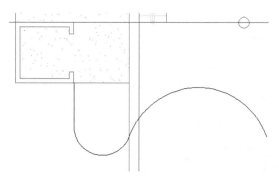

3. In the Design palette, right-click the Railing tool (refer to Figure 12.4). Choose Apply Tool Properties To ➢ Polyline. Select the polyline you drew previously and press Enter. The command line says the following:

```
Erase layout geometry? [Yes/No] <No>:
```

Type **Y** and press Enter. A freestanding railing object replaces the polyline. In the Properties palette, verify that Elevation is 13′. Press Esc to deselect.

4. Click the Railing tool in the Design palette. In the Properties palette under Basic > Location, change Attached To to Stair. You can attach a railing to an entire stair or just to a flight within the stair object. Set Side Offset to 2″ (an inward offset) and Automatic Placement to Yes.

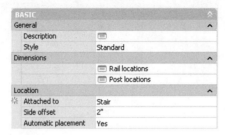

5. Attach two railings to every stair (and ramp) in the sample file. Each stair requires two clicks—one on each side. Figure 12.56 shows the result.

TIP You can adjust the position of a railing with respect to the stair it is attached to by using the Anchor worksheet in the Properties palette.

Working with Railing Styles

We will create nine railing styles that represent a wide range of real world railings. Figure 12.57 shows the styles that we'll create in this section. The railings are descriptively named using plus symbols to delimit components included in each style. I recommend following this naming convention in your own projects to keep railing styles clearly differentiated.

IMPORTING PROFILES AND CREATING RAILING STYLES

Some of the railing styles we'll create use profiles for their components. You already learned how to define profiles in many earlier chapters, so let's not belabor the point. You will load profiles from a content drawing in the Style Manager to speed the process along.

FIGURE 12.56
Railings attached to every stair

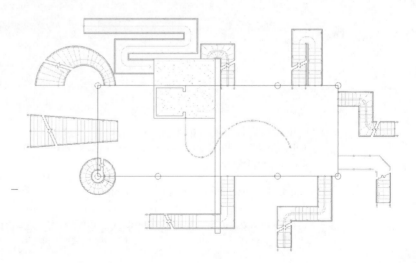

FIGURE 12.57
Railing styles

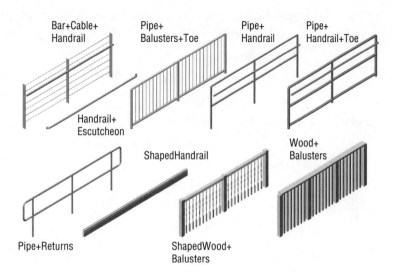

1. Choose Format ➤ Style Manager. Inside the Style Manager dialog box, choose File ➤ Open Drawing. In the Open Drawing dialog box that appears, navigate to this chapter's folder on the companion DVD, select `Profiles.dwg`, and click Open. The Open Drawing dialog box disappears, and the Profiles.dwg node appears in the Style Manager's tree pane.

2. In the tree pane, expand the Profiles.dwg, Multi-Purpose Objects, and Profiles nodes. In the content pane, hold down Ctrl and select the following profile definitions: Baluster, EscutcheonPlan, GuardrailCap, GuardrailReturnPlan, and HandrailGrip. Drag these profile definitions into the tree pane and drop them on the StairStyles.dwg node. The profiles are copied to our working drawing.

3. Right-click the Profiles.dwg node in the tree pane and choose Close from the shortcut menu.

4. Expand the StairStyles.dwg, Architectural Objects, and Railing Styles nodes in the tree pane.

5. Right-click the Railing Styles node and choose New from the shortcut menu. Rename the new style **Bar+Cable+Handrail**.

6. Repeat the previous step, creating the following new railing styles: **Handrail+Escutcheon**, **Pipe+Balusters+Toe**, **Pipe+Handrail**, **Pipe+Handrail+Toe**, **Pipe+Returns**, **ShapedHandrail**, **ShapedWood+Balusters**, and **Wood+Balusters**.

Setting Rail Locations

Each railing style has three possible kinds of horizontal rail components: Guardrail, Handrail, and Bottomrail. Each has a check box in the Rail Locations tab that turns it on. The Bottomrail component can be repeated as many times as you specify. You can specify different values for each rail in both horizontal and sloping conditions. Handrails are usually offset some distance from posts, perpendicular to the railing direction. Let's specify rail locations for all the styles at once to maximize efficiency.

1. Select the Bar+Cable+Handrail style in the tree pane of the Style Manager. In the content pane, click the Rail Locations tab. Study the illustrations and their labeled parameters. Check

Guardrail, Handrail, and Bottomrail to enable these components (see Figure 12.58). Set the following values:

Rail Locations Settings	Value
Guardrail Horizontal and Sloping Heights	3′-6″
Guardrail Side for Offset	Auto
Guardrail Offset From Post	0″
Handrail Horizontal and Sloping Heights	2′-10″
Handrail Side for Offset	Auto
Handrail Offset From Post	3″
Bottomrail Horizontal and Sloping Heights	6″
Bottomrail Side for Offset	Auto
Bottomrail Offset From Post	0″
Number of Rails	6
Spacing of Rails	6″

TIP After changing the Number Of Rails to 2 or more, click in another text box to enable the Spacing Of Rails text box or press Enter to shift focus to the next text box.

2. Select the Handrail+Escutcheon style in the tree pane. In the content pane, verify that Handrail is checked, whereas Guardrail and Bottomrail are unchecked. Set the following values:

Rail Locations Settings	Value
Handrail Horizontal and Sloping Heights	2′-10″
Handrail Side for Offset	Auto
Handrail Offset From Post	3″

FIGURE 12.58
Setting rail locations for
railing styles

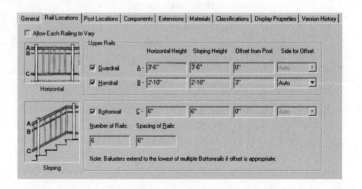

3. Select the Pipe+Balusters+Toe style in the tree pane. In the content pane, uncheck Handrail and check both Guardrail and Bottomrail. Set the following values:

Rail Locations Settings	Value
Guardrail Horizontal and Sloping Heights	3'
Guardrail Side for Offset	Auto
Guardrail Offset From Post	0"
Bottomrail Horizontal and Sloping Heights	3"
Bottomrail Side for Offset	Auto
Bottomrail Offset From Post	0"
Number of Rails	1

4. Select the Pipe+Handrail style in the tree pane. In the content pane, check Guardrail and Bottomrail, and verify that Handrail is also checked. Set the following values:

Rail Locations Settings	Value
Guardrail Horizontal and Sloping Heights	3'-6"
Guardrail Side for Offset	Auto
Guardrail Offset From Post	0"
Handrail Horizontal and Sloping Heights	2'-10"
Handrail Side for Offset	Auto
Handrail Offset From Post	3"
Bottomrail Horizontal and Sloping Heights	1'-10 $1/2$"
Bottomrail Side for Offset	Auto
Bottomrail Offset From Post	0"
Number of Rails	1

5. Select the Pipe+Handrail+Toe style in the tree pane. In the content pane, check Guardrail and Bottomrail, and verify that Handrail is also checked. Set the following values:

Rail Locations Settings	Value
Guardrail Horizontal and Sloping Heights	3'-6"
Guardrail Side for Offset	Auto
Guardrail Offset From Post	0"
Handrail Horizontal and Sloping Heights	3'
Handrail Side for Offset	Auto

Handrail Offset From Post	3″
Bottomrail Horizontal and Sloping Heights	3″
Bottomrail Side for Offset	Auto
Bottomrail Offset From Post	0″
Number of Rails	2
Spacing of Rails	1′-7 1/2″

6. Select the Pipe+Returns style in the tree pane. In the content pane, uncheck Handrail and check both Guardrail and Bottomrail. Set the following values:

Rail Locations Settings	Value
Guardrail Horizontal and Sloping Heights	3′-6″
Guardrail Side for Offset	Auto
Guardrail Offset From Post	0″
Bottomrail Horizontal and Sloping Heights	1′-10 1/2″
Bottomrail Side for Offset	Auto
Bottomrail Offset From Post	0″
Number of Rails	1

7. Select the ShapedHandrail style in the tree pane. Verify that Handrail is the only component that is checked. Set the following values:

Rail Locations Settings	Value
Handrail Horizontal and Sloping Heights	2′-10″
Handrail Side for Offset	Auto
Handrail Offset From Post	3″

8. Select the ShapedWood+Balusters style in the tree pane. In the content pane, check Guardrail and uncheck Handrail. Verify that Bottomrail is unchecked. Set the following values:

Rail Locations Settings	Value
Guardrail Horizontal and Sloping Heights	2′-11 1/4″
Guardrail Side for Offset	Center

9. Finally, select the Wood+Balusters in the tree pane. In the content pane, check Guardrail and uncheck Handrail. Verify that Bottomrail is unchecked. Set the following values:

Rail Locations Settings	Value
Guardrail Horizontal and Sloping Heights	3′-6″

| Guardrail Side for Offset | Auto |
| Guardrail Offset From Post | 1″ |

Click the Apply button at the bottom of the Style Manager.

SETTING POST LOCATIONS

Each railing style has three possible kinds of vertical components: Fixed Posts, Dynamic Posts, and Balusters. Each one of these components is optional, so each has a check box in the Post Locations tab that turns it on. The Baluster component can be repeated as many times as you specify, either by setting a maximum center to center spacing or by specifying a certain number per tread with a stair tread length override. A check box controls whether fixed posts will appear at railing corners—that is, in addition to the fixed posts that appear at start and endpoints of the railing object. Once again, we specify post locations for the all styles at once.

1. Select the Bar+Cable+Handrail style in the tree pane of the Style Manager. In the content pane, click the Post Locations tab. Study the illustration and its labeled parameters (see Figure 12.59). Uncheck Balusters to disable this component. Verify that Fixed Posts and Dynamic Posts are checked. Set the following values:

Post Locations Settings	Value
Extension Of ALL Posts From Top Railing	1 1/2″
Fixed Posts At Railing Corners	Check
Maximum Center To Center Spacing	5′

2. Select the Handrail+Escutcheon style in the tree pane. Uncheck Fixed Posts and Balusters. Notice that Dynamic Posts are grayed-out because they are dependent upon Fixed Posts. Now all vertical components are disabled.

NOTE   You cannot have Dynamic Posts without Fixed Posts. You can have Fixed Posts without Dynamic Posts, however.

FIGURE 12.59
Setting post locations for railing styles

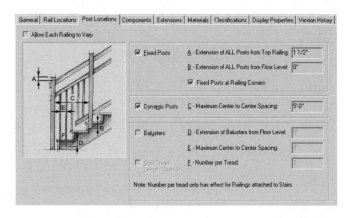

3. Select the Pipe+Balusters+Toe style in the tree pane. Verify that Fixed Posts, Dynamic Posts, and Balusters are enabled. Set the following values:

Post Locations Settings	Value
Extension Of ALL Posts From Top Railing	0″
Fixed Posts At Railing Corners	Check
Maximum Center To Center Spacing	5′

4. Select the Pipe+Handrail style in the tree pane. Uncheck Balusters. Verify that Fixed Posts and Dynamic Posts are enabled. Set the following values:

Post Locations Settings	Value
Extension Of ALL Posts From Top Railing	0″
Fixed Posts At Railing Corners	Check
Maximum Center To Center Spacing	5′

5. Repeat the previous step for the Pipe+Handrail+Toe and Pipe+Returns styles.

6. Select the ShapedHandrail style in the tree pane. Uncheck Fixed Posts and Balusters. This style will float without visible support. Although it is a bit more abstract, using a floating railing might be acceptable if you plan to specify its attachment conditions in detail drawings.

7. Select the ShapedWood+Balusters style in the tree pane. Verify that Fixed Posts, Dynamic Posts, and Balusters are enabled. Set the following values:

Post Locations Settings	Value
Extension Of ALL Posts From Top Railing	2″
Fixed Posts At Railing Corners	Check
Maximum Center To Center Spacing	5′

8. Select the Wood+Balusters style in the tree pane. Verify that Fixed Posts, Dynamic Posts, and Balusters are enabled. A negative value for Extension Of ALL Posts From Top Railing means that the fixed posts will stop short of the full railing height. Set the following values:

Post Locations Settings	Value
Extension Of ALL Posts From Top Railing	-3/4″
Fixed Posts At Railing Corners	Check
Maximum Center To Center Spacing	4′

Click the Apply button at the bottom of the Style Manager.

TIP You can alter post placement using the railing object's shortcut menu.

SPECIFYING COMPONENTS

Each railing style has six components: Guardrail, Handrail, Bottomrail, Fixed Post, Dynamic Post, and Baluster. Each of these components has a profile that can be circular, rectangular, or a custom shape. You will set the width, depth, rotation, and justification for each component's profile. As you are getting accustomed, you'll specify component profiles and dimension for the all styles at once.

1. Select the Bar+Cable+Handrail style in the tree pane of the Style Manager. In the content pane, click the Components tab. Study the illustration and its labeled parameters (see Figure 12.60).

   For all the railing styles, the following parameters are always the same:

Parameter	Value
Scale	Scale To Fit
Rotation	0 for those components where it's relevant (Fixed Post, Dynamic Post, and Baluster)
Justification	Middle Center

2. In the content pane, for the Bar+Cable+Handrail style, set the "always" parameters listed in step 1; then enter the following:

Component	Profile Name	Width	Depth
Guardrail	*Circular*	$1/4''$	$1/4''$
Handrail	*Circular*	$1\,1/2''$	$1\,1/2''$
Bottomrail	*Circular*	$1/4''$	$1/4''$
Fixed Post	*Rectangular*	$3''$	$1/4''$
Dynamic Post	*Rectangular*	$3''$	$1/4''$
Baluster	*Circular*	$1''$	$1''$

FIGURE 12.60

Setting component properties for railing styles

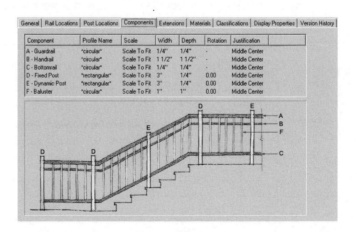

3. Select the Handrail+Escutcheon style in the tree pane. Set the "always" parameters listed in step 1; then enter the following in the content pane:

Component	Profile Name	Width	Depth
Guardrail	*Rectangular*	5 1/2"	1 1/2"
Handrail	*Circular*	1 1/2"	1 1/2"
Bottomrail	*Rectangular*	1 1/2"	3/4"
Fixed Post	*Rectangular*	3 1/2"	3 1/2"
Dynamic Post	*Rectangular*	3 1/2"	3 1/2"
Baluster	*Rectangular*	1 1/2"	1 1/2"

4. Select the Pipe+Balusters+Toe style in the tree pane. Set the "always" parameters listed in step 1, and set Profile Name for all components to *Circular*. Then enter the following in the content pane:

Component	Width	Depth
Guardrail	1 1/2"	1 1/2"
Handrail	1 1/2"	1 1/2"
Bottomrail	2"	2"
Fixed Post	2"	2"
Dynamic Post	2"	2"
Baluster	1/2"	1/2"

5. Select the Pipe+Handrail style in the tree pane. Set the "always" parameters listed in step 1. For all components, set Profile Name to *Circular* and set Width and Depth to 1 1/2".

6. Select the Pipe+Handrail+Toe style in the tree pane. Set the "always" parameters listed in step 1, and set Profile Name for all components to *Circular*. Then enter the following in the content pane:

Component	Width	Depth
Guardrail	2"	2"
Handrail	1 1/2"	1 1/2"
Bottomrail	2"	2"
Fixed Post	2"	2"
Dynamic Post	2"	2"
Baluster	1/2"	1/2"

7. Select the Pipe+Returns style in the tree pane. Set the "always" parameters listed in step 1. For all components, set Profile Name to *Circular* and set Width and Depth to 1 1/2".

8. Select the ShapedHandrail style in the tree pane. Set the "always" parameters listed in step 1; then enter the following in the content pane:

Component	Profile Name	Width	Depth
Guardrail	*Rectangular*	1 1/2″	1 1/2″
Handrail	HandrailGrip	1 1/2″	5 1/2″
Bottomrail	*Rectangular*	1 1/2″	3/4″
Fixed Post	*Rectangular*	3 1/2″	3 1/2″
Dynamic Post	*Rectangular*	3 1/2″	3 1/2″
Baluster	*Rectangular*	1 1/2″	1 1/2″

9. Select the ShapedWood+Balusters style in the tree pane. Set the "always" parameters listed in step 1; then enter the following in the content pane:

Component	Profile Name	Width	Depth
Guardrail	GuardrailCap	3 3/8″	3″
Handrail	*Rectangular*	1″	1″
Bottomrail	*Rectangular*	1 1/2″	3/4″
Fixed Post	*Rectangular*	2 1/2″	2 1/2″
Dynamic Post	*Rectangular*	2 1/2″	2 1/2″
Baluster	Baluster	1″	1″

10. Select the Wood+Balusters style in the tree pane. Set the "always" parameters listed in step 1, and set Profile Name for all components to *Rectangular*. Then enter the following in the content pane:

Component	Width	Depth
Guardrail	5 1/4″	1 1/2″
Handrail	1 1/2″	1 1/2″
Bottomrail	1 1/2″	3/4″
Fixed Post	3 1/2″	3 1/2″
Dynamic Post	3 1/2″	3 1/2″
Baluster	1 1/2″	1 1/2″

RAILING EXTENSIONS AND MATERIALS

Railings that are attached to stairs follow the shape of the stair itself. Building codes often require that railings extend some distance beyond the start and end of the stair itself. You can use the Extensions tab of a railing style to control this behavior. Figure 12.61 shows the controls available for extending railing beyond stair flights, both at floor levels and at landings.

FIGURE 12.61
Railing extensions

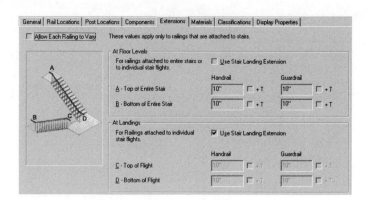

We aren't concerned with extending our railing styles in this tutorial, although the way to do so is straightforward. You don't need to change anything on the Extensions tab in the Style Manager.

TIP If railing extensions are allowed to vary at the object level, the railing endpoint can be grip-edited.

Railings can accept different materials on each of their six possible components. You'll need to assign only two different materials to all the railing styles. You'll first need to load one material definition from the Material content drawing in the Style Manager. Then you can assign materials to all the railing style components very easily.

1. In the tree pane, expand the Material Definitions (Imperial).dwg, Multi-Purpose Objects nodes. In the content pane, select the `Metals.Metal Handrails and Railings.Stainless Steel.Satin` material definition.

2. Drag the material definition from the content pane to the StairStyles.dwg node in the tree pane and release the mouse button. I'll refer to this material as Steel.

3. Right-click the Material Definitions (Imperial).dwg node and choose Close from the shortcut menu.

4. Click the Material tab in the content pane and assign Steel to all the components of the following railing styles:

   ♦ Bar+Cable+Handrail

   ♦ Handrail+Escutcheon

   ♦ Pipe+Handrail

   ♦ Pipe+Handrail+Toe

   ♦ Pipe+Returns

5. Assign Paint to all the components of the Pipe+Balusters+Toe railing style.

6. Assign Wood to all the components of the following railing styles:

   ♦ ShapedHandrail

- ShapedWood+Balusters
- Wood+Balusters

7. Click OK to close the Style Manager dialog box.

NOTE You don't need to assign any classifications to the railing styles for the purposes of this tutorial. See Chapter 3, "Object Styles," for more on classifications.

ASSIGNING RAILING STYLES

Now that you have mostly finished designing all nine railing styles, it is time to assign them to the generic railing objects you made earlier. This approach yielded the greatest efficiency when you were following the steps of the tutorial. When you design your own railing style from scratch, you'll probably want to assign the new style to a railing immediately and observe the changes on the object as you make changes to its style in stages. It's more convenient to right-click an object and choose Edit Railing Style from its shortcut menu than it is to use the Style Manager when you are focusing on a single style. However, working in the Style Manager is preferable when editing multiple styles or when you're comparing styles in two or more drawing files.

1. Assign the styles as shown in Figure 12.62 to the generic railing objects in your scene.

FIGURE 12.62
Railing styles

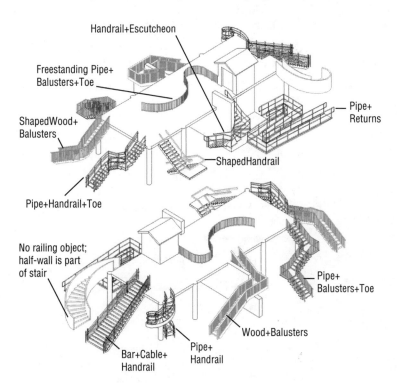

2. Delete any railing objects added to the HalfWallRail stair because its "railings" are already an integral part of its stair style.

3. Turn layer A-Roof back on.

4. Notice that the landing on the straight stair causes the Bar+Cable+Handrail railing's cables to jog, which is clearly an impossible situation for cables under tension. Remove the flight height rule on the straight stair.

SETTING DISPLAY PROPERTIES

You can add custom display blocks that can add or replace components in railing styles. You can save time by first inserting a drawing containing blocks of the escutcheon and guardrail return objects. You'll add the 3D blocks to Model representations in selected railing styles. Several profiles were added to the drawing file earlier, and these will be used as custom blocks in several plan representations.

1. Choose Insert ➢ Block and click the Browse button in the Insert dialog box. Navigate to this chapter's folder on the companion DVD and choose `RailingReturns.dwg`. Click OK to close the Select Drawing File dialog box.

2. In the Insert dialog box, verify that Specify On-Screen is checked in the Insertion Point group. Check Explode and click OK. Click a point off to the side of the training structure. Two blocks were inserted into the drawing called GuardrailReturn and Escutcheon—they were made using mass elements (see Figure 12.63).

3. By inserting this geometry you also brought their block definitions into the drawing database. Delete the geometry that you just inserted—you need only the blocks.

4. Choose Format ➢ Style Manager. Expand the StairStyles.dwg, Architectural Objects, and Railing Styles nodes in the tree pane. Select the Handrail+Escutcheon railing style in the tree pane. This style has two escutcheons at either end of the railing that must be added as custom blocks to the Model and Plan display representations. Click the Display Properties tab in the content pane of the Style Manager.

5. Place a check in the Style Override column for the Model display representation. The Display Properties dialog box appears; select the Other tab.

6. Click the Add button in the Custom Block Display group. The Custom Block dialog box appears. Click the Select Block button. Choose Escutcheon from the list that appears in the Select a Block dialog box; click OK to close it.

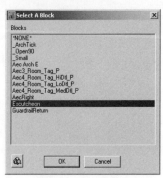

7. In the Insertion Point group, change X to Left and Z to Middle. In the Component group, uncheck Baluster and then check Handrail (see Figure 12.64). Click OK to close the dialog box.

8. You need to add a second custom block for the escutcheon on the right side of the railing. Click the Add button in the Custom Block Display group. Click the Select Block button. Choose Escutcheon from the list and click OK.

9. In the Insertion Point group, change X to Right and Z to Middle. In the Component group, uncheck Baluster and check Handrail. Check Mirror X in the Mirror In group and click OK.

10. Back in the Display Properties dialog box, check both settings in the Cleanup group. You need to disable cleanup because the escutcheon must stand on its own without being merged into other geometry. Click OK to close the Display Properties dialog box.

FIGURE 12.63
Inserting 3D blocks:
GuardrailReturn (left)
and Escutcheon (top
right)

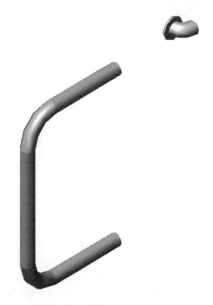

FIGURE 12.64
Editing a Custom Block

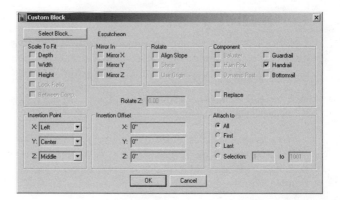

11. You need to also make a style override for the Plan display representation that uses a profile as a custom block. Repeat steps 5–10 for the Plan display representation, choosing the EscutcheonPlan profile in place of the Escutcheon block you used in the Model display representation.

12. Switch to the Top viewpoint and 2D Wireframe display mode. Zoom in on the U-shaped 1/2 Turn stair. Select its inner railing and change Side Offset to -1 1/2″ in the Properties palette. The railing abuts the wall.

13. Switch to the NE Isometric viewpoint and zoom in on the railing you have been working on. You may need to change Side Offset to 0″ to correct the railing if it appears crooked in isometric viewpoints (see Figure 12.65).

14. Following a similar procedure to steps 1–11, create custom display blocks and profiles for the Pipe+Returns railing style—use the GuardrailReturn block and GuardrailReturnPlan profile and attach them to the Guardrail. You'll need to align GuardrailReturn to the Top in Z and use a -³/₄″ offset in Z.

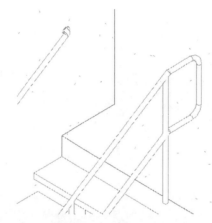

15. Save your work as **StairsRailings.dwg** if you want to keep the styles developed in this chapter for future reference. This file is also provided on the companion DVD for your convenience.

Generating a Stair Tower

Use the Stair Tower Generate tool when you want to create a series of stacked stairs that connect multiple levels. Stair towers can be created within a project only inside a spanning construct. We will use the project developed in Chapter 5 to explore the stair tower feature.

WARNING   You cannot create a stair tower with spiral stairs. Instead, make spiral stairs manually on each level.

You create a stair tower from one stair (and can optionally include railings and/or slabs) that is replicated on multiple levels. As the stair tower is generated, each individual stair height will be automatically adjusted to match its corresponding level's floor-to-floor height. Changes made to floor-to-floor heights propagate to stairs in the tower.

FIGURE 12.65
Escutcheon custom
display block and profile

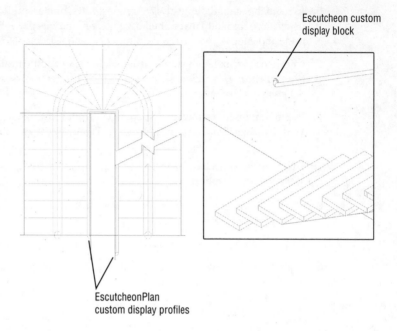

Escutcheon custom
display block

EscutcheonPlan
custom display profiles

1. Click the Project Browser button on the Navigation toolbar. Make the Chapter 05 project current either from your hard drive or from the Chapter 5 folder on the companion DVD. Close the Project Browser.

2. Click the Constructs tab of the Project Navigator that appears. Expand the Architectural and Shells categories and double-click the Tower Shell spanning construct. Zoom to the extents of the drawing—a cylindrical space boundary filled with a space. Select and hide the space object but leave the space boundary visible.

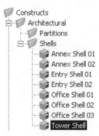

3. Choose Format ➢ Style Manager. Click the Open Drawing button on the toolbar inside the Style Manager. In the Open Drawing dialog box, navigate to this chapter's folder on your hard drive or the companion DVD, select StairsRailings.dwg and click OK.

4. Expand the StairsRailings.dwg, Architectural Objects, and Stair Styles nodes. Drag the Cantilever style into the Tower Shell.dwg node in the tree pane.

5. Expand the StairsRailings.dwg, Architectural Objects, and Railing Styles nodes. Drag Pipe+Balusters+Toe into the Tower Shell.dwg node in the tree pane. Right-click the StairsRailings.dwg node and choose Close from the shortcut menu. Click OK to close the Style Manager.

6. Click the Stair tool in the Design palette. In the Properties palette, set Shape to U-shaped, Shape to 1/2 Landing, Horizontal Orientation to Counterclockwise, and Vertical Orientation to Up. Set style to Cantilever.

7. In the Dimensions subcategory, change Height to 13′. Change Justify to Center and Terminate With Landing. Set Calculation Rules to Tread. Verify that Tread is set to 11″.

WARNING   If you include a slab in a stair tower (instead of a terminating landing), it must be at the top of the stair to be replicated.

8. Click two points along a horizontal line to create the stair. Center it in the round space boundary, as shown in Figure 12.66.

9. Attach railings to the stair and assign them the Pipe+Balusters+Toe railing style.

10. Click the Stair Tower Generate tool in the Design palette. Select the stair object and press Enter. The Select Levels worksheet appears. Check Include Anchored Railings and Keep Landing Location When Adjusting U-Shaped Stair. Check Floor 2 and click OK. The stair tower appears (see Figure 12.67).

11. Close the file without saving and then close the project in the Project Browser.

FIGURE 12.66
Creating a stair object in a spanning construct

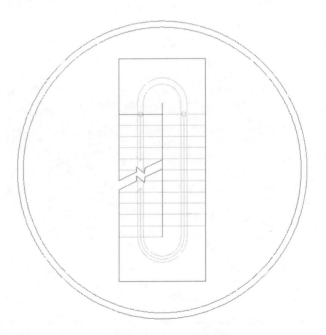

FIGURE 12.67
Stair tower generated
on two levels

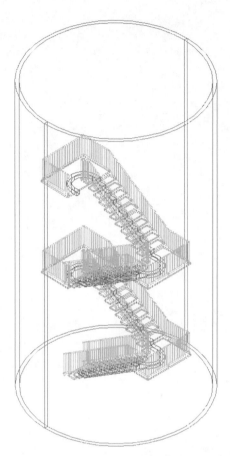

Selecting any of the stairs, slabs, or railings in a stair tower merely brings up the individual object properties—there are not any special properties for the stair tower. If you want to modify the stair tower itself, change the original stair, slab, and/or railing objects and then reapply the Stair Tower Generate tool. It will revise the existing objects, rather than deleting the existing stairs. Any VIZ Render customization you might have done (see Chapter 18, "Using VIZ Render") is preserved because the objects in the tower are modified, not deleted and re-created.

Summary

This chapter has exposed you to everything you need to know about stairs, ramps, and railings. You created every object type and examined all the options these objects have to offer. Most importantly, you built complex stair and railing styles from scratch. Armed with this knowledge, you should now be able to style your own real-world objects with a little practice.

Congratulations on completing Part 3 of this book! You have now learned everything necessary to develop your own designs using ADT's intelligent objects. In the next part of this book, we sharpen the focus on detail in construction documentation.

Part 4

Construction Documentation

Chapter 13

Annotating, Tagging, and Dimensioning

We start the process of documenting designs for construction by looking at how to *annotate* in Architectural Desktop: a skill that includes labeling drawings with descriptive text, drawing *leaders* (lines that lead the attention to noteworthy features), and adding a wide variety of symbolic documentation content.

Tagging is the process of adding symbols to a drawing that reference invisible data stored in the project. For example, a door tag might be a circular symbol that has a number inside that you insert adjacent to a door. The number identifies the door as belonging to a particular room. You don't enter the room number in the tag—it is referenced instead from invisible data. The invisible data attached to objects can be *scheduled*, or brought together and displayed on the drawing in table form (see Chapter 14, "Schedules, Display Themes, and Areas").

The third topic in this chapter deals with *dimensioning*, which is the art of illustrating the sizes of objects in two dimensions. You'll find that the process of adding dimensions is streamlined in ADT as compared with AutoCAD. ADT uses architecture, engineering, and construction (AEC) dimension styles that are separate from—but built on top of—AutoCAD dimension styles. AEC dimensions have many advantages for illustrating the sizes of AEC objects: Their size depends on drawing scale, they have display control, and they work across XRefs. You may have to relearn everything you knew about dimensioning in AutoCAD to get the most out of ADT's highly evolved dimensioning system. This chapter's topics include:

◆   Adding Annotation

◆   Tagging Objects

◆   Dimensioning

Adding Annotation

You'll be working on a sample project that's provided on the companion DVD throughout this chapter. Annotation should always be added to views in the project structure (refer to Chapter 5, "Project Management"). If you annotate constructs or elements, the changes you make will carry through to all views that reference those constructs and/or elements.

However, when you annotate a view, the changes made are specific to that view. In this section, you'll learn how to use ADT's annotation tool to write text and draw leaders. In addition, you'll see how to access a wide variety of ready-made symbolic AEC content that you can add to views.

Writing Text

Instead of using AutoCAD's TEXT, DTEXT, or MTEXT commands to write text, you will use a different tool in ADT: technically it is the `AecDtlAnnoLeaderAdd` command. Thankfully you never have to type that long string of characters on the command line. Instead, you can click ADT's text tool on the Annotation palette (in the Documentation palette group).

The great advantage that ADT's text tool has over AutoCAD's text commands is that text size is set by the current drawing scale. No longer will you have to calculate how large text objects should be in a given scale because ADT's text tool handles it automatically. In addition, text tool properties let you assign a layer key, so you can be sure that the text you write will always be on the correct layer.

INVESTIGATING THE SAMPLE PROJECT

1. Copy all the files and subfolders within this chapter's folder on the companion DVD to your hard drive under the following:

   ```
   C:\Documents and Settings\<username>\My Documents\Autodesk\My Projects\Chapter 13
   ```

   Substitute your Windows username for `<username>` in the preceding path.

TIP The completed Chapter 13 project is provided on the companion DVD for your reference as a ZIP file. Extract it into a separate folder from the project you have developed in this chapter. You can load the completed project for comparison with your own work.

2. Click the Project Browser button on the Navigation toolbar. Double-click the Chapter 13 project to make it current (see Figure 13.1). Click the Yes button when asked if you want to repath the project. The project is a single level of a high-rise building, as you can see in the bulletin board's thumbnail image. Click the Close button to close the Project Browser.

3. The Project Navigator palettes appear as soon as the Project Browser is closed. Select the Project tab (see Figure 13.2). The project contains a single level and division. Level 23 uses 0 (zero) as its base elevation. This fact simplifies the situation and is appropriate in tenant improvement work when you are not concerned with modeling an entire building.

FIGURE 13.1
Setting the Chapter 13 project current in the Project Browser

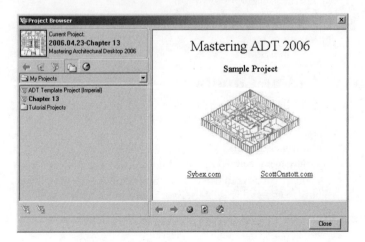

FIGURE 13.2

Investigating the Project Navigator's Project, Constructs, Views, and Sheets tabs

4. Click the Constructs tab. There are four constructs and four elements. Click each node to view its preview image in the lower pane to get an idea of what information is contained in each drawing file. The Shell construct has the Core element as an XRef attachment. The Partitions construct has the Shell and Tenant Stair constructs as XRef overlays and multiple instances of the WorkstationCluster elements attached. The Spaces construct has Partitions and Shell constructs as XRef overlays.

5. Click the Views tab. There are two views: Construction Plan and Space Plan. Each view drawing has a model space view defined and title mark inserted. Double-click Space Plan to open this view drawing.

6. Click the Sheets tab. There is one sheet defined in the sheet set that has two sheet views corresponding to the two view drawings. Click the Auto-hide button on the Project Navigator if necessary to hide the palette when you move the cursor away from it.

USING THE ANNOTATION TOOL TO WRITE TEXT

Before you use ADT's text tool, take a moment and verify that you are in a view drawing—in this project you'll start annotating the Space Plan. Views were specifically designed within ADT's overall project structure to hold annotation, tags, and dimensions (refer to Chapter 5)—it is best to use them rather than constructs, elements, or sheets.

1. Click the Drawing menu icon at the extreme left end of the drawing status bar. Choose Drawing Setup from the drawing menu. Select the Scale tab in the Drawing Setup dialog box. Verify that Scale is set to 1/8″=1′-0″ and that Annotation Plot Size is set to 3/32″. Annotation plot size is the actual size text will appear when printed on physical media in the real world. ADT will automatically scale text created with the text tool to maintain the annotation plot size, no matter which scale is chosen. Click OK.

TIP If the scale you want to use does not appear in the Scale list in the Drawing Setup dialog box, you can click the Edit Scale List button and add a custom scale. This is a new feature in ADT 2006. You'll have to enter scale factors for custom scales to relate paper and drawing sizes.

2. In the Tool Palettes, open the palette menu and make the Document palette group current. The Annotation, Callouts, Scheduling, and Drafting palettes appear. Select the Annotation palette if it is not already selected.

3. Right-click Text Tool and choose Properties from the shortcut menu. The Tool Properties worksheet appears. Notice that ANNOBJ is set as the Layer Key and Content Type is MText. Leader Type is set to None in the Leader subcategory when you want to write text only. Change Prompt For Width to No (to avoid having to set the paragraph width) and Mask Background to Yes (see Figure 13.3). Click OK to close the worksheet.

4. Zoom in on the tenant stair area near the bottom of the space plan. Click the Text Tool in the Annotation palette and click an insertion point for the MText entity in the circulation space below the tenant stair. The command line says the following:

```
Enter first line of text <Mtext>:
```

Type **Open To Below** and press Enter twice to end the command. Text appears with a mask that hides the hatching in the circulation space (see Figure 13.4). Move the text entity if necessary to match the figure.

5. Double-click the text you just created. The In-Place Text Editor appears (this is a new feature in AutoCAD 2006 that ADT inherits; see Figure 13.5). Highlight the text by dragging your cursor across all the letters. Click the leftmost drop-down list, choose the Title-Normal text style from the list, and click the OK button in the Text Formatting toolbar. The text appears in a different font and is bold. Move the text if necessary to center it below the staircase.

NOTE A number of improvements have been made to MText in AutoCAD 2006. Refer to the AutoCAD Help by pressing F1 to learn more.

FIGURE 13.3
Adjusting Text Tool
Properties

FIGURE 13.4
Creating text with
the Text Tool

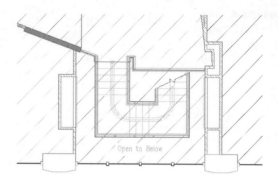

FIGURE 13.5
Using the Text
Formatting toolbar

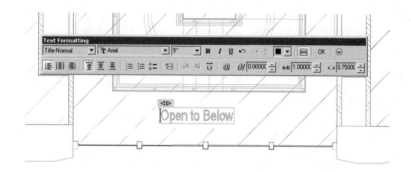

Drawing Leaders

Leaders are made with the same command as text—AecDtlAnnoLeaderAdd. Like text, leaders are made by clicking a tool in the Annotation palette. The only difference is how you configure the tool properties. Keynotes are also made by customizing the same tool properties, but we will hold off on learning about keynotes until Chapter 17, "Details and Keynotes." Leaders can be drawn with either straight segments or curved splines.

1. In the Annotation palette, right-click the Text (Straight Leader) tool and choose Properties from the shortcut menu. The Tool Properties worksheet appears. Notice that Leader Type is set to Straight—this option shows additional choices in the Text subcategory below.

2. Change Limit points to Yes and Maximum Points to 3. These settings affect how many points may be clicked to define straight segments before placing the MText entity.

3. In the Text subcategory, notice that Default Text is set to double dashes (--). Two dashes mean that the property has been intentionally set with no value. Set Prompt For Width to No. Set Left Side Attachment and Right Side Attachment to Middle Of Multi-Line Text. Finally, set Mask Background to Yes (see Figure 13.6). Click OK to close the worksheet.

FIGURE 13.6

Setting Text (Straight Leader) tool properties

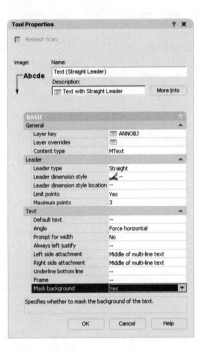

TIP Copy and paste tools within the Tool palettes to create new tools. You can customize each set of properties separately to fashion different tools.

4. Click the Text (Straight Leader) tool in the Annotation palette. Press Shift and right-click to open the object snap menu. Click Nearest and then specify first point of leader line, as shown in Figure 13.7—snap it along the corridor edge of the wooden wall adjacent to the tenant stair. This is where the point of the arrowhead will appear.

5. Specify next point of leader line above the first point somewhere in the middle of the corridor. Using Polar object tracking mode, click the third point a short distance horizontally and to the left of the second point. The command line says the following:

```
Enter first line of text <Mtext>:
```

Type **Feature Wall** and press Enter twice to end the command. The Leader and annotation appear.

6. Select the MText object and the leader you just created. Click its one blue grip and move it up and to the left slightly. Press Esc to deselect.

7. Press Ctrl+S to save your work.

The behavior of leaders and text works much the same as in AutoCAD—only the tools you use to make them and the way you set their creation options in tool properties has changed. Overall, creating text and leaders in ADT is very intuitive and straightforward.

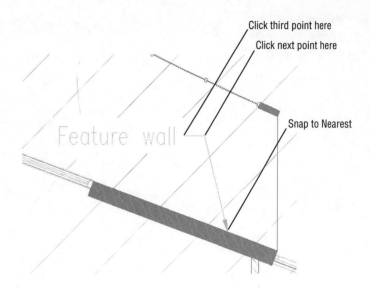

FIGURE 13.7
Drawing a leader and
annotating it with text

Click third point here

Click next point here

Snap to Nearest

Feature wall

Adding AEC Content

ADT ships with much AEC content that you can use to document your designs. AEC content includes North arrows, a bar scale, match lines, column bubbles, a datum point, fire rating lines, chases, revision clouds, and many other common architectural symbols. More than just drafting symbols, AEC content has intelligence built in, as you have come to expect when using ADT.

You can access AEC content from either the Content Browser or the AEC Content tab in DesignCenter. The DesignCenter is an older interface as compared with the Content Browser. In most cases, you'll want to use the Content Browser because it has the most comprehensive collection of AEC content. The DesignCenter still remains useful to create AEC Content.

ADDING A NORTH ARROW

Let's add a North arrow to the Construction Plan view.

1. Double-click the Construction Plan view node in the Project Navigator to open it.

2. Click the Content Browser button in the Navigation toolbar. Open the Documentation Tool Catalog and navigate to Miscellaneous > North Arrows. Click the Page 2 link and drag the i-drop icon from North Arrow M into the drawing window in ADT. Leave the Content Browser open unless otherwise noted.

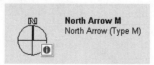

North Arrow M
North Arrow (Type M)

3. Click a point to place the North arrow in the lower-right corner of the Construction Plan. Move the cursor up vertically by using polar object tracking and click to set the North direction. Move the North bubble so that the quadrants of the circle are tangent to both the right edge of the building, and the lower quadrant of the title mark's bubble (see Figure 13.8).

FIGURE 13.8
Placing a North arrow in
Construction Plan view

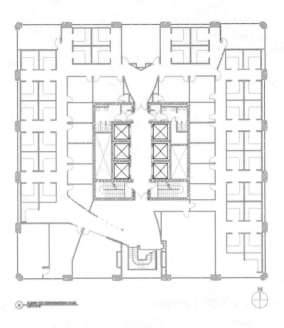

ADDING FIRE RATING LINES

Although color is an effective means to differentiate items on the screen, this level of information is lost when the drawing is printed in grayscale. In addition, fire-rating lines graphically draw attention because they use thick polylines (an old AutoCAD trick) to identify wall type. Let's add fire-rating lines to some of the walls using an AEC content routine.

1. Zoom in on the walls shown in the construction plan. Notice that many of the walls have hatch patterns in different colors that indicate different wall styles. To add fire rating lines, you'll have to open the construct that contains the walls themselves. This is a rare example of adding documentation content directly to a construct. Be aware that doing so will carry this change forward into all views and sheets.

2. Select the Constructs tab in the Project Navigator. Double-click the Partitions construct to open it. Zoom in on the walls coming off the upper-right corner of the core—they have a purple hatch pattern. Select one of these walls and verify that its style reads InteriorPartitions-2 Hour in the Properties palette.

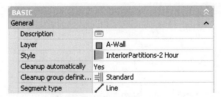

3. Right-click and choose Edit Wall Style from the shortcut menu. Click the Display Properties tab in the Wall Style Properties dialog box that appears. Double click the Plan display representation icon to open its Display Properties dialog box. Click the yellow light bulb adjacent to

the Shrink Wrap Hatch component to toggle it off. Click OK and OK again to close all open dialog boxes. The InteriorPartitions-2 Hour walls appear hollow now that the hatch pattern has been turned off.

NOTE 2-hour walls are fire-rated, meaning they should contain a fire burning on one side for 2 hours before they are penetrated.

4. Switch to the Content Browser. Click the word North Arrows in the navigation pane to go up one level in the catalog. Click Fire Rating Lines to enter this subcategory. Drag the 2 Hr tool's i-drop icon into the drawing window in ADT.

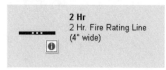

5. The AEC content tool executes code on the command line. The command line says the following:

```
Command: _AecAnnoRatingLineAdd
Adding: 2 Hr. Fire Rating Line (4" wide)
Select first end or intersection of rated wall or [Width/Color/Linetype]: _WIDTH
Specify polyline width<4">: 4
Select first end or intersection of rated wall or [Width/Color/Linetype]:
_COLOR Specify polyline color<BYLAYER>_ByLayer
Select first end or intersection of rated wall or [Width/Color/Linetype]:
_LINETYPE
Specify polyline linetype or [?]<Aec_Rating_2Hr>: Aec_Rating_2Hr
Select first end or intersection of rated wall or [Width/Color/Linetype]:
_Endofparam
Select first end or intersection of rated wall or [Width/Color/Linetype]:
```

Click the first end near the lower end of the 2-hour rated wall where it meets the core. Specify the next end near the end of this wall segment and press Enter. A thick polyline appears, as shown in Figure 13.9.

TIP Use Regen if you don't see the fire rating lines after creating them.

6. Press the Spacebar to repeat the AecAnnoRatingLineAdd command. It maintains the same options as set in the previous step, so you can add another 2-hour line. Click the start and end of the adjacent 2-hour wall and press Enter. The fire rating line passes through the door. Click the fire rating line and move its start and end grips back so it does not obscure other objects.

TIP Do not worry about adding fire rating lines to very short line segments. The walls are already identified by style and can be scheduled as such—fire-rating lines are used only as a visual aid.

7. Continue adding fire-rating lines on all 2-hour rated walls, as shown in Figure 13.10. Select the graphline to add fire-rating lines to walls.

FIGURE 13.9
Drawing a 2-hour rated
wall fire rating line

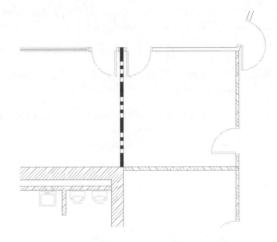

FIGURE 13.10
Adding fire rating lines
to 2-hour rated walls at
upper-right corner of
core (left) and lower-
right corner (right)

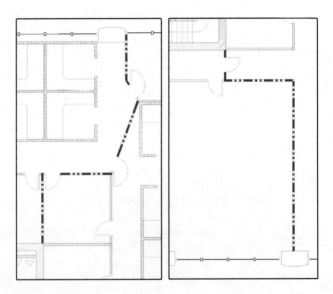

8. Save and close the Partitions construct.

9. Switch back to the Construction Plan view and reload its XRefs to see the changes you have just made to the Partitions construct.

REVISION CLOUDS

Revision clouds are a graphic convention used to document an area of a drawing that has been changed after the original drawings were submitted. The *cloud* portion of the symbol is a series of connected arcs that surround and draw attention to the affected area. The cloud may optionally have a revision triangle symbol placed along the cloud edge to indicate the revision number. Numbering revisions is essential if you want to keep track of changes by date on a title block, for example.

WARNING　The revision cloud tool in ADT is different from the REVCLOUD AutoCAD command. ADT's version has automatic scaling, layer keying, and the optional revision triangle.

1. Pan and zoom to the tenant stair area on the construction plan view.

2. In the Content Browser, click Fire Rating Lines in the navigation pane to go up a level in the catalog. Click Miscellaneous to go up another level. Click the Revision Clouds category.

3. Drag the Small Arcs & Tag i-drop icon into the drawing window in ADT.

4. The command line says the following:

```
Command: _ContentTool
Command: _AecAnnoRevisionCloudAdd
Adding: Revision Cloud with Tag (1/2" Arcs)
Specify cloud starting point or [Symbol block/pline Color/Arc length/pline
Width]: _SYMBOL
Specify symbol block or [?]<NONE>: Anno_Revision_A
Specify cloud starting point or [Symbol block/pline Color/Arc length/pline
Width]: _ARCLENGTH
Specify arc length <1">: .5
Specify cloud starting point or [Symbol block/pline Color/Arc length/pline
Width]: _WIDTH
Specify cloud polyline width<0">: .03125
Specify cloud starting point or [Symbol block/pline Color/Arc length/pline
Width]: _COLOR Specify cloud color<BYLAYER>_ByLayer
Specify cloud starting point or [Symbol block/pline Color/Arc length/pline
Width]: _Endofparam
Specify cloud starting point or [Symbol block/pline Color/Arc length/pline Width]:
```

Click the cloud start point somewhere very close to the tenant stair.

5. Carefully move the cursor counterclockwise around the stair. As you start to move the cursor, connected arcs will appear where the cursor has been. As you come full circle and get close to the point you clicked previously, the cloud will close automatically.

6. The command line says the following:

```
Specify center point of revision tag <None>:
```

If you want a revision tag, click a point near the edge of the cloud. If not, pressing Enter would skip this option. Go ahead and insert a revision tag.

7. The Edit Attributes dialog box appears, prompting you for a revision number to put inside the triangular symbol. Click OK to accept 1 as the default. Figure 13.11 shows the result.

FIGURE 13.11
Creating a revision cloud

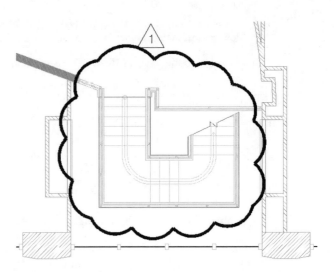

NOTE The revision tag is an old-school attributed block, unlike the more common multiview block tags referencing property data that you'll learn about later on in this chapter. The revision tag is not tied to any other data in the project.

8. Save and close the Construction Plan.dwg view and close the Content Browser. Close Space Plan.dwg.

EDITING AEC CONTENT

There are things you can do in the DesignCenter that aren't possible in the Content Browser—for example, editing AEC content. From time to time, you may have unique pieces of construction that you want to turn into AEC content. In addition, managers may want to customize existing AEC content to suit their company standards. Before planning your own custom AEC content, it's a good idea—and a learning experience—to inspect the existing AEC content that ships with ADT. We will inspect a *chase*—a vertical penetration through a building that is defined as a piece of AEC content.

1. Click the DesignCenter button on the Navigation toolbar.

2. Select the AEC Content tab in the DesignCenter if it's not already selected. Expand Custom Applications > Architectural Desktop > Imperial > Documentation nodes. Click the Chases folder on the left.

3. The right side of the DesignCenter palette is divided into three panes. The top pane contains the actual content nodes. Click the Chase (6) node. A preview of this node appears in the middle pane, and a description appears in the bottom pane (see Figure 13.12).

4. Right-click the Chase (6) node in the top pane and choose Edit from the shortcut menu. The Create AEC Content Wizard appears. This is the same wizard you can access by choosing Format ➤ AEC Content Wizard to create new content. You can inspect all the settings used to create existing AEC content and take notes to learn how you might make your own. The first page of the wizard reveals that the Content Type is Custom Command. The command string is the following:

```
_aecannomvblockinterferenceadd Chase-6_I
```

This custom command inserts the chase as a multiview block and adds an interference condition to any walls or spaces that the chase penetrates (see Figure 13.13).

5. Page through the AEC Content Wizard and study its interface. Click Cancel when done and close the DesignCenter.

Obviously, you'll have to do your homework before you can create your own custom AEC content. A detailed explanation for this feature goes beyond the scope of this book. Refer to the ADT Help to learn more on your own.

FIGURE 13.12
Accessing AEC content in the DesignCenter

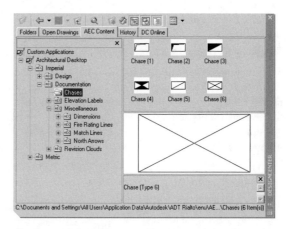

FIGURE 13.13
Editing AEC Content

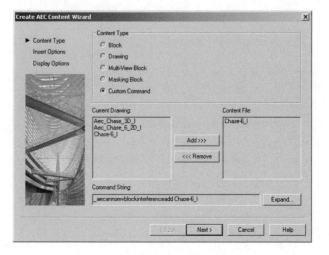

Tagging Objects

Tags are symbols that are inserted into views and associated with individual objects. Tags are the bridge between objects and the visible data appearing in schedules. However, it is important to understand that tags do not contain any data themselves. When you tag an object, one or more *property sets* are automatically attached; they act as containers for the actual property data associated with the object. Tags may visibly display a small portion of the invisible property data associated with objects.

To make matters even more complicated, property sets are attached to objects across XRefs; for example, you'll usually attach tags in a view, reaching through to the XRef and attaching property sets to objects stored in constructs. If all this sounds too abstract, it is; but read on, and the examples you'll work through in the tutorials will make it clear.

In this section you'll learn how to add schedule tags, edit referenced property set data, create schedule tag tools, and renumber tags. Tagging objects is really a lot easier than it might sound.

NOTE   Tagging objects is really the first step in generating schedules, which you'll learn how to create in the next chapter.

Adding Schedule Tags

Schedule tags are multiview blocks whose view blocks have attribute definitions inside them. We'll deconstruct a schedule tag later on to really understand how it works, but for now, let's just add some tags. We'll add space tags to the space plan first to gain some basic experience and then add room tags to the construction plan.

ADDING SPACE TAGS

The Documentation Tool Catalog contains a ready-made space tag tool that you'll use to identify spaces in the space plan.

1. Double-click the Space Plan view in the Project Navigator to open it.

2. Click the Content Browser button in the Navigation toolbar. Open the Documentation Tool Catalog. Click the Schedule Tags category and then the Room & Finish Tags subcategory.

3. Click the Scheduling tab in the Tool palettes. Drag the Space Tag's i-drop icon from the Content Browser to the Scheduling palette. Drop the tool just above the Browse Property Data tool in the Scheduling palette. Close the Content Browser.

4. Click the Space Tag tool in the Scheduling palette. The command line says the following:

```
Select object to tag:
```

Click the hatch pattern of the space in the elevator lobby.

5. The command line says the following:

```
Specify location of tag <Centered>:
```

You could click any point to insert the tag, but press Enter for centered in this case and press Enter until the command ends. The space tag appears centered in the elevator lobby space. Note that the space tag is visibly displaying data related to the space object to which it is associated (see Figure 13.14).

6. Click the space object in the elevator lobby. All the spaces highlight. Check the Properties palette and verify that what you have selected is an external reference of the `spaces.dwg` file.

You know that objects live in constructs and elements, not in views (refer to Chapter 5). When you tagged the elevator lobby in the Space Plan view, you actually attached property sets to the object in the Spaces construct. Confused? It will make more sense to you the more you practice and think about it. Let's tag the remaining spaces in the space plan view.

FIGURE 13.14
Adding a space tag to the elevator lobby space

7. Click the Space Tag tool in the Scheduling palette. Move the cursor over the reception space, which is just below the elevator lobby: It highlights. Isn't that a bit strange? Remember that the spaces live in the Spaces construct, which is XRefed into the view. Normally you wouldn't be able to individually select an externally referenced object—but you can when inserting schedule tags because they work across XRefs. Click the reception space to select it and then click again to locate the tag somewhere in the middle of the space.

8. The command line says the following:

```
Select object to tag [Multiple]:
```

Type **M** for multiple and press Enter. Click several spaces and press Enter when you are done. Space tags appear centered in the spaces you selected with the Multiple option.

9. Continue working your way around the floor tagging spaces, but tag only one workstation (cubicle) because they all share the same typical dimensions. Figure 13.15 shows the result.

FIGURE 13.15
Space tags added to
spaces in space plan

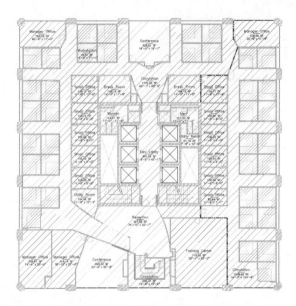

10. To demonstrate that space tags display data coming from the space objects, let's change the name of one of its space styles. Click the Constructs tab in the Project Navigator and double-click the Spaces construct to open it.

11. Select the magenta-colored corner office space in the lower-left corner of the building, right-click, and choose Edit Space Style from the shortcut menu. In the Space Style Properties dialog box that appears, select the General tab and rename the style from Manager Office to **Large Office**. Click OK.

12. Save and close the Spaces.dwg construct file. You will now see the Space Plan view open in the drawing window. Notice that the corner office's space tag still says Manager Office. A balloon informs you that the External Reference File Has Changed.

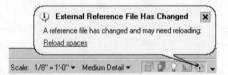

13. Right-click the Manager XRefs icon in the drawing tray (where the balloon is emanating from) and choose Reload XRefs from the shortcut menu. All Manager Office spaces now display as Large Office in the space tags. Data is not stored in the tags themselves, but in property sets stored in the construct. The property sets automatically read data from the space styles and pass them to tags in views.

TIP Clicking the Reload Spaces link in the balloon will reload just that XRef, rather than reloading all XRefs, and can be faster if there are large XRefs that do not require reloading.

14. Save and close the Space Plan.dwg view file.

ADDING ROOM TAGS

There are two ready-made room tag tools in the Scheduling palette: the Room Tag (proper), and the Room Tag - Project Based. We'll use the project-based version because it has extra intelligence built in that reads which floor we are on from project data and numbers rooms accordingly. Let's add room tags to the construction plan.

1. Click the Views tab in the Project Navigator and double-click the Construction Plan view to open it.

2. As you learned with space tags, tags are attached to objects. Room tags must be attached to spaces. So let's change the content of the construction plan view to include the Spaces construct. Right-click the Construction Plan node in the Project Navigator and choose Properties from the shortcut menu.

3. Click the Content node in the left pane of the Modify General View worksheet that appears. In the right pane, check the Spaces construct and click OK (see Figure 13.16). Spaces appear as an XRef in the construction plan. None of the space tags you added to the space plan appear here because those tags are stored in a different view.

4. Click the Room Tag - Project Based tool in the Scheduling palette. Click the space in the elevator lobby. Type **C** for the centered option and press Enter: The Edit Property Set Data worksheet appears. This worksheet displays the property sets that you are attaching to the space object in the construct. Collapse the GeoObjects and RoomFinishObjects property sets. Edit the Name property in the RoomObjects property set. Change its value from ROOM to **Elevator Lobby**. Notice that Data Source for the property set is Spaces (a construct). Click OK to close the worksheet and press Enter. The room tag appears centered in the space displaying room number 2301; the floor number prefixes an increment number (see Figure 13.17).

5. So you'll see how property data is stored separately from tags, delete the room tag you just added.

6. Repeat step 4 to add the project-based room tag back to the same space. When the Edit Property Set Data worksheet reappears, notice that the name ELEVATOR LOBBY is already entered in the Name property within the RoomObjects property set.

FIGURE 13.16

Changing the content of the Construction Plan view to include the Spaces construct

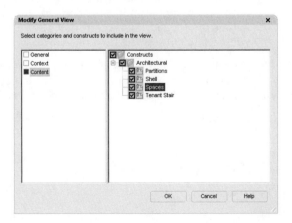

FIGURE 13.17

Editing property set data as tag is attached to space (left) and resulting room tag (right)

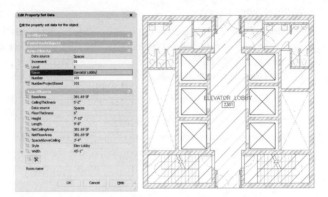

Think about what you just experienced—the original room tag attached property sets to the space object. Property data was still there after the tag was deleted and was read by the new tag when you reinserted it. This exposes the truth about property sets: They work invisibly behind the scenes storing data. Let's add room tags to the rest of the construction plan.

7. Click the Room Tag - Project Based tool. Click the reception space to select it and click again to locate its room tag. In the Edit Property Set Data worksheet, give this room the name **Reception** in the RoomObjects property set. Click OK to close the worksheet. Press Enter to end the command.

NOTE You'll create a room tag later that automatically takes its name from its associated space style.

8. There's an option that controls whether you can edit property set data immediately after inserting a new tag. Choose Format ➤ Options and click the AEC Content tab. Uncheck Display Edit Property Data Dialog During Tag Insertion and click OK. Not having to enter property data every time you add a tag saves time if you are simply concerned with attaching tags and/or property sets.

9. Click the Room Tag - Project Based tool. Click the next space in a clockwise fashion and press Enter to center the tag. Notice that the Edit Property Set Data worksheet does not appear, and the name of the room remains as the default:ROOM. Don't worry about editing names right now. Type **M** for the multiple option and press Enter. Click several spaces in a clockwise fashion and press Enter when you are done. Room tags appear centered in the spaces you selected with the Multiple option. Each room tag is incrementally numbered.

10. Continue working your way around the floor, adding room tags to spaces. Do not tag any workstations, however, because they are part of open office "rooms." The room numbers that appear depend on the order you tag the spaces. You'll learn to renumber them later.

11. Save the Construction Plan.dwg view file.

TIP Use the Renumber Data tool in the Scheduling palette to renumber any property set that uses an automatic increment property.

ADDING DOOR TAGS

Your next task is to add door tags to the construction plan. Remember that when you tag objects, property sets are attached behind the scenes. It is the property set data that you will actually schedule in Chapter 14.

Unlike the other tags you have added thus far, the door tag is attached to—you guessed it—door objects. The doors in this project are stored in the Partitions construct—the property sets that you add by attaching door tags will be stored there.

You'll use the project-based door tag because it will show the same room numbers as the room tags that were added earlier. The door tag can display the proper room numbers because it references the RoomObjects property set that was already attached to the spaces by the project-based room tag.

WARNING   Although you can tag doors before rooms, it is best not to do so. Door tags reference property data stored in property sets added to spaces by room tags.

1. Click the Views tab in the Project Navigator and double-click the Construction Plan view to open it if it is not already open.

2. Zoom in on the Utility Room near Reception (refer to the space plan if necessary). Click the Door Tag - Project Based tool on the Scheduling palette.

3. Select the door and then click a point to insert the tag inside the utility room. Press Enter to complete the command. The number on the door tag should match the number in the room tag (see Figure 13.18).

4. Continue adding door tags to all the remaining doors in the tenant space. Do not tag any of the doors in the core yet.

FIGURE 13.18
Adding a project-based
door tag

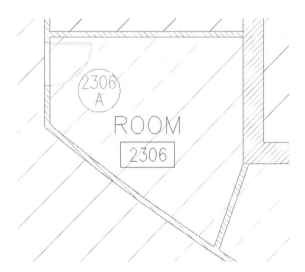

Modifying the Objects that Tags Reference

The design process is never perfectly organized, and chances are you'll be redesigning at least some aspects of your projects while you're in the construction documentation phase. Let's see what happens to the tags you added to the view when we move or delete objects in a construct.

1. Zoom in on the training room just to the right of reception. Notice that its door is very close to the fire-rated door in the corridor. This close proximity between doors might cause problems that we can avoid by moving the training room door to the left (see top of Figure 13.19).

2. Select the Constructs tab in the Project Navigator and double-click the Partitions construct to open it. Zoom in on the training room door (shown as 2323A in Figure 13.19). Select this door and click its location grip. Move the cursor to the left and type **10′**. Click the flip grip on the door panel to flip the hinge. Press Esc to deselect.

3. Save the Partitions.dwg construct file. Press Ctrl+Tab to switch to the construction plan view file. Right-click the Manage Xrefs icon in the drawing tray and choose Reload XRefs from the shortcut menu. As you can see, tags are intelligent in more ways than one; the tag automatically moved over and maintained its position relative to the door. The bottom of Figure 13.19 shows the condition after the door was moved in the construct.

FIGURE 13.19
Before (top) and after (bottom) door object is moved in construct

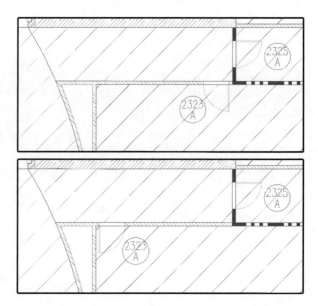

4. Zoom into the rooms just above the core. There are four rooms that each has two doors (see Figure 13.20). Let's delete one door from each room. Switch to the partitions construct, by pressing Ctrl+Tab. (You may have to press Ctrl+Tab again if you have the blank Drawing1.dwg open. Each time you press Ctrl+Tab, you cycle to the next open drawing.)

5. Press Ctrl+Tab again to switch back to the Construction Plan.dwg view file. Right-click the Manage XRefs icon in the drawing tray and choose Reload XRefs from the shortcut menu. The four doors and their associated tags are gone. You didn't have to erase the tags in the view—that was done automatically when the XRef was reloaded.

FIGURE 13.20
Identifying doors to delete in the construction plan

Delete these doors in the construct

Once you tag objects, you don't have to worry about keeping them up-to-date with the objects they reference. If you modify objects in constructs that have already been tagged in a view, the tags will automatically move or delete themselves as necessary, so you don't have to think about it.

Door tags are automatically associated with the space on their swing side—however, this is not always appropriate in every situation. You can control which space a door tag references by adjusting the door's *Property Data Location* grip. Of course, you have to open the construct where the door object lives to adjust its grips.

1. Zoom in on the door into the large office in the lower-left corner of the building. Notice that its door tag refers to the number of the adjacent room—the door is associated with the space on its swing side.

2. Select the Constructs tab of the Project Navigator and double-click the Partitions construct to open it.

3. Zoom into the same door, select it, and look closely at its grips. A new grip appears! You never saw this grip in Chapter 9, "Doors, Windows, and Openings," because it appears only after a door has a location-based property assigned. Move the Property Data Location grip into the room on the left (see Figure 13.21).

4. Save and close the Partitions.dwg construct file. Press Ctrl+Tab to switch back to the Construction Plan.dwg view file.

5. Right-click the Manage XRefs icon in the drawing tray and choose Reload XRefs from the shortcut menu. Zoom into the large office in which the door that you just modified is located. Notice that now the door's tag matches the room in which it is located.

6. Save the Construction Plan.dwg view file.

FIGURE 13.21
Moving the Property
Data Location grip before
(left) and after (right) in
the construct

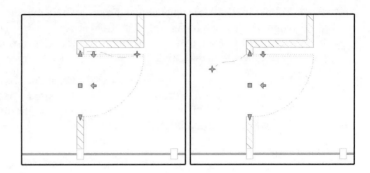

Attaching Property Sets to Objects without Tags

Perhaps the most confounding aspect of dealing with tags is when you want to tag objects that reside in elements. For example, let's say that we want to tag the fire-rated doors in the core. Normally in tenant improvement work, the objects in the core are outside the scope of work. However, that is not the case with new construction. Let's assume that we are dealing with new construction, at least for the two pairs of fire-rated doors on either side of the elevator lobby. Everything else in the core we'll consider to be existing construction outside the scope of work.

You'll attach the DoorObjects property set to the fire-rated doors in the core element. When the Core element is Xrefed into the Shell construct, any property sets it has will receive *property set data overrides* in the construct. It is these overrides that will be referenced by the project-based door tag in the view. To accomplish this, we'll fashion a tool that inserts property set data without inserting a tag at all.

1. Select the Scheduling tab in the Tool Palettes if it is not already selected. Right-click the Door Tag - Project Based tool and choose Copy from the shortcut menu.

2. Right-click in the body of the Scheduling palette and choose Paste from the shortcut menu. A new tool appears at the bottom of the palette. Drag this tool up and drop it just below the tool you just copied it from.

3. Right-click the new tool and choose Properties from the shortcut menu. In the Tool Properties worksheet, rename the tool **DoorObjects Property Data Set**. In the General subcategory, select the Type property and change the value by clicking the down arrow at the right and selecting Property set data from the drop-down list. Then click the Property Data worksheet icon. The Add Property Sets worksheet appears. Check DoorObjects in the list of property set definitions that appear (see Figure 13.22). Click OK to close this worksheet.

NOTE See Chapter 14 to learn how to create property set definitions.

4. In the Tool Properties worksheet, click the Description worksheet icon and type **Attaches Property Data Only** and click OK (see Figure 13.23). Click OK again to close the Tool Properties worksheet.

5. Click the freshly customized **DoorObjects Property Data Set** tool, select both fire-rated double door objects in the core, and press Enter to end the command.

6. Save and close the Core.dwg element file. Switch back to the Construction Plan.dwg view file. Reload its XRefs.

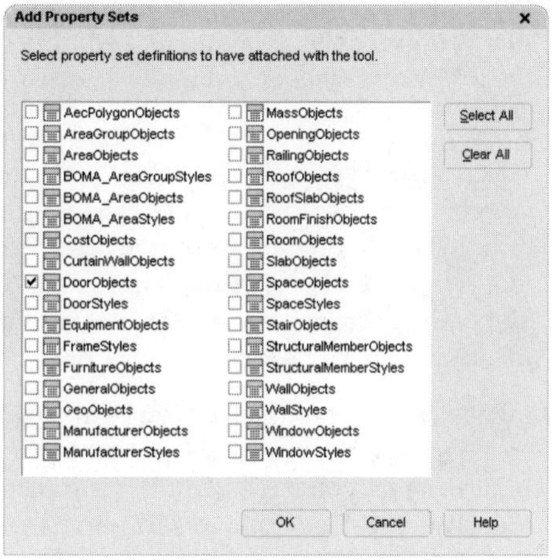

FIGURE 13.22
Selecting a property set definition to have attached with a tool

FIGURE 13.23
Fashioning a tool that attaches property set data without a tag

7. Click the Door Tag - Project Based tool and tag both of the fire-rated double doors in the core. This time the door tags appear without displaying an error—the tags now properly show the room number.

8. Save the Construction Plan.dwg view file.

WARNING Only data that lives in constructs can be scheduled. This includes property set data overrides from externally referenced elements.

Browsing and Editing Property Set Data

There are several ways to browse and edit property set data. Let's take a look at each method in turn so you'll have many different techniques in your repertoire.

1. Open the Spaces construct, zoom in on the elevator lobby, and select its space.

2. Look at the Properties palette and notice that it actually has another tab called Extended Data that you probably have overlooked until this moment. Click this tab and you'll be looking at the property sets attached to the selected object (and possibly to its style).

3. First of all, notice that the top of the Properties palette indicates that you have a Space object selected (see Figure 13.24)—this is what the property sets are attached to. In the Property Sets category, collapse the GeoObjects and RoomFinishObjects property sets so you can more easily examine the RoomObjects properties. Increment, Name, and Number are manual properties that you can edit here (we don't use number in project-based tags). Level comes from project data, and NumberProjectBased is calculated by a formula. All the SpaceObjects properties are automatically calculated from the space object itself (BaseArea, for example). Press Esc to deselect.

4. Switch back to the construction plan view. This time, select the Elevator Lobby space tag and look again at the Extended Data tab in the Properties palette. The top of the Properties palette indicates that you have a Multi-View Block Reference selected. A key piece of information is found in the category name: Property Sets From Referenced Objects. Collapse both GeoObjects and RoomFinishObjects property sets and observe that none of the RoomObjects properties are editable—they are all grayed-out because you are merely viewing the properties of the object this tag references. Press Esc to deselect.

5. Click the Elevator Lobby space to select the Spaces.dwg XRef in the construction plan view. Right-click and choose Edit Referenced Property Set Data from the shortcut menu. Select the Elevator Lobby space (it highlights individually) and press Enter. The Edit Referenced Property Set Data worksheet appears. Collapse the GeoObjects and RoomFinishObjects categories. The same properties that were editable in the RoomObjects property set in step 3 are editable here. Notice there is one additional property: Data Source. This reveals where this property set data lives: in the Spaces construct (see Figure 13.25). Click Cancel.

FIGURE 13.24
Viewing Extended Data in the Properties palette for the source object (left) and a tag that references it (right)

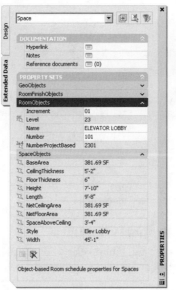
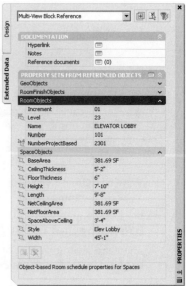

FIGURE 13.25
Editing referenced
property set data from
a view

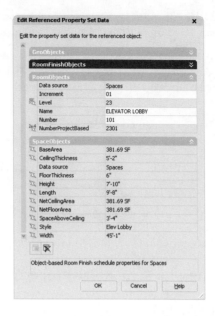

NOTE   Using the Edit Property Set Data tool in the Scheduling palette is equivalent to the procedure described in step 5.

6. Click the Browse Property Data tool in the Scheduling palette. The worksheet that appears is one-stop shopping for all the property data in this drawing and all its external references. Expand Spaces in the tree and select Space (1C75). (See Figure 13.26.) Check Highlight and notice the elevator lobby highlight in the drawing window (you may have to drag the worksheet out of the way to see this). You can use the Browse Property Data worksheet for information only; to edit property data; to delete or reassign property set definitions to specific objects. You can edit property values on the right side of the worksheet. Click Cancel.

FIGURE 13.26
Browsing property data

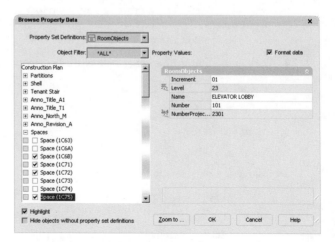

WARNING   If you uncheck anything in the Browse Property Data worksheet, manually entered values are lost. Undo immediately if this is not your intention.

Now that you know how to edit property set data, you can apply this knowledge to solve a problem with the door tags in the construction plan. The closet doors for the break rooms and the conference room at the top of the plan have two doors each. The second door should have a B in its NumberSuffix property.

7. Using the method of your choice, change the NumberSuffix property value from A to B for selected doors.

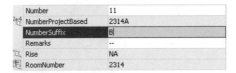

8. Save the Construction Plan.dwg view file.

Working with Style-Based Property Sets

So far you have been working with property sets attached to objects. It is also possible to attach property sets to styles. It makes sense to record information common to all members of a style through style-based property set data. For example, you might record the manufacturer, model, color, and cost for a particular style so this information can be scheduled later on.

1. Open the Partitions construct. Select one of the doors in the tenant space, right-click and choose Edit Door Style from the shortcut menu.

2. Choose the General tab in the Door Style Properties dialog box and then click the Property Sets button. In the Edit Property Set Data worksheet that appears there are three property sets already attached to this style: DoorStyles, FrameStyles, and ManufacturerStyles. Click the Remove Property Sets button at the bottom of the worksheet.

3. The Remove Property Sets worksheet appears, listing three available style-based property sets; you can remove property sets attached to the style here. Click Cancel. If there were additional style-based property sets that applied to doors in this file, the Add Property Sets button would be enabled and you could select that to add the sets in the Add Property Sets worksheet.

4. Back in the Edit Property Set Data worksheet, enter the following property data:

Property Set	Property	Enter
FrameStyles	FrameMaterial	**WOOD**
ManufacturerStyles	Color	**NATURAL**
ManufacturerStyles	Cost	**259.00**
ManufacturerStyles	Manufacturer	**PELLA**

Figure 13.27 shows the result. Click OK to close the worksheet. Click OK again to close the Door Style Properties dialog box. Save the `Partitions.dwg` construct file.

5. Select a tenant door and check the Extended Data tab of the Properties palette. Collapse the Documentation and Property Sets categories to reveal the Property Sets From Style category. All the data you see in this category is for your information only. However, a new feature in ADT 2006 now allows you to edit this data. Click the worksheet icon on the Property Sets From Style category title bar. The same Edit Property Set Data worksheet that you just used in step 4 appears. This is merely a convenient shortcut instead of having to edit the style to access this information. Press Esc to deselect.

6. Close all files without saving.

Creating Schedule Tag Tools

There are a number of schedule tag tools in the Documentation Tool Catalog. Be sure to study them in the Content Browser before deciding that you want to create a new schedule tag. If there is nothing in the catalog that is quite what you are looking for, you can use the Define Schedule Tag worksheet to assist you in generating a new tag—an excellent new feature in ADT 2006. But first, we will unravel the mystery of an existing schedule tag to understand how it works.

FIGURE 13.27
Editing property set data
for a style

DECONSTRUCTING A SCHEDULE TAG

Let's start at the top level and work our way down through nested data structures to understand the mystery of how schedule tags work.

Multiview blocks are AEC objects that have display control and therefore scale awareness. Schedule tags must be multiview blocks—to take advantage of ADT's display system. Multiview blocks themselves contain standard AutoCAD blocks—which are called view blocks in reference to the multiview block. So unraveling the first layer of the mystery is to identify which view blocks make up a particular schedule tag.

1. Open the Construction Plan view. Zoom in on the room tag in Reception.

2. Select the project-based room tag in the Reception space. Make a mental note of where its insertion point is (where the single grip is located). Click the Design tab of the Properties palette and verify that it is a Multi-View Block Reference with the Definition name of Aec6_ Room_Tag_Project.

3. Right-click and choose Edit Multi-View Block Definition from the shortcut menu. Select the View Blocks tab in the Multi-View Block Definition Properties dialog box that appears. This particular definition uses only one view block, called Aec6_Room_Tag_P. Click each one of the display representations to see that this view block is present only in General and Reflected (see Figure 13.28).

TIP Add different view blocks to the Plan, Plan High Detail, and/or Plan Low Detail display representations instead of General to make a tag scale-dependent schedule tag. Then the tag will change sizes when you change display configurations, provided you create view blocks to do so.

FIGURE 13.28
Editing Multi-View
Block Definition
Properties

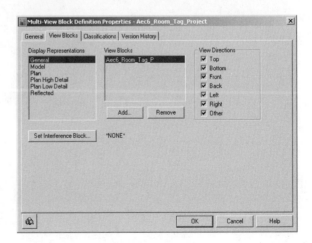

4. Now that you know the name of the view block that underpins the schedule tag's multiview block, insert it off to the side for a closer look. Choose Insert ➤ Block. In the Insert dialog box, click the name drop-down list and select Aec6_Room_Tag_P. Check Specify On-Screen in the Insertion Point group, uncheck Explode, and click OK. Pan over to one side, beyond the building, and click to insert the attributed block. Click OK in the Edit Attributes dialog box that appears.

The way data is made visible through blocks is through *attributes*—a well-known AutoCAD concept. Attribute definitions are wrapped into blocks when the blocks are defined. The second layer of the mystery is exposed when you explode an attributed block to reveal its attribute definitions. By examining the attribute definitions, you'll finally understand how the link is made between the schedule tag and property sets.

5. Type **X** for explode on the command line and press Enter. Select the attributed block and press Enter. The attribute definitions appear after the block is exploded. The attribute tag names reveal the link to property sets (see Figure 13.29).

Schedule tags do more than insert a multiview block; they also attach property set data to the objects they tag. The attribute tag names are what ADT reads when it automatically attaches property set data. The attribute tag names take the following form:

```
PropertySetDefinitionName:PropertyDefinitionName
```

So the first attribute definition in Figure 13.29 has the tag name RoomObjects:Name, which refers to the Name property within the RoomObjects property set. Now this should make sense to you; the attribute's name actually causes ADT to attach the corresponding property set to the object. Then the named property set data fills in the attribute value, making the hidden data visible.

CREATING A SCHEDULE TAG

New! You can build schedule tags by working in reverse through the previous deconstruction procedure, or you can follow a simpler path by using regular text as a placeholder for attribute definitions. We'll take the easy route and use placeholder text and the new define schedule tag worksheet.

FIGURE 13.29
Attributed block (top) and exploded version revealing attribute definitions (bottom)

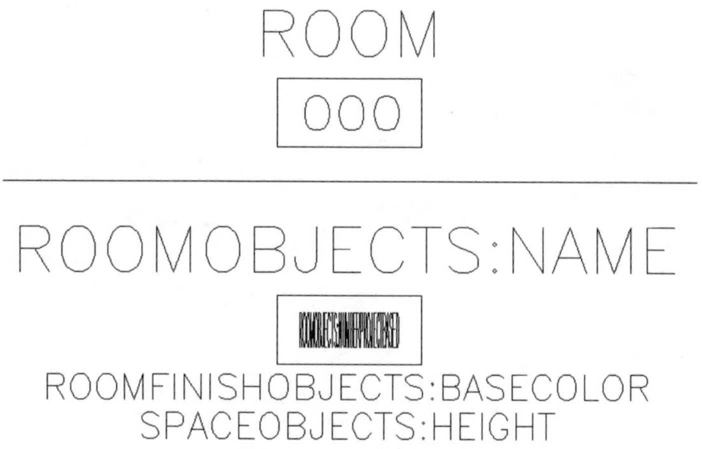

ROOM

000

ROOMOBJECTS:NAME

ROOMFINISHOBJECTS:BASECOLOR
SPACEOBJECTS:HEIGHT

1. Erase all the attribute definitions but leave the rectangle from the exploded view block. The rectangle is the correct size for a room tag. Rather than try and calculate what this size ought to be, it is easier to deconstruct an existing tag and use parts of it to build a new schedule tag.

2. Choose Format ➢ Text Style and choose RomanS-Narrow from the Style Name drop-down list in the Text Style dialog box. Click Cancel to close the dialog box (this doesn't actually cancel the changes because this dialog box has no OK button).

3. Now you can create the placeholder text. Type **DTEXT** on the command line and press Enter. Type **J**↵ for Justify and **F**↵ for Fit. Click two points inside the rectangle, leaving a small whitespace. Type **1** and press Enter to set the room number to the annotation plot size. Type **Number** and press Enter twice to end the command.

4. Press Enter to repeat the command. Press **J**↵ for Justify and **C**↵ for Center. Click the center point above the rectangle, centered on its midpoint. Press **1**↵ to specify the height and press **0**↵ to set the rotation. Type **Name** and press Enter twice more to end the command (see Figure 13.30).

5. Choose Format ➢ Define Schedule Tag. Click the Name placeholder text object first; then Number. Click the rectangle also and press Enter; the Define Schedule Tag worksheet appears. Type **Room Tag - Space And Project Based** in the Name text box. In the Name row, change Type to Property, Property Set to SpaceObjects, and Property Definition to Style. In the Number row, change Type to Property, Property Set to RoomObjects, and Property Definition to NumberProjectBased (see Figure 13.31). Click OK to close the worksheet.

FIGURE 13.30
Creating placeholder
text for new schedule tag

Name

Number

FIGURE 13.31
Defining a schedule tag

6. Click the insertion point for this schedule tag in the same place as the tag you deconstructed: the midpoint of the top edge of the rectangle. The new schedule tag is complete.

7. Save the `ConstructionPlan.dwg` view file. You must save before you can make a tool from this schedule tag.

CREATING AND CUSTOMIZING TOOLS

The last procedure in the schedule tag making process is to create a tool from the tag and then customize its tool properties.

1. Drag the schedule tag you just completed into the Scheduling palette. Right-click the new tool that appears and then choose Properties.

2. In the Tool Properties worksheet that appears, change Property Def Location to the following path:

```
C:\Documents and Settings\All Users\Application Data\Autodesk\ADT
2006\enu\Styles\Imperial\Schedule Tables (Imperial).dwg
```

Change Layer Key to ROOMNO, Attribute Text Style to Target Drawing Text Style, and Attribute Text Angle to Right Reading (see Figure 13.32). Click OK to close the worksheet.

3. Delete the original Multiview Block that you dragged into the Scheduling palette—the prototype is no longer needed.

FIGURE 13.32
Customizing properties of new schedule tag tool

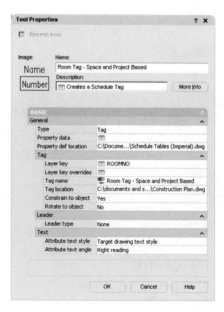

The limitation of the out-of-the box tag is the fact that you must manually enter a room name in the associated RoomObjects:Name property for each tag. If you didn't name space styles in conceptual design, or if you want to use room names that differ from their space style names, using the out-of-the-box project-based room tag is fine. However, we want to use the space style names in our room tags, so we'll use the custom tag that was just developed.

4. Select one of the existing project-based room tags. Right-click and choose Select Similar from the shortcut menu. Press Delete; all the room tags are gone.

5. Click the Room Tag - Space And Project Based tool in the Scheduling palette and tag all the rooms in the construction plan, except for the workstations (see Figure 13.33).

FIGURE 13.33
Adding custom room tags that display the space style name and project-based room numbers

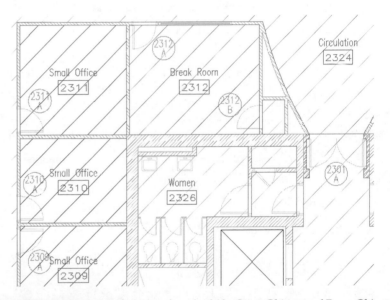

The room tag that you made is a hybrid that reads data from both the SpaceObjects and RoomObjects property sets. When you replaced the tags, the property set data remained, and the new tags simply read and display it through their attributes.

6. You can't detach the Spaces XRef without breaking the connection the schedule tags have with the property set data stored in this construct. Instead, you can turn off the layer containing the hatch patterns of the spaces; turn off the `Spaces|A-Area-Spce` layer.

7. Save the `Construction Plan.dwg` view file.

Dimensioning

If you are a veteran AutoCAD user, you probably have quite a few opinions on how to dimension—a complex feature set has evolved in AutoCAD over decades to address these needs. To fully take advantage of ADT, try setting aside what you might already know about dimensions, at least for awhile.

Architectural Desktop uses its own version of dimensions called AEC dimensions, which naturally have display control and scale awareness built-in. In addition, AEC dimensions work across XRefs, unlike the dimensions of old. Like all other forms of annotation, always add AEC dimensions to views within the project structure. That way, the dimensions that you do add will be specific to the view that you put them in—period. No more worries about trans-spatial dimensions, paper space, viewport layers, scale overrides, and so on.

Making AEC Dimensions

There are just two types of AEC dimensions: automatic and manual. You'll first learn to create and edit both types and then explore AEC dimension styles. Unfortunately, AEC dimensions are not the end of the subject in ADT. AutoCAD dimensions must still be used for certain types of dimensions. In fact, all AEC dimensions are ultimately based on AutoCAD dimension styles. In the end, all the knowledge packed away in your brain regarding AutoCAD dimensions is not entirely lost because you'll need this fuller understanding to get the most out of dimensioning in ADT.

AUTOMATIC DIMENSIONING

Automatic dimensions are the most advanced way to add dimensions, and you will probably use them the most. You create automatic dimensions by selecting linework and/or objects. AEC dimensions reach through XRefs and associate themselves with the objects stored in constructs. Any changes made to source objects in constructs are automatically reflected in dimension objects in views.

1. Click the Views tab in the Project Navigator and double-click the Construction Plan view to open it if it's not already open. Zoom in on the break room and small office just off the upper-left corner of the core.

2. Verify that the scale pop-up menu on the drawing status bar reads 1/8"=1'-0". AEC dimensions automatically scale themselves to the appropriate size based on the scale you have chosen in the view. The scale must be set prior to creating the dimensions.

NOTE   There is a setting in Drawing Setup dialog box that controls whether dimensions will automatically scale. Verify that Automatically Create Dimscale Override is set (it will be by default) if you want this behavior.

3. When working with AEC dimensions, you don't need to use AutoCAD's Dimension toolbar. Instead select the Annotation palette and click the AEC Dimension (2) tool. The number in the parentheses means that the tool will create a dimension object with 2 *chains*—or linked dimension lines.

4. Click the upper wall of the Small Office adjacent to the break room (number 2311 in Figure 13.34; although your number may be different, I'll refer to this room using this number). Press Enter and then click a point just above the wall to insert the dimension object. It appears with loads of information, showing extension lines that reach many significant points.

5. Click the AEC Dimension (2) tool again. Select the vertical wall on the left side of Small Office 2311 and press Enter. Click a point a short distance to the left of the wall, and another dimension object appears.

6. Select the dimension object and look at the Properties palette. There's almost nothing there; only Description, Layer, and Style properties appear. Press Esc to deselect—you don't edit AEC dimensions with properties.

FIGURE 13.34

Adding an automatic AEC dimension to a wall

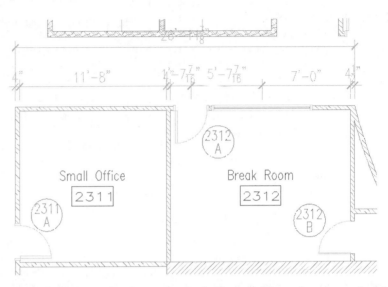

Let's fashion a new dimension tool that makes an automatic single chain. The easiest way to do this is to copy and paste an existing tool.

1. Right-click the AEC Dimension (2) tool in the Annotation palette and choose Copy from the shortcut menu.

2. Right-click the body of the Annotation tool palette and choose Paste. Drag the new tool from the bottom of the palette just below the tool it was copied from.

3. Right-click the new tool and give it the name AEC Dimension (1) in the Tool Properties worksheet. Change the description text, replacing "2 chains" with "1 chain". Change Style to 1 Chain. Verify that Specify Using is set to Linework And Objects—this is what makes the style "automatic" (see Figure 13.35). If you set Specify Using to Points, it would be a manual dimension (don't do that here). Click OK to close the worksheet.

4. Click the AEC Dimension (1) tool in the Annotation palette and then click the right wall in Small Office 2311. Click a short distance to the left of the wall to locate a new dimension object having one chain (see Figure 13.36). The dimension reads 11'-8".

MANUAL DIMENSIONING

Some situations call for manual AEC dimensions. For example, if you want to dimension the space between objects, use a manual AEC dimension. Manual dimension requires that you click all the points you want to include in the dimension chain.

1. Pan over to the circulation space between the curved walls coming out of the top of the core. Let's dimension the distance between the corners of the curved walls.

2. Click the AEC Dimension (1) - Manual tool in the Annotation palette.

FIGURE 13.35
Creating an AEC
dimension tool

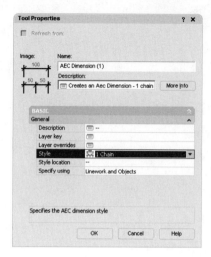

FIGURE 13.36
Creating a single chain
automatic dimension
with new tool

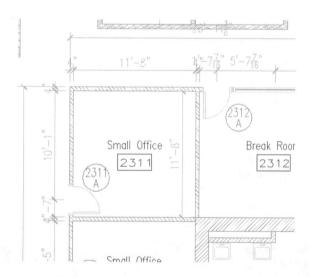

3. Click the two endpoints shown in Figure 13.37 and press Enter.

4. The command line says the following:

```
Pick side to dimension or [Style]:
```

Click a point a short distance above the horizontal line implied by the two dimension points you just clicked. Click again a short distance above the last point. The dimension chain appears. Don't worry right now if its dimension line doesn't align with the others.

FIGURE 13.37
Creating a manual AEC
dimension

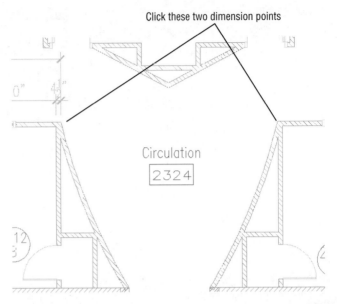

Manual dimensions are not associated with objects as automatic dimensions are. Instead, manual dimensions are configured by default to create point entities that the dimension object is associated with. Moving the points transforms the manual dimension object. You can't see these points by default because the point style is set to a single pixel.

1. Choose Format ➢ Point Style to open the Point Style dialog box. Click the symbol of a circle with an X through it and click OK.

2. Points appear where you added manual dimension points before. The manual dimension is associated with these points (see Figure 13.38).

WARNING   Point entities appear on the same layer as the AEC dimension object, not on the Defpoints layer as with AutoCAD dimensions.

FIGURE 13.38
Reformatting point
style (left) to make the
points appear that are associated with a manual
dimension object (right)

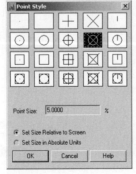
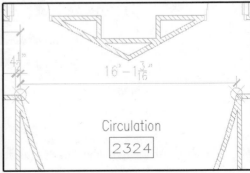

3. Move one of the points to the tip if the triangular wall above the dimension chain. The manual dimension immediately updates.

There are two types of manual dimensions: transformable and static. The transformable type inserts point entities as you have seen, and the static type does not. Static dimension points cannot be adjusted, and are useful if you really want to lock a manual dimension down.

4. Type **DimPointMode** on the command line and press Enter. The command line says the following:

```
Enter mode [Transformable] <Static>:
```

Type **S** for Static and press Enter.

5. Create another manual dimension, clicking one dimension point at the tip of the triangular wall and the other at the right endpoint of the curved wall (see Figure 13.39). The static dimension cannot be adjusted because it has no transformable point entities that it is associated with.

6. Set the dimension point mode back to its default setting. Type **DimPointMode** on the command line and press Enter. Type **T** for Transformable and press Enter.

7. Set the point style back to the single pixel symbol. Use the DDPTYPE command this time.

FIGURE 13.39
Static and transformable manual AEC dimensions

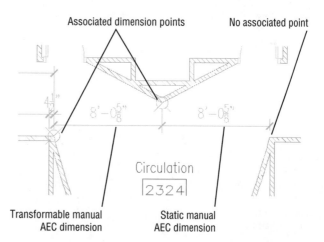

Editing AEC Dimensions

Editing AEC dimension objects is straightforward—all its editing modes are listed in the shortcut menu. Let's make the automatic dimension object you first created more presentable.

1. Select the AEC dimension object above the Small Office 2311. Right-click and choose Edit In Place (you can also enter this mode by clicking the trigger grip).

2. Many more grips appear while you are in this mode. The triangular grips on the dimension lines allow you to move the chains while the triangular grips on the extension lines allow you

to change their offsets. The square grips are used to move the dimension text. Move things around as best you can to make the dimension more readable.

3. Right-click and choose Remove Dimension Points. Select the four extension lines shown in Figure 13.40. The extension lines highlight in red as you select them. Press Enter to revise the dimension.

4. Select the dimension again, right-click, and choose Add Dimension Points. Click the corner of the conference room wall and press Enter. The command line says the following:

```
Select Dimension chain:
```

Click the top chain and press Enter. The dimension is revised to include the additional dimension point. Move the dimension text over if necessary to make it readable.

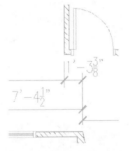

FIGURE 13.40
Removing dimension points by selecting extension lines (top) and the result (bottom)

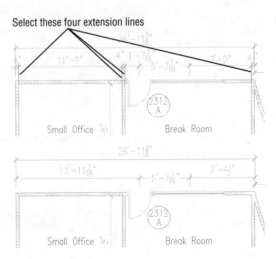

NOTE Attach and Detach Objects are editing options in the shortcut menu that affect all chains together. Use Add And Remove Dimension Points when you want finer control and the ability to affect one chain at a time.

5. Create a manual AEC dimension that shows the clear dimension between cubicles. It should read 5'-3".

6. Select the new dimension, right-click, and choose Override Text & Lines to open a dialog box of the same name. Type **<space>CLR** in the Suffix text box. Typing a space before the abbreviation for clear will separate the suffix from the dimension text it follows (see Figure 13.41). Click OK to close the dialog box. Notice the marker that appears, indicating that the dimension text has been overridden—this marker will not print and is for your information only.

FIGURE 13.41
Overriding Text & Lines

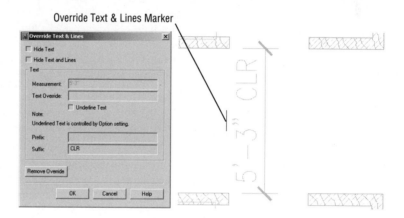

Editing AEC Dimension Styles

Amazingly, AEC Dimension styles have only one property, called the Number Of Chains, with an obvious function. All the interesting content within AEC dimension styles is hidden in their display properties. It is probably best to make new AEC dimension styles for every type of object that you want to dimension. For example, curtain walls might deserve their own AEC dimension style, but the styles you decide to make will have to grow out of the type of work that you are doing.

1. Select one of the double-chain dimension objects you have already made. Right-click and choose Edit AEC Dimension Style from the shortcut menu.

2. Select the Chains tab in the AEC Dimension Style Properties dialog box that appears. There is only one property here: Number Of Chains. You can have up to 10 chains, although I doubt you'll ever need to dimension an object with such detail.

3. Click the Display Properties tab. Notice that most of the display representations have style overrides already applied. Do not remove them; the style overrides are necessary for the normal functioning of AEC dimensions. Instead, you can edit the existing style overrides if you want to make changes. Double-click the Plan display representation icon.

4. In the Display Properties dialog box that appears, click the Layer/Color/Linetype tab if it's not already selected. Turn all the display components on and click OK in each open dialog box.

Display Component	Function
AEC Dimension Group	The dimension object itself—never turn this off
AEC Dimension Group Marker	Helpful nonplotting symbol that identifies Move All Chains grip
Removed Points Marker	Nonplotting symbol that shows where points have been removed
Override Text & Lines Marker	Bar that shows up on layer Defpoints when overrides are present

5. Zoom into one of the double-chain AEC dimensions that you have made. The red circle with an X through it is the Removed Points Marker. The double # symbol is the AEC Dimension Group Marker. Remember that these symbols do not plot, so there is really no problem in leaving their display components on, unless you are giving an on-screen presentation.

6. Go back to the Display Properties dialog box for the Plan display representation. Click the Contents tab (see Figure 13.42). There is really a wealth of information to study on this tab. Each listed object has different settings that appear when you select it in the Apply To list. Click each object type in turn. Refer to the ADT help for more information.

7. Click the Other tab. This is where you assign an AutoCAD dimension style that underlies the style override for this display representation. Notice that the Aec-Arch-I-96 AutoCAD dimension style is assigned to the Plan representation (see Figure 13.43). In other words, an $1/8''$ scale AutoCAD dimension style is assigned to the Plan display representation. Click Cancel.

8. Double-click the Plan High Detail display representation icon in the AEC Dimension Style Properties dialog box. Notice that the Aec-Arch-I-48 AutoCAD dimension style is assigned on the Other tab. In other words, a $1/4''$ scale AutoCAD dimension style is assigned to the Plan High Detail display representation—this should make sense to you by now (refer to Chapter 2, "Display Systems," if you are confused about the display system).

TIP You can access underlying AutoCAD dimension styles by clicking the convenient Edit button on the Other tab in the Display Properties dialog box.

9. Notice that the Other tab is the home to several important AEC Dimension settings, including Distance Between Chains, the layer (set to 0 by default), and an override to use a fixed-length extension line. Show Height Of Openings is mainly used in Europe to dimension this information in plan. Click Cancel. Click Cancel again to close all dialog boxes.

10. Choose Format ➤ Options. Click the AEC Dimension tab. Study this tab if you want complete control over how your AEC dimensions appear (see Figure 13.44). Click Cancel.

AutoCAD dimension styles are responsible for many features—including the appearance of dimension and extension lines, the shape and size of arrowheads, the dimension units and precision, and much more. Refer to the AutoCAD Help if you need to refresh your dimension style knowledge.

USING THE AEC DIMENSION STYLE WIZARD

If you are new to ADT and don't want to learn about the complexities of AutoCAD dimension styles, you are in luck. There is a wizard that can make changes to both AEC dimension styles and associated AutoCAD dimension styles through one convenient interface. The wizard is a quick way to make common alterations.

Choose Format ➢ AEC Dimension Style Wizard. Shown here are the four pages of properties you can set by using this wizard. Use the wizard as a convenient alternative to setting both AEC dimension style properties and AutoCAD dimension style properties.

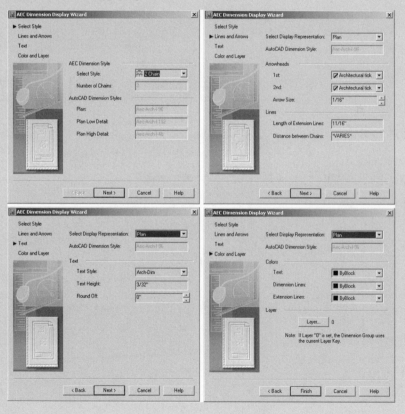

WARNING Use AutoCAD dimension tools to create angular, arc length, radius, and diameter dimensions. AEC dimensions cannot handle these types.

11. Close all files without saving. Open the Project Browser, right-click Chapter 13 in the tree, and choose Close Project from the shortcut menu. Close the Project Browser. Congratulations— you made it!

FIGURE 13.42

Other tab of AEC Dimension display properties style override

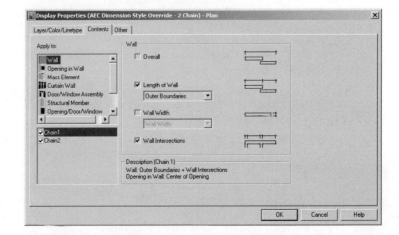

FIGURE 13.43

Contents tab of AEC Dimension display properties style override

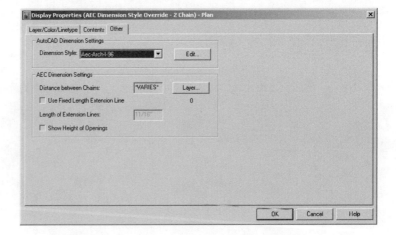

FIGURE 13.44
AEC dimension options

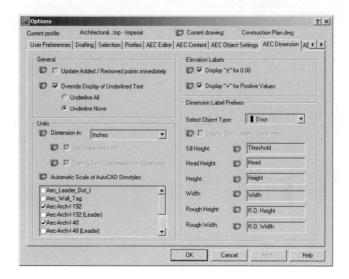

Summary

In this chapter you learned how to annotate, tag, and dimension view drawings. These skills are essential to master if you plan to make readable construction documents. It is well worth your time to practice the skills taught in this chapter to improve your understanding and productivity using the complex tools that ADT has to offer. In the next chapter you will deepen your understanding of property sets while generating schedules. In addition, you'll learn a powerful system for tracking building areas and generating detailed reports on the building information model.

Chapter 14

Schedules, Display Themes, and Areas

Schedules make important nongraphical object data in your project visible in tabular form. Although you can generate schedule tables in any project phase to extract information that might feed back into the design process, the most common use is in the construction documentation phase to list and tabulate object quantities and add up costs.

Similar to the schedule tags you learned about in the last chapter, the data appearing in schedule tables comes from property sets attached to architecture, engineering, and construction (AEC) objects, not the objects themselves. Schedule tables can themselves be used to add property sets to any objects appearing in schedules that do not already have the relevant property sets attached. Then the cells of the schedule table can be edited—much like a spreadsheet—but the data itself is always stored in property sets and displayed in the schedule table.

Schedule tables can read property set data across XRefs, from an external file containing XRefs, and even from within block definitions if you so choose. Therefore, schedule tables are typically added to view files, like other documentation content. This chapter takes a tutorial approach to learning schedule tables: You will create a complex Furniture Schedule, its classifications, and properties from scratch—and you'll ultimately add it to a Furniture Plan view file.

Display themes are specialized schedules that act as legends on drawings that they affect. Instead of displaying property set data inside the display theme schedule itself, display themes alter the way objects are displayed, based on property set data. In other words, display themes make invisible property set data visible by affecting the display of the objects they are attached to.

Area objects and the toolset they belong to were designed specifically to accommodate the complexity associated with calculating areas for building codes and leasing standards. In the chapter's final tutorial, you'll use the area toolset to design an area group template that will be used as a framework for calculating the gross, rentable, usable, common, and vertical penetration areas of the highrise building in the tutorial, ultimately generating an Excel spreadsheet known as an area evaluation document. This chapter's topics include:

◆   Generating Schedules

◆   Using Display Themes

◆   Working with Areas

Generating Schedules

This section takes you through a tutorial that teaches you how to generate a custom Furniture Schedule in a particular sequence. I believe that working straight through the tutorial is the easiest way to wrap your mind around the complexities of generating schedules, which includes creating and assigning classifications, property data formats, property set definitions and properties, and schedule table styles. Although you do not necessarily have to perform every step in the order shown, it is perhaps the most efficient sequence. Once you understand how everything fits together, you can approach the task of generating schedules in whichever order that suits you.

1. Copy this chapter's folder on the companion DVD into the following folder on your hard drive:

   ```
   C:\Documents and Settings\<username>\My Documents\Autodesk\My Projects
   ```

   This is the standard path for storing local projects on your hard drive. You will probably store projects on a file server if working in a networked environment.

2. Click the Project Browser button on the Navigation toolbar.

3. Navigate to the folder you copied the files into in step 1. Double-click the Chapter 14 project folder to make it current. In a few moments the Project Navigator palettes appear. This chapter picks up where the last chapter left off in regards to the high-rise floor project.

4. In the Tool Palettes, make the Document palette group current.

5. Choose the Constructs palette and double-click the Furniture construct to open it (see Figure 14.1). Investigate the file: It contains furniture multiview blocks on two different layers. The Partitions, Shell, and Tenant Stair constructs are overlaid as XRefs. The I-Furn-E layer holds existing furniture, and the I-Furn layer holds new furniture.

6. Leave the project open for the duration of this chapter.

Creating Classifications

Classifications were introduced in Chapter 3, "Object Styles," in which you learned how to create classification definitions and used them to filter the object display system. In this chapter you'll use classifications in different ways—to filter schedule table data, and to actually appear as columns in a schedule table as well.

Using classifications is an entirely optional but extremely effective way to track extra data by style. Let's create a Vendor classification that simply lists all the vendors from which furniture will be purchased in the project.

1. Choose Format ➢ Style Manager. Expand the current drawing, Multi-Purpose Objects, and Classification Definitions nodes. Click the Uniformat II classification definition node in the tree pane.

2. In the content pane, there is only one classification defined: E2020 - Movable Furnishings. This classification is attached by default to all the furnishings in the DesignCenter. The Furniture construct contains AEC content from the DesignCenter plus several custom multiview blocks.

We will use this classification later on to filter the schedule table to display only movable furniture.

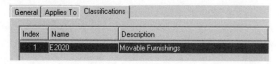

TIP You can access the full list of Uniformat classifications in the `Uniformat II Classifications (1997 ed).dwg` file in the following folder: `C:\Documents and Settings\All Users\Application Data\Autodesk\ADT 2006\enu\Styles\Imperial`.

3. Right-click the Classification Definitions node in the tree pane and choose New from the shortcut menu. Give the new classification definition the name **Vendor**.

4. We're building a classification for furniture objects that are all multiview block (MVB) definitions. Click the Applies To tab in the content pane and check Multi-View Block Definition.

5. Click the Classifications tab in the content pane. Click the Add button to create a classification with the vendor name **Acme**. Create two more classifications called **Greene** and **FurnCo** (see Figure 14.2). Click OK to close the Style Manager.

FIGURE 14.1
Furniture construct

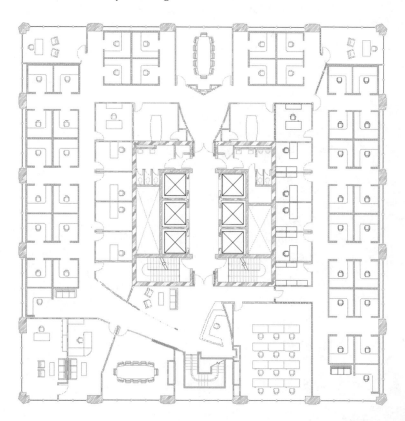

FIGURE 14.2
Creating a classification
definition

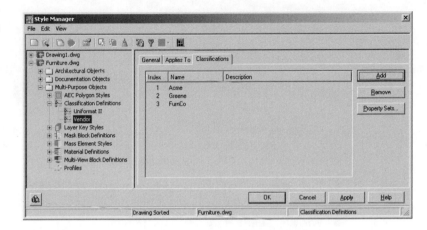

Assigning Classifications

Every object style has a Classifications tab. Classifications are assigned on a style basis—not to individual objects. Now that you have created a classification definition, the next step is to assign its classifications to the furniture styles present in the Furniture construct.

1. Choose Format ➤ Style Manager. Expand the current drawing, Multi-Purpose Objects, and Multi-View Block Definitions nodes in the tree pane. Select the Coffee Table node.

2. Click the Classifications tab in the Content pane. Two classifications are present: Uniformat II and Vendor. Currently Vendor is *Unspecified*. Change this to Acme (see Figure 14.3). Click OK.

3. Repeat the previous steps and assign classifications for each of the following pieces of furniture:

Multi-View Block	Acme	Greene	FurnCo
Conference Table		X	
Credenza			X
Desk	X		
File Cabinet			X
Lounge Chair		X	
Sofa	X		
Table			X
Task Chair		X	

WARNING   Do not assign a classification to the Reception Desk. It will remain with an *Unspecified* value because it is custom millwork not purchased from a vendor.

4. Save and close the Furniture.dwg construct file.

FIGURE 14.3
Assigning a classification to an MVB Definition

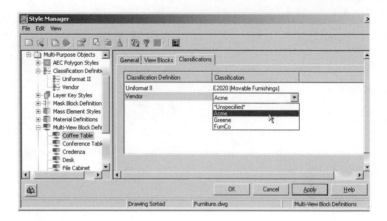

Creating Property Data Formats

Property data formats control how data in property sets appear. Schedules show property set data in tabular form, so if you are building a schedule table from scratch, it makes sense to decide on property data formats early on.

Ultimately, the schedule table we are building will live in a view file like other annotation content. The reason for this is clear—the objects placed in a view file remain specific to that view. If you place a schedule table in a construct, it will appear in every view because views reference constructs (refer to Chapter 5, "Project Management," if you are confused about project structure). Therefore, we will open the Furniture Plan view to begin building the precursors to the schedule table, which is the goal of this section.

1. Select the Views tab in the Project Navigator and double-click the Furniture Plan view to open it. Room tags (space- and project-based) have already been added to the view.

2. Choose Format ➤ Style Manager. Expand the current drawing, Documentation Objects, and Property Data Formats nodes in the tree pane. Click the Property Data Formats node and read the descriptions in the content pane. Many common property data formats are supplied in the drawing template, so you'll have to make only one new property data format.

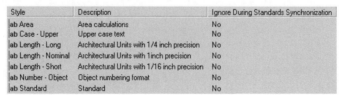

3. Right-click the Property Data Format node in the tree pane, choose New from the shortcut menu, and type the name **Case - Title**. Click the Formatting tab in the content pane and locate the Text group. Select Title in the Case drop-down list (see Figure 14.4). Title text capitalizes the first letter of each word, such as This Is Title Text. Click the Apply button and leave the Style Manager open.

FIGURE 14.4
Creating a new property
data format

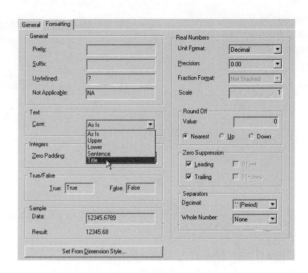

TIP   It is better to create a different property set format for each type of formatting you want to use, rather than try and make one property data format to suit all situations.

Notice all the possibilities for formatting data that appear on the Formatting tab: Options exist for text, integers, true/false variables, and real numbers. In the General group, a question mark and the letters NA appear in text boxes—these are characters that appear in schedule tables when properties are undefined or not applicable, as we'll see later on.

Working with Property Set Definitions

If property data formats are used to control the appearance of property data, property set definitions hold the property definitions that store that data. If you follow this chain of reasoning, you are becoming fluent in the language of ADT. In other words, after you've settled on formats, the next step is to build the properties that you want to appear as columns in the schedule table.

INVESTIGATING DEFAULT PROPERTY SET DEFINITIONS

You can learn a lot by investigating some of the default property set definitions. In particular, we'll look at the SpaceObjects and RoomObjects property set definitions.

TIP   You can access the full list of default property set definitions in the Schedule Tables (Imperial).dwg file in the following folder: C:\Documents and Settings\All Users\ Application Data\Autodesk\ADT 2006\enu\Styles\Imperial.

   1. In the tree pane of the Style Manager, expand the Property Set Definitions node. Select the SpaceObjects node. Choose the Applies To tab in the content pane. Notice that there are two radio buttons: Objects, and Styles and Definitions. Radio buttons offer an either/or choice. SpaceObjects applies to area and space objects (see Figure 14.5).

FIGURE 14.5

Viewing which objects a property set definition applies to

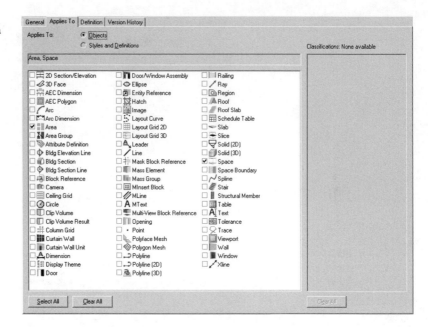

You can create property set definitions that apply to AutoCAD entities as well as AEC objects. In addition, a property set can be further limited to apply only to objects whose styles are assigned a particular classification if the property set definition applies to the exact same object types as the style types to which the classification definition applies. The classification can apply to the styles of more object types than the property set definition, but not the other way around.

2. Select the Definition tab in the content pane; a list of property definitions appears. The buttons along the right edge allow you to create new property definitions of the following types: manual, automatic, formula, location, classification, material, and project. All the properties in SpaceObjects are automatic, as you can see by their icons (see Figure 14.6).

3. Select the RoomObjects node in the tree pane. The Definition tab shows that this property set has five property definitions: Increment, Level, Name, Number, and NumberProjectBased. Increment, Name, and Number are manual properties. Level is a project-based property, and NumberProjectBased is a formula property. Select the Increment property and click the Type drop-down list. It shows the six variable types that are available: Integer, Real, Text, True/False, and Auto Increment data types for both integers and characters (see Figure 14.7). Do not change anything—you are just investigating to understand how property definitions are defined.

When you added the Room Tag - Project Based schedule tag in Chapter 13, "Annotating, Tagging, and Dimensioning," the reason why each tag displayed a different room number was because its associated property set's Increment Property was using the Auto Increment - Integer variable type. The number that appeared in the tag actually came from the NumberProjectBased property definition (2301, for example).

FIGURE 14.6
Examining property
definitions

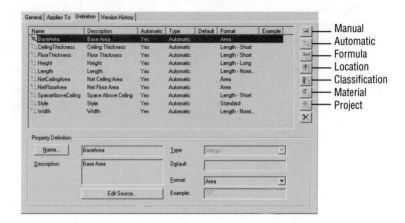

FIGURE 14.7
Investigating property
variable types

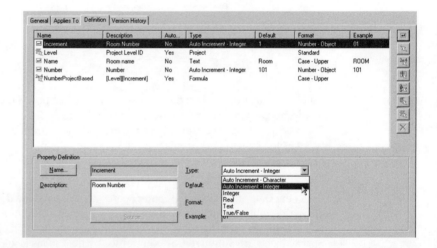

4. Double-click the NumberProjectBased node in the Definition list; the Formula Property Definition dialog box appears (see Figure 14.8). The formula shown is a simple one—it is the concatenation of two other properties:

```
[Level][Increment]
```

The formula was created by double-clicking property definitions from the list below into the Formula list box. In this case the Level property definition reads the Level ID from the project, which is 23 in our tutorial. This is concatenated with an integer that is automatically incremented, so the first tag would show 2301, the next 2302, and so on. If you remember adding project-based room tags in Chapter 13—that is exactly what happened. Click Cancel to close the Formula Property Definitions dialog box.

FIGURE 14.8
Formula Property
Definitions

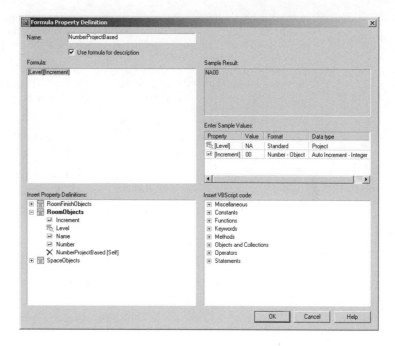

NOTE   You can create more complex formulas by dragging VBScript code into your property definition formulas. Refer to ADT and Visual Basic help to learn more.

CREATING PROPERTY SET DEFINITIONS AND PROPERTIES

Now that you have investigated some property definitions, you are in a better position to create new
ones. The furniture schedule table that we are building requires two new property set definitions:
MVBObjects and VendorClass.

NOTE   Each property definition has the potential to act as a column in a schedule table.

The MVBObjects property set definition will contain three properties: Number, Room, and Item.
The Number property will show the project-based room number that a scheduled piece of furniture
is in. The Room property will list the room name that the piece of furniture is in, which in this project
comes from a space style name. Both Number and Room must be location-based properties because
the data they show depends on which space the furniture is in. The Item property must be automatic
because it will read the MVB style name to identify a particular piece of furniture.

1. Right-click the Property Set Definitions node in the tree pane, choose New from the shortcut
menu, and type **MVBObjects** as the name.

2. Select the Applies To tab in the content pane of the Style Manager dialog box. Verify that the
Objects radio button is selected because we ultimately want the schedule to reflect object quantities. Click the Clear All button and then check both Multi-View Block Reference and Space.

3. Click the Definition tab and click the Add Location Property Definition button. The Location Property Definition dialog box appears. Type **Number** in the Name text box and then expand the RoomObjects property definition (under Space). Check NumberProjectBased (see Figure 14.9). Click OK.

4. Select the new Number property definition, open the Format drop-down list, and choose Number - Object from the list of property data formats.

5. Click the Add Location Property Definition button again. In the Location Property Definition dialog box, type **Room** in the Name text box and then expand the SpaceObjects property definition (under Space). Check Style and click OK.

6. Select the Room property definition, open the Format drop-down list, and choose Case - Title from the list of property data formats.

7. Click the Add Automatic Property Definition button; the Automatic Property Source dialog box appears. Choose the Categorized tab if it's not already selected. Check the Name property under Multi-View Block Reference and click OK (see Figure 14.10).

8. Select the new property definition and click the Name button. Type **Item** in the Name worksheet that appears and click OK. Open the Format drop-down list and choose Case - Title from the list of property data formats.

9. Click the Apply button and leave the Style Manager open.

Creating a Classification-Based Property Definition

The VendorClass property set definition will contain two properties: Vendor and Delivery Date. Vendor will be a classification-based property that reads the data inside the Vendor classification. Delivery Date will simply be a manual property that one can type a date into.

Before you can create a property definition based upon a classification, the classification it references must be in the file. Therefore, you'll have to import classifications from the Furniture construct.

1. Choose File ➢ Open Drawing from the Style Manager menu. In the Open Drawing dialog box that appears, navigate to the following folder:

   ```
   C:\Documents and Settings\<username>\My Documents\Autodesk\My Projects\Chapter 14\
   Constructs\Architectural
   ```

   Select the Furniture.dwg file and click Open.

2. Expand Furniture.dwg, Multi-Purpose Objects, and Classification Definitions in the tree pane. Click the Classification Definitions node. In the content pane, select both Vendor and Uniformat II. Drag both nodes into the Furniture Plan.dwg node above and then click the Apply button.

3. Right-click the Furniture.dwg node and choose Close from the shortcut menu.

4. Right-click the Property Set Definitions node in the tree pane, choose New from the shortcut menu, and type **VendorClass** as the name.

FIGURE 14.9
Setting a location property definition

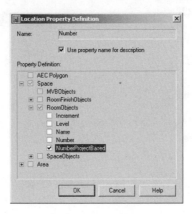

FIGURE 14.10
Selecting an automatic property source

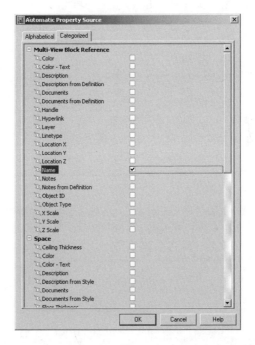

5. Select the Applies To tab in the content pane of the Style Manager dialog box. Choose the Styles and Definitions radio button. Click the Clear All button and then check Multi-View Block Definition.

6. Click the Definition tab and click the Add Classification Property Definition button. The Classification Property Definition dialog box appears. Type **VendorProperty** in the Name text box and then check the Vendor classification definition (see Figure 14.11). Click OK.

FIGURE 14.11
Creating a classification
property definition

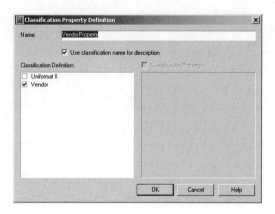

7. In the Classification Property Definition dialog box, click the Add Manual Property Definition button.

8. Type **DeliveryDate** in the Name text box of the small New Property dialog box that appears and click OK. Type a double dash (--) in the Default text box so that the cell can be edited in the schedule table. Click Apply.

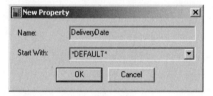

WARNING Property names that use spaces in their names cannot be used in schedule tags because spaces are not allowed in attribute definitions.

Importing an Existing Property Set Definition

There is one other property definition that you'll need to create the furniture schedule table. It's a default property definition called ManufacturerStyles. There's no sense in reinventing the wheel; it's quicker to get this property definition from a content drawing rather than re-create it.

1. Choose File ➢ Open Drawing from the Style Manager menu. In the Open Drawing dialog box that appears, click the Content button in the Favorites pane. Double-click the Styles and Imperial folders. Select the `Schedule Tables (Imperial).dwg` file and click Open.

2. Expand the Schedule Tables (Imperial).dwg, Documentation Objects, and Property Set Definitions nodes. Drag the ManufacturerStyles node up in the tree pane, and hold it at the top of the tree—the pane will automatically scroll down. Drop the node onto the Furniture Plan.dwg node.

3. Right-click the Schedule Tables (Imperial).dwg node and choose Close from the shortcut menu.

4. Expand the Furniture Plan.dwg, Documentation Objects, and Property Set Definitions nodes. Click the ManufacturerStyles node. Select the Definition tab in the Content pane. There are four manual property definitions: Color, Cost, Manufacturer, and Model.

5. Change the formats of the Color, Cost, and Model property definitions to Case - Title. Notice that Cost uses the Costing format—this is not one of the original property data formats. It was also brought in by the ManufacturerStyles property set definition when you imported it from the content drawing.

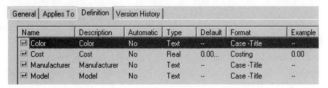

6. Click the Apply button and leave the Style Manager open.

Creating a Schedule Table Style

Once you have created all the property set definitions that you will need for a schedule table, it is time to start building the schedule table style. Property definitions form the columns of the schedule table, and objects will form its rows. Property set data fills in the cells of a schedule table.

1. Right-click the Schedule Table Styles node in the tree pane, just under Property Set Definitions. Choose New from the shortcut menu and type **Furniture Schedule** as its name.

2. Click the Default Format tab in the content pane. This is where you control the way the data appearing in the cells of the schedule table will appear. Click the Style drop-down list in the Text Appearance group and choose the Schedule-Data text style. Verify that Alignment is set to Middle Center. Type **3/32"** in the Height text box, and enter **1/16"** in the Gap text box if it isn't already entered (see Figure 14.12). Height is the height of the data text, and Gap is the white space separating data text from its cell borders

3. Select the Applies To tab. Notice that there are no radio buttons for selecting Objects or Styles and Definitions, as there were in other Applies To tabs. Schedule tables always apply to objects. Click the Clear All button and then check Multi-View Block Reference.

WARNING Property set definitions must apply to everything a schedule table style applies to in order to be available for use in the schedule table.

FIGURE 14.12
Setting the default
format of schedule
table data

4. In the Classifications pane on the right side of the Applies To tab, expand the Uniformat II node and check E2020 (Movable Furnishings). By selecting a specific classification that the schedule table will apply to, you are filtering the data that appears in the schedule. Now, only movable furnishings will appear—built-in millwork such as the Reception Desk MVB will not be scheduled.

TIP You might create a Construction Status classification definition that has New Construction and Existing Construction To Remain classifications. By checking the New Construction classification in the schedule table's Applies To tab, you can filter the schedule to show only new work.

5. Select the Columns tab. Click the Add Column button; the Add Column dialog box appears. Click the Categorized tab if it's not already selected. Three property set definitions appear: ManufacturerStyles, MVBObjects, and VendorClass. These appear because they are bound to the same object types as the schedule table, namely Multi-View Blocks in this case. Click the MVBObjects:Number property definition. Type **Number** in the Heading text box to match its property definition name (see Figure 14.13). Click OK to close the Add Column dialog box.

TIP Resize the Style Manager slightly to get the information in the Columns tab to fill the pane.

6. Continue repeating the last step, adding columns in the following order:

Column No.	Property Set Definition	Property Definition	Heading
2	MVBObjects	Room	Room
3	MVBObjects	Item	Item
4	ManufacturerStyles	Manufacturer	Manufacturer
5	ManufacturerStyles	Model	Model
6	ManufacturerStyles	Color	Color
7	VendorClass	VendorProperty	Vendor
8	VendorClass	DeliveryDate	Delivery Date
9	ManufacturerStyles	Cost	Cost

7. Check Include Quantity Column. Drag the new Quantity column to the right until it appears as the tenth column. Check Include Product Column; it appears as the eleventh and last column.

8. Select the Quantity column and click the Modify button; the Edit Quantity Column dialog box appears. Check Total and click OK. Select the Product column and click the Modify button. Change the Header to Total and choose ManufacturerStyles:Cost from the Data Column dropdown list. Click the Override Cell Format button, change Alignment to Middle Right in the Cell Format Override dialog box, and click OK. In the Edit Product Column dialog box, check Total and click OK (see Figure 14.14). The last column shows the product of cost and quantity.

9. You have the option of formatting data in a matrix with symbols instead of in text form—let's do this for the vendors. We'll create a matrix of subcolumns, one for each vendor, and use a

symbol to indicate which vendor supplied a particular object. Select the Vendor column and click the Modify button. In the Modify Column dialog box, check Matrix and verify that Max Columns is set to 3 because there are three vendor classifications that will be scheduled.

10. Click the Override Cell Format button; the Cell Format Override dialog box appears. In the Matrix Symbol group, click the Symbol drop-down list and choose Dot. It appears in red to indicate that this default format parameter has been overridden (see Figure 14.15).

FIGURE 14.13
Adding a column to the schedule table style

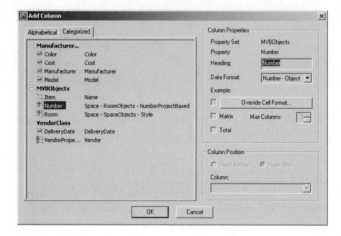

FIGURE 14.14
Modifying Quantity (left) and Product columns (right)

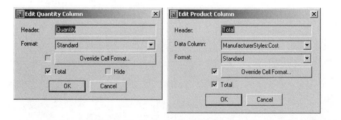

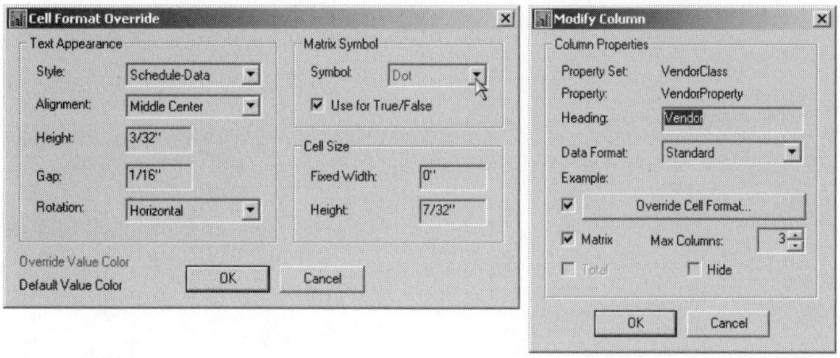

FIGURE 14.15
Overriding cell format (left) in Modify Column dialog box (right)

11. Click OK and OK again to close both dialog boxes. Click the Apply button in the Style Manager dialog box that remains open. Figure 14.16 shows the completed columns for the furniture schedule table style. Verify that your columns match the figure—if they do not, go back and fix them.

12. Select the Sorting tab. Click the Add button, select MVBObjects:Number from the small Select Property dialog box that appears, and click OK. This will sort the rows in the schedule by room number in ascending order.

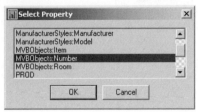

13. Click the Add button again and add the second sorting criterion of MVBObjects:Item (see Figure 14.17).

14. Select the Layout tab. Change the Table Title to **FURNITURE SCHEDULE** (uppercase). The title of a schedule table is not controlled by property data formats and will appear exactly as you type it (see Figure 14.18).

15. In the Format group, click the Override Cell Format button next to Title. In the Cell Format Override dialog box that appears, change Style to Schedule-Title, set Height to **1/4"**, and Gap to **1/8"**. Click OK. Click the Override Cell Format button next to Column Headers. In the Cell Format Override dialog box that appears, change Style to Schedule-Header, set Height to **1/8"** and click OK.

FIGURE 14.16
Completed columns

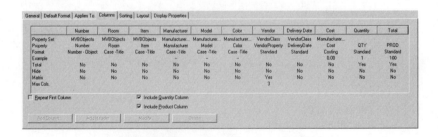

FIGURE 14.17
Adding sorting criteria

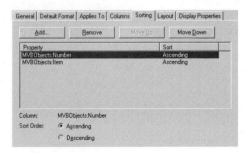

WARNING Text styles are not automatically copied from one drawing to another when you drag schedule tables between nodes in the Style Manager. Use the DesignCenter to transfer text styles between drawings.

16. Finally, select the Display Properties tab. There is only one display representation: General. Instead of making a style override, you will change the drawing default display property source that affects all schedule tables. Double-click the General display representation icon; the Display Properties dialog box appears. Select the Title Row Line display component. Change its properties to match the Outer Frame: change Color to 234, Lineweight to 0.70mm, and Plot Style to Extra Wide (see Figure 14.19). Click OK to close the dialog box.

TIP It is best to leave the Out Of Date Marker display component on. This component draws a diagonal line across the schedule table when any of its data is not displaying the latest changes.

17. Click OK to close the Style Manager. Save the `Furniture Plan.dwg` view file.

Working with Schedule Tables

You'll need to create a tool to insert the furniture schedule table whose style you have already labored to define. The easiest way to create a tool is to copy and paste an existing tool.

1. Choose the Scheduling palette and scroll down until you locate the Door Schedule. Right-click and choose Copy from the shortcut menu.

FIGURE 14.18
Setting layout options for schedule table style

FIGURE 14.19
Adjusting Display Properties

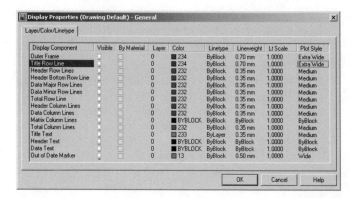

2. Make the Chapter 14 palette group current. It contains only one palette, called Project Tools. You can also create a blank palette in the current palette group, if you prefer.

WARNING If you do not see a project palette group, it is because ADT can't find the tool palette file location. Since this location will vary according to your username and drive letter, you must specify this location in the project properties (see Chapter 5, "Project Management").

3. Right-click the body of the Project Tools palette and choose Paste from the shortcut menu; the Door Schedule tool appears.

4. Right-click the Door Schedule tool and choose Properties from the shortcut menu; the Tool Properties worksheet appears. Type **Furniture Schedule** in the Name text box and change the Description to **Create A Furniture Schedule Table**. Click the Style Location drop-down list and select Browse. In the Select A Location File dialog box that appears, navigate to the following folder:

```
C:\Documents and Settings\<username>\My Documents\Autodesk\My Projects\Chapter
14\Views
```

Double-click the `Furniture Plan.dwg` file. Choose Furniture Schedule from the Style drop-down list and set Scan XRefs to Yes (see Figure 14.20). Click OK to close the worksheet.

NOTE Schedule Tables that scan XRefs from a view file can extract property data from all attached construct files.

5. Click the new Furniture Schedule tool. Click a piece of furniture; the entire Furniture construct highlights. Press Enter and then click a point to the right of the entire building to locate the upper-left corner of the schedule table itself. Press Enter again to complete the command; the schedule table object appears (see Figure 14.21).

There are question marks appearing in the cells of the schedule because the objects referenced in the schedule (MVBs from the Furniture construct) do not have property sets attached yet. It would be quite tedious to have to attach property sets to each MVB in the Furniture construct. Fortunately, there is a way to use the schedule table itself to attach property sets to the objects it schedules.

6. Select the furniture schedule, right-click, and choose Add All Property Sets. After a few moments, the schedule updates and fills in with lots of data.

The Layer Wildcard property lets you filter what appears in the schedule table by using wildcard characters to specify which layers to include. The asterisk character means that any string of characters and the vertical bar (called a *pipe*) is what separates XRef filenames from their layers. So a layer wildcard of `*|I-Furn` means to include the I-Furn layer from any XRefed drawing in the schedule. By typing this layer wildcard, you are effectively excluding the `Furniture|I-Furn-E` layer. XRefs reside on layer 0 (zero), so you should also include this layer in the layer wildcard. Multiple wildcards can be used simultaneously be separating them with commas.

FIGURE 14.20
Setting properties for
Furniture Schedule tool

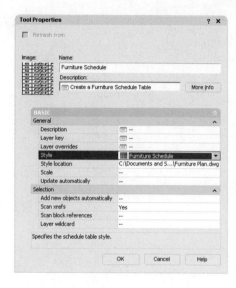

FIGURE 14.21
Furniture Schedule
after it is first inserted
into view

FURNITURE SCHEDULE										
Number	Room	Item	Manufacturer	Model	Color	Vendor ?	Delivery Date	Cost	Quantity	Total
?	?	?	?	?	?	●	?	?	130	?
									130	?

7. Select the furniture schedule again, and open the Properties palette. Type the following text into the Layer Wildcard property: **0,*|I-Furn.** Then press Enter (see Figure 14.22).

8. Look at the other options in the Properties palette (see Figure 14.23):

◆ Update Automatically keeps the schedule table up-to-date, but adversely affects system performance, so be careful about using this feature in complex projects. Leave this set to No.

◆ Set Add New Objects Automatically to Yes.

◆ Scan XRefs is already set to Yes because the schedule table is in a view file referencing property set data from an externally referenced construct.

◆ Set Scan Block References to Yes if you want the schedule table to access property set data inside block definitions. Leave it set to No in this tutorial.

◆ Leave Schedule External Drawing set to No. Set it to Yes if you insert the schedule table on a sheet and want to reference property set data through a view file.

◆ The Table Breaks controls affect how long tables appear when broken into two parts. Moving the schedule table's Maximum Page Height grip up does this.

FIGURE 14.22
Furniture schedule using layer wildcard to include new furniture only

FURNITURE SCHEDULE

Number	Room	Item	Manufacturer	Model	Color	Vendor			Delivery Date	Cost	Quantity	Total
						Acme	FurnCo	Greene				
2302	Reception	Coffee Table	---	---	---	●			---	0.00	1	0
2302	Reception	Lounge Chair	---	---	---			●	---	0.00	2	0
2302	Reception	Sofa	---	---	---	●			---	0.00	1	0
2302	Reception	Task Chair	---	---	---			●	---	0.00	1	0
2303	Conference	Conference Table	---	---	---			●	---	0.00	1	0
2304	Large Office	Coffee Table	---	---	---	●			---	0.00	1	0
2304	Large Office	Credenza	---	---	---		●		---	0.00	1	0
2304	Large Office	Desk	---	---	---	●			---	0.00	2	0
2304	Large Office	Sofa	---	---	---	●			---	0.00	1	0
2304	Large Office	Task Chair	---	---	---			●	---	0.00	1	0
2305	Large Office	Coffee Table	---	---	---	●			---	0.00	1	0
2305	Large Office	Credenza	---	---	---		●		---	0.00	2	0
2305	Large Office	Desk	---	---	---	●			---	0.00	1	0
2305	Large Office	Lounge Chair	---	---	---			●	---	0.00	2	0
2305	Large Office	Sofa	---	---	---	●			---	0.00	1	0
2305	Large Office	Task Chair	---	---	---			●	---	0.00	1	0
2307	Small Office	Desk	---	---	---	●			---	0.00	1	0
2307	Small Office	Task Chair	---	---	---			●	---	0.00	1	0
2308	Small Office	Desk	---	---	---	●			---	0.00	1	0
2308	Small Office	Task Chair	---	---	---			●	---	0.00	1	0
2309	Small Office	Desk	---	---	---	●			---	0.00	1	0
2309	Small Office	Task Chair	---	---	---			●	---	0.00	1	0
2310	Small Office	Desk	---	---	---	●			---	0.00	1	0
2310	Small Office	Task Chair	---	---	---			●	---	0.00	1	0
2311	Small Office	Credenza	---	---	---		●		---	0.00	1	0
2311	Small Office	Desk	---	---	---	●			---	0.00	1	0
2311	Small Office	Task Chair	---	---	---			●	---	0.00	1	0
2312	Break Room	Table	---	---	---		●		---	0.00	1	0
2313	Large Office	Desk	---	---	---	●			---	0.00	1	0
2313	Large Office	Lounge Chair	---	---	---			●	---	0.00	2	0
2313	Large Office	Task Chair	---	---	---			●	---	0.00	1	0
2314	Conference	Conference Table	---	---	---			●	---	0.00	1	0
2315	Large Office	Desk	---	---	---	●			---	0.00	1	0
2315	Large Office	Lounge Chair	---	---	---			●	---	0.00	2	0
2315	Large Office	Task Chair	---	---	---			●	---	0.00	1	0
2316	Break Room	Table	---	---	---		●		---	0.00	1	0
2323	Training Center	Desk	---	---	---	●			---	0.00	12	0
2323	Training Center	Task Chair	---	---	---			●	---	0.00	12	0
2324	Open Office	Sofa	---	---	---	●			---	0.00	1	0
2337	Workstation	Task Chair	---	---	---			●	---	0.00	21	0
											88	0

FIGURE 14.23
Schedule Table Properties

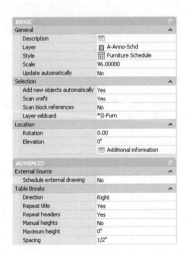

If you want to include multiple floors in one schedule, it is possible to add the schedule table to a sheet and have it reference a remote view drawing. This doesn't violate the rule of keeping specific data out of sheet files because the data in a schedule table is generated anew each time the sheet file is opened for printing or publishing. In such a case, create a composite view file that references multiple levels. When a schedule table on a sheet references a composite view, the view passes the property set data referenced in its constructs to the table.

Editing Scheduled Property Set Data

At this point much of the data has appeared in the furniture schedule, but there are double dashes (--) in numerous cells. Double dashes indicate that although property sets have been attached to the scheduled objects, no data is yet stored in them. Cells will be blank if double dashes haven't been set as the default in the property set definitions. We'll rectify this situation by editing the property set data directly in the cells of the schedule table.

1. Select the furniture schedule, right-click, and choose Edit Table Cell from the shortcut menu. Click the double dash in the Manufacturer column for the coffee table in reception (room number 2302). A warning dialog box appears, informing you that data from this cell comes from a referenced style or definition. In this case it comes from the style-based ManufacturerStyles property set definition. Click Yes to continue (you wouldn't see this warning if the referenced property set definition were object-based).

WARNING Be careful not to select the border of the schedule table while in Edit Table Cell mode or you'll be editing all the items at once.

2. The Edit Property Set Data worksheet appears. Under ManufacturerStyles, set Color to Slate, Cost to 495, Manufacturer to Hill Inc., and Model to Classic. Under VendorClass, set Delivery-Date to 4/23/06 and click OK. Notice that VendorProperty is set to Acme and cannot be edited here—remember this was already chosen as a classification for the MVB Coffee Table style (see Figure 14.24).

FIGURE 14.24
Editing property set data within a table cell

3. Continue repeating the last step, entering the following data (or data you make up) into the schedule table cells:

Item	Manufacturer	Model	Color	Delivery Date	Cost
Lounge Chair	Barker	Bentwood	Sandstone	5/15/06	1295
Sofa	Lemon Mfg.	Italian	Black	4/12/06	2250
Task Chair	Barker	Freedom	Red	4/23/06	750
Conference Table	Barker	EX-453	Ash	6/01/06	3500
Credenza	Lemon Mfg.	Corbu	Walnut	5/15/06	1800
Desk	Modern Design	Drafting	Charcoal	4/12/06	1250
Table	Lemon Mfg.	TL-194	Ash	6/01/06	750

Item	Color	Cost	Manufacturer	Model	Delivery Date
Lounge Chair	Sandstone	1295	Barker	Bentwood	5/15/06
Sofa	Black	2250	Lemon Mfg.	Italian	4/12/06
Task Chair	Red	750	Barker	Freedom	4/23/06
Conference Table	Ash	3500	Barker	EX-453	6/01/06
Credenza	Walnut	1800	Lemon Mfg.	Corbu	5/15/06
Desk	Charcoal	1250	Modern Design	Drafting	4/12/06
Table	Ash	750	Lemon Mfg.	TL-194	6/01/06

Press Enter when you are done to complete the ScheduleCellEdit command.

4. Observe that there are 88 items at the bottom of the Quantity column. Save the Furniture Plan.dwg view file and leave it open.

5. Select the Constructs tab in the Project Navigator. Double-click the Furniture construct to open it.

6. So you can see the effect of changing a classification assignment, select one of the sofa objects, right-click, and choose Edit Multi-View Block Definition from the shortcut menu. In the Multi-View Block Definition Properties dialog box, select the Classifications tab, change the Vendor classification to FurnCo, and click OK.

7. Copy a new credenza into the conference room at the bottom of the plan. Rotate it and move it into a suitable location. Save and close the Furniture.dwg construct file.

8. Switch back to the Furniture Plan.dwg view file. Right-click the Manage XRefs icon in the drawing tray and choose Reload XRefs from the shortcut menu.

9. Notice that nothing has changed in the schedule table. This may be surprising because you set Add New Objects Automatically to Yes earlier. However, the table was not updated because Update Automatically is set to No. Select the furniture schedule, right-click, and choose Update Schedule Table. Some Vendor matrix dots change position because of the change you made to the sofa's classification in the construct. Also notice there are now 89 items listed at the bottom of the Quantity column. The total cost is also listed at the bottom of the Total column as $98,095. Toggle LWT on in the drawing status bar to show lineweights. Figure 14.25 shows the completed furniture schedule.

FIGURE 14.25
Completed furniture schedule

						Vendor						
Number	Room	Item	Manufacturer	Model	Color	Acme	FurnCo	Greene	Delivery Date	Cost	Quantity	Total
2302	Reception	Coffee Table	Hill Inc.	Classic	Slate	●			4/23/06	495.00	1	495
2302	Reception	Lounge Chair	Barker	Bentwood	Sandstone			●	5/15/06	1295.00	2	2590
2302	Reception	Sofa	Modern Design	Italian	Black		●		4/12/06	2250.00	1	2250
2302	Reception	Task Chair	Barker	Freedom	Red			●	4/23/06	750.00	1	750
2303	Conference	Conference Table	Barker	Ex-453	Ash			●	6/01/06	3500.00	1	3500
2303	Conference	Credenza	Lemon Mfg.	Corbu	Walnut		●		5/15/06	1800.00	1	1800
2304	Large Office	Coffee Table	Hill Inc.	Classic	Slate	●			4/23/06	495.00	1	495
2304	Large Office	Credenza	Lemon Mfg.	Corbu	Walnut		●		5/15/06	1800.00	1	1800
2304	Large Office	Desk	Modern Design	Drafting	Charcoal	●			4/12/06	1250.00	2	2500
2304	Large Office	Sofa	Modern Design	Italian	Black		●		4/12/06	2250.00	1	2250
2304	Large Office	Task Chair	Barker	Freedom	Red			●	4/23/06	750.00	1	750
2305	Large Office	Coffee Table	Hill Inc.	Classic	Slate	●			4/23/06	495.00	1	495
2305	Large Office	Credenza	Lemon Mfg.	Corbu	Walnut		●		5/15/06	1800.00	2	3600
2305	Large Office	Desk	Modern Design	Drafting	Charcoal	●			4/12/06	1250.00	1	1250
2305	Large Office	Lounge Chair	Barker	Bentwood	Sandstone			●	5/15/06	1295.00	2	2590
2305	Large Office	Sofa	Modern Design	Italian	Black		●		4/12/06	2250.00	1	2250
2305	Large Office	Task Chair	Barker	Freedom	Red			●	4/23/06	750.00	1	750
2307	Small Office	Desk	Modern Design	Drafting	Charcoal	●			4/12/06	1250.00	1	1250
2307	Small Office	Task Chair	Barker	Freedom	Red			●	4/23/06	750.00	1	750
2308	Small Office	Desk	Modern Design	Drafting	Charcoal	●			4/12/06	1250.00	1	1250
2308	Small Office	Task Chair	Barker	Freedom	Red			●	4/23/06	750.00	1	750
2309	Small Office	Desk	Modern Design	Drafting	Charcoal	●			4/12/06	1250.00	1	1250
2309	Small Office	Task Chair	Barker	Freedom	Red			●	4/23/06	750.00	1	750
2310	Small Office	Desk	Modern Design	Drafting	Charcoal	●			4/12/06	1250.00	1	1250
2310	Small Office	Task Chair	Barker	Freedom	Red			●	4/23/06	750.00	1	750
2311	Small Office	Credenza	Lemon Mfg.	Corbu	Walnut		●		5/15/06	1800.00	1	1800
2311	Small Office	Desk	Modern Design	Drafting	Charcoal	●			4/12/06	1250.00	1	1250
2311	Small Office	Task Chair	Barker	Freedom	Red			●	4/23/06	750.00	1	750
2312	Break Room	Table	Lemon Mfg.	TI-194	Ash		●		6/01/06	750.00	1	750
2313	Large Office	Desk	Modern Design	Drafting	Charcoal	●			4/12/06	1250.00	1	1250
2313	Large Office	Lounge Chair	Barker	Bentwood	Sandstone			●	5/15/06	1295.00	2	2590
2313	Large Office	Task Chair	Barker	Freedom	Red			●	4/23/06	750.00	1	750
2314	Conference	Conference Table	Barker	Ex-453	Ash			●	6/01/06	3500.00	1	3500
2315	Large Office	Desk	Modern Design	Drafting	Charcoal	●			4/12/06	1250.00	1	1250
2315	Large Office	Lounge Chair	Barker	Bentwood	Sandstone			●	5/15/06	1295.00	2	2590
2315	Large Office	Task Chair	Barker	Freedom	Red			●	4/23/06	750.00	1	750
2316	Break Room	Table	Lemon Mfg.	TI-194	Ash		●		6/01/06	750.00	1	750
2323	Training Center	Desk	Modern Design	Drafting	Charcoal	●			4/12/06	1250.00	12	15000
2323	Training Center	Task Chair	Barker	Freedom	Red			●	4/23/06	750.00	12	9000
2324	Open Office	Sofa	Modern Design	Italian	Black		●		4/12/06	2250.00	1	2250
2337	Workstation	Task Chair	Barker	Freedom	Red			●	4/23/06	750.00	21	15750
											89	98095

FURNITURE SCHEDULE

TIP To export a schedule table to another application, select the table, right-click, and choose Export. The Export Schedule Table dialog box that appears has options for saving in Microsoft Excel 97 (*.xls) format, plus tab-delimited (*.txt) and comma-delimited (*.csv) formats. The exported schedule will not be linked to the data in ADT, but might be useful in business studies or reports you may make with other software.

10. Toggle LWT off. Save and close the Furniture Plan.dwg view file. Congratulations, you have completed the schedules tutorial. You should be able to create any kind of schedule if you practice what you have learned in this section.

Using Display Themes

New!

Display themes are new in ADT 2006 and affect how objects are displayed based upon the property data that is attached to them. ADT's out-of-the-box display theme styles include themes by space size and fire rating. These display themes colorize spaces according to their sizes, and colorize walls and doors according to their fire ratings, respectively. You can create your own display themes by setting rules that control how objects are shown based on their property set data. To explore display themes, let's apply some out-of-the-box display theme styles and investigate their effects.

1. Select the Views tab in the Project Navigator. Double-click the Construction Plan to open it.

2. Set the Document palette group current and select the Scheduling palette. Click the Theme By Fire Rating tool. Click a point to the right of the entire building to locate the upper-left corner of the display theme legend. Press Enter to complete the command. Portions of the drawing immediately appear with solid fill colors that correspond to the swatches in the Fire Rating Legend (see Figure 14.26).

FIGURE 14.26
After adding a display theme by fire rating

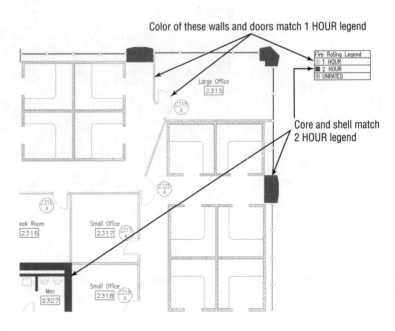

Color of these walls and doors match 1 HOUR legend

Core and shell match 2 HOUR legend

Adding the display theme object immediately altered the way selected walls and doors appear. These objects were altered because they have property set definitions attached with data that matches rules defined in the display theme style. To understand how this works, let's edit the display theme style.

3. Select the Fire Rating Legend, which is actually a Display Theme object. Right-click and choose Edit Display Theme Style from the shortcut menu (see Figure 14.27).

   Each theme setting in the top pane has its own set of rules in the bottom pane. Theme index 1 is selected in the top pane—it has two rules defined in the bottom pane with indices 1.1 and 1.2. The first theme setting is for the fire rating 1 HOUR; it will be shown in color 41 with a solid hatch pattern. None of the other columns in the top pane apply to solid hatch patterns, so you can ignore them. The bottom pane reveals any objects having the WallStyles:FireRating or DoorObjects:FireRating property, and property set definitions will be affected if their values equal 1 HOUR. If affected, the objects display according to the theme settings in the upper pane.

4. Click Index 2 in the upper pane. The dialog box looks the same, except the lower pane indices are 2.1 and 2.2 and the Value column reads 2 HOUR in its two cells.

NOTE   Objects that do not have property set values matching display theme rules are not affected—they will continue to display as they did prior to the insertion of the display theme legend.

5. Select the Legend Format tab. The display theme legend format controls (see Figure 14.28) are quite simple and straightforward compared with schedule tables. The Symbol drop-down list allows you to choose a square or circle swatch that appears in the legend. The Legend Display Properties are likewise very simple, so there is no need to belabor the point. Click OK to close the dialog box. Save and close the `Construction Plan.dwg` view file.

6. To really understand the whole picture, open the Core element and check out its walls and doors. Select the Constructs tab in the Project Navigator and double-click the Core element to open it. Select one of the core walls, right-click, and choose Edit Wall Style from the shortcut menu. Select the General tab and click the Property Sets button; the Edit Property Set Data worksheet appears. The core walls have the very property set data that was referenced by the display theme rule—this is why the fire rating display theme changes the core walls' appearance in the construction plan view. Click Cancel and Cancel again.

FIGURE 14.27
Display theme
design rules

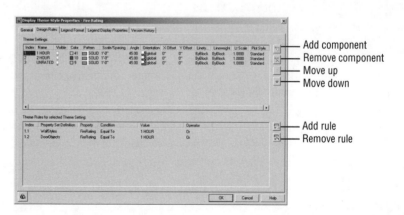

FIGURE 14.28
Display theme legend
format controls

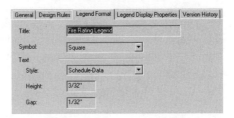

FIGURE 14.29
Core walls (left) and
doors (right) have Fire–
Rating property set to
2 HOUR.

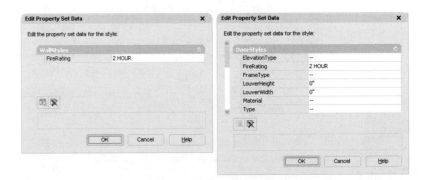

7. Select one of the double doors, right-click, and choose Edit Door Style from the shortcut menu. Select the General tab and click the Property Sets button; the DoorStyles property set also has a FireRating property that is set to 2 HOUR (see Figure 14.29). Click Cancel and Cancel again. Close the `Core.dwg` element file without saving.

Let's investigate another out-of-the-box display theme in the Space Plan. This time, we'll have to add property sets to get the display theme to affect space objects.

1. Click the Views tab in the Project Navigator and double-click the Space Plan to open it.

2. Click the Theme By Space Size tool in the Scheduling palette. Click a point to the right of the entire building to locate the upper-left corner of the display theme legend. Press Enter to complete the command. Although the Space Size Legend appears, it doesn't seem to affect any of the spaces (see Figure 14.30).

3. Select the Space Size Legend, right-click, and choose Edit Display Theme Style from the shortcut menu. Select the Design Rules tab and investigate the theme settings and theme rules. All the theme rules are based on the SpaceStyles property set definition. This is the key—you must attach this property set definition to all the space objects for them to be affected by the display theme. Click Cancel.

4. Select the Constructs tab in the Project Navigator and double-click the Spaces construct to open it. Choose Format ➢ Style Manager. Expand the Spaces.dwg, Architectural Objects, and Spaces Styles nodes in the tree pane. Select the first space style—Break Room.

5. In the content pane, select the General tab and click the Property Sets button; the Edit Property Set Data worksheet appears. Click the Add Property Sets button; the Add Property Sets worksheet appears, listing all the property sets that apply to space styles—in this case, there is only one—but it is what we need: SpaceStyles (see Figure 14.31). Click OK in both worksheets to close them.

6. Repeat the last step for each space style in the Spaces construct. Click OK when you're done to close the Style Manager. Save and close the `Space.dwg` construct file.

7. Switch back to the Space Plan view and reload its XRefs. The spaces show solid hatching colors controlled by the display theme style (see Figure 14.32). You'll see colors on screen but not in the figures of this book. Now you should understand how display themes work! Save the `Space Plan.dwg` view file.

FIGURE 14.30
Space Size Legend

Space Size Legend
0–50
51–100
101–150
151–200
201–250
251–300
301–350
351–400
401–450
451–500
501–550
551–600
601–650
651–700
701–750
751–800
801–850
851–900
901–950
951–1000
1001–

FIGURE 14.31
Adding the SpaceStyles property set to a space style

FIGURE 14.32
Space Plan showing
space size display theme

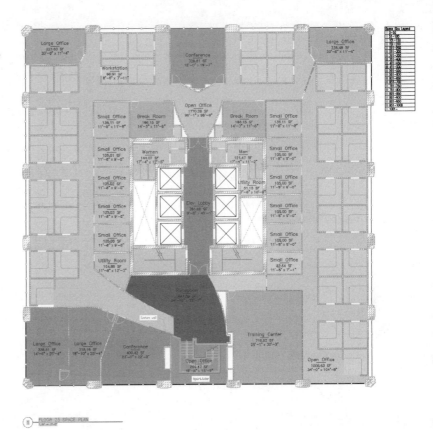

8. Select the Space Size Legend, right-click, and choose Disable Display Theme from the shortcut menu. The solid hatch colors disappear, and a diagonal line is drawn through the Space Size Legend to show that it is defunct. This can be helpful if you want to temporarily turn off the display theme without erasing its legend. You can reapply the display theme at any time through the Space Size Legend shortcut menu. Close the Space Plan without saving.

Working with Areas

Although space objects calculate their own areas, they are not ideally suited to the task of calculating more complex areas that span more than one space. The area toolset was expressly designed for this purpose—to calculate floor areas for government plan approval, calculate leasing rates, and other facility management uses. Area objects are best used concurrently in a project with space objects.

The area toolset includes area objects and their styles, plus many other tools that work together for the purpose of ultimately generating an area evaluation document in Microsoft Excel (*.xls) or text form (*.txt). In this tutorial, you'll learn how to create calculation modifier styles, name definitions, and area group styles—all for the purpose of creating an area group template that provides a structure to attach area objects. After you have attached area objects to the group template, it will be used to generate the area evaluation document. The group template you'll build can easily be adapted and reused in your future projects.

You can make calculating areas as easy or as complex as the project requires. You might use the area toolset to generate an area evaluation document and stop there, or you might continue and create an area plan with area tags and area schedules that can be included in your published sheet set.

TIP   Check the Document Tool Catalog in the Content Browser for some basic area schedule tags, along with area and area group styles. You will also find area property set definitions and area schedule table styles in the `Schedule Table (Imperial).dwg` content file.

Here you will simply learn the area toolset and generate an area evaluation document. You will create an area plan for this purpose, but will not include it in a sheet set.

1. Select the Views tab in the Project Navigator. Right-click the View category and choose New View Drawing ➢ General from the shortcut menu.

2. Type the name **Area Plan** on the first page of the Add General View worksheet. Click the Next button.

3. Check Level 23 Division 1 and click the Next button. Uncheck the Furniture and Spaces constructs and click the Finish button.

4. Double-click the Area Plan node in the Project Navigator to open it and then zoom to the extents of the drawing. Leave the `Area Plan.dwg` view file open until the end of this section.

Creating a Calculation Modifier Style

Some governmental jurisdictions require common areas to be adjusted by multiplying their areas with a scalar factor. Calculation Modifier Styles are used to fulfill this particular requirement. You can ignore this feature if the building codes in your region do not require such modification.

WARNING   Check your local building codes for specific instructions to calculate building areas. Do not use this book as a guide to building codes or calculating specific areas.

1. Choose Format ➢ Style Manager. Expand the Area Plan.dwg and Documentation Objects nodes in the tree pane. Right-click the Calculation Modifier Styles node and choose New from the shortcut menu.

2. Type **15 Percent Commons Factor** as the name of the new calculation modifier style and press Enter.

3. Click the Apply To tab in the content pane. Uncheck Perimeter so the style applies only to modifying area calculations.

4. Click the Definition tab. In the Parameters group, click the Add button. Type **CommonsFactor** as the variable name. Double-click the value and type **1.15** to enter a 15% increase.

5. In the Formula group, notice that the Data variable is AreaValue. Type **AreaValue* CommonsFactor** in the Expression text box (see Figure 14.33).

6. Click the Apply button and leave the Style Manager open.

Creating Name Definitions

Name definitions are an optional way to identify area objects. You can manually type in names for area objects, but predefined name definitions make naming many area objects more efficient. This feature is especially useful if you are preparing area plans for numerous floors and/or buildings. Name definitions are an entirely optional feature and are extremely simple.

1. Right-click the Name Definitions node in the tree pane and choose New from the shortcut menu. Give the new node the name **TenantNames**.

2. Click the Content tab and click the New button. Type the name **Chases**.

3. Repeat the last step, creating the following names in the TenantNames definition: **Core**, **Empty Space**, **Entire Building**, and **Tenant** (see Figure 14.34). That's it; rejoice because you have discovered the simplest object in all of ADT.

4. Click the Apply button and leave the Style Manager open.

Defining Area Group Styles

Area groups are styled objects that you will attach area objects to later on. Each area group can have multiple area objects attached. Area groups report the sum of the floor areas of their attached objects. Area groups are used as an organizational tool to categorize types of areas such as gross, usable, and rentable floor areas.

FIGURE 14.33
Defining a calculation modifier style

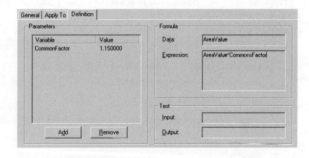

FIGURE 14.34
Creating name definitions

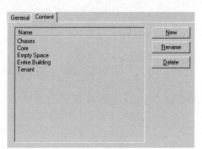

Area groups have display properties that control both how they appear and how their attached entities appear. You will create a series of style overrides to customize the way each area group style (and its attached areas) appears.

1. Right-click the Area Group Styles node and choose New from the shortcut menu. Give the new node the name **Gross**.

2. Choose the Display Properties tab in the content pane. Place a check in the Style Override column of the Plan display representation; the Display Properties dialog box appears. Toggle on its Hatch display component and change its color to Green. In addition, toggle on the Area Connection Line display component and change its color to Green (see Figure 14.35). Click OK to close the dialog box.

3. It can be useful to use the Presentation display configuration when working with area groups (see Chapter 2, "Object Display"). We will create the appropriate style override for this eventuality; place a check in the Style Override column for the Plan Presentation display configuration. Toggle on its Hatch display component and make it Green. Click OK to close the dialog box.

4. Repeat steps 1–3, creating style overrides for both the Plan and Plan Presentation display representations for each of the following area group styles (and their override colors):

Area Group Style	Override Color
Commons	Cyan
Usable	Blue
Vertical Penetrations	Magenta

5. Click the Apply button and leave the Style Manager open.

FIGURE 14.35
Creating display property style overrides for area group styles

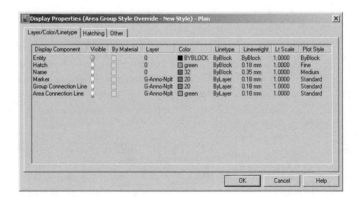

Working with Group Templates

The Building Owners and Managers Association (BOMA) publishes guidelines for calculating floor areas in North America. There are BOMA group templates, property set definitions, schedule tags, and area schedules in content drawings that ship with ADT. On other continents, there are different guidelines to follow that conform to your local building codes. Group templates provide a means to organize the particular requirements of your locale into a hierarchical structure that is used to facilitate area calculations. In this section you will build a hypothetical group template to become familiar with the area toolset. It is up to you to research your local requirements and apply the area toolset to them.

CREATING A GROUP TEMPLATE

After you have a calculation modifier style, name definitions, and area group styles, you are in the position to design a group template. Group templates define a hierarchical structure that controls how area groups are related to one another. Although group templates are again an optional feature, it is worth defining one because it saves time; you can reuse the group template for multiple floors and projects.

1. Right-click the Group Templates node in the tree pane and choose New from the shortcut menu. Give the new node the name **Hypothetical** because you will have to adapt it to meet your local building code requirements.

2. Select the Content tab and type **Gross Floor Area** in the Name text box in the General group. Choose Gross from the Style drop-down list and TenantNames from the Name Definition drop-down list.

3. Right-click the new Gross Floor Area node in the left pane on the Content tab and choose New from the shortcut menu. Type **Common Floor Area** as the name of the new child node. Choose Commons from the Style drop-down list and TenantNames from the Name Definition drop-down list.

4. Right-click the Gross Floor Area node in the left pane on the Content tab and choose New from the shortcut menu. Type **Usable Floor Area** as the name of the new child node. Choose Usable from the Style drop-down list and TenantNames from the Name Definition drop-down list.

5. Right-click the Gross Floor Area node in the left pane on the Content tab and choose New from the shortcut menu. Type **Vertical Penetration Area** as the name of the new child node. Choose Vertical Penetrations from the Style drop-down list and TenantNames from the Name Definition drop-down list.

6. Right-click the Usable Floor Area node (not Gross Floor Area, as you have done before) and choose New from the shortcut menu. Type **Rentable Space** as the name of the new child node. Choose Usable from the Style drop-down list and TenantNames from the Name Definition drop-down list. Click the Attach button in the Calculation Modifier Styles group. In the dialog box that appears, click OK to attach the 15 Percent Commons Factor calculation modifier style that you made earlier.

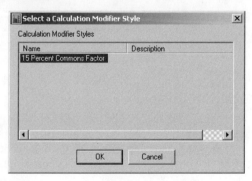

7. Right-click the Usable Floor Area node again and choose New from the shortcut menu. Type **Vacant Space** as the name of the new child node. Choose Usable from the Style drop-down list and TenantNames from the Name Definition drop-down list. Click the Attach button in the Calculation Modifier Styles group. In the dialog box that appears, click OK to attach the 15 Percent Commons Factor calculation modifier style that you made earlier (see Figure 14.36).

8. Click the OK button to close the Style Manager. Save and close the `Area Plan.dwg` view file.

INSERTING THE GROUP TEMPLATE

Inserting the group template is easy—you'll add it to the area plan. There is also a specialized command—AreaGroupLayout—you'll use to control the spacing between area group nodes in the group template.

1. Reopen the Area Plan view.

2. Make the Document palette group current in the Tool Palettes. Select the Scheduling palette.

3. Click the Area Group From Template tool and look in the Properties palette. Set Group Template to Hypothetical. Click a point off to the left side of the entire building. Six connected area group nodes appear.

4. Select the Gross Floor Area group. Right-click and choose Area Group Layout from the shortcut menu. The command line says the following:

```
Specify layout offset [Distance/Row offset/Column offset]:
```

Type **R** for row offset and press Enter. Type **5′** and press Enter. Type **C** for column offset. Type **5′** and press Enter twice to complete the command. The nodes appear farther apart for clarity (see Figure 14.37).

FIGURE 14.36
Designing a group template

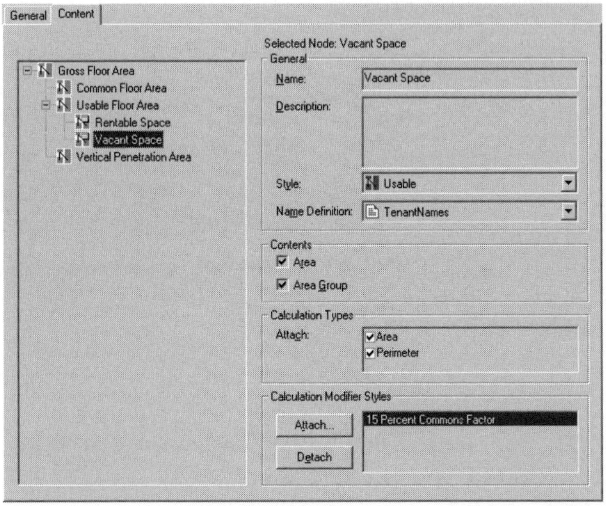

FIGURE 14.37
Inserting the area group template (left) after adjusting area group layout (right)

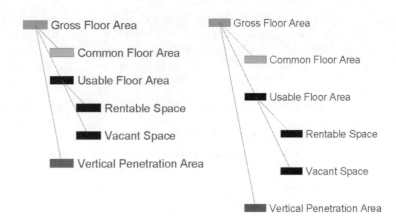

TIP You can move area group nodes individually, and they will remain connected to the other nodes in the group template with group connection lines.

   5. Save the Area Plan.dwg view file and leave it open.

Using Area Objects

The process we will follow in this tutorial is to create area objects and then attach them to area groups. However, you can also work the other way around—if you want to start with area objects and build a group template as you go, that is an equally valid approach.

CREATING AREA OBJECTS

Creating area objects works exactly like creating closed polylines. In addition, area objects are edited the same way that AEC Polygons and Space objects are: by using vertex and edge grips. You can also create area objects by applying Area tool properties to linework and AEC objects. This is a good option to use if you want to create areas from existing spaces and/or wall objects, for example. Here you will create new area objects from scratch.

   1. Select the Scheduling palette and click the Area tool. Zoom in on the building core and click its four corners. Type **C** for close and press Enter twice to end the command.

   2. Select the new area object by clicking its edge that passes by each set of double doors in the core. In the Properties palette, Calculated Area reads 2074 SF (square feet).

   3. Create another two area objects that trace the perimeters of the large chases in the core. Create six more square area objects that trace the elevator shafts.

   4. Create an area object that traces the outside edges of the entire building. You will have to zoom in and carefully select all the outer endpoints of the shell.

TIP Use the BOUNDARY command to create complex closed polylines that you can use to generate area objects.

5. Create an area object to enclose the spaces inside the 1 HOUR fire-rated partitions on the right side of the floor plan.

6. Create an area object to enclose the tenant space on the left side of the 1 HOUR fire-rated partitions.

MODIFYING AREA OBJECTS

Use vertex and edge grips to add and remove vertices along the closed perimeter of the area object if necessary. You can also use AEC Modify tools to change area object shapes. When you subtract one area from another, the subtracted object forms a hole in the enclosing area object, and the floor area of the subtraction is deducted from the total.

1. Select one of the area objects that trace a chase, right-click, and choose AEC Modify ➢ Merge from the shortcut menu.

2. Select the other chase and all six elevator shaft area objects and press Enter. Type **Y** to erase the existing linework and press Enter. All the vertical penetration areas are joined into a single area object.

3. Select the newly merged vertical penetration area in the core and look in the Properties palette. The Calculated Area should be 652 SF.

4. Select the first area object that you made—the one tracing the square building core. Right-click and choose AEC Modify ➢ Subtract from the shortcut menu. Select the vertical penetration area and press Enter. Type **N** to not erase the existing linework and press Enter.

5. Select the subtracted area and read its Calculated Area in the Properties palette—it should be 1422 SF (2074 − 652 = 1422 SF).

NOTE   Area styles have a Decomposed display representation that is useful in Germany and Japan, in which proof of areas must be visually represented.

ATTACHING AREA OBJECTS TO AREA GROUPS

The final step before generating an area evaluation document is to attach the area objects you made to the area group nodes that were placed into the drawing earlier.

1. Select the Gross Floor Area node, right-click, and choose Attach Areas/Area Groups. Select the appropriate area object and press Enter. A green line connects the area object and the area group node (see Figure 14.38).

2. Select the area object that is attached to the Gross Floor area group. In the Properties palette, change Name to Entire Building. The Name definition assigned in the group template is now available to the attached area object. Press Esc to deselect.

3. Attach all the appropriate area objects to their corresponding area group nodes. The Rentable space is the larger area that includes both conference rooms. The Vacant Space is the area to the right of the 1 HOUR fire rated partitions. Do not attach any area object to the Usable Floor Area group node (see Figure 14.39).

4. Save the Area Plan.dwg view file.

FIGURE 14.38
Attaching area object
to area group

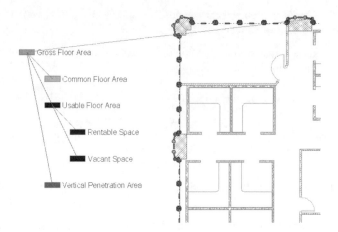

FIGURE 14.39
Area objects attached
to area group nodes

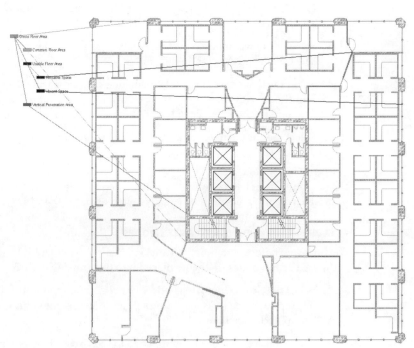

Generating an Area Evaluation Document

After you have attached area objects to area groups, you are finally ready to generate an area evaluation document. Creating this document is straightforward, although there are a number of options that you can set if so inclined.

1. Click the Area Evaluation tool in the Scheduling palette; the Area Evaluation dialog box appears. Place a check in the top node in the tree on the left to indicate that you want to generate an evaluation of all this drawing's area groups and area objects (see Figure 14.40).

2. Click the Evaluation Options button; the Evaluation Properties dialog box appears (see Figure 14.41). Read the ADT Help for details about any that are unfamiliar. Click Cancel.

3. Back in the Area Evaluation dialog box, click the Export Evaluation To Microsoft Excel button. The Open Template dialog box appears. Navigate to the following folder:

```
C:\Documents and Settings\All Users\Application Data\Autodesk\ADT 2006\enu\
Template\Evaluation Templates
```

Select the `Area Evaluation Template (1) - Portrait.xlt` template file and click Open.

FIGURE 14.40
Area Evaluation
dialog box

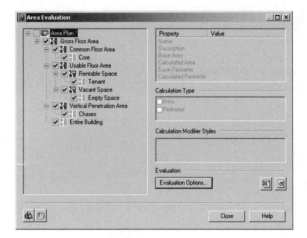

FIGURE 14.41
Evaluation Properties
dialog box

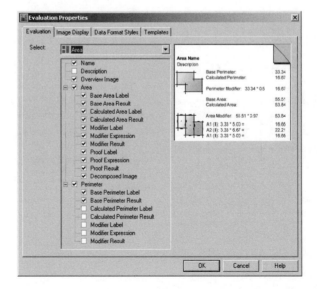

4. If you see a small dialog box that asks if you want to use the template as the default for Area Evaluation, click Yes.

5. The Save Excel Evaluation File dialog box appears. Save a file called `Area.xls` in your project folder. After a few moments a progress bar will appear in the Area Evaluation dialog box. When it finishes, click the Close button.

6. Open Microsoft Excel if you have it installed and open the `Area.xls` file (see Figure 14.42). The evaluation lists decomposed areas in the shape of triangles for proof of area reports. This file is not linked to ADT—you will have to re-create it if areas in your project change.

As you can see, the area toolset is extensive and allows for a great variety of area calculations. You should now be able to generate useful area evaluations that will help with government approval, leasing calculations, and facility-management tasks.

FIGURE 14.42

Area Evaluation in Excel

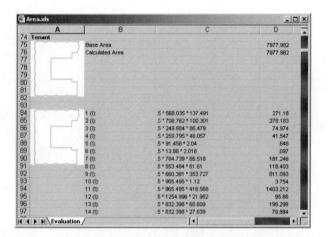

Summary

This chapter taught you about schedules by having you create a complex furniture schedule. Having that experience, you possess the skills to generate any type of schedule you want to create. In addition, you can now take advantage of the new display theme feature to make property set data visible in graphical form. Finally, you explored the area toolset and generated a hypothetical area evaluation for the sample project. Armed with this knowledge, you should be able to fashion area tools that apply to your jurisdiction and building codes, so you can create area evaluations for your own projects.

Chapter 15

Floor and Ceiling Plans

In addition to the space, construction, and furniture plans made in previous chapters, construction drawing sets often include a number of additional types of plans—including power and signal, finish, equipment, and reflected ceiling plans. This chapter's tutorial continues where we left off in the previous chapter and teaches you how to set up a power and signal floor plan.

After creating the appropriate elements, constructs, views and sheets in the sample project, you'll access and insert power and communication symbols that ship with ADT. You'll also learn how to create your own intelligent symbols that are sized according to the drawing scale and automatically inserted on the correct layer.

Later on you'll set up a reflected ceiling plan and make the necessary changes to the project structure. Then you'll create ceiling grids in the Reflected display configuration and clip them with space objects. In addition, you'll insert lighting as mask block references—you'll attach them to ceiling grids to hide portions of the grid that are obscured by the addition of the ceiling fixtures. This chapter's topics include:

◆   Creating Floor Plans

◆   Creating Reflected Ceiling Plans

Creating Floor Plans

Before you create plans, you must ask yourself how they will fit into the overall project structure. Would it be better to create a construct or a view? The answer depends on the content of the plan you wish to make. For example, let's consider the case of a finish plan.

Finish plans do not typically introduce new building components. Instead, they usually employ schedule tags to identify floor, wall, base, and ceiling surface finishes. Depending on the complexity of your project, you might choose to separate floor and wall finishes into different drawings, or combine them into one. On the other hand, you might choose to include finish tags on the construction plan in a simple project and forgo creating a separate finish plan altogether.

In either case, finish plans are really an exercise in adding (and possibly designing) schedule tags that make hidden property set data visible, a process you learned in the previous two chapters. Therefore, we can conclude that finish plans should always be created as views because they are yet another form of documentation that references the property set data stored in constructs.

Now let's consider the case of an equipment plan. The term *equipment* might refer to many different types of objects, depending upon the class of architecture involved. For example, equipment might include generators, networking hardware, computers, fax machines, copiers, clothes washers and dryers, water heaters, vending machines, dishwashers, refrigerators, ranges, kitchen appliances, and so on.

Equipment is not a form of documentation, and therefore belongs in a construct. However, you probably don't want equipment to show up in every view, so it is usually best to save equipment in a separate construct. You can then overlay other constructs within the equipment construct to help you locate equipment relative to other objects, such as partitions.

Ultimately you'll also need an Equipment Plan view that references the Equipment construct in addition to other constructs. If you design schedule tags and/or schedules to document equipment, they belong in the view instead of the construct, just as the furniture schedules you created in Chapter 14, "Schedules, Display Themes, and Areas," belonged with the Furniture Plan view.

Before you make a new plan drawing, step back and think through the repercussions it will have on the project structure. Work through your own thought experiment to guide you in deciding whether to create only a view, or both a construct and a view.

NOTE   As a further alternative for creating plans, in the "Creating Reflected Ceiling Plans" section you'll use the display system to compartmentalize information within a construct.

Setting Up a Power and Signal Plan

Aside from adding symbols and creating a symbol legend, no further documentation is anticipated for a typical power and signal plan. None of the power and signal symbols typically references property set data stored in constructs. It makes the most sense to add symbols directly to a view rather than a construct.

You will approach the process of creating a view in a different order than you learned in Chapter 5, "Project Management": First you'll make a sheet, then an element, and finally a view and a model space view. In the end you'll drop the model space view on the sheet, and it will fit perfectly. This technique allows you to measure space available for drawings on a sheet and transfer this information to a view via an element. This tutorial uses the same project you have been using in previous chapters.

1. Copy this chapter's folder from the companion DVD into the following folder on your hard drive:

   ```
   C:\Documents and Settings\<username>\My Documents\Autodesk\My Projects
   ```

2. Choose File ➤ Project Browser. Navigate to the folder listed in the previous step and double-click the Chapter 15 project to set it current. Choose to repath the project files if prompted. Right-click Chapter 15 node in the Project Browser and choose Project Properties. Repath each of the templates and close the Project Properties worksheet. Click the Close button to close the Project Browser.

WARNING   Repathing templates is necessary when opening projects made by different users and/or when projects are stored on different drive letters (when relative pathing is turned off).

3. Select the Sheets tab in the Project Navigator. Verify that you are in Sheet Set View by clicking the button at the top of the Sheets palette. Expand the Architectural node, right-click the Plans subset and choose New ➤ Sheet. If you are prompted to browse for a new template, choose the AEC Sheet (Imperial Stb).dwt template with the Arch F (30 x 42) layout. (In the New Sheet dialog box, type **A103** in the Number text box and **Power & Signal Plan** in the Sheet Title text box. Click OK to close the New Sheet dialog box. The A103 Power & Signal Plan sheet node appears in the Project Navigator (see Figure 15.1).

FIGURE 15.1
Creating a new sheet
(left) that appears in
Project Navigator (right)

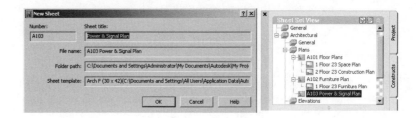

4. Double-click the A103 Power & Signal Plan sheet to open it. Click the Polygon button on the Shapes toolbar. The command line says the following:

```
Enter number of sides <3>:
```

Type **4** to make a square and press Enter. The command line says the following:

```
Specify center of polygon or [Edge]:
```

Type **E** for edge mode and press Enter. Click the lower-left corner of the title block and then click the polygon's second endpoint along a horizontal line between the 3 and 4 labels on the title block (see Figure 15.2).

5. Select the new square (actually a polyline entity) and change it to layer G-Anno-Nplt.

You are using this layer because it is used for general annotation and does not plot. I'll refer to the polyline just drawn as a *frame*—ultimately used to transfer the dimensions of the drawing area on the sheet to the view file. We will use an element as the mechanism to transfer this graphical information within the project structure.

FIGURE 15.2
Drawing a square that
fills half the allotted
space on the title block

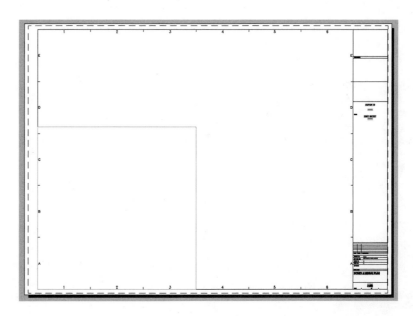

6. Reselect the frame, right-click, and choose Clipboard ➤ Cut from the shortcut menu.

7. Select the Constructs tab of the Project Navigator. Right-click the Elements category and choose New ➤ Element from the shortcut menu. In the Add Element worksheet that appears, type **Frame** in the Name text box (see Figure 15.3). Click OK to close the worksheet.

8. Double-click the Frame element to open it. Right-click in the drawing window and choose Clipboard ➤ Paste to Original Coordinates. Zoom to the extents of the drawing. The frame polyline appears.

9. It is necessary to scale the frame up to match the drawing scale of the view you will be creating. Select the frame polyline, right-click, and choose Basic Modify Tools ➤ Scale. Click the lower right corner of the frame polyline as the base point. The command line says the following:

```
Specify scale factor or [Copy/Reference] <0'-1">:
```

Type **96** (the scale factor for $1/8"=1'-0"$ scale) and press Enter. Zoom to the extents of the drawing again. Save and close the Frame element.

10. Choose the Views tab of the Project Navigator. Right-click the Views category and choose New View Drawing ➤ General. Type **Power & Signal Plan** in the Name text box in the Add General View worksheet. Click the Next button. Check division 1 on the 23rd floor (the only choice possible in this project) and click Next. Uncheck the Spaces construct (see Figure 15.4) and click Finish to close the Add General View worksheet.

FIGURE 15.3
Creating an element (left) that appears on the Constructs tab (right)

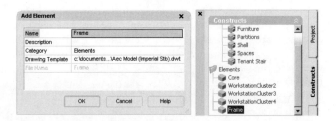

FIGURE 15.4
Adding the Power & Signal Plan view in the worksheet (left) and in the Project Navigator (right)

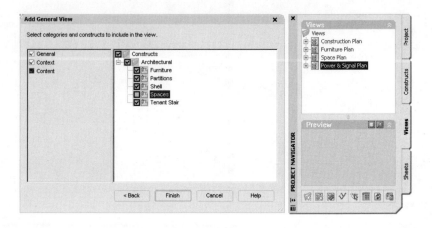

11. Double-click the Power & Signal Plan view to open it. Select the Constructs tab in the Project Navigator. Right-click the Frame element and choose XRef Overlay from the shortcut menu. Zoom to the extents of the drawing.

12. Use object snaps and object tracking to move the frame so it surrounds and is centered on the building—do not move any of the building constructs from their original coordinates (see Figure 15.5). Save the `Power & Signal Plan.dwg` view drawing.

The overlaid frame element in the view represents the drawing area on the sheet in $1/8''$-$1'$-$0''$ scale. You will match the size of a new model space view (MSV) to the frame element in the view. Next add a title mark and drag and drop the MSV into the sheet. The sheet view will then perfectly fit the sheet.

1. Right-click the Power & Signal Plan view node in the Project Navigator and choose New Model Space View from the shortcut menu.

2. Type **Floor 23 Power & Signal Plan** in the Name text box in the Add Model Space View worksheet. Click the Define View Window button and click two opposite endpoints of the frame element in the drawing window. Click OK to close the worksheet, and the MSV is created (see Figure 15.6).

3. Make the Document palette group current in the Tool Palettes. Choose the Callouts palette. Click the Title Mark tool, that adds a title mark with number.

Move the cursor over the MSV in the drawing window and notice that a large title mark symbol highlights. Click the first point just below the lower left corner of the building within the MSV. Click the second point a short distance horizontally from the previous point. The title mark with number appears (see composite Figure 15.7).

FIGURE 15.5
Centering the overlaid frame element on the building in the view

FIGURE 15.6
Creating a Model Space
View in the worksheet
(left) causes a child node
to appear in the Project
Navigator (right).

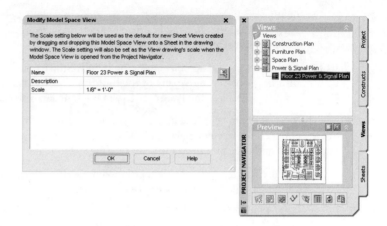

FIGURE 15.7
Choosing a Title Mark
tool (top left), locating
symbol (top right), and
the resulting title mark
(bottom)

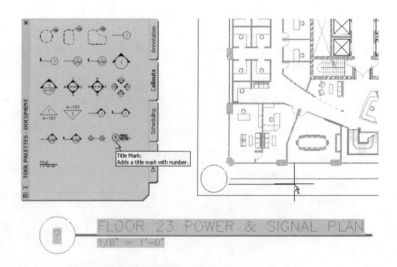

4. Notice that there is a question mark in the number field inside the title mark symbol. The number that goes in the title bubble will be automatically resolved when you convert the MSV to a sheet view. Save the `Power & Signal Plan.dwg` view file. Choose Window ➢ A103 Power & Signal Plan.dwg to switch to the sheet drawing.

5. Drag the Floor 23 Power & Signal Plan MSV node from the Views palette to the sheet drawing. Click a point on the sheet to convert the MSV to a sheet view. Move the sheet view so it is centered on the available space inside the title block (see Figure 15.8).

FIGURE 15.8
Converting a model
space view to a sheet
view by inserting it
onto a sheet

Drag MSV from View palette...

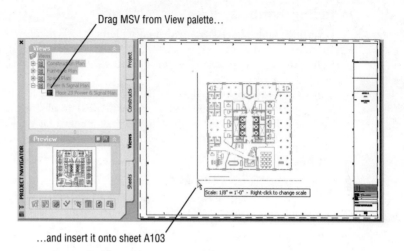

...and insert it onto sheet A103

6. Select the Sheets tab in the Project Navigator. Notice that a sheet view child node appears below the A103 Power & Signal Plan sheet you made earlier. The sheet view is called 1 Floor 23 Power & Signal Plan because it is drawing number one on the sheet and it was inserted from the Floor 23 Power & Signal Plan MSV.

Save and close the A103 Power & Signal Plan.dwg sheet file.

7. Switch back to the Power & Signal Plan.dwg view file if it did not automatically appear after closing the sheet. Zoom in on the title mark and verify that it has a one in its title bubble. If it does not, select the title mark and drag it onto the sheet view node in the Project Navigator. This process is called *post-linking*, and is occasionally necessary when ADT loses track of field associations. It is hard to predict when you might need to post-link title marks, so it is good to understand how to do it should the need arise.

8. Save the Power & Signal Plan.dwg view file. You have successfully registered the Power & Signal drawing in the project. Other plans can be added to the project by following the same procedures.

Adding Symbols

Power and signal plans typically display a plethora of symbols representing electrical power, telecommunications, and heating/ventilation/air conditioning (HVAC) devices. Examples of these symbols might include power receptacles, junction boxes, phone and data jacks, light switches, occupancy sensors, and thermostats.

Many symbols are available in the Design Tool Catalog, accessible via the Content Browser. Symbols in ADT are made either as multiview blocks (MVBs) or mask blocks (see "Creating Reflected Ceiling Plans" later in this chapter), so they can take advantage of the object display system. Let's insert the appropriate symbols from the Design Catalog to start designing the Power & Signal Plan.

1. Open the `Power & Signal Plan.dwg` view file if it is not already open. Verify that the scale pop-up on the drawing status bar reads $^1/8''=1'-0''$.

2. Open the Content Browser by pressing Ctrl+4. Click the Design Tool Catalog - Imperial to open it in the Content Browser.

3. In the navigation pane choose Electrical ➤ Power. Click the Receptacle subcategory and locate the Duplex Receptacle tool. Drag its i-drop icon into the drawing window.

4. In the Properties palette, verify that Specify Scale On Screen is set to No. The size of the symbol will automatically match the drawing scale. Change Specify Rotation On Screen to Yes. You will click a point to specify the symbol's orientation.

5. Zoom in on the Break Room above and to the left of the building core. Click a point along the right wall of the Break Room to locate the symbol (see Figure 15.9). Using polar object tracking, move the cursor horizontally to the left and click a point to set the rotation to 180 degrees.

6. Press Enter, and the symbol changes from the black of layer 0 to a cyan color. Click the symbol and look in the Properties palette. It is identified as a Multi-View Block Reference on layer E-Wall-Powr. As you can see, you do not have to worry about layers or scaling when inserting symbols designed as AEC Content. Press Esc to deselect.

NOTE It is acceptable to copy symbols within a view. Symbols do not attach property set data to objects in constructs, so copying them has no adverse effects. However, inserting symbols from a tool might be more convenient because you have the opportunity to specify the symbol's rotation interactively on-screen.

7. When you open projects created by other users, it is necessary to repath the tool palette file location. Select the Project tab of the Project Navigator and click the Edit Project button. Click the Tool Palette File Location's ellipsis button to open the Browse for Folder dialog box. Expand the Standards folder within the project folder, select the Workspace ToolPalettes folder and click OK. Click OK to close the Modify Project worksheet and click OK if you see a message informing you that the tool palettes are being rebuilt.

FIGURE 15.9
Inserting a duplex power
symbol in the Power &
Signal view

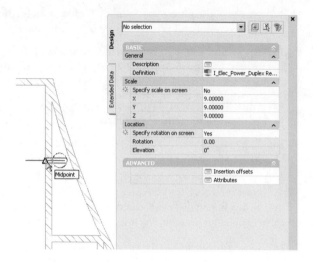

8. Drag symbol tools you plan to use repeatedly into a palette for added convenience. Set the Chapter 15 palette group current in Tool Palettes. In the Content Browser, navigate to the Electrical ➢ Communications subcategory. Drag the Phone Jack tool's i-drop icon from the Content Browser to the Project Tools palette.

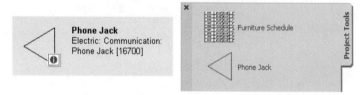

9. Click the Phone Jack tool in the Project Tools palette. Snap to a Nearest point along the wall adjacent to and just above the duplex receptacle you inserted earlier. Click a point to set the rotation to 180 degrees in this case. Press Enter to complete the routine, and the phone jack will appear on the T-Comm layer in cyan.

10. Select the phone jack symbol. Click the Attributes worksheet icon in the Properties palette. In a power and signal plan, attributes are used to differentiate different circuits or phone lines in rooms that have more than one. Type a Subscript value of **A** in the Multi-View Block Attributes worksheet (see Figure 15.10). Click OK to close the worksheet. The letter appears on the lower

corner of the phone jack symbol. Unfortunately, the attribute interferes with the duplex receptacle symbol and is rotated so it is hard to read.

11. Right-click in the drawing window and choose Edit Attribute Orientations from the shortcut menu. Two grips appear. Click the Rotation of Attribute: Subscript grip. Move the cursor up and around to the right and click a point to rotate the attribute approximately 90 degrees.

12. Click the Location of Attribute: Subscript grip and move the attribute up so it does not interfere with the other symbol (see Figure 15.11).

13. Explore all the subcategories and symbol tools available in the Design Tool Catalog in the Content Browser.

TIP Most symbols have 2D representations only, but some symbols have 3D representations that are visible in oblique, isometric, and perspective views. Use 2D symbols everywhere unless you plan to make 3D presentation images. Use 3D symbols sparingly to conserve computer resources.

14. Drag appropriate tools onto the Project Tools palette and continue adding symbols to the view. Save the `Power & Signal Plan.dwg` view file when you are comfortable with how the symbol tools work. You do not have to complete the whole Power & Signal Plan unless you want to take this opportunity to practice.

FIGURE 15.10
Entering a subscript attribute value in a communications symbol

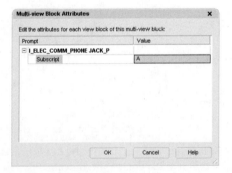

FIGURE 15.11
Rotating attribute (left), relocating attribute (middle), and the result (right)

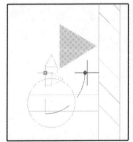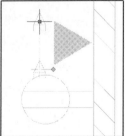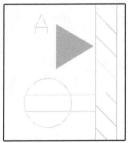

Designing Symbols

The default symbols are not likely to fit your documentation needs in every situation. For example, there is no combination data and phone jack symbol included by default.

This tutorial teaches how to design an intelligent symbol by using an existing symbol as a starting point. To be fully compliant with ADT's layer and display system, the new intelligent symbol will be defined as an attributed block wrapped in a multiview block definition, which is then defined as AEC Content–accessible through the DesignCenter. In the end, you'll add the new symbol as a tool to the Project Tool palette. Use this procedure to design any symbol you might need in your own projects.

1. Open the `Power & Signal Plan.dwg` view file if it is not already open.

2. Click the Phone Jack tool in the Project Tools palette. Add a phone jack to the left wall of the office adjacent to the break room you were working on in the last section.

3. Select the new phone jack symbol, right-click, and choose Edit Multi-View Block Definition from the shortcut menu. Choose the View Blocks tab in the Multi-View Block Definition Properties dialog box that appears. Click each display representation in turn to learn which view blocks are used in the MBV definition. The `I_ELEC_COMM_PHONE JACK_P` view block is used in both the General and Model display representations (make a mental note of the view block name). This means that the same 2D block will be shown in all viewpoints. Click Cancel.

4. Designing a new symbol is often easier when basing it on an existing symbol. We will create a symbol that represents both a phone jack and data jack on the same cover plate. To insert the view block into the drawing, choose Insert ➤ Block: the Insert dialog box appears. Choose `I_ELEC_COMM_PHONE JACK_P` from the Name drop-down list. Verify that Specify On-screen is checked for insertion point and Explode is not checked. Click OK in the Insert dialog box. Snap the view block to a nearest point adjacent and above the MVB definition you inserted in step 2 (see Figure 15.13) and then click OK again in the Enter Attributes dialog box that appears. The view block is much smaller than the MVB because the MVB was scaled up to fit the drawing scale.

FIGURE 15.12

Finding the name of a view block within a MVB definition

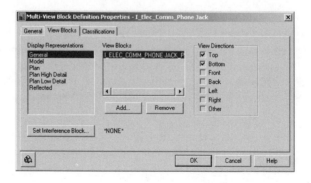

FIGURE 15.13
Inserting view block
above Multi-View block

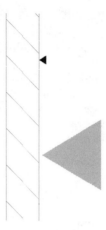

NOTE View blocks created with a size of approximately one unit (one inch in architectural units) will be automatically scaled when inserted to match the annotation plot size.

5. Zoom in and select the view block reference you just inserted. Right-click and choose Copy Block Definition And Assign from the shortcut menu. Type the new name **I_ELEC_COMM_ PHONE_DATA JACK_P** in the New Block Definition worksheet and click OK.

6. Select the new view block, right-click, and choose Block Editor from the shortcut menu. The Block Editor is a new feature in AutoCAD 2006 that ADT has inherited. It works very much like the older RefEdit interface: Both provide separate interfaces for designing block definitions. If you see a dialog box asking if you want to learn about the new features, click No for now.

TIP Search the AutoCAD User's Guide for "Block Editor" to learn more about the new block editor environment. It can be used to author blocks that can have parameters and actions built-in that define dynamic block behavior. However, dynamic blocks will not maintain dynamic behavior as view blocks within a Multi-View block definition.

7. The block was isolated, and the screen turned pale yellow to indicate that you are inside the block editor interface. Additional palettes appear, and there is a special block editor toolbar that appears at the top of the drawing window. Draw a polyline along half of the phone symbol, as shown in Figure 15.14. Snap the third vertex to the midpoint of the triangular symbol.

FIGURE 15.14

Draw three vertex polylines along edge of phone symbol.

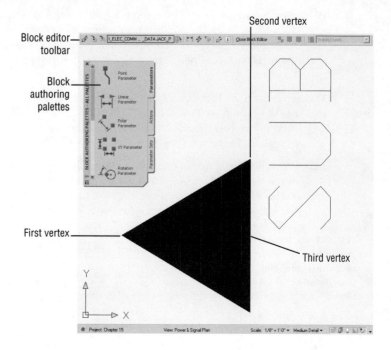

8. Select the lower half of the triangular symbol. Notice in the Properties palette that the selected entity is a Solid. Select its top vertex grip and snap it to the third vertex of the polyline you just drew. Select the attribute definition and change Style to RomanS in the Properties palette. Press Esc to deselect.

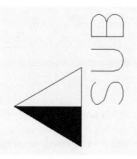

9. Click the Close Block Editor button on the Block editor toolbar. A small warning dialog box will appear, asking you if you want to save changes to I_ELEC_COMM_PHONE_DATA JACK_P? Click Yes. You exit block editor mode and return to the drawing window. Delete the view block from the drawing window; it is now defined in the drawing database.

10. Select the phone jack MVB reference you inserted in step 2, right-click, and choose Copy Multi-View Block Definition And Assign. Select the General tab of the Multi-View Block Definition Properties dialog box that appears and rename the definition to **I_Elec_Comm_ Phone_Data Jack**. Change the description to **Electric: Communication: Combo Phone and Data Jack**.

11. Select the View Blocks tab and click the Remove button to drop the original view block. Click the Add button, and select the I_ELEC_COMM_PHONE_DATA JACK_P block (see Figure 15.15). Click OK to close the Select A Block dialog box. Uncheck all the view directions in the Multi-View Block Definition Properties dialog box except for Top and Bottom.

12. Select the Model display representation. Click the Remove button and then click the Add button. Select the I_ELEC_COMM_PHONE_DATA JACK_P block and click OK. Uncheck the Top and Bottom view directions and click OK to close the Multi-View Block Definition Properties dialog box. The MVB appears with the updated geometry of the redefined view block.

FIGURE 15.15
Selecting a new view block for copied and reassigned Multi-View block

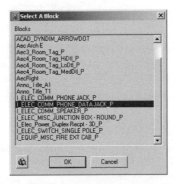

You have successfully created a new MVB that encapsulates a new attributed view block in two of its display representations. The next procedure defines the symbol as AEC Content; this gives the MVB the capability to choose a layer and scale when it is inserted.

1. Select the MVB and change it to layer 0 (zero). Do this to ensure that the MVB will assume the layer assigned to it by the AEC Content routine.

2. Choose Format ➤ AEC Content Wizard, and the Create AEC Content Wizard dialog box appears. Choose the Multi-View Block radio button in the Content Type group. Select I_Elec_Comm_Phone_Data Jack in the Current Drawing list and click the Add >>> button to move the MVB to the Content File list on the right (see Figure 15.16). Click the Next button.

3. Choose the Annotation radio button in the Additional Scaling group. Also check Enable AEC Unit Scaling. In the Attribute Text Angle group, choose the Right Reading radio button. Click the Select Layer Key button to open a dialog box of the same name. Scroll down and select the COMMUN layer key—it will place the symbol on layer T-Comm for telecommunication devices (see Figure 15.17). Click OK and Next.

4. Click the Browse button on the Display Options page of the AEC Content Wizard. The Save Content File dialog box appears. Navigate to the following folder, in which AEC Content is stored:

```
C:\Documents and Settings\All Users\Application Data\Autodesk\ADT 2006\enu\AEC
Content\Imperial\Design\Electrical\Communications
```

Type the name **PhoneData.dwg** in the File Name text box and click Save.

5. Type **Combo Phone and Data Jack** in the Detailed Description text box (see Figure 15.18). Click the Finish button to close the AEC Content Wizard. Delete the MVB reference in the drawing window. You will insert it again from a tool you make shortly.

6. Press Ctrl+2 to open the DesignCenter. Select the AEC Content tab. Expand the Custom Applications, Architectural Desktop, Imperial, Design, and Electrical nodes and click the Communication node. The PhoneData symbol appears on the upper-right pane in the DesignCenter (see Figure 15.19). The icon doesn't look correct—you will remedy that once you make PhoneData a tool.

FIGURE 15.16
Selecting a content type and MVB definition in AEC Content wizard

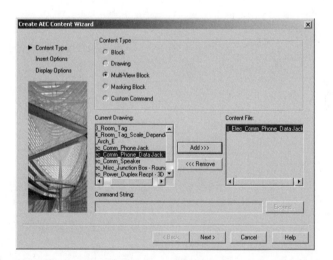

FIGURE 15.17
Selecting insert options for MVB in AEC Content Wizard (left) and selecting a layer key (right)

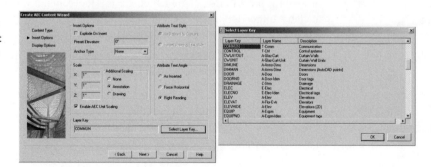

FIGURE 15.18
Saving symbol with
other AEC Content

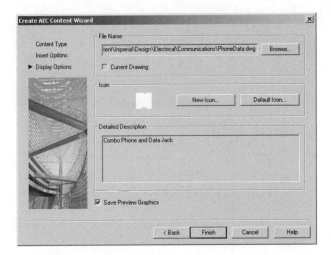

FIGURE 15.19
Custom AEC
Content appearing
in DesignCenter

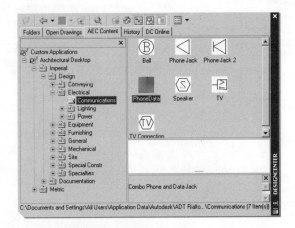

7. Drag the PhoneData symbol from the DesignCenter and drop it onto the Project Tools palette. A new tool appears that's called PhoneData; this tool contains the AEC Content routine that you created in addition to the MVB. Close the DesignCenter. Right-click the new tool and choose Properties. Type **Phone/Data Jack** as the tool name and click OK to close the Properties worksheet.

8. Click the Phone/Data Jack tool and insert a symbol into the drawing window. It automatically appears in the correct scale and on the correct layer.

9. Right-click the Phone/Data Jack tool and choose Set Image from Selection from the shortcut menu. Select the symbol you just inserted and press Enter. The tool's icon is updated (see Figure 15.20). The custom symbol tool is complete.

10. Save and close the Power & Signal Plan.dwg view file.

Congratulations on creating a custom AEC Content tool. You should be able to make every custom symbol you might need by following the preceding procedures.

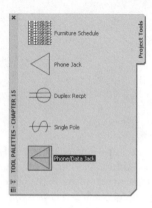

FIGURE 15.20
Project Tools palette
showing custom-made
Phone/Data Jack tool

Creating Reflected Ceiling Plans

A reflected ceiling plan (RCP) is a special type of plan that must be created in a specific way to get the most out of ADT's tools. RCPs very often show ceiling grids that represent the tiles hung from a suspended ceiling system reflected back onto the floor plan. In AutoCAD, drawing ceiling grids can be a very tedious task. Fortunately, ADT's intelligent ceiling grids are easy to use because their boundaries can be set very quickly using space objects. In addition, lighting, air distribution, and life safety symbols can be attached to ceiling grids with relative ease. You'll learn how mask blocks are used to hide the geometry they cover by attaching lighting fixtures to a ceiling grid.

Setting up the Project

RCPs are best made in the file that contains space objects because ceiling grids are most efficiently clipped by those objects. In addition, mask blocks do not work across XRefs. These facts determine how we will approach setting up the project. The entire reflected ceiling plan will be made in the same construct in which the space objects live. All the ceiling fixtures will also be added to the construct.

Of course, we will need to make a Reflected Ceiling Plan view and sheet. As always, use the view if you want to add dimensions or annotation to the RCP. Do not put anything in the sheet except for the sheet view so it will be ready to print at any time. We will use the display system to compartmentalize information, so that the ceiling grids and fixtures stored in a construct do not appear on views other than the RCP.

1. Choose the Constructs tab of the Project Navigator. Right-click the Spaces construct and choose Rename from the shortcut menu. Give it the name **Spaces And Ceiling** to indicate the additional content you will add to this construct.

2. Click the Repath XRef button in the Project Navigator. Click the Re-path button in the Reference File Re-path Queue worksheet that appears (see Figure 15.21). After a few moments, all the files in the project will be updated to reference the renamed construct.

3. Now you will create a RCP view. Choose the Views tab in the Project Navigator. Right-click the Views category node and choose New View Drawing ➢ General from the shortcut menu. Give the new view the name **Reflected Ceiling Plan** in the Add General View worksheet and click Next. Check division 1 on Level 23 and click Next. Uncheck the Furniture and Tenant Stair constructs and click Finish.

FIGURE 15.21
Repathing files after
renaming a construct

4. Double-click the Reflected Ceiling Plan node to open the view file. Change the display configuration to Reflected. Notice that you can see the workstations and spaces in the view—these should not appear on an RCP. Remember that the workstations are elements that are attached to the Partitions construct, which this view references. You cannot detach the nested workstation elements without detaching the Partitions construct (which we need). Therefore, the solution to hiding the workstations is through layers. Click the Layer Manager button on the Layer Properties toolbar.

5. Click the XRef node in the tree pane. Toggle off the following XRef nodes in the content pane: WorkstationCluster2, WorkstationCluster3, and WorkstationCluster4. Scroll down and turn off the `Spaces and Ceiling|A-Area-Spce` layer (see Figure 15.22).

6. You'll need to save a layer snapshot to transfer the XRef layer states from the MSV to the sheet view. Still in the Layer Manager, click the Snapshots button. Click the New button and type the name **MySnapshot** (see Figure 15.23). Click OK in all three dialog boxes, closing them all.

NOTE The current display configuration and layer state will be used in any MSVs that you create.

7. Select the Constructs tab of the Project Navigator. Right-click the Frame element and choose Overlay XRef from the shortcut menu. Move the Frame element so that it is centered on the building.

FIGURE 15.22
Turning off the workstation and space layers

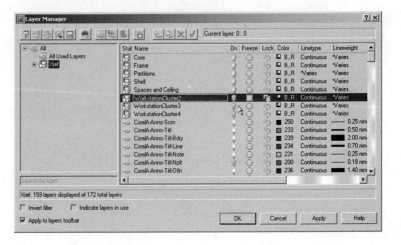

FIGURE 15.23

Saving a snapshot of
layer state

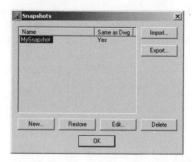

8. Select the View tab of the Project Navigator. Right-click the Reflected Ceiling Plan view and choose New Model Space View from the shortcut menu. Give the MSV the name **Floor 23 Reflected Ceiling Plan** in the Add Model Space View worksheet. Verify that Scale is set to $1/8''=1'-0''$ (see Figure 15.24). Click the Define View Window button and click two opposite corners of the frame element. Click OK to close the worksheet.

9. Add a title mark to the lower-left corner of the MSV as you have done before. Save and close the `Reflected Ceiling Plan.dwg` view file.

10. Select the Sheet tab of the Project Navigator. Create a new sheet with the number **A104** and the name **Reflected Ceiling Plan**. Open the new sheet drawing. Select the Views tab of the Project Navigator and drag the Floor 23 Reflected Ceiling Plan MSV onto the sheet.

11. Center the sheet view on the sheet. Save and close the `A104 Reflected Ceiling Plan.dwg` sheet file. The project setup is complete.

FIGURE 15.24

Saving an RCP MSV

Working with Ceiling Grids

The actual work of developing the RCP happens in the Spaces and Ceiling construct. The next task is to add and modify ceiling grids.

1. Double-click the Spaces and Ceiling construct to open it. Switch to the Reflected display configuration by using the pop-up on the drawing status bar.

2. Zoom in on the Conference Room at the top of the plan. Set the Design palette group current in the Tool palettes. Click the Ceiling grid tool. In the Properties palette, change X-Depth and Y-Depth to 20′. Verify that the Layout Types are set to Repeat with a Bay Size of 2′ in both X and Y axes. Snap the ceiling grid to the lower left outside corner of the conference room and press Enter twice to accept the default rotation and to end the command (see Figure 15.25).

3. Select the ceiling grid object and click its lower-right grip. Move it down a bit until you see a new row of tiles appear. Click to enlarge the grid so it extends beyond the lower border of the conference room.

TIP Create a space style override for the Reflected display representation to alter grid spacing or hatch pattern angle so as not to visually conflict with ceiling grids.

4. Repeat the previous step using the upper-right grip to enlarge the ceiling grid again. Make sure that the grid covers the entire space by stretching it up and to the right.

5. Select the ceiling grid, right-click, and choose Clip from the shortcut menu. The command line says the following:

```
Ceiling grid clip [Set boundary/Add hole/Remove hole]:
```

Type **S** for set boundary and press Enter. Select the space inside the conference room and press Enter. The ceiling grid is clipped to the boundaries of the space (see Figure 15.26).

6. Press F3 to toggle object snap off. Select the ceiling grid and click its lower-left grip. Move the grip slowly and watch as the ceiling grid moves within its clipped boundary. You can change the registration of the grid by moving the grip. Click to set the grid in a new location. As long as you do not move the grip too far up or to the right, the grid will continue to fill its boundary. Press Esc to deselect.

7. There is a more efficient way to set ceiling grids to their boundaries—by using an option of the ceiling grid tool.

   This way, a ceiling grid can be centered and set into a boundary as the ceiling grid is created. Click the Ceiling Grid tool on the Design palette. The command line says the following:

```
Insertion point or [WIdth/Depth/XSpacing/YSpacing/XDivide by toggle/YDivide by
toggle/Set boundary/SNap to center/Match]:
```

Type **S** for Set boundary and press Enter. Select the small office space protruding beyond the upper-left corner of the building core. Right-click and choose Snap To Center from the shortcut menu. Press Enter twice to complete the command. The ceiling grid is set to the boundary of the space and centered within it (see Figure 15.27).

TIP You can also set the boundary of ceiling grids with linework and layout grids. Right-click the Ceiling Grid tool, choose Apply Tool Properties To, and make a selection. Selecting a closed polyline does not create a grid clipped by that polyline, but creates a custom shape ceiling grid that matches the polyline boundary.

8. Continue adding ceiling grids and setting their boundaries to fit within all the enclosed rooms as you see fit. Do not put ceiling grids in the open offices, workstations, reception, stairs, or building core spaces. Save the `Spaces and Ceiling.dwg` construct when you are done.

Ceiling grids are two-dimensional. If you want a ceiling grid to appear in a perspective drawing, you can move it up in the Z direction. If you use a space to clip the ceiling grid, the grid will be placed at the space height of the space object. Be aware that it will appear only in line drawings but not in renderings done in ADT or VIZ Render. If you want to show ceilings in 3D it is better to use the ceiling component of space objects, which can accept rendering materials. You can simulate tiled ceilings by adjusting the tiling of material mapping coordinates in VIZ Render (see Chapter 18, "Using VIZ Render").

WARNING   ADT maintains the full grid size for each ceiling grid object, even when clipped. File size can increase and display performance suffer from too many overly large ceiling grids. Minimize ceiling grid size to maximize performance and decrease file size.

FIGURE 15.25
Setting ceiling grid creation properties (left) and inserting the ceiling grid in the construct (right)

 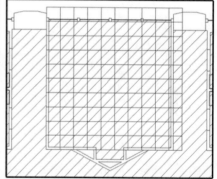

FIGURE 15.26
Clipping ceiling grid with space

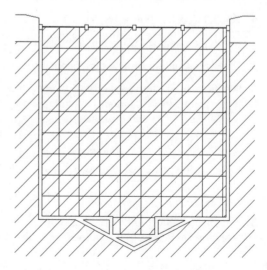

FIGURE 15.27
Setting a ceiling grid to a
boundary and centering
it within

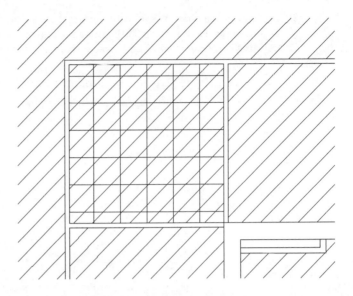

Adding Ceiling Fixtures and Attaching Mask Blocks

Many ceiling fixtures can be found in the Design Tool Catalog. Symbols that are appropriate for a reflected ceiling plan are located in the following subcategories:

♦ Electrical ➢ Lighting ➢ Fluorescent: Fixtures that fit into common ceiling grid tile sizes

♦ Electrical ➢ Lighting ➢ Incandescent: Downlights and emergency flashers

♦ Electrical ➢ Lighting ➢ Track Light: Fixtures for hard ceilings

♦ Mechanical ➢ Air Distribution: Air supply and return diffusers and access panel symbols

♦ Special Construction ➢ Detection and Alarm: Exit signs and smoke detector symbols

Now you'll add some fluorescent light fixtures to the ceiling grids.

1. Open the Content Browser if it is not already open. Explore the categories listed above.

2. Navigate to Electrical ➢ Lighting ➢ Fluorescent subcategory. Drag the 2x4 tool to the Project Tools palette in the Chapter 15 palette group. Notice that the tool says it is in a masking block— you'll learn what that means in the next section.

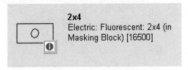

2x4
Electric: Fluorescent: 2x4 (in
Masking Block) [16500]

3. Toggle on OSNAP on the drawing status bar if it is not already. Click the 2X4 tool. Set Specify Rotation On Screen to Yes in the Properties palette.

4. Zoom into the conference room at the top of the plan. Click an intersection point on the ceiling grid. Using polar object tracking, move the cursor vertically down and click a point to orient the fixture vertically within the grid and press Enter to end the command (see Figure 15.28).

TIP Anchor downlights to a layout curve to control their spacing parametrically (refer to Chapter 7, "Parametric Layouts, Anchors, and Structural Members").

5. Freeze layer A-Area-Spce to get a clearer picture of the ceiling grids—this will help you to add ceiling fixtures. Remember that you'll have to thaw this layer (if VISRETAIN is set to 0) before saving because there are views that reference this construct for spaces in addition to its ceilings.

6. Continue adding fluorescent fixtures, air supply and return diffusers, and a smoke detector symbol to the conference room.

Some people prefer to show electrical switches on the RCP along with the lighting fixtures that they control. The switches in the Design Tool Catalog were not designed to appear on the RCP. You can design custom switch MVBs whose view blocks appear in the Reflected display configuration so that they will appear on the RCP, or modify the default switch MVB by adding a view block to the Reflected display configuration.

7. Select one of the 2x4 fluorescent light fixtures you have attached to the ceiling grid in the conference room. Right-click and choose Select Similar. All the 2x4 fixtures are selected. Right-click again and choose Attach Objects. Select the ceiling grid in the conference room; the Select Display Representation dialog box appears. Click OK to select the Reflected display representation of the ceiling grid object to mask. Press Enter twice to complete the command. The ceiling grid is masked underneath the fluorescent fixtures (see Figure 15.29).

FIGURE 15.28
Snapping a fluorescent lighting fixture to ceiling grid

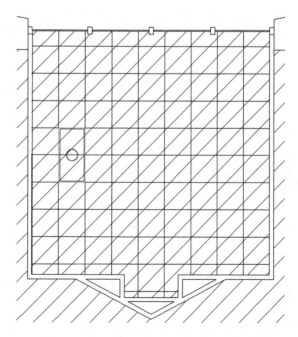

FIGURE 15.29
Selecting a display
representation to mask
(left), and the result
hiding the ceiling grid
underneath the lighting
fixtures (right)

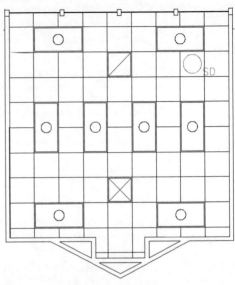

TIP If you add ceiling fixtures directly from the DesignCenter (instead of from the Tool palettes), they will be automatically anchored to the ceiling grid.

8. Thaw layer A-Area-Spce and then save the Spaces and Ceiling.dwg construct file. Open sheet A104 and take a look at the evolving RCP that is ready to be printed at any time.

9. Switch back to the construct and continue adding ceiling fixtures as you see fit. Save and close all files when you have finished practicing. The completed chapter is provided in a zip file in this chapter's folder on the companion DVD for you to compare your work.

NOTE Create custom mask blocks by first drawing a closed polyline to serve as the mask block boundary. Then create a new Mask Block Definition in the Style Manager. Right-click the new definition, choose Set From, select the polyline, and then select the MVB to be encapsulated within the mask block. Use the AEC Content Wizard as you have done before to save additional information with the mask block such as scale and layer information.

Summary

Through the experience of creating a power and signal plan and a reflected ceiling plan, you have learned how to design floor and ceiling plans that fit within the project structure. Although the techniques shown in this chapter are not the only way to organize project information, they represent perhaps the most efficient approach that takes full advantage of ADT's project system. You will need to practice what you have learned in this chapter by creating additional plans to really own the skills presented—and this will happen naturally as you work on your own projects. Use this chapter as a reference in the future when you are designing floor and ceiling plans. In the next chapter, you'll learn how to create section and elevation drawings.

Chapter 16

Sections and Elevations

No drawing set would be complete without sections and elevations. Although traditional plan and elevation drawings are together sufficient to document all three dimensions of a design in two dimensions, section drawings are most helpful for visualizing architectural interior spaces.

In Chapter 2 you learned how to use ADT 2006's new Edit In Section and Edit In Elevation display modes. Don't confuse these temporary editing modes with true sections and elevations that actually become part of the construction documentation drawing set—the subjects of this chapter. Architectural Desktop (ADT) orthogonally projects plan, section, and elevation drawings from a single building model (SBM), sourced from a logical project framework.

Although elevations are always linked from the SBM, sections may be either linked or live. Linked projections function somewhat like external references and must be refreshed when the design changes. Unlike XRefs, which automatically refresh when you reopen the host drawing, linked projections of the SBM must always be manually refreshed and regenerated.

Live Section mode is a special mode that lets you cut away part of the three-dimensional SBM itself to reveal its interior spaces. Live Section mode is for interactive visualization on-screen and is not intended to be documented. To use the visualization, you'll project both isometric and perspective sections from a live-sectioned SBM in this chapter.

Later on, you'll use powerful callout tools to create linked sections and elevations that are called 2D Section/Elevation objects. The callout tools automate a long series of steps that are necessary to integrate the projections into the project structure. You'll learn how to customize 2D Section/Elevation styles and edit them as objects to control their linework's appearance. This chapter's topics include:

◆ Working with Sections

◆ Adding Section and Elevation Callouts

◆ Editing 2D Section/Elevation Styles

◆ Working with 2D Section/Elevation Objects

Working with Sections

Section drawings cut through a building to reveal its interior. The Bldg Section Line object usually represents a vertical plane that slices completely through a building. However, the Bldg Section Line can be jogged to bypass certain areas of a building or it can represent a true 3D volume (with both vertical and horizontal cut planes) inside of which the section is defined.

In the tutorial that follows, you'll learn to use the Bldg Section Line object and understand its display properties before enabling Live Section mode. Once in that mode, you'll be able to visualize the interior of the building in three dimensions. You can optionally display the portion of the building that was cut away by the Bldg Section Line transparently in renderings. Later on, you'll learn how to control the appearance of live-sectioned geometry using material definition display properties.

In the end you'll use Live Section mode to create a perspective section drawing that is a two-dimensional projection of the 3D geometry. In addition, you'll generate a 3D linked section that is based on, but separate from, the Live Section SBM.

Using the Bldg Section Line

The tutorials in this chapter use the gambrel roof house that you built in Chapter 11, "Roofs and Slabs."

The single file that you worked on before has been elaborated upon and converted into a project framework. You'll open a composite view in this chapter's project and proceed to add a Bldg Section Line using a tool on the Design palette.

1. Copy this chapter's folder from the DVD to the following folder on your hard drive or to the equivalent folder on a networked file server:

   C:\Documents and Settings\<username>\My Documents\Autodesk\My Projects

2. Click the Project Browser button on the Navigation toolbar. In the Project Browser, double-click the Chapter 16 node in the tree pane to set the project current (see Figure 16.1). Re-path the templates and tool palette file locations. Click Close.

3. Choose the Views tab in the Project Navigator. Double-click the Composite View node to open the view file. The file opens in the SW Isometric viewpoint (see Figure 16.2). 3D Orbit around the structure to visualize its exterior from all sides. When you are done, switch to the Top viewpoint.

4. Choose the Design palette group in the Tool palettes, if it is not already current. Select the Design palette and click the Vertical Section tool (see Figure 16.3).

FIGURE 16.1

Setting the project current in the Project Browser

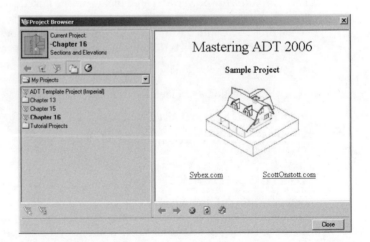

FIGURE 16.2
Composite view

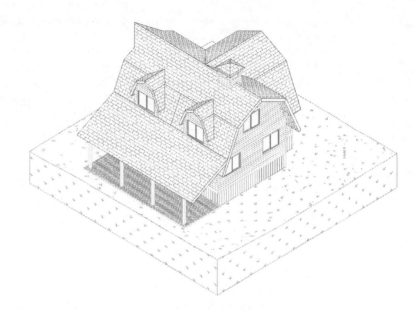

FIGURE 16.3
Section tools on
the Design palette

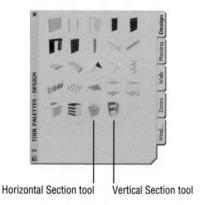

Horizontal Section tool   Vertical Section tool

NOTE   Notice that there is also a Horizontal Section tool on the Design palette. Use this tool to cut plans from the SBM. Normally this is not necessary because the SBM is itself created from objects placed in plan, after all. However, you might find horizontal sections useful as analysis tools to study plans at different cut plane heights. They work the same as vertical sections; they are just oriented so the section cut happens horizontally.

   5. Using object tracking, acquire the tip of the roof extension at the top of the plan, move the cursor up vertically and click the start point above the terrain object. Move the cursor straight down and click the next point below the terrain and press Enter (see Figure 16.4). These two points are on the *defining line*—where the building is actually cut by the section. The command line says the following:

```
Enter length <20'-0">:
```

The length is how far the section extends away from the Bldg Section Line. Type **40'** and press Enter. The defining line passes along the ridgeline of the main roof.

TIP You can create a jogged Bldg Section Line by clicking more than two points when drawing the defining line.

6. Switch to the SW Isometric viewpoint and notice that the Bldg Section Line is on top of the roof. Select the Bldg Section Line and change Elevation to 0 (zero) in the Properties palette to move the Bldg Section Line to ground level.

7. Adding subdivisions will allow you to vary the lineweight of objects as they recede from the Bldg Section Line. Click the Subdivisions worksheet icon in the Dimensions subcategory. Click the Add button three times in the Subdivisions worksheet that appears and click OK. You will adjust the position and display of subdivisions later on.

NOTE The Bldg Elevation Line works the same as the Bldg Section Line. You'll create Bldg Elevation Lines in "Adding Section and Elevation Callouts."

8. With the Bldg Section Line still selected, click the trigger grip to choose not to use the model extents for the height. The object suddenly appears as a volume with additional grips. Click the Lower Extension grip and move it down below the terrain object (see Figure 16.5). Now the section volume cuts through the entire building and the terrain that it sits on.

9. The Bldg Section Line and Bldg Elevation Line objects are not style-based. However, they do have display properties accessible through object display. There are only three display components for section lines: the Defining line, Subdivision lines, and Boundary. Switch back to the Top viewpoint. Notice that in plan, the Bldg Section Line appears as a series of vertical lines. Select the Bldg Section Line and notice that it is on layer A-Sect-Line, a nonplotting layer by default.

10. Right-click and choose Edit Object Display from the shortcut menu. The Display Properties dialog box appears. Choose the Display Properties tab. Double-click the Plan representation to edit the Drawing Default property source.

FIGURE 16.4
Drawing the Bldg
Section Line using the
Vertical Section tool

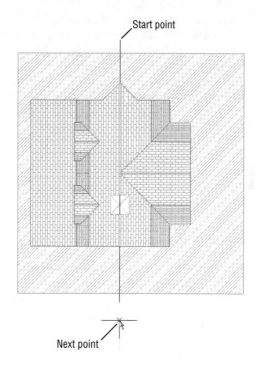

Start point

Next point

FIGURE 16.5
Adjusting sectional
volume with grips

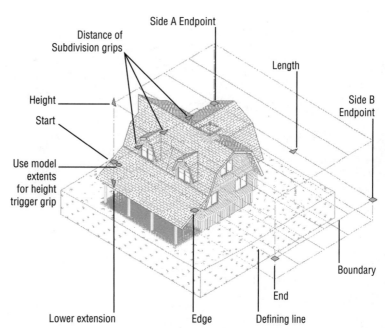

Side A Endpoint

Distance of
Subdivision grips

Length

Side B
Endpoint

Height

Start

Use model
extents
for height
trigger grip

Lower extension

Edge

Defining line

End

Boundary

11. Toggle on the Boundary display component. Notice that none of the three components plots. Defining Line is on layer 0, so it inherits the layer the object is on (A-Sect-Line). Subdivision Lines and Boundary are on layer G-Anno-Nplt by default. Click OK in each dialog box to close them. The boundary appears in plan. There is no harm in displaying all three components on-screen because none of them plots, after all.

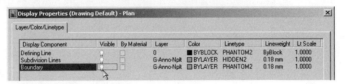

Enabling Live Section Mode

Live section mode is useful to visualize the interior of any building. You can use it at any time, not just in construction documention, to aid in the design process. Live section mode is also used to project 2D perspective section drawings from the 3D model.

Live Section mode is enabled from the shortcut menu of the Bldg Section Line object. Once enabled, everything outside the Bldg Section Line will be hidden by default, making it possible to see inside the building.

1. Switch into the Left viewpoint. Select the Bldg Section Line, right-click, and choose Enable Live Section from the shortcut menu. You can look into the building interior (see Figure 16.6).

2. Select the Bldg Section Line and move its Height grip up above the building so you do not cut off the top of the building. Press Esc to deselect.

3. Switch into the SW Isometric viewpoint and observe the result of the live section. Select the Bldg Section Line, right-click, and choose Reverse from the shortcut menu. Switch to the SE Isometric viewpoint to see the other side (see Figure 16.7). Portions of some of the furniture Multi-View blocks (MVBs) overhang the cut line—unfortunately, there's nothing you can do about that. Although MVBs do not obey Live Section mode properly, it won't matter when you generate orthogonal section drawings.

FIGURE 16.6
Live Section mode
enabled

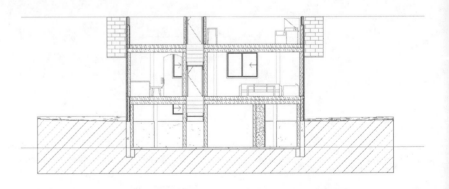

NOTE   After Live Section mode is enabled, any changes you make to the Bldg Section Line's shape or orientation are immediately visible in the cutaway model.

4. Switch to the Low Detail display configuration. The entire building reappears and the surface hatching disappears in the Low Detail configuration (see Figure 16.8). Live Section mode is specific to the display configuration where it is applied. Switch back to the Medium Detail display configuration.

TIP   Use Live Section mode to accelerate display performance in the composite view of a complex model. The geometry that is hidden is not sent to the graphics card for display.

FIGURE 16.7
Viewing the live section in SE Isometric viewpoint (left) and SW Isometric viewpoint (right)

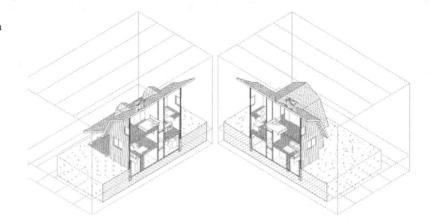

FIGURE 16.8
Changing display configurations disables Live Section mode

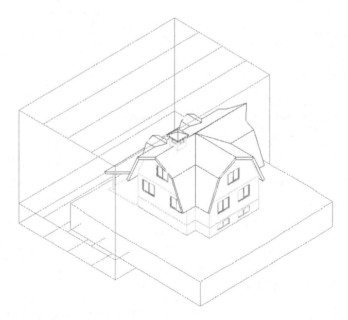

DISPLAYING THE SECTIONED BODY

The *sectioned body* is defined as everything outside the volume contained within the Bldg Section Line. Normally this geometry is hidden in a section, but it is possible to display the sectioned body transparently for presentation purposes.

1. Select the Bldg Section Line, right-click, and choose Toggle Sectioned Body Display from the shortcut menu. The portion of the building outside the Bldg Section Line appears in (almost black) wireframe in Hidden display mode. Most importantly, you can see through the sectioned body wireframe, even if you are using Hidden display mode.

2. Switch to Gouraud Shaded display mode. After a few moments, the sectioned body will display in transparent blue (see Figure 16.9).

TIP Rendering a transparent sectioned body can be a very compelling way to present a perspective section. You'll learn how to render in Chapter 18, "Using VIZ Render."

3. Select the Bldg Section Line, right-click, and choose Toggle Sectioned Body Display from the shortcut menu. The blue geometry disappears. Switch back to Hidden display mode. Click the Surface Hatch Toggle icon in the drawing tray to turn it off.

FIGURE 16.9
Displaying the sectioned body in Hidden (left) and Gouraud shaded (left) display modes

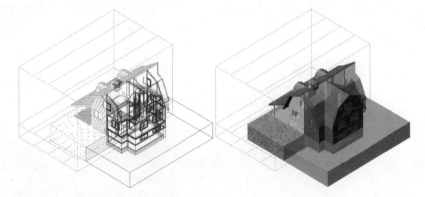

UNDERSTANDING LIVE SECTION DISPLAY PROPERTIES

The Bldg Section Line does not control how objects appear in Live Section mode. In this situation, the materials assigned to the objects control the appearance. In Chapter 3, "Object Styles," you learned the uses of material definition display components. We will revisit this topic here in an effort to understand how objects are displayed in Live Section mode.

1. Zoom in on the laundry room in the basement. Select the basement wall behind the clothes dryer. All the basement walls are selected because we are working in the Composite view, which references constructs. Look in the Properties palette and discover that the selected XRef is Basement Foundation Walls.dwg.

2. Select the Constructs tab in the Project Navigator. Expand the Exterior Walls category if it is not already expanded. Double-click the Basement Foundation Walls construct to open it. Again, select the wall behind the laundry machines—this time only the one wall object selects (see Figure 16.10).

FIGURE 16.10
Opening a construct and
selecting a wall object

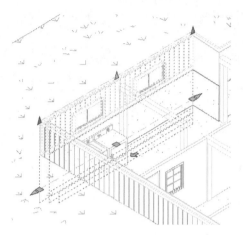

3. Right-click and choose Edit Wall Style from the shortcut menu. Select the Materials tab in the Wall Style Properties dialog box and select the Concrete component. Click the Edit Material button—the Material Definition Properties dialog box appears. Select the Display Properties tab and double-click the General Medium Detail display representation—the Display Properties dialog box for the material definition override appears. Select the Layer/Color/Linetype tab (see Figure 16.11).

   The display properties for a selected material are listed by the components of Live Section mode. The Sectioned Boundary component is linework that outlines the cut line defined by Bldg Section Line. Notice that the Sectioned Boundary displays in red in typical material definitions to draw your attention to the actual cut plane. The Section Hatch component displays inside the Sectioned Boundary. The Sectioned Body component is set to color 251 (almost black). Remember that it appeared this way in Hidden display mode when the Sectioned Body Display was toggled on previously. The 2D Section/Elevation Linework and Surface Hatch components controls all the linework in the 2D Section/Elevation objects that you'll learn about later in this chapter.

4. Select the Hatching tab. The Section Hatch pattern (displayed in Live Section mode) is assigned and controlled here, along with the Plan Hatch and Surface Hatch components.

5. Select the Other tab (see Figure 16.12). Notice that in Live Section mode you can assign render materials for cut surfaces and the sectioned body. Materials that ship with ADT use the General.Sectioned Surface and General.Sectioned Body render materials by default.

FIGURE 16.11
Accessing material
definition display
properties

Display Component	Visible	Layer	Color	Linetype	Lineweight	Lt Scale	Plot Style
Plan Linework		0	11	ByBlock	0.25 mm	1.0000	Thin
2D Section/Elevation Linework		0	BYBLOCK	ByBlock	ByBlock	1.0000	ByBlock
3D Body		0	252	ByBlock	ByBlock	1.0000	ByBlock
Plan Hatch		0	30	ByBlock	0.18 mm	1.0000	Fine
Surface Hatch		0	30	ByBlock	0.18 mm	1.0000	Fine
Section Hatch		0	30	ByBlock	0.18 mm	1.0000	Fine
Sectioned Boundary		0	red	ByBlock	0.18 mm	1.0000	Fine
Sectioned Body		0	251	ByBlock	0.35 mm	1.0000	Medium Screened

Display Properties (Material Definition Override - Concrete.Cast-in-Place.Flat.Grey) - General Medium Detail

Layer/Color/Linetype | Hatching | Other

FIGURE 16.12
Other tab in Material
Definition Override
Display Properties

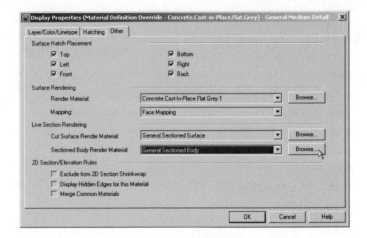

6. Click the Browse button next to the General.Sectioned Body render material to open the Select Rendering Material dialog box. Notice that its preview image shows a transparent blue. This is the render material that appeared earlier in Gouraud Shaded display mode. You'll learn how to edit render materials in Chapter 18. You might create a new render material that is more or less transparent and/or reflective, or change its tint color to something other than blue, for example. Click Cancel in every open dialog box.

NOTE   Choose View ➤ Regen Model if you make any changes to material definition display properties.

7. Close the Basement Foundation Walls construct without saving.

Creating Perspective Sections

So far you have been viewing isometric sections in the Composite view. It is convenient to use isometric viewpoints while adjusting a live section. However, perspective sections are arguably more compelling for presentation where dimensions and annotation are not required. You'll learn how to quickly create a perspective section using the 3D Orbit command and how to project the geometry from the SBM to 2D linework that is more efficiently stored. In addition, you'll create a "napkin sketch" from the hidden line projection, to give the perspective section a more hand-drawn look. Drawings made in this way are not linked to the SBM, so you'll have to delete and recreate them should the design change.

1. Open the Composite View if it is not already open. Switch to the Right viewpoint.

2. Right-click in the drawing window and choose 3D Orbit from the shortcut menu. A green circle appears in the viewport. Move the cursor inside the top constraint grip at the top quadrant of the green circle and drag down slightly. This orbits the model down a bit to give a slightly elevated point of view.

3. Right-click again and choose Projection ➤ Perspective from the 3D Orbit shortcut menu.

4. Right-click and choose More ➤ Adjust Distance. Drag the cursor down to move the point of view backward until you can see the whole building on-screen (see Figure 16.13). Press Enter to end the 3D Orbit command.

TIP Use the Zoom option in the 3D Orbit command to adjust the field of view. Zooming out creates a wide-angle shot, whereas zooming in simulates a telephoto camera lens.

5. Saving a named view allows you to switch back to this perspective point of view after changing viewpoints. Choose View ➤ Named Views to open the View dialog box. Click the New button and type **Perspective Section** as the View Name in the New View dialog box (see Figure 16.14). Click OK and OK again to close both dialog boxes.

FIGURE 16.13
Creating a perspective section

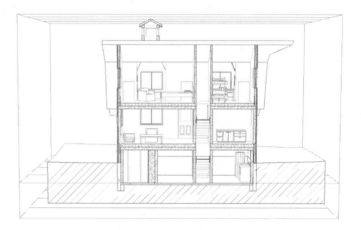

FIGURE 16.14
Saving the Perspective Section named view

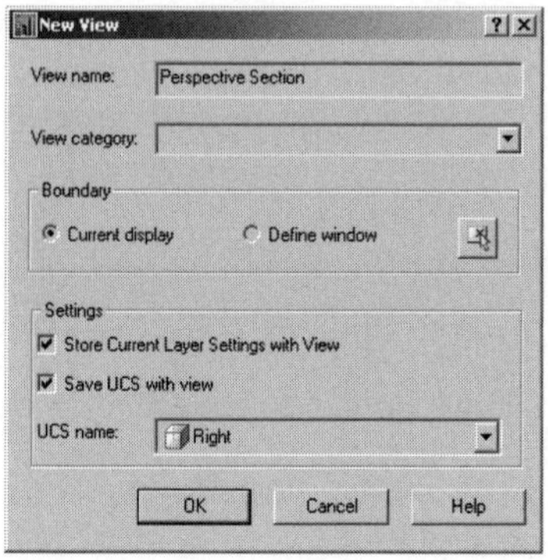

6. Set the Chapter 16 palette group current in the Tool palettes. Remember you'll have to re-path the tool palette file location in the project properties to see the Chapter 16 palette group. Two tools have already been added to the Project Tools palette from the Stock Tool Catalog: Hidden Line Projection and Napkin Sketch. You can add these tools to a new palette if you prefer.

7. Click the Hidden Line Projection tool, which will project the 3D geometry of the SBM to flat 2D linework. Type **ALL** on the command line and press Enter twice to select all the objects. You cannot pick points in perspective. Type **0,0** as the block insertion point and press Enter. The command line says the following:

```
Insert in plan view [Yes/No] <Yes>:
```

Press Enter to insert the projected linework in plan.

8. Switch to the Top viewpoint. The 2D projected linework appears correctly in plan, adjacent to the 3D SBM (see Figure 16.15). The projected linework is a block reference, not linked to the geometry in the SBM. If you make any changes to the design, they will not appear in the hidden line projection, and you will have to repeat the projection process to re-create the 2D linework.

9. Now that you have projected linework from the SBM, move it into an element, so it can eventually appear on a sheet. On the Constructs tab in the Project Navigator, right-click the Elements category and choose New ➢ Element from the shortcut menu. Type **Western Perspective Section** as the name and click OK to close the Add Element worksheet.

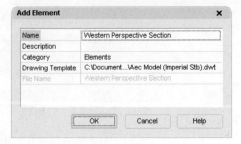

10. Click the hidden line projection block reference to select it. Drag it into the Project Navigator and drop it on the Western Perspective Section element. The linework disappears. Save the `Composite View.dwg` view file.

11. Double-click the Western Perspective Section element to open the file. Zoom to the extents of the drawing. Freeze the `A-Sect-Line` and `G-Anno-Nplt` layers to hide the linework representing the Bldg Section Line (see Figure 16.16).

FIGURE 16.15
Hidden line projection (left) and single building model (right)

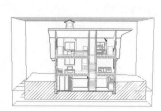
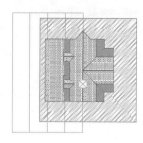

FIGURE 16.16
Freezing hidden line projection layers in element file

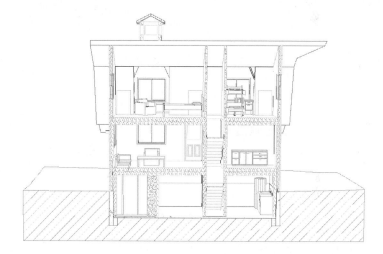

12. You could leave the perspective section as it is at this point or go a step further to make a napkin sketch—we'll go the extra mile. Click the Napkin Sketch tool on the Project Tools palette. Select the block reference and press Enter. The Napkin Sketch worksheet appears. Choose the Messy radio button and choose $1/8$"=1'-0" as the intended plot scale, even though the perspective section is actually not to scale (see Figure 16.17). The Napkin Sketch tool needs a ballpark estimate so it can make squiggles at a particular size. Click OK.

13. Press **M** and then Enter to execute the Move command. Press **L** and then Enter to select the last object that was created, which is the napkin sketch in this case. Move it down some arbitrary distance so you can see the original hidden line projection underneath. Erase the hidden line projection block reference and zoom in closely on the napkin sketch to examine its linework—there are numerous squiggles. Finally, zoom to the extents of the drawing (see Figure 16.18).

14. Save and close the `Western Perspective Section.dwg` element file. You'll place this element on a sheet later on.

FIGURE 16.17
Making a napkin
sketch of the hidden
line projection

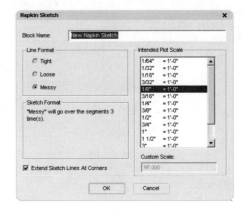

FIGURE 16.18
Completed napkin
sketch of western
perspective section
(left) and a detail (right)

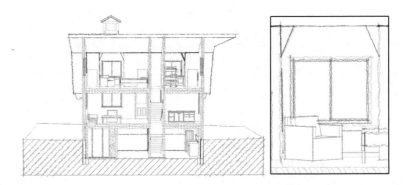

Generating Linked Section Objects

It is possible to generate separate Bldg Section objects that stay linked to the geometry in the SBM (unlike a hidden line projection). When the design changes, you'll be able to update the linked Bldg Section object without having to delete and re-create it.

Bldg Section objects are separate from the SBM and therefore are not controlled by material definitions assigned to the actual objects in constructs. Instead, the Bldg Section object itself has display properties that control its appearance.

1. Reopen the Composite View if it is not already open. Switch to the Top viewpoint. Select the Bldg Section Line, right-click, and choose Generate 2D Section from the shortcut menu. By the way, the name of this command is a bit of a misnomer because you can also generate 3D Bldg Section objects using it—that is what we will do now.

2. Choose the 3D Section/Elevation object radio button in the Generate Section/Elevation worksheet that appears. Click the Select Objects button, type **ALL,** and press Enter to select everything. Verify that the New Object radio button is selected and click the Pick Point button. Click a point well away from the SBM (it doesn't matter exactly where). Verify that Section_Elev is selected as the display set that this object will use and click OK to close the worksheet (see Figure 16.19).

3. Switch to the SE Isometric viewpoint. You can't see the Bldg Section object yet because Live Section mode is still enabled. Select the Bldg Section Line, right-click, and choose Disable Live Section. The SBM returns to displaying the entire structure while the linked Bldg Section object appears some distance off to the side. You can think of the Bldg Section object as a moment in time captured from the SBM. Zoom in on the Bldg Section object (see Figure 16.20).

FIGURE 16.19
Generating a linked 3D
Bldg Section object

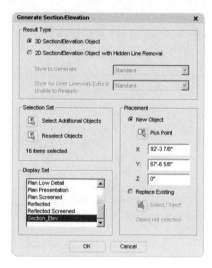

FIGURE 16.20
Examining the Bldg
Section object

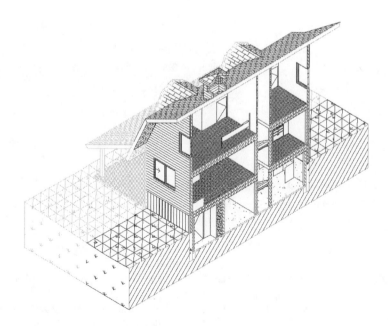

4. Notice that there are different colors in the wireframe of the Bldg Section object—they are controlled by the subdivisions you made earlier. Select the Bldg Section object, right-click, and choose Edit Object Display from the shortcut menu; the Display Properties dialog box appears. Double-click the Sub-divisions display representation to access the display components (see Figure 16.21). Here is where you control the appearance of each subdivision separately. Click Cancel in each open dialog box.

WARNING Changing material definition component display properties has no effect upon linked sections and elevation objects. Edit the Bldg Section object display instead.

5. Save and close the Composite View.dwg view drawing. It contains the linked Bldg Section object in addition to the SBM.

Subdivisions are typically used to fade lineweight as geometry recedes from the defining line of the cut plane. More often used in elevations, subdivisions allow closer surfaces to appear with bolder lines and more distant surfaces to appear less-emphasized. You can have up to a maximum of ten subdivisions, although one or two will probably suffice in most situations.

You might have noticed that 2D Section/Elevation Object With Hidden Line Removal was an option for generating a linked section object. Although it is possible to manually create a 2D linked section in this way, it is more common to use callout tools to automate this process. The next topic describes how to use callout tools to generate linked sections, elevations, and much more.

FIGURE 16.21
Editing the Sub-divisions representation's display properties

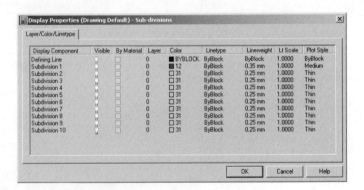

Adding Section and Elevation Callouts

Section and elevation callout tools automate a long series of steps that lead to integrating a section or elevation drawing into your project. Callout tools are used in plan views. Just as you might draw a section or elevation symbol in a plan that references another drawing in your sheet set, the callout tools start in the same way by inserting a callout tag into a plan view. The callout tag is an attributed block that uses fields that coordinate data appearing in the symbol itself (such as drawing and sheet number) with the actual drawing and sheet number you will ultimately place the drawing on.

After inserting the callout tag, you are prompted to create either a Bldg Section Line or Bldg Elevation Line, as the case may be. Following that procedure, the callout automation creates a model space view (MSV) and adds a title mark. Finally, the tool generates a 2D Section/Elevation object and gives you the opportunity to place it in a view drawing. Although callout tools have a huge amount of automation built in, they are quite easy to use.

Creating Exterior Elevations with Callout Tools

The procedure to create an exterior elevation has two major parts. In the first part you create a callout tag, view drawing, 2D Section/Elevation object, title mark, and MSV. In the second phase you adjust the size of the MSV to fit a frame, create a sheet, and place the MSV on the sheet.

CREATING THE ELEVATION OBJECT

Remember that the section and elevation callouts are to be placed in plan views. Let's start by using an exterior elevation callout tool in the first floor plan of our continuing tutorial.

1. Choose the View tab of the Project Navigator and double-click the First Floor Plan to open it. You will elevate the western exterior wall first.

2. Set the Document palette group current in the Tool palettes and choose the Callouts palette (see Figure 16.22). Study the callout tools.

FIGURE 16.22
Callout tools

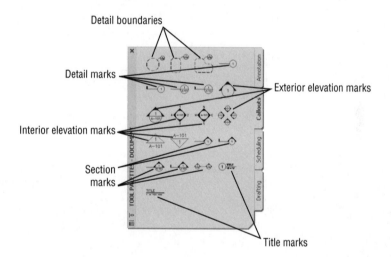

3. Hover the cursor over the second exterior elevation mark to see its ToolTip, which identifies the tool as Elevation Mark A2. The mark has both a drawing and sheet number and is designed to work within a project. Click the Elevation Mark A2 tool.

4. Click a point on the left side of the building inside the frame but outside the building. This specifies the location of the elevation tag. Using polar object tracking, move the cursor horizontally to the right and click again to specify the direction of the elevation. The tag points toward the east but elevates the western side of the building.

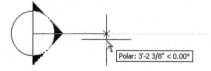

5. The Place Callout worksheet appears. Type **Western Exterior Elevation** as the New Model Space View Name. Verify that Generate Section/Elevation and Place Titlemark are checked. Click the Scale drop-down list and select $1/4''=1'-0''$; this scale will be the scale of the new elevation you are generating (see Figure 16.23).

TIP If you want to place the same callout in another floor plan, for example, uncheck Generate Section/Elevation and Place Titlemark and choose Callout Only in the Place Callout worksheet.

6. Click the New View Drawing button in the Place Callout worksheet. The Add Section/Elevation View worksheet appears in place of the Place Callout worksheet, which has disappeared. Type **Exterior Elevations** as the new view name and click the Next button.

7. Verify that all three levels are checked on the Context page of the Add Section/Elevation View worksheet. Click the Next button.

8. On the Content page, check the Exterior Walls and Roof Structures categories. Uncheck Interior Partitions, Stairs, and all constructs in the Slabs category except for Deck (see Figure 16.24). Click Finish to close the Add Section/Elevation View worksheet.

9. The command line says the following:

```
Specify first corner of elevation region:
```

Click a point just outside the building's lower-left corner. Specify the opposite corner of the elevation region above and to the right of the entire building (see Figure 16.25).

10. The final step is to locate the new 2D Section/Elevation object in the Exterior Elevations view drawing. Quite unusually, you are prompted to specify the position for this object in the new view while you are still in the floor plan view. The command line says the following:

```
** You are being prompted for a point in a different view drawing **
Specify insertion point for the 2D elevation result:
```

FIGURE 16.23
Filling out the Place
Callout worksheet

Click a point some distance off the right side of the frame element. You'll see a progress bar appear while the new 2D Section/elevation object is being generated.

11. Save the First Floor Plan.dwg view file.

FIGURE 16.24
Creating the Exterior
Elevations view

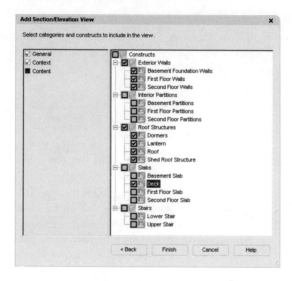

FIGURE 16.25
Specifying the
elevation region

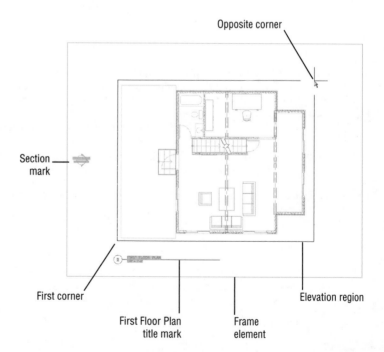

PLACING THE ELEVATION ON A SHEET

After the MSV has been created in the new view drawing, the field placeholders in the section mark change to question marks. To resolve the missing data, the Exterior Elevation's MSV needs to be placed onto a sheet. You will create a sheet and drop the Western Exterior Elevation MSV onto it to complete the whole process of creating and integrating the exterior elevation into the project.

1. Before you create the sheet, it is helpful to adjust the MSV boundaries in the new view that was just created so it will fit perfectly on the sheet. Double-click the Exterior Elevations node in the Project Navigator to open it.

2. The Exterior Elevations.dwg view file opens in Top viewpoint. The Western Exterior Elevation appears next to the externally referenced constructs to which it is linked. You chose these constructs when making the view file previously. Notice that the elevation does not take in the whole building. Select the Bldg Elevation Line in the XRefed constructs. Move its start and end grips outward beyond the building (see Figure 16.26). Press Esc to deselect.

3. Select the elevation—verify that you have selected a 2D Section/Elevation object in the Properties palette. Right-click and choose Refresh from the shortcut menu. In a few moments, the Western Exterior Elevation is updated to encompass the entire building, including the roof overhangs.

WARNING If you see solid hatching appear on an elevation (with the exception of a terrain), adjust the Bldg Elevation Line in the view so that its defining line is in front of the building, not cutting through its interior. Otherwise, you will make a section.

4. Choose the Constructs tab in the Project Navigator. Drag the Frame element into the drawing window. Move the frame so it is roughly centered on the Western Exterior Elevation, but do not move the elevation. We used the frame element technique in Chapter 15, "Floor and Ceiling Plans," to match the available space on the sheet with the MSV.

5. Click the elevation and look in the Properties palette—verify that you have selected a 2D Section/Elevation object. Four magenta grips appear on the MSV boundary. Move each grip in turn to match the size of the frame element (see Figure 16.27). Press Esc to deselect.

6. Save the Exterior Elevations.dwg view file.

7. Select the Sheets tab in the Project Navigator. Right-click the Elevations subset and choose New ➤ Sheet from the shortcut menu. Type **A201** as the Number and **Exterior Elevations** as the Sheet Title (see Figure 16.28). Click OK.

FIGURE 16.26
Moving 2D Section/
Elevation object's MSV
grips to match frame size

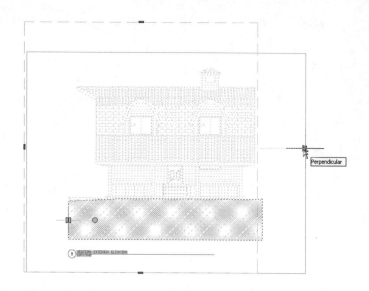

FIGURE 16.27
Adjusting Bldg Elevation
Line in view

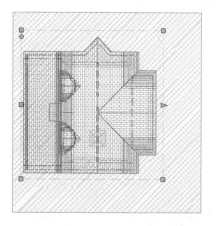

FIGURE 16.28
Creating a new sheet

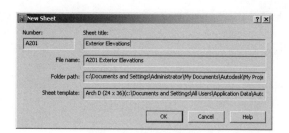

8. Double-click the A201 Exterior Elevations sheet node in the Project Navigator to open it.

9. Select the Views tab in the Project Navigator. Expand the Exterior Elevations view node to reveal its MSV. Drag the Western Exterior Elevation MSV into the sheet and snap it to the middle of the title block as a sheet view (see Figure 16.29). It fits perfectly because you preadjusted the MSV to fit the frame.

10. Save the A201 Exterior Elevations.dwg sheet file.

11. Switch back to the First Floor Plan view and zoom in on the elevation callout tag. The fields in the tag have been automatically updated so the tag is coordinated with the appropriate drawing and sheet number. Save the First Floor Plan.dwg view file. This completes the process of creating an exterior elevation.

12. Create the remaining three other exterior elevations on your own. Because you already have created a view drawing to hold all exterior elevations, click the Existing View Drawing button in the Place Callout worksheet this time. Place each exterior elevation MSV on the same sheet A201 (see Figure 16.30).

TIP Use Exterior Elevation Mark A3 to generate four exterior elevations simultaneously. Do not use this tool if you have already created an exterior elevation, however.

FIGURE 16.29
Placing elevation
on sheet

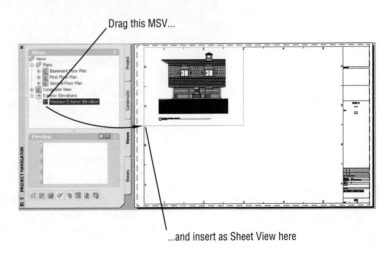

Drag this MSV...

...and insert as Sheet View here

FIGURE 16.30
Completed exterior
elevations placed
on sheet

Creating Interior Elevations with Callout Tools

Interior elevations are also made with callout tools that automate a long list of steps. You have the option of creating singular interior elevations or four interior elevations at once. Let's start by creating a single interior elevation of the living room in the first floor plan. You will elevate the southern wall first.

1. Open the First Floor Plan view if it is not already open.

2. Hover the cursor over the Elevation mark tools in the Callouts palette to read their ToolTips. Click Interior Elevation Mark C2. Click a point in the middle of the living room, above the furniture and to the left of the overhead beam. Use polar object tracking and specify the direction of the tag vertical downward, so you'll create an elevation of the southern interior wall.

3. Type **Living Room Elevation** as the New Model Space View Name in the Place Callout worksheet that appears. Notice that 3/8"-1'-0" scale is already selected—ADT does this for all interior elevations. Click the New View Drawing button.

4. Type **First Floor Interior Elevations** as the Name on the General page of the Add Section/Elevation View worksheet. Click Next.

5. Uncheck Basement and Second Floor levels on the Context page. Click Next.

6. On the Content page, uncheck the Roof Structure and Stairs categories. Uncheck the Slabs category and then check the First Floor Slab construct (see Figure 16.31). Click Finish.

7. Select two points that surround the southern wall of the living room and the furniture grouping. Then click a point off to the right side of the entire first floor plan to locate the new 2D Section/Elevation object in the First Floor Interior Elevations view drawing.

Selecting constructs for
the First Floor Interior
Elevations view

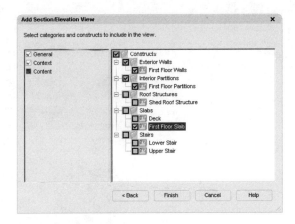

8. Choose the Views tab of the Project Navigator and double-click the First Floor Interior Elevations view to open it. The interior elevation object appears adjacent to the externally referenced constructs that it is linked to.

9. You need to adjust the boundaries of the elevation to encompass the volume of the living room. Switch to the SW Isometric viewpoint and toggle surface hatching off to increase display performance.

   Select the Bldg Elevation Line object and snap its Start grip perpendicular to the interior face of the exterior wall (see Figure 16.32). Snap the End grip to the interior face of the opposite wall. Press Esc to deselect.

FIGURE 16.32
Adjusting Bldg Elevation
Line in view

10. Select the interior elevation, right-click, and choose Refresh from the shortcut menu. The sides of the elevation are adjusted to match the boundary of the Bldg Elevation Line.

11. It isn't desirable to show the floor slab in the elevation. If we had the foresight to predict this, we might not have selected the First Floor Slab construct when we created this view earlier. Because you can't always make accurate predictions about how elevations will ultimately appear, you need to learn how to regenerate existing elevations. Select the elevation, right-click, and choose Regenerate. Click the Reselect Objects button in the Generate Selection/Elevation worksheet (see Figure 16.33). Select the exterior walls and interior partition constructs, but do not select the floor slab. Click OK to close the worksheet.

12. After a few moments the floor slab disappears from the elevation as it is regenerated (see Figure 16.34). Right-click the Manage XRefs icon in the drawing tray and detach the First Floor Slab construct. Select the elevation and adjust its MSV boundary, if necessary, so that the boundary is larger than the elevation and its title mark together. Click OK and save the `First Floor Interior Elevations.dwg` view file.

13. Create a new sheet using number A301 and name it **Interior Elevations**. Place the Living Room Elevation MSV onto the sheet. Save the `A301 Interior Elevations.dwg` sheet file.

14. Generate an interior elevation of the northern wall of the living room on your own. Place it onto sheet A301 (see Figure 16.35). Save the sheet file.

NOTE If you want to hide furniture in sections and elevations, move all pieces of furniture to separate constructs for each level. Then do not include the furniture constructs when generating or regenerating sections and elevations.

FIGURE 16.33
Reselecting the objects that generate an interior elevation

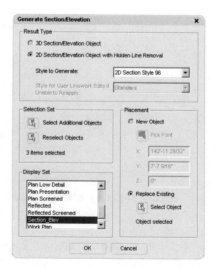

FIGURE 16.34
Completed Living Room elevation

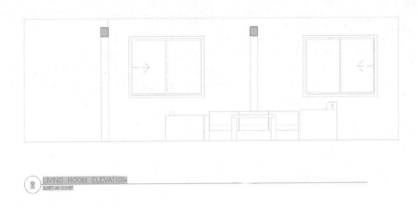

FIGURE 16.35
Completed First Floor interior elevations placed on sheet

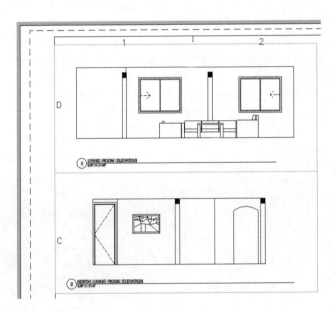

Creating Sections with Callout Tools

Section callout tools function much like the elevation callout tools. Let's create a longitudinal section through the entire building using section callout tool A2T—the callout tag has drawing and sheet number, a section line, and a tail. You will initiate the process in the Second Floor Plan in which the callout tag will live. In addition, you'll make a jogged Bldg Section Line to explore this possibility.

1. Select the Views tab of the Project Navigator and double-click the Second Floor Plan to open it.

2. Set the Document palette group current and choose the Callouts palette. Click the Section Mark A2T tool.

GENERATING MULTIPLE INTERIOR ELEVATIONS SIMULTANEOUSLY

If you have to make numerous interior elevations within a room or rooms, it is more efficient to use one of the callout tools designed for this purpose. These tools need to "know" the boundary of the room they are placed into, and you can use Space or Area objects to give the callout tool this information. You can create temporary spaces (or areas) if necessary to aid in this process, and delete them after the elevations have been created.

Use the Space Auto Generate tool on the Design palette (in the Design palette group) to quickly create spaces in existing rooms. It is easier to create spaces in this way rather than try and draw areas vertex by vertex. Create spaces before generating interior elevations.

Interior Elevation Mark B1 uses four numbered elevations. You can always delete one or more of these if you don't want to elevate all four interior walls. Use Interior Elevation Mark B2 if you want to identify the elevations by cardinal direction (N, E, S, and W) instead of by number on the plan.

Remember that you'll probably have to adjust the Bldg Elevation Line for each of your elevations to get their scopes exactly as you intend. Refresh the linked 2D Section/Elevation objects after making changes to the Bldg Elevation line.

3. Click the start point above the window in the north wall. Use polar object tracking and click the second point vertically down, inside the bedroom but above the bunk beds. Move the cursor horizontally to the right and click the next point above the door. Click three more points as shown on the left of Figure 16.36. Press Enter to complete drawing the section line. Move the cursor to the left and click a point outside the building to specify the section extents (see Figure 16.36, right).

4. Type **Longitudinal Building Section** as the New MSV Name in the Place Callout worksheet. Change the Scale drop-down list to $1/4''=1'-0''$. Verify that both check boxes are set and click the New View Drawing button.

5. Type the name **Building Sections** as the new view name on the General page of the Add Section/ Elevation View worksheet. Click Next.

FIGURE 16.36
Drawing section line (left) and specifying section extents (right)

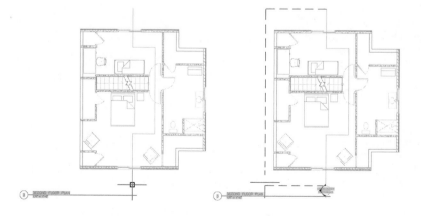

6. Leave all three levels checked on the Context page and click Next. Leave all constructs checked on the Content page except for Shed Roof Structure and Deck, which you can uncheck. These two constructs will not be visible in the section. Click Finish to close the worksheet.

7. The command line says the following:

```
** You are being prompted for a point in a different view drawing **
Specify insertion point for the 2D section result:
```

Click a point off to the right side of the second floor plan to locate the new 2D Section/Elevation object in the Building Sections view.

8. Double-click the Building Sections node that has just appeared in the Project Navigator to open it. Zoom in on the section drawing and notice that you can see the surface hatching on the underside of the roof and the inside of the dormer walls. This surface hatching should appear only on the exterior face of the roof, not on its underside. To hide this surface hatching, you'll have to create material surface hatch overrides in the constructs that the section was generated from.

9. Select the Constructs tab in the Project Navigator and double-click the Roof construct in the Roof Structures category to open it. Use the 3D Orbit command to rotate underneath the roof. Select one of the roof slabs, right-click, and choose Materials ➤ Add Surface Hatch Override from the shortcut menu. Click the surface hatch on the underside of the roof slab. Choose All Bottom Faces from the Faces drop-down list in the Surface Hatch Override worksheet that appears (see Figure 16.37). Check Hide Surface Hatching and click OK. The surface hatching disappears on the underside of the roof slab. Monolithic slabs have only one bottom face.

TIP Set UCS to world prior to 3D orbiting for more intuitive control.

10. Repeat the last step for each of the roof slabs. Save and close the Roof.dwg construct file.

11. Double-click Dormers in the Roof Structures category to open it. Switch to the SE Isometric viewpoint. Hide the surface hatching on the backside of the walls that contain the dormer windows. Save and close the Dormers.dwg construct file.

FIGURE 16.37
Hiding bottom faces' surface hatching in construct (left) and the result on underside of roof slab (right)

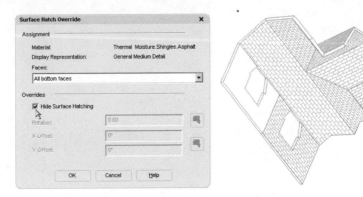

12. Switch back to the Building Sections view. Notice that a balloon informs you that XRefs may have changed. Right-click the Manage XRefs icon in the drawing tray and choose Reload XRefs from the shortcut menu. The Longitudinal Building Section has not changed.

13. Select the Longitudinal Building Section, right-click, and choose Refresh. The surface hatching disappears from the underside of the roof and from the backside of the dormer walls in the section (see Figure 16.38).

NOTE Remember that even if XRefs may have changed and been reloaded in a view, you still have to manually refresh section and elevation objects for the changes to take effect.

14. Save and close the Building Sections.dwg view file. Choose the Sheets tab in the Project Navigator and create a new sheet inside the Sections subset. Type **A401** as Number and **Building Sections** as Sheet Title in the New Sheet dialog box and click OK. Double-click A401 Building Sections to open the new sheet.

15. Choose the Views tab in the Project Navigator. Expand the Building Sections view node and drag the Longitudinal Building Section MSV into the sheet.

16. Select the Constructs tab in the Project Navigator and drag the Western Perspective Section element into the sheet. Zoom to the extents of the sheet and scale the element down so it fits on the sheet. Move the element to an appropriate place on the sheet.

17. Adapt the preceding steps to create a Transverse Building Section on your own and add it to the same sheet (see Figure 16.39). Save and close all open files (except for Drawing1.dwg).

WARNING Always leave one blank drawing open or else ADT will go into the "zero doc" state, in which it cannot display palettes and menus.

FIGURE 16.38
Matching MSV boundary
to frame dimensions
in view

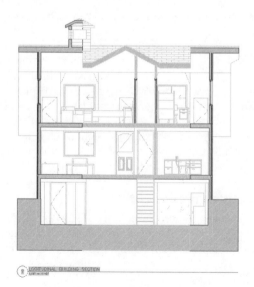

LONGITUDINAL BUILDING SECTION

FIGURE 16.39
Completed building
sections

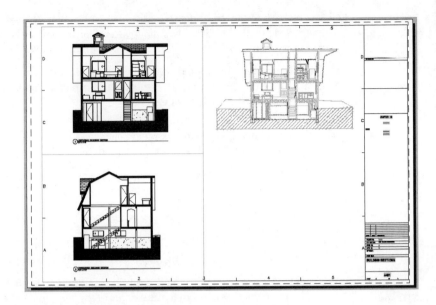

Editing 2D Section/Elevation Styles

Sections and elevations—technically known as 2D Section/Elevation objects—have styles that help to control their appearance. Let's explore 2D Section/Elevation styles with the goal of understanding how they work.

Consider that sections and elevations are generated from objects that might have materials assigned to their component parts. These materials interact with the 2D Section/Elevation style to determine the ultimate appearance of the linework in section and/or elevation drawings.

For example, in this tutorial the roof slabs have an asphalt shingle material assigned to their slab component. The asphalt shingle material definition has display properties such as the `Roofing_Shingles_3-Tab` surface hatch pattern that is inherited by the linework in the 2D Section/Elevation object.

The 2D Section/Elevation styles have custom components that are subject to design rules that determine how linework is assigned to its display components, and thus control how linework will ultimately appear. Design rules work by color, so it behooves you to study object colors in constructs before coming up with new design rules for 2D Section/Elevation styles.

In this topic, you'll edit a 2D Section/Elevation style to improve the appearance of the linework shown in your elevations. In addition, you'll open constructs and adjust material definition options to tweak some of the finer points relating to 2D Section/Elevation objects.

Creating Components

In this context, the term *components* refers to user-defined display components belonging to a 2D Section/Elevation style. Components are used in conjunction with design rules, which you'll learn about shortly. Let's examine the default components that have already been set up for you.

1. Select the Views tab of the Project Navigator and double-click Exterior Elevations to open it.

2. Zoom in on the Western Exterior Elevation 2D Section/Elevation object. On the application status bar, toggle on LWT to display lineweights on-screen. This will help you to visualize how this drawing will ultimately be published (see Chapter 19, "Printing and Publishing"). The title mark is the only portion of the drawing that gets a thicker lineweight at present.

3. Select the 2D Section/Elevation object, right-click, and choose Edit 2D Elevation/Section Style from the shortcut menu. Choose the Components tab of the 2D Section/Elevation Style Properties dialog box that appears (see Figure 16.40). Leave the dialog box open.

There are two components defined already: Medium-Weight Objects and Swing Lines. As you can see, these components have an index number, name, and description. Obviously, there must be more to the story because by themselves components have no effect unless they are assigned to design rules.

FIGURE 16.40

2D Section/Elevation style components

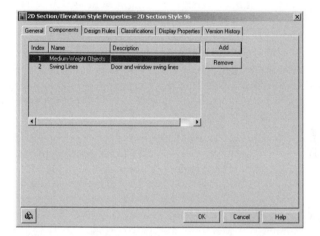

Setting Design Rules

Design rules are based on color. Design rules map objects that display in particular colors to specific display components that are controlled by the 2D Section/Elevation style's display properties. Let's take a look at predefined design rules to understand how they work.

Select the Design Rules tab (see Figure 16.41). Rule 1 can be summarized as follows: Any visible objects with color 54 will be assigned to the Swing Lines component. This rule maps windows and door swings to the user-defined Swing Lines component you saw in Figure 16.40. The rule works because window and door swings have Swing components that use color 54 in their Elevation display representations. You would have to investigate this issue to know which color the Swing component used in the drawing default display properties for door and window styles. Thus, setting design rules can be a very deep exercise that requires careful planning.

With design rule 1 in effect, the ultimate appearance of door and window swings is now controlled by the display properties of the custom component in the 2D Section/Elevation style. Click OK to close the 2D Section/Elevation Style Properties dialog box.

FIGURE 16.41

Design rules of 2D
Section/Elevation style

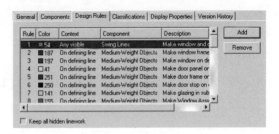

Controlling Display Properties

2D Section/Elevation styles have numerous permanent and user-defined display components that
control the appearance of the linework in section and elevation drawings. Let's examine and adjust
these components to improve the way the elevation drawings appear.

UNDERSTANDING DISPLAY COMPONENTS

Both permanent and user-defined display components appear in the General display representation's
display properties. The General display representation has a style override by default. Before you get
started adjusting display properties of the various display components, it helps to examine the layers
in the current drawing.

1. Click the Layer Manager button on the Layer Properties toolbar. Scroll down in the Layer Manager and locate the A-Elev layer. Notice that it is greenish (color 111) and has a lineweight of
   0.25mm. Layer A-Elev-Line is not plottable and is not seen in elevations because it is the layer
   the Bldg Elevation Line resides on. Scroll a bit farther down and study the A-Sect layers. Pay
   attention to their colors and lineweights because they can appear in the elevation object (see
   Figure 16.42). After you finish examining the settings, click Cancel.

2. Select the 2D Section/Elevation object and observe that it resides on layer A-Elev. Right-click
   and choose Edit 2D Elevation/Section Style from the shortcut menu. Choose the Display Properties tab of the 2D Section/Elevation Style Properties dialog box.

FIGURE 16.42

Examining relevant
layers for sections and
elevations

3. Double-click the General display representation's icon to open the Display Properties Style Override dialog box.

4. Choose the Layer/Color/Linetype tab if it is not already selected (see Figure 16.43). Change the Outer Shrinkwrap display component's lineweight to 0.50 mm. This will thicken the border that wraps around cut objects, which in this elevation is the terrain only.

NOTE Use 2D Section/Elevation styles to specify which components will have their display controlled by materials and which will not (by checking the By Material column). User-defined components cannot use materials because they exist only within the 2D Section/Elevation styles.

5. Toggle off the visibility of the Shrinkwrap Hatch component—this is the light gray solid hatch that filled the terrain.

6. Notice that the Surface Hatch Linework display component's color is set to ByBlock. The surface hatching you see in the elevation is greenish (color 111) because the ByBlock assignment causes this linework to inherit the color of the layer the 2D Section/Elevation object is on (A-Elev).

7. Change the layer assignment of the Subdivision 1 display component to A-Sect-Medm to embolden the major lines in the elevation.

8. Toggle off the visibility of the Swing Lines component to hide door and window swings. Click OK in each open dialog box. The appearance of the elevation is improved (see Figure 16.44). Be aware that the LWT toggle exaggerates the actual printed lineweights on-screen.

TIP Use the Style Manager to overwrite the 2D Section Style 96 in the Building Sections view with the same style from the Exterior Elevation view to save time customizing display properties.

9. Save and close the `Exterior Elevations.dwg` view file.

FIGURE 16.43
Adjusting style override display properties

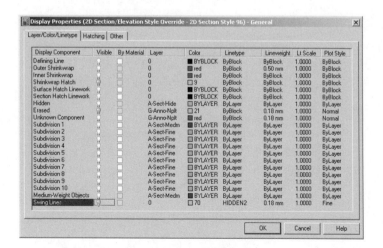

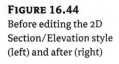

FIGURE 16.44
Before editing the 2D
Section/Elevation style
(left) and after (right)

Working with 2D Section/Elevation Objects

Aside from editing styles, there are several things you can do with 2D Section/Elevation objects. You'll learn the distinction between refreshing, batch refreshing, and regenerating elevations and sections. You can also edit individual linework within 2D Section/Elevation objects for the ultimate in customizability. In addition, you'll learn how to limit the display of surface hatching within a specific boundary.

OTHER OPTIONS AND 2D SECTION/ELEVATION MATERIAL RULES

The display properties dialog box for the 2D Section/Elevation style override has an Other tab in which there are two check boxes that control how material components intermingle:

◆ Use Subdivision Properties For Surface Hatching—check this box to get subdivision components to use the surface hatch of the material while using all the remaining display properties of the subdivision. By Material must be cleared for this to work.

◆ Use 3D Body Display Component For By Material Linework—checking this box causes the Defining Line and Subdivision components to display according to the 3D Body component of materials. This is off by default, so the display properties in the 2D Section/Elevation style take precedence.

Material definitions have several rules that apply to 2D Section/Elevation objects. You can find these rules on the Other tab in the material definition display properties dialog box:

◆ Exclude from 2D Section Shrinkwrap—choose this setting when you want to exclude certain components, such as glass or air gap, from the typically bold shrinkwrap linework that appears in 2D Section/Elevation objects.

◆ Display Hidden Edges For This Material—select this setting to display components that are typically hidden, such as foundation walls, footings, and structural members that you want to have in a 2D Section/Elevation object.

◆ Merge Common Materials—choosing this setting removes edges between adjacent coplanar faces on objects that share the same material. You might use this to merge linework between footings and foundation walls in a section, or to merge the lines between floors, for example.

Refreshing, Batch Refreshing, and Regenerating

Whenever the design changes, with alterations made to objects and material definitions stored in construct files, you have to reload the affected external references in section and elevation view files. In addition, you must refresh individual 2D Section/Elevation objects for design changes to appear. If your project contains dozens of section and elevation objects, this might be a daunting task. Fortunately, there is a batch refresh command that automates this process across multiple drawing files.

Choose View ➤ Refresh Sections and Elevations. Choose the Current Project radio button to process every file in the project. Choose Folder if you want to be more specific. Click Start and watch the drawing window as each drawing file is opened in turn and its 2D Section/Elevation objects refreshed. Figure 16.45 shows batch refreshing in process.

Regenerating is different from refreshing because it allows you to go back and re-create the section or elevation object from first principles. When regenerating, you have the opportunity to reselect the objects that will be linked to the replacement 2D Section/Elevation object. In other words, regenerating is an opportunity to add or remove objects that are linked into the 2D Section/Elevation object.

For example, if you decide that you don't want to include a furniture construct in a section, regenerate it and don't reselect the XRefed furniture construct in the view file when you replace the existing 2D Section/Elevation object. You can then detach any unused XRefs from the view file because they are no longer needed.

You can also change the result type between 2D Section/Elevation object with Hidden Line Removal and a 3D Section/Elevation object by regenerating. This process can be useful if you want to convert a traditional 2D section that is viewed orthogonally to a 3D section that is viewed isometrically, or vice versa.

FIGURE 16.45
Batch refreshing 2D
Section/Elevation
objects

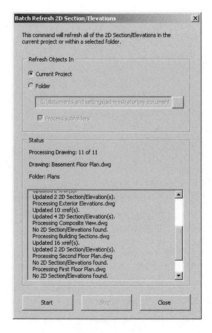

Editing Linework

New!

Sometimes the way an elevation or section appears isn't as you intend, even after you've adjusted its display properties and edited its material definitions. You can edit linework within a 2D Section/ Elevation object, and using a trigger grip to enter an In Place Editing mode is new to ADT 2006. Editing linework offers the maximum control over section and elevation display. It works regardless of what subdivision lines are assigned to. You can even draw new lines and merge them into the 2D Section/Elevation object and assign components to individual lines that alter a section or elevation object's appearance.

1. Choose the Views tab in the Project Navigator and double-click Exterior Elevations to open it.

2. Zoom in on the Western Exterior Elevation and select it. Click its Edit Linework trigger grip. An In-Place Edit floating toolbar appears.

3. Select the vertical line dividing roof slabs in between the two dormers. This edge appears because this roof surface was created with separate roof slab objects in the Roofs construct. Right-click and choose Modify Component from the shortcut menu.

4. The Select Linework Component worksheet appears. Choose Erased Vectors from the Linework Component drop-down list (see Figure 16.46). Click OK and the vertical line disappears because it was reassigned to the Erased display component (visibility off by default). Click the Save All Changes button in the In-Place Edit toolbar.

5. Zoom in on the region between the two dormers. Draw five short vertical line segments to complete the missing surface hatch pattern. Select the 2D Section/Elevation object, right-click, and choose Linework ➤ Merge from the shortcut menu. Select all five line segments and press Enter. Choose Surface Hatch from the drop-down list in the Select Linework Component worksheet (see Figure 16.47). Click OK; the lines you drew turn greenish (color 111) in this case as they become part of the 2D Section/Elevation object.

TIP Lines merged on the Erased Vectors linework component hide lines they overlap. This allows you to add lines on top of existing lines to erase them.

FIGURE 16.46

Modifying component assignment of individual line within the 2D Section/Elevation object

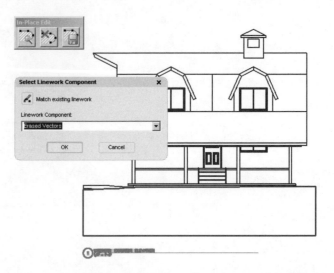

FIGURE 16.47
Merging linework and
assigning a linework
component

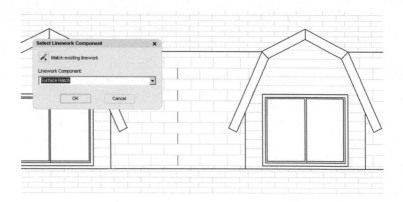

Adding a Material Boundary

Displaying surface hatching all over an elevation can make it seem too busy and might detract from
the readability of the drawing. However, showing at least some surface hatching can be beneficial to
convey the impression of materiality without going overboard. Surface hatch patterns are assigned to
objects by material definitions. Adding a material boundary to a 2D Section/Elevation object solves
the problem of selectively displaying surface hatching.

1. Open `Exterior Elevations.dwg` if it is not already open. Zoom in on the Northern Exterior
   Elevation.

2. Draw a closed polyline like the one shown in Figure 16.48 to define a boundary that you'll add
   to the 2D Section/Elevation object in a moment. Don't worry about matching your boundary
   exactly to the figure—its exact dimensions are of no consequence.

FIGURE 16.48
Drawing a closed bound-
ary to limit material
display

3. Select the 2D Section/Elevation object, right-click, and choose Material Boundary ➤ Add. Select the polyline you just drew. Press **Y** and then Enter to erase the polyline.

4. The 2D Section/Elevation Material Boundary worksheet appears. Leave everything else with its default settings. You have the opportunity to select individual materials that the material boundary will apply to, among other things. Click OK and the surface hatching is limited to the boundary you drew previously. Figure 16.49 shows the worksheet and the result in the 2D Section/Elevation object.

5. Save and close all files. Open the Project Browser and close the project. Congratulations on completing another chapter.

FIGURE 16.49
Adding a 2D Section/Elevation Material Boundary (left) and the result (right)

ANNOTATING SECTIONS AND ELEVATIONS

Annotations should be treated the same way in sections and elevations as in other drawings in the project hierarchy. That is, you should add dimensions and notes to view files, directly to the 2D Section/Elevation objects. Do not dimension the live section or 3D XRefed constructs in the view files, however. Make a hidden-line projection or linked section or elevation object when you want to add annotation and/or dimensions.

Special elevation labels are located in the Documentation Tool Catalog (accessible via the Content Browser). Elevation labels are provided that show heights in plans, in 2D sections, and in 3D model viewpoints. You can also access these symbols in the DesignCenter under the following folder on the AEC Content tab:

```
Custom Applications > Architectural Desktop > Imperial > Documentation > Elevation
Labels
```

Summary

You have learned how to generate section and elevation drawings from the single building model (SBM) stored in a project's elements and constructs. You started by visualizing the SBM by cutting a live section in a composite view. Then you made a hidden-line projection and generated 2D and 3D linked section and elevation objects. You learned everything necessary to integrate the linked sections and elevations into the project structure so they can be printed on sheets. You also learned how to customize the appearance of 2D Section/Elevation styles and objects to get drawings exactly as you want them. In the next chapter, you'll explore the last facets of construction documentation: details and keynotes.

Chapter 17

Details and Keynotes

Architectural Desktop (ADT) has robust detailing and keynoting systems that are based on Microsoft Access databases. The databases that ship with ADT have a great deal of content that will get you started both with detailing and keynotes. However, you'll eventually need to add new content to suit your specific needs because of the virtually limitless content shown in detail drawings.

In ADT 2006, you can add and edit data stored in the databases from within ADT without having to use Access to perform this work. You might create different databases for each project or allow one set of detail and keynote databases to evolve with every project taken on by your organization.

This chapter uses databases that are based on the Construction Specifications Institute (CSI) Master-Format system, which is used widely in the United States and Canada. MasterFormat is a hierarchical system of numbers and titles that classify building components. ADT also ships with additional detail and keynote databases that are commonly used in other parts of the world, and they are used in the same ways.

Detail callout tools add detail bubbles that are automatically coordinated with appropriate drawing and sheet numbers in the sheet set, just like the elevation and section callout tools you learned how to use in the last chapter. Unlike the other callout tools, however, detail callouts generate 2D Section/Elevation objects that do not plot because they are used merely as tracing templates for detail components. You'll learn how to add detail components from the default database by using various detail tools and by using the Detail Component Manager.

Detail components are stored as "recipes" in Extensible Markup Language (XML) files. In this chapter you'll learn how to create a custom detail component without hand-coding XML. However, greater functionality for designing detail components is available to managers who can write XML code.

As a last stage, you'll learn how to add reference and sheet keynotes to detail drawings that you have created. You'll use the new Keynote Editor to interface with ADT's keynote database, in which you will make necessary adjustments. Finally, you'll generate keynote legends from the added keynotes and learn how to edit their table styles and cells. This chapter's topics include the following:

◆ Using Detail Callouts

◆ Adding Detail Components to a Drawing

◆ Creating Custom Components

◆ Working with Keynotes

Using Detail Callouts

Detail callout tools are used in views, just like the elevation and section callout tools you used in Chapter 16, "Sections and Elevations." Detail callouts can be added to plans, elevations, and/or section views to indicate areas that have corresponding detail drawings. A detail callout tool potentially adds a callout tag, view drawing, 2D Section/Elevation object, title mark, and model space view (MSV). After using a detail callout tool, you'll be left with a 2D Section Elevation object whose display components are preconfigured on a nonplotting layer.

The 2D Section Elevation object forms a kind of tracing template onto which you'll add detail components to create a particular detail drawing. The detail drawing itself will be added to a sheet using the MSV generated by the detail callout tool. The process for creating detail drawings is quite straightforward and easy to understand once you experience it.

A very simple project has been created for this chapter so you can focus on detailing without distraction. You will create a typical wall section detail. Let's open the project and get started.

1. Copy this chapter's folder from the DVD to the following folder on your hard drive or to the equivalent folder on a networked file server:

   `C:\Documents and Settings\<username>\My Documents\Autodesk\My Projects`

2. Click the Project Browser button on the Navigation toolbar. In the Project Browser, double-click the Chapter 17 node in the tree pane to set the project current (see Figure 17.1). Click Close.

3. Choose the Views tab in the Project Navigator. Expand the Sections node and double-click the Exterior Wall Section MSV node to open the file and zoom to the named view.

4. Set the Document palette group current in the Tool palettes and choose the Callouts palette. There are three detail callout tools located at the top of the palette with round, rectangular, and free form-shaped detail boundaries. Move the cursor over the tools and read their ToolTips. Click the Detail Boundary B tool (with a rectangular boundary). Draw a detail box in which the exterior wall and first floor intersect (see Figure 17.2). The detail boundary will appear after you click two opposite corners of the detail box.

FIGURE 17.1
Setting the project current in the Project Browser

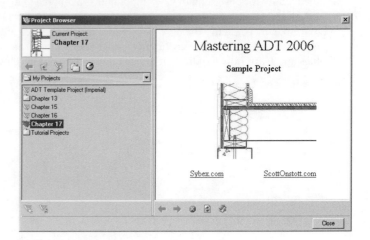

FIGURE 17.2
Drawing detail box

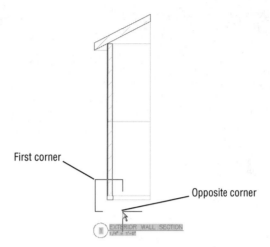

First corner

Opposite corner

5. Using polar object tracking, move the cursor above and to the left of the detail boundary along a 135-degree vector and click the first point of the leader line. Move the cursor horizontally to the left and click the next point (see Figure 17.3). Press Enter to end the leader line.

6. The Place Callout worksheet appears. Type **Typical Wall Section At First Floor** in the New Model Space View Name text box. Change the Scale drop-down list to 1"=1'-0". Verify that Generate Section/Elevation and Place Titlemark are checked (see Figure 17.4).

7. For the Create In option, click the Current Drawing button; the Place Callout worksheet disappears. Specify the insertion point off to the right side of the section drawing.

NOTE Alternatively, you might create a new Detail view drawing in a more complex project in which you want to separate sections from details.

FIGURE 17.3
Drawing a leader line

First point of leader line

Next point

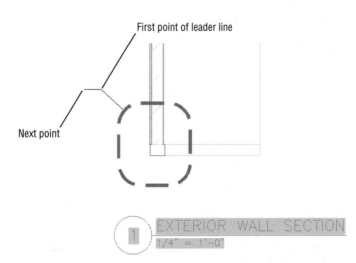

FIGURE 17.4
Filling in the Place
Callout worksheet

8. Switch to the SW Isometric viewpoint and toggle off surface hatching. The XRefed constructs have a Bldg Section Line object that is associated with the Exterior Wall Section drawing (the old 2D Section/Elevation object). The Bldg Elevation Line object is associated with the new 2D Section/Elevation object (refer to Figure 17.5) that will act as a tracing template for a detail you will draw shortly. The Bldg Elevation Line looks three-dimensional because it is not using model extents for its height. Instead, the 3D wireframe of the Bldg Elevation Line determined the size of the new 2D Section/Elevation object that was generated from it. The X and Z dimensions of the Bldg Elevation Line were determined when you placed the callout. The Y dimension isn't relevant because it is perpendicular to the plane of the detail. You can easily adjust the dimensions of the Bldg Elevation Line using its grips.

9. At this point you have the basis for tracing a new detail drawing over the new 2D Section/Elevation object. Switch back to the Top viewpoint. Save the Sections.dwg view file.

FIGURE 17.5
Examining the relationship between Bldg
Lines and 2D Section/
Elevation objects

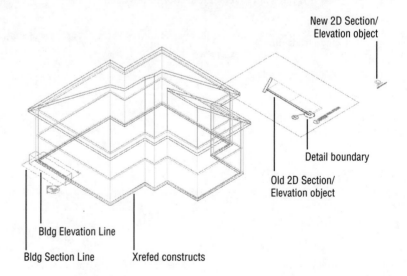

10. The sheet and drawing number fields in the detail callout tag and Typical Wall Section At First Floor title mark will not be resolved until you place the detail on a sheet. Select the Sheets tab in the Project Navigator and double-click the A601 Details node to open the file.

11. Choose the View tab in the Project Navigator and drag the Typical Wall Section At First Floor MSV onto the sheet and click a point to insert the detail sheet view. Save and close the A601 `Details.dwg` sheet file. Now the question mark fields are resolved in the callout tag and title mark on the Sections view (see Figure 17.6).

FIGURE 17.6
Detail callout tag (left) and detail title mark (right) referenced as drawing 1 on sheet A601

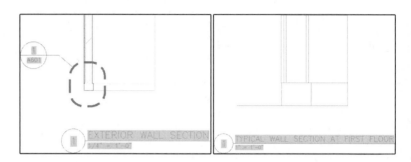

Adding Detail Components to a Drawing

Although detail components are not intelligent architecture, engineering, and construction (AEC) objects, they are still "smarter" than AutoCAD entities because extra information in the form of extended entity data (Xdata) is automatically attached. The Xdata makes it possible to quickly add similar components and to replace existing detail components with ease.

Detail components might appear as anonymous blocks, linework, or hatch patterns, depending on which type of component was inserted. Detail components follow *recipes* that describe which orientations (plan, elevation, and/or section) are available for a chosen detail component and how to draw it using *jigs*—programming constructs that control how objects are added to a drawing.

Recipes are stored in XML files and are customizable. You'll learn how to let ADT create a generic recipe for you in the section "Creating Custom Components" later in this chapter.

NOTE Describing how to hand-code recipes in XML goes beyond the scope of this book. If you're experienced with XML, refer to the ADT help system for recipe specifications.

Before you start adding detail components, you'll need to choose a detail component database. Right-click the command line and choose Options from the shortcut menu. Navigate to and choose the AEC Content tab in the Options dialog box.

Click the Add/Remove Detail Component Databases button. Verify that the AEC Detail Component Database (US) appears in the Configure Detail Component Databases dialog box (see Figure 17.7). This would be the place to add your own custom Access database (`.mdb` file) if so inclined, or if working outside the US. The databases that ship with ADT are located in the following folder:

```
C:\Documents and Settings\All Users\Application Data\Autodesk\ADT
2006\enu\Details
```

Please use the US database in this chapter. Click OK twice to return to the drawing.

FIGURE 17.7
Checking detail
component database

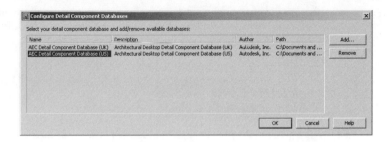

TIP The databases that ship with ADT are nested within the following folder: `C:\Documents and Settings\All Users\Application Data\Autodesk\ADT 2006\enu\Details`

There are two methods for adding detail components: using detail tools and using the Detail Component Manager. There are a number of detail tools stored in the Detailing palette group. You can add additional detail tools to the Tool palettes by dragging and dropping entities from the drawing window or the Content Browser. The Detail Component Manager offers the most comprehensive list of components, but isn't quite as convenient as using the detail tools.

Using Detail Tools to Add Detail Components

Detail tools offer the most convenient interface for accessing detail component content. The Detailing palette group comes preconfigured with numerous commonly used detail components. Customize the palettes in the Detailing palette group as your projects evolve.

1. Choose the Views tab in the Project Navigator and double-click the Typical Wall Section At First Floor MSV to open the file and zoom to the named view. Open the Properties palette if it is not already open.

2. Set the Detailing palette group current in the Tool palettes. Select the Basic palette and examine its tools; there are tools that range from 02 - Sitework to 16 - Electrical. These tools mirror the major divisions of the CSI MasterFormat (see Figure 17.8). Click the 03 - Concrete tool.

3. Properties will appear in the Properties palette in a few moments. Spend some time experimenting with the available properties but do not click in the drawing window to avoid placing a detail component yet. When you are satisfied, select Walls from the Type drop-down list. Set Show Reinforcing to No in the Specifications subcategory.

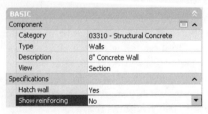

4. The command line says the following:

```
Start point or [Xflip/Yflip/Left/Center/Right]:
```

FIGURE 17.8
Basic detailing tools

Type **R** for right justification and press Enter. Click the first point shown in Figure 17.9 to insert the concrete detail component on top of the 2D Section/Elevation object. Move the cursor vertically down a short distance, click again to specify the next point, and press Enter to end the command.

5. A concrete wall appears in the section filled with a concrete hatch pattern. Select the concrete detail component and look again at the Properties palette. Notice that the properties you set earlier have disappeared, and the Properties palette shows the selected component as a Block Reference. The Name parameter has a code that identifies it as an anonymous block. Select the Extended Data tab and notice that the Detail Component Data category: this is Xdata (see Figure 17.10). The Xdata remains attached to the object but is not editable. Press Esc to deselect.

6. Click the 06 - Woods & Plastics tool on the Basic palette. Choose the Design tab of the Properties palette and change the Category to 06110 - Wood Framing. Verify that Type is set to Nominal Cut Lumber and change the Description property to 2x6.

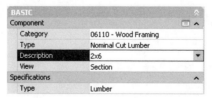

FIGURE 17.9
Drawing a concrete wall
component in section

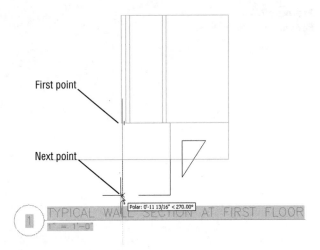

FIGURE 17.10
Examining the Properties
palettes after inserting
a detail component:
Design tab (left) and
Extended Data tab (right)

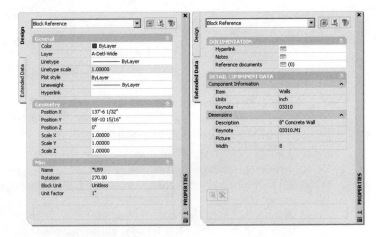

7. The command line says the following:

```
Insert point or [Base point/Rotate/Xflip/Yflip]:
```

Type **R** for Rotate, press Enter, type **90**, and press Enter. Type **Y** to flip the component across its y-axis and then click the endpoint shown in Figure 17.11 to insert the sill plate on top of the concrete wall. Press Enter to end the command.

FIGURE 17.11
Inserting a 2x6 sill plate

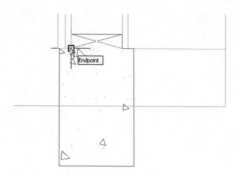

8. Choose the Exterior palette. Select the 2x6 component in the drawing window and drag it to the Exterior palette. A new 2x6 tool is created. Make specific tools like this when you anticipate adding multiple similar components.

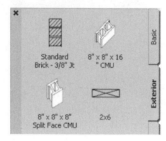

Using the Detail Component Manager

Another way to add detail components is through the Detail Component Manager. The Detail Component Manager has direct access to the database and offers the maximum number of components. You will start by adding a thin layer of joint sealant between the concrete wall and the 2x6 sill plate.

1. Toggle on LWT on the application status bar—it can be helpful to preview lineweight as you are adding detail components. Choose Insert ➢ Detail Component Manager to open a dialog box of the same name. Verify that AecDtlComponents (US).mdb is selected in the Current Detail Component Database drop-down list. In the tree pane, expand Division 07 - Thermal and Moisture Protection > 07900 - Joint Sealers > 07915 - Joint Sealer and click the Joint Sealant node (see Figure 17.12). There is only one detail component listed in the bottom pane; notice that it has a specific keynote assigned (07915.D1). The Image tab shows a preview of the component, and the Information tab might have additional data (not in this case, however).

NOTE   Each detail component has a corresponding keynote that is stored in the keynote database.

FIGURE 17.12
Detail Component
Manager

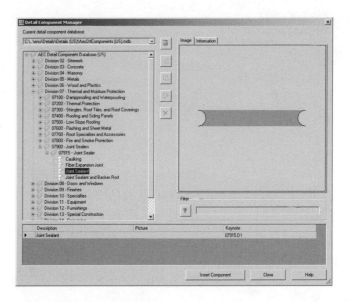

2. Click the Insert Component button, and the Detail Component Manager dialog box closes. Change the Joint Size property to $^1/_4$″ in the Properties palette. Notice the worksheet icon in the title bar of the Component subcategory: It reopens the Detail Component Manager when clicked.

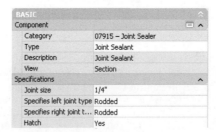

3. The command line says the following:

```
Start point or [Xflip/Yflip]:
```

Type **X** to flip the component across the x-axis. Click the start point on the lower-left corner of the 2x6. Click the endpoint at the lower-right corner and press Enter. Move the 2x6 up $^1/_4$″ vertically (see Figure 17.13). It is no problem to move, copy, and rotate components after they have been inserted.

4. Now you will create a platform framing condition by adding a header joist and a floor joist. Click the 2x6 tool and change Description to 2x8. Click the upper-left corner of the sill plate to insert the header joist. Change View to Elevation and click the lower-right corner of the header joist as the start point and click again perpendicular to the right edge of the 2D Section/Elevation object to draw the floor joist (see Figure 17.14). Press Enter to end the command.

FIGURE 17.13
Adding joint sealer
between concrete and
sill plate

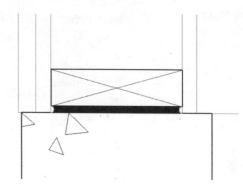

FIGURE 17.14
Adding joist and
header joist

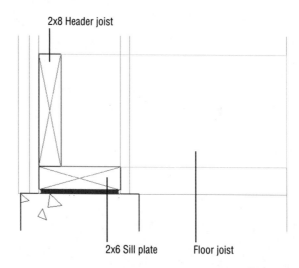

2x8 Header joist

2x6 Sill plate   Floor joist

5. Next up is the plywood subfloor that goes on top of the platform. Choose Insert ➤ Detail Component Manager. Type **plywood** in the Filter text box and click the adjacent filter button. The tree view is immediately filtered to show components having the entered keyword only. This is the fastest way to access a component. Select the Plywood node under 06160 - Sheathing. Click the cell adjacent to $3/4$" Plywood in the bottom pane to select it (see Figure 17.15).

6. Click the Insert Component button and click the first point on the upper-left corner of the header joist. Click the endpoint on the upper-right corner of the floor joist. Plywood extends across the platform. Press Enter to end the command.

7. Now you will add a 2x6 sole plate on top of the subfloor and a wall stud on top of the sole plate. Select the sill plate, right-click, and choose Add Selected from the shortcut menu. Click the upper-left corner of the plywood flooring to add the sole plate. Change View to Elevation to look at this piece of lumber from the side. Click the upper-left corner of the sill plate and type **L** to left-justify the new component. A triangular symbol indicates the length dimension of the stud. Move the cursor up vertically and click a point some distance above the top of the 2D Section/Elevation object (see Figure 17.16). Press Enter to end the command.

FIGURE 17.15
Filtering the detail
component database

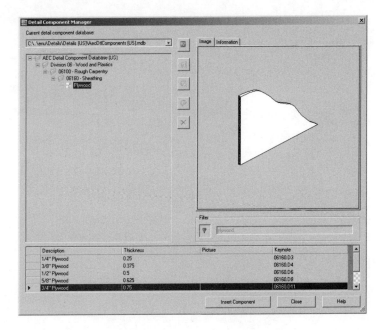

FIGURE 17.16
Adding sole plate
and wall stud

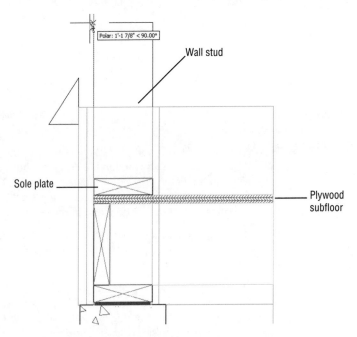

TIP Use Replace Selected on the shortcut menu to quickly change a selected component without having to open the Detail Component Manager. Replace selected deletes the original component and restarts its recipe in the Properties palette.

8. Add $^5/_8''$ plywood sheathing to the exterior face of the wall. Use the Detail Component Manager and add one layer of $^5/_8''$ gypsum wallboard (MasterFormat 09250) to the interior face of the wall stud on top of the platform. Hide the 2D Section/Elevation object for clarity (see Figure 17.17).

9. The wall needs an anchor bolt to connect it with the concrete foundation wall. Choose Insert ➢ Detail Component Manager. Type **Anchor Bolt** in the Filter text box and click the filter button. Select the Anchor Bolts Hook node in the tree pane. Choose $^1/_2''$ Hooked Anchor Bolt in the bottom pane and click the Insert Component button. Click the projection point at the midpoint of the top edge of the concrete wall. Click the nut location at the top of the sill plate. Click a point below and to the left of the bottom of the bolt to specify the hook location (see Figure 17.18). Click Enter to end the command.

10. The AEC Modify Obscure command is quite helpful when inserting detail components. Make a crossing selection and select the joint sealer, sill plate, and floor joist. Right-click and choose AEC Modify ➢ Obscure. Select the hooked anchor bolt and press Enter. Red lines appear inside the boundary of the anchor shaft: These are hidden lines. Freeze the A-Detl-Hide layer, and these red lines disappear.

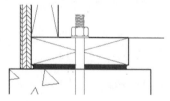

FIGURE 17.17
Adding exterior plywood sheathing and interior gypsum wallboard

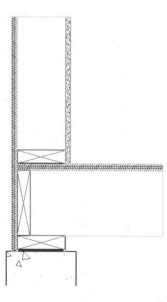

FIGURE 17.18
Inserting a hooked
anchor bolt

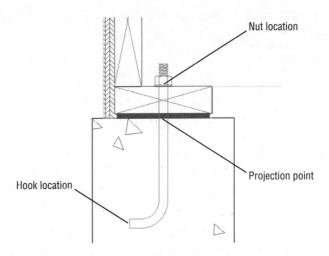

11. Use the Detail Component Manager to insert 1x4 wood strip tongue and groove flooring on top of the subfloor (MasterFormat 09640). Click the start point on the lower-right edge of the interior gypsum wallboard and the endpoint some distance beyond the right edge of the floor joist.

12. Add $5/8''$ X $31/2''$ Base Molding (MasterFormat 06450) to the interface between the wood strip flooring and the gypsum wallboard.

13. The wall still needs insulation. Open the Detail Component Manager again. type **Batt** in the text box, and press the filter button. Add 5-$1/2''$ R-21 Fiberglass Batt Insulation in between the wall studs. Click the start point at the midpoint along the upper edge of the sole plate and the next point at the top of the stud. Press Enter to complete the command.

14. Insulation also needs to be placed behind the header joist on top of the sill plate. Add more of the same type of insulation there by using left justification and snapping the start and endpoints to the corners of the header joist. When the command line says the following, click the upper-right corner of the sill plate and then click a point perpendicular to the subfloor:

```
Select first point of first taper boundary or ENTER for none:
```

Press Enter to end the command. The insulation is tapered to fit within the compressed space. Use the Obscure command to hide the batt insulation behind the anchor bolt threads (see Figure 17.19).

NOTE   You will design exterior siding in the "Creating Custom Components" section later in this chapter.

15. You can add a vapor barrier by drawing a line and assigning a specific detail component to it. Then the line will be easy to keynote later on. Set layer A-Detl-Thin current. Draw vertical line along the exterior face of the gypsum wallboard facing the insulation.

FIGURE 17.19
Adding insulation

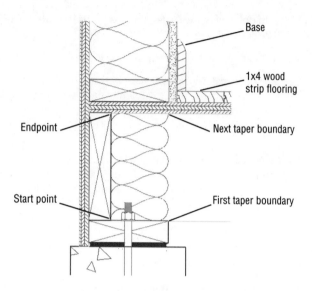

Base

1x4 wood strip flooring

Endpoint

Next taper boundary

Start point

First taper boundary

16. Type **DtlComp** on the command line and press Enter. The command line says the following:

```
Detail component [Add/Manager/ASsign id/Remove id]:
```

Type **AS** to assign identifying Xdata to the linework. Press Enter, and the Select Component dialog box appears. Type **Vapor** in the filter text box and click the filter button. Click the Vapor Barriers node in the tree pane and select Vapor Retarder in the bottom pane. Click the Select component button and press Enter to end the command.

17. To verify that Xdata was indeed assigned to the line you just drew, select it and click the Extended Data tab in the Properties palette. Detail Component Data appears; click Esc to deselect. The detail is almost complete. There are just a few remaining issues to attend to.

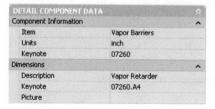

Adding Break Marks

Following long-standing graphic tradition, you will add break marks to the edges of components that continue beyond the scope of the detail. The Break Mark tool is new in ADT 2006. It applies both a break mark symbol and an AEC Polygon that is set to use a background mask. The AEC Polygon is what hides detail components beyond the break mark symbol. The Break Mark tool uses drawing scale to determine the size of the break mark symbol. Always verify the drawing scale prior to using the break mark tool.

1. Verify that the Scale pop-up menu is set to 1"=1'-0" on the drawing status bar.

2. The Break Mark tool is not in the Detailing palette group; it's in the Document palette group instead. Make the Document palette group current in the Tool palettes. Choose the Annotation palette. Scroll down in the palette and click the Cut Line (1) tool, which executes the AecBreakMarkAdd command.

WARNING   The break mark tool has size limitations based upon the drawing scale. You won't see a break mark in a given scale if you make it too small. What "too small" is varies with the scale, so it is best to draw a larger break mark than you think you might need, and then use grips to make it smaller afterward.

3. Click the first point of the break line a short distance on the exterior side of the stud wall. Click the second point of the break line an equal distance on the interior side of the wall. The command line says the following:

```
Specify break line extents:
```

Click a point above the remaining portion of the wall that you are trying to hide. Everything above the break line disappears, and the geometry is neatly trimmed above the Z of the break mark itself (see Figure 17.20).

TIP   You can add double break marks by setting the tool properties of the Cut Line tool to a type of dual break.

4. Add two additional break marks to the floor joists and concrete wall, as shown in Figure 17.21. Save the Sections.dwg view file.

FIGURE 17.20
Adding a break mark

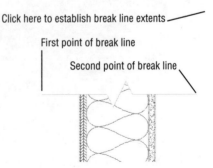

Click here to establish break line extents

First point of break line

Second point of break line

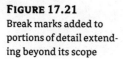

FIGURE 17.21
Break marks added to
portions of detail extending beyond its scope

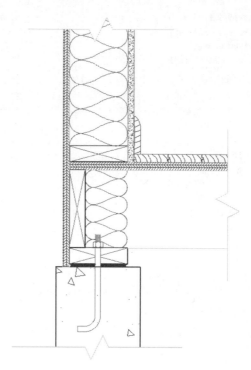

Creating Custom Components

The last component needed to complete the detail drawing you have been developing is exterior siding. To do this, you will create a custom detail component and add it to the detail component database by using a block provided on the companion DVD. The block is a polyline representing the cross-section of *shiplap* horizontal wood siding. Shiplap is a traditional profile shape given to overlapping boards.

1. Open the WoodShape.dwg from this chapter's folder on the companion DVD. Select the shape and select the Design tab on the Properties palette. The selected shape is a closed polyline defined as block reference called Shiplap (see Figure 17.22). Press Esc to deselect.

2. Choose File ➢ Save As. Save the file in the following folder on your hard drive:

   ```
   C:\Documents and Settings\All Users\Application Data\Autodesk\ADT
   2006\enu\Details\Details (US)\07 - Thermal and Moisture Protection\dwgs
   ```

   Close Woodshape.dwg.

FIGURE 17.22
Shiplap shape (left) and
its information on the
Properties palette (right)

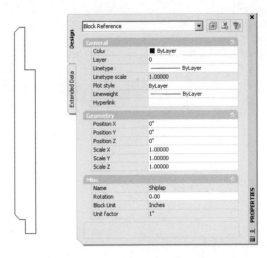

3. I provided a preview image of shiplap siding in this chapter's folder on the companion DVD. Using a preview image is entirely optional. Copy Shiplap.png to the following folder on your hard drive:

```
C:\Documents and Settings\All Users\Application Data\Autodesk\ADT
2006\enu\Details\Details (US)\07 - Thermal and Moisture Protection\images
```

4. Choose Insert ➢ Detail Component Manager. Navigate to 07460 - Siding in the tree view, which is where you will create a new component. Click the Edit Database button. Notice that additional groups appear in the tree pane—you see the entire MasterFormat when in Edit Database mode. Click the Add component button (see Figure 17.23).

5. Click the blank image thumbnail in the New Component dialog box. Select Shiplap.png from the SelectImageFile dialog box that appears and click OK. On the General tab of the New Component dialog box, type **Horizontal Shiplap Siding** as the Display Name. Type **ShiplapSiding** as the Table Name, **HorizontalShiplapSiding.xml** as the Recipe, and **6" Horizontal Wood Board Siding** as the Description. Type **Siding, Shiplap** as the Filter Keywords and type **Scott Onstott** as Author (see Figure 17.24).

TIP You can Edit a component's recipe XML file to hand-code more complex behavior into components.

6. Choose the Parameters tab in the New Component dialog box. In the General subcategory, set Jig Type to Linear Array. Click the Layer Key worksheet icon and choose MED from the Select Layer Key worksheet. Click in the Block Drawing Location field and choose Browse from its drop-down list. Select WoodShape.dwg in the Select Block Library dialog box from the path given in step 2.

FIGURE 17.23
Creating a component in
the Detail Component
Manager

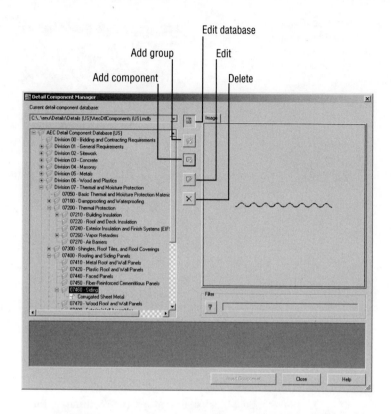

FIGURE 17.24
Selecting an image (left)
and entering data for the
new component (right)

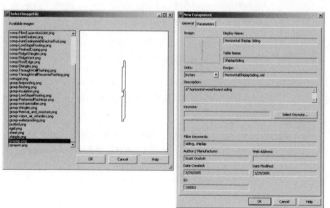

FIGURE 17.25
Specifying component
parameters

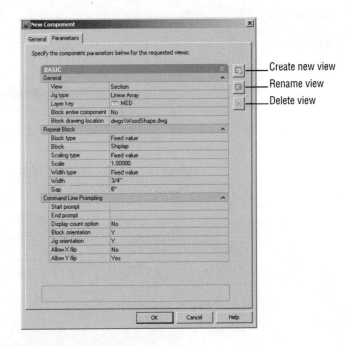

— Create new view
— Rename view
— Delete view

NOTE Use the buttons on the Parameters tab of the New Component dialog box to create additional views (such as Plan and/or Elevation). You can enter different sets of parameters for each view.

7. In the Repeat Block subcategory, type **Shiplap** in the Block text box. Change Width Type to Fixed and type **3/4"** in the Width text box. Type **6"** in the Gap text box to set the distance between items in the linear array (see Figure 17.25).

8. In the Command Line Prompting subcategory, change Allow Y Flip to Yes. Click OK to close the New Component dialog box.

9. In the bottom pane of the Detail Component Manager, type **1x6 Horizontal Shiplap Siding** in the Description text box. Toggle the Edit Database button off. A small dialog box appears, asking the question "Save Changes To Detail Component Table 'ShiplapSiding'?" Choose Yes.

10. Click the Insert Component button. Click the lower-left corner of the exterior plywood sheathing as the insertion point for the shiplap siding. Type **Y** to flip the component about the Y-axis. Move the cursor up vertically and click again after enough boards appear to extend beyond the upper break line. Erase the upper break line and create a new one to hide the siding as well (see Figure 17.26).

TIP Instead of erasing and recreating a break line to hide additional components, you can alternatively select the detail component you wish to hide, right-click and choose Basic Modify Tools ➢ Send To Back. Then grip edit the breakline's polyline and AEC Polygon as necessary to cover the detail component.

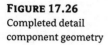

FIGURE 17.26
Completed detail
component geometry

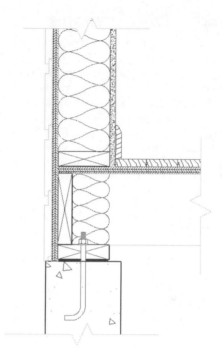

11. Save the Sections.dwg view file and leave it open.

JIG TYPES

Jigs are programming constructs used to control how detail components are added to a drawing. The following are examples of common jigs:

- Stamp—Inserts a block reference
- Bookends—Array of blocks with the provision for a different block on each end
- Linear Array—Array of blocks in a line appearing across a given distance
- Countable Linear Array—Array of a specific number of blocks in a line
- Surface—Rectangular boundary filled with a hatch pattern
- Surface Linetype—Rectangular boundary surrounded by wide polyline with specified linetype
- Surface Top—Rectangular boundary with bottom side missing filled with a hatch pattern
- Bolt—Allows you to locate nut on bolt threads like anchor bolt
- ApplyToLinework—Brands existing linework with Xdata and keynote; does not create any geometry

Refer to the "Customizing and Adding New Content for Detail Components" topic in the ADT help system for more specific information.

Working with Keynotes

After you have created a detail drawing by adding specific components, adding keynotes is quick and easy. There are three types of keynotes to choose from: reference, sheet, and manual. Reference keynotes use text to identify selected detail components, and sheet keynotes use numbers. Manual keynotes also use numbers, but they are not tied into the keynoting database.

Reference and sheet keynotes have legends that can be automatically generated after you add specific keynotes to detail drawings. As with other annotation tasks, keynoting is done in view drawings within the project framework.

Like detail components, keynotes are stored in a centralized database. The continuing tutorial uses a keynote database that is based on CSI MasterFormat's numbers and titles. Detail components, object styles, and material definitions all have keynotes preassigned. Now in ADT 2006, you can add and edit keynotes in the database without using Access.

Adding Keynotes

Before you add keynotes, you might want to inspect the objects in your detail drawings to learn which keynotes will be referenced. The new Object Inspector tool allows you to do this by providing information in ToolTips that appear when you hover the cursor over objects.

Click the Object inspector button on the Standard toolbar or type **AecInspect** on the command line. Hover the cursor over a detail component and observe the large ToolTips that appear. For example, hover the cursor over the batt insulation to learn that its keynote uses MasterFormat 07210 (see Figure 17.27). Because you used the taper option when creating this particular batt, it is compressed smaller than its default 5.5", so its R value is likewise lessened. The object inspector merely reads the Xdata associated with detail components; you must evaluate whether the information is correct given the situation.

Let's add reference and sheet keynotes to the same detail drawing to explore these features. In your own projects you'll probably want to use one type or the other exclusively. Sheet keynotes require less space on a drawing and can be more suitable to larger projects.

TIP   In addition to details, you can keynote plans, elevations, and section views.

FIGURE 17.27
Using the object inspector to glean component information

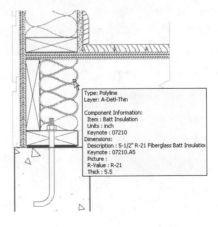

REFERENCE KEYNOTES

It is helpful to add a construction line prior to keynoting so that the keynotes that you add will line up with one another. In this tutorial, you'll add reference keynotes to the right side of the detail drawing.

1. Click the Construction Line tool on the Shapes toolbar. Hold the cursor over the vertical break line that hides the right edges of the floor joists to establish a vertical orientation. Click, move the cursor a short distance to the right, and click again to insert a construction line. Press Esc to end the command.

2. Choose the Annotation palette if it is not already selected. Click the Reference Keynote (Straight Leader) tool. The cursor turns into a selection box. Click the gypsum wallboard to select it. The command line says the following:

   ```
   Select first point of leader:
   ```

   Click the midpoint of the interior face of the wallboard. Then click a point perpendicular to the construction line and press Enter twice to complete the command. A reference keynote appears, showing both a number and text (see Figure 17.28). The keynote is an MText entity displaying a field linked to the keynote database. The beauty of this system is evident: You didn't have to type anything in to add the keynote.

NOTE The Reference Keynote tool adds text without a leader.

3. Repeat steps 1 and 2 to add additional reference keynotes for the following components on the right side of the detail drawing: vapor retarder, batt insulation, base, wood strip flooring, and floor joist.

4. Sometimes you might want to add additional descriptive text to a reference keynote. Double-click the text referencing the floor joist. Place the cursor after the field, type **FLOOR JOIST**, and click OK in the floating Text Formatting toolbar. Appending text to a keynote in this way does not add information to the keynote database. Figure 17.29 shows the result.

WARNING Keynotes display information stored in the database at the moment the keynote is inserted. If the database changes, the keynote will not be updated. You will have to re-keynote if you alter a keynote's database source—such as changing material assignments, for example. Select a keynote, right-click, and choose Re-keynote.

FIGURE 17.28
Adding a reference keynote

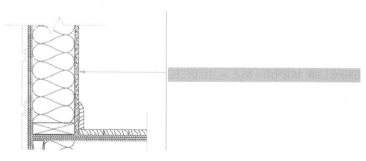

FIGURE 17.29
Additional reference
keynotes added

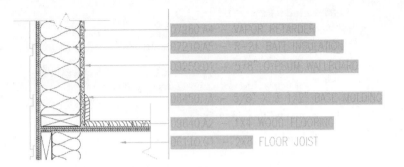

SHEET KEYNOTES

Sheet keynotes use numbers to identify components and appear with question marks in their tags until they are referenced in a sheet legend. Sheet keynotes are numbered sequentially in the order they are added to a drawing. You will add sheet keynotes to the left side of the detail drawing.

1. Add another construction line to the left side of the detail drawing so that the sheet keynotes you are about to add will all be aligned with each other.

2. Click the Sheet Keynote tool in the Annotation palette. Select one of the shiplap components. The Select Keynote dialog box appears because this is a custom component and does not already have a keynote assigned to it. Navigate to MasterFormat 07460 - Siding and click the Edit Keynote database button (see Figure 17.30).

3. Click the Create New Keynote button. Type **07460.B1** in the Key text box. Type **Shiplap Cedar Horizontal Siding** in the Note text box and click OK.

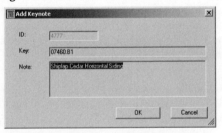

4. Toggle the Edit Keynote Database button off. Click Yes if prompted to save the database. Select the new keynote node **07460.B1**, and click OK. The command line says the following:

```
Select first point of leader:
```

Type **NEA** and press Enter to use the nearest object snap. Click the edge of the shiplap siding and then click the next point perpendicular to the construction line you drew in step 1. Press Enter to end the command, and the keynote tag appears at the end of the leader with a question mark as expected.

5. Continue adding sheet keynotes to the following components: plywood sheathing, sole plate, header joist, sill plate, anchor bolt, and the concrete wall. Figure 17.31 shows the result.

FIGURE 17.30
Adding a keynote to the keynote database

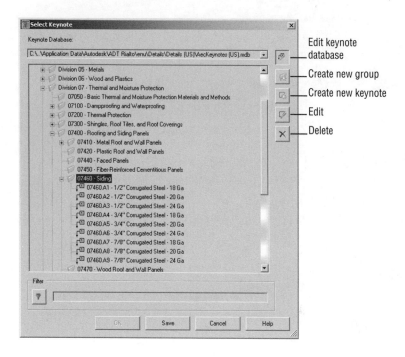

Edit keynote database

Create new group

Create new keynote

Edit

Delete

FIGURE 17.31
Additional sheet keynotes added

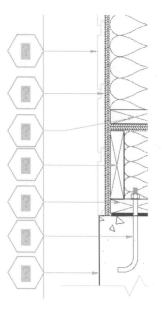

MANUAL KEYNOTES

Manual keynotes are attributed blocks with leaders. Manual keynotes are not connected to databases. In most cases, you will not need to use manual keynotes, but they are available if you decide not to use the database features. The following steps demonstrate the basic procedure by adding a manual keynote for the joint sealant in our detail drawing.

1. Click the Square (Straight Leader) tool in the Annotation palette.

2. Zoom into the area in which the sill plate meets the concrete wall. Click the first point of the leader at the midpoint of the right edge of the joint sealant. Click the next point perpendicular to the right construction line and press Enter.

3. Type **8** as the ID number in the Edit Attributes dialog box and click OK.

Figure 17.33 shows the result. Note that manual keynotes use a square symbol by default. You will have to add descriptive text that corresponds to number 8 to a keynote legend later on.

ADJUSTING MSV

After you add keynotes, check to see if the keynotes fit within the MSV's border. Right-click the red light bulb icon in the drawing status bar and choose End Object Isolation from the shortcut menu. Select the MSV and adjust its edge grips to surround the detail drawing, all its keynotes, and its title mark (see Figure 17.32). You will still have to adjust the size of the viewport on the sheet to match the revised MSV border.

FIGURE 17.32
Adjusting MSV border to encompass keynotes

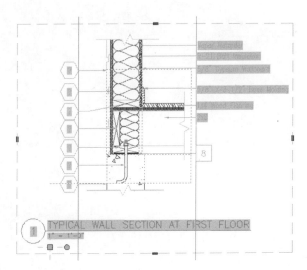

Toggle off LWT on the application status bar and delete the construction lines for a cleaner look. Hide the 2D Section/Elevation object after you have made the necessary adjustments. Save the view file where your detail drawing is located. You might have to adjust the viewport size in any details you have adjusted on sheets in which they were previously referenced.

Editing Keynotes

You can change the way keynotes are displayed globally within a drawing file. Keynotes can display with the key (number), note, or both simultaneously. By default, sheet keynotes display the key only, and reference keynotes display both key and note.

Choose View ➢ Keynote Display ➢ Reference Keynotes. Choose the Reference Keynote - Note Only radio button in the Select Reference Keynote Display dialog box that appears. Choose Title Case in the Format list box and click OK (see Figure 17.33). The keynote numbers disappear. and the formatting changes for the notes.

WARNING   Notice that the extra text previously appended to the 2x8 disappeared when you changed keynote display. Text appended to MText fields is always in danger of being lost, so it is best to avoid adding text in that way. Instead, edit the keynote database for robust alterations that will always remain linked to keynotes. For example, not every 2x8 will be a floor joist. You can create a new keynote for 2x8 floor joists to differentiate them from other 2x8 framing members.

In ADT 2006, you can edit the keynote database directly by using the Keynote Editor. In previous versions, you had to edit the database in Access. As you saw before, the Keynote Editor appears automatically whenever you try to keynote an object that does not already have a keynote assigned. You can also edit existing keynotes at any time by using a pull-down menu.

Choose Window ➢ Pulldowns ➢ CAD Manager Pulldown. Choose CAD Manager ➢ Keynote Editor. Use the Keynote Dtatebase drop down list to browse for the AecKeynotes (US).mdb database if it is not already selected. You can select existing keynotes and click the edit button to change their key numbers and/or the notes associated with them. Check with your CAD Manager before saving changes to the keynote database. It might be the case that everyone in your organization shares one keynote database, so you'll want to be sure that it is acceptable to make changes to it.

Another alternative a CAD Manager might choose is to use a different keynote database for each project. That way, designers can alter their databases without affecting other teams working on different projects. Use the AEC Content tab of the Options dialog box to add and remove keynote databases if you elect to exercise this option. Close the Keynote Editor dialog box. Save and close the Sections.dwg view file.

FIGURE 17.33
Changing keynote display (left) and the result (right)

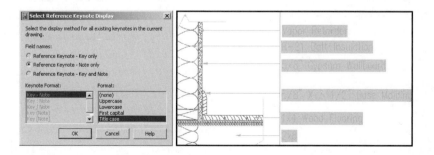

Generating Keynote Legends

You can create two types of keynote legends: reference keynote legends and sheet keynote legends. Although reference keynote legends can be thought of as optional—because reference keynotes already spell out what you are trying to convey—sheet keynote legends are required. Sheet keynotes get enumerated after a sheet keynote legend is generated, so only then can you make the correspondence between the number and the annotated information.

1. Open the A601 Details sheet file. Click the Reference Keynote Legend tool in the Annotation palette. Right-click and choose Sheets from the shortcut menu. In the Select Sheets to Keynote worksheet, select the A601 Details node in the tree and click the Add button to move it to the right side (see Figure 17.34).

2. Click OK to close the worksheet and then click an insertion point for the Reference Keynote Legend adjacent to the detail. The Reference Keynote Legend is organized by CSI MasterFormat groups (see Figure 17.35).

FIGURE 17.34
Selecting sheets to keynote

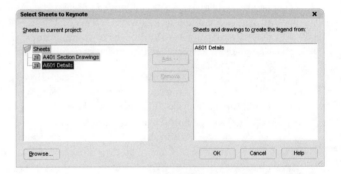

FIGURE 17.35
Generating a Reference Keynote Legend and inserting it on a sheet

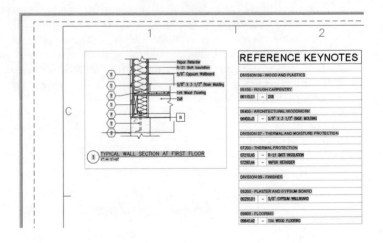

WARNING   Close view files prior to adding a sheet keynote legend to a sheet. The field codes showing sheet numbers in the view must be updated, which is not possible when file locks exist.

3. Adding a Sheet Keynote Legend is just as easy. Click the Sheet Keynote Legend tool on the Annotation palette. Select each one of the sheet keynotes inside the viewport showing the Typical Wall Section at First Floor detail drawing. Strangely enough, you can select sheet keynotes within XRefed drawings, even while in the paper space of the sheet.

4. Press Enter to stop selecting sheet keynotes and click a point just under the detail drawing to insert the Sheet Keynote Legend. In a few moments numbers appear in the field codes in the Xrefed detail drawing that match the numbers in the legend (see Figure 17.36).

NOTE   Notice that sheet keynote number 3 is repeated. This happened because these sheet keynotes refer to two occurrences of the same detail component (2x6).

5. Save the A601 Details.dwg sheet file.

FIGURE 17.36
Generating a Sheet
Keynote Legend and
inserting it on a sheet

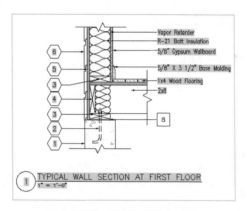

EDITING LEGENDS

Keynote legends use AutoCAD tables to format the information contained within them. AutoCAD tables are different from the schedule tables you learned about in Chapter 14, "Schedules, Display Themes, and Areas." Keynote legends have fields within their table cells that are linked to data in the keynote database. AutoCAD tables do not have display control or property sets associated with them. Instead, AutoCAD tables are controlled by table styles that function much like text styles to control appearance.

Choose Format ➢ Table Style to adjust the appearance of keynote legends. Select individual table cells and use the shortcut menu to adjust alignment, columns, rows, borders, and so on. Refer to the AutoCAD help to learn more about tables.

Selecting the border of the table and right-clicking opens a different shortcut menu, in which you will find Update Sheet Keynote Legend and the Selection submenu. Choose Update Sheet Keynote Legend if you have made changes to the keynote database and/or sheet keynote assignments in the view file. The Selection submenu contains choices for adding, reselecting, applying keys, and showing all instances of a selected keynote in the drawing. Be aware that the reselect option causes any customizations made to the table to be lost.

Summary

In this chapter you learned how to use detail callout tools to set up detail drawings. You used detail tools and the Detail Component Manager to generate detail drawings by inserting components sourced from a database. Later on you added reference and sheet keynotes to the detail drawing and watched as the information once again got linked from yet another database. You learned how to create a custom detail component, and you generated reference and sheet keynote legends to complete the detailing cycle.

This chapter completes Part 4 of the book. Congratulations on your achievements up to this point—with practice you will possess the skills needed to generate construction documents using ADT. Part 5 contains two chapters that explore options for communicating all your hard work to others.

Part 5

Design Communication

Chapter 18

Using VIZ Render

VIZ Render is a stand-alone program used to generate presentation imagery—photorealistic render-ings—based on designs developed in ADT. Bundled with ADT, VIZ Render is basically a simplified version of Autodesk VIZ, the more powerful architecture, engineering, and construction (AEC) visu-alization product that is sold separately. The major difference from Autodesk VIZ is that you cannot create geometry in VIZ Render alone. Instead, you create the geometry in ADT and link the building models into VIZ Render. VIZ Render is much more powerful than AutoCAD's native renderer, which has been around for many years and is also a part of ADT.

In this chapter you'll add cameras in VIZ Render that allow you to fine-tune your point of view within the perspective of three-dimensional space. To achieve higher levels of realism, you'll learn how to merge 3D assets from Autodesk VIZ and/or discreet 3ds max into VIZ Render—then you'll substitute these assets for placeholder content linked from ADT.

You'll also add light sources in VIZ Render that illuminate the model by emitting both natural sun-light and artificial light. Materials assigned to objects and styles in ADT are linked into VIZ Render in which you'll have the ability to adjust and refine materials for even greater levels of realism.

Geometry, cameras, lights, and materials are the necessary ingredients you'll be using to create photorealistic renderings. In the end you'll be able to produce still images of your work that are sure to impress your audience. This chapter's topics include the following:

◆ Getting Started with VIZ Render

◆ Adding Cameras

◆ Performing Substitutions

◆ Emitting Light

◆ Working with Materials

◆ Rendering

Getting Started with VIZ Render

Although VIZ Render is a simplified version of Autodesk VIZ, it still has more features than this book has space to document. This chapter focuses on the most important issues, and the tutorials provided will get you up and running and making renderings very quickly. Look to the VIZ Render help to answer additional specific questions you may have.

The features of VIZ Render are by and large a subset of the features of Autodesk VIZ. If you want to get the most out of VIZ Render, I recommend reading portions of *Mastering Autodesk VIZ 2005*

(Sybex, 2005), written by George Omura and me. In addition, I have video courses available at ScottOnstott.com that you might want to investigate.

Understanding File Linking

Before you dive into using VIZ Render, it is helpful to understand how file linking works. You usually won't launch VIZ Render by itself, even though it is a stand-alone application because VIZ Render cannot open or import ADT's native drawing files (.dwg). Instead, you'll first launch ADT and open a drawing as usual. When you choose to link the current drawing to VIZ Render, that application will launch, and the current drawing and all of its XRefs will appear in the viewport.

NOTE Objects that are hidden or on frozen layers in ADT do not get linked into VIZ Render. Use this fact to intentionally exclude objects from file linking.

It takes some time for VIZ Render to launch and link drawing files, and you'll see a progress bar appear in VIZ Render that tracks the linking process by a percentage. To avoid unnecessary waiting (and rendering time), in more complex projects you should plan carefully to determine how much of the building model should be linked from ADT to VIZ Render. In general, avoid linking content that will not be seen by the camera in the imagery you are planning to create.

If you are linking a project view file, make sure that all the constructs and elements that the view references are needed in VIZ Render. Sometimes it makes sense to create an additional view in ADT that contains only the constructs you are interested in visualizing before linking it to VIZ Render. For example, if you are planning to make an interior rendering on the third floor, attach only third floor constructs to a view file that you link to VIZ Render. On the other hand, you might link a single drawing file outside of a project structure that contains all the objects to be included in your visualization—this is the approach that this chapter's tutorials take.

TIP Live sectioned views appear correctly in VIZ Render (see Chapter 16, "Sections and Elevations"). Use live sections to make photorealistic perspective section imagery in VIZ Render.

1. Copy this chapter's folder from the companion DVD to the following folder on your hard drive:

   ```
   C:\Documents and Settings\<username>\My Documents\Autodesk\My Projects
   ```

2. Launch ADT and open the file Room.dwg from that folder. The drawing file contains a room and an adjacent space with a stair that will be included in visualizations that you will make in this chapter. Figure 18.1 shows the room's floor plan. Only content anticipated to be included in the visualization is included in the drawing file.

WARNING Do not link a drawing file into VIZ Render from read-only media like a DVD. VIZ Render needs to be able to save a drf (discreet render format) file in the same folder in which you link the drawing.

FIGURE 18.1
Floor plan of drawing file
in ADT

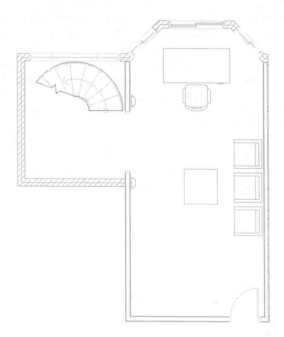

3. Open the drawing menu by clicking the arrow button on the extreme left side of the drawing status bar and choose Link to VIZ Render. You can also initiate the linking process by choosing File ➢ Link to Autodesk VIZ Render or by typing **VizRender.↵** on the command line.

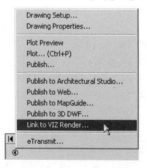

4. You'll have to wait a minute or two for VIZ Render to launch and link this simple drawing file—complex drawings might take much longer. A new file is automatically created in the same folder in which you linked the drawing file. In this example, the new file is called `Room.drf`.

You'll usually want to leave both ADT and VIZ Render running simultaneously, memory permitting. Often, visualizing the model in VIZ Render will identify problems that need to be corrected in ADT.

The procedure for using ADT and VIZ Render together is as follows: After making changes to objects, styles, and/or material definitions in ADT, save the drawing file. Then switch back to VIZ Render by clicking its task on the Windows taskbar (or by pressing Alt+Tab) and reload the linked file—changes made to the geometry and materials then appear in VIZ Render. You can repeat the process of switching between applications, saving, and reloading as many times as necessary as your design evolves.

The link between ADT and VIZ is a one-way link; changes you make in VIZ Render never affect the drawing in ADT. Furthermore, subsequent changes you make in ADT do not have to appear in VIZ Render unless you choose them to be by manually reloading the link. The link to the ADT drawing can be updated in VIZ Render with or without using the drawing's material definitions and/or material assignments.

NOTE It is possible to transfer render materials from VIZ Render to ADT using the Content Browser (see "Working with Materials" later in this chapter).

It is possible to break the link between ADT and VIZ Render—it is called *binding the model*. When you bind a linked model in VIZ Render, changes made in ADT can no longer be reloaded into VIZ Render. Unlike linked geometry, bound geometry can be erased or moved to different layers in VIZ Render—these are the main reasons to bind.

There can be only one ADT drawing linked to any VIZ Render session and one model open in VIZ Render at any time. It is also possible to bring additional content developed in Autodesk VIZ and/or 3ds max into VIZ Render through the .max file format. In fact, Autodesk VIZ is the perfect complement to VIZ Render that you might naturally graduate to if advanced visualizations are important to you.

TIP Save often to prevent data loss. VIZ Render tends to crash more often than ADT.

Understanding the User Interface

Because VIZ Render is an application in its own right, it makes sense that it has its own user interface. Not surprisingly, VIZ Render's user interface has much in common with both ADT and Autodesk VIZ. Figure 18.2 shows the VIZ Render user interface.

New!

The Tool palettes have been streamlined in VIZ Render 2006. Click the Auto-hide toggle in the Tool palettes if necessary to make them appear constantly. Hold your cursor over the tabs in the Tool palettes to read the full palette names or enlarge the Tool palettes to read the full names if you have enough screen real estate. Click each palette and investigate its contents. The top palette reveals which materials are used in the *scene*—VIZ Render's term for the model. The second palette shows which materials are defined, but not assigned to objects in the scene. The Doors & Windows, Flooring, Masonry, and Concrete palettes contain some commonly used materials in these categories. The Cameras and Light palette has tools for creating both types of objects (you'll use these later in the chapter).

The toolbars identified in Figure 18.2 are docked. Toolbars in VIZ Render function much as they do in ADT: Drag their handles to move them. There are also many floating toolbars that aren't visible by default. Choose Customize ➤ Show UI ➤ Show Floating Toolbars. Figure 18.3 shows the toolbars floating.

Close all but View Shading and View Orientation toolbars: you'll use them later in this chapter.

Drag these two toolbars to the upper-right corner of the viewport. Hold down the Ctrl key to avoid docking them.

FIGURE 18.2
VIZ Render user interface

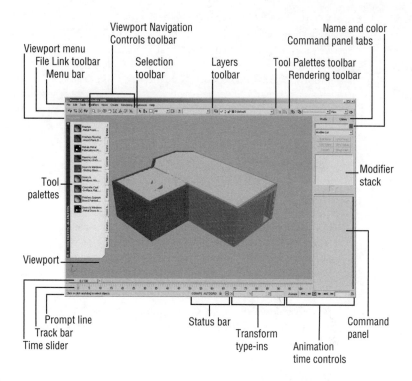

FIGURE 18.3
Floating toolbars

Navigating in Viewports

The first skill you will learn is how to navigate in viewports so you can get around a 3D model in VIZ Render. Figure 18.4 shows the Viewport Navigation Tools toolbar, shown floating with its flyout menus expanded for clarity. All the navigation tools work a bit differently from their counterparts in ADT.

1. The buttons that have "mode" in their name indicate modes that you stay in until you use another tool. Click the Zoom Mode button, and drag up to zoom in and down to zoom out.

2. Click the Field of View mode tool; drag up and then down to alter the field of view of the viewport, which is analogous to changing the focal length of a camera lens. Dragging upward in Field of View mode zooms in like a telephoto lens, and dragging downward changes to a wide-angle field of view (without "fisheye" spherical distortion).

FIGURE 18.4
Viewport navigation tools

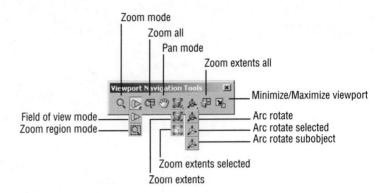

NOTE Zoom mode is for moving your point of view closer or farther away from the model while working. Although it might appear that you are getting closer or farther away from objects by adjusting the field of view, it is different than zooming. You should adjust the field of view only when setting up a composition for rendering. Viewports with extreme field of view (either wide or narrow) appear distorted.

3. Hold down the Field of View tool and choose the Zoom Region mode button. It works much like Zoom window does in ADT, but you use Zoom Region mode by dragging instead of clicking two discrete points. Zoom into the large arched window. You might need to arc rotate the view so you can see the arched window.

4. Click the Minimize/Maximize viewport button and the single viewport VIZ Render starts with is divided into four viewports: Top, Front, Left, and Perspective.

5. Click the Zoom Extents All button to do a zoom extents in all the viewports simultaneously.

6. Choose the Zoom All button and drag upward in a viewport; all the viewports zoom in.

7. Choose Pan mode and drag the mouse around in the Top viewport. Press and hold the wheel button if your mouse is so equipped. Move the cursor, and you are panning. You can enter pan mode by dragging the wheel button at any time.

8. Click on the desk to select it. Click Zoom Extents button, and the entire floor plan fills the viewport. Click Zoom Extents Selected and you zoom into the extents of the desk.

9. Right-click the Perspective viewport to select it: the viewport edges highlight in yellow to indicate that it is active. Click the Arc Rotate tool and drag within the yellow circle to rotate your point of view in 3D.

TIP Hold down the Alt key and drag the wheel button to arc rotate. You can do this without clicking the Arc Rotate tool in the toolbar. Turn the mouse wheel to zoom.

10. Click the Maximize viewport button again (or press Alt+W) to return the Perspective viewport to its original size. It is best to use four viewports only when comparing different points of view simultaneously. A single viewport allows geometry to appear larger on the screen.

11. Click the Top button on the floating View Orientation toolbar: you should recognize these icons from ADT. The viewport immediately displays the top point of view. Press Alt+Ctrl+Z to zoom to the extents of the model. Also notice that the display mode has changed to wireframe so you can see into the model.

12. Click the Default Southwest View button and notice that the viewport menu now says "User". This term indicates that you are looking at an axonometric viewport—not in perspective. Press Alt+Ctrl+Z.

Adding Cameras

Cameras fix your point of view at a particular location in space, and determine the settings for perspective that mimic those of a traditional single lens reflex camera. Use cameras to fine tune perspective and compose the scene for a rendering. Named views automatically become cameras when a drawing is linked in VIZ Render. You'll have to create your own cameras in VIZ Render to view interior spaces from the inside. Looking through a camera is the way to view the interior of a space as if you were standing there, or to frame the exterior of a building as if you were taking a photograph of it from the street, or perhaps from a helicopter (and it's a lot less expensive).

There are two types of cameras in VIZ Render: target and free. Target cameras have two objects that always remain connected: the camera itself and the target it looks at. You cannot rotate a target camera itself. Instead, moving the target causes the camera to rotate because it must always point directly at its own target. In contrast, free cameras have no target and can be rotated on their own.

TIP You can animate the position of a camera and its target separately to create more complex motion.

1. Select the Cameras and Lights tab in the Tool palettes. Click the Target Camera tool.

2. Click and hold the mouse button inside the room in front of the door to locate the camera. Drag the mouse over to the left and release the mouse button in front of the cased opening, as shown in Figure 18.5. Move the mouse upward and click to set the elevation at approximately eye level. The target camera is created.

3. To look through the camera you just created, click the Camera View button on the View Orientations toolbar or press C.

4. Verify that the Modify tab is selected and examine the Parameters rollout in the command panel. Click the 35mm button in the Stock Lenses group. This simulates a slightly wide-angle camera lens so you can see more of the interior.

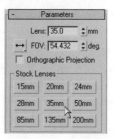

FIGURE 18.5
Creating a target camera

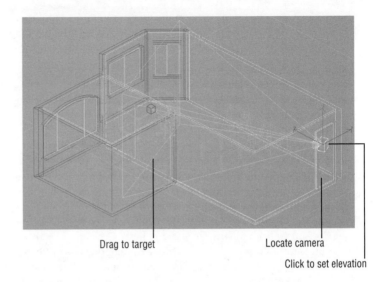

Drag to target   Locate camera

Click to set elevation

5. Click the Wireframe / Smooth+Highlights Toggle button on the View Shading toolbar. Congratulations! You have composed your first scene (see Figure 18.6).

6. You will also place a free camera. Click the Front view button on the View Orientations toolbar. Press Alt+Ctrl+Z to zoom extents. You are looking at the room from the outside. Click the Wireframe / Smooth+Highlights Toggle button on the View Shading toolbar. Click the Free Camera tool in the Tool palettes. Click a point at eye level to the left of the door, as shown in Figure 18.7.

7. Switch to the Top viewport by pressing T and press Alt+Ctrl+Z. The free camera is some distance in front of the room. Click on the free camera to select it. Right-click and choose Move from the Edit/Transform quad menu (see Figure 18.8). The quad menus can display up to four menus simultaneously, depending on the context in which you invoke them.

FIGURE 18.6
Looking through a camera in the room's interior

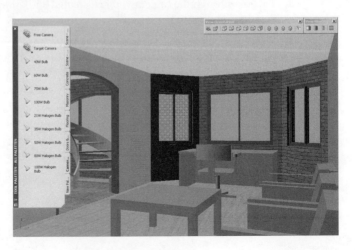

FIGURE 18.7
Placing a free camera in the Front viewport

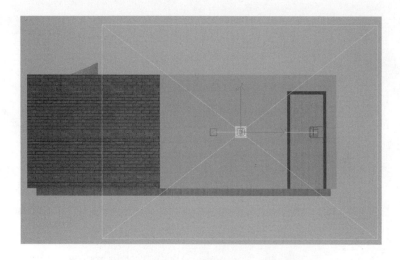

FIGURE 18.8
Moving free camera into room

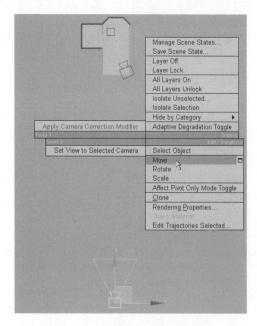

8. Move the cursor over the y-axis transform gizmo to constrain motion in that direction and drag upward. Release the mouse button when the camera is centered in the room.

9. Right-click the viewport menu and choose Views ➢ Camera01. You are looking through the target camera again and can now see the free camera in the space. Position the free camera (Camera02) on your own to create another composition.

10. Save the file by pressing Ctrl+S. Remember that the file was automatically named and saved when you linked the drawing from ADT. It is important to save often in case VIZ Render crashes.

TIP You can simulate two-point perspective when your camera angle is tilted upward. This is especially helpful for exterior shots of tall buildings. To do this, apply the Camera Correction modifier (see the VIZ Render help).

Performing Substitutions

ADT is not very well-suited to modeling complex geometry such as furniture and light fixtures to be used in photorealistic visualizations. The furniture that was linked from ADT is quite blocky and not very realistic (refer to Figure 18.6). You can improve these basic 3D representations by substituting more refined models made in Autodesk VIZ and/or discreet 3ds max. If you don't have access to these programs, do not worry. I have modeled a number of pieces of furniture and light fixtures and provided them on the companion DVD for you to use in this tutorial and in your own work.

TIP Check out `ScottOnstott.com` for more free designer furniture models.

1. Switch to the Top viewport by pressing T and then Alt+Ctrl+Z.

2. Click the Wireframe/Smooth+Highlights Toggle button on the View Shading toolbar.

3. Select the desk object; it appears as a Multi-View Block (MVB) in the Name and Color area of the user interface. It is the standard I_Furn_Desk_72x36 Right MVB inserted in ADT from the DesignCenter.

4. Click the Utilities tab of the command panel. Click the Substitute Manager button in the Utilities rollout. The Substitution rollout appears below in the command panel. Click the Create Substitute button, and the Merge File dialog box appears. Select the `Desk.max` file and click the Open button. An Obsolete File dialog will appear; click OK to dismiss. You'll see this message anytime you merge files made in previous version of Autodesk VIZ and/or 3ds max. You can use "obsolete" files without any problems.

5. The substitute model has a different insertion point and rotation, so the model jumps over to the right, outside of the room. Select the new desk; notice that its name says Desk01 now. Press **W** to enter Move mode. Position the cursor over the XY plane handle of the transform gizmo and move the desk into the room.

NOTE The letters Q, W, E, and R are adjacent letters on the keyboard. These keys correspond to the Select, Move, Rotate, and Scale modes, respectively.

6. Press **E** to enter Rotate mode. Right-click the Z transform type-in to reset the value to 0 (zero). Press **W** and move the desk into position above the chair, in which its original MVB stood before the substitution (see Figure 18.9).

FIGURE 18.9
Substituting a 3D model
for an MVB (left) and
transforming it (right)

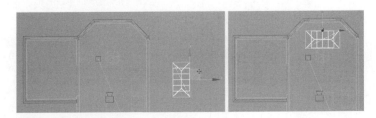

WARNING   VIZ Render cannot accept anything but Editable Meshes for substitution. If you model objects in Autodesk VIZ and/or 3ds max, collapse the objects' modifier stacks prior to substitution in VIZ Render.

7. Substitute the Chair, Coffee, Lounge, and WallLamp `.max` files for their corresponding blocks in VIZ Render. Transform the substituted objects back into position (see Figure 18.10). Switch into the Camera01 viewport and move the WallLamps upward in the Z direction so they are mounted at approximately eye level.

8. Notice that you can't see much of the nearest lounge chair—perhaps we don't need it. Select the nearest Lounge object and press Delete. A message appears, informing you that substitutions cannot be deleted—without binding, that is—and we don't want to lose the link between ADT and VIZ Render, so binding is not an option. Click OK to close the warning dialog box.

9. Switch back to ADT and delete the lounge chair MVB closest to the door. Also move the other two lounge chairs and the coffee table upward about a foot. Center the coffee table between the lounge chairs in the Y direction. Save the file in ADT.

10. Switch back to VIZ Render by pressing Alt+Tab.

11. Click the Reload Geometry and Materials button on the File Link toolbar. The changes you made in ADT appear in VIZ Render. The composition looks good and is acceptable for making a rendering. Press Ctrl+S to save in VIZ Render.

FIGURE 18.10
After substitution in Top (left) and Camera01 (right) viewports

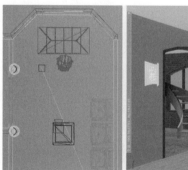

Emitting Light

You have already substituted 3D WallLamps in VIZ Render for the 2D lighting blocks drawn in ADT. The WallLamp 3D model includes a light source. In fact, the WallLamp model is a *photometric luminaire*, a light fixture assembly that contains a physically accurate artificial light source with a simplified user interface. Although it is not possible to create photometric luminaires in VIZ Render, you can find many such models online.

TIP   See www.erco.com for hundreds of photometric luminaires that you can use as substitutions in Viz Render.

The WallLamp models will illuminate the interior of the room, and the light they emit will wash over the walls they are mounted on. This would be enough to create a nighttime rendering. However, you will create a daytime rendering in this tutorial with the artificial lights switched on to get the best of both worlds.

The daylight system is used to simulate both sunlight and the ambient illumination in the sky. You can perform accurate shadow studies with the daylight system because it uses a sun angle calculator that is based upon the site's location on the earth, the building's orientation to North, and the exact time.

1. Press T to switch to the Top viewport and Alt+Ctrl+Z to zoom extents. Choose Create ➢ Daylight System.

2. A warning dialog box appears, asking if you want to set the Exterior Daylight Flag. Click No because you are not making an exterior rendering. Instead, you'll be using daylight to illuminate an interior through windows.

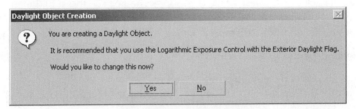

3. Position your cursor just outside the building, underneath the space containing the stair, so you can easily see it. It actually doesn't matter where the daylight system is placed because the sun's rays are essentially parallel (because the sun is so far away from the earth). Drag the mouse outward from the point you select until you can see a compass rose appear. Release the mouse button and then drag upward to create the sun itself. Again, it doesn't matter how far the "sun" is away from the building—just make it far enough so the sun is above the ceiling (see Figure 18.11). You might need to switch into the Front viewport to verify that the sun is above the ceiling.

4. Click the Modify tab of the command panel. Scroll down and locate the Control Parameters rollout. Click the Get Location button. A map appears in a dialog box. Click about where you think Los Angeles ought to be on the map. Its name highlights in the list on the left because Nearest Big City is checked (see Figure 18.12). Maps from other continents are provided in the drop-down list. Click OK.

5. The latitude and longitude of Los Angles have been entered in the Location group. You can type specific GPS coordinates of your site for greater accuracy. Change North Direction to 180 to rotate the compass rose to align with the orientation of your buildings on site. Increase the Orbital Scale to move the sun farther away from the compass rose if you like. The height of the sun doesn't affect the lighting.

6. Change the time to 11 o'clock on September 21, 2005. Check Daylight Savings Time. Now the sun is oriented specifically for the site, the building's orientation, and an exact moment in time. You don't need to adjust the sun's brightness because it is controlled by the daylight system based upon time and location.

7. Examine the IES Sky Parameters rollout. You have three options to choose from in the Coverage group: Clear, Partly Cloudy, and Cloudy. Choose the Partly Cloudy radio button. Light is more diffuse and even with some cloud cover.

8. Press Ctrl+S to save.

FIGURE 18.11
Creating the daylight system

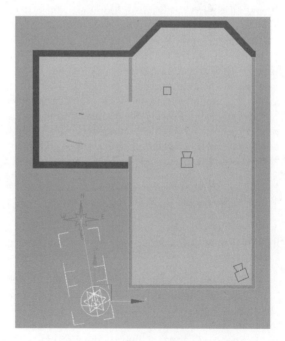

FIGURE 18.12
Choosing a geographic
location

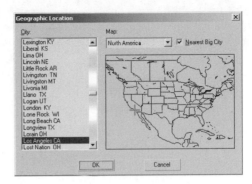

Working with Materials

Material definitions in ADT specify many properties, including plan linework, surface hatching, 2D Section/Elevation rules, render materials, and many others. The *render material* is what you see in ADT when in a shaded display mode. In VIZ Render, render materials are just called materials.

You can drag materials back and forth between VIZ Render and ADT. Although it is possible to drag a material directly between applications (from Tool palette to Tool palette), the Content Browser is often used to facilitate the exchange of material data because it makes that data available to your team.

To simulate surfaces with great realism, materials in VIZ Render have more parameters than render materials do in ADT. When render materials are stored in ADT, they retain all the extra parameters necessary to fully describe surfaces in VIZ Render, even though much of that data is not visible in ADT. No data is lost when transferring materials between VIZ Render and ADT (and vice versa)—that is why materials and render materials truly are exchangeable.

You can design entirely new materials in VIZ Render and apply them to surfaces directly prior to rendering. If you think a new material you've designed deserves to be used in future projects, you might transfer it to a standards drawing to complete a material definition in ADT (see Chapter 3, "Object Styles" for materials and Chapter 5, "Project Management" for standards).

NOTE Designing new materials goes beyond the scope of this book. Refer to the VIZ Render help for more information.

More often, standard materials are usually very close to what you might want to use in a rendering. You can tweak existing materials very easily to achieve the look you desire by using the Material Editor.

1. Click the second button from the left of the Selection toolbar or press **H** to launch the floating selection dialog box. The term *floating* means that the dialog box will stay open until you close it. Scroll down and double-click the second Space <Standard> Floor node to select it. There are two space objects in the scene (one in each room), so that is why there are two Space <Standard> nodes. The word in angled brackets refers to the space style name from ADT. The word following the angled brackets identifies the component. Notice that components are indented (in what is called a *subtree*) in the Selection Floater (see Figure 18.13). Click Close.

FIGURE 18.13
Selecting a specific
component

FIGURE 18.13
Selecting a specific
component

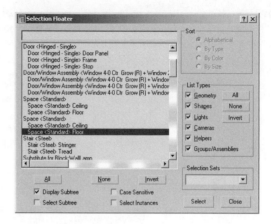

2. Right-click in the viewport and choose Query Material in the Edit/Transform quad menu. The material assigned to the main room's floor is highlighted in the Tool palettes. More specifically, it is called Finishes.Flooring.Wood.Plank.Beech.

3. Open the Material Editor by clicking the first button in the Render toolbar or by pressing **M**. Click the just-identified material in the Scene-InUse palette and notice that it appears in the Material Editor (see Figure 18.14).

4. The Material Editor shows a preview of the material on a sphere on the left and a preview of its diffuse map on the right. In this case the diffuse map is a bitmap image of wood. The specular highlight on the sphere looks a bit too shiny—it would render as a mirror-like polished floor. Change the Shininess spinner to 50 to tone down the specular highlight slightly.

FIGURE 18.14
Selecting a material
for editing

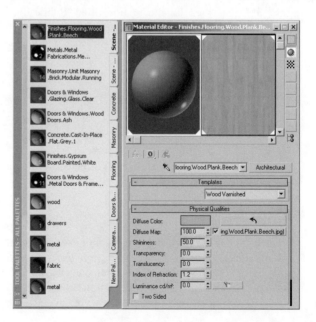

WARNING VIZ Render has only one type of material: Architectural. AutoCAD VIZ and 3ds max have many more types of materials and maps for even greater levels of realism. Materials brought in on geometry merged or substituted from these programs will render correctly in VIZ Render, but you won't be able to tweak their materials.

5. Click the button adjacent to the Diffuse Map component (it has a long name with the `.jpg` extension). This opens the diffuse map in the Material Editor. Click the View Image button. A dialog box appears, revealing a photograph of beech flooring that is the basis of this material. Sometimes it is helpful to view the image you are using to determine if it is an acceptable simulation of the surface you wish to render. Click the close box.

6. The map appears a bit dark in the Material Editor as compared with the image you just opened. In the Texture Tiling and Output rollout, change Brightness to 0.85 to lighten up the floor slightly.

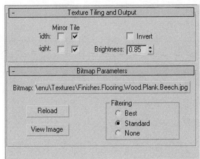

7. Click the Go to Parent button ⬆ to return to the top level of the material hierarchy. Scroll down and open the Adjust Radiosity rollout. This is where you set physical qualities that affect *radiosity* (see the following section, titled "Rendering") such as how much light energy is reflected or transmitted, and how much color bleeds onto adjacent surfaces. Change Color Bleed Scale to 50 and Reflectance Scale to 50. This will tone down the large floor surface's influence of the rest of the room.

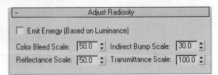

8. Close the Material Editor by clicking its close box in the upper-right corner and save your work by pressing Ctrl+S.

Rendering

Rendering is the process of calculating photorealistic imagery based upon the camera, lights, geometry, and materials of a scene. However, the imagery you see on the screen is also a form of rendering that takes place in real time to give you visual feedback. When you make a rendering for output, you are essentially asking the computer to turn the entire scene description into a pretty picture, often with much higher quality and finer resolution than you can see on the screen, to be suitable for printing.

Processing renderings in complex projects can take a great deal of time, even with a fast computer. The best strategy to achieving acceptable imagery is to do a series of renderings of ever-increasing realism. You'll usually notice some problems with some parts of the scene after you do a quick *draft* (low-quality) rendering. After fixing any outstanding issues seen in your test rendering, you can invest more time into making another rendering with greater realism. With experience you might realize that there are still things you can do at that point to improve the image. So you make some tweaks and render again, repeating this process until acceptable output is produced.

Radiosity is a particular rendering algorithm that produces high-quality imagery. Light energy is bounced around the scene in a radiosity simulation, and indirect illumination is actually stored in the geometry of the model in what is called a *radiosity mesh*. After you have indirect illumination stored in a radiosity mesh, you can make a final rendering that combines the radiosity data with direct illumination. So in summary, you'll choose environment settings, calculate a radiosity solution, and finally make a rendering. You'll learn how to render still images later in this section.

Making a Draft Rendering

New! Preset rendering options, which control numerous settings that affect rendering, are new in VIZ Render 2006. You can use the default presets quickly, without learning much about rendering. You can also save your own presets after learning how you want everything set after much study and experimentation.

1. Switch into the Camera01 viewport. Open the Render Presets drop-down list in the Rendering toolbar and select Draft.

2. A small dialog box appears in which you can choose which preset categories you wish to load (see Figure 18.15). Leave all categories selected and click Load.

3. Now numerous settings have been configured to make a draft rendering. Click the Quick Render button on the right side of the Rendering toolbar. Its icon is that of a teapot—the mascot of computer graphics. After about a minute, a draft rendering appears in what is called the rendered frame window (RFW). Figure 18.16 shows the result. No maps or indirect illumination have been processed, so the rendering doesn't look very realistic. You might catch glaring problems here, such as missing objects, or other obvious problems with the composition. In this case our test render looks OK, and we've invested only about two minutes of rendering time to find out. Close the RFW.

FIGURE 18.15
Loading selected preset
rendering categories

FIGURE 18.16
Completed draft
rendering

Working with the Environment

In the context of rendering, the *environment* is everything outside the model. The environment in VIZ Render includes the background, which might be a solid color or a bitmap image. In addition, the dynamic range of the image is part of the environment and is adjusted with exposure control. As part of our preparation for a high-quality final rendering, let's work with the environment controls to give the sky some color.

1. Open the Render Presets drop-down list in the Rendering toolbar and select Quality-Interior. Leave all categories selected and click Load in the small dialog box that appears.

2. Open the Render Scene dialog box by clicking the second button on the Rendering toolbar, or press F10 and click the Environment tab (see Figure 18.17).

3. Click the color swatch in the Background group to open the color selector. Choose a very pale blue color to simulate the sky environment that we'll see outside the windows. Close the Color Selector.

NOTE   The Effects tab of the Render Scene dialog box allows you to apply Blur, Color Balance, and/ or Film Grain effects within VIZ Render.

Calculating a Radiosity Solution

Calculating a radiosity solution is a separate process from rendering output. The draft rendering you made earlier did not use a radiosity solution, and the quality level was correspondingly low (see Figure 18.16). Now you'll learn how to improve the quality of your renderings greatly by using the radiosity algorithm to calculate indirect illumination.

FIGURE 18.17

Environment tab of
Render Scene dialog box

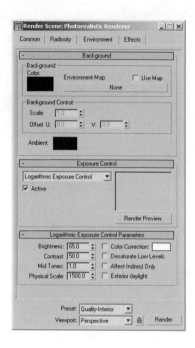

1. Click the Radiosity tab in the Render Scene dialog box. To better store lighting data, you can create a radiosity mesh that subdivides itself to adapt to the most intense changes in lighting intensity.

2. Expand the Radiosity Meshing Parameters rollout and check Use Adaptive Subdivision. In the Mesh Settings group, change Maximum Mesh Size to 12′ and Minimum Mesh Size to 6″. Now the radiosity mesh will automatically adapt to the lighting intensity (within the ranges you set) and a higher-quality solution will be generated.

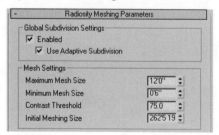

3. Scroll up and click the Start button at the top of the Radiosity Processing Parameters rollout. Watch as the progress bar moves across the Render Scene dialog box, just below the start button. The progress bar will move repeatedly from left to right as light energy is bounced around the scene. After the solution quality reaches 85%, four more refine iterations will be performed

on all the objects to further improve the solution. Calculating the radiosity solution takes about three minutes in this simple scene (processing time is a function of processor speed).

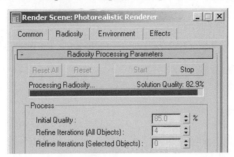

The colors in the viewport change as a rough approximation of the radiosity solution data is displayed. It already looks better than the draft rendering. Making a final rendering will actually give much better results compared to what you see in the viewport.

4. Right-click the viewport menu and choose Wireframe display mode. The mesh reveals additional subdivisions generated by the radiosity algorithm (see Figure 18.18). Notice that there is more topology closer to the light sources—that is the result of adaptive subdivision.

After a radiosity solution has been generated you cannot move objects or adjust lights or materials without invalidating the solution. The prompt line will inform you if the solution is invalid. If this happens, click the Reset All button in the Radiosity Processing Parameters rollout on the Radiosity tab and then click Start to recalculate the solution.

NOTE You can still adjust brightness and contrast after a radiosity solution has been generated without invalidating the solution. Do so in the Logarithmic Exposure Control Parameters rollout on the Environment tab of the Render Scene dialog box.

Save your work by pressing Ctrl+S. The file size will grow much greater now because the radiosity data is included—Roof.drf is now almost 7 MB. Now you are ready to create a rendering.

FIGURE 18.18
Camera viewport after radiosity solution was generated (left) and radiosity mesh revealed (right)

Rendering Stills

Most of the time when using VIZ Render you will probably want to create still images that you can print out for presentation. Remember that for the best quality results, calculate a radiosity solution prior to rendering stills. The print quality of stills depends on resolution, which is defined as the number of pixels—also known as dots—per inch (dpi). Therefore, to get higher quality or larger prints, render more pixels.

NOTE   You can make simple animations in VIZ Render. For example, you can move the camera in time to make a walkthrough or flyby animation, or keyframe the daylight system to animate the sun moving overhead as in a time-lapse video. Refer to the VIZ Render help for more information.

Choose the Common tab of the Render Scene dialog box.

You choose the number of pixels in the Common Parameters rollout in the Output Size group. You can specify the pixel dimension of your output by typing values in the Width and Height text boxes. The numbered buttons to the right of these parameters are common preset sizes. Click the 800x600 button.

Rendering time depends partly on the number of pixels rendered. Rendering a 1600x1200 image takes four times as long as an 800x600 image because there are four times as many pixels in the larger image.

TIP   Choose small output size if you are doing a quality test rendering. Increase pixel size only after you are certain that everything in the scene is ready for final output.

Click the Render button, and the RFW window will appear. The RFW gets progressively filled in with pixels as the rendering is calculated. In this tutorial, the process should take about 10 minutes to render an 800x600 image. You might want to take a break while your computer processes the rendering (see Figure 18.19).

After the image has rendered you can save it in your choice of image formats by clicking the Save Image button in the RFW. I recommend saving images for print in the .tif format as it preserves the full quality of the image. Each image format has its own options. Choose 8-bit Color and No Compression in the TIF Image Control dialog box for standard color images suitable for printing.

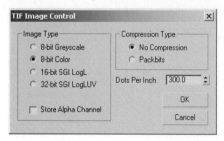

FIGURE 18.19
Completed radiosity
rendering

You can click the Print button in the RFW to print to your default printer. Render another image looking through Camera02 if you want. You don't have to recalculate the radiosity solution to render additional images from different viewpoints.

Summary

In this chapter you have just scratched the surface of what VIZ Render offers. You have learned how to link your model from ADT into VIZ Render, add cameras and lighting, substitute geometry, calculate radiosity, and render still images. You can create truly stunning presentation imagery the more you practice with VIZ Render.

Chapter 19

Printing, Publishing, and Data Exchange

Before you can print or publish, you need to set up your system to work with output devices. Although that configuration usually falls under the purview of CAD managers, this chapter begins with an overview of the setup process for those who work in small organizations and might need to do the setup themselves.

The term *plotting* has been used for many years in AutoCAD—it derives from the old output devices that physically printed lines with technical pen tips on print media. When we use this term today, it usually refers to printing on raster output devices—including most modern printers—or to completely electronic forms of "output" such as Autodesk's design web format (DWF). In addition, we more specifically use the term *plotting* for generating output from a single drawing.

When we speak of publishing in ADT, we are talking about plotting multiple drawings together. In Chapter 5, "Project Management," you learned that sheets form the top level of the drawing hierarchy; and that views, constructs, and elements are referenced into them. As long as you haven't added any content to sheets (other than the XRefs that actually store the content), you can publish sheets at any time and rest assured that they contain the most current and coordinated project information.

In Chapter 1, "The Basics," I discussed how ADT is built on the philosophy of building information modeling (BIM) and its efficient approach to building design, construction, and management. Part of the BIM approach is the commitment to keeping information digital. By exchanging data rather than physical drawings, you can increase the overall efficiency of your organization and help the environment by saving trees and transportation costs. There are many ways to exchange data that you'll learn in this chapter. This chapter's topics include the following:

◆ Setting Up

◆ Plotting

◆ Publishing

◆ Exchanging Data

Setting Up

As you are probably aware, a physical printing device—such as an inkjet printer—requires installing special software called a *driver* to interface with Windows. When you install a driver, a system printer is created in Windows. For most applications, this system printer contains all the information required for successful printing.

Although it is possible to plot directly to system printers in ADT, it is not recommended. ADT has its own set of plotter drivers that stand between the application and the system printers. Each ADT plotter driver controls a set of paper sizes, graphics settings, and custom properties that go beyond what is available in the system printer. You will get the best results by setting up and using plotter drivers in ADT.

Some plotter drivers are *logical printers*, meaning they have no physical analogue. These printers are used for "printing" to different output formats. As an exercise, you will set up a logical plotter driver to output raster images in the Tagged Image File Format (TIFF). The TIFF format supports lossless compression for highest quality printing. You might, for example, use the TIFF plotter driver to create images that can be enhanced and printed in Adobe Photoshop.

NOTE   See my book *Enhancing CAD Drawings with Photoshop* (Sybex, 2004) to learn powerful techniques for making presentations starting with images output from AutoCAD and/or ADT.

Adding Plotter Drivers

In this section you will create two plotter drivers: one physical and one logical. The physical driver I will show you how to install is for the popular HP DesignJet 500 large format inkjet printer. The logical plotter driver you'll make is used for outputting TIFF images from ADT.

ADDING A PLOTTER DRIVER FOR A PHYSICAL DEVICE

Follow along with the tutorial, substituting your own printer model where appropriate (you are likely to own a different device).

1. If you have not already done so, install a Windows system printer for the printer model that you own. Usually printers ship with a CD that contains a program you run prior to physically connecting the device to your computer or network. Follow the instructions that come with your printer. I have installed the HP DesignJet 500 24 system printer.

TIP   You might want to check the printer manufacturer's website for your device's latest drivers. Sometimes drivers are available that are newer than the ones on the installation CD that came with the product.

2. Launch ADT and choose Format ➤ Plotter Manager, or type **PLOTTERMANAGER**↵ on the command line. A Windows Explorer window appears (see Figure 19.1). The window that appears shows files and folders in the following path:

```
C:\Documents and Settings\All Users\Application Data\Autodesk\ADT
2006\enu\Plotters
```

The files you see are preconfigured plotter drivers that ship with ADT.

3. Double-click the Add-A-Plotter Wizard icon. An Add Plotter wizard dialog box appears. Read the introductory message and click the Next button.

4. The Begin page offers you three choices: My Computer, Network Plotter Server, or System Printer. Choose My Computer when a device is physically connected to your computer, and Network Plotter when the device is a node on your local area network (LAN), accessible to others on the LAN.

FIGURE 19.1
Exploring Plotters folder

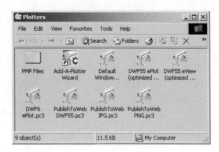

5. Choose System Printer in this case (see Figure 19.2). The ADT driver hands off the plot job to the Windows system printer after applying different default values as compared with other Windows applications. Click Next.

6. Choose your device's system printer from the list on the System Printer page. I will choose HP DesignJet 500 24 (setup in step 1). Click Next.

7. On the Import PCP or PC2 page, the Import File button allows you to bring in legacy plotter configuration parameter files from old versions of AutoCAD and/or ADT. We don't need this; click Next.

8. The Plotter Name page suggests the system printer name as the name for your plotter driver. Click Next.

9. On the Finish page, click the Edit Plotter Configuration button to open the Plotter Configuration Editor (see Figure 19.3).

10. Select the Device and Document Settings tab and verify that the Custom Properties node is selected in the tree pane. Click the Custom Properties button to open the HP DesignJet 500 24 Properties dialog box. You'll see a different dialog box if you are setting up a different device. Every device has its own properties that control its specific hardware features. In this case, I will choose Arch D paper size (see Figure 19.4) and click OK. You should choose settings appropriate to your configuration and click OK.

FIGURE 19.2
Choosing to configure a plotter as a system printer

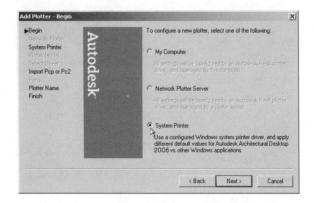

FIGURE 19.3
Plotter Configuration
Editor

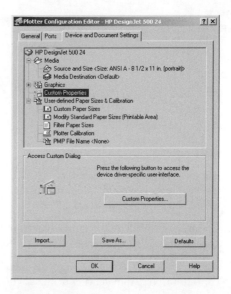

FIGURE 19.4
Specific driver
properties

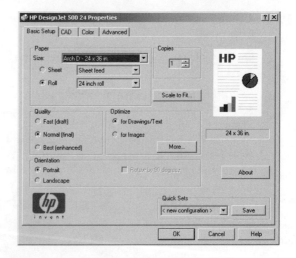

11. Select the Filter Paper Sizes node in the tree pane. The Filter Paper Sizes group lists all the paper sizes that are available within this driver. Click the Uncheck All button. The list usually includes sizes used in many countries including US, ISO, ANSI, DIN, JIS, and Arch. I will select only Arch D - 24 x 36 (see Figure 19.5) and click OK to close the dialog box. Go through the list and check only the sizes that you intend to use. Click Finish to close the wizard, and a new plotter driver is created.

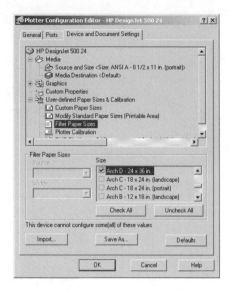

FIGURE 19.5
Filtering paper sizes

ADDING A LOGICAL PLOTTER DRIVER

The logical plotter driver you'll create does not go through a Windows system printer. Instead, it goes through what is called an Autodesk Heidi plotter driver (Hierarchical object-oriented pipeline system Device Interface, or more popularly known as Heidi). The Heidi driver is Autodesk's version of the Windows system printer.

You will set this up using the same wizard you used to add the physical plotter driver.

1. Choose Format ➢ Plotter Manager again to bring the same Windows Explorer window to the front. This time you should see the plotter driver you made earlier (HP DesignJet 500 24, in my case). Double-click the Add-A-Plotter Wizard icon.

2. When the wizard dialog box appears, click Next and choose the My Computer radio button on the Begin page. Click Next.

3. On the Plotter Model page, choose Raster File Formats in the Manufacturers list. Select TIFF Version 6 (Uncompressed) from the Models list (see Figure 19.6). Click Next.

4. Click Next three more times to accept the defaults on the next three pages. When you get to the Finish page, click the Edit Plotter Configuration button.

5. You will set up a new "paper" size, which in this case is actually a pixel size for the raster plotter driver. In the Plotter Configuration Editor, select the Custom Paper Sizes node. Click the Add button to launch the Custom Paper Size Wizard. Leave the Start From Scratch radio button selected on the Begin page and click Next.

6. You'll create a large "paper" size, so you'll have lots of resolution to make clear prints in an image-editing program such as Adobe Photoshop. Enter a Width of 3000 and Height of 2000 pixels on the Media Bounds page (see Figure 19.7). Click Next.

FIGURE 19.6
Choosing a raster file
format in Heidi driver

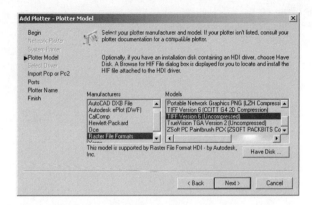

FIGURE 19.7
Creating a custom
"paper" size

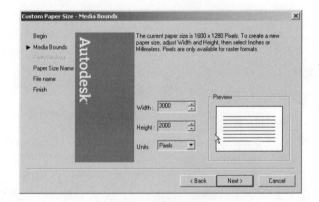

7. Click Next three more times to accept the defaults on the next three pages of the wizard. Click Finish to close the Custom Paper Size Wizard and click OK to close the Plotter Configuration Editor. Click Finish to close the Add Plotter Wizard. A new PC3 and PMP file have been created on your hard drive. The PC3 file is the plotter driver, and the PMP file stores the custom paper size.

8. Close the Plotters Windows Explorer window.

Setting Plot and Publish Options

After you have created one or more plotter drivers in ADT, there are several plot and publish options you may also want to set. These are accessible in the Options dialog box. Before you change any options, check with your CAD manager (if you have one).

1. Right-click the command line and choose Options from the shortcut menu.

2. Select the Plot and Publish tab. I recommend checking Hide System Printers in the General Plot Options group (see Figure 19.8). Only the ADT plotter drivers will then be available inside ADT, so you will avoid making the mistake of plotting directly to a system printer when you have corresponding plotter drivers available.

FIGURE 19.8

Plot and Publish options

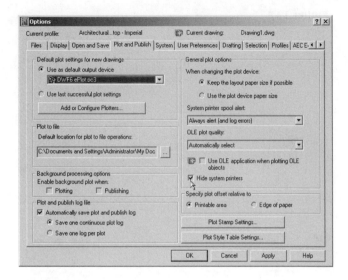

3. In the Use as Default Output Device drop-down list, choose the plotter driver you expect to use the most often. I will leave DWF6 ePlot.pc3 selected because I expect to use this digital format most often.

4. Notice the Default Location for Plot To File Operations path in the Plot To File group. This feature used to be in the Plot dialog box in previous versions, so it's important to be aware of where your plotted files will appear. You might want to change this path to your project folder, for example.

NOTE   Read the AutoCAD help to learn more about the Plot and Publish options.

5. Click the Plot Stamp Settings button. This feature allows you to stamp each plotted sheet with text information. You might want to use this feature when printing physical sheets so you can identify the drawing name, date and time, and device name, for example (see Figure 19.9). You can also choose to include a plot stamp when you plot or publish later on. For this exercise, click Cancel.

6. Click the Plot Style Table Settings button. There are two types of plot style tables: color dependent and named plot styles. ADT uses named plot styles in its templates, so I recommend that you select the Use Named Plot Styles radio button. This choice affects new drawings that you create from scratch only. Older drawings that use color tables are not affected by this choice. You might use color tables if migrating from plotting standards based upon pen number (common in the early 1990s but rare today).

7. Choose AIA Standard.stb from the Default Plot Style Table drop-down list if you are using Imperial units (see Figure 19.10). Click OK. Click OK again to close the Options dialog box.

TIP   You can configure plot style tables themselves by clicking the Add or Edit Plot Style Tables button in the Plot Style Table Settings dialog box. Otherwise, choose Format ➢ Plot Style Manager or type **STYLESMANAGER.**⏎ on the command line to access plot style tables in Windows Explorer.

FIGURE 19.9
Plot Stamp settings

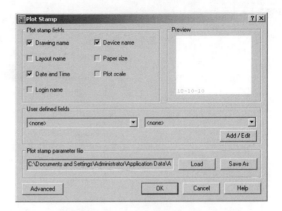

FIGURE 19.10
Plot Style Table Settings

Plotting

Previewing your plots prior to printing can save time as well as paper. Use the Plot dialog box to generate output from a single drawing. View plot and publish details to debug any errors that might occur. You'll learn to work with named page setups to save time setting up plot details on multiple layouts and/or across drawing files. We'll use the project developed in Chapter 16, "Sections and Elevations," to explore plotting and publishing.

Copy the sample files from the Chapter 16 folder on the companion DVD onto your hard drive if you haven't already done so. Included in these files is a zip archive called Completed Chapter 16. Extract these files in the archive to the following folder on your hard drive, overwriting other files that might already be there:

```
C:\Documents and Settings\<username>\My Documents\Autodesk\My Projects\Chapter 16
```

Open the Project Browser and navigate to the above path. Double-click the Chapter 16 project node and close the Project Browser. Choose the Sheets tab in the Project Navigator: There are numerous sheets already defined for you to explore plotting issues in this chapter.

Previewing Prior to Printing

How many times have you printed essentially the same sheet, tweaking minor details, until you generate the output you intend? All too often this is the case, and even if you are charging your client for your "mistakes," the printing costs can add up quickly and adversely affect your project budget.

First of all, consider that because the information exists digitally you may not need paper plots at all during much of a project's review cycle. Instead, using the information-exchange techniques presented at the end of this chapter, you can realize considerable gains in efficiency. Realistically, generating electronic plots instead of paper ones will require discussion with your team members, manager, and consultants before all parties buy into such a strategy. It is really worth checking out: We have the technology.

If you must print on paper, making a preview is a good way to catch potential last-minute mistakes and save resources. Of course, this strategy works only if you really study the preview to notice anything gone awry. Let's try an example.

1. Open the A201 Exterior Elevations sheet. Click the Plot Preview button on the Standard toolbar, or type **PREVIEW**↵ on the command line. Figure 19.11 shows the preview window.

2. All the palettes disappear so you can study the preview while in this mode. What you see is what you get. Linetypes and lineweights appear exactly as they will plot while in preview mode.

3. There is a single docked toolbar at the top of the interface with buttons letting you pan and zoom. Navigate around the sheet and make sure that it looks as you intend. If you did find any mistakes, you would most likely have to correct them in other files (views, constructs, and/or elements).

4. Save any changes, return to the sheet and reload its XRefs before making another plot preview.

5. Repeat this cycle until what you see passes your visual inspection. You can then either click the Plot button or Close Preview Window button on the toolbar. Click the latter in this case.

FIGURE 19.11
Plot preview interface

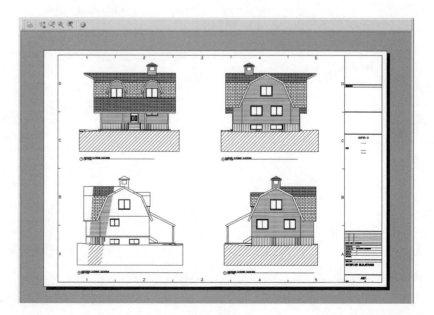

TIP Try post-linking field codes if you see number signs in any of the title marks on sheets (see Chapter 5). Reload XRefs and the title marks will update with coordinated information.

Using the Plot Dialog Box

Use the Plot dialog box to choose a plotter driver, paper size, and plot style table, and to set up numerous options for printing.

1. Choose File ➤ Plot, type **PLOT↵** or press **Crtl+P** to open the Plot dialog box (see Figure 19.12). Click the More Options button (>) in the lower-right corner to expand the dialog box.

2. Choose a plotter driver from the Name drop-down list in the Printer/Plotter group. I'll choose HP DesignJet 500 24.pc3 to use the plotter driver I made earlier. You should choose the plotter driver you set up. Notice that Arch D appears in the Paper Size drop-down list because I filtered the paper sizes in the plotter driver to show only the relevant sizes used on this device.

3. The plot style table is assigned on the upper right. I recommend leaving AIA Standard.stb if you are working with Imperial units in North America. Otherwise, choose the plot style table that matches your drawing templates.

   Notice that there is a Preview button in the lower-left corner of the Plot dialog box. This is an alternative way to access preview mode. The Page Setup group offers you a way to save all the settings in the Plot dialog box under a name.

4. Click the Add button if you like and give your setting a name. When you are done, click OK to generate the plot. That's it! Click the Help button if you want to learn more about each setting in the Plot dialog box.

TIP Check out www.bluebeam.com if you want to output PDF files from ADT. Some consultants find working with Autodesk's DWF format cumbersome, and PDF is a popular format that most people understand.

FIGURE 19.12
Plot dialog box

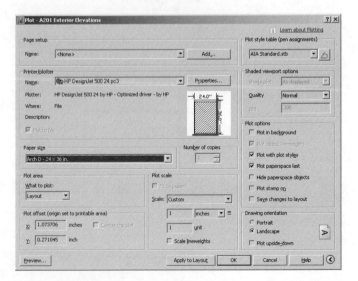

Viewing Plot and Publish Details

After you send a plot, you'll see a progress bar, and after a few moments a balloon message will appear in the lower-right corner of the ADT interface. In the example it says no errors or warnings found, so you typically would click the close box to dismiss the balloon. In this case, let's see what happens, so click to view plot and publish details.

The Plot and Publish Details dialog box appears with text information relating to this sheet (see Figure 19.13). By reading the text, you can investigate when and where the plot file was sent. This information is critical to debugging plotting errors when they occur. For example, if you have confirmation that a plot file was sent to your plot spooler, but it still hasn't emerged from the printer, you have a place to start looking for the bottleneck in your plot system. Click the Close button when you are finished reviewing the information.

TIP The Plot and Publish options contain a setting for saving a log file as either one continuous plot log, or one log per plot.

Working with Page Setups

Page setups store the information in the Plot dialog box for repeated use. You can use named page setups on multiple paper space layouts. You can even import page setups from a different drawing file into your current drawing. That way, you won't have to be bothered by the details of setting up plots, and you can simply select a page setup and send the plot.

1. Choose File ➤ Page Setup Manager or right-click the Model/Layout tab and choose Page Setup Manager from the context menu (see Figure 19.14). A list of preconfigured page setups appear that ship with ADT. Any page setups you save from the Plot dialog box will appear here as well.

FIGURE 19.13
Plot and Publish Details

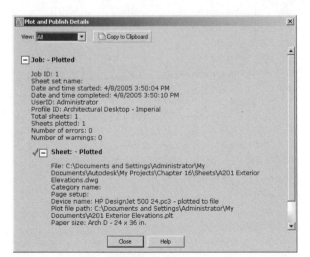

FIGURE 19.14

Page Setup Manager

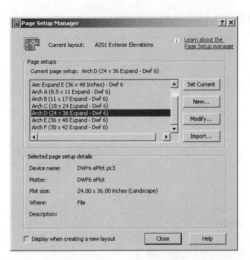

2. Select Arch D (24 x 36 Expand - Dwf 6) from the list and click the Modify button. The Page Setup dialog box appears, configured with all the settings stored in the page setup. For example, this page setup uses the DWF 6 ePlot.pc3 plotter driver and ARCH Expand D paper size. Notice that the Page Setup group does not have a drop-down list now because you are editing a specific page setup. Any changes you make are saved in the named page setup. Click Cancel when you are finished reviewing the Page Setup options. The Import button in the Page Setup Manager is used to bring in named page setups from other drawing files.

3. Click Close to close the dialog box.

Publishing

The Publish command is typically used to plot more than one drawing. You can publish named sheet selections, all the sheets in a sheet subset, or the entire sheet set in a project. See Chapter 5 for more on sheet mechanics.

You should probably make at least one test plot before deciding to publish the entire sheet set in your project. Of course, the potential for loss of plot media is great when you are asking to plot numerous sheets at once. Be sure that you are getting acceptable plots with the Plot command before attempting to publish.

New!

Now in ADT 2006, 3D DWF files are a publishing option. Three-dimensional design web format files are a great way to share your single building model with others who do not have access to ADT (AutoDesk's DWF Viewer can be downloaded free of charge). Viewing a design in 3D is the fastest way to visualize its spatial qualities. It may be worth exploring this exciting publishing option as an alternative to, or as an addition to, other presentation imagery you might have prepared.

Publishing to DWF and Plotter

You can choose to publish to a DWF or to a plotter using the Publish dialog box, which lists the drawings you select on the Sheets tab of the Project Navigator. You can select a single drawing or make a selection of sheets by Ctrl-clicking.

To select the entire sheet set, right-click the top node in the sheet hierarchy on the Sheets tab of the Project Navigator. Choose Publish ➢ Publish Dialog Box from the shortcut menu (see Figure 19.15). Notice that the cascading shortcut menu also has options to publish directly to DWF or to a plotter, use a page setup override, include a plot stamp, and more.

The Publish dialog box appears, listing all the sheets in the sheet set (four sheets in this example). Choose the Arch D page setup in each drop-down menu in the Page Setup column. Note that you could choose different page setups for each sheet—to send plots to different devices or use different paper sizes. In this case, just choose Arch D for each sheet (see Figure 19.16).

The *sheet list* is what you develop in the Publish dialog box. It contains the sheet names and the page setups associated with them. You can save the sheet list for future use and load it later on. The sheets are processed in the order they appear in the list (from the top down). You can move sheets up and down in the list to affect the order in which they are plotted.

Choose the Plotter Named In Page Setup radio button in the Publish To group. You can force a page setup that contains a physical plotter driver to output a DWF file by choosing the DWF File radio button.

Uncheck the Model Tab option in the Include When Adding Sheets group. If you are plotting sheets, you only need to include paper space layout tabs because that is where the sheets are stored.

Click the Publish button to start the entire batch process.

Click Yes if you are presented with a small dialog box asking if you want to save the list of sheets. The sheet list is saved as a Drawing Set Description file (DSD). Save this in your project folder if you ever want to reprint all these sheets again.

FIGURE 19.15
Choosing to publish a sheet set

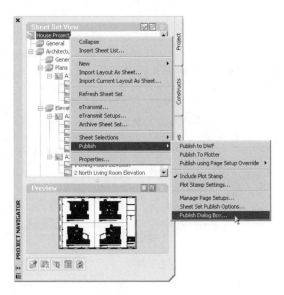

FIGURE 19.16
Selecting Page Setups in
the Publish dialog box

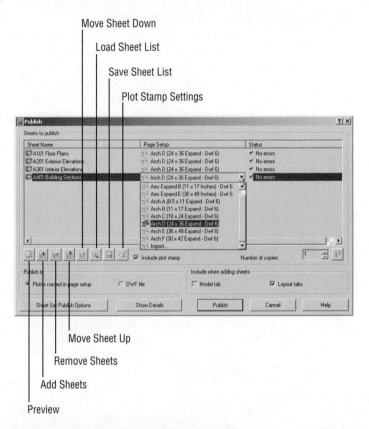

You'll see progress bars showing sheet and job status. After about a minute this simple publishing
job will be complete. If you chose to publish to DWF, check the folder specified in the Plot and Publish
options for the DWF output files (My Documents by default). The DWF files published in this way are
two-dimensional. If you publish to a plotter, printing will being immediately.

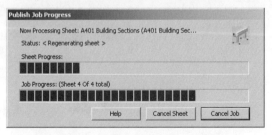

Publishing to 3D DWF

3D DWF files are published through a separate interface. Before you choose to publish 3D DWF files,
you must be in model space within a drawing file that contains 3D geometry.

1. Unlike 2D DWF files, 3D DWF files are published one file at a time. Choose the Views tab in
   the Project Navigator and open the Composite view file. Choose File ➢ Publish to 3D DWF.

2. The AEC 3D DWF Publishing Options dialog box (see Figure 19.17) appears. Select a filename for your output in the DWF File Name box. You can choose to organize the 3D DWF file by XRef and whether you want to group objects in the 3D DWF file by object type and style or by layer.

3. The Properties group allows you to select which property sets (if any) you'd like to export with the DWF file. Click the Edit AEC DWF Options button to open the AEC DWF Publishing Options dialog box. The property sets available to be published are stored in a Published Properties List (PPL) file. A PPL file is loaded by default called AEC DWF List.ppl. You can browse for another PPL file, or create a new one using the buttons in the dialog box (see Figure 19.18). Individual property set definitions can be added or removed from the list as needed. Click OK.

NOTE Property set data can be published with both 2D and 3D DWF files. Choose File ➢ Export Property Data to choose property sets prior to publishing a 2D DWF file.

4. Check Include Properties from AEC DWF Options. Finally, click OK, and the 3D DWF is generated.

FIGURE 19.17
Publishing options for a 3D DWF file

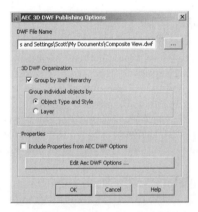

FIGURE 19.18
AEC DWF Publishing Options

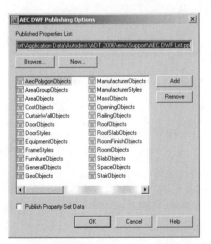

CONTINUING THE DESIGN PROCESS: REVIEW, MARK UP, AND REVISE

Autodesk has three different DWF viewing products to choose from. The oldest product, which is called Volo View, also supports Autodesk Inventor and DXF files. Choose Volo View only if you need to interchange data with mechanical engineers who use Inventor, for example.

Autodesk's more recent viewing product is called the DWF Viewer, and it was automatically installed on your computer when you installed ADT. The DWF Viewer is free for others to download from www.autodesk.com. This is the best choice to recommend to consultants who want to view and print your DWF content. The new version supports 3D objects and textures.

Autodesk offers another product called DWF Composer, which is a low-priced piece of software that acts both as a DWF viewer and redliner. Members of your team can mark up DWF files in Composer and then they can be brought back into ADT (making a round trip) for integration into the project dataset. This is a good option for members of your team (or consultants) who do not need or want to pay for the full functionality of ADT, but who want to keep information digital.

Exchanging Data

There are numerous ways to exchange data with other people and other programs. You can send a single drawing as an email attachment using an automated feature called Send within ADT. If you want to exchange more than one file, create an eTransmittal that conveniently packages multiple drawings and their dependent files. Then you can transfer the package over the Internet using file transfer protocol (FTP) or burn it on a CD or DVD.

If you have a project website, ADT allows you to publish drawings to the web in DWF form through a wizard interface that provides options to create a web page with i-drop ActiveX controls. In addition, ADT supports numerous file formats that allow you to export data to other programs.

Sending Drawings by Email

The most basic way to get a single drawing to someone electronically is by including it as an attachment in an email message. Pay special attention to the attachment's file size, however, because most people have limited mailbox size.

Open the Windows Explorer and check out the attachment's file size prior to sending the message. If the drawing you want to send is small enough (probably less than 5 MB), choose File ➢ Send to have ADT create a new message in your default mail program and attach the current drawing to the message.

Creating an eTransmittal

When you want to transfer drawings to another party who is using ADT, using eTransmit is the best option. Projects in ADT involve numerous files, including drawings and their XRefs, XML documents, plotter drivers, plot style tables, plotter configuration files, project files, and many others. Trying to manually keep track of all the dependent files is no small task. eTransmit makes this easy.

1. If you want to package a single drawing and its dependent files choose File ➢ eTransmit. If you want to transfer an entire sheet set, right-click the top node on the Sheets tab of the

Project Navigator and choose eTransmit from the shortcut menu (do this now). Figure 19.19 shows the Create Transmittal dialog box.

2. Use the tabbed interface to select the files you are interested in packaging for transfer. If you need multiple transmittal setups for different purposes, click the Transmittal Setups button to open a smaller dialog box that allows you to manage those setups.

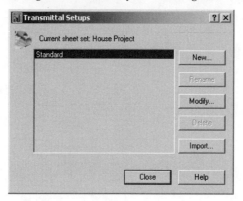

3. After you select the files to package, click the New button. Type **Self Extracting** in the New Transmittal Setup dialog box and click Continue.

4. The Modify Transmittal Setup dialog box allows you to choose how you want the data packaged. Change the Transmittal Package Type drop-down list from Zip to Self-Extracting Executable (*.exe). The recipient just has to double-click your package to extract its files to their hard drive (see Figure 19.20).

WARNING Some corporate firewalls do not permit executable files to pass through.

FIGURE 19.19
Creating an electronic
transmittal

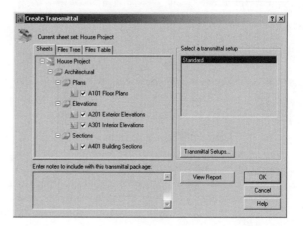

FIGURE 19.20
Setting transmittal
options

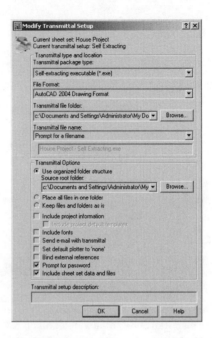

5. As you can see from studying Figure 19.20, there are numerous transmittal options. In this example, check Prompt For Password, which provides security for your package if it is intercepted during transfer. Enter a filename and then a password and confirm it again in the Password Confirmation textbox and click OK.

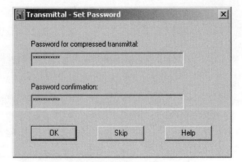

6. Click the Self Extracting transmittal setup and click OK to close the Modify Transmittal Setup dialog box. Click Save, and after a few moments `House Project - Self Extracting.exe` is created. Now you can transfer this single file to your recipient using an FTP program, or burn it on a CD or DVD and messenger it or ship it to them. You don't need to worry about including instructions (except for the password) because it couldn't be easier for the recipient to double-click the self-extracting program and receive your data.

NOTE You can archive the sheet set by choosing this option in the shortcut menu within the Sheets tab of the Project Navigator. Archiving works just like the eTransmittal feature. Instead of transmitting the archive, store it on magnetic tape or optical media for long-term storage.

Publishing to the Web

If you have a project website, publishing drawings to the Web might be just the ticket. Your network administrator or website designer can provide password protection and security if desired for the web pages you make with ADT.

1. First save the current drawing and then choose File ➤ Publish to Web.

   The Publish To Web Wizard appears. Leave the Create New Web Page radio button selected and click Next.

2. Type **Elevations** in the first text box. Click the ellipsis button and select a folder to store the web page in. Type **House Elevations** as the description (see Figure 19.21). Click Next.

3. The Select Image Type page offers you a choice of DWF, JPEG, or PNG formats. Use DWF when you want a vector "image" that allows you to navigate using an ActiveX control, JPEG for color renderings, and PNG for linework. In this example, leave DWF selected and click Next.

4. In subsequent pages of the wizard, you'll select a template, apply a theme, enable i-drop, and select drawings. Notice that you can add multiple drawing files as "images" on the Select Drawings page of the wizard. You can post the files to your website via FTP by clicking the Post Now button on the Preview and Post page of the wizard. Click Finish.

Notice that the Publish To Web Wizard creates numerous files in the folder you selected to store the web page in. The files include drawings, hypertext markup language web pages, JavaScript, cascading styles sheets, thumbnail images, and more.

NOTE Refer to the ADT help to learn more about how you (or your web designer) can customize the Publish To Web templates.

FIGURE 19.21
Using the Publish To Web Wizard

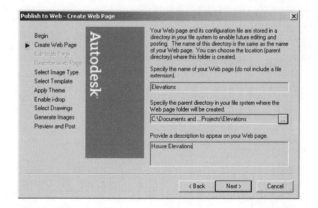

Exporting Data to Other Programs

You can prepare data in ADT for export to many other programs. How you prepare depends on what program you are exporting data to. For example, if you are exporting data to AutoCAD, you can still view ADT's intelligent objects by using an object enabler.

Autodesk provides free object enablers (download them from www.autodesk.com) that allow users of other Autodesk products to view and print intelligent architecture, engineering, and construction (AEC) object data that was created in ADT.

If you are exporting data for a consultant who does not have access to an object enabler (using Bentley Microstation, for example), you might need to explode the AEC objects prior to export to reduce them to "dumb" 2D blocks. First save a copy of the file you wish to export (so you don't inadvertently alter your source file in ADT). Then type **AECObjExplode** on the command line and press Enter (see Figure 19.22). Select how you want to explode the objects and click OK. Export the drawing to DWG or DXF and be sure not to save the drawing when closing it in ADT!

ADT supports the formats shown in Table 19.1 through File ➢ Export.

FIGURE 19.22

Exploding AEC Objects

TABLE 19.1: Export File Formats

FILE TYPE	EXTENSION
Windows Metafile	.wmf
ACIS	.sat
Stereolithography	.stl
Encapsulated Postscript	.eps
DXX Extract	.dxx
Bitmap	.bmp
3D Studio	.3ds
Block	.dwg

TIP You can also publish to Autodesk MapGuide using an option on the File menu. You'll have to have MapGuide installed to do so.

Exploring ADT Web Sites and Web Logs

I thought I'd leave you with a few web links to connect you with the online ADT community. Happy surfing!

URL	DESCRIPTION
www.autodesk.com	Autodesk
discussion.autodesk.com	ADT Forum
autodesk.blogs.com/between_the_walls	Autodesk's official ADT blog
autodesk.blogs.com/between_the_lines	Autodesk's official AutoCAD blog
www.archidigm.com	Source for ADT consulting and training
www.cgarchitect.com	Great computer graphics resource for architects
architects-desktop.blogspot.com	David Koch's blog (technical editor of this book)

Summary

Printing and publishing are essential skills to master in ADT and fortunately they are quite straightforward. You have learned how to set up plotter drivers and plot with them. You learned how to publish and studied the many options for exchanging data. This brings us to the end of *Mastering Architectural Desktop 2006*. It's been a long and complex trip learning ADT. I hope you have enjoyed the journey, and also that you'll find this book an essential tool in your ongoing work with ADT.

Scott Onstott

http://ScottOnstott.com

Appendix

Stand-Alone Utilities

Architectural Desktop (ADT) ships with several stand-alone utility applications that aid in a variety of tasks. This appendix contains descriptions of the following utilities:

- Batch Standards Checker
- Attach Digital Signatures Utility
- Portable License Utility
- Detail Component - Keynote Database Migration Utility
- Keynote Editor

Batch Standards Checker

The Batch Standards Checker is a utility that was designed to audit multiple drawing files and report on their compliance or non-compliance with AutoCAD standards (see Chapter 5, "Project Management"). Use the Batch Standards Checker to compare dimension styles, layers, linetypes, and text styles in selected drawings with those saved in standards drawings (with the dws extension).

WARNING The Batch Standards Checker does not audit ADT standards. Use the CAD Manager pull-down menu's AEC Project Standards submenu to access tools to audit ADT standards.

Launch this utility by clicking the Windows Start menu ➤ All Programs ➤ Autodesk ➤ Autodesk Architectural Desktop 2006 ➤ Batch Standards Checker. Figure A.1 shows this utility's tabbed dialog box interface. Use the Drawings tab to load multiple drawing files for review. Use the Standards tab to load the project's AutoCAD standards file.

Choose Check ➤ View Report to audit the selected drawings. As its name suggests, this utility only checks drawings; it does not "fix" them. Use the information in the report to make any adjustments needed in ADT.

Attach Digital Signatures Utility

Digital signatures are an optional part of a robust security system that is built into ADT. Using a digital signature (also known as a digital ID or digital certificate) is a much more secure way of identifying yourself than including a scanned handwritten signature, which could be copied or forged. Digital signatures are a form of identification containing your name, serial number, and expiration date. Digital signatures must be renewed every year from a certificate authority. You must have a digital signature installed on your computer before you can attach it via ADT.

TIP Research digital signatures on the Internet if you are interested in learning more about this feature.

Digital signatures are typically used as part of an overall security system that often includes password-protected encryption of drawing files to maintain privacy when transmitted over the Internet.

In addition to positively identifying you, a digital signature time-stamps a drawing and ensures that its data has not been changed since it was signed. Therefore, digital signatures should be applied only after drawing files are password-protected. If a password is assigned after a drawing has been digitally signed, the signature will be invalidated.

The Attach Digital Signatures utility is used to attach your signature to multiple drawing files. You can launch this utility from the Start menu ≻ All Programs ≻ Autodesk ≻ Autodesk Architectural Desktop 2006 ≻ Attach Digital Signatures, or you can use the following procedure to access the same options via the Security Options dialog box.

Password-Protecting a Drawing File

Before you launch Attach Digital Signatures, it is helpful to understand the process used to secure one drawing file in ADT.

1. Open a drawing file in ADT and choose Format ≻ Options and select the Open and Save tab.

2. Click the Security Options button in the File Safety Precautions group. Figure A.2 shows the Security Options dialog box that appears.

FIGURE A.2

Security Options
dialog box

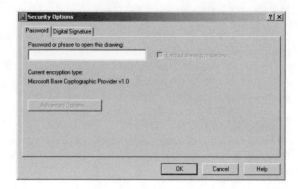

3. Type a password in the text box. If you lose this password, you lose the drawing file—there is no way around it.

TIP Make a copy of each drawing before you password-protect it and store the copies in a safe place (such as a DVD). You will need these files if you ever lose the passwords used to encrypt drawing files.

Attaching a Digital Signature

Once you've assigned a password to a drawing, you are ready to attach a digital signature.

1. Click the Digital Signature tab of the Security Options dialog box. If a digital signature isn't yet installed on your computer, the Valid Digital ID Not Available dialog box appears (see Figure A.3).

2. Click the Get A Digital ID button and you will be brought to a website in which you can purchase a digital certificate. Check with your manager to see if your firm already has a digital signature that you can use.

   After you purchase and install a digital certificate on your computer, you'll have access to the Digital Signature tab shown in Figure A.2.

3. Use this tab to select your signature to attach to the drawing file and a time server to be used to time-stamp the drawing. The Attach Digital Signatures utility works in exactly the same way as the Digital Signature tab of the Security Options dialog box, except that you have the ability to select multiple drawing files to attach signatures to. This utility makes attaching digital signatures more efficient.

For more information about security, I suggest reading the extensive notes in the AutoCAD help regarding protecting and signing drawings.

FIGURE A.3

You must purchase a
digital ID before you
can sign drawings.

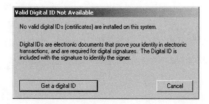

Portable License Utility

You can use the stand-alone version of ADT on more than one computer without purchasing additional licenses, but only on one computer at a time.

To do this, you must use the Portable License Utility. For example, you might want to transfer your ADT license from your desktop to a notebook computer when you're on the road. You may use a stand-alone license on only one computer at a time.

Access this program by clicking the Start menu ➢ All Programs ➢ Autodesk ➢ Autodesk Architectural Desktop 2006 ➢ Portable License Utility.

For the sake of this tutorial, let's assume that you want to transfer your ADT license from a desktop to notebook computer, and you've installed ADT on both machines.

1. Launch the Portable License Utility on the notebook and write down the identification code for the notebook computer on a piece of paper. This code appears at the bottom of the Portable License Utility dialog box (see Figure A.4). Each computer has a unique identification code.

WARNING   Adding, removing, or reformatting hard drives can affect your computer's unique identification code and therefore damage your ADT license and make it unusable. Transfer your license to another computer prior to making hardware changes.

2. Launch the Portable License Utility on the desktop computer and click the Computers tab. Click the Add button and enter the code you wrote down earlier and the notebook computer's name.

3. Select the Licenses tab of the Portable License Utility dialog box (see Figure A.5). Click the Export License button. You are prompted to save the license as a file with the PLU extension. Move this file to any memorable location on your notebook computer.

FIGURE A.4

Portable License Utility's Computers tab

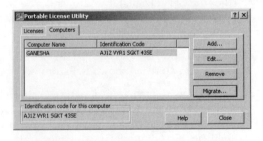

FIGURE A.5

Portable License Utility's Licenses tab

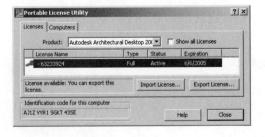

4. Switch to the Portable License Utility on the notebook computer and choose the Licenses tab. Click the Import License button and select the PLU file you just transferred.

That's it; now you can use ADT on your notebook computer. Reverse the process to move the file back to the desktop computer.

Detail Component - Keynote Migration Utility

New!

This utility is new to ADT 2006. Use it if you developed detail component and/or keynote databases (see Chapter 5) from earlier versions of ADT and want to migrate these databases into ADT 2006.

The Detail Component - Keynote Migration Utility performs only one function: migrating databases. The nice thing about this feature is you don't have to know anything about Access to migrate databases.

1. To launch the utility, choose Start menu ➢ All Programs ➢ Autodesk ➢ Autodesk Architectural Desktop 2006 ➢ Detail Component - Keynote Migration Utility. Figure A.6 shows the interface.

2. Click the ellipsis button next to Merge From, and select your old detail component database or your old keynote database (both are Access MDB files).

3. Click the ellipsis button next to Merge Into and select ADT's current detail component or keynote database, as the case may be. Do not mix database types in the Merge From and Merge Into fields.

4. Click the Start button, and the data from the old database will be migrated into the new database schemas and tables.

TIP   Check inside the following folder for ADT 2006's databases: `C:\Documents and Settings\All Users\Application Data\Autodesk\ADT 2006\enu\Details`.

FIGURE A.6
Detail Component -
Keynote Migration
Utility

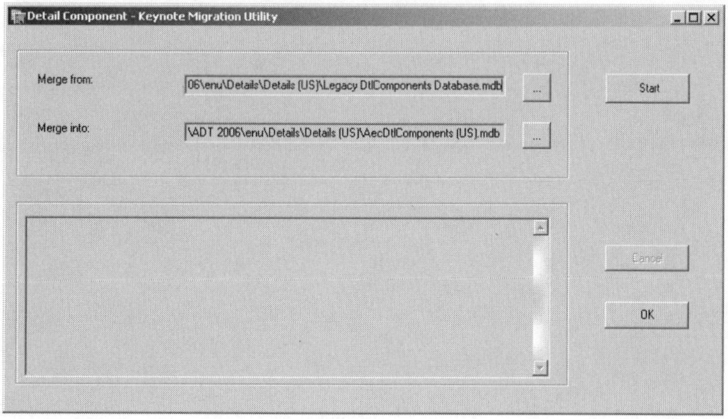

Keynote Editor

In Chapter 17, "Details and Keynotes," you learned how to edit keynotes from within ADT. The Keynote Editor is another new feature in ADT 2006 that is available as a stand-alone utility. The stand-alone version has similar functionality but is more convenient when you want to compare or edit keynotes in different databases. Unlike ADT's internal keynote editor, the external Keynote Editor program allows you to edit keynotes in multiple keynote databases in the same dialog box.

1. Choose Start menu ➢ All Programs ➢ Autodesk ➢ Autodesk Architectural Desktop 2006 ➢ Keynote Editor to launch the Keynote Editor. Figure A.7 shows its dialog box.

2. Click the Keynote Database drop-down list and select Browse to select a keynote Access database. You can load multiple databases into the drop-down list for the ability to quickly toggle between them for comparison. You can also create a new keynote database by clicking the New Database button at the bottom of the dialog box.

3. Expand groups in the keynote tree until you locate the actual keynote nodes. Double-click any keynote node to edit both its key and note.

FIGURE A.7

Stand-alone Keynote Editor

Index

Note to the reader: Throughout this index **boldfaced** page numbers indicate primary discussions of a topic. *Italicized* page numbers indicate illustrations.

Even though all of this may sound like utopian thinking, we might recall that the American educational system was founded not as a consumer or an economic good but as a public good—one designed to foster citizenship in the young republic. Over time, our schools have also been asked to serve many other purposes, and we cannot simply wish those other functions away. But we must not forget that the public school system was designed to make Americans. Across lines of race, class, ethnicity, and language, our best schools have done just that; they have been instruments of alchemy.[2]

Our first step forward in reviving this foundational vision must be to remember what we value and to align our measurement systems with those values. This will require political will and civic energy. It will require leadership and activism. It will require experimentation, trial and error, and missteps. And beyond the first summit is another mountain to climb—the work of acting on that information, of pursuing a broader set of goals for all schools. We are well down a path that has narrowed our view of education and reduced our understanding of what it means to be a good school, and we must not follow it any further.

Measurement, insofar as it explicitly identifies goals and tracks our progress toward those goals, shapes how we think and act. As I hope the preceding chapters have made clear, this is true for schools. It is also generally true for the world beyond schools—from police work to medicine to environmental conservation. When done effectively, measurement can foster engagement, appreciation, care, and support. It can keep us on track. When done poorly, however, it can warp our vision and undermine our ideals. It can lead us astray. Perhaps considering an example from outside education, then, can most clearly bring this point home.[3]

Two years ago a storm ravaged a red maple in our yard. Twelve months later, the electric company nearly hacked it to death, trimming it back from the power lines according to corporate directive.

We considered cutting the tree down, but then we began thinking about what it would cost to save it, what it would cost to replace it, and what the tree itself was worth. As I calculated it, our maple would produce roughly 300 board feet of quality lumber. That's about $150 in salable hardwood—a nice, concrete measure of our tree's value. To value the tree solely for its lumber, though, would be like valuing a school only on the basis of its test scores; it would miss almost the whole story of what makes a tree a tree.

So I flipped the paper over and began a new calculation.

We love our maple because each fall it turns gold, the color of the sun, a few weeks before it goes deep crimson. We love it because at the end of winter we tap it for syrup, right in the middle of the most densely populated city in New England. And in the summer we sit beneath its shade. I built a swing for my daughter and hung it from that tree. I use the tree as a landmark when I give directions. I regularly find myself staring out the window at it, lost in thought.

By the measure of board feet, it isn't a particularly good tree. Log buyers usually measure tree height from the ground to the first major defect, such as a large branch or fork. Part of what makes our tree good for climbing is that it splits in several directions at roughly five feet. It's also full of knots and healed wounds, which I think give it character, but which are otherwise classified as defects in the wood.

So by one measure, our tree isn't worth a tremendous amount—about the cost of an expensive dinner. If we valued board feet, we would sell our maple for its lumber and invest the proceeds in something that grows taller, faster, and smoother.

Yet that hardly captures the value of our tree. To act on such a calculation would be a terrible mistake.

Ultimately, schools are ecosystems. And because a healthy ecosystem will find its own distinct balance and become its own unique place, there is no perfect measure to deploy—no one set of standards to put in place. As the ecologist Aldo Leopold sagely put it: "A thing is right when it tends to preserve the integrity, stability, and beauty of the biotic community. It is wrong when it tends otherwise."[4]

Whatever our progress in measuring school quality, then, it is essential that we keep this simple truth in mind, because without such an ethos we will create an educational future that is narrow, homogeneous, and uninspiring, however advanced our information systems. Measurement, after all, is merely a means to an end. The deeper purpose of education is the pursuit of goodness, truth, beauty, and justice. However we try get there, we must not forget where we are trying to go.

Postscript

IN 2014, I had coffee with my state senator, Pat Jehlen, who represents Somerville, Cambridge, and Winchester in the Massachusetts state legislature. Pat is a strong supporter of public education, as is her husband, Alain, who is a board member of Citizens for Public Schools. Pat and I were writing an op-ed in the *Boston Globe* outlining our opposition to the state's method for identifying "low-performing" schools. It didn't seem fair to us that, given the relationship between socioeconomic status and test scores, the schools with the largest share of low-income and minority students were the most likely to be branded as failures.

The state could easily change its calculation, we argued, by looking at test score growth rather than raw test scores. Doing so would create a more level playing field across lines of race and class. That isn't to say that we thought that growth scores fully measured school quality; but we saw it as a simple and straightforward improvement. As we wrote: "Neither of us has much confidence in the exclusive or near-exclusive reliance on test scores in any permutation to measure something as complex as school quality. In fact, what we favor is a multi-dimensional model that goes far beyond such narrow measures."[1] Of course, we knew that if we wanted a better system for measuring school quality, we'd have to get the ball rolling ourselves. Test scores had been the coin of the realm in Massachusetts for nearly a quarter-century, and there was little sign of change on the horizon, so we began planning a consortium of districts that would show proof of concept for a new way of assessing school quality.

One big hole in my team's previous work was our lack of expertise in performance assessment. If we truly wanted to get beyond standardized test scores, we would have to establish some kind of alternate assessment system—perhaps via student portfolios—to accompany or replace standardized test results in our Academic Learning category. It so happened that Dan French, of the Center for Collaborative Education (CCE), had a strong working relationship with Pat and Alain and that CCE had just done some very promising work on performance assessment in New Hampshire.[2]

Over the next year, Dan, Pat, Alain, and I talked with district superintendents, school committees, and teachers, gauging interest in a consortium. Our goal was to assemble a large enough and diverse enough group of districts to allow for claims about generalizability—something that might lead the way to state-level change. At the same time, we wanted to keep our group small enough to produce something democratic and of high quality.

Ultimately, six districts came on board: Attleboro, Boston, Lowell, Revere, Somerville, and Winchester. The newly created Massachusetts Consortium for Innovative Education Assessment would be governed jointly by superintendents and teacher union presidents from member districts. And it would seek funding from both public and private sources, beginning with $350,000 from the state legislature.

The going wasn't easy. Union leaders, for instance, had questions about how much teachers would be asked to do on top of their substantial existing workloads. Three districts that had originally expressed interest in the consortium eventually decided not to join. Limited funding necessitated some creative thinking about day-to-day operations.[3] Nevertheless, the group began to move forward, and did so by taking the same first step we had taken in Somerville: figuring out what was worth measuring. So we got to work, conducting focus groups with students, teachers, administrators, parents, and community members in all member districts—incorporating their feedback into our evolving school quality framework.

Meanwhile, because Somerville was already two years ahead of the curve, our team continued working there to pilot practices that might be adopted by the rest of the consortium. We planned a parent survey, which would be built into the district's new online school registration system. We began designing a short form of our student survey—with perhaps twenty to twenty-five questions—for third and fourth graders. We set about building a feature into our web tool that would allow teachers to text message responses to questions from their principals. We also worked with the district to begin rolling the new data out to the public. As superintendent Mary Skipper put it: "We didn't cooperate on this project so we could keep it on a shelf. Let's put it out there and see how it does."

In short: we continue moving forward. We still don't have all the answers. But the ground beneath our feet is firm.

Although the future of this work is unwritten, it is hardly uncertain. There is mounting desire among parents and educators for better information about how our schools are doing. And there is increasing acceptance among policymakers that the era of test scores is coming to a close. That doesn't mean that we will create perfect replacement systems overnight. It has, however, created the space to begin moving slowly toward our goal. New tools are coming off the shelf—we'll see how they do.

Notes

Acknowledgments

Index

Notes

Introduction

1. See, for instance, the annual survey of public attitudes toward education conducted by Phi Delta Kappa and Gallup. See also the Gallup Poll Social Series: Work and Education; polling from 2005 to 2010 indicates that roughly 80 percent of respondents are "completely satisfied" or "somewhat satisfied" with their children's schools. Later chapters discuss small-scale polling in Somerville.

2. I am referring here to average scores, by grade level, on the Massachusetts Comprehensive Assessment System (MCAS).

3. The connection between test scores and family background is discussed in much greater detail in Chapters 2 and 3.

4. See, for instance, Micere Keels, Julia Burdick-Will, and Sara Keene, "The Effects of Gentrification on Neighborhood Public Schools," *City and Community* 12, no. 3 (2013): 238–259; David R. Garcia, "The Impact of School Choice on Racial Segregation in Charter Schools," *Educational Policy* 22 (2008): 805–829.

5. Jesse Rothstein, "College Performance Predictions and the SAT," *Journal of Econometrics* 121, nos. 1–2 (2004): 297–317; Donald C. Orlich and Glenn

Gifford, "The Relationship of Poverty to Test Scores," *Leadership Informa-tion* 4, no. 3 (2005): 34–38; Catherine Rampell, "SAT Scores and Family Income," *New York Times,* August 27, 2009, http://economix.blogs.nytimes .com/2009/08/27/sat-scores-and-family-income/?_r=0.

6. It is worth noting here that the Educational Testing Service is revamping the SAT to remain relevant.

7. The practice is so standard that Microsoft offers a Microsoft Office Business Scorecard Manager with Balanced Scorecard Templates. For more, see Robert S. Kaplan and David P. Norton, *The Balanced Scorecard: Translating Strategy into Action* (Cambridge, MA: Harvard Business School Press, 1996).

8. See, for instance, David Scharfenberg, "Boston's Struggle with Income Segregation," *Boston Globe,* March 6, 2016, https://www.bostonglobe.com /metro/2016/03/05/segregation/NiQBy000TZsGgLnAT0tHsL/story.html.

9. Thomas Dee, Brian A. Jacob, and Nathaniel Schwartz, "The Effects of NCLB on School Resources and Practices," *Educational Evaluation and Policy Analysis* 35, no. 2 (2013): 252–279; Dana Markow, Lara Macia, and Helen Lee, *MetLife Survey of the American Teacher*: Challenges for School Leadership (New York: Metropolitan Life Insurance Company, 2013).

10. Amy S. Finn, Matthew A. Kraft, Martin R. West, Julia A. Leonard, Crystal E. Bish, Rebecca E. Martin, Margaret A. Sheridan, Christo-pher F. O. Gabrieli, and John D. E. Gabrieli, "Cognitive Skills, Student Achievement Tests, and Schools," *Psychological Science* 25, no. 3 (2014): 736–744.

11. Massachusetts Department of Elementary and Secondary Education, "Indicators of School Quality or Student Access," http://www.doe.mass .edu/boe/docs/FY2017/2016–09/item3-ESSASuggestedIndicators.pdf.

12. Hunter is now at the University of California, Santa Barbara.

13. As later discussion in the book reveals, generating support for this work once we had results to show was quite easy. The Massachusetts Consor-tium for Innovative Education Assessment came together in a matter of months, despite the need to coordinate across multiple districts. Neverthe-less, with little to show for ourselves other than theoretical knowledge and civic commitment, it isn't hard to imagine that other cities would not have been particularly inclined to partner with us.

14. These racial categories are taken from the U.S. Census.

15. National Center for Education Statistics, "Characteristics of Public and Private Elementary and Secondary Schools in the United States: Results from the 2011–12 Schools and Staffing Survey," August 2013, http://nces .ed.gov/pubs2013/2013312.pdf; National Center for Education Statistics, "Racial / Ethnic Enrollment in Public Schools," http://nces.ed.gov /programs/coe/indicator_cge.asp.

16. It is important to note here that Somerville represents a case study rather than a "sample." As Robert K. Yin has argued, case studies are generalizable to theoretical propositions rather than to populations. So although Somerville's demographics do roughly match those of the United States as a whole, we must still treat the city as a site for expanding and generalizing theories rather than as one for generating more statistical generalizations.

17. Focus groups conducted between 2014 and 2016 included meetings with all school principals, all district administrators, parent liaisons for each school, and roughly 10 percent of teachers in the district. Additional focus groups, organized and facilitated with the help of the Somerville Family Learning Collaborative and the Welcome Project, elicited the feedback of over thirty parents whose native languages include Spanish, Portuguese, Haitian Creole, and Arabic. Surveys were also conducted in Somerville— with all principals and administrators, with roughly 100 community members, and with roughly 400 parents. As discussed in detail in Chapter 5, a deliberative poll was also conducted with forty-five parents and community members.

Chapter 1 Wrong Answer

1. For those unfamiliar, "English Language Arts" is simply another way of describing what was once simply called "English." MCAS results can be accessed electronically through the state Department of Elementary and Secondary Education "School and District Profiles" website: http://profiles .doe.mass.edu/.

2. Pamela E. Davis-Kean, "The Influence of Parent Education and Family Income on Child Achievement: The Indirect Role of Parental Expectations and the Home Environment," *Journal of Family Psychology* 19, no. 2

(2005): 294–304; Sean F. Reardon, "The Widening Academic Achievement Gap between the Rich and the Poor: New Evidence and Possible Explanations," in *Whither Opportunity*, Greg J. Duncan and Richard J. Murnane, eds. (New York: Russell Sage Foundation, 2011), 91–116.

3. Donald J. Hernandez, "Double Jeopardy: How Third-Grade Reading Skills and Poverty Influence High School Graduation," Annie E. Casey Foundation, Baltimore, MD, 2011; Joy Lesnick, Robert Goerge, Cheryl Smithgall, and Julia Gwynne, "Reading on Grade Level in Third Grade: How Is It Related to High School Performance and College Enrollment?," Chapin Hall at the University of Chicago, 2010.

4. Lee Shulman, "Counting and Recounting: Assessment and the Quest for Accountability," *Change* 39, no. 1 (2007): 20–25. Bloom's Taxonomy is a hierarchically-structured device for organizing cognitive acts in education.

5. Morgan S. Polikoff, Andrew C. Porter, and John Smithson, "How Well Aligned Are State Assessments of Student Achievement with State Content Standards?," *American Educational Research Journal* 48, no. 4 (2011): 965–995; Edward Haertel, "Reliability and Validity of Inferences about Teachers Based on Student Test Scores," report based on the 14th William H. Angoff Memorial Lecture at the National Press Club, Educational Testing Service, Princeton, NJ, 2013.

6. Ronald P. Carver, "What Do Standardized Tests of Reading Comprehension Measure in Terms of Efficiency, Accuracy, and Rate?," *Reading Research Quarterly* 27, no. 4 (1992): 346–359; Janice M. Keenan, Rebecca S. Betjemann, and Richard K. Olson, "Reading Comprehension Tests Vary in the Skills They Assess: Differential Dependence on Decoding and Oral Comprehension," *Scientific Studies of Reading* 12, no. 3 (2008): 281–300.

7. Nel Noddings, "Identifying and Responding to Needs in Education," *Cambridge Journal of Education* 35, no. 2 (2005): 147–159; Theresa Perry and Lisa D. Delpit, *The Real Ebonics Debate: Power, Language, and the Education of African-American Children* (Boston: Beacon Press, 1998).

8. For a good primer on psychometrics, see John Rust and Susan Golombok, *Modern Psychometrics: The Science of Psychological Assessment* (London: Routledge, 2014).

9. Robin B. Howse, Garrett Lange, Dale C. Farran, and Carolyn D. Boyles, "Motivation and Self-Regulation as Predictors of Achievement in Economically Disadvantaged Young Children," *Journal of Experimental Education* 71, no. 2 (2003): 151–174; Greg J. Duncan, Chantelle J. Dowsett, Amy Claessens, Katherine Magnuson, Aletha C. Huston, Pamela Klebanov, Linda S. Pagani, et al., "School Readiness and Later Achievement," *Developmental Psychology* 43, no. 6 (2007): 1428.

10. See, for example, Claude Steele, *Whistling Vivaldi: How Stereotypes Affect Us and What We Can Do* (New York: W. W. Norton, 2011). Steele's book provides an overview of his extensive work in this area.

11. Reardon, "The Widening Academic Achievement Gap," 91–116; Jeanne Brooks-Gunn and Greg J. Duncan, "The Effects of Poverty on Children," in *Consequences of Growing Up Poor*, ed. Greg J. Duncan and Jeanne Brooks-Gunn (New York: Russell Sage Foundation), 596–610; Karl L. Alexander, Doris R. Entwisle, and Samuel D. Bedinger, "When Expectations Work: Race and Socioeconomic Differences in School Performance," *Social Psychology Quarterly* 57, no. 4 (1994): 283–299; Valerie E. Lee and Robert G. Croninger, "The Relative Importance of Home and School in the Development of Literacy Skills for Middle-Grade Students," *American Journal of Education* 102, no. 3 (1994): 286–329.

12. Betty Hart and Todd R. Risley, "The Early Catastrophe: The 30 Million Word Gap by Age 3," *American Educator* 27, no. 1 (2003): 4–9. For more on the relationship between family income and child development, see Robert Haveman and Barbara Wolfe, "The Determinants of Children's Attainments: A Review of Methods and Findings," *Journal of Economic Literature* 33, no. 4 (1995): 1829–1878; Jean W. Yeung, Miriam R. Linver, and Jeanne Brooks-Gunn, "How Money Matters for Young Children's Development: Parental Investment and Family Processes," *Child Development* 73, no. 6 (2002): 1861–1879; Mark M. Kishiyama, W. Thomas Boyce, Amy M. Jimenez, Lee M. Perry, and Robert T. Knight, "Socioeconomic Disparities Affect Prefrontal Function in Children," *Journal of Cognitive Neuroscience* 21, no. 6 (2009): 1106–1115.

13. For a much more thorough account of what standardized tests do and don't tell us, see Daniel Koretz, *Measuring Up: What Educational Testing Really Tells Us* (Cambridge, MA: Harvard University Press, 2009).

14. For more, see Jason L. Endacott and Christian Z. Goering, "Assigning Letter Grades to Public Schools? The Danger of the Single Performance Indicator," *Teachers College Record,* December 11, 2015, http://www .tcrecord.org/Content.asp?ContentID=18834.

15. In compliance with No Child Left Behind, states began administering science tests at three grade levels in the 2007–8 school year. No stakes were attached to these, however.

16. For more on the role of history, see David Tyack and Larry Cuban, *Tinkering toward Utopia: A Century of Public School Reform* (Cambridge, MA: Harvard University Press, 1995); Jack Schneider and Ethan Hutt, "Making the Grade: A History of the A–F Marking Scheme," *Journal of Curriculum Studies* 46, no. 2 (2014): 201–224.

17. Much of the following history of standardized testing was researched in partnership with my colleague Ethan Hutt.

18. William J. Reese, *Testing Wars in the Public Schools: A Forgotten History* (Cambridge, MA: Harvard University Press, 2013).

19. "Blame Regents Test for Faulty Teaching," *New York Times,* November 14, 1927, 14.

20. "Linville Assails Tests by Regents," *New York Times,* February 26, 1930, 19.

21. Educational Policies Commission, *The Purposes of Education in American Democracy* (Washington, DC: National Education Association of the United States and the American Association of School Administrators, 1938).

22. Ibid.

23. For more on the thinking behind this initiative, see Wilford M. Aikin, *The Story of the Eight-Year Study* (New York: Harper and Brothers, 1942).

24. For a history of meritocracy, see Joseph F. Kett, *Merit: The History of a Founding Ideal from the American Revolution to the Twenty-First Century* (Ithaca, NY: Cornell University Press, 2012).

25. See, for instance, Lawrence Cremin, *The Republic and the School: Horace Mann on the Education of Free Men* (New York: Teachers College Press, 1957).

26. J. B. Canning, "The Meaning of Student Marks," *School Review* 24, no. 3 (1916): 196.

27. Denton L. Geyer, *Introduction to the Use of Standardized Tests* (Chicago: Plymouth Press, 1922), 8.

28. "Need Better School Test, Says Bachman," *New York Times,* November 22, 1912, 8.

29. William K. Stevens, "Once-Feared Regents Tests Face Hazy Future," *New York Times,* June 18, 1971, 41.

30. James C. Scott, *Seeing Like a State* (New Haven, CT: Yale University Press, 1999).

31. Leonard Buder, "Educators Split on Regents Tests," *New York Times,* September 28, 1954, 31.

32. Glenn R. Snider, "The Secondary School and Testing Programs," *Teachers College Record* 65, no. 1 (1963): 57–67.

33. *New York State Pupil Evaluation Program: School Administrator's Manual* (Albany: New York State Education Department, 1970), 10.

34. Stephen Jay Gould, *The Mismeasure of Man* (New York: W. W. Norton, 1981).

35. Philander P. Claxton, "Army Psychologists for City Public School Work," *School and Society* 9, no. 216 (1919): 203–204.

36. Burdette Ross Buckingham, *Bureau of Educational Research Announcement, 1918–1919* (Urbana: University of Illinois Press), 46.

37. Joan Cook, "Unrelenting Pressure on Students Brings Varied Assessment of Tests for Intelligence and Ability," *New York Times,* September 24, 1964, 51.

38. See, for instance, Valerie Strauss, "Big Education Firms Spend Millions Lobbying for Pro-Testing Policies," *Washington Post,* March 30, 2015, https://www.washingtonpost.com/news/answer-sheet/wp/2015/03/30/report-big-education-firms-spend-millions-lobbying-for-pro-testing-policies/.

39. Harlan C. Hines, "Measuring the Achievement of School Pupils," *American School Board Journal* 65, (1922): 37.

40. Michael Capuano, "With Test Resistance Rising Nationwide, What's Next for Federal Education Policy?," Citizens for Public Schools Forum, Tufts University, Medford, MA, October 6, 2014.

41. Ethan Hutt, "Certain Standards: How Efforts to Establish and Enforce Minimum Educational Standards Transformed American Schooling (1870–1980)" (doctoral diss., Stanford University, 2013); Walter Haney, George Madaus, and Robert Lyons, *The Fractured Marketplace for Standardized Testing* (Boston: Kluwer, 1993).

42. For evidence of this constancy, see Larry Cuban, *How Teachers Taught: Constancy and Change in American Classrooms, 1890–1990* (New York: Teachers College Press, 1993).

43. Marshall Smith and Jennifer O'Day, "Systemic School Reform," in *The Politics of Curriculum and Testing*, ed. Susan Fuhrman and Betty Malen (Bristol, PA: Falmer, 1991).

44. National Commission on Excellence in Education, *A Nation at Risk: The Imperative for Educational Reform* (Washington, DC: Government Printing Office, 1983).

45. Committee for Economic Development, *Investing in Our Children: Business and the Public Schools* (New York: Committee for Economic Development, 1985), 2.

46. National Governors' Association, *Time for Results: The Governors' 1991 Report on Education* (Washington, DC: National Governors' Association, 1986).

47. Reagan Walker, "Bush: Capturing the 'Education' Moment?," *Education Week,* October 19, 1988.

48. H.R. 1804, Goals 2000: Educate America Act, 103rd Congress of the United States of America, January 25, 1994, http://www2.ed.gov /legislation/GOALS2000/TheAct/index.html.

49. Ethan Bronner, "Texas School Turnaround: How Much Bush Credit?," *New York Times,* May 28, 1999.

50. Ibid.

51. For a good primer on school funding, see Bruce D. Baker, David G. Sciarra, and Danielle Farrie, *Is School Funding Fair? A National Report Card* (Newark, NJ: Rutgers University Education Law Center, 2014).

52. Marga Mikulecky and Kathy Christie, *Rating States, Grading Schools: What Parents and Experts Say States Should Consider to Make School Accountability Systems Meaningful* (Washington, DC: Education Commission of the States, 2014).

53. According to a U.S. Department of Education report, funding increased roughly 10 percent between 1998–99 and 2001–2, when adjusted for inflation: U.S. Department of Education, "10 Facts about K–12 Education Funding," http://www2.ed.gov/about/overview/fed/10facts/index.html ?exp; for an excellent analysis of NCLB and the tutoring industry, see Jill

Koyama, *Making Failure Pay: For-Profit Tutoring, High-Stakes Testing, and Public Schools* (Chicago: University of Chicago Press, 2010).

54. See, for instance, Kris Axtman, "When Tests' Cheaters Are the Teachers," *Christian Science Monitor,* January 11, 2005, http://www.csmonitor.com /2005/0111/p01s03-ussc.html.

55. Kathryn A. McDermott, "Incentives, Capacity, and Implementation: Evidence from Massachusetts Education Reform," *Journal of Public Administration Research and Theory* 16, no. 1 (2006): 45–65.

56. Some states had done this already, as a part of their Race to the Top proposals.

57. Thomas Ahn and Jacob Vigdor, *Were All Those Standardized Tests for Nothing?* (Washington, DC: American Enterprise Institute, 2013); Jaekyung Lee and Todd Reeves, "Revisiting the Impact of NCLB High-Stakes School Accountability, Capacity, and Resources: State NAEP 1990–2009 Reading and Math Achievement Gaps and Trends," *Educational Evaluation and Policy Analysis* 34, no. 2 (2012): 209–231; Sean F. Reardon, Erica H. Greenberg, Demetra Kalogrides, Kenneth A. Shores, and Rachel A. Valentino, *Left Behind? The Effect of No Child Left Behind on Academic Achievement Gaps* (Stanford, CA: Center for Education Policy Analysis, 2013).

58. Lee and Reeves, "Revisiting the Impact of NCLB," 209–231; Jennifer L. Jennings and Jonathan Marc Bearak, "'Teaching to the Test' in the NCLB Era: How Test Predictability Affects Our Understanding of Student Performance," *Educational Researcher* 43, no. 8 (2014): 381–389.

59. U.S. Department of Education, "Every Student Succeeds Act (ESSA)," http://www.ed.gov/essa.

60. Melissa Lazrin, *Testing Overload in America's Schools* (Washington, DC: Center for American Progress, 2014).

61. For a more detailed history of the SAT, see Nicholas Lemann, *The Big Test: The Secret History of the American Meritocracy* (New York: Farrar, Straus and Giroux, 1999).

62. Maria V. Santelices and Mark Wilson, "Unfair Treatment? The Case of Freedle, the SAT, and the Standardization Approach to Differential Item Functioning," *Harvard Educational Review* 80, no. 1 (2010): 106–134; Josh Zumbrun, "SAT Scores and Income Inequality," *Wall Street Journal,*

October 7, 2014, http://blogs.wsj.com/economics/2014/10/07/sat-scores
-and-income-inequality-how-wealthier-kids-rank-higher/.

63. Although the College Board claims that coaching raises scores by only
fifteen to twenty points on the verbal section and twenty to thirty points
on the math section, evidence suggests that effective coaching can have an
impact two to three times as great. See, for instance, Derek C. Briggs,
"Evaluating SAT Coaching: Gains, Effects, and Self-Selection," in
*Rethinking the SAT: The Future of Standardized Testing in University
Admissions,* ed. Rebecca Zwick (New York: Routledge, 2004): 217–233;
and Jack Kaplan, "An SAT Coaching Program That Works," *Chance* 15,
no. 1 (2002): 12–22.

64. William W. Turnbull, *Student Change, Program Change: Why the SAT
Scores Kept Falling,* College Board Report no. 85–2 (New York: ETS, 1985).

65. "The ACT: Biased, Inaccurate, and Misused," National Center for Fair and
Open Testing, August 20, 2007, http://www.fairtest.org/act-biased
-inaccurate-and-misused.

66. Education Commission of the States, "High School Exit Exams,"
http://www.ecs.org/html/issue.asp?issueid=108&subIssueID=159;
Thomas S. Dee and Brian A. Jacob, "Do High School Exit Exams Influence
Educational Attainment or Labor Market Performance?," NBER Working
Paper 12199, National Bureau of Economic Research, Cambridge, MA,
May 2006; Nanette Asimov, "Judge Says California Exit Exam Is Unfair,"
San Francisco Chronicle, May 9, 2006.

67. "Why Other Countries Teach Better," *New York Times,* December 17,
2013, http://www.nytimes.com/2013/12/18/opinion/why-students-do
-better-overseas.html?_r=2&.

68. Stefan Thomas Hopmann, Gertrude Brinek, and Martin Retzl, *PISA
according to PISA* (New Brunswick, NJ: Transaction, 2007), http://www
.univie.ac.at/pisaaccordingtopisa/pisazufolgepisa.pdf; Daniel Tröhler,
Heinz-Dieter Meyer, David F. Labaree, and Ethan L. Hutt, "Accountability:
Antecedents, Power, and Processes," *Teachers College Record* 116, no. 9
(2014): 1–12.

69. Russell W. Rumberger and Gregory J. Palardy, "Test Scores, Dropout
Rates, and Transfer Rates as Alternative Indicators of High School
Performance," *American Educational Research Journal* 42, no. 1 (2005):

3–42; Stephen B. Billings, David J. Deming, and Jonah E. Rockoff, *School Segregation, Educational Attainment and Crime: Evidence from the End of Busing in Charlotte-Mecklenburg*, no. w18487 (Cambridge, MA: National Bureau of Economic Research, 2012).

70. Michael B. Henderson, Paul E. Peterson, and Martin R. West, "The 2015 EdNext Poll on School Reform," *Education Next* 16, no. 1 (2016), 8–20, http://educationnext.org/2015-ednext-poll-school-reform-opt-out -common-core-unions/; 47th Annual PDK/Gallup Poll of the Public's Attitudes toward the Public School, September 2015, http:// pdkpoll2015.pdkintl.org/wp-content/uploads/2015/08/pdkpoll47_2015 .pdf.

71. Kwame Anthony Appiah, "Do We Have to Send Our Kid to a Bad Public School?," The Ethicist, *New York Times Magazine*, January 6, 2016, http://www.nytimes.com/2016/01/10/magazine/do-we-have-to-send-our -kid-to-a-bad-public-school.html?_r=0.

Chapter 2 Through a Glass Darkly

1. Christine Armario, "82 Percent of U.S. Schools May Be Labeled 'Failing,'" *Washington Post*, March 9, 2011, http://www.washingtonpost.com/wp-dyn /content/article/2011/03/09/AR2011030903226.html.

2. Marga Mikulecky and Kathy Christie, *Rating States, Grading Schools: What Parents and Experts Say States Should Consider to Make School Account-ability Systems Meaningful* (Washington, DC: Education Commission of the States, 2014).

3. California Office to Reform Education, Local Educational Agencies' Request for Waivers under Section 9401 of the Elementary and Secondary Education Act of 1965 (2013), https://www2.ed.gov/policy/eseaflex /approved-requests/corerequestfullredacted.pdf.

4. Quoted in Joy Resmovits, "These California Districts Are Measuring Schools in a New Way," *Los Angeles Times*, December 4, 2015, http://www .latimes.com/local/education/standardized-testing/la-me-edu-core -districts-new-accountability-index-nclb-waiver-20151203-story.html.

5. Quoted in Joy Resmovits, "California Schools Won't Be Judged Only by Their Test Scores, School Board Votes," *Los Angeles Times*, September 8,

2016, http://www.latimes.com/local/education/la-me-california-school
-accountability-20160908-snap-story.html.

6. "ESEA Flexibility," U.S. Department of Education, http://www2.ed.gov
/policy/elsec/guid/esea-flexibility/index.html; Sarah Reckhow and Megan
Tompkins-Stange, "'Singing from the Same Hymnbook': Education Policy
Advocacy at Gates and Broad," American Enterprise Institute, February 5,
2015, http://www.aei.org/publication/singing-hymnbook-education
-policy-advocacy-gates-broad/.

7. Eileen Lai Horng, Daniel Klasik, and Susanna Loeb, "Principal's Time Use
and School Effectiveness," *American Journal of Education* 116, no. 4
(2010): 491–523.

8. Linda Darling-Hammond, "What Matters Most: A Competent Teacher for
Every Child," *Phi Delta Kappan* 78, no. 3 (1996): 193–200; Donald L.
Haefele, "Evaluating Teachers: A Call for Change," *Journal of Personnel
Evaluation in Education* 7, no. 1 (1993): 21–31; New Teacher Project,
Teacher Hiring, Assignment, and Transfer in Chicago Public Schools
(Brooklyn, NY: New Teacher Project, 2007).

9. Lauren Sartain, Sara Ray Stoelinga, and Eric R. Brown, *Rethinking Teacher
Evaluation in Chicago,* Consortium on Chicago School Research, Univer-
sity of Chicago (2011), http://www.joycefdn.org/assets/1/7/Teacher-Eval
-Report-FINAL1.pdf.

10. Readers interested in thorough treatment of value-added measures of
teacher quality should read Douglas Harris, *Value-Added Measures in
Education: What Every Educator Needs to Know* (Cambridge, MA:
Harvard Education Press, 2011).

11. Noelle A. Paufler and Audrey Amrein-Beardsley, "The Random
Assignment of Students into Elementary Classrooms: Implications for
Value-Added Analyses and Interpretations," *American Educational
Research Journal* 51, no. 2 (2014): 328–362; Kun Yuan, "A Value-Added
Study of Teacher Spillover Effects across Four Core Subjects in Middle
Schools," *Educational Policy Analysis Archives* 23, no. 38 (2015): 1–24;
Edward Haertel, "Reliability and Validity of Inferences about Teachers
Based on Student Test Scores," report based on the 14th William H.
Angoff Memorial Lecture at the National Press Club, Educational
Testing Service, Princeton, NJ, 2013; Derek Briggs and Ben Domingue,

Due Diligence and the Evaluation of Teachers (Boulder, CO: National Education Policy Center, 2011), http://nepc.colorado.edu/files/NEPC -RB-LAT-VAM_0.pdf; Eva L. Baker, Paul E. Barton, Linda Darling-Hammond, Edward Haertel, Helen F. Ladd, Robert L. Linn, Diane Ravitch, Richard Rothstein, Richard J. Shavelson, and Lorrie A. Shepard, *Problems with the Use of Student Test Scores to Evaluate Teachers*, EPI Briefing Paper 278 (Washington, DC: Economic Policy Institute, 2010).

12. Valerie Strauss, "Master Teacher Suing New York State over 'Ineffective' Rating Is Going to Court," *Washington Post,* August 9, 2015, https://www.washingtonpost.com/news/answer-sheet/wp/2015/08/09 /master-teacher-suing-new-york-state-over-ineffective-rating-is-going -to-court/.

13. One example of this, and one of the earliest of these models, is the IMPACT system in use in Washington, DC. For an overview of IMPACT, see Susan Headden, *Inside IMPACT: DC's Model Teacher Evaluation System* (Washington, DC: Education Sector, 2011).

14. Susanna Loeb, "How Can Value-Added Measures Be Used for Teacher Improvement?," Carnegie Foundation for the Advancement of Teaching, 2013, https://cepa.stanford.edu/sites/default/files/CKN-Loeb_Teacher -Improvement.pdf; Haertel, "Reliability and Validity of Inferences about Teachers."

15. David Shenk, *Data Smog: Surviving the Information Glut* (San Francisco: HarperCollins, 1997).

16. Mikulecky and Christie, *Rating States, Grading Schools.*

17. To say *U.S. News* is the leader in this practice is not to say it does it well. For criticism, see Nicholas A. Bowman and Michael N. Bastedo, "Getting on the Front Page: Organizational Reputation, Status Signals, and the Impact of *U.S. News and World Report* on Student Decisions," *Research in Higher Education* 50, no. 5 (2009): 415–436; Michael N. Bastedo and Nicholas A. Bowman, "*U.S. News and World* Report College Rankings: Modeling Institutional Effects on Organizational Reputation," *American Journal of Education* 116, no. 2 (2010): 163–183.

18. As one Boston Latin parent remarked to me: "It's a good school. But my daughter is stressed out all the time. And all she does is study for tests."

19. Zillow.com, "Zillow Now Exclusive Real Estate Search Partner of Great-Schools," http://www.zillow.com/blog/zillow-now-exclusive-real-estate-search-partner-of-greatschools-126514/, accessed February 18, 2016.

20. Separately, polling has found that 51 percent of parents report utilizing websites that rate and compare schools. See, for instance, Trevor Tompson, Jennifer Benz, and Jennifer Agiesta, "Parents' Attitudes on the Quality of Education in the United States," Associated Press–NORC Center for Public Affairs Research, 2013, http://www.apnorc.org/PDFs/Parent%20 Attitudes/AP_NORC_Parents%20Attitudes%20on%20the%20Quality%20 of%20Education%20in%20the%20US_FINAL_2.pdf

21. Dan A. Black and Jeffrey A. Smith, "How Robust Is the Evidence on the Effects of College Quality? Evidence from Matching," *Journal of Econometrics* 121, no. 1 (2004): 99–124; Stacy Berg Dale and Alan B. Krueger, "Estimating the Payoff to Attending a More Selective College: An Application of Selection on Observables and Unobservables," NBER Working Paper No. 7322 (Cambridge, MA: National Bureau of Economic Research, 1999).

22. ACT, "College Enrollment by Student Background and School Location," information brief, 2014–2015, http://www.act.org/research/researchers /briefs/pdf/2014-15.pdf.

23. Justine S. Hastings, Thomas J. Kane, and Douglas O. Staiger, "Parental Preferences and School Competition: Evidence from a Public School Choice Program," NBER Working Paper 11805, National Bureau of Economic Research, 2005; Carol Ascher, *Hard Lessons: Public Schools and Privatization* (New York: Twentieth Century Fund Press, 1996); Jeffrey R. Henig, *Rethinking School Choice: Limits of the Market Metaphor* (Princeton, NJ: Princeton University Press, 1995); Jeffrey Henig, "Race and Choice in Montgomery County, Maryland, Magnet Schools," *Teachers College Record* 96, no. 4 (1995): 729–734; Jack Dougherty, Jeffrey Harrelson, Laura Maloney, Drew Murphy, Russell Smith, Michael Snow, and Diane Zannoni, "School Choice in Suburbia: Test Scores, Race, and Housing Markets," *American Journal of Education* 115, no. 4 (2009): 523–548; Courtney A. Bell, "Space and Place: Urban Parents' Geographical Preferences for Schools," *Urban Review* 39, no. 4 (2007): 375–404.

24. Hastings, Kane, and Staiger, *Parental Preferences and School Competition*; Courtney Bell, "Geography in Parental Choice," *American Journal of Education* 115, no. 4 (2009): 493–521.

25. Carl Bagley, Philip A. Woods, and Ron Glatter, "Rejecting Schools: Towards a Fuller Understanding of the Process of Parental Choice," *School Leadership and Management* 21, no. 3 (2001): 309–325; Ernest Boyer, *School Choice* (Princeton, NJ: Carnegie Foundation, 1992); Jennifer Jellison Holme, "Buying Homes, Buying Schools: School Choice and the Social Construction of School Quality," *Harvard Educational Review* 72, no. 2 (2002): 177–206.

26. Holme, "Buying Homes, Buying Schools"; Mark Schneider, Paul Teske, Christine Roch, and Melissa Marschall, "Networks to Nowhere: Segregation and Stratification in Networks of Information about Schools," *American Journal of Political Science* 41, no. 4 (1997): 1201–1223; Arne Duncan, "Remarks at the Statehouse Convention Center in Little Rock, Arkansas," U.S. Department of Education, August 25, 2010, http://www.ed.gov/news /speeches/secretary-arne-duncans-remarks-statehouse-convention-center -little-rock-arkansas.

27. Tiffany A. Ito, Jeff T. Larson, N. Kyle Smith, and John T. Cacioppo, "Negative Information Weighs More Heavily on the Brain: The Negativity Bias in Evaluative Categorization," *Journal of Personality and Social Psychology* 75, no. 4 (1998): 887–900; Daniel Kahneman, *Thinking Fast and Slow* (New York: Farrar, Straus and Giroux, 2013).

28. Miller McPherson, Lynn Smith-Lovin, and James Cook, "Birds of a Feather: Homophily in Social Networks," *Annual Review of Sociology* 27, no. 1 (2001): 420; Peter V. Marsden, "Core Discussion Networks of Americans," *American Sociological Review* 52, no. 1 (1987): 122–131; Miller McPherson, Lynn Smith-Lovin, and James M. Cook, "Birds of a Feather: Homophily in Social Networks," *Annual Review of Sociology* 27, no. 1 (2001): 415–444.

29. Stephen J. Ball, Richard Bowe, and Sharon Gewirtz, "Circuits of Schooling: A Sociological Exploration of Parental Choice of School in Social Class Contexts," *Sociological Review* 43, no. 1 (1995): 52–78; Mark Schneider, Paul Teske, and Melissa Marschall, *Choosing Schools: Consumer Choice*

and the Quality of American Schools (Princeton, NJ: Princeton University Press, 2000), 133.

30. Schneider, Teske, Roch, and Marschall, "Networks to Nowhere," 1220; Peter Rich and Jennifer Jennings, "Choice, Information, and Constrained Options: School Transfers in a Stratified Educational System," *American Sociological Review* 80, no.5 (2015): 1069–1098.

31. Jeffrey Henig, "Race and Choice in Montgomery County, Maryland, Magnet Schools," *Teachers College Record* 96, no. 4 (1995): 729–734; Salvatore Saporito and Annette Lareau, "School Selection as a Process: The Multiple Dimensions of Race in Framing Educational Choice," *Social Problems* 46 (1999): 418–435.

32. David Sikkink and Michael O. Emerson, "School Choice and Racial Segregation in US Schools: The Role of Parents' Education," *Ethnic and Racial Studies* 31, no. 2 (2008): 267–293; Saporito and Lareau, "School Selection as a Process"; Ryan Holeywell, "The Troubling Ways Wealthy Parents Pick Schools," Kinder Institute, July 30, 2015, http://urbanedge .blogs.rice.edu/2015/12/24/the-troubling-ways-wealthy-parents-pick -schools/#.VuBUrvkrJD8.

33. Schneider, Teske, and Marschall, *Choosing Schools*.

34. For a much more thorough discussion of how such heuristics are developed, see Kahnemann, *Thinking Fast and Slow.*

35. Jon Hurwitz and Mark Peffley, "Public Perceptions of Race and Crime: The Role of Racial Stereotypes," *American Journal of Political Science* 41, no. 2 (1997): 375–401; Patricia G. Devine and Andrew J. Elliot, "Are Racial Stereotypes Really Fading? The Princeton Trilogy Revisited," *Personality and Social Psychology Bulletin* 21, no. 11 (1995): 1139–1150; Lincoln Quillian and Devah Pager, "Black Neighbors, Higher Crime? The Role of Racial Stereotypes in Evaluations of Neighborhood Crime," *American Journal of Sociology* 107, no. 3 (2001): 717–767; Mahzarin R. Banaji and Anthony G. Greenwald, *Blindspot: Hidden Biases of Good People* (New York: Delacorte Press, 2013).

36. Ann Owens, "Inequality in Children's Contexts: Income Segregation of Households with and without Children," *American Sociological Review* 81, no. 3 (2016): 549–574. It is also worth noting here that segregation by race is also higher among households with children than among other households.

37. Douglas Lee Lauen and S. Michael Gaddis, "Exposure to Classroom Poverty and Test Score Achievement: Contextual Effects or Selection?," *American Journal of Sociology* 118, no. 4 (2013): 943–979; Robert A. Garda, "The White Interest in School Integration," *Florida Law Review* 63 (2011): 605–660; Aprile D. Benner and Robert Crosnoe, "The Racial / Ethnic Composition of Elementary Schools and Young Children's Academic and Socioemotional Functioning," *American Educational Research Journal* 48, no. 3 (2011): 621–646; National Center for Education Statistics, *School Composition and the Black-White Achievement Gap* (Washington, DC: U.S. Department of Education, 2015).

38. For a good discussion of the relationship between fictional narrative in film and reality in schools, see Marshall Gregory, "Real Teaching and Real Learning vs. Narrative Myths about Education," *Arts and Humanities in Higher Education* 6, no. 1 (2007): 7–27.

39. Linda Darling-Hammond, "Third Annual Brown Lecture in Education Research: The Flat Earth and Education; How America's Commitment to Equity Will Determine Our Future," *Educational Researcher* 36, no. 6 (2007): 318–334; Matthew Ronfeldt, Susanna Loeb, and James Wyckoff, "How Teacher Turnover Harms Student Achievement," *American Educational Research Journal* 50, no. 1 (2013): 4–36; Christopher Jencks and Meredith Phillips, eds., *The Black-White Test Score Gap* (Washington, DC: Brookings Institution Press, 2011); Russell J. Skiba, Robert H. Horner, Choong-Geun Chung, M. Karega Rausch, Seth L. May, and Tary Tobin, "Race Is Not Neutral: A National Investigation of African American and Latino Disproportionality in School Discipline," *School Psychology Review* 40, no. 1 (2011): 85.

40. It is worth noting that there are clear and powerful exceptions to this, where ethnic or racial pride infuse a school with an ethos of community.

41. Zillow.com, "Zillow Now Exclusive Real Estate Search Partner of GreatSchools."

42. Ryan Dezember, "Blackstone Gains from Banks' Financial-Crisis Pain," *Wall Street Journal,* January 21, 2016, http://www.wsj.com/articles /blackstone-gains-from-banks-financial-crisis-pain-1453408139.

43. In most intradistrict choice plans, preference is given to students who live within a short walk of the school, as well as to students with siblings at the

school. If more students wish to attend a school than there are spots available, students are usually admitted via a lottery. This might seem to present a complicated scenario for a district, but parental preference for proximity usually ensures that schools are not underenrolled.

44. Allison Roda and Amy Stuart Wells, "School Choice Policies and Racial Segregation: Where White Parents' Good Intentions, Anxiety, and Privilege Collide," *American Journal of Education* 119, no. 2 (2013): 261–293.

45. See, for instance, Christopher A. Lubienski and Sarah Theule Lubienski, *The Public School Advantage: Why Public Schools Outperform Private Schools* (Chicago: University of Chicago Press, 2013).

46. Those with greater financial resources are best positioned to consider multiple places for their homes. Still, polling indicates that the connection between schools and home selection is fairly common. See, for instance, Editorial Projects in Education, *Accountability for All: What Voters Want from Education Candidates,* January 2002, from the iPOLL Databank, Roper Center for Public Opinion Research, University of Connecticut, retrieved June 9, 2014, http://files.eric.ed.gov/fulltext /ED464190.pdf.

47. Rhema Thompson, "Poll: School Grades Important but Not Understood," *WJCT 89.9 News,* December 11, 2014.

48. Saporito and Lareau, "School Selection as a Process."

49. Gallup, "In U.S., Private Schools Get Top Marks for Educating Children," August 29, 2012, http://www.gallup.com/poll/156974/private-schools-top -marks-educating-children.aspx.

50. Groton Matriculations, https://www.groton.org/page/academics/college -counseling/matriculations.

51. Jed Kolko, "Where Private School Enrollment Is Highest and Lowest across the U.S.," *CityLab,* August 13, 2012, http://www.citylab.com /housing/2014/08/where-private-school-enrollment-is-highest-and-lowest -across-the-us/375993/.

52. National Center for Education Statistics, *Digest of Education Statistics* (Washington, DC: NCES, IES, U.S. Department of Education, 2016), table 302.30: Percentage of Recent High School Completers Enrolled in 2-Year and 4-Year Colleges, by Income Level: 1975 through 2013.

53. Simone Robers, Anlan Zhang, Rachel E. Morgan, and Lauren Musu-Gillette, *Indicators of School Crime and Safety: 2014* (Washington, DC: U.S. Department of Education and U.S. Department of Justice Office of Justice Programs, 2015); U.S. Department of Education, National Center for Education Statistics, Schools and Staffing Survey (SASS), "Private School Teacher Data File," 2007–8; U.S. Department of Education, National Center for Education Statistics, Schools and Staffing Survey (SASS), "Public School Teacher Data File," 2007–8.

54. Douglas Lee Lauen, Bruce Fuller, and Luke Dauter, "Positioning Charter Schools in Los Angeles: Diversity of Form and Homogeneity of Effects," *American Journal of Education* 121, no. 2 (2015): 213–239; Christina Clark Tuttle, Bing-ru Teh, Ira Nichols-Barrer, Brian P. Gill, and Philip Gleason, *Student Characteristics and Achievement in 22 KIPP Middle Schools: Final Report* (Washington, DC: Mathematica Policy Research, 2010); CREDO, National Charter School Study, 2013, http://credo.stanford.edu /documents/NCSS%202013%20Final%20Draft.pdf; Devora H. Davis and Margaret E. Raymond, "Choices for Studying Choice: Assessing Charter School Effectiveness Using Two Quasi-Experimental Methods," *Economics of Education Review* 31, no. 2 (2012): 225–236; Caroline M. Hoxby and Sonali Murarka, "Charter Schools in New York City: Who Enrolls and How They Affect Their Students' Achievement," NBER Working Paper No. 14852, National Bureau of Economic Research, Cambridge, MA, 2009; Lauen, Fuller, and Dauter, "Positioning Charter Schools in Los Angeles," 213–239; RAND, *Charter School Operations and Performance: Evidence from California* (2003), http://www.rand.org/pubs/monograph _reports/MR1700.html.

55. Ron Zimmer, Brian Gill, Kevin Booker, Stéphane Lavertu, and John Witte, "Examining Charter Student Achievement Effects across Seven States," *Economics of Education Review* 31, no. 2 (2012): 213–224.

56. Stephen Worchel, Jerry Lee, and Akanbi Adewole, "Effects of Supply and Demand on Ratings of Object Value," *Journal of Personality and Social Psychology* 32, no. 5 (1975): 906–914.

57. Ashley Morris and Brittany Landsberger, "Charter School Operators Use Key Words to Entice Families away from Public Schools," *Akron Beacon Journal,* May 27, 2014, http://www.ohio.com/news/local/charter-school

-operators-use-key-words-to-entice-families-away-from-public-schools-1
.491420; Nora Kern and Wentana Gebru, "Waiting Lists to Attend Charter
Schools Top One Million Names," National Alliance for Public Charter
Schools, May 2014, http://www.publiccharters.org/wp-content/uploads
/2014/05/NAPCS-2014-Wait-List-Report.pdf.

58. Edith K. McArthur, Kelly Colopy, and Beth Schlaine, *Use of School Choice*,
NCES 95–742R (Washington, DC: U.S. Department of Education,
National Center for Educational Statistics, 1995); Simona Botti, "The Dark
Side of Choice: When Choice Impairs Social Welfare," *Journal of Public
Policy and Marketing* 25, no. 1 (2006), http://www.columbia.edu/~ss957
/articles/dark_side_of_choice.pdf.

59. Research has raised questions about the accuracy of these calculations for
very-high-achieving and very-low-achieving students, due to scaling
issues. For a concise discussion of this, see Haertel, "Reliability and
Validity of Inferences about Teachers."

60. Basmat Parsad and Maura Spiegelman, *A Snapshot of Arts Education in
Public Elementary and Secondary Schools: 2009–10* (Washington, DC: U.S.
Department of Education, 2011).

61. Robert Balfanz and Vaughan Byrnes, *The Importance of Being There: A
Report on Absenteeism in the Nation's Public Schools* (Baltimore, MD:
Johns Hopkins University School of Education, Everyone Graduates
Center, 2012).

62. Kathryn R. Wentzel and Kathryn Caldwell, "Friendships, Peer
Acceptance, and Group Membership: Relations to Academic Achievement in Middle School," *Child Development* 68, no. 6 (1997): 1198–
1209; Kathryn R. Wentzel, Carolyn McNamara Barry, and Kathryn A.
Caldwell, "Friendships in Middle School: Influences on Motivation
and School Adjustment," *Journal of Educational Psychology* 96, no. 2
(2004): 195–203; Thomas J. Berndt, Ann E. Laychak, and Keunho
Park, "Friends' Influence on Adolescents' Academic Achievement
Motivation: An Experimental Study," *Journal of Educational Psychology*
82, no. 4 (1990): 664; Allison M. Ryan, "Peer Groups as a Context for
the Socialization of Adolescents' Motivation, Engagement, and
Achievement in School," *Educational Psychologist* 35, no. 2 (2000):
101–111.

63. Mary A. Burke and Tim R. Sass, "Classroom Peer Effects and Student Achievement," *Journal of Labor Economics* 31, no. 1 (2013): 51–82; Caroline Hoxby, *Peer Effects in the Classroom: Learning from Gender and Race Variation,* NBER Working Paper No. w7867, National Bureau of Economic Research, 2000; Michael A. Gottfried and Jennifer Graves, "Peer Effects and Policy: The Relationship between Classroom Gender Composition and Student Achievement in Early Elementary School," *BE Journal of Economic Analysis and Policy* 14, no. 3 (2014): 937–977; Michael A. Gottfried, "Peer Effects in Urban Schools: Assessing the Impact of Classroom Composition," *Educational Policy* 28, no. 5 (2014): 607–647; Caroline M. Hoxby and Gretchen Weingarth, "Taking Race out of the Equation: School Reassignment and the Structure of Peer Effects," working paper, 2005, http://isites.harvard.edu/fs/docs/icb.topic185351 .files/hoxby_weingarth_taking_race.pdf; Eric A. Hanushek, John F. Kain, and Steven G. Rivkin, *New Evidence about Brown v. Board of Education: The Complex Effects of School Racial Composition on Achievement,* NBER Working Paper No. w8741, National Bureau of Economic Research, 2002; Roslyn Arlin Mickelson, Martha Cecilia Bottia, and Richard Lambert, "Effects of School Racial Composition on K–12 Mathematics Outcomes: A Metaregression Analysis," *Review of Educational Research* 83, no. 1 (2013): 121–158; Michael A. Gottfried, "The Positive Peer Effects of Classroom Diversity: Exploring the Relationship between English Language Learner Classmates and Socioemotional Skills in Early Elementary School," *Elementary School Journal* 115, no. 1 (2014): 22–48.
64. It is important to note here that adverse peer effects can manifest in many different ways, and in every kind of school. Issues such as bullying or drug use are hardly confined to schools with low levels of academic achievement, despite popular perceptions.
65. Dan D. Goldhader, Dominic J. Brewer, and Deborah J. Anderson, "A Three-Way Error Components Analysis of Educational Productivity," *Education Economics* 7, no. 3 (1999): 199–208; Barbara Nye, Spyros Konstantopoulos, and Larry V. Hedges, "How Large Are Teacher Effects?," *Educational Evaluation and Policy Analysis* 26, no. 3 (2004): 237–257; Steven G. Rivkin, Eric A. Hanushek, and John F. Kain, "Teachers, Schools, and Academic Achievement," *Econometrica* 73, no. 2 (2005): 417–458;

Brian Rowan, Brian, Richard Correnti, and Robert Miller, "What Large-Scale Survey Research Tells Us about Teacher Effects on Student Achievement: Insights from the Prospects Study of Elementary Schools," *Teachers College Record* 104, no. 8 (2002): 1525–1567.

66. Jennifer Glass, Vern L. Bengtson, and Charlotte Chorn Dunham, "Attitude Similarity in Three-Generation Families: Socialization, Status Inheritance, or Reciprocal Influence?," *American Sociological Review* 51, no. 5 (1986): 685–698.

67. Betty Hart and Todd R. Risley, *Meaningful Differences in the Everyday Experience of Young People* (Baltimore, MD: Paul H. Brookes, 1995); Carol Sue Fromboluti, Diane Magarity, and Natalie Rinck, *Early Childhood: Where Learning Begins; Mathematics: Mathematical Activities for Parents and Their 2- to 5-Year-Old Children* (Washington, DC: U.S. Department of Education, Office of Educational Research and Improvement, 1999).

68. Kara S. Finnigan and Betheny Gross, "Do Accountability Policy Sanctions Influence Teacher Motivation? Lessons from Chicago's Low-Performing Schools," *American Educational Research Journal* 44, no. 3 (2007): 594–630.

69. Sandra E. Black and Stephen J. Machin, "Housing Valuations of School Performance," *Handbook of Economics of Education* 3 (2011): 485–516; Steve Bogira, "Three Families Tell Us Why They Ditched CPS," *Chicago Reader,* September 24, 2013; Rebecca Jacobsen, Andrew Saulz, and Jeffrey W. Snyder, "When Accountability Strategies Collide: Do Policy Changes That Raise Accountability Standards Also Erode Public Satisfaction?," *Educational Policy* 27, no. 6 (2013): 360–389.

Chapter 3 What Really Matters

1. Philip W. Jackson, Robert E. Boostrom, and David T. Hanson, *The Moral Life of Schools* (San Francisco: Jossey-Bass, 1993), xii.

2. Blue Three, Comment on Anya Kamenetz's "To Measure What Tests Can't, Some Turn to Surveys," NPR, December 2, 2015, http://www.npr.org /sections/ed/2015/12/02/457281686/how-schools-are-using-surveys-to -measure-what-tests-can-t.

3. Richard Rothstein, Rebecca Jacobsen, and Tamara Wilder, *Grading Education: Getting Accountability Right* (Washington, DC: Economic Policy Institute, 2008).

4. For more on these efforts, see discussion of the Massachusetts Consortium for Innovative Education Assessment in this book's postscript.

5. George A. Miller, "The Magical Number Seven, Plus or Minus Two: Some Limits on Our Capacity for Processing Information," *Psychological Review* 63, no. 2 (1956): 81–97; Alan Baddeley, "Working Memory," *Science* 255, no. 5044 (1992): 556–559; Nelson Cowan, "Metatheory of Storage Capacity Limits," *Behavioral and Brain Sciences* 24, no. 1 (2001): 154–176.

6. Thirty-nine teachers and support staff participated in four focus groups; they were recruited through e-mails sent by district administrators and were offered stipends to attend; teachers from all schools in the district were represented. Five additional teachers participated in a separate Special Education focus group, which was conducted to learn more about the particular issues of importance to teachers working with that student population. All principals and key district administrators participated in focus groups organized by the district. Thirty-three parents attended two open focus groups; recruitment for these was conducted via e-mails sent by the principals of each K–8 school and the high school. A separate focus group was conducted with the eight community liaisons who have been contracted by the Somerville Family Learning Collaborative (SFLC) to reach out to families at each of the city's schools—particularly members of racial and ethnic minorities; two staff from the SFLC also participated in this focus group, which was designed to elicit feedback around tradition-ally underserved communities. Thirty non-English-speaking parents attended focus groups facilitated with the help of the SFLC and Somer-ville's Welcome Project. We conducted one focus group with high school students, recruited with assistance from the district. Generally speaking, participants in focus groups were introduced to the project with the following statement: "The goal of this study is to better understand the way people think about issues of school quality and evaluation. In thinking beyond standardized test scores as the only way to judge school performance, we've identified some major categories of inputs and outputs that people might think about in evaluating schools. We're hoping to

receive feedback about these categories. In general, we would like to hear your thoughts on whether our categories and sub-categories make sense and measure the right things. We'll talk briefly about each of the main categories until we have discussed all of them. Are there any questions before we begin?" The basic categories for these discussions were established by our team's review of polling data and educational research. In discussing the various major categories, participants were asked whether particular draft subcategories seemed more important than others, whether anything was missing, and whether anything seemed unclear. Our team also solicited feedback about values and priorities that might not fit into the major categories that were used to guide the discussion.

7. Memo from David Casalaspi, October 1, 2014.

8. After analysis of year one data, we found positive between-category Pearson correlation coefficients, with magnitudes varying from 0.18 to 0.70. Overall, these findings suggest that categories used to construct the framework exhibit meaningful associations while not being deterministically related. We believe that this lends support to their combined use as more valid representation of school quality.

9. Matthew A. Kraft, William H. Marinell, and Darrick Yee, *Schools as Organizations: Examining School Climate, Turnover, and Student Achievement in New York City* (New York: Research Alliance for New York City Schools, 2016); Matthew A. Kraft and Sarah Grace, "Teaching for Tomorrow's Economy? Teacher Effects on Complex Cognitive Skills and Social-Emotional Competencies" (working paper, Brown University, 2016), http://scholar.harvard.edu/files/mkraft/files/teaching_for _tomorrows_economy_-_final_public.pdf.

10. This is not to say that parental engagement is entirely outside the control of schools. Research does, however, suggest that the way parents engage— with their children and with schools—is mediated by factors such as social class. See, for instance, Annette Lareau, "Invisible Inequality: Social Class and Childrearing in Black Families and White Families," *American Sociological Review* 67, no. 5 (2002): 747–776.

11. This would not necessarily invalidate the measures. Instead, it would suggest that the measures are telling users something that they already know, which they can learn simply by examining the school's demography.

12. Philip Elliott and Jennifer Agiesta, "AP-NORC Poll: Parents Back High-Stakes Testing," August 17, 2013, http://www.apnorc.org/news-media /Pages/News+Media/ap-norc-poll-parents-back-high-stakes-testing.aspx.

13. Eric A. Hanushek, "The Economic Value of Higher Teacher Quality," *Economics of Education Review* 30, no. 3 (2011): 466–479. See also Steven G. Rivkin, Eric A. Hanushek, and John F. Kain, "Teachers, Schools, and Academic Achievement," *Econometrica* 73, no. 2 (2005): 417–458; Linda Darling-Hammond, "Teacher Quality and Student Achievement," *Education Policy Analysis Archives* 8 (2000): 1.

14. Mark Schneider, Paul Teske, and Melissa Marschall, *Choosing Schools: Consumer Choice and the Quality of American Schools* (Princeton, NJ: Princeton University Press, 2000), 108.

15. Jack Jennings and Diane Stark Rentner, "Ten Big Effects of the No Child Left Behind Act on Public Schools," *Phi Delta Kappan* 88, no. 2 (2006): 110; Leslie S. Kaplan and William A. Owings, "No Child Left Behind: The Politics of Teacher Quality," *Phi Delta Kappan* 84, no. 9 (2003): 687; Laura Goe, "The Link between Teacher Quality and Student Outcomes: A Research Synthesis," National Comprehensive Center for Teacher Quality, 2007, http://files.eric.ed.gov/fulltext/ED521219.pdf; Joshua D. Angrist and Jonathan Guryan, "Does Teacher Testing Raise Teacher Quality? Evidence from State Certification Requirements," *Economics of Education Review* 27, no. 5 (2008): 483–503.

16. Suzanne M. Wilson, Robert E. Floden, and Joan Ferrini-Mundy, "Teacher Preparation Research: An Insider's View from the Outside," *Journal of Teacher Education* 53, no. 3 (2002): 190–204; Thomas J. Kane, Jonah E. Rockoff, and Douglas O. Staiger, "What Does Certification Tell Us about Teacher Effectiveness? Evidence from New York City," *Economics of Education Review* 27, no. 6 (2008): 615–631; Richard Buddin and Gema Zamarro, "Teacher Qualifications and Student Achievement in Urban Elementary Schools," *Journal of Urban Economics* 66, no. 2 (2009): 103–115; Andrew J. Wayne and Peter Youngs, "Teacher Characteristics and Student Achievement Gains: A Review," *Review of Educational Research* 73, no. 1 (2003): 89–122; Charles T. Clotfelter, Helen F. Ladd, and Jacob L. Vigdor, "Teacher Credentials and Student Achievement: Longitudinal Analysis with Student Fixed Effects," *Economics of Education Review*

26, no. 6 (2007): 673–682; Douglas N. Harris and Tim R. Sass, "Teacher Training, Teacher Quality and Student Achievement," *Journal of Public Economics* 95, no. 7 (2011): 798–812.

17. Daniel D. Goldhaber and Dominic J. Brewer, "Does Teacher Certification Matter? High School Teacher Certification Status and Student Achievement," *Educational Evaluation and Policy Analysis* 22, no. 2 (2000): 129–146; Daniel D. Goldhaber and Dominic J. Brewer, "Why Don't Schools and Teachers Seem to Matter? Assessing the Impact of Unobservables on Educational Productivity," *Journal of Human Resources* 32, no. 3 (1997): 505–523; David H. Monk and Jennifer A. King, "Multilevel Teacher Resource Effects in Pupil Performance in Secondary Mathematics and Science: The Case of Teacher Subject Matter Preparation," in *Choices and Consequences: Contemporary Policy Issues in Education,* ed. R. G. Ehrenberg (Ithaca, NY: ILR Press, 1994); Jacob M. Marszalek, Arthur L. Odom, Steven M. LaNasa, and Susan A. Adler, "Distortion or Clarification: Defining Highly Qualified Teachers and the Relationship between Certification and Achievement," *Education Policy Analysis Archives* 18, no. 27 (2010).

18. Charlotte Danielson and Thomas L. McGreal, *Teacher Evaluation to Enhance Professional Practice* (Alexandria, VA: ASCD, 2000); Linda Darling-Hammond, *Getting Teacher Evaluation Right: What Really Matters for Effectiveness and Improvement* (New York: Teachers College Press, 2013); Helen Ladd and Susanna Loeb, "The Challenges of Measuring School Quality: Implications for Educational Equity," in *Education, Justice, and Democracy*, Denielle Allen and Rob Reich, eds. (University of Chicago Press, 2013), 18–42; Heather Hill and Pam Grossman, "Learning from Teacher Observations: Challenges and Opportunities Posed by New Teacher Evaluation Systems," *Harvard Educational Review* 83, no. 2 (2013): 371–384.

19. For more on the development of survey questions and scales, see Chapter 4.

20. Jason J. Teven, "Teacher Temperament: Correlates with Teacher Caring, Burnout, and Organizational Outcomes," *Communication Education* 56, no. 3 (2007): 382–400; Kathleen Buss, James Gingles, and Jay Price, "Parent-Teacher Temperament Ratings and Student Success in Reading,"

Reading Psychology: An International Quarterly 14, no. 4 (1993): 311–323; Jason J. Teven and James C. McCroskey, "The Relationship of Perceived Teacher Caring with Student Learning and Teacher Evaluation," *Communication Education* 46, no. 1 (1997): 1–9; Nel Noddings, "An Ethic of Caring and Its Implications for Instructional Arrangements," *American Journal of Education* 96, no. 2 (1988): 215–230.

21. Matthew A. Kraft and John P. Papay, "Can Professional Environments in Schools Promote Teacher Development? Explaining Heterogeneity in Returns to Teaching Experience," *Educational Evaluation and Policy Analysis* 36, no. 4 (2014): 476–500; Helen F. Ladd and Lucy C. Sorensen, "Returns to Teacher Experience: Student Achievement and Motivation in Middle School," Working Paper 112, Center for Analysis of Longitudinal Data in Education Research, 2014; Michael Fullan, ed., *Teacher Development and Educational Change* (New York: Routledge, 2014); Andy Hargreaves and Michael Fullan, *Professional Capital: Transforming Teaching in Every School* (New York: Teachers College Press, 2012).

22. Linda Darling-Hammond, "Policy and Professionalism," in *Building a Professional Culture in Schools,* ed. Ann Lieberman (New York: Teachers College Press, 1988), 55–77; Wayne K. Hoy and Megan Tschannen-Moran, "The Conceptualization and Measurement of Faculty Trust in Schools," in *Essential Ideas for the Reform of American Schools,* ed. Wayne K. Hoy and Michael D. Paola (Charlotte, NC: Information Age, 2007), 87–114. Richard Ingersoll, "Teacher Turnover and Teacher Shortages: An Organizational Analysis," *American Educational Research Journal* 38, no. 3 (2001): 499–534; Susanna Loeb, Linda Darling-Hammond, and John Luczac, "How Teaching Conditions Predict Teacher Turnover in California," *Peabody Journal of Education* 80, no. 3 (2005): 44–70; Matthew Ronfeldt, Susanna Loeb, and James Wyckoff, "How Teacher Turnover Harms Student Achievement," *American Educational Research Journal* 50, no. 1 (2013): 4–36.

23. Mike Taylor, Anne Yates, Luanna H. Meyer, and Penny Kinsella, "Teacher Professional Leadership in Support of Teacher Professional Development," *Teaching and Teacher Education* 27, no. 1 (2011): 85–94; Kwang Suk Yoon, Teresa Duncan, Silvia Wen-Yu Lee, Beth Scarloss, and Kathy L. Shapley, "Reviewing the Evidence on How Teacher Professional Development

Affects Student Achievement, " Issues & Answers, REL 2007-No. 033, Regional Educational Laboratory Southwest (NJ1), October 2007, https://ies.ed.gov/ncee/edlabs/regions/southwest/pdf/REL_2007033.pdf; John M. Foster, Eugenia F. Toma, and Suzanne P. Troske, "Does Teacher Professional Development Improve Math and Science Outcomes and Is It Cost Effective?," *Journal of Education Finance* 38, no. 3 (2013): 255–275.

24. Heather E. Price, "Principal-Teacher Interactions: How Affective Relationships Shape Principal and Teacher Attitudes," *Educational Administration Quarterly* 48, no. 1 (2012): 39–85; Philip Hallinger and Ronald H. Heck, "Exploring the Principal's Contribution to School Effectiveness: 1980–1995," *School Effectiveness and School Improvement* 9, no. 2 (1998): 157–191; Anthony S. Bryk, Penny Bender Sebring, Elaine Allensworth, John Q. Easton, and Stuart Luppescu, *Organizing Schools for Improvement: Lessons from Chicago* (Chicago: University of Chicago Press, 2010); Thomas M. Smith and Richard M. Ingersoll, "What Are the Effects of Induction and Mentoring on Beginning Teacher Turnover?," *American Education Research Journal* 41, no. 3 (2004): 681–714; Anthony S. Bryk and Barbara Schneider, *Trust in Schools* (New York: Russell Sage Foundation, 2002).

25. To say that these variables are not dependent on demography is not to say that they are completely independent. Demography shapes almost every aspect of life in schools.

26. In the literature, the research on "school culture" often bleeds together with that on "school climate." I have opted for the phrase "school culture," though I have included many of the perspectives from the work on "school climate." See Education Week Research Center, *Engaging Students for Success: Findings from a National Survey,*2014, http://www.edweek.org/media/ewrc_engagingstudents_2014.pdf; Wayne K. Hoy, John Hannum, and Megan Tschannen-Moran, "Organizational Climate and Student Achievement: A Parsimonious and Longitudinal View," *Journal of School Leadership* 8, no. 4 (1998): 336–359; Talisha Lee, Dewey Cornell, Anne Gregory, and Xitao Fan, "High Suspension Schools and Dropout Rates for Black and White Students," *Education and Treatment of Children* 34, no. 2 (2011): 167–192; Kathleen Fulton, Irene Yoon, and Christine Lee, "Induction into Learning Communities," National Commission on

Teaching and America's Future, 2005; Jessica L. Grayson and Heather K. Alvarez, "School Climate Factors Relating to Teacher Burnout: A Mediator Model," *Teaching and Teacher Education* 24, no. 5 (2008): 1349–1363; Ann Higgins-D'Alessandro, "The Necessity of Teacher Development," *New Directions for Child and Adolescent Development,* no. 98 (2002): 75–84.

27. Grayson and Alvarez, "School Climate Factors Relating to Teacher Burnout"; Bryk et al., *Organizing Schools for Improvement.*

28. Heather P. Libbey, "Measuring Student Relationships to School: Attachment, Bonding, Connectedness, and Engagement," *Journal of School Health* 74, no. 7 (2004): 274–283. For examples of toxic academic culture, see Denise Clark Pope, *Doing School: How We Are Creating a Generation of Stressed Out, Materialistic, and Miseducated Students* (New Haven, CT: Yale University Press, 2001). For examples of toxic social culture, see Jess Bidgood, "Students Say Racial Hostilities Simmered at Historic Boston Latin School," *New York Times,* January 30, 2016, http://www.nytimes.com /2016/01/31/education/students-say-racial-hostilities-simmered-at -historic-boston-latin-school.html?_r=0; and Jeannie Suk, "St. Paul's School and a New Definition of Rape," *New Yorker,* November 3, 2015, http://www.newyorker.com/news/news-desk/st-pauls-school-and-a-new -definition-of-rape.

29. Michael B. Ripski and Anne Gregory, "Unfair, Unsafe, and Unwelcome: Do High School Students' Perceptions of Unfairness, Hostility, and Victimization in School Predict Engagement and Achievement?," *Journal of School Violence* 8, no. 4 (2009): 355–375; Ron Avi Astor, Nancy Guerra, and Richard Van Acker, "How Can We Improve School Safety Research?," *Educational Researcher* 39, no. 1 (2010): 69–78; Jaana Juvonen, Adrienne Nishina, and Sandra Graham, "Ethnic Diversity and Perceptions of Safety in Urban Middle Schools," *Psychological Science* 17, no. 5 (2006): 393–400; Russell Skiba, Ada B. Simmons, Reece Peterson, Janet McKelvey, Susan Forde, and Sarah Gallini, "Beyond Guns, Drugs and Gangs: The Structure of Student Perceptions of School Safety," *Journal of School Violence* 3, nos. 2–3 (2004): 149–171; Lee Shumow and Richard G. Lomax, "Predicting Perceptions of School Safety," *School Community Journal* 11, no. 2 (2001): 93–112.

30. Skiba et al., "Beyond Guns, Drugs and Gangs," 149–171; Salvatore Saporito and Annette Lareau, "School Selection as a Process: The Multiple Dimensions of Race in Framing Educational Choice," *Social Problems* 46 (1999): 418–435; Juvonen, Nichina, and Graham, "Ethnic Diversity," 393–400; Johanna R. Lacoe, "Unequally Safe: The Race Gap in School Safety," *Youth Violence and Juvenile Justice* 13, no. 2 (2015): 143–168.

31. Tonja R. Nansel, Mary Overpeck, Ramani S. Pilla, W. June Ruan, Bruce Simons-Morton, and Peter Scheidt, "Bullying Behaviors among US Youth: Prevalence and Association with Psychosocial Adjustment," *Journal of the American Medical Association* 285, no. 16 (2001): 2094–2100; Ian Rivers, V. Paul Poteat, Nathalie Noret, and Nigel Ashurst, "Observing Bullying at School: The Mental Health Implications of Witness Status," *School Psychology Quarterly* 24, no. 4 (2009): 211.

32. Bryk and Schneider, *Trust in Schools.*

33. Adena M. Klem and James P. Connell, "Relationships Matter: Linking Teacher Support to Student Engagement and Achievement," *Journal of School Health* 74, no. 7 (2004): 262–273; Karen F. Osterman, "Students' Need for Belonging in the School Community," *Review of Educational Research* 70, no. 3 (2000): 323–367; Eric M. Anderman, "School Effects on Psychological Outcomes during Adolescence," *Journal of Educational Psychology* 94, no. 4 (2002): 795; Marti Rice, "Importance of School Connectedness," *Pediatrics for Parents* 25 (2009): 20; Andrea E. Bonny, Maria T. Britto, Brenda K. Klostermann, Richard W. Hornung, and Gail B. Slap, "School Disconnectedness: Identifying Adolescents at Risk," *Pediatrics* 106, no. 5 (2000): 1017–1021; Lyndal Bond, Helen Butler, Lyndal Thomas, John Carlin, Sara Glover, Glenn Bowes, and George Patton, "Social and School Connectedness in Early Secondary School as Predictors of Late Teenage Substance Use, Mental Health, and Academic Outcomes," *Journal of Adolescent Health* 40, no. 4 (2007): 357-e9.

34. Xin Ma, "Sense of Belonging to School: Can Schools Make a Difference?," *Journal of Educational Research* 96, no. 6 (2003): 340–349.

35. Ellen A. Skinner and Michael J. Belmont, "Motivation in the Classroom: Reciprocal Effects of Teacher Behavior and Student Engagement across the School Year," *Journal of Educational Psychology* 85, no. 4 (1993): 571; Theresa M. Akey, *School Context, Student Attitudes and Behavior, and*

Academic Achievement: An Exploratory Analysis (New York: MDRC, 2006); Bronwyn E. Becker and Suniya S. Luthar, "Social-Emotional Factors Affecting Achievement Outcomes among Disadvantaged Students: Closing the Achievement Gap," Educational Psychologist 37, no. 4 (2002): 197–214; Anne Gregory and Rhona S. Weinstein, "Connection and Regulation at Home and in School: Predicting Growth in Achievement for Adolescents," Journal of Adolescent Research 19, no. 4 (2004): 405–427; Klem and Connell, "Relationships Matter," 262–273.

36. Clea McNeely and Christina Falci, "School Connectedness and the Transition into and out of Health-Risk Behavior among Adolescents: A Comparison of Social Belonging and Teacher Support," Journal of School Health 74, no. 7 (2004): 284–292; Stephanie H. Schneider and Lauren Duran, "School Climate in Middle Schools," Journal of Research in Character Education 8, no. 2 (2010): 25–37.

37. Education Week Research Center, Engaging Students for Success; Nan Marie Astone and Sara S. McLanahan, "Family Structure, Parental Practices and High School Completion," American Sociological Review 56, no. 3 (1991): 309–320; Richard J. Murnane, U.S. High School Graduation Rates: Patterns and Explanations, NBER Report w18701 (Cambridge, MA: National Bureau of Economic Research, 2013).

38. Wayne K. Hoy, Scott R. Sweetland, and Page A. Smith, "Toward an Organizational Model of Achievement in High Schools: The Significance of Collective Efficacy," Educational Administration Quarterly 38, no.1 (2002): 77–77; Valerie Lee, Julia B. Smith, Tamara E. Perry, and Mark A. Smylie, Social Support, Academic Press, and Student Achievement: A View from the Middle Grades in Chicago (Chicago: Consortium on Chicago School Research, 1999); Meredith Phillips, "What Makes Schools Effective? A Comparison of the Relationships of Communitarian Climate and Academic Climate to Mathematics Achievement and Attendance during Middle School," American Educational Research Journal 34, no. 4 (1997): 633–662.

39. Student standardized test scores can also reveal gaps, but represent less actionable information. Insofar as that is the case, it is critical to measure inputs alongside outcomes, despite a propensity among policymakers to look exclusively at the latter.

40. Per-pupil expenditure can be calculated by taking a school's total spending and dividing by the number of students. These expenditures vary dramatically across states but average out to roughly $12,000 per student nationwide.

41. Howard Blume and Stephen Ceasar, "L.A. Unified's iPad Rollout Marred by Chaos," *Los Angeles Times,* October 1, 2013, http://articles.latimes.com /2013/oct/01/local/la-me-1002-lausd-ipads-20131002; Howard Blume, "L.A. School District Demands iPad Refund from Apple," *Los Angeles Times,* April 16, 2015, http://www.latimes.com/local/lanow/la-me-ln-ipad -curriculum-refund-20150415-story.html. Calculating the additional cost of Special Education students is challenging, given the facts that services differ across populations and price differs across states, but a reasonable estimate is that Special Education students require an addition $10,000 per pupil.

42. Bruce D. Baker, "Revisiting the Age-Old Question: Does Money Matter in Education?," Albert Shanker Institute, 2012, http://www.shankerinstitute .org/resource/does-money-matter-second-edition; Rob Greenwald, Larry V. Hedges, and Richard D. Laine, "The Effect of School Resources on Student Achievement," *Review of Educational Research* 66, no. 3 (1996): 361–396; C. Kirabo Jackson, Rucker C. Johnson, and Claudia Persico, "The Effects of School Spending on Educational and Economic Outcomes: Evidence from School Finance Reforms," *Quarterly Journal of Economics* 131, no. 1 (2015): 157–218.

43. Jack Buckley, Mark Schneider, and Yi Shang, "Fix It and They Might Stay: School Facility Quality and Teacher Retention in Washington, DC," *Teachers College Record* 107, no. 5 (2005): 1107–1123; Cynthia Uline and Megan Tschannen-Moran, "The Walls Speak: The Interplay of Quality Facilities, School Climate, and Student Achievement," *Journal of Educational Administration* 46, no. 1 (2008): 55–73; Valkiria Durán-Narucki, "School Building Condition, School Attendance, and Academic Achievement in New York City Public Schools: A Mediation Model," *Journal of Environmental Psychology* 28, no. 3 (2008): 278–286.

44. Peter Blatchford, Paul Bassett, and Penelope Brown, "Examining the Effect of Class Size on Classroom Engagement and Teacher-Pupil Interaction: Differences in Relation to Pupil Prior Attainment and Primary vs.

Secondary Schools," *Learning and Instruction* 21, no. 6 (2011): 715–730; Diane Whitmore Schanzenbach, *Does Class Size Matter?* (Boulder, CO: National Education Policy Center, 2014).

45. Valerie E. Lee and Ruth B. Ekstrom, "Student Access to Guidance Counseling in High School," *American Educational Research Journal* 24, no. 2 (1987): 287–310; Richard T. Lapan, Norman C. Gysbers, and Yongmin Sun, "The Impact of More Fully Implemented Guidance Programs on the School Experiences of High School Students: A State-wide Evaluation Study," *Journal of Counseling and Development* 75, no. 4 (1997): 292–302; Jenni Jennings, Glen Pearson, and Mark Harris, "Implementing and Maintaining School-Based Mental Health Services in a Large, Urban School District," *Journal of School Health* 70, no. 5 (2000): 201–205; Laura A. Nabors and Matthew W. Reynolds, "Program Evaluation Activities: Outcomes Related to Treatment for Adolescents Receiving School-Based Mental Health Services," *Children's Services: Social Policy, Research, and Practice* 3, no. 3 (2000): 175–189.

46. James Catterall, "The Arts and Achievement in At-Risk Youth: Findings from Four Longitudinal Studies," Research Report no. 55, (Washington, DC: National Endowment for the Arts, 2012; James Catterall, Richard Chapleau, and John Iwanaga, "Involvement in the Arts and Human Development: General Involvement and Intensive Involvement in Music and Theater Arts," in *Champions of Change: The Impact of the Arts on Learning*, Edward B. Fiske, ed. (Washington, DC: President's Committee on the Arts and the Humanities, 1999): 1–18; Kristin D. Conklin, Bridget K. Curran, and Matthew Gandal, *An Action Agenda for Improving America's High Schools. National Education Summit on High Schools* (Washington, DC: National Governors Association, 2005); Michael Chajewski, Krista D. Mattern, and Emily J. Shaw, "Examining the Role of Advanced Placement Exam Participation in 4-Year College Enrollment," *Educational Measurement: Issues and Practice* 30, no. 4 (2011): 16–27; Kristin Klopfenstein and M. Kathleen Thomas, "The Link between Advanced Placement Experience and Early College Success," *Southern Economic Journal* 75, no. 3 (2009): 873–891; Dan Willingham, *Why Don't Students Like School?* (San Francisco: Jossey-Bass, 2010); Thomas Dee, Brian A. Jacob, and Nathaniel Schwartz, "The Effects of NCLB on School

Resources and Practices," *Educational Evaluation and Policy Analysis* 35, no. 2 (2013): 252–279.

47. It is worth noting that this concern was also articulated by focus group participants in other districts in our work through the Massachusetts Consortium for Innovative Education Assessment.

48. For more about core knowledge, see E. D. Hirsch Jr., *Cultural Literacy: What Every American Needs to Know* (New York: Houghton Mifflin, 1987). For culturally responsive curricula, see Lisa Delpit, *Other People's Children: Cultural Conflict in the Classroom* (New York: New Press, 1995); James A. Banks, "A Curriculum for Empowerment, Action, and Change," in *Empowerment through Multicultural Education*, ed. Christine E. Sleeter (Albany: State University of New York Press, 1991); Ana María Villegas and Tamara Lucas, "Preparing Culturally Responsive Teachers: Rethinking the Curriculum," *Journal of Teacher Education* 53, no. 1 (2002): 20–32.

49. Joyce L. Epstein, Mavis G. Sanders, Beth S. Simon, Karen Clark Salinas, Natalie Rodriguez Jansorn, and Frances L. Van Voorhis, *School, Family, and Community Partnerships: Your Handbook for Action* (Thousand Oaks, CA: Corwin Press, 2002); Nancy E. Hill and Lorraine C. Taylor, "Parental School Involvement and Children's Academic Achievement: Pragmatics and Issues," *Current Directions in Psychological Science* 13, no. 4 (2004): 161–164; Robert Pianta and Daniel Walsh, *High-Risk Children in Schools: Constructing Sustaining Relationships* (New York: Routledge, 2014); Anne T. Henderson and Karen L. Mapp, "A New Wave of Evidence: The Impact of School, Family, and Community Connections on Student Achievement; Annual Synthesis 2002," National Center for Family and Community Connections with Schools, 2002, http://files.eric.ed.gov /fulltext/ED474521.pdf.

50. Education Week Research Center, *Engaging Students for Success*.

51. Bryk et al., *Organizing Schools for Improvement*; Henderson and Mapp, "A New Wave of Evidence."

52. Bryk et al., *Organizing Schools for Improvement*; ETS, Ready for the World: *Americans Speak Out on High School Reform* (Princeton, NJ: ETS, 2005), https://www.ets.org/Media/Education_Topics/pdf/2005highschoolreform .pdf; Atelia Melaville, Amy C. Berg, and Martin J. Blank, "Community-Based Learning: Engaging Students for Success and Citizenship," Coalition

for Community Schools, 2006, http://files.eric.ed.gov/fulltext/ED490980 .pdf; Susan Moore Johnson, Matthew A. Kraft, and John P. Papay, "How Context Matters in High-Need Schools: The Effects of Teachers' Working Conditions on Their Professional Satisfaction and Their Students' Achievement," *Teachers College Record* 114, no. 10 (2012): 1–39; Elliot Washor and Charles Mojkowski, *Leaving to Learn* (Portsmouth, NH: Heinemann, 2013); Ron Ferguson and Eric Hirsch, "How Working Conditions Predict Teaching Quality and Student Outcomes," in *Designing Teacher Evaluation Systems: New Guidance from the Measures of Effective Teaching Project,* ed. Thomas Kane, Kerri Kerr, and Robert Pianta (San Francisco: Jossey-Bass, 2014).

53. ETS, *Americans Speak Out;* Richard Rothstein and Rebecca Jacobsen, "The Goals of Education," *Phi Delta Kappan* 88, no. 4 (2006): 264–272.

54. Doug Shapiro, Afet Dundar, Phoebe K. Wakhungu, Xin Yuan, Angel Nathan, and Youngsik Hwang, *Completing College: A National View of Student Attainment Rates—Fall 2008 Cohort,* Signature Report no. 8 (Herndon, VA: National Student Clearinghouse, 2014).

55. Gauging student growth will take a significant amount of research. To be successful in this enterprise, we must first answer basic questions about when it is appropriate to take baseline measures, how many years should pass between baseline and output measures, and how much growth measures can account for out-of-school factors.

56. Douglas Harris, *Value-Added Measures in Education: What Every Educator Needs to Know* (Cambridge, MA: Harvard Education Press, 2011).

57. Ray Hart, Michael Casserly, Renata Uzzell, Moses Palacios, Amanda Corcoran, and Liz Spurgeon, *Student Testing in America's Great City Schools: An Inventory and Preliminary Analysis* (Washington, DC: Council of the Great City Schools, 2015).

58. Youb Kim and Lisa Sensale Yazdian, "Portfolio Assessment and Quality Teaching," *Theory into Practice* 53, no. 3 (2014): 220–227; Betty Mc-Donald, "Portfolio Assessment: Direct from the Classroom," *Assessment and Evaluation in Higher Education* 37, no. 3 (2012): 335–347; Elliott Asp, "Assessment in Education: Where Have We Been? Where Are We Headed?," Association for Supervision and Curriculum Development Yearbook (Alexandria, VA: Association for Supervision and Curriculum

Development, 2000), 123–157; Bette S. Bergeron, Sarah Wermuth, and Rebecca C. Hammar, "Initiating Portfolios through Shared Learning: Three Perspectives," *Reading Teacher* 50, no. 7 (1997): 552–562; Judith H. Cohen and Roberta B. Wiener, *Literacy Portfolios: Improving Assessment, Teaching, and Learning* (Merrill, WI: Merrill Publishing, 2003); Kathleen Blake Yancey, "Dialogue, Interplay, and Discovery: Mapping the Role and the Rhetoric of Reflection in Portfolio Assessment," in *Writing Portfolios in the Classroom: Policy, Practice, Promise and Peril,* ed. Robert Calfee and Pamela Perfumo (Mahwah, NJ: Lawrence Erlbaum Associates, 1996), 83–102.

59. Klem and Connell, "Relationships Matter," 262–273. See also: Maria R. Reyes, Marc A. Brackett, Susan E. Rivers, Mark White, and Peter Salovey, "Classroom Emotional Climate, Student Engagement, and Academic Achievement," *Journal of Educational Psychology* 104, no. 3 (2012): 700–712; John Mark Froiland and Emily Oros, "Intrinsic Motivation, Perceived Competence and Classroom Engagement as Longitudinal Predictors of Adolescent Reading Achievement," *Educational Psychology* 34, no. 2 (2014): 119–132; Margaret Beale Spencer, Elizabeth Noll, Jill Stoltzfus, and Vinay Harpalani, "Identity and School Adjustment: Revisiting the 'Acting White' Assumption," *Educational Psychologist* 36, no. 1 (2001): 21–30.

60. Donald J. Hernandez, "Double Jeopardy: How Third-Grade Reading Skills and Poverty Influence High School Graduation," Annie E. Casey Foundation, 2011, http://www.aecf.org/m/resourcedoc/AECF-DoubleJeopardy -2012-Full.pdf; Christine A. Christle, Kristine Jolivette, and C. Michael Nelson, "School Characteristics Related to High School Dropout Rates," *Remedial and Special Education* 28, no. 6 (2007): 325–339; Nan Marie Astone and Sara S. McLanahan, "Family Structure, Parental Practices and High School Completion," *American Sociological Review* (1991): 309–320; Russell W. Rumberger and Gregory J. Palardy, "Test Scores, Dropout Rates, and Transfer Rates as Alternative Indicators of High School Performance," *American Educational Research Journal* 42, no. 1 (2005): 3–42.

61. Rothstein and Jacobsen, "The Goals of Education," 264–272; James Hiebert, Thomas P. Carpenter, Elizabeth Fennema, Karen Fuson, Piet

Human, Hanlie Murray, Alwyn Olivier, and Diana Wearne, "Problem Solving as a Basis for Reform in Curriculum and Instruction: The Case of Mathematics," *Educational Researcher* 25, no. 4 (1996): 12–21.

62. An excellent example of this is "progressive" teaching—an incredibly abstract aim that has primarily impacted the way educators talk about pedagogy. For an in-depth treatment of this, see Larry Cuban, *How Teachers Taught: Constancy and Change in American Classrooms, 1880–1990* (New York: Teachers College Press, 1993).

63. Stephen P. Norris, "Synthesis of Research on Critical Thinking," *Educational Leadership* 42, no. 8 (1985): 40–45.

64. Stephen I. Brown and Marion I. Walter, eds., *Problem Posing: Reflections and Applications* (Mahwah, NJ: Lawrence Erlbaum Associates, 1993); Carolyn N. Hedley, Patricia Antonacci, and Mitchell Rabinowitz, eds., *Thinking and Literacy: The Mind at Work* (New York: Routledge, 2013); Louis Alfieri, Patricia J. Brooks, Naomi J. Aldrich, and Harriet R. Tenenbaum, "Does Discovery-Based Instruction Enhance Learning?," *Journal of Educational Psychology* 103, no. 1 (2011): 1; Timothy R. Elliott, Frank Godshall, John R. Shrout, and Thomas E. Witty, "Problem-Solving Appraisal, Self-Reported Study Habits, and Performance of Academically At-Risk College Students," *Journal of Counseling Psychology* 37, no. 2 (1990): 203; Thomas J. D'Zurilla and Collette F. Sheedy, "The Relation between Social Problem-Solving Ability and Subsequent Level of Academic Competence in College Students," *Cognitive Therapy and Research* 16, no. 5 (1992): 589–599.

65. Susan L. Hersperger, John R. Slate, and Stacey L. Edmonson, "A Review of the Career and Technical Education Research Literature," *Journal of Education Research* 7, no. 3 (2013): 157–179; ACT, Inc., *Ready for College and Ready for Work: Same or Different?* (Iowa City, IA: Act, Inc., 2006); Michael Bangser, *Preparing High School Students for Successful Transitions to Postsecondary Education and Employment* (New York: MDRC, 2008), http://www.mdrc.org/sites/default/files/PreparingHSStudentsforTransition_073108.pdf.

66. Horace Mann, *Twelfth Annual Report to the Secretary of the Massachusetts State Board of Education* (N.p. 1848).

67. "The 48th Annual PDK Poll of the Public's Attitudes toward the Public Schools," *Phi Delta Kappan* 98, no. 1 (2016); NPR / Kaiser Family Foundation / Kennedy School Education Survey, 1999, http://www.npr.org /programs/specials/poll/education/education.results.html.

68. Joseph E. Zins, ed., *Building Academic Success on Social and Emotional Learning: What Does the Research Say?* (New York: Teachers College Press, 2004); James P. Comer, ed., *Rallying the Whole Village: The Comer Process for Reforming Education* (New York: Teachers College Press, 1996); Bryk et al., *Organizing Schools for Improvement*; Higgins-D'Alessandro, "The Necessity of Teacher Development," 75–84.

69. Rothstein and Jacobsen, "The Goals of Education," 264–272.

70. Jack Schneider and Michael Fuerstein, "Thinking Civically," *Social Education*, September, 2013.

71. See, for instance, C. Kirabo Jackson, "Non-cognitive Ability, Test Scores, and Teacher Quality: Evidence from 9th Grade Teachers in North Carolina," NBER Working Paper 18624, National Bureau of Economic Research, December 2012; Jennifer L. Jennings and Thomas A. DiPrete, "Teacher Effects on Social / Behavioral Skills in Early Elementary School," CPRC Working Paper 09–11, Columbia Population Research Center, New York, 2009.

72. Carnegie Corporation of New York and CIRCLE: The Center for Information & Research on Civic Learning and Engagement, *The Civic Mission of Schools* (New York: Carnegie Corporation of New York and CIRCLE, 2003); David E. Campbell, Meira Levinson, and Frederick M. Hess, eds., *Making Civics Count: Citizenship Education for a New Generation* (Cambridge, MA: Harvard Education Press, 2012).

73. Joseph J. Ellis, *Founding Brothers: The Revolutionary Generation* (New York: Knopf, 2001), 154.

74. Dara Zeehandelaar and Amber M. Winkler, eds., *What Parents Want: Education Preferences and Trade-Offs* (Washington, DC: Thomas B. Fordham Institute, 2013). See also Amy Stuart Wells, Lauren Fox, and Diana Cordova-Cobo, *How Racially Diverse Schools and Classrooms Can Benefit All Students* (New York: Century Foundation, 2016).

75. John J. Heldrich Center for Workforce Development, *Attitudes about Work, Employers, and Government Survey* (New Brunswick, NJ: Rutgers

University, 2000); Rothstein and Jacobsen, "The Goals of Education," 264–272.

76. Camille A. Farrington, Melissa Roderick, Elaine Allensworth, Jenny Nagaoka, Tasha Seneca Keyes, David W. Johnson, and Nicole O. Beechum, *Teaching Adolescents to Become Learners: The Role of Noncognitive Factors in Shaping School Performance—A Critical Literature Review* (Chicago: Consortium on Chicago School Research, 2012), https://consortium .uchicago.edu/sites/default/files/publications/Noncognitive%20Report .pdf; Angela L. Duckworth, Christopher Peterson, Michael D. Matthews, and Dennis R. Kelly, "Grit: Perseverance and Passion for Long-Term Goals," *Journal of Personality and Social Psychology* 92, no. 6 (2007): 1087; Angela L. Duckworth and David Scott Yeager, "Measurement Matters: Assessing Personal Qualities Other Than Cognitive Ability for Educational Purposes," *Educational Researcher* 44, no. 4 (2015): 237–251.

77. Lisa S. Blackwell, Kali H. Trzesniewski, and Carol Sorich Dweck, "Implicit Theories of Intelligence Predict Achievement across an Adolescent Transition: A Longitudinal Study and an Intervention," *Child Development* 78, no. 1 (2007): 246–263; Carol S. Dweck, *Self-Theories: Their Role in Motivation, Personality, and Development* (Philadelphia: Psychology Press, 1999); Carol S. Dweck, "The Perils and Promises of Praise," *Educational Leadership* 65, no. 2 (2007): 34–39; Joshua Aronson, Carrie B. Fried, and Catherine Good, "Reducing the Effects of Stereotype Threat on African American College Students by Shaping Theories of Intelligence," *Journal of Experimental Social Psychology* 38, no. 2 (2002): 113–125; Carol S. Dweck, "Who Will the 21st-Century Learners Be?," *Knowledge Quest* 38, no. 2 (2009): 8.

78. Rothstein and Jacobsen, "The Goals of Education," 264–272.

79. Catterall, "The Arts and Achievement in At-Risk Youth"; E. B. Fiske, ed., *Champions of Change: The Impact of the Arts on Learning* (Washington, DC: Arts Education Partnership and the President's Committee on Arts and Humanities, 1999), http://www.aep-arts.org/files/publications /ChampsReport.pdf; Douglas Israel, *Staying in School: Arts Education and New York City High School Graduation Rates* (New York: Center for Arts Education, 2009); Bill Lucas, Guy Claxton, and Ellen Spencer, "Progression in Student Creativity in School: First Steps towards New Forms of

Formative Assessments," OECD Education Working Paper 86, OECD Publishing, 2013; James C. Kaufman, "Counting the Muses: Development of the Kaufman Domains of Creativity Scale," *Psychology of Aesthetics, Creativity, and the Arts* 6, no. 4 (2012): 298–308; Ronald A. Beghetto, James C. Kaufman, and Juliet Baxter, "Answering the Unexpected Questions: Exploring the Relationship between Students' Creative Self-Efficacy and Teacher Ratings of Creativity," *Psychology of Aesthetics, Creativity, and the Arts* 5, no. 4 (2011): 342.

80. Rothstein and Jacobsen, "The Goals of Education," 264–272.

81. Sonja Lyubomirsky, Laura King, and Ed Diener, "The Benefits of Frequent Positive Affect: Does Happiness Lead to Success?," *Psychological Bulletin* 131, no. 6 (2005): 803–855; Greg J. Duncan, Chantelle J. Dowsett, Amy Claessens, Katherine Magnuson, Aletha C. Huston, Pamela Klebanov, Linda S. Pagani, et al., "School Readiness and Later Achievement," *Developmental Psychology* 43, no. 6 (2007): 1428; Rothstein and Jacobsen, "The Goals of Education," 264–272.

82. James F. Sallis, Thomas L. McKenzie, Bohdan Kolody, Michael Lewis, Simon Marshall, and Paul Rosengard, "Effects of Health-Related Physical Education on Academic Achievement: Project SPARK," *Research Quarterly for Exercise and Sport* 70, no. 2 (1999): 127–134; Roy J. Shephard, "Curricular Physical Activity and Academic Performance," *Pediatric Exercise Science* 9 (1997): 113–126; Roy J. Shephard, M. Volle, H. Lavallee, R. LaBarre, J. C. Jequier, and M. Rajic, "Required Physical Activity and Academic Grades: A Controlled Study," in *Children and Sport* (Berlin: Springer, 1984), 58–63; Cynthia Wolford Symons, Bethann Cinelli, Tammy C. James, and Patti Groff, "Bridging Student Health Risks and Academic Achievement through Comprehensive School Health Programs," *Journal of School Health* 67, no. 6 (1997): 220–227; Duncan et al., "School Readiness and Later Achievement," 1428–1446.

Chapter 4 But How Do We *Get* That Kind of Information?

1. Each of our focus groups lasted for approximately one hour. As a general rule, we tried to limit focus groups to ten people or fewer. There are also financial costs associated with focus groups. Teachers were paid stipends of thirty to forty dollars per focus group.

2. One promising technique for addressing reference bias is the inclusion of anchoring vignettes. For more on this, see Patrick C. Kyllonen and Jonas P. Bertling, "Innovative Questionnaire Assessment Methods to Increase Cross-Country Comparability," in *Handbook of International Large-Scale Assessment: Background, Technical Issues, and Methods of Data Analysis*, ed. Leslie Rutkowski, Matthias von Davier, and David Rutkowski (Boca Raton, FL: Chapman and Hall, 2013); Gary King, Christopher J. L. Murray, Joshua A. Salomon, and Ajay Tandon, "Enhancing the Validity and Cross-Cultural Comparability of Measurement in Survey Research," *American Political Science Review* 98, no. 1 (2004): 191–207. That said, there is evidence from the CORE districts in California that reference bias may be more of an imagined concern than a practical one. These districts have chosen not to use anchoring vignettes, despite having cooperated with ETS to develop and pilot them for use in student perception surveys.

3. To be clear: there are methods for dealing with all of these problems. In this case, creating a "skip pattern" in the survey can create different kinds of questions for different audiences who are taking the same survey.

4. Jon A. Krosnick, "Survey Research," *Annual Review of Psychology* 50, no. 1 (1999): 537–567; Brian S. Connelly and Deniz S. Ones, "An Other Perspective on Personality: Meta-analytic Integration of Observers' Accuracy and Predictive Validity," *Psychological Bulletin* 136, no. 6 (2010): 1092; Joshua J. Jackson, James J. Connolly, S. Mason Garrison, Madeleine M. Leveille, and Seamus L. Connolly, "Your Friends Know How Long You Will Live: A 75-Year Study of Peer-Rated Personality Traits," *Psychological Science* 26, no. 3 (2015): 335–340.

5. Thomas J. Kane and Douglas O. Staiger, "Gathering Feedback for Teaching: Combining High-Quality Observations with Student Surveys and Achievement Gains" (research paper, MET Project, Seattle, WA: Bill & Melinda Gates Foundation, 2012); David J. Wilkerson, Richard P. Manatt, Mary Ann Rogers, and Ron Maughan, "Validation of Student, Principal, and Self-Ratings in 360 Feedback® for Teacher Evaluation," *Journal of Personnel Evaluation in Education* 14, no. 2 (2000): 179–192.

6. Ronald F. Ferguson, "Can Student Surveys Measure Teaching Quality?," *Phi Delta Kappan* 94, no. 3 (2012): 24–28; George G. Bear, Clare Gaskins, Jessica Blank, and Fang Fang Chen, "Delaware School Climate Survey—

Student: Its Factor Structure, Concurrent Validity, and Reliability," *Journal of School Psychology* 49, no. 2 (2011): 157–174.

7. Michael Eid and Ed Diener, eds., *Handbook of Multimethod Measurement in Psychology* (Washington, DC: American Psychological Association, 2006); J. Philippe Rushton, Charles J. Brainerd, and Michael Pressley, "Behavioral Development and Construct Validity: The Principle of Aggregation," *Psychological Bulletin* 94, no. 1 (1983): 18; Angela L. Duckworth and David Scott Yeager, "Measurement Matters Assessing Personal Qualities Other Than Cognitive Ability for Educational Purposes," *Educational Researcher* 44, no. 4 (2015): 237–251.

8. Information about Ron Ferguson's survey assessments for early elementary grades can be requested directly from Tripod Education Partners.

9. Anthony S. Bryk, Penny Bender Sebring, Elaine Allensworth, John Q. Easton, and Stuart Luppescu, *Organizing Schools for Improvement: Lessons from Chicago* (Chicago: University of Chicago Press, 2010); University of Chicago, Chicago Consortium for School Research, "5Essentials," https://uchicagoimpact.org/5essentials, accessed February 11, 2016.

10. For more, see Hunter Gehlbach and Maureen E. Brinkworth, "Measure Twice, Cut Down Error: A Process for Enhancing the Validity of Survey Scales," *Review of General Psychology* 15, no. 4 (2011): 380–387.

11. See, for instance, Gordon B. Willis, *Cognitive Interviewing: A Tool for Improving Questionnaire Design* (Thousand Oaks, CA: Sage, 2005).

12. Chiefly, we wondered if the questions would offer any discriminative power. That is, would we get different results across teachers, or would all teachers issue themselves high ratings? The former turned out to be the case.

13. For more, see Julianne Viola, Joe McIntyre, and Hunter Gehlbach, "Teachers' Interest in Students' Personal Development: The Creation of a New Survey Scale," *SAGE Research Methods Cases*, 2016, http://methods .sagepub.com/case/teachers-interest-students-personal-development -creation-new-survey-scale.

14. Sally M. Weinstein, Robin J. Mermelstein, Benjamin L. Hankin, Donald Hedeker, and Brian R. Flay, "Longitudinal Patterns of Daily Affect and Global Mood during Adolescence," *Journal of Research on*

Adolescence 17, no. 3 (2007): 587–600; Sally M. Weinstein and Robin Mermelstein, "Relations between Daily Activities and Adolescent Mood: The Role of Autonomy," *Journal of Clinical Child and Adolescent Psychology* 36, no. 2 (2007): 182–194; Eddie M. W. Tong, George D. Bishop, Hwee Chong Enkelmann, Yong Peng Why, Siew Maan Diong, Majeed Khader, and Jansen Ang, "The Use of Ecological Momentary Assessment to Test Appraisal Theories of Emotion," *Emotion* 5, no. 4 (2005): 508–512.

15. U.S. Department of Education, Office of Research, "Education Consumer Guide," no. 2, September 1993, https://www2.ed.gov/pubs/OR/Consumer-Guides/perfasse.html.

16. John O'Neil, "Putting Performance Assessment to the Test," *Educational Leadership* 49, no. 8 (1992): 14–19.

17. New York Performance Standards Consortium, *Educating for the 21st Century: Data Report on the New York Performance Standards Consortium,* New York, n.d., http://performanceassessment.org/articles/DataReport_NY_PSC.pdf.

18. U.S. Department of Education, Office of Research, "Education Consumer Guide," no. 2.

19. Ronald A. Berk, "National Trends in Student and Teacher Assessment: Issues in Performance Assessment," in National Evaluation Systems, *Performance Assessment in Teacher Certification Testing* (Amherst, MA: National Evaluation Systems, 1993), 17–33.

20. Desmond L. Nuttall, "Performance Assessment: The Message from England," *Educational Leadership* 49, no. 8 (1992): 54–57.

21. Linda Darling-Hammond and Frank Adamson, *Beyond Basic Skills: The Role of Performance Assessment in Achieving 21st Century Standards of Learning* (Stanford, CA: Stanford Center for Opportunity Policy in Education, 2010).

22. Ibid.

23. For a longer explanation of this, see Jack Schneider, Joe Feldman, and Dan French, "The Best of Both Worlds," *Phi Delta Kappan* 98, no. 3 (2016): 60–67.

24. For more on teacher performance assessment, see Irena Nayfeld, Raymond L. Pecheone, Andrea Whittaker, Ben Shear, and Heather Klesch,

Educative Assessment and Meaningful Support: 2014 edTPA Administrative Report, Stanford Center on Assessment, Learning and Equity, September 2015.

25. New Teacher Project, *The Mirage: Confronting the Hard Truth about Our Quest for Teacher Development* (New York: New Teacher Project, 2015); Allison Gulamhussein, *Teaching the Teachers: Effective Professional Development in an Era of High Stakes Accountability* (Alexandria, VA: Center for Public Education, 2013); Ruth Chung Wei, Linda Darling-Hammond, Alethea Andree, Nikole Richardson, and Stelios Orphanos, *Professional Learning in the Learning Profession: A Status Report on Teacher Development in the U.S. and Abroad* (Washington, DC: National Staff Development Council, 2009).

Chapter 5 An Information Superhighway

1. Thom File and Camille Ryan, "Computer and Internet Use in the United States: 2013," *American Community Survey Reports* (Washington, DC: U.S. Census Bureau, U.S. Department of Commerce, 2014).

2. Susan Cooper Loomis and Mary Lyn Bourque, eds., *National Assessment of Educational Progress Achievement Levels, 1992–1998 for Mathematics* (Washington, DC: National Assessment Governing Board, July 2001).

3. Illinois State Board of Education, "FAQs Illinois 5Essentials Survey," August 2014, http://www.isbe.net/5essentials/pdf/2014–15/faq1408.pdf.

4. Data courtesy of the Massachusetts Department of Elementary and Secondary Education and the *Boston Globe.*

5. For a more detailed account of this experiment, see Jack Schneider, Rebecca Jacobsen, Rachel S. White, and Hunter Gehlbach, "The (Mis) Measure of Schools: How Data Affect Stakeholder Knowledge and Perceptions of Quality," *Teachers College Record* 120, no. 6 (2018).

6. James Fishkin, *When the People Speak: Deliberative Democracy and Public Consultation* (New York: Oxford University Press, 2009); Jane Mansbridge, "Deliberative Polling as the Gold Standard," *The Good Society* 19, no. 1 (2010): 55.

7. For a much more thorough discussion of the experimental poll and its results, see Schneider et al., "The (Mis)Measure of Schools."

8. Baseline rates of "I don't know" responses for randomly assigned schools were 67 percent for control and 69 percent for treatment. For familiar schools, they were 24 percent for control and 23 percent for treatment.

9. Phi Delta Kappan / Gallup, *The 47th Annual PDK / Gallup Poll of the Public's Attitudes toward the Public Schools* (Bloomington, IN: PDK International, 2015).

10. Ibid.

11. Jonathan Sandy and Kevin Duncan, "Examining the Achievement Test Score Gap between Urban and Suburban Students," *Education Economics* 18, no. 3 (2010): 297–315; Suzanne E. Graham and Lauren E. Provost, *Mathematics Achievement Gaps between Suburban Students and Their Rural and Urban Peers Increase over Time,* Issue Brief 52 (Durham, NH: Carsey Institute, 2012); Christy Lleras, "Race, Racial Concentration, and the Dynamics of Educational Inequality across Urban and Suburban Schools," *American Educational Research Journal* 45, no. 4 (2008): 886–912; Selcuk R. Sirin, "Socioeconomic Status and Academic Achievement: A Meta-analytic Review of Research," *Review of Educational Research* 75, no. 3 (2005): 417–453.

Chapter 6 A New Accountability

1. James Vaznis, "After Stagnant MCAS Results, Six More Schools 'Under-performing,'" *Boston Globe,* September 19, 2014, https://www.bostonglobe .com/2014/09/19/mcas/1dq3cKgyvElF7XR6A10vLO/story.html; Will Pinkston, "Failing Schools Demand Board Response," *Tennessean* (Nashville), August 27, 2014, http://www.tennessean.com/story/opinion /contributors/2014/08/27/pinkston-failing-schools-demand-board -response/14680021/; "City to Address Failing Schools," WROC (Rochester, NY), August 4, 2015, http://www.rochesterhomepage.net/story/d /story/city-to-address-failing-schools/20847 /eGV1JzYPTUWJKVSB8nRHEw.

2. Lowell C. Rose and Alec M. Gallup, *The 34th Annual PDK / Gallup Poll of the Public's Attitudes toward the Public Schools* (Bloomington, IN: PDK International, 2002); William J. Bushaw and Shane J. Lopez, *The 45th Annual PDK / Gallup Poll of the Public's Attitudes toward the Public Schools* (Bloomington, IN: PDK International, 2013).

3. Also compelling is the fact that while Americans have long rated their own congressional representatives more highly than Congress as a whole, the two ratings move almost in lockstep with each other, with a 0.93 correlation. Ratings of the schools are different in this regard, suggesting that the same mechanism is not at work in both fields. For more on ratings of Congress, see Harry Enten, "Disliking Congress as a Whole, and as Individuals," FiveThirtyEight, July 1, 2014, http://fivethirtyeight.com/datalab/disliking-congress-as-a-whole-and-as-individuals/.

4. Martin R. West, "Why Do Americans Rate Their Local Public Schools So Favorably?," *Education Next,* October 27, 2014; see also Mark Schneider, Paul Teske, and Melissa Marschall, *Choosing Schools: Consumer Choice and the Quality of American Schools* (Princeton, NJ: Princeton University Press, 2000); Joseph L. Bast and Herbert J. Walberg, "Can Parents Choose the Best Schools for Their Children?," *Economics of Education Review* 23, no. 4 (2004): 431–440.

5. National Center for Education Statistics, *The Nation's Report Card: Trends in Academic Progress, 2012* (Washington, DC: U.S. Department of Education, 2013).

6. For more on the rhetoric of crisis, see Ethan L. Hutt and Jack Schneider, "The Rhetoric of Reform," *Teachers College Record*—Commentary (December 14, 2012).

7. This is not to suggest that the schools are, therefore, models of perfection. Instead, it seems that the schools, over time, are improving slowly, and possibly even at an insufficient pace. The logical policy response to slow improvement, however, is likely quite different from the logical response to precipitous decline.

8. For a more in-depth discussion of accountability and its constituent parts, see Andreas Schedler, "Conceptualizing Accountability," in *The Self-Restraining State: Power and Accountability in New Democracies*, ed. Andreas Schedler, Larry Diamond, and Marc F. Plattner (Boulder, CO: Lynne Rienner, 1999). It is also worth exploring the approach taken by the CORE districts in California, where the state pairs low-performing districts with higher-performing districts; the aim is to build capacity rather than to impose punitive sanctions.

9. For a discussion of local knowledge, see James C. Scott, *Seeing Like a State* (New Haven, CT: Yale University Press, 1999).

10. This does not mean that, even in the long run, all students will achieve at equal levels. It is to suggest, rather, that particular opportunity variables might someday become equal or close to equal, as well as to suggest that levels of student growth on outcomes—when aggregated across the whole school—might be close to equal.

11. The Every Student Succeeds Act, signed into law in December of 2015, does allow for states to determine their own targets, though a number of rules apply to how this is done.

12. For more detail, see Chapter 3.

13. For more, see Andrew Saultz, Kristin M. Murphy, and Brittany Aronson, "What Can We Learn from the Atlanta Cheating Scandal?," *Phi Delta Kappan* 97, no. 6 (2016): 48–52.

14. See, for instance, the resistance to state takeover of the Holyoke Public Schools in Massachusetts, described in "Holyoke: The Schools Our Children Deserve," Massachusetts Teachers Association, 2016, http://www .massteacher.org/issues_and_action/ongoing_issues/holyoke.aspx.

15. U.S. Department of Education, "Teaching American History," archived information, http://www2.ed.gov/programs/teachinghistory/index .html.

16. Rick Shenkman, "OAH 2009: Sam Wineburg Dares to Ask If the Teaching American History Program Is a Boondoggle," History News Network, April 19, 2009, http://historynewsnetwork.org/article/76806; Daniel C. Humphrey, Christopher Chang-Ross, Mary Beth Donnelly, Lauren Hersh, and Heidi Skolnik, *Evaluation of the Teaching American History Program* (Washington, DC: SRI International, 2005).

17. In Massachusetts, an annual PPI is calculated for all student subgroups, and is made up of several indicators. These indicators include proficiency gaps in standardized test scores, test score growth, and dropout / graduation rates.

18. MCAS is the state standardized test for K–12 schools in Massachusetts.

19. Professional development fails for other reasons, too. See Hilda Borko, "Professional Development and Teacher Learning: Mapping the Terrain," *Educational Researcher* 33, no. 8 (2004): 3–15; Suzanne M. Wilson and

Jennifer Berne, "Teacher Learning and the Acquisition of Professional Knowledge: An Examination of Research on Contemporary Professional Development," *Review of Research in Education* 24 (1999): 173–209; New Teacher Project, *The Mirage: Confronting the Hard Truth about Our Quest for Teacher Development* (New York: New Teacher Project, 2015).

20. Thanks to Dan French and members of the Massachusetts Consortium for Innovative Education Assessment governing board for their input on these.

21. It is also important to note here that schools are not like products conducive to free market consumption. Schools, for instance, are quite different from a product such as breakfast cereal, which can be purchased conveniently, tasted quickly, judged easily, and tossed aside with virtually no consequences; consumers can then repeat this process at a very low cost, and in short order, until they find something they like. Schools, by contrast, require great effort to enroll in, take a long time to reveal their strengths and weaknesses, are deeply affected by community turnover, and can be difficult to leave for students who have formed attachments.

22. Elizabeth N. Farley-Ripple, Kelly Sherretz, and Chris Kelly, *School Success Reports, Stakeholder Feedback: Final Report* (Newark: University of Delaware, 2015).

23. Leadership Conference on Civil and Human Rights, "Civil Rights Groups: 'We Oppose Anti-testing Efforts,'" press release, May 5, 2015, http://www.civilrights.org/press/2015/anti-testing-efforts.html.

24. American Federation of Teachers, "AFT's Weingarten on the U.S. Education Department's 'Testing Action Plan,'" press release, October 24, 2014, http://www.aft.org/press-release/afts-weingarten-us-education-departments-testing-action-plan.

25. Students Matter, "About Us," http://studentsmatter.org/about/, accessed February 4, 2016; *Vergara v. California-Tentative Decision,* Superior Court of the State of California, County of Los Angeles, June 10, 2014; California Teachers Association, "*Vergara v. State of California,*" Issues and Action, http://www.cta.org/vergara, accessed February 4, 2016.

26. Joanne W. Golann, "The Paradox of Success at a No-Excuses School," *Sociology of Education* 88, no. 2 (2015): 103–119.

27. "More Than 620,000 Refused Tests in 2015," press release, FairTest, February 3, 2016, http://www.fairtest.org/more-500000-refused-tests -2015; Katie Zahedi, "Those Phony, Misleading Test Scores: A NY Principal Reacts," http://dianeravitch.net/2013/08/08/those-phony -misleading-test-scores-a-ny-principal-reacts/.

Conclusion

1. For a deeper discussion of private versus public goods in education, see David F. Labaree, "Public Goods, Private Goods: The American Struggle over Educational Goals," *American Educational Research Journal* 34, no. 1 (1997): 39–81. See also Denise Clark Pope, *Doing School: How We Are Creating a Generation of Stressed Out, Materialistic, and Miseducated Students* (New Haven, CT: Yale University Press, 2001).
2. For a history of the early American school system, see Carl Kaestle, *Pillars of the Republic: Common Schools and American Society, 1780–1860* (New York: Macmillan, 2011).
3. For more on the examples of police work, medicine, and environmental conservation, see John A. Eterno and Eli B. Silverman, "The New York City Police Department's Compstat: Dream or Nightmare?," *International Journal of Police Science and Management* 8 (2006): 218; Gwyn Bevan and Christopher Hood, "What's Measured Is What Matters: Targets and Gaming in the English Public Health Care System," *Public Administration* 84, no. 3 (2006): 517–538; Anne D. Guerry, Stephen Polasky, Jane Lubchenco, Rebecca Chaplin-Kramer, Gretchen C. Daily, Robert Griffin, Mary Ruckelshaus, et al., "Natural Capital and Ecosystem Services Informing Decisions: From Promise to Practice," *Proceedings of the National Academy of Sciences* 112, no. 24 (2015): 7348–7355.
4. Aldo Leopold, *A Sand County Almanac* (New York: Oxford University Press, 1949), 224–225.

Postscript

1. Jack Schneider and Pat Jehlen, "A Fairer Test Score Measure," *Boston Globe,* May 6, 2014.

2. For more on performance assessment, see Chapter 4.

3. Funding for the consortium was originally vetoed by Governor
   Charlie Baker. After a legislative override of the veto, the governor
   called back funds through midyear "9C" budget cuts in December
   2016.

Acknowledgments

Several years ago, I was at work on what I believed would become my third book when I was drawn into, and consumed by, a new research project. That project eventually led to a different book—this one.

I was swept up in this work because I found it intellectually stimulating and politically important, particularly as the parent of a child just beginning her journey through the school system. But I was also deeply moved by the community in which this research was conducted—the city of Somerville, Massachusetts. Insofar as that is the case, any acknowledgment must begin with the people who make our 4.2 square miles feel quite a bit larger than it really is. I continue to be grateful to live in a city as diverse, vibrant, and engaged as ours.

I was also drawn into this project by forward-looking civic leaders who were willing to experiment. Mayor Joseph Curtatone, former superintendent Tony Pierantozzi, superintendent Mary Skipper, assistant superintendent Vince McKay, and members of the Somerville school committee have been consistently supportive of this work, as have been the district's principals, teachers, staff, and families. To say that this project would not have been possible without them, though a platitude, is also a fact.

Thanks are also due to a rotating corps of collaborators and assistants whose labors made much of this work possible, and whose insights made all of the work stronger. Among collaborators, particular thanks are due to Rebecca Jacobsen and Hunter Gehlbach—outstanding scholars who are as generous with their wisdom as they are with their friendship. Chapters 4 and 5, particularly, could not have been written without them. Special thanks are also due to Jared Cosulich, who served as the lead web developer on the project, as well as to the staff at the Somerville Family Learning Collaborative, who at every stage helped us include traditionally underrepresented members of the community.

Like the research project in general, this book is also the product of a small-scale solidarity movement. I am grateful to Jennifer Berkshire, Larry Cuban, Elizabeth Farley-Ripple, Scott Gelber, Bob Hampel, Ethan Hutt, Alain Jehlen, David Labaree, and Trey Popp for their careful reading of the manuscript. From my second-rate first drafts through the final edit, they kept me alert as both a scholar and a writer. I am especially grateful to my friend Sivan Zakai, who somehow never tires of offering clear, helpful, and encouraging feedback.

Given the subject of this book, it would be careless not to thank my teachers. From my first day of kindergarten through my last day of graduate school, I have been blessed with compassionate and committed teachers. As both a scholar and a person, I owe them a tremendous debt of thanks. The largest debt, of course, is owed to my first teachers—my mother and father. They taught me to read and write, to love ideas, to seek knowledge, and to work hard. More importantly, though, my parents taught me to laugh and to love, to live with integrity, and to seek justice. The hardest work of all has been showing them my gratitude, which is boundless.

Finally, I want to acknowledge the two loves of my life. My daughter Annabelle, for whom I want school to be a great joy, is the reason I wrote this book. Along with her mother, Katie—who just happens to be the best high school English teacher I know—she is the reason I get up each morning. They are the beginning, the middle, and the end. Everything else is just footnotes.

Index

Performance standards, 131, 178. *See also* Benchmarks

Perseverance, 141

Persico, Claudia, 122

Phi Delta Kappa, 139, 212, 221

Physical activity, 144

Pierantozzi, Tony, 8, 19, 68, 97, 129

PISA (Programme for International Student Assessment), 48–49

Policy, and testing, 29–30

Political influence, and testing, 33

Polling, deliberative, 206–207

Portfolios, 131–132, 261. *See also* Performance assessments

Poverty, 256. *See also* Class; Demographics; Income

Princeton Review, 45

Principals, control over, 25

Private schools, 78, 80–81

Problem-solving skills, 134

Professional development (PD), 109, 181–182, 238

Proficiency, 14–15, 41, 194

Programme for International Student Assessment (PISA), 48–49

Protective factors, 133

Psychological health, 143–144

Punishment, 226, 232, 240

Purpose of Education in American Democracy, The (EPC), 26–27

Questionnaires. *See* Surveys

Race: and perceptions of school quality, 72–76; as proxy for school quality, 3, 114; and test scores, 9, 21. *See also* Demographics

Ranking/rating, of schools: effects of, 218, 240; problems with, 193–194, 196, 204–205; by for-profit entities, 63–68, 224

Reading comprehension, and content knowledge, 19

Real estate, 77–79

Reality, reflected in data, 245

Realtors, 77

Reference bias, 305n2

Regents exam, 29

Relationships, 88–89, 115–117, 285n64

Resources: community support, 124–126; described, 120–121; measuring, 121–127; physical spaces, 122–123; questions to ask about, 128–129; and school quality, 242. *See also* Curriculum; Funding

Rothstein, Richard, 10, 97, 141

Safety: emotional, 114–115; physical, 113–114; survey questions for, 167–168. *See also* Health

Sanctions, 226, 231, 232

SAT, 3, 45–46

Schneider, Mark, 70

School councils, 237

School culture, 57; academic orientation, 117–118; described, 112–113; evaluating, 113–119; positive, 117; questions to ask about, 119–120; relationships, 115–117; safety, 113–115; and school quality, 242; survey questions for, 167–168

School environment, 108–110

School improvement plans, 237–238